One hot guy + One funny-looking guy = One hilarious couple!

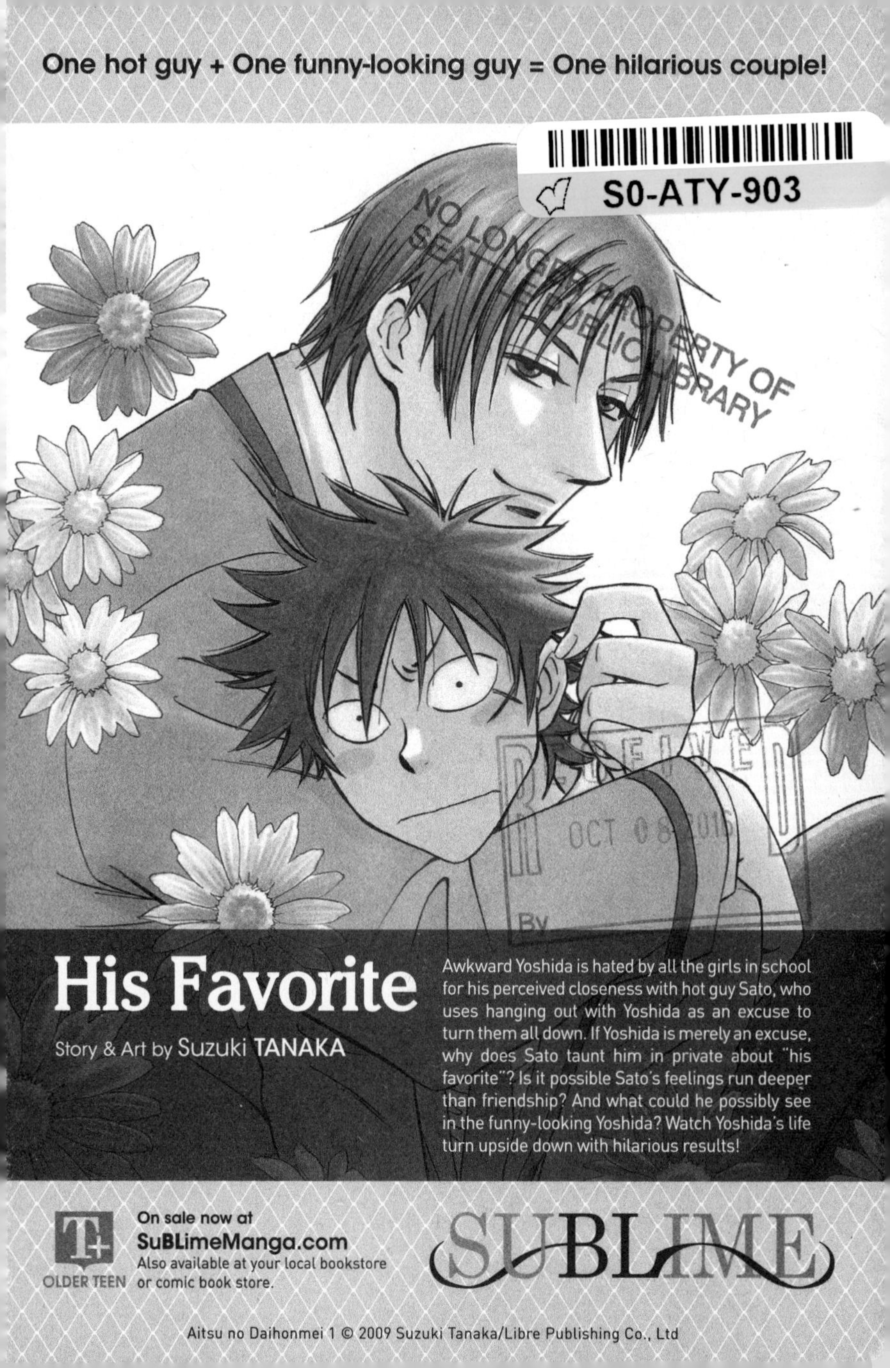

His Favorite

Story & Art by Suzuki TANAKA

Awkward Yoshida is hated by all the girls in school for his perceived closeness with hot guy Sato, who uses hanging out with Yoshida as an excuse to turn them all down. If Yoshida is merely an excuse, why does Sato taunt him in private about "his favorite"? Is it possible Sato's feelings run deeper than friendship? And what could he possibly see in the funny-looking Yoshida? Watch Yoshida's life turn upside down with hilarious results!

T+ OLDER TEEN

On sale now at
SuBLimeManga.com
Also available at your local bookstore or comic book store.

SUBLIME

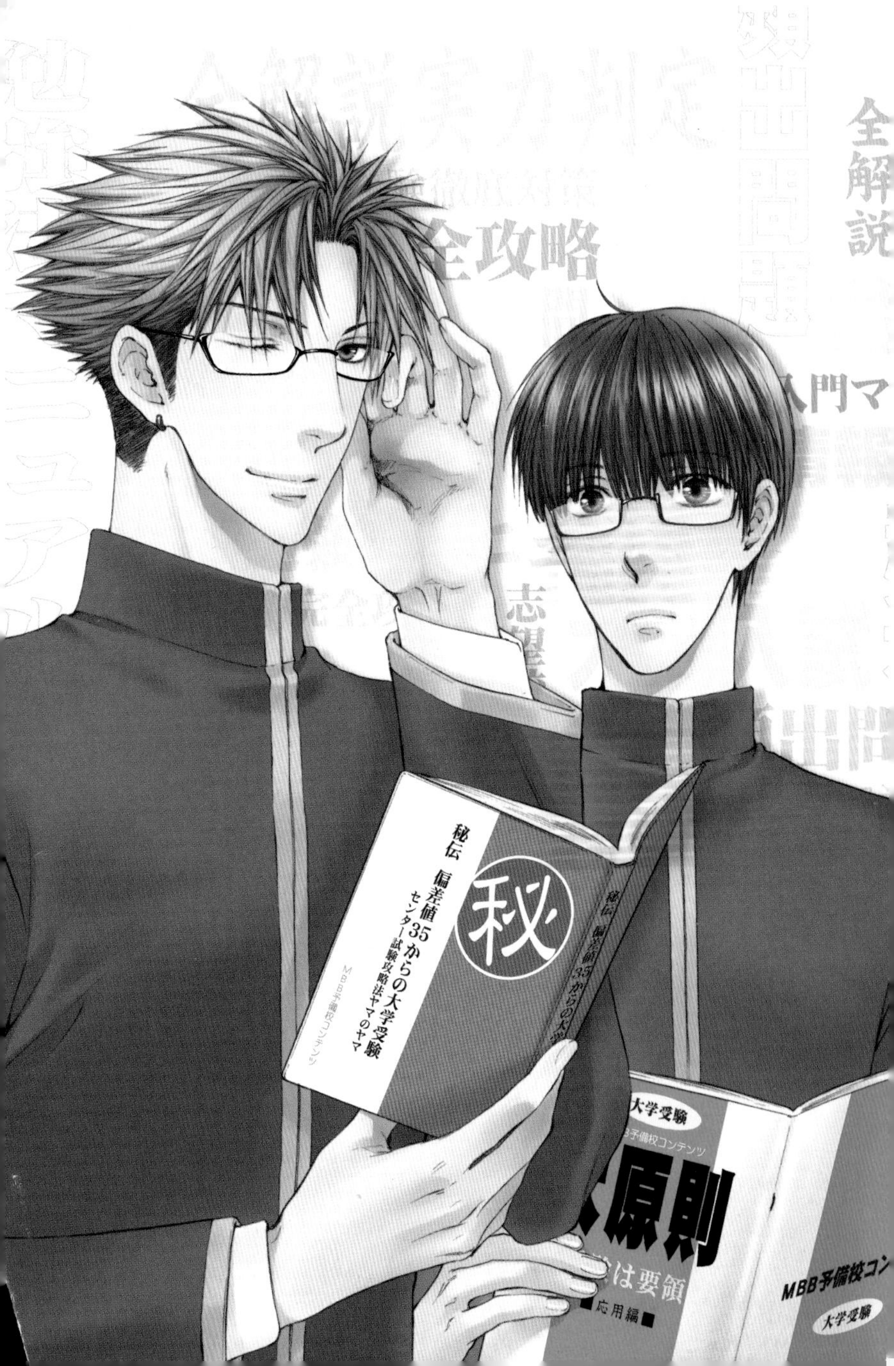

全解説
全攻略
入門マ
秘伝　偏差値35からの大学受験
センター試験攻略法ヤマのヤマ
MBB予備校コンテンツ
秘
大学受験
原則
は要領
■応用編■
MBB予備校コン
大学受験

Don't Be Cruel

Story and Art by **Yonezou Nekota**   volumes **3&4**

CONTENTS

SUBLIME
SuBLime Manga Edition

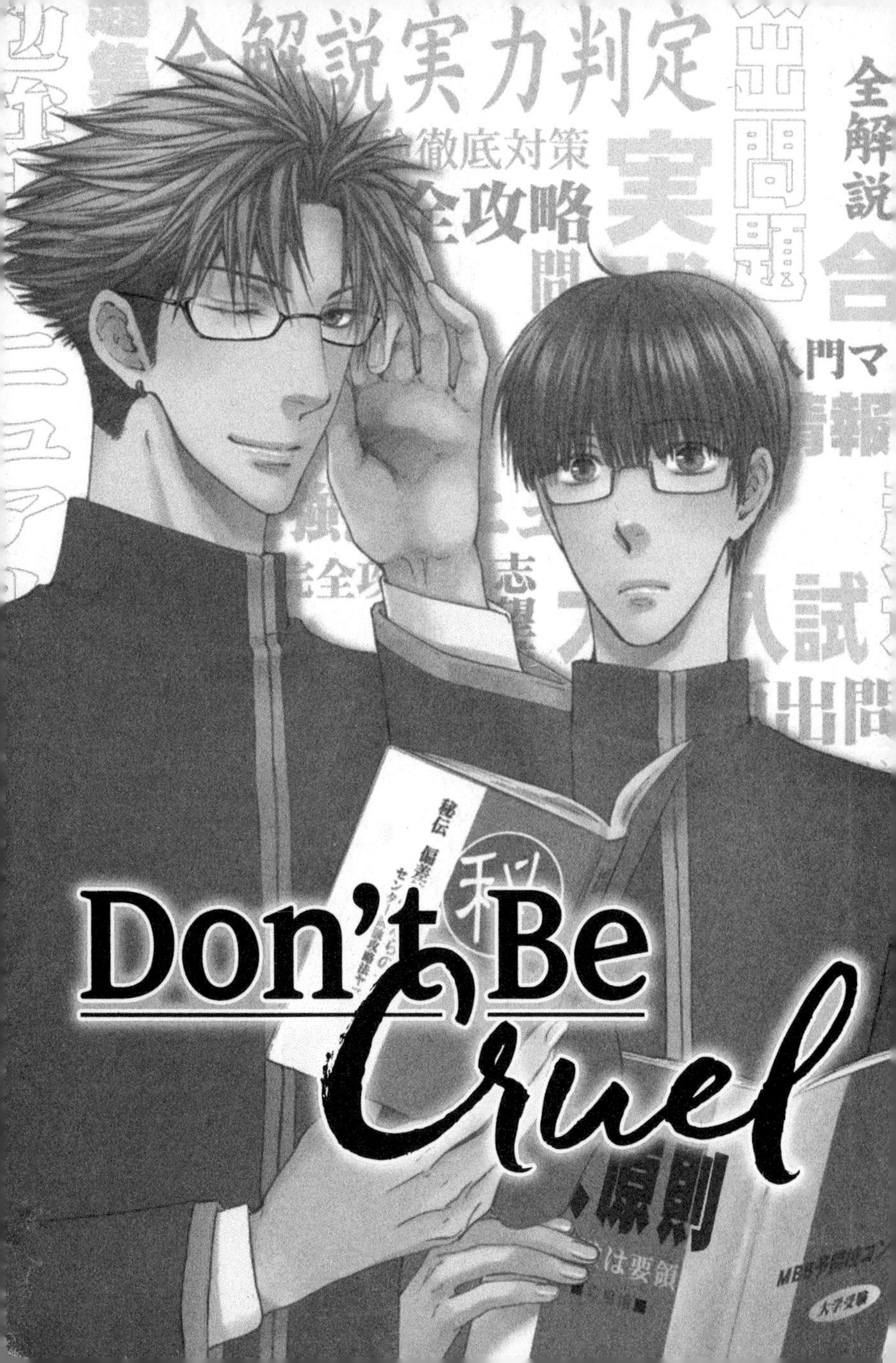
Don't Be
Cruel

THAT'S TWO NOT-TOO-EMBARRASSING-TO-TAKE-TO-THE-

REGISTER COVER ILLUSTRATIONS IN A ROW! YAY! AND

HELLO! STARTING WITH VOLUME 3, NEMUGASA FINALLY—OH, WAIT.

SPOILER ALERT! DON'T READ ANY FURTHER UNTIL AFTER YOU

FINISH THE MAIN STORY IN THIS VOLUME. 😄

AHEM! AS I WAS SAYING, IN THIS VOLUME, NEMUGASA FINALLY GETS A

TURN AT BEING THE BLUSHING DERE. WE'RE JUST ONE STEP AWAY FROM

HIM REALIZING THAT HE CAN'T LIVE WITHOUT MAYA. I'M SURE THERE

ARE SOME READERS OUT THERE WHO STILL FIND THIS UNEXPECTED.

FALLING IN LOVE CAN REALLY CHANGE A PERSON THOUGH.

I HOPE YOU ALL ENJOY READING HOW THIS

RELATIONSHIP IS CHANGING

ALL THOSE INVOLVED.

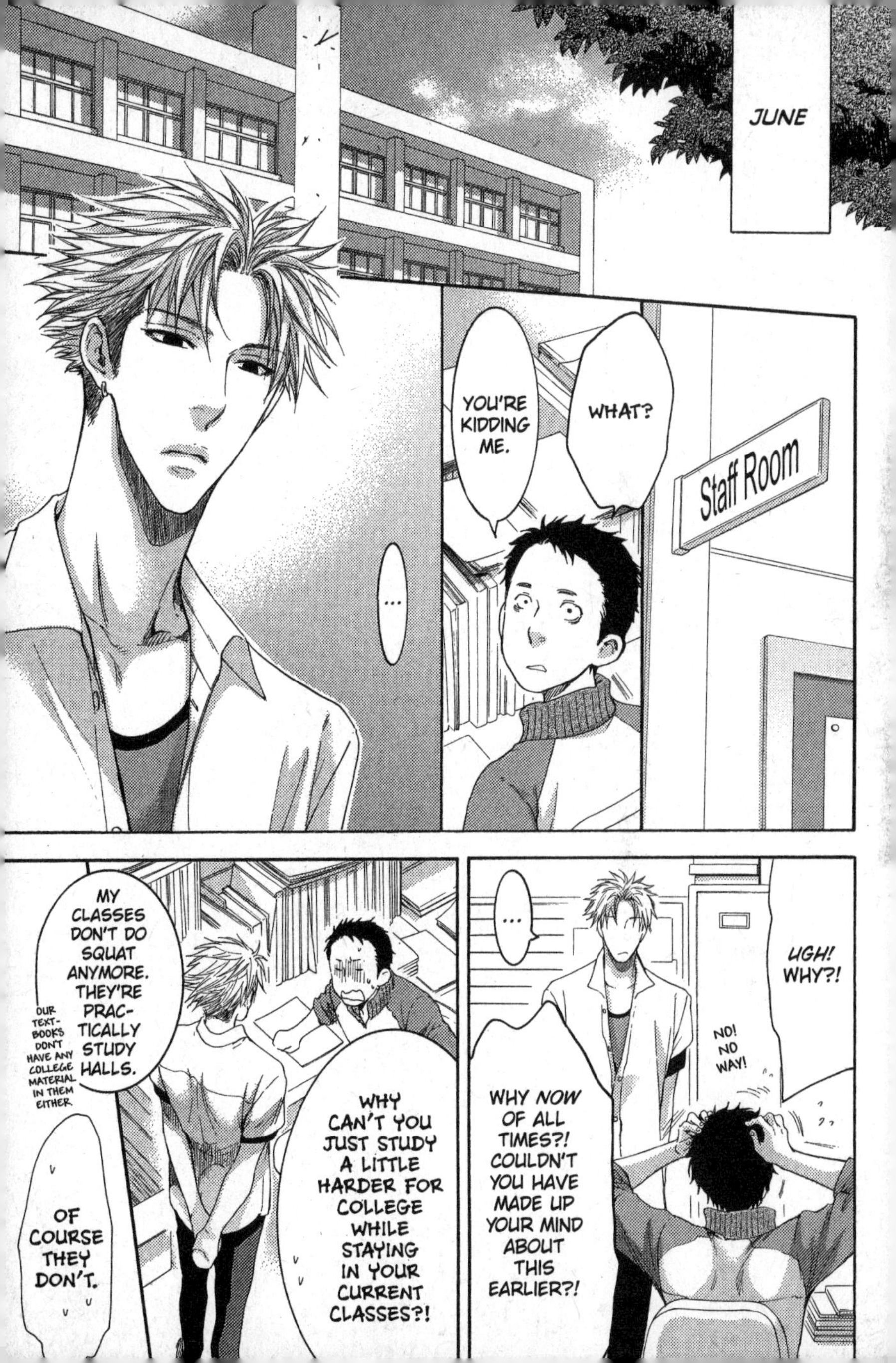
JUNE
WHAT?
YOU'RE KIDDING ME.
...
...
UGH! WHY?!
NO! NO WAY!
WHY NOW OF ALL TIMES?! COULDN'T YOU HAVE MADE UP YOUR MIND ABOUT THIS EARLIER?!
WHY CAN'T YOU JUST STUDY A LITTLE HARDER FOR COLLEGE WHILE STAYING IN YOUR CURRENT CLASSES?!
MY CLASSES DON'T DO SQUAT ANYMORE. THEY'RE PRAC-TICALLY STUDY HALLS.
OUR TEXT-BOOKS DON'T HAVE ANY COLLEGE MATERIAL IN THEM EITHER.
OF COURSE THEY DON'T.
Staff Room

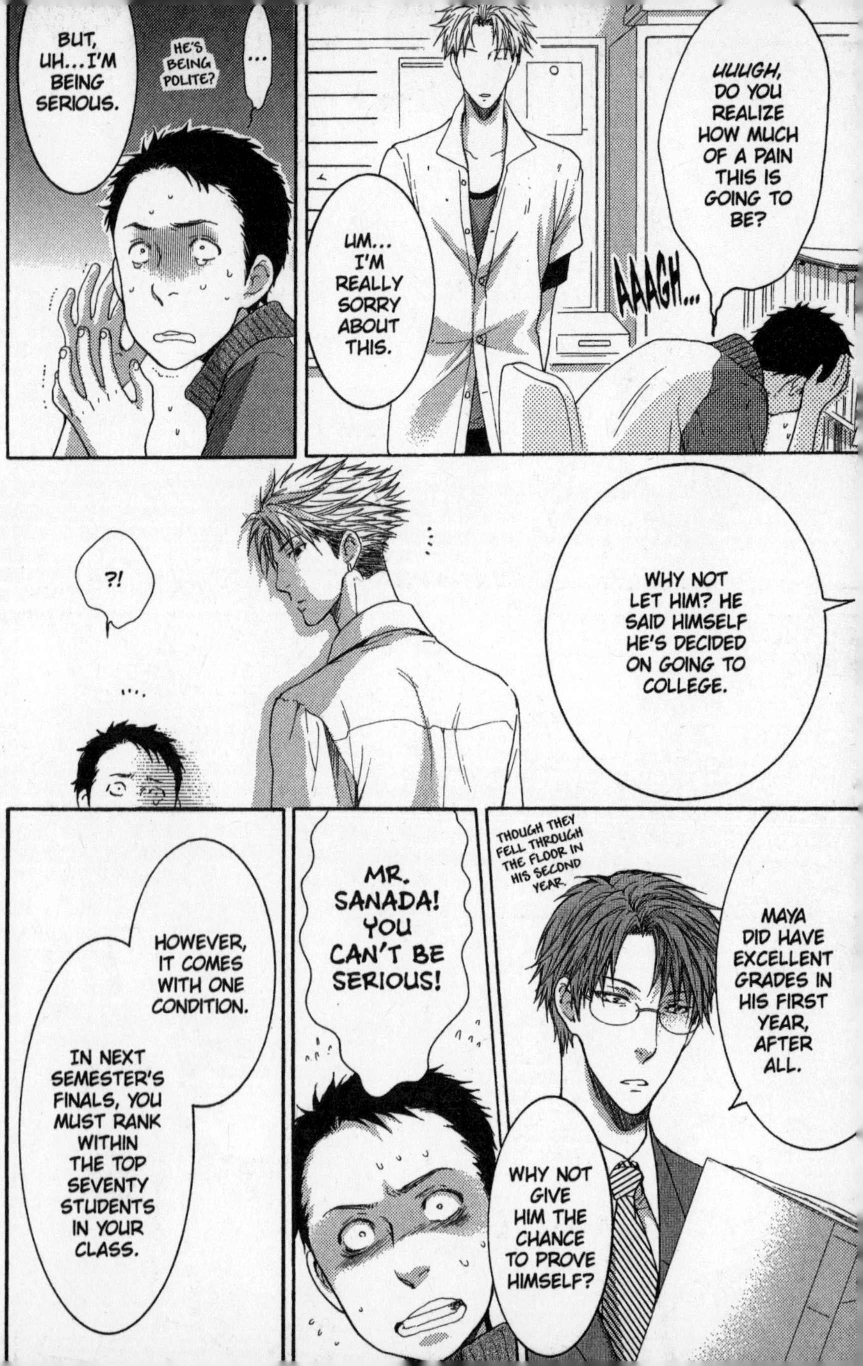
UUUGH, DO YOU REALIZE HOW MUCH OF A PAIN THIS IS GOING TO BE?
AAAGH...
UM... I'M REALLY SORRY ABOUT THIS.
...
HE'S BEING POLITE?
BUT, UH...I'M BEING SERIOUS.
WHY NOT LET HIM? HE SAID HIMSELF HE'S DECIDED ON GOING TO COLLEGE.
?!
...
MAYA DID HAVE EXCELLENT GRADES IN HIS FIRST YEAR, AFTER ALL.
THOUGH THEY FELL THROUGH THE FLOOR IN HIS SECOND YEAR.
WHY NOT GIVE HIM THE CHANCE TO PROVE HIMSELF?
MR. SANADA! YOU CAN'T BE SERIOUS!
HOWEVER, IT COMES WITH ONE CONDITION.
IN NEXT SEMESTER'S FINALS, YOU MUST RANK WITHIN THE TOP SEVENTY STUDENTS IN YOUR CLASS.

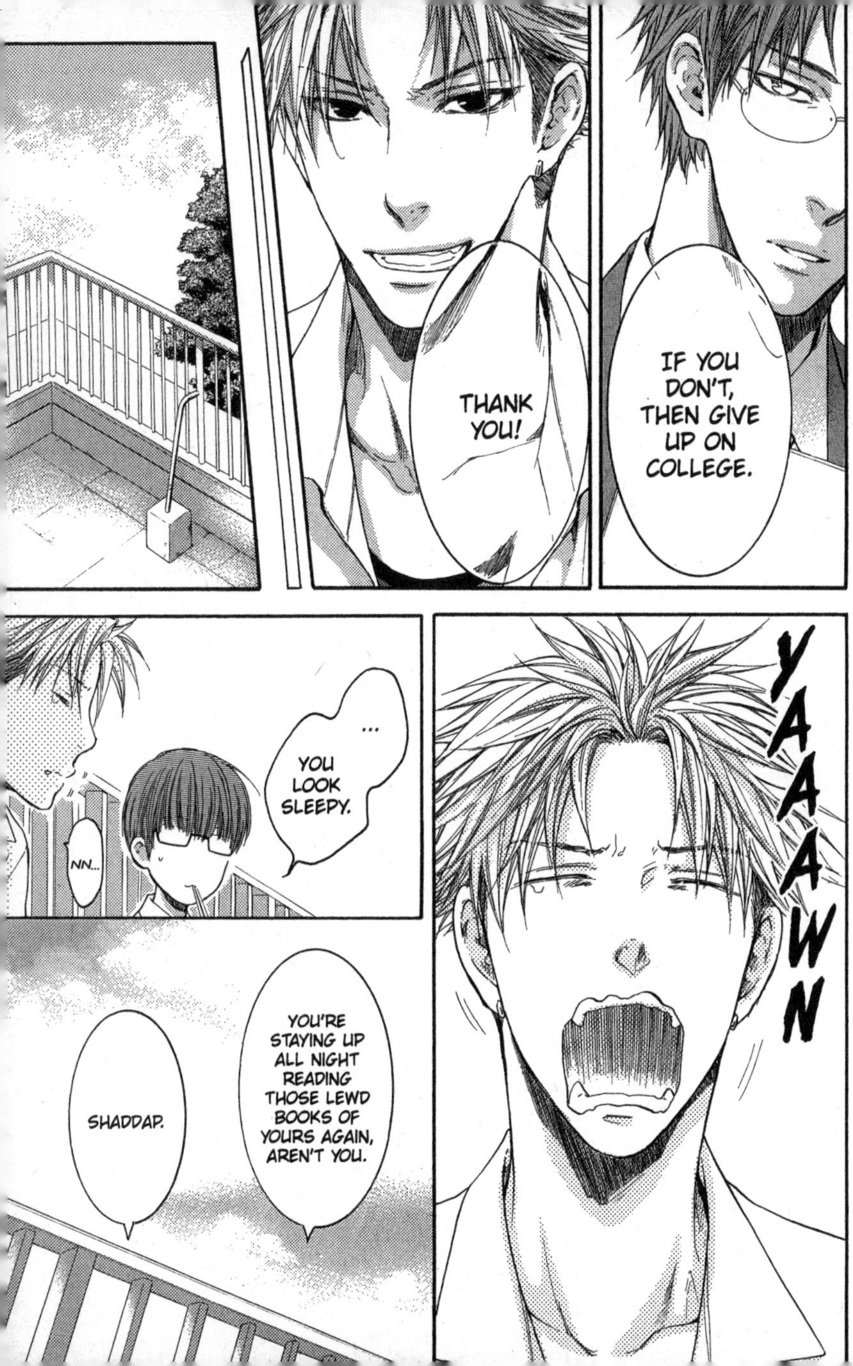
IF YOU DON'T, THEN GIVE UP ON COLLEGE.
THANK YOU!
YAAAWN
... YOU LOOK SLEEPY.
NN...
YOU'RE STAYING UP ALL NIGHT READING THOSE LEWD BOOKS OF YOURS AGAIN, AREN'T YOU.
SHADDAP.

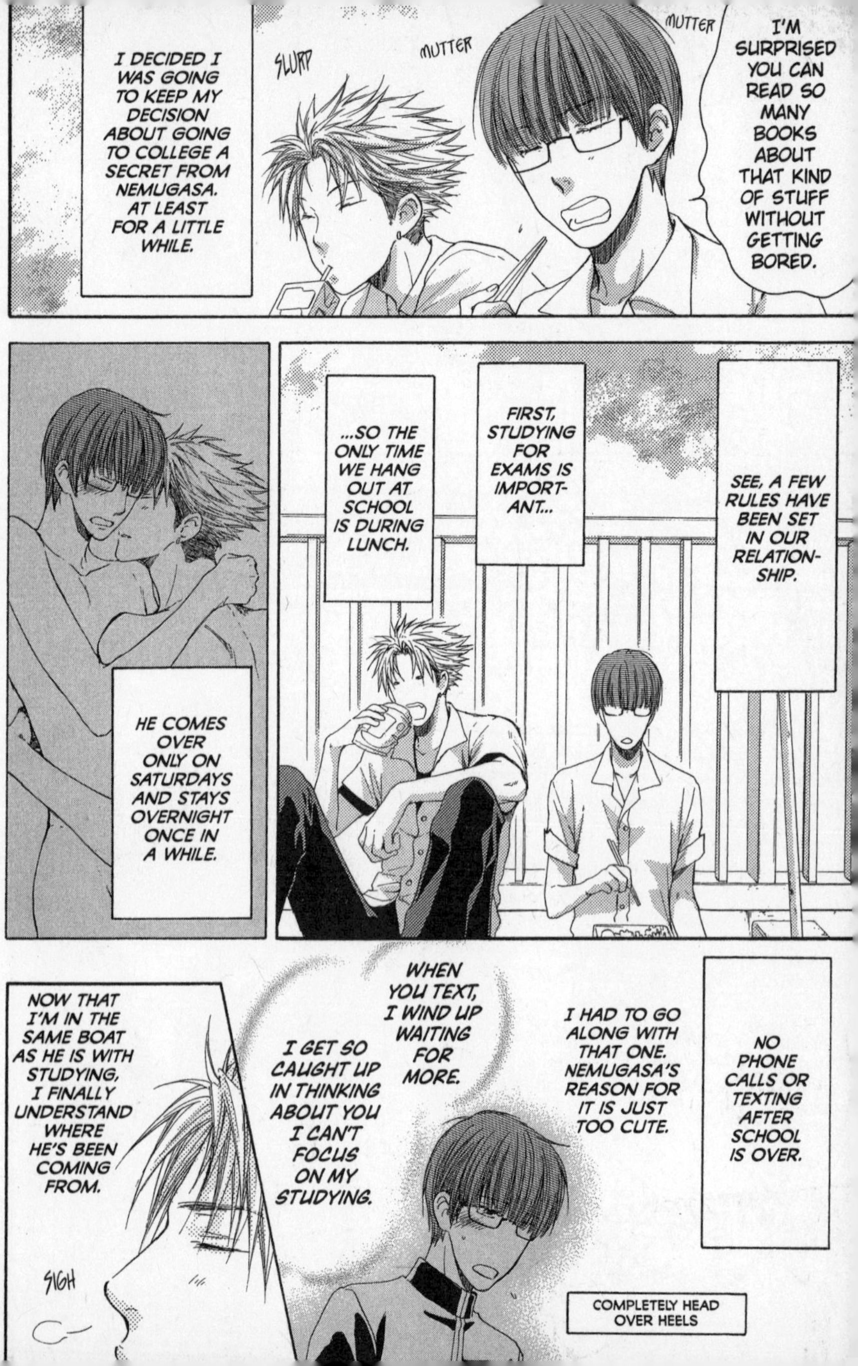
MUTTER
I'M SURPRISED YOU CAN READ SO MANY BOOKS ABOUT THAT KIND OF STUFF WITHOUT GETTING BORED.
MUTTER
SLURP
I DECIDED I WAS GOING TO KEEP MY DECISION ABOUT GOING TO COLLEGE A SECRET FROM NEMUGASA. AT LEAST FOR A LITTLE WHILE.
SEE, A FEW RULES HAVE BEEN SET IN OUR RELATIONSHIP.
FIRST, STUDYING FOR EXAMS IS IMPORTANT...
...SO THE ONLY TIME WE HANG OUT AT SCHOOL IS DURING LUNCH.
HE COMES OVER ONLY ON SATURDAYS AND STAYS OVERNIGHT ONCE IN A WHILE.
NO PHONE CALLS OR TEXTING AFTER SCHOOL IS OVER.
I HAD TO GO ALONG WITH THAT ONE. NEMUGASA'S REASON FOR IT IS JUST TOO CUTE.
WHEN YOU TEXT, I WIND UP WAITING FOR MORE.
I GET SO CAUGHT UP IN THINKING ABOUT YOU I CAN'T FOCUS ON MY STUDYING.
NOW THAT I'M IN THE SAME BOAT AS HE IS WITH STUDYING, I FINALLY UNDERSTAND WHERE HE'S BEEN COMING FROM.
SIGH
COMPLETELY HEAD OVER HEELS

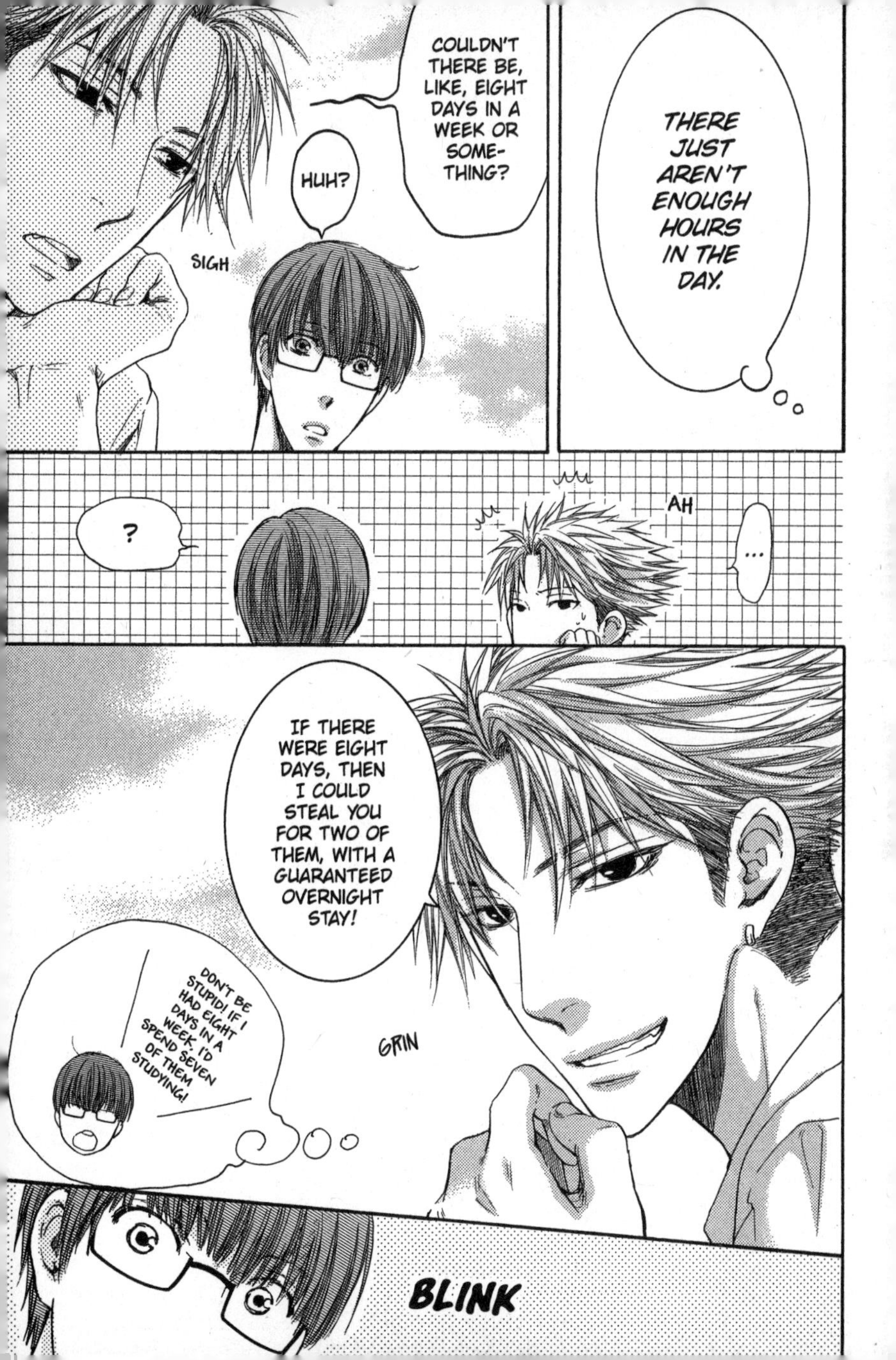
THERE JUST AREN'T ENOUGH HOURS IN THE DAY.
COULDN'T THERE BE, LIKE, EIGHT DAYS IN A WEEK OR SOME-THING?
HUH?
SIGH
...
AH
?
IF THERE WERE EIGHT DAYS, THEN I COULD STEAL YOU FOR TWO OF THEM, WITH A GUARANTEED OVERNIGHT STAY!
GRIN
DON'T BE STUPID! IF I HAD EIGHT DAYS IN A WEEK I'D SPEND SEVEN OF THEM STUDYING!
BLINK

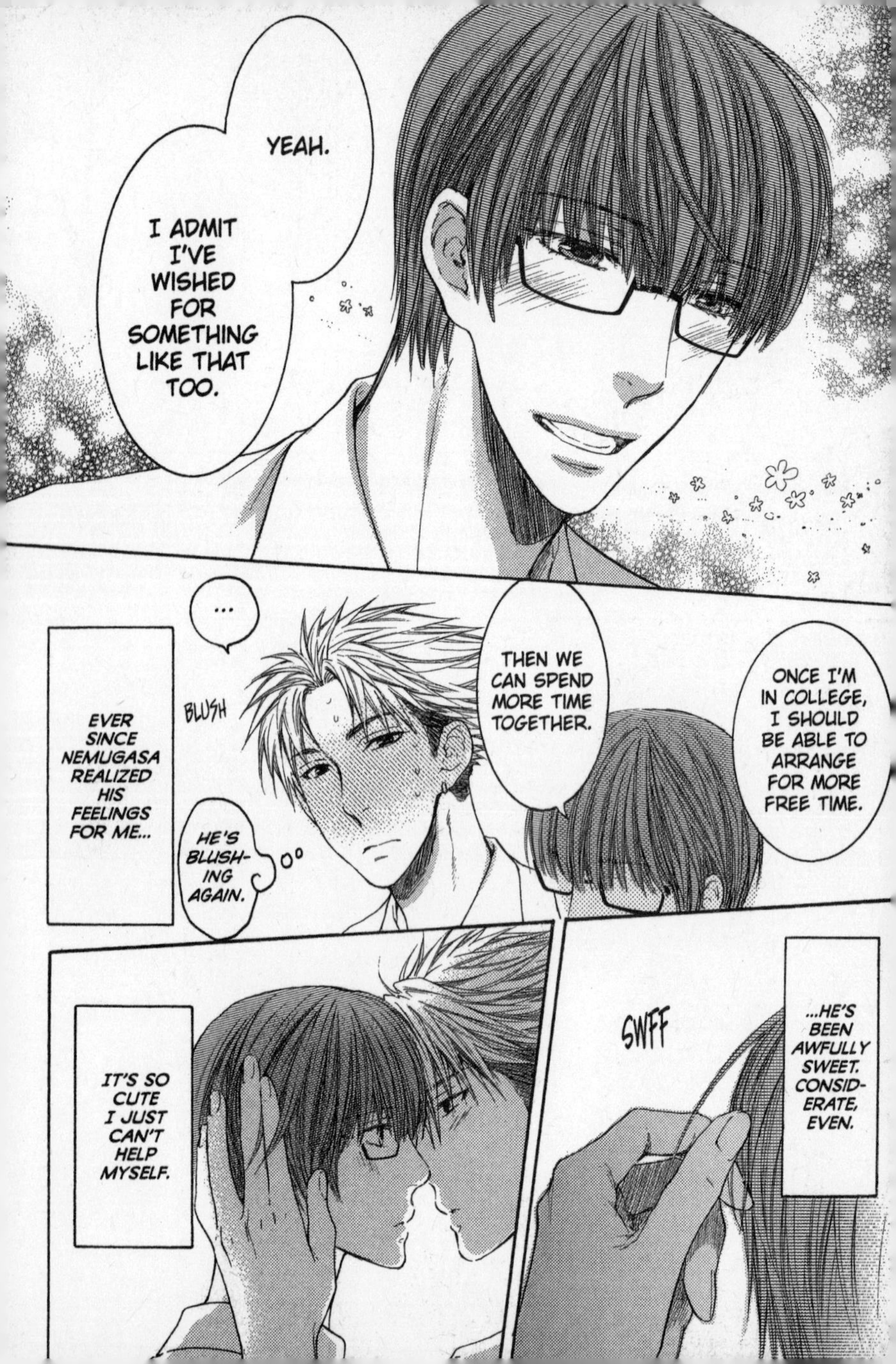
YEAH.
I ADMIT I'VE WISHED FOR SOMETHING LIKE THAT TOO.
ONCE I'M IN COLLEGE, I SHOULD BE ABLE TO ARRANGE FOR MORE FREE TIME.
THEN WE CAN SPEND MORE TIME TOGETHER.
...
BLUSH
EVER SINCE NEMUGASA REALIZED HIS FEELINGS FOR ME...
HE'S BLUSHING AGAIN.
SWFF
...HE'S BEEN AWFULLY SWEET. CONSIDERATE, EVEN.
IT'S SO CUTE I JUST CAN'T HELP MYSELF.

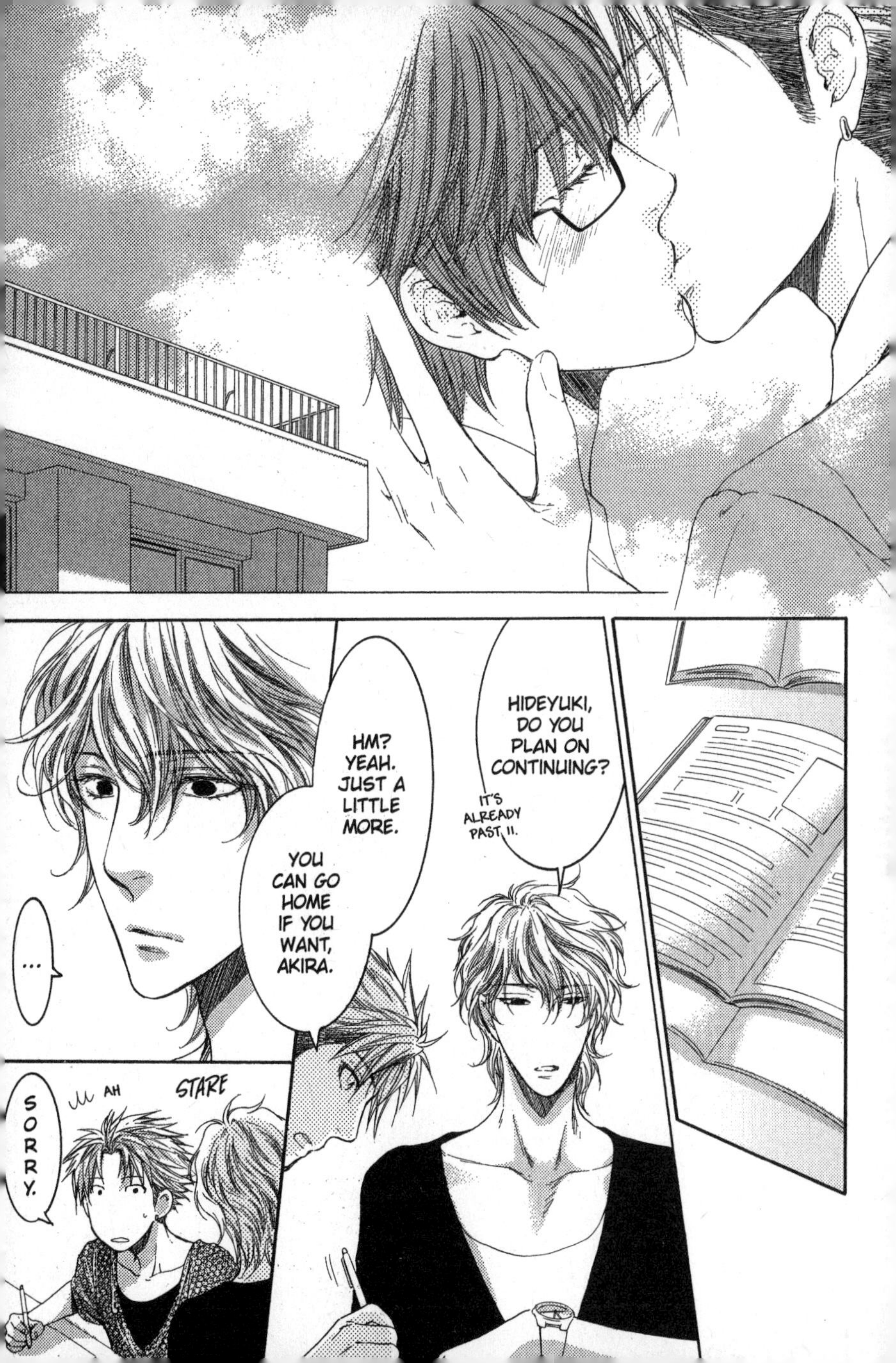
HIDEYUKI, DO YOU PLAN ON CONTINUING?
IT'S ALREADY PAST 11.
HM? YEAH. JUST A LITTLE MORE.
YOU CAN GO HOME IF YOU WANT, AKIRA.
...
STARE
AH
SORRY.

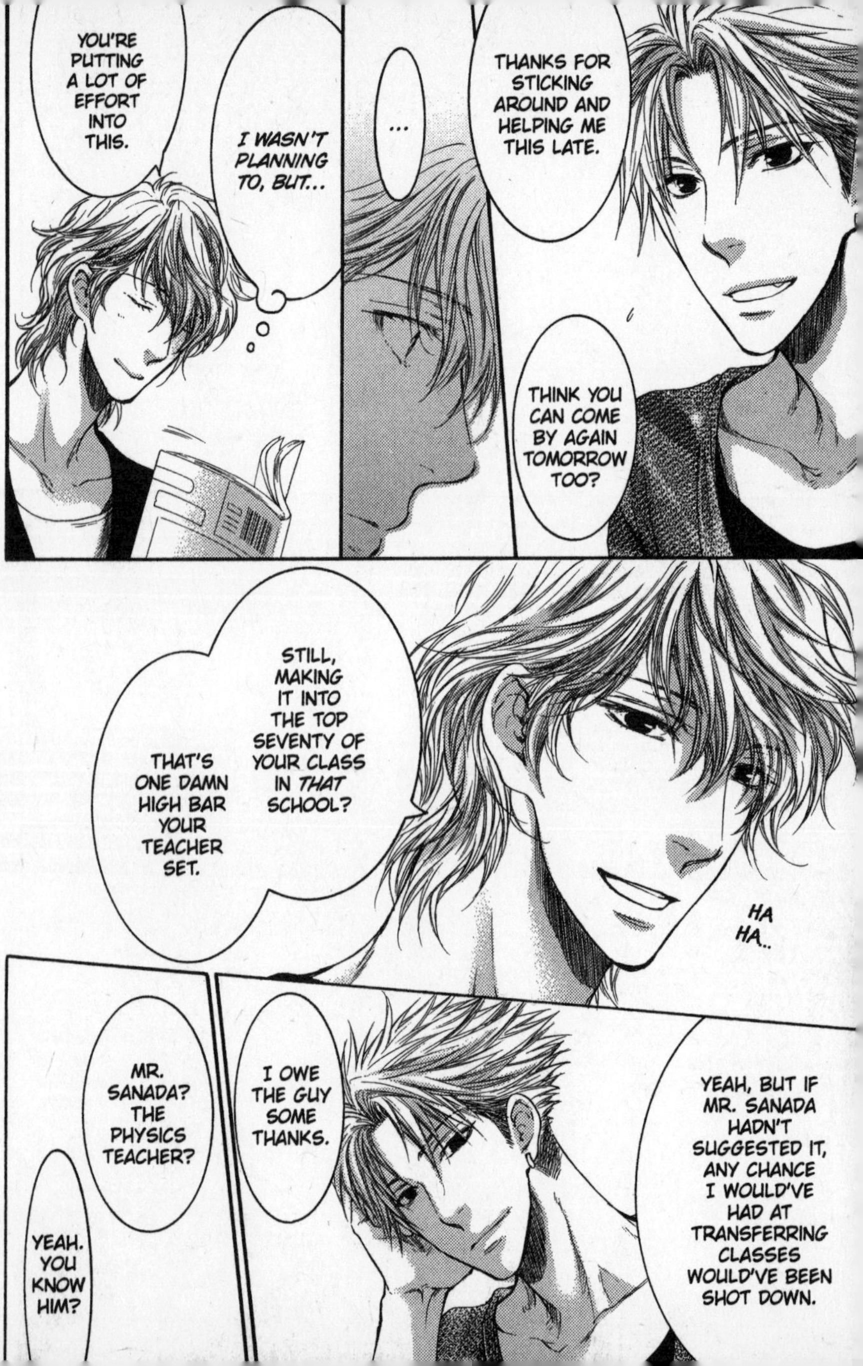
THANKS FOR STICKING AROUND AND HELPING ME THIS LATE.
THINK YOU CAN COME BY AGAIN TOMORROW TOO?
...
I WASN'T PLANNING TO, BUT...
YOU'RE PUTTING A LOT OF EFFORT INTO THIS.
HA HA..
STILL, MAKING IT INTO THE TOP SEVENTY OF YOUR CLASS IN *THAT* SCHOOL?
THAT'S ONE DAMN HIGH BAR YOUR TEACHER SET.
YEAH, BUT IF MR. SANADA HADN'T SUGGESTED IT, ANY CHANCE I WOULD'VE HAD AT TRANSFERRING CLASSES WOULD'VE BEEN SHOT DOWN.
I OWE THE GUY SOME THANKS.
MR. SANADA? THE PHYSICS TEACHER?
YEAH. YOU KNOW HIM?

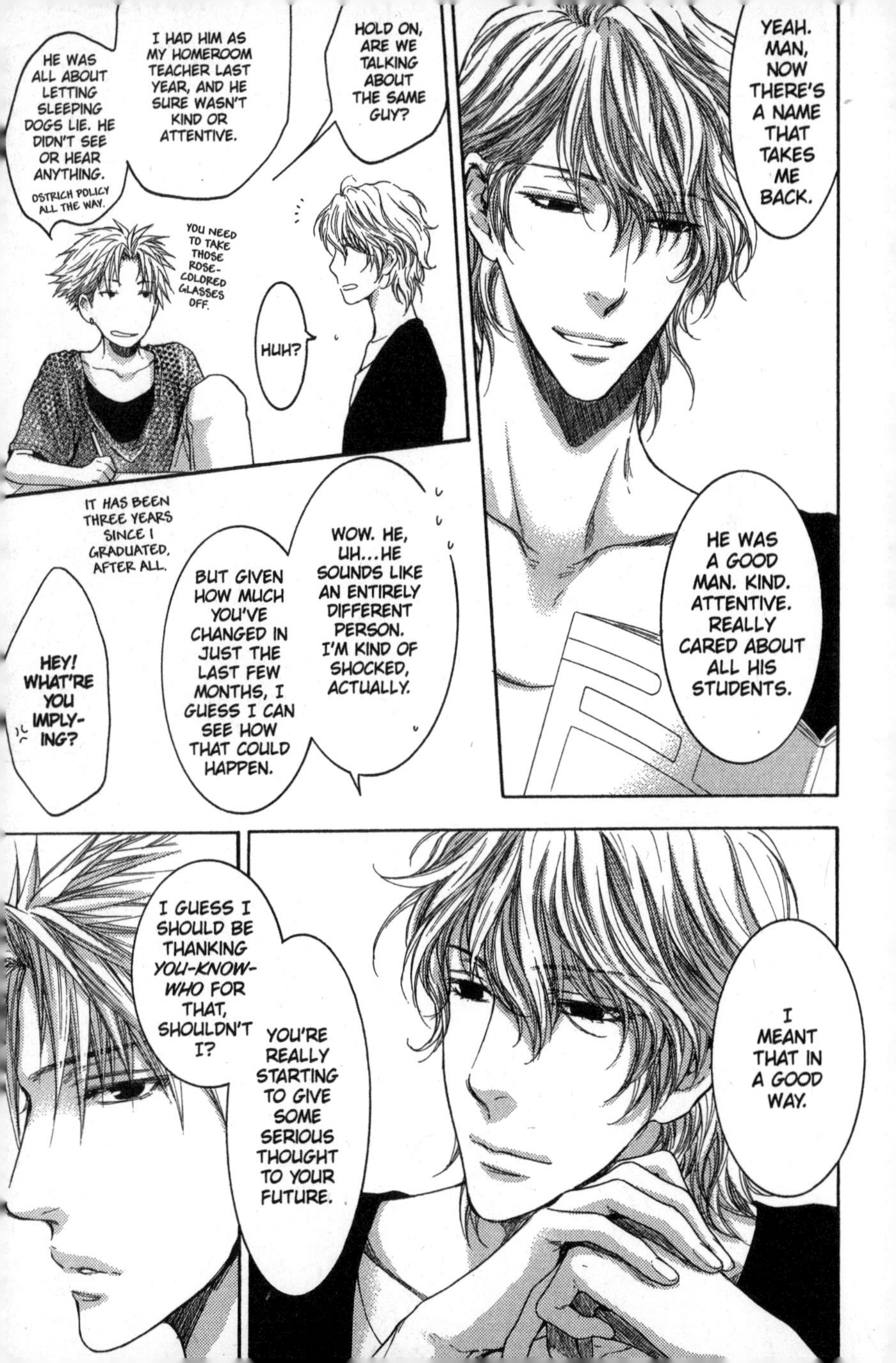

YEAH. MAN, NOW THERE'S A NAME THAT TAKES ME BACK.
HE WAS A GOOD MAN. KIND. ATTENTIVE. REALLY CARED ABOUT ALL HIS STUDENTS.
HOLD ON, ARE WE TALKING ABOUT THE SAME GUY?
I HAD HIM AS MY HOMEROOM TEACHER LAST YEAR, AND HE SURE WASN'T KIND OR ATTENTIVE.
HE WAS ALL ABOUT LETTING SLEEPING DOGS LIE. HE DIDN'T SEE OR HEAR ANYTHING.
OSTRICH POLICY ALL THE WAY.
YOU NEED TO TAKE THOSE ROSE-COLORED GLASSES OFF.
HUH?
WOW. HE, UH...HE SOUNDS LIKE AN ENTIRELY DIFFERENT PERSON. I'M KIND OF SHOCKED, ACTUALLY.
BUT GIVEN HOW MUCH YOU'VE CHANGED IN JUST THE LAST FEW MONTHS, I GUESS I CAN SEE HOW THAT COULD HAPPEN.
IT HAS BEEN THREE YEARS SINCE I GRADUATED, AFTER ALL.
HEY! WHAT'RE YOU IMPLY-ING?
I MEANT THAT IN A GOOD WAY.
YOU'RE REALLY STARTING TO GIVE SOME SERIOUS THOUGHT TO YOUR FUTURE.
I GUESS I SHOULD BE THANKING *YOU-KNOW-WHO* FOR THAT, SHOULDN'T I?

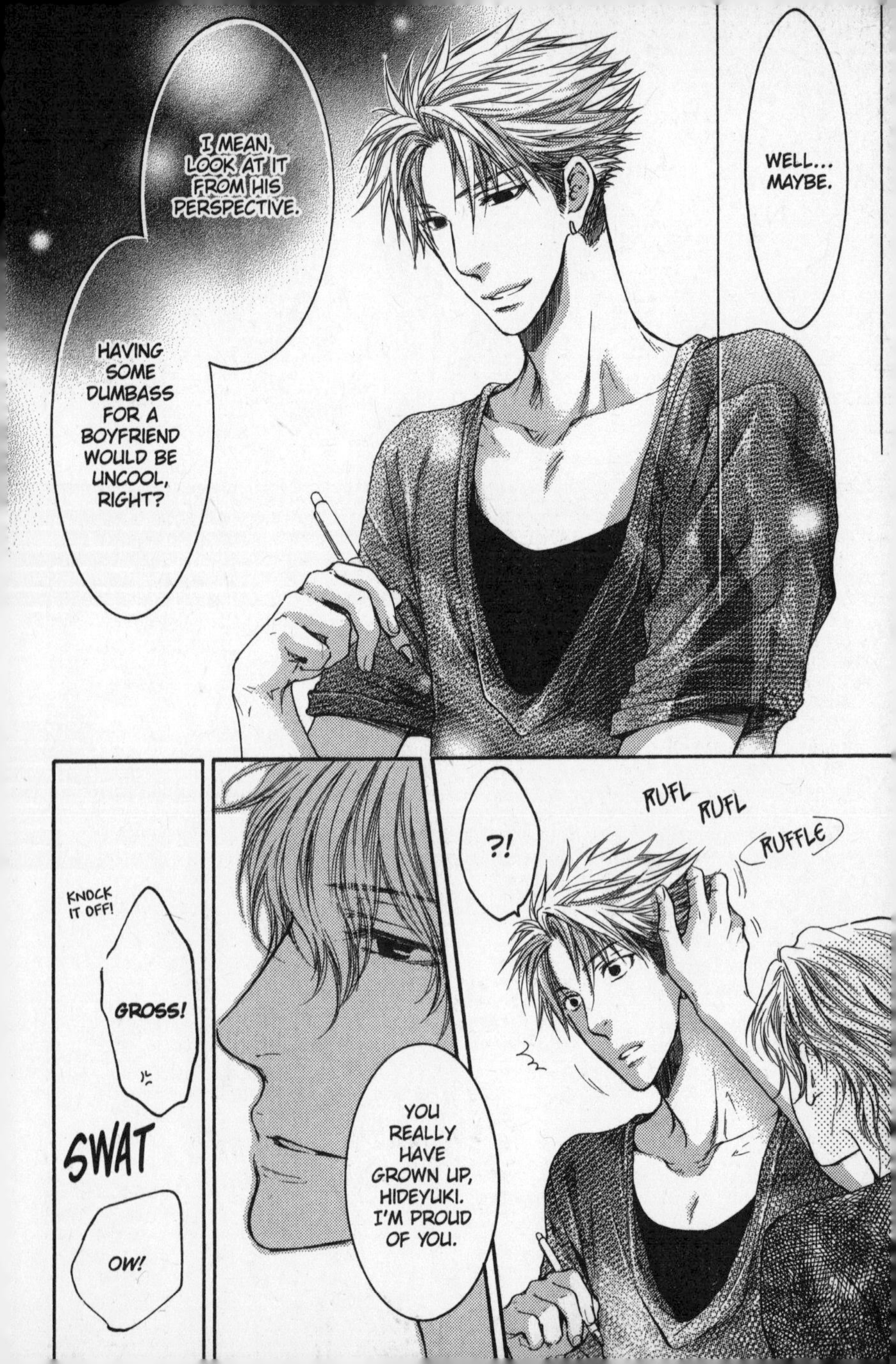
WELL... MAYBE.
I MEAN, LOOK AT IT FROM HIS PERSPECTIVE.
HAVING SOME DUMBASS FOR A BOYFRIEND WOULD BE UNCOOL, RIGHT?
?!
RUFL
RUFL
RUFFLE
YOU REALLY HAVE GROWN UP, HIDEYUKI. I'M PROUD OF YOU.
KNOCK IT OFF!
GROSS!
SWAT
OW!

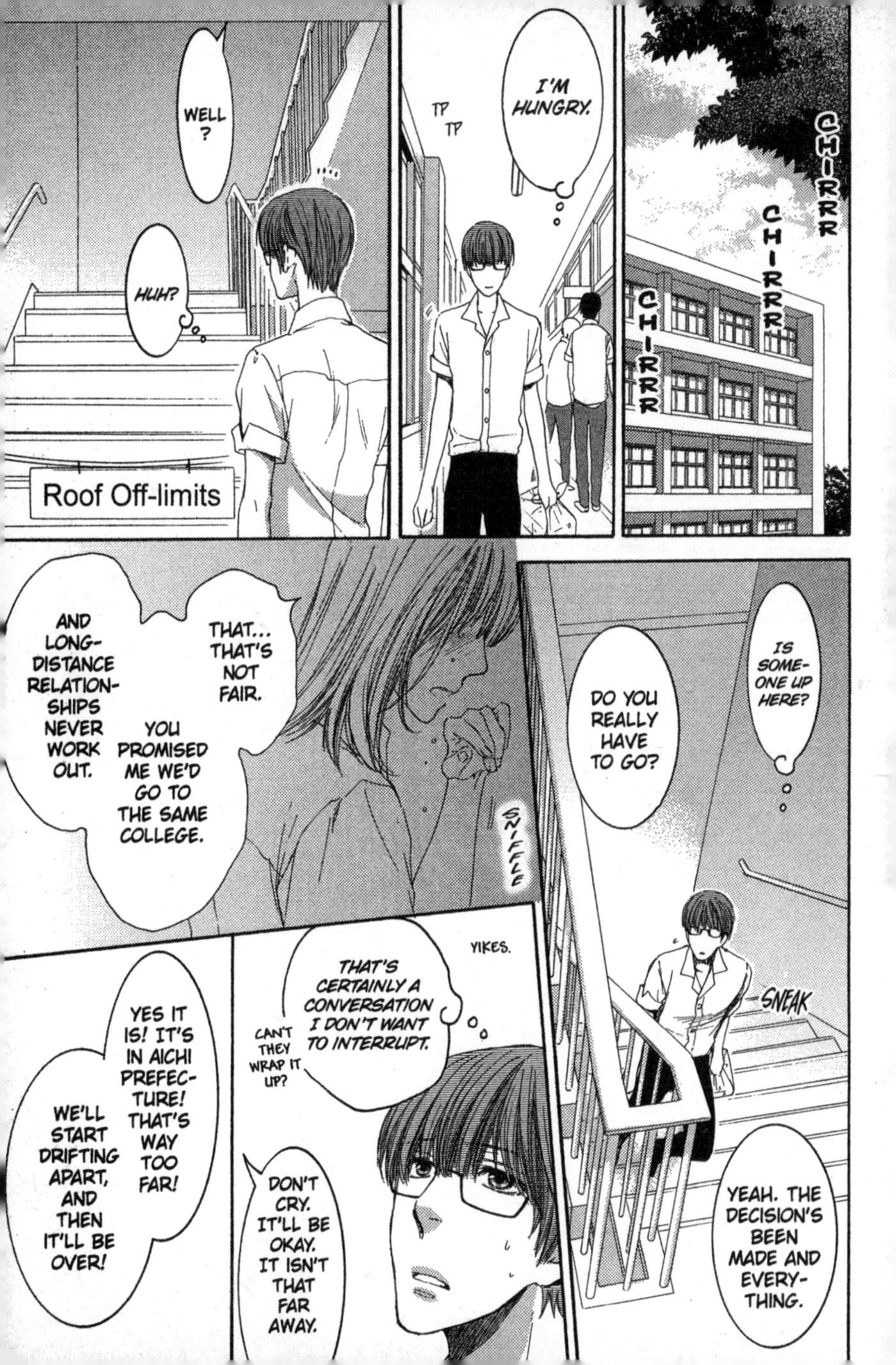
CHIRRR
CHIRRR
CHIRRR
I'M HUNGRY.
TP TP
WELL?
...
HUH?
Roof Off-limits
IS SOMEONE UP HERE?
DO YOU REALLY HAVE TO GO?
SNEAK
YEAH. THE DECISION'S BEEN MADE AND EVERYTHING.
THAT... THAT'S NOT FAIR.
YOU PROMISED ME WE'D GO TO THE SAME COLLEGE.
AND LONG-DISTANCE RELATIONSHIPS NEVER WORK OUT.
SNIFFLE
YIKES.
THAT'S CERTAINLY A CONVERSATION I DON'T WANT TO INTERRUPT.
CAN'T THEY WRAP IT UP?
DON'T CRY. IT'LL BE OKAY. IT ISN'T THAT FAR AWAY.
YES IT IS! IT'S IN AICHI PREFECTURE! THAT'S WAY TOO FAR!
WE'LL START DRIFTING APART, AND THEN IT'LL BE OVER!

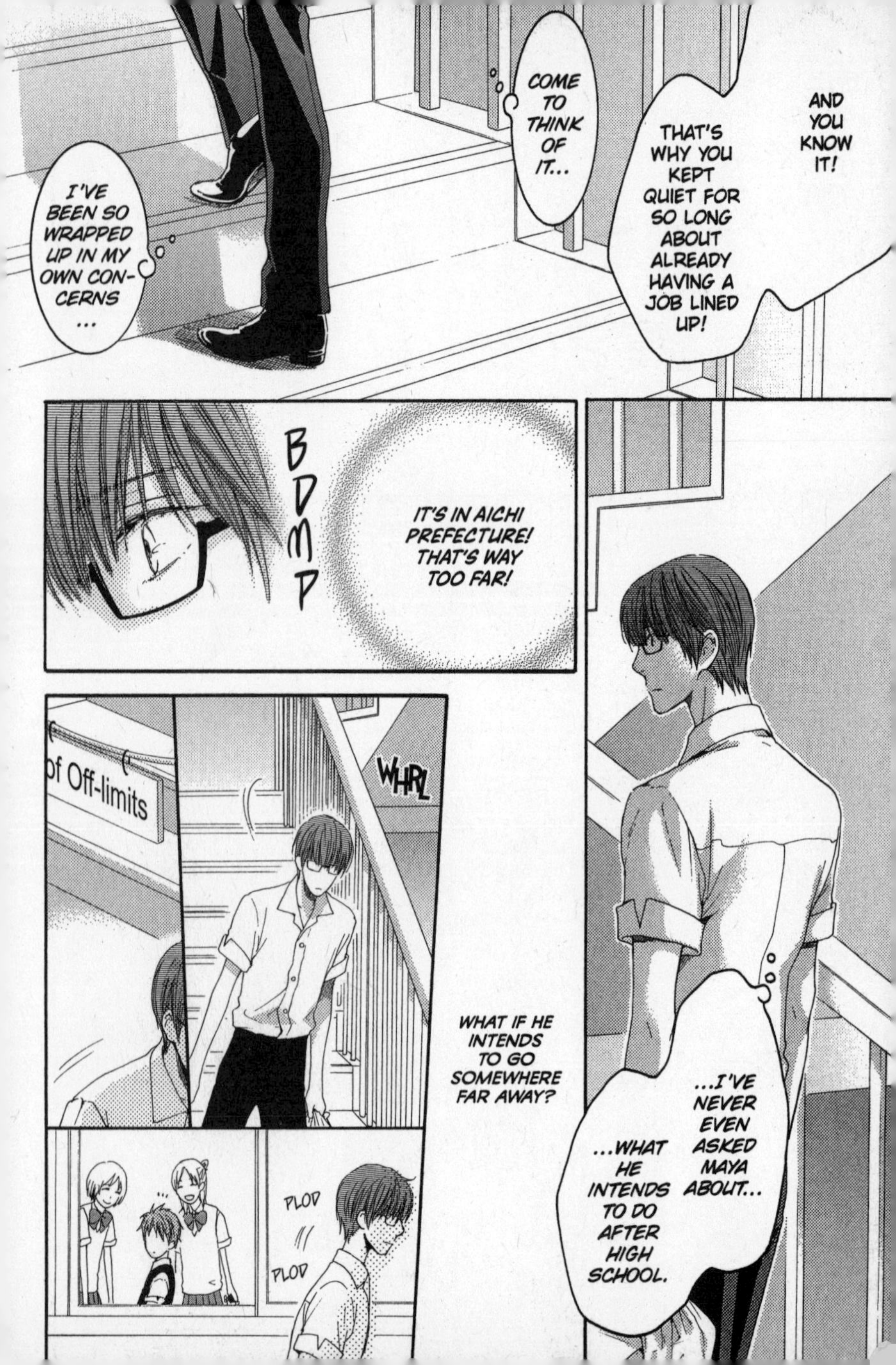
AND YOU KNOW IT!
THAT'S WHY YOU KEPT QUIET FOR SO LONG ABOUT ALREADY HAVING A JOB LINED UP!
COME TO THINK OF IT...
I'VE BEEN SO WRAPPED UP IN MY OWN CON-CERNS ...
...I'VE NEVER EVEN ASKED MAYA ABOUT...
...WHAT HE INTENDS TO DO AFTER HIGH SCHOOL.
BDMP
IT'S IN AICHI PREFECTURE! THAT'S WAY TOO FAR!
WHRL
of Off-limits
WHAT IF HE INTENDS TO GO SOMEWHERE FAR AWAY?
PLOD
PLOD

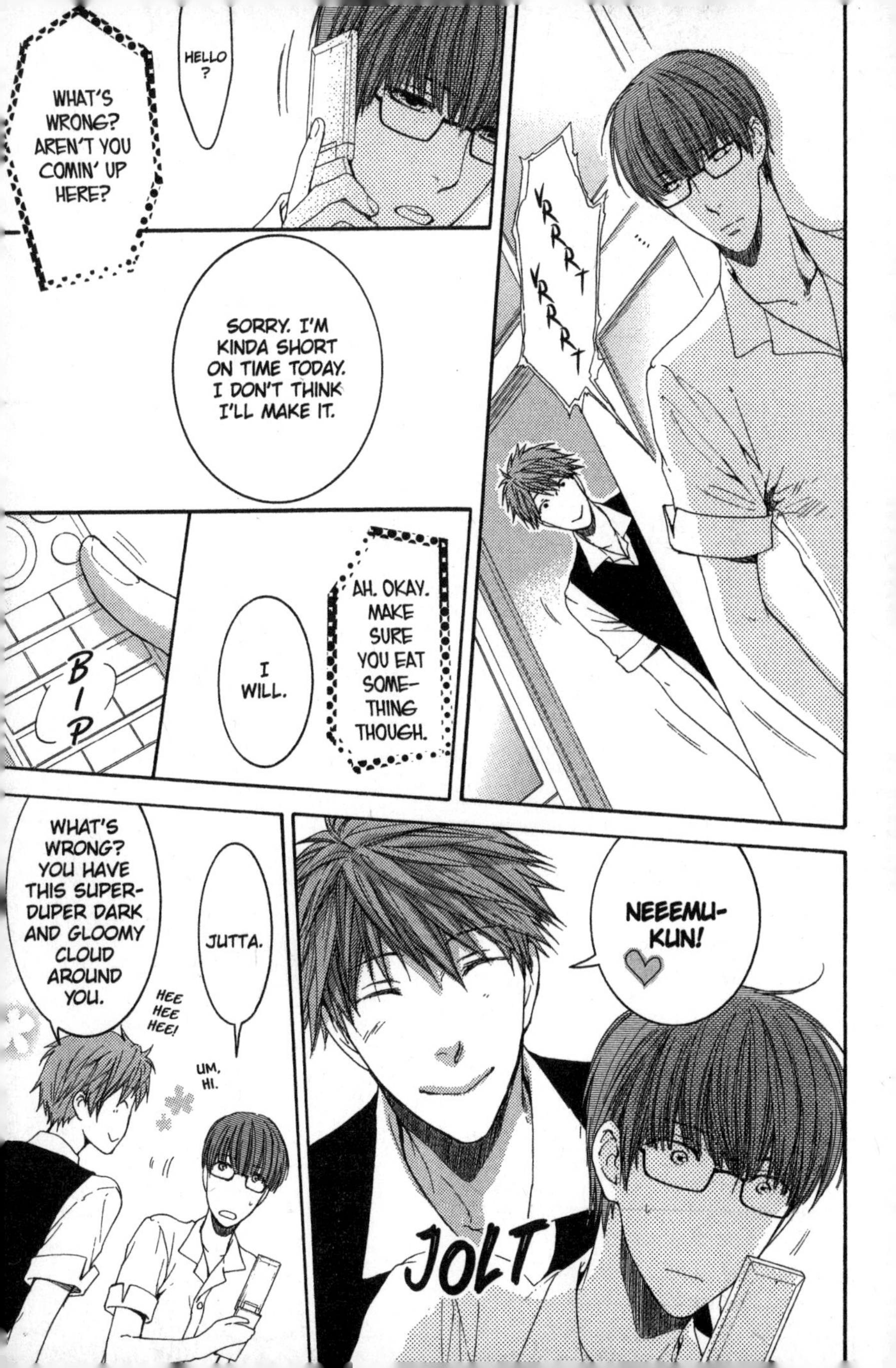
VRRRRT VRRRRT
...
HELLO?
WHAT'S WRONG? AREN'T YOU COMIN' UP HERE?
SORRY. I'M KINDA SHORT ON TIME TODAY. I DON'T THINK I'LL MAKE IT.
AH. OKAY. MAKE SURE YOU EAT SOMETHING THOUGH.
I WILL.
BIP
NEEEMU-KUN!
JOLT
JUTTA.
WHAT'S WRONG? YOU HAVE THIS SUPER-DUPER DARK AND GLOOMY CLOUD AROUND YOU.
HEE HEE HEE!
UM, HI.

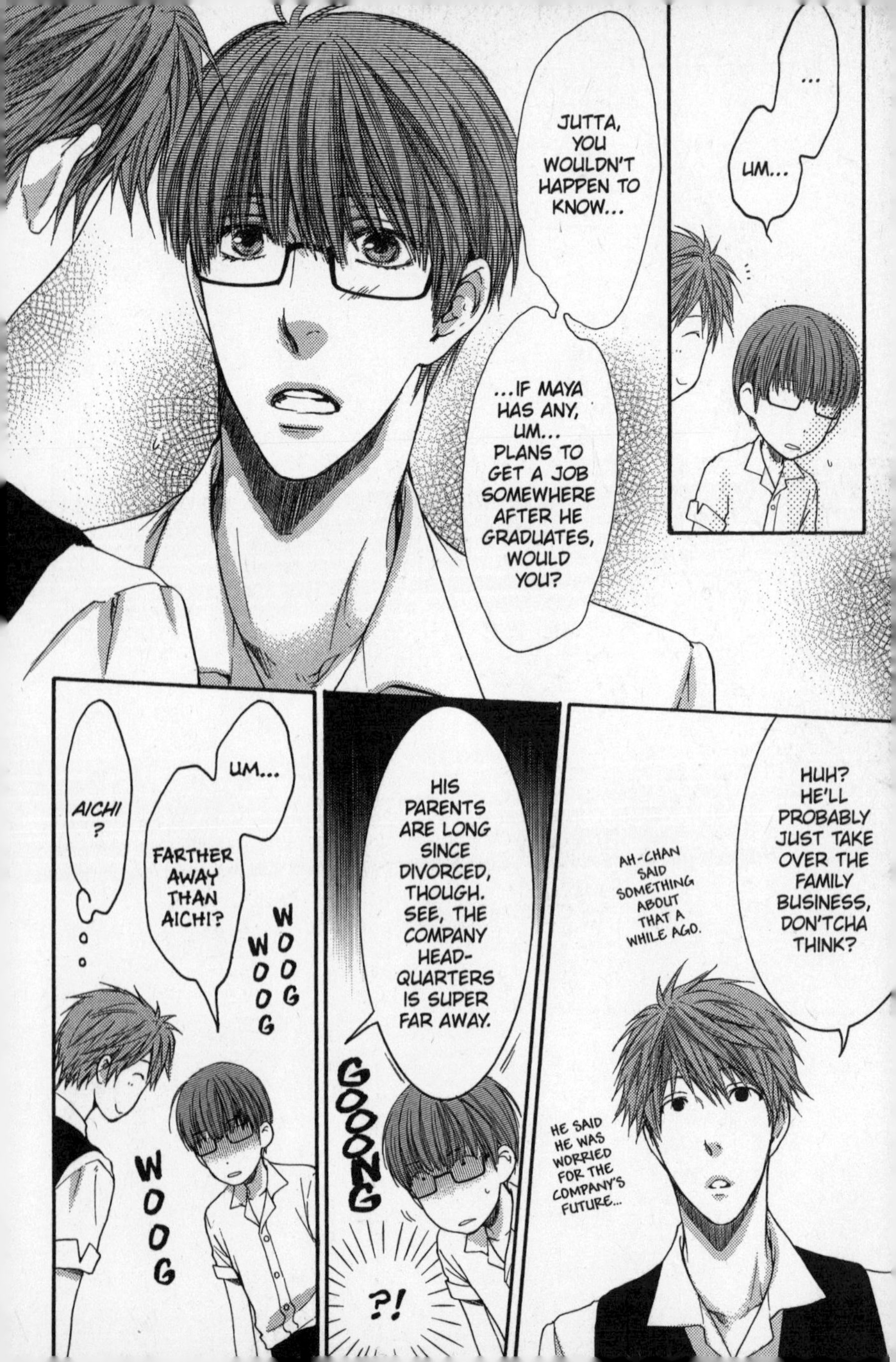
...
UM...
JUTTA, YOU WOULDN'T HAPPEN TO KNOW...
...IF MAYA HAS ANY, UM... PLANS TO GET A JOB SOMEWHERE AFTER HE GRADUATES, WOULD YOU?
HUH? HE'LL PROBABLY JUST TAKE OVER THE FAMILY BUSINESS, DON'TCHA THINK?
AH-CHAN SAID SOMETHING ABOUT THAT A WHILE AGO.
HE SAID HE WAS WORRIED FOR THE COMPANY'S FUTURE...
HIS PARENTS ARE LONG SINCE DIVORCED, THOUGH. SEE, THE COMPANY HEAD-QUARTERS IS SUPER FAR AWAY.
GOOOONG
?!
UM... FARTHER AWAY THAN AICHI?
AICHI?
WOOG WOOG WOOG
WOOG

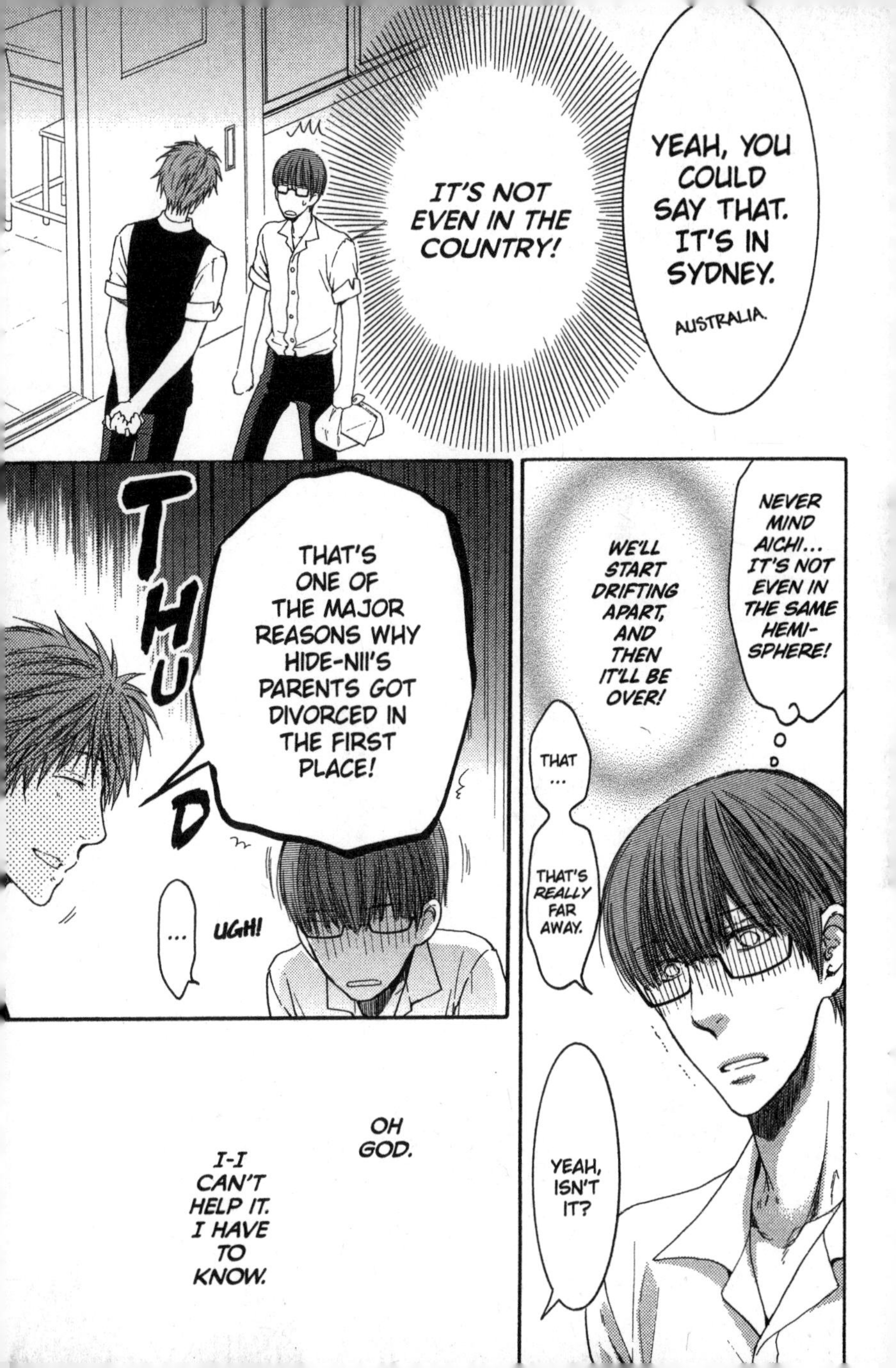
YEAH, YOU COULD SAY THAT. IT'S IN SYDNEY.
AUSTRALIA.
IT'S NOT EVEN IN THE COUNTRY!
NEVER MIND AICHI... IT'S NOT EVEN IN THE SAME HEMI-SPHERE!
WE'LL START DRIFTING APART, AND THEN IT'LL BE OVER!
THAT... THAT'S REALLY FAR AWAY.
YEAH, ISN'T IT?
THUD
THAT'S ONE OF THE MAJOR REASONS WHY HIDE-NII'S PARENTS GOT DIVORCED IN THE FIRST PLACE!
UGH!
...
OH GOD.
I-I CAN'T HELP IT. I HAVE TO KNOW.

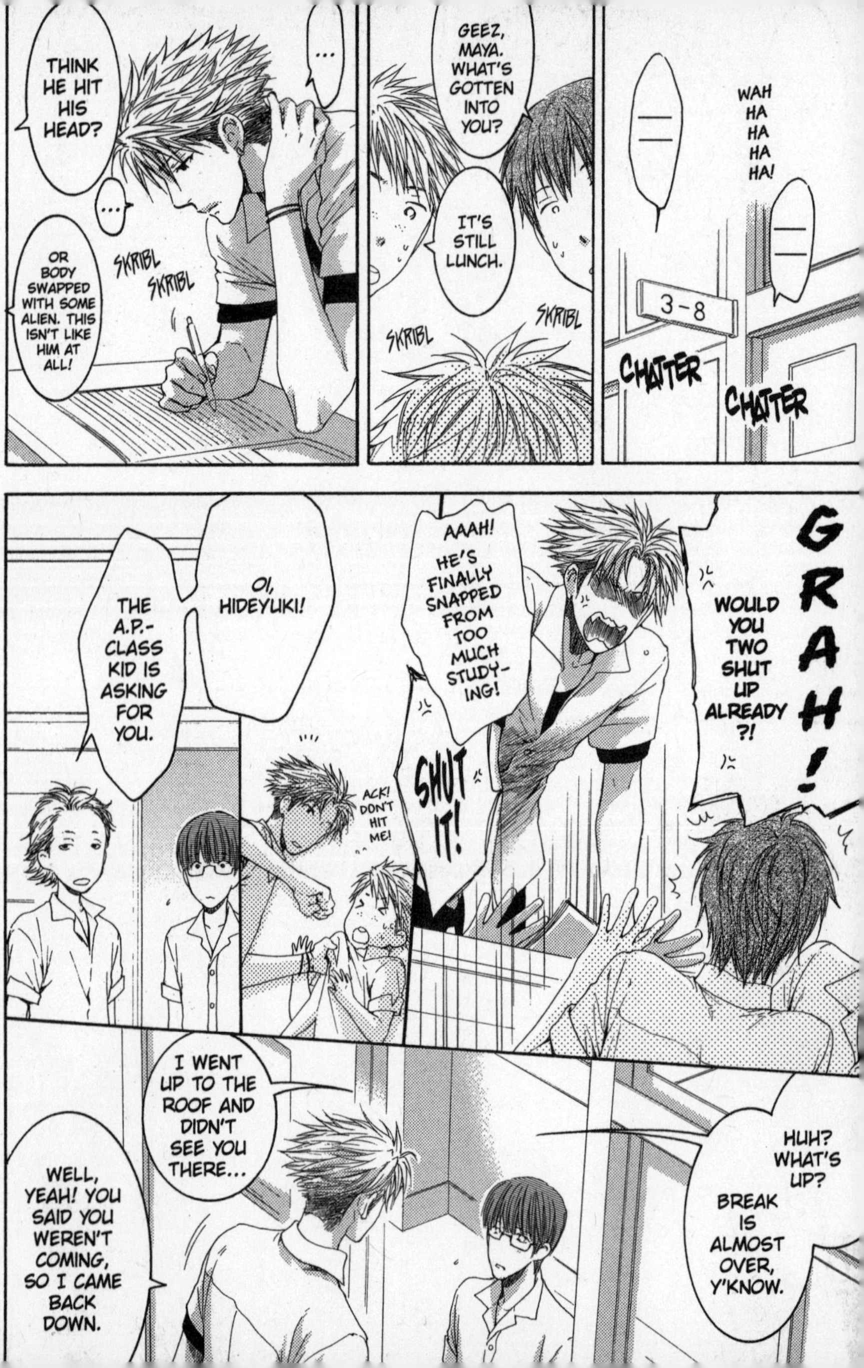
——
WAH HA HA HA HA!
——
3-8
CHATTER
CHATTER
GEEZ, MAYA. WHAT'S GOTTEN INTO YOU?
IT'S STILL LUNCH.
SKRIBL
SKRIBL
...
THINK HE HIT HIS HEAD?
...
OR BODY SWAPPED WITH SOME ALIEN. THIS ISN'T LIKE HIM AT ALL!
SKRIBL
SKRIBL
GRAH!
WOULD YOU TWO SHUT UP ALREADY?!
AAAH! HE'S FINALLY SNAPPED FROM TOO MUCH STUDYING!
SHUT IT!
ACK! DON'T HIT ME!
OI, HIDEYUKI!
THE A.P.-CLASS KID IS ASKING FOR YOU.
HUH? WHAT'S UP?
BREAK IS ALMOST OVER, Y'KNOW.
I WENT UP TO THE ROOF AND DIDN'T SEE YOU THERE...
WELL, YEAH! YOU SAID YOU WEREN'T COMING, SO I CAME BACK DOWN.

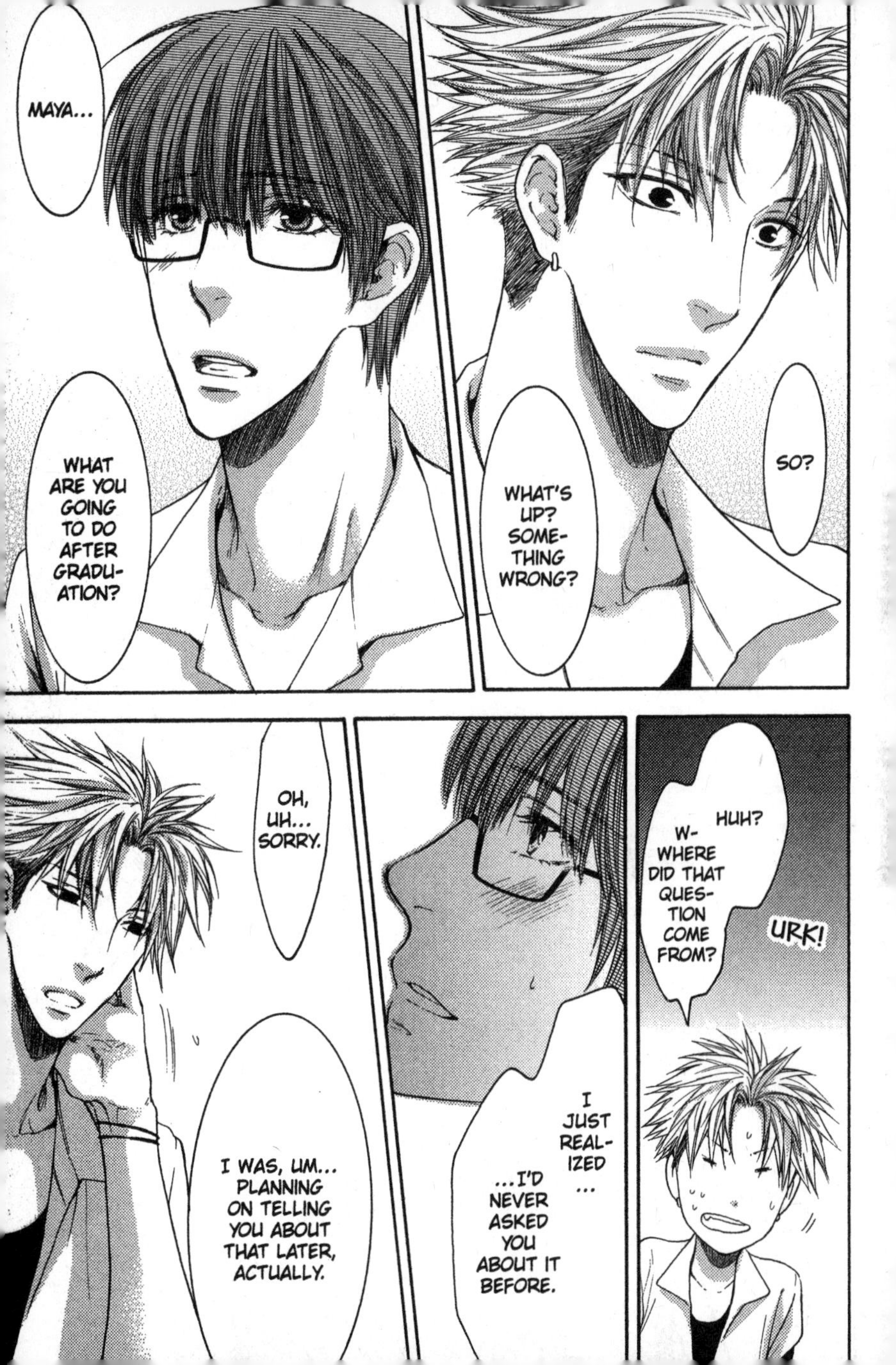
SO?
WHAT'S UP? SOME-THING WRONG?
MAYA...
WHAT ARE YOU GOING TO DO AFTER GRADU-ATION?
HUH? W-WHERE DID THAT QUES-TION COME FROM?
URK!
I JUST REAL-IZED...
...I'D NEVER ASKED YOU ABOUT IT BEFORE.
OH, UH... SORRY.
I WAS, UM... PLANNING ON TELLING YOU ABOUT THAT LATER, ACTUALLY.

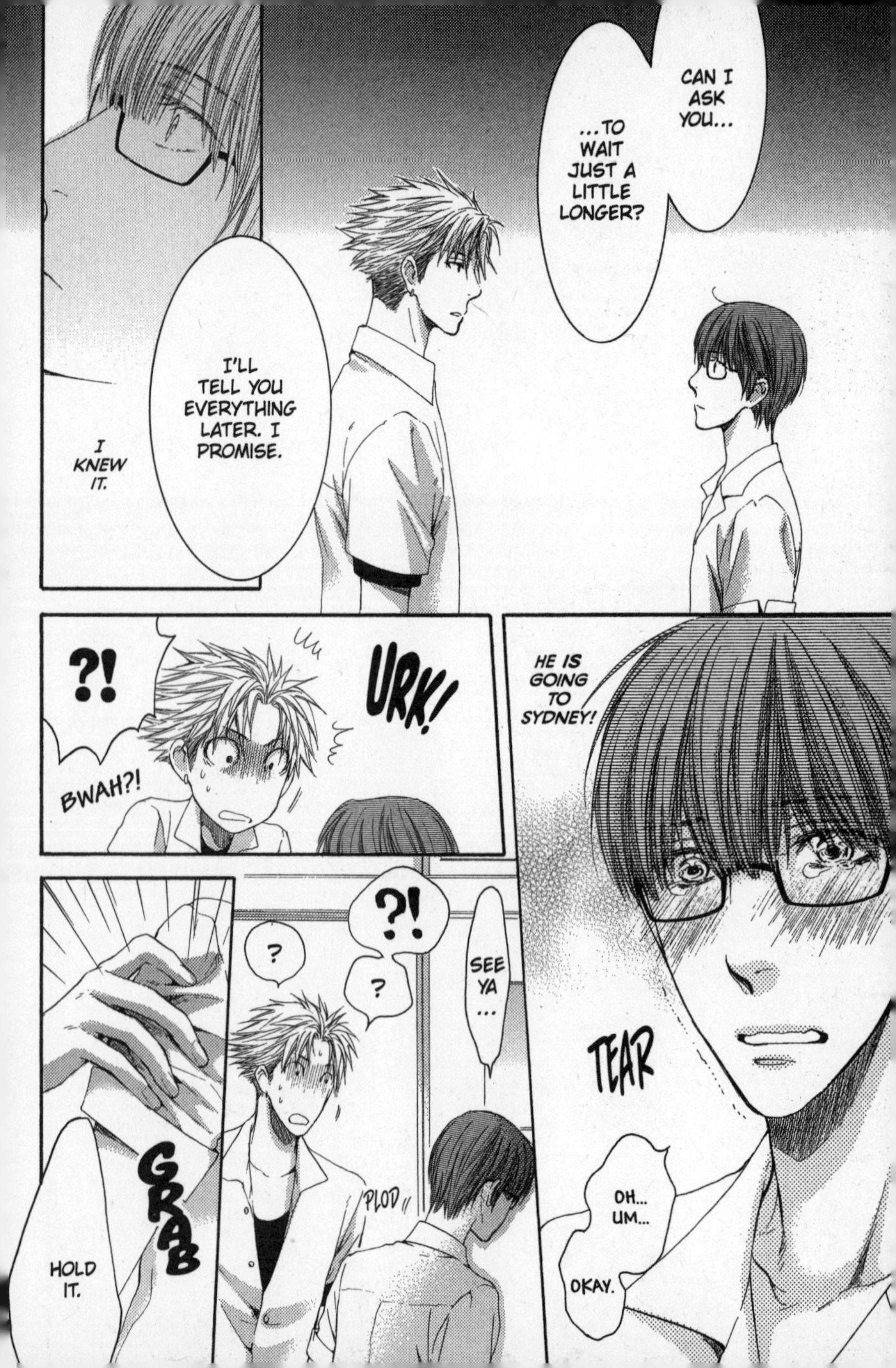
CAN I ASK YOU...
...TO WAIT JUST A LITTLE LONGER?
I'LL TELL YOU EVERYTHING LATER. I PROMISE.
I KNEW IT.
HE IS GOING TO SYDNEY!
TEAR
OH... UM...
OKAY.
URK!
?!
BWAH?!
SEE YA...
?!
?
?
PLOD
GRAB
HOLD IT.

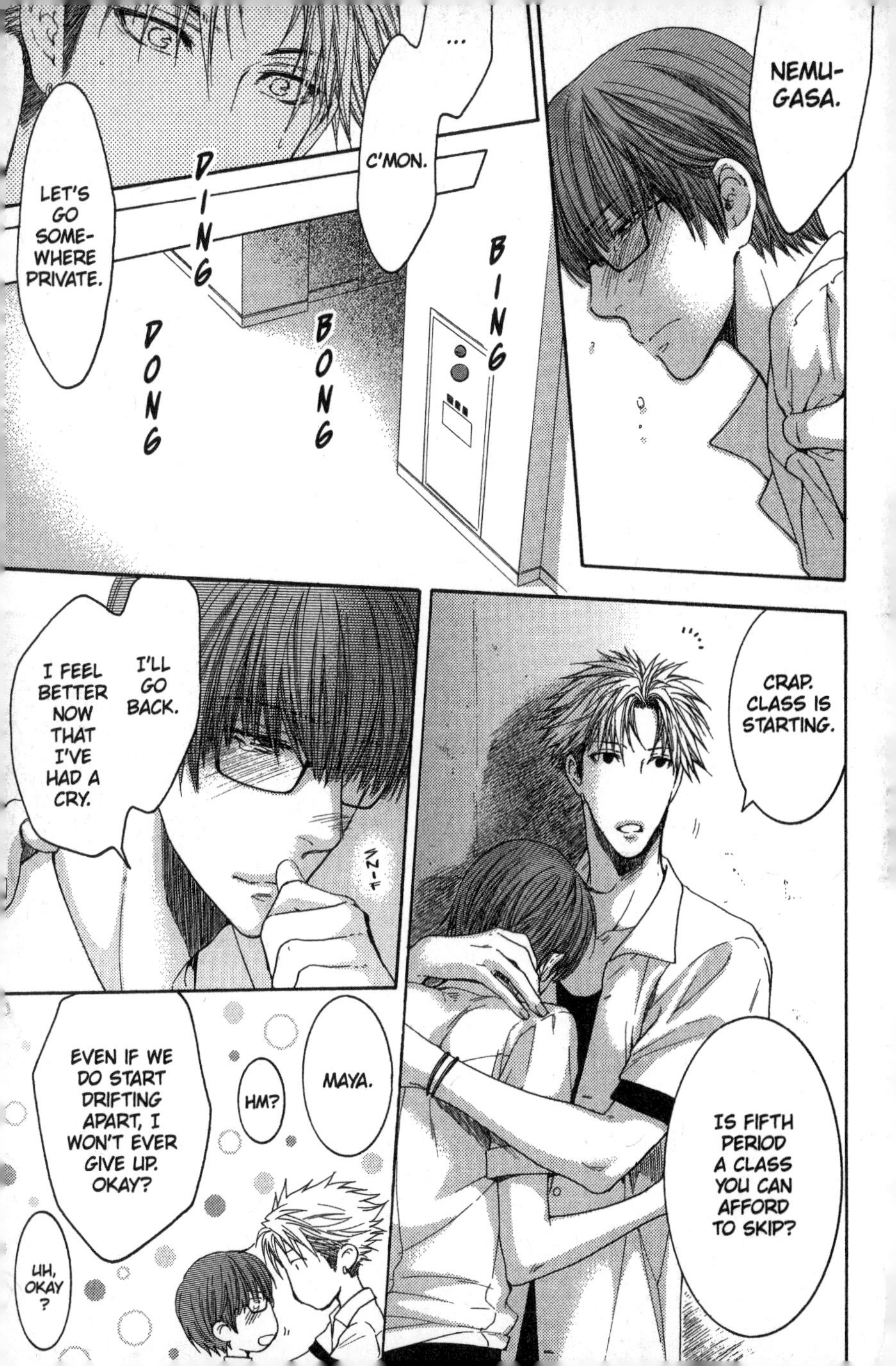
NEMU-GASA.
...
BING BONG
C'MON.
DING DONG
LET'S GO SOMEWHERE PRIVATE.
CRAP. CLASS IS STARTING.
IS FIFTH PERIOD A CLASS YOU CAN AFFORD TO SKIP?
I'LL GO BACK.
I FEEL BETTER NOW THAT I'VE HAD A CRY.
SNIF
MAYA.
HM?
EVEN IF WE DO START DRIFTING APART, I WON'T EVER GIVE UP. OKAY?
UH, OKAY?

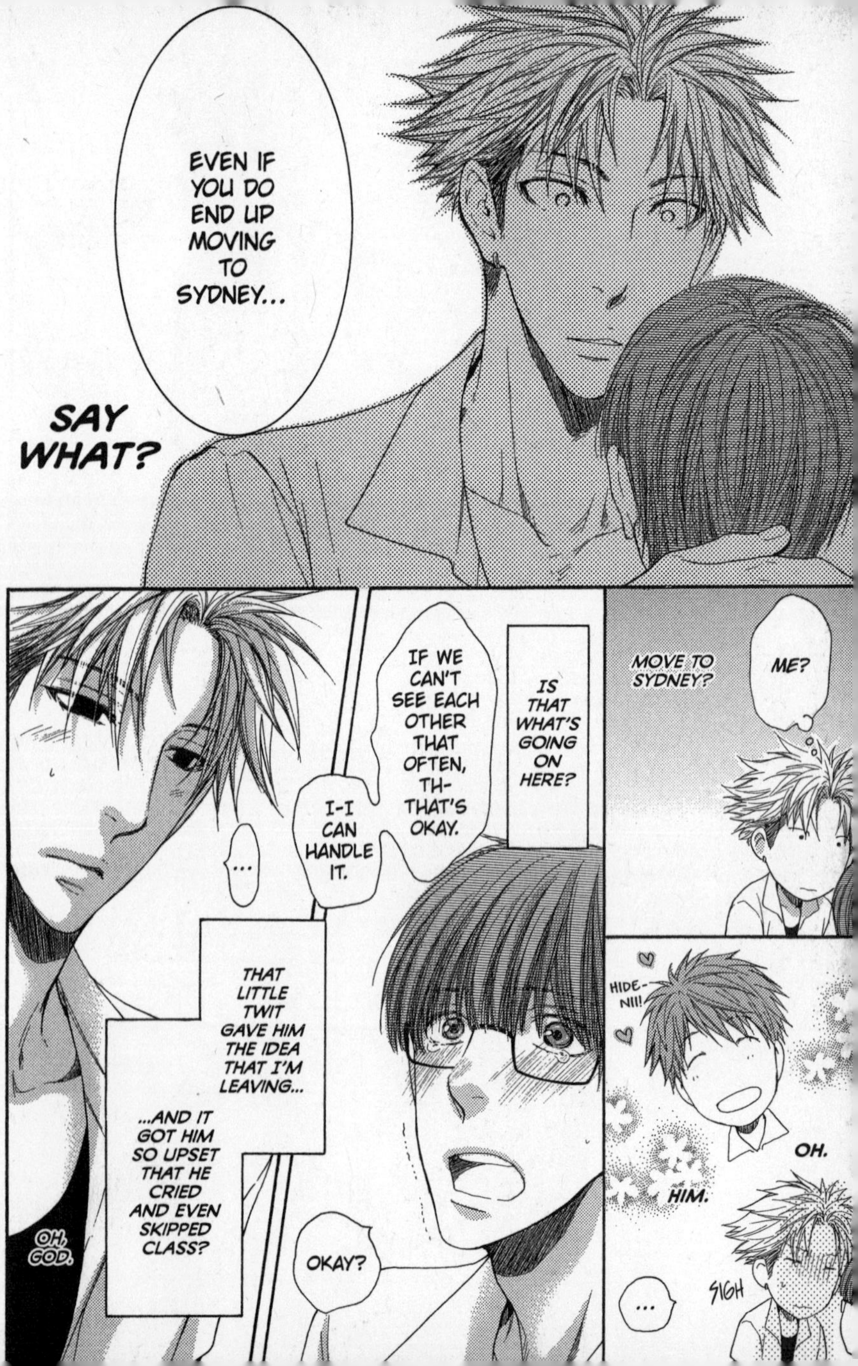

EVEN IF YOU DO END UP MOVING TO SYDNEY...
SAY WHAT?
ME?
MOVE TO SYDNEY?
HIDE-NII!
OH.
HIM.
SIGH
...
IS THAT WHAT'S GOING ON HERE?
IF WE CAN'T SEE EACH OTHER THAT OFTEN, TH-THAT'S OKAY.
I-I CAN HANDLE IT.
THAT LITTLE TWIT GAVE HIM THE IDEA THAT I'M LEAVING...
...AND IT GOT HIM SO UPSET THAT HE CRIED AND EVEN SKIPPED CLASS?
OKAY?
...
OH, GOD.

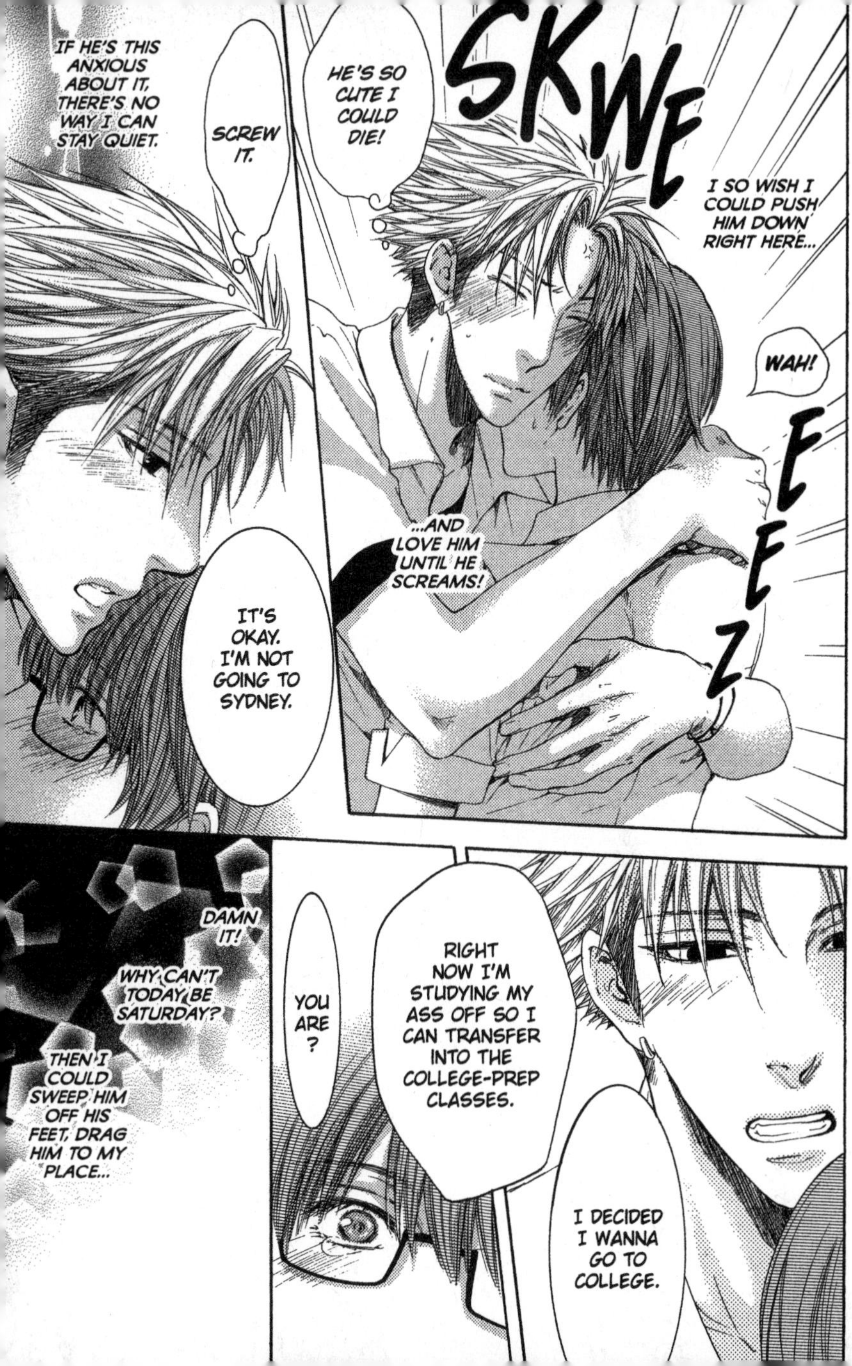
SKWEEEZ
HE'S SO CUTE I COULD DIE!
I SO WISH I COULD PUSH HIM DOWN RIGHT HERE...
WAH!
...AND LOVE HIM UNTIL HE SCREAMS!
SCREW IT.
IF HE'S THIS ANXIOUS ABOUT IT, THERE'S NO WAY I CAN STAY QUIET.
IT'S OKAY. I'M NOT GOING TO SYDNEY.
I DECIDED I WANNA GO TO COLLEGE.
RIGHT NOW I'M STUDYING MY ASS OFF SO I CAN TRANSFER INTO THE COLLEGE-PREP CLASSES.
YOU ARE?
DAMN IT!
WHY CAN'T TODAY BE SATURDAY?
THEN I COULD SWEEP HIM OFF HIS FEET, DRAG HIM TO MY PLACE...

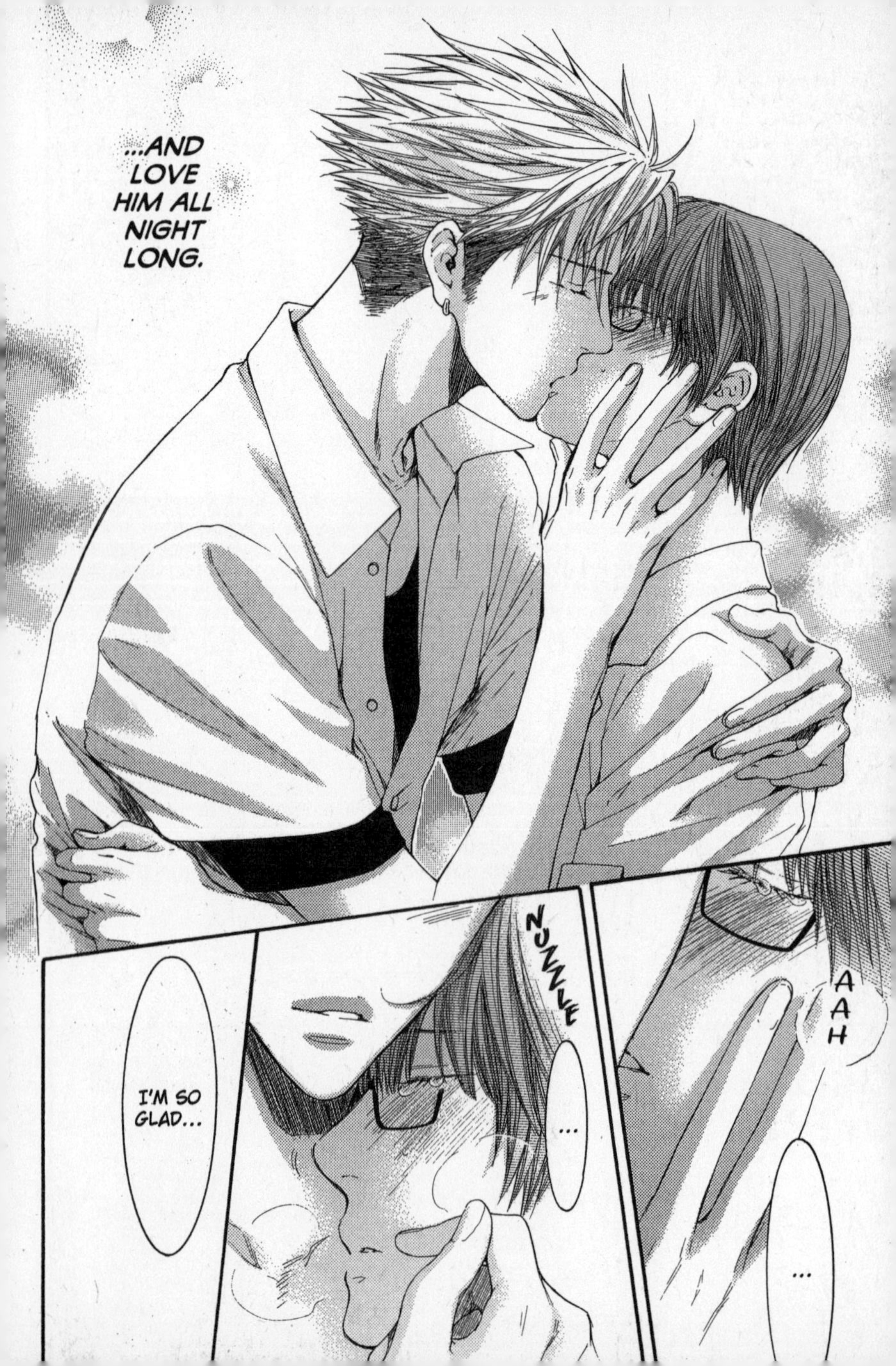
...AND LOVE HIM ALL NIGHT LONG.
AAH
...
NUZZLE
...
I'M SO GLAD...

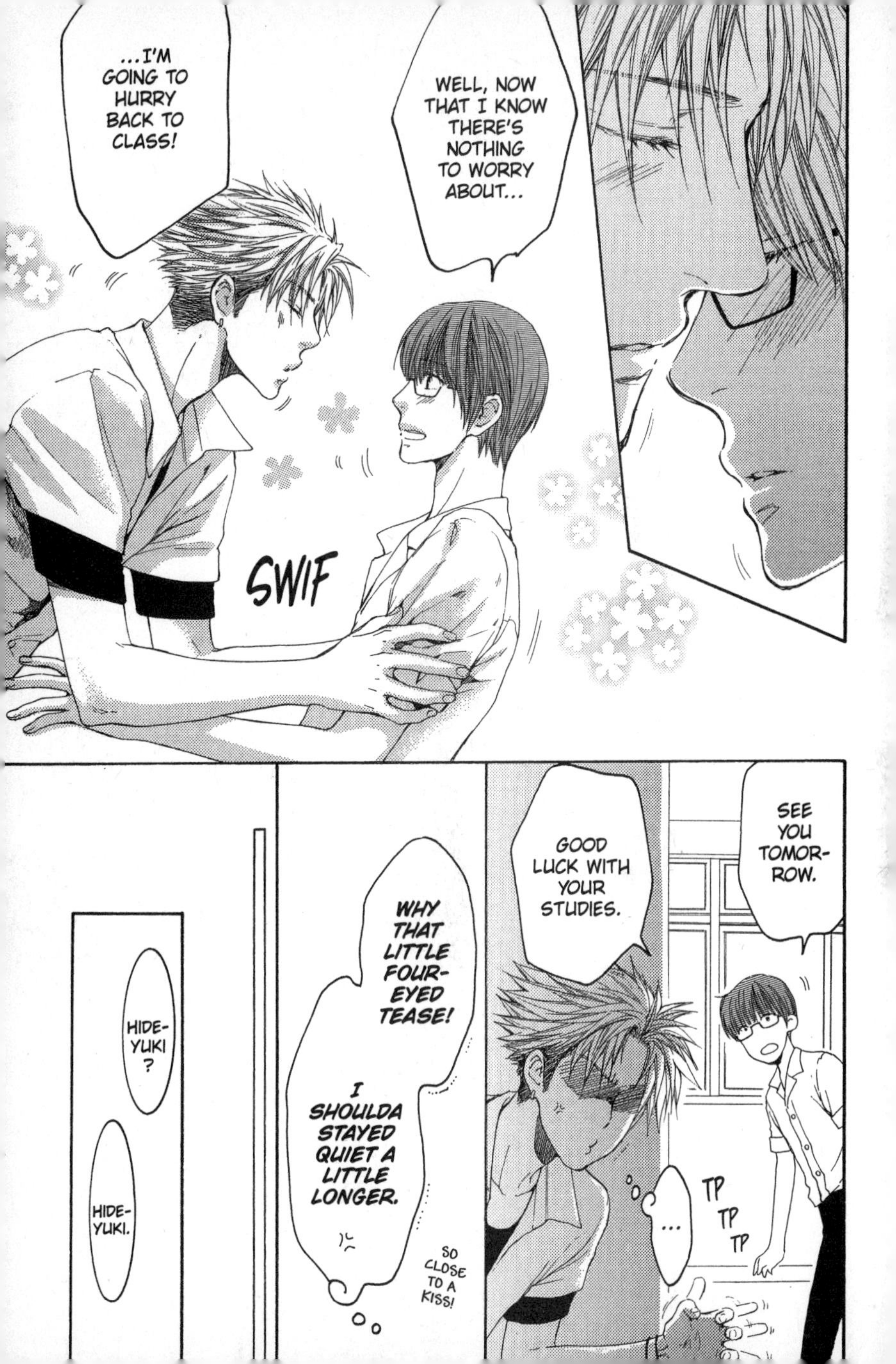
WELL, NOW THAT I KNOW THERE'S NOTHING TO WORRY ABOUT...
...I'M GOING TO HURRY BACK TO CLASS!
SWIF
SEE YOU TOMORROW.
GOOD LUCK WITH YOUR STUDIES.
...
TP TP TP
WHY THAT LITTLE FOUR-EYED TEASE!
I SHOULDA STAYED QUIET A LITTLE LONGER.
SO CLOSE TO A KISS!
HIDEYUKI?
HIDEYUKI.

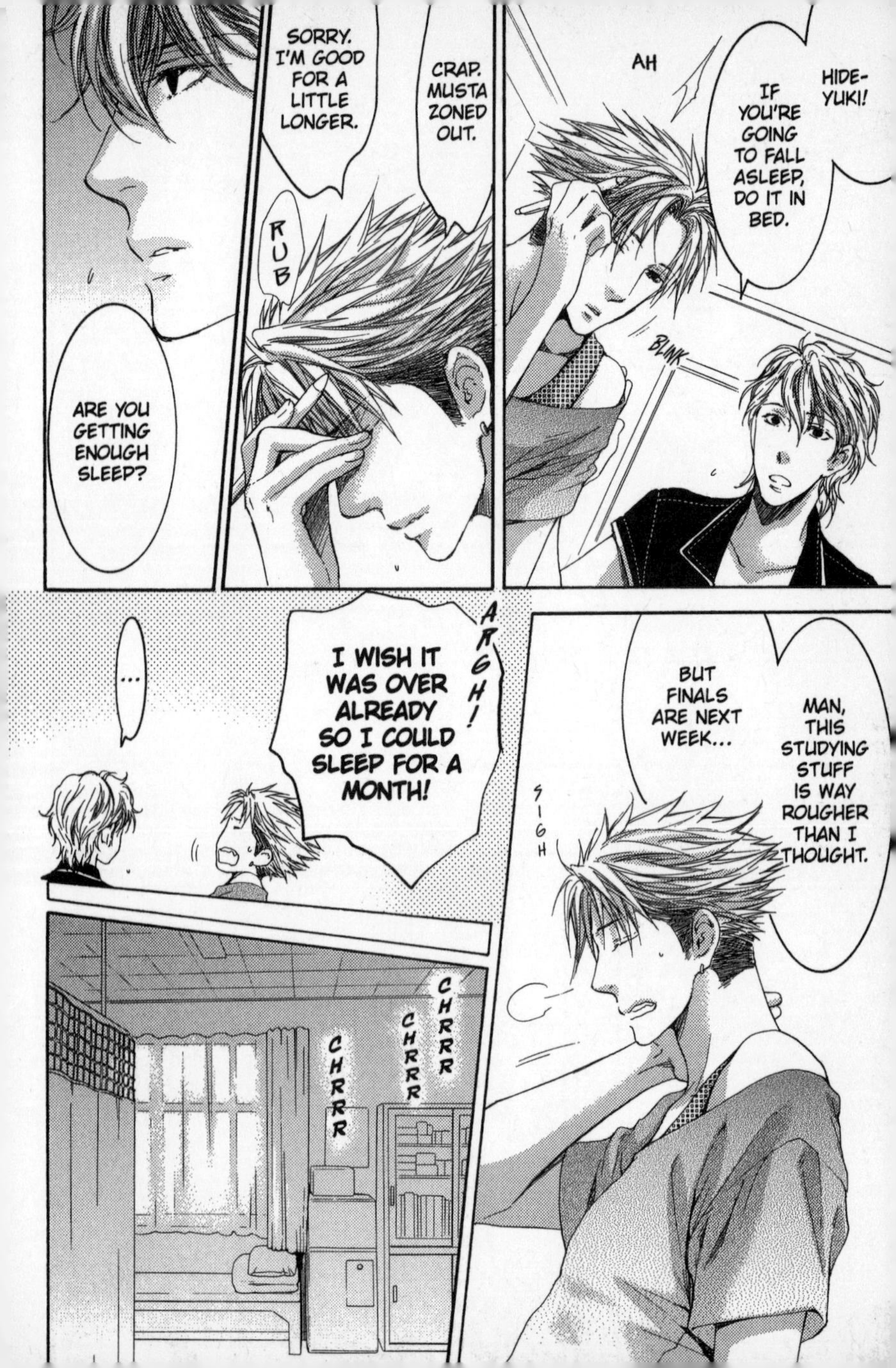
HIDE-YUKI!
IF YOU'RE GOING TO FALL ASLEEP, DO IT IN BED.
AH
BLINK
CRAP. MUSTA ZONED OUT.
SORRY. I'M GOOD FOR A LITTLE LONGER.
RUB
ARE YOU GETTING ENOUGH SLEEP?
MAN, THIS STUDYING STUFF IS WAY ROUGHER THAN I THOUGHT.
BUT FINALS ARE NEXT WEEK...
SIGH
ARGH!
I WISH IT WAS OVER ALREADY SO I COULD SLEEP FOR A MONTH!
...
CHRRR
CHRRR
CHRRR
CHRRR

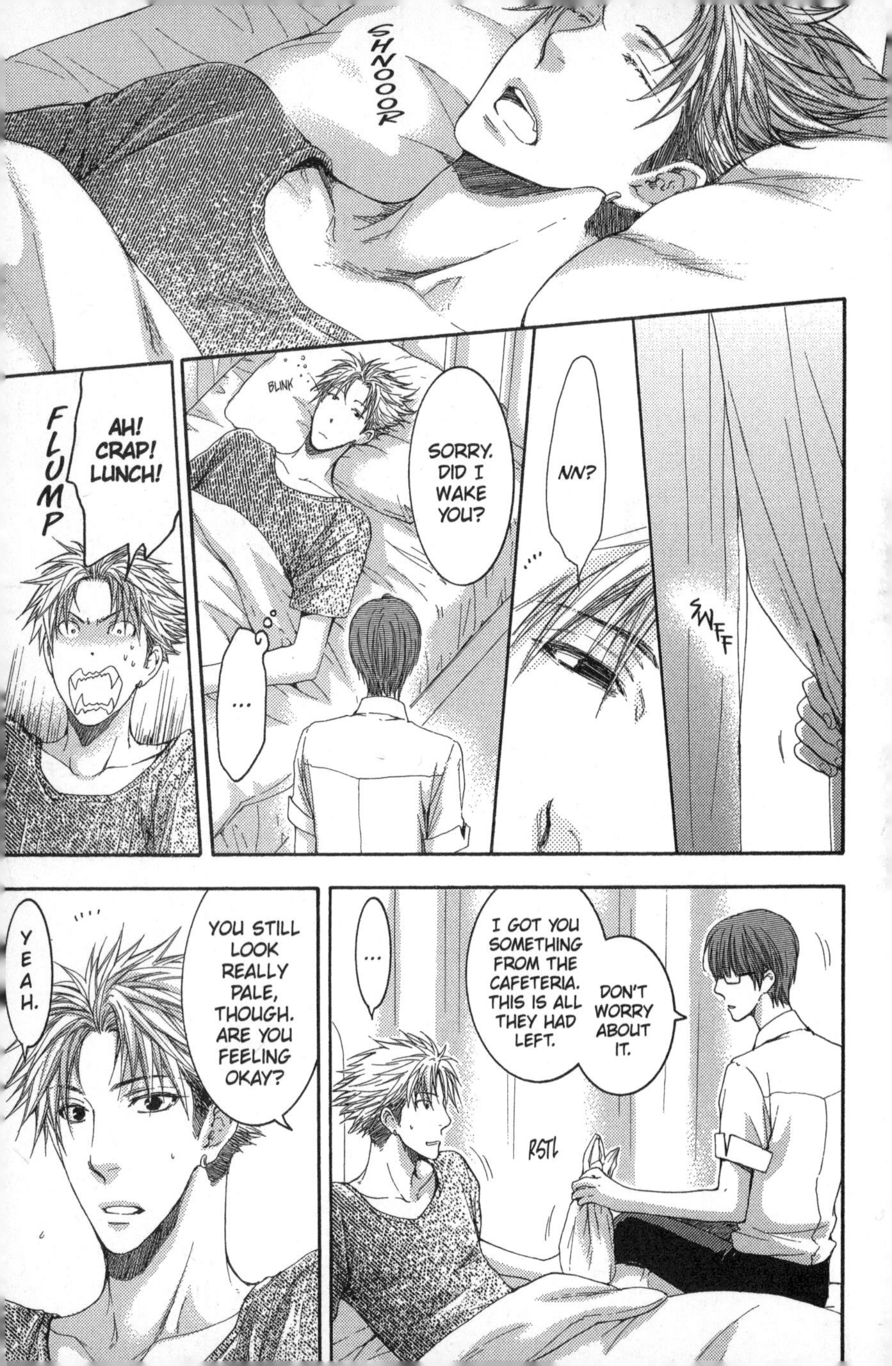
SHNOOOR
SWFF
NN?
...
SORRY. DID I WAKE YOU?
BLINK
...
AH! CRAP! LUNCH!
FLUMP
I GOT YOU SOMETHING FROM THE CAFETERIA. THIS IS ALL THEY HAD LEFT.
DON'T WORRY ABOUT IT.
...
RSTL
YOU STILL LOOK REALLY PALE, THOUGH. ARE YOU FEELING OKAY?
...
YEAH.

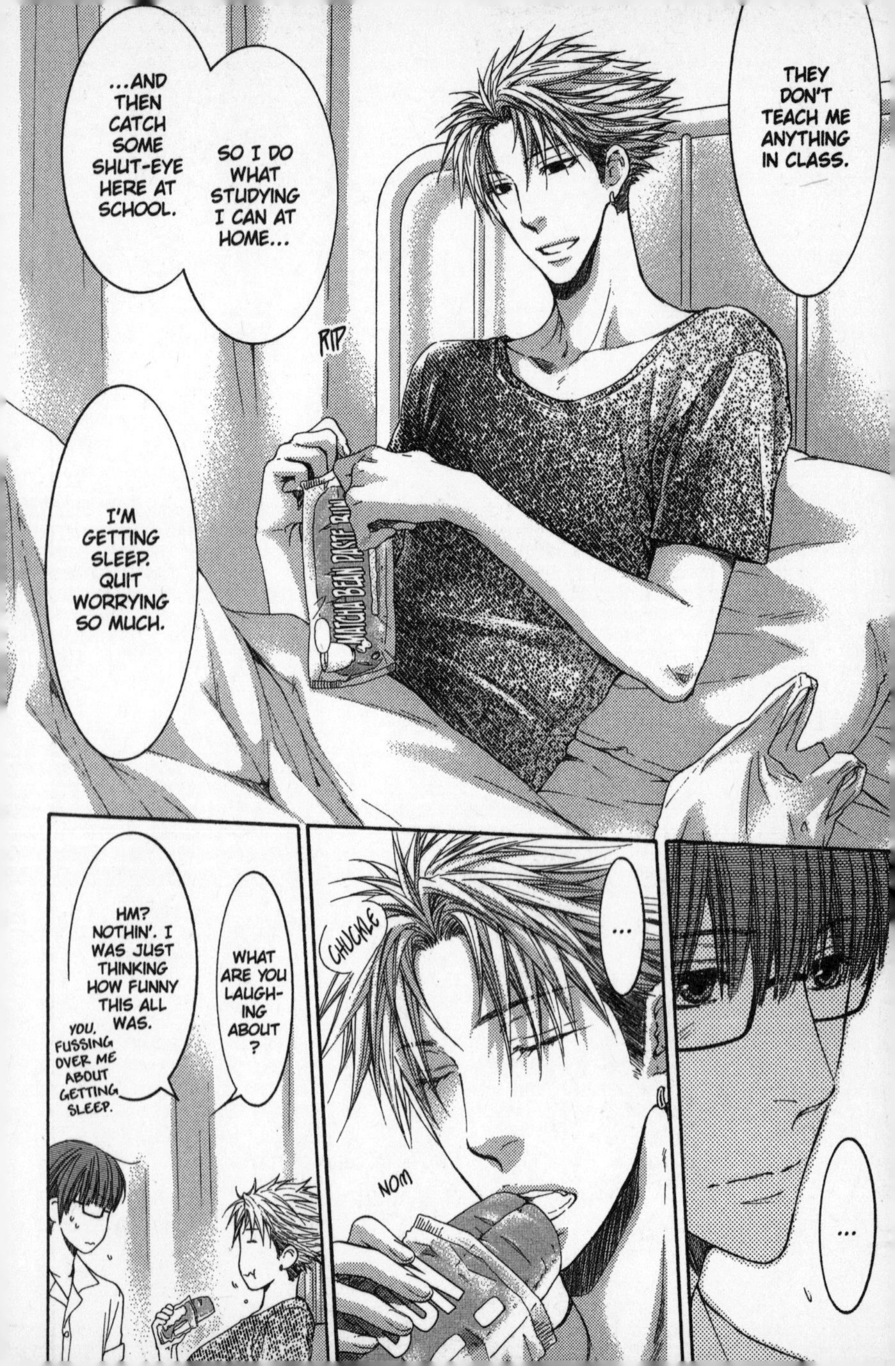

THEY DON'T TEACH ME ANYTHING IN CLASS.
SO I DO WHAT STUDYING I CAN AT HOME...
...AND THEN CATCH SOME SHUT-EYE HERE AT SCHOOL.
RIP
MATCHA BEAN PASTE BUN
I'M GETTING SLEEP. QUIT WORRYING SO MUCH.
...
...
CHUCKLE
NOM
WHAT ARE YOU LAUGH-ING ABOUT?
HM? NOTHIN'. I WAS JUST THINKING HOW FUNNY THIS ALL WAS.
YOU, FUSSING OVER ME ABOUT GETTING SLEEP.

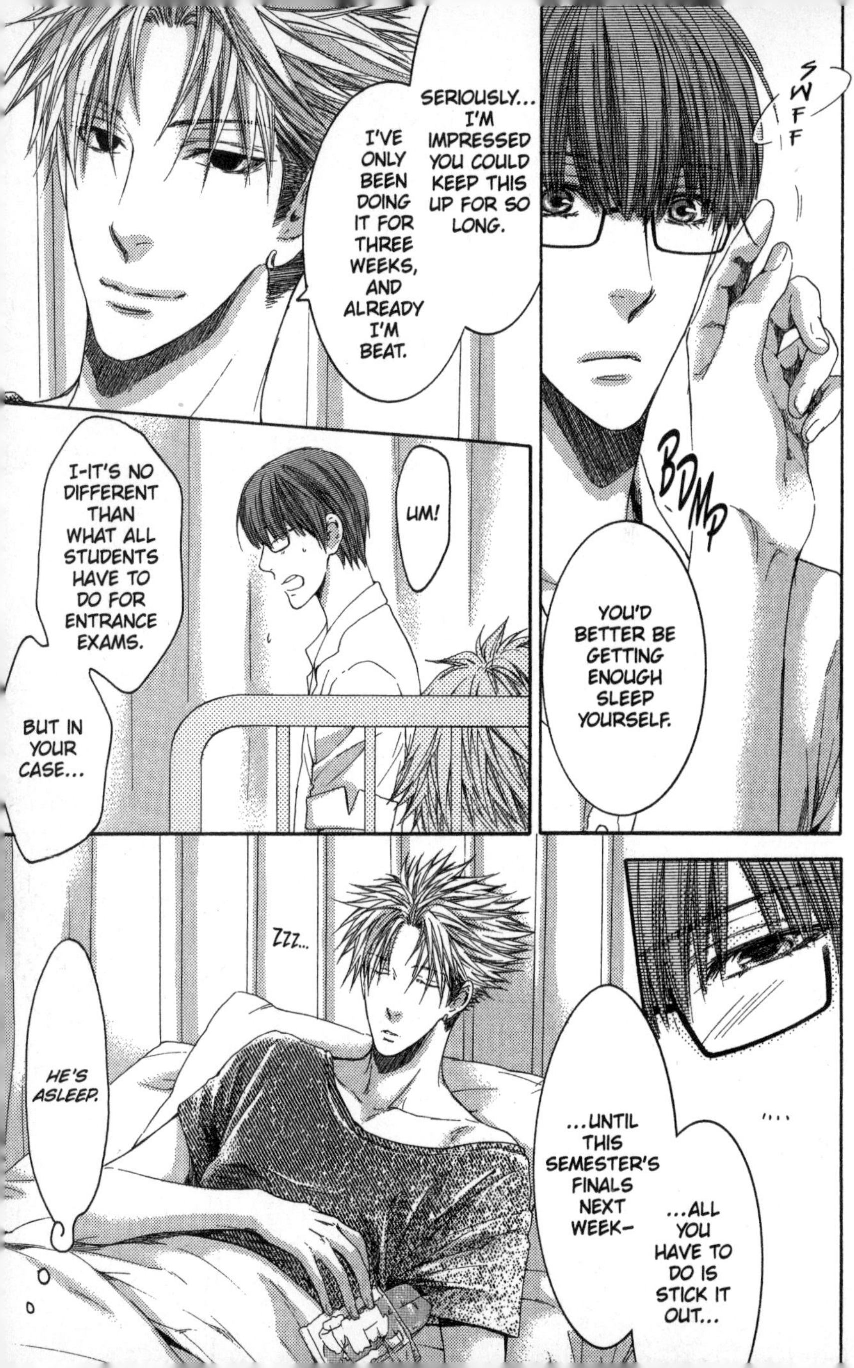
SWFF
BDMP
YOU'D BETTER BE GETTING ENOUGH SLEEP YOURSELF.
SERIOUSLY... I'M IMPRESSED YOU COULD KEEP THIS UP FOR SO LONG.
I'VE ONLY BEEN DOING IT FOR THREE WEEKS, AND ALREADY I'M BEAT.
UM!
I-IT'S NO DIFFERENT THAN WHAT ALL STUDENTS HAVE TO DO FOR ENTRANCE EXAMS.
BUT IN YOUR CASE...
...
...UNTIL THIS SEMESTER'S FINALS NEXT WEEK-
...ALL YOU HAVE TO DO IS STICK IT OUT...
ZZZ...
HE'S ASLEEP.

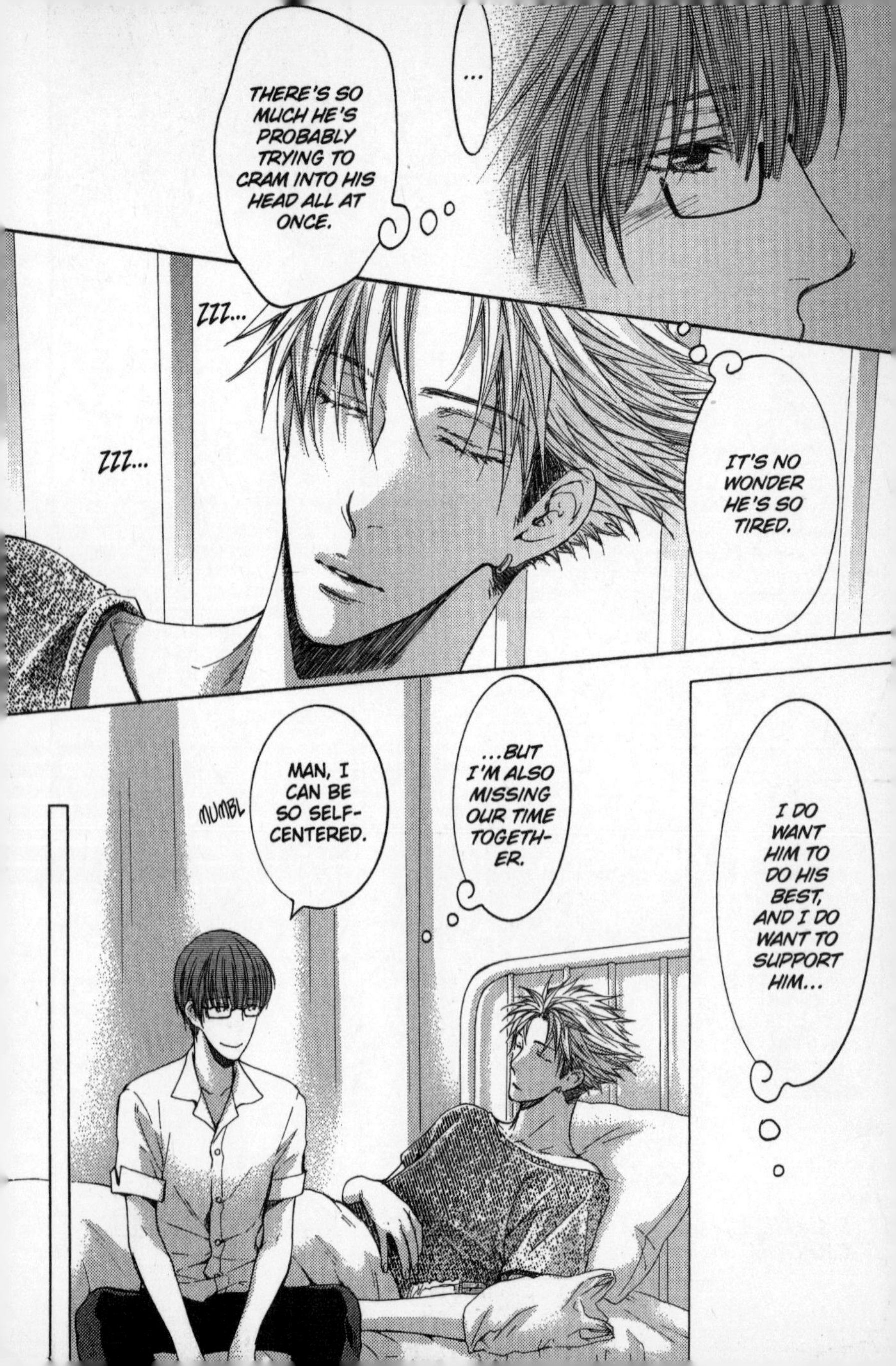
...
THERE'S SO MUCH HE'S PROBABLY TRYING TO CRAM INTO HIS HEAD ALL AT ONCE.
IT'S NO WONDER HE'S SO TIRED.
ZZZ...
ZZZ...
I DO WANT HIM TO DO HIS BEST, AND I DO WANT TO SUPPORT HIM...
...BUT I'M ALSO MISSING OUR TIME TOGETH-ER.
MAN, I CAN BE SO SELF-CENTERED.
MUMBL

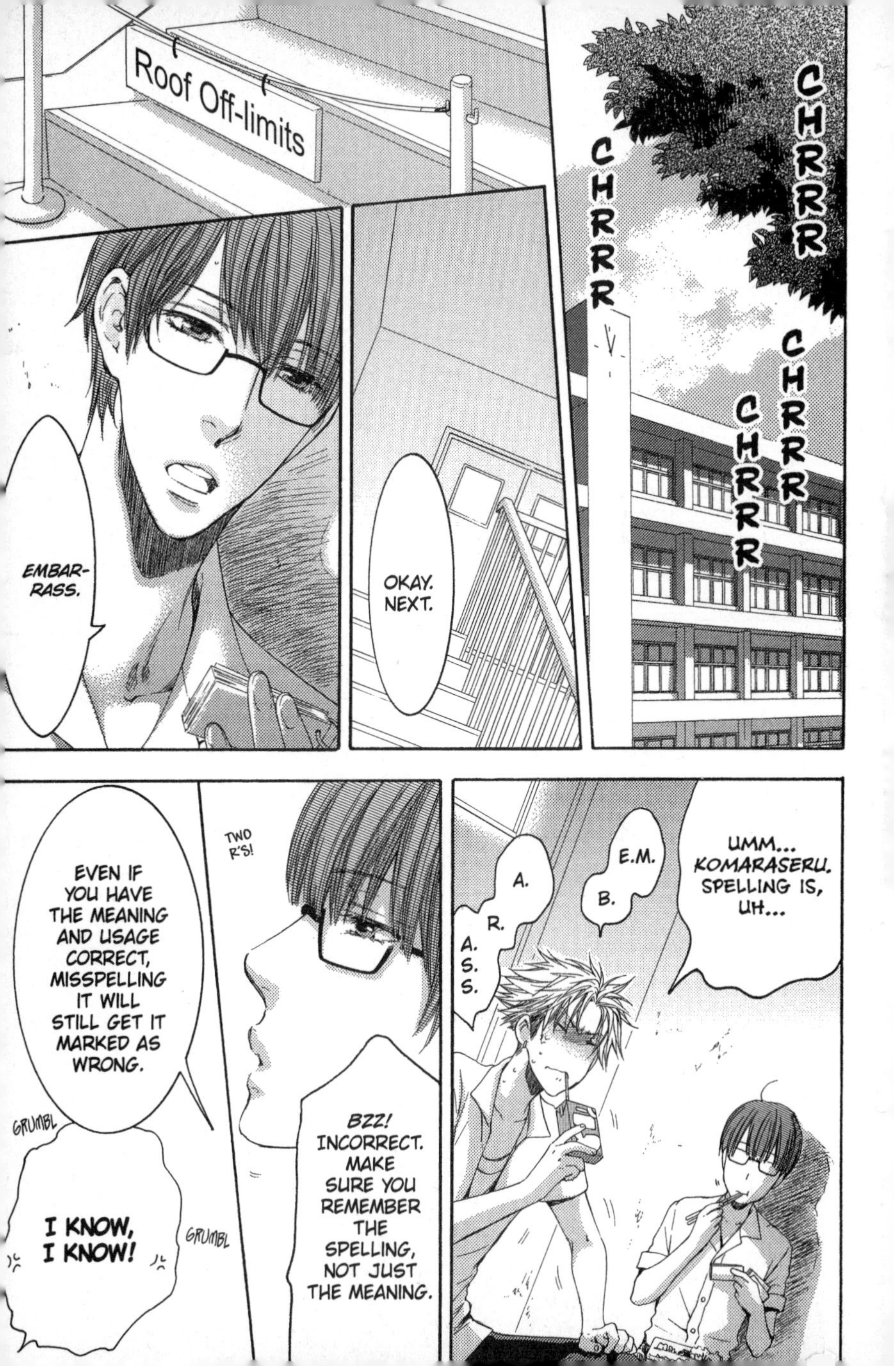
CHRRR
CHRRR
CHRRR
CHRRR
Roof Off-limits
OKAY. NEXT.
EMBARRASS.
UMM... KOMARASERU. SPELLING IS, UH...
E.M. B.
A. R. A. S. S.
BZZ! INCORRECT. MAKE SURE YOU REMEMBER THE SPELLING, NOT JUST THE MEANING.
TWO R'S!
EVEN IF YOU HAVE THE MEANING AND USAGE CORRECT, MISSPELLING IT WILL STILL GET IT MARKED AS WRONG.
GRUMBL
I KNOW, I KNOW!
GRUMBL

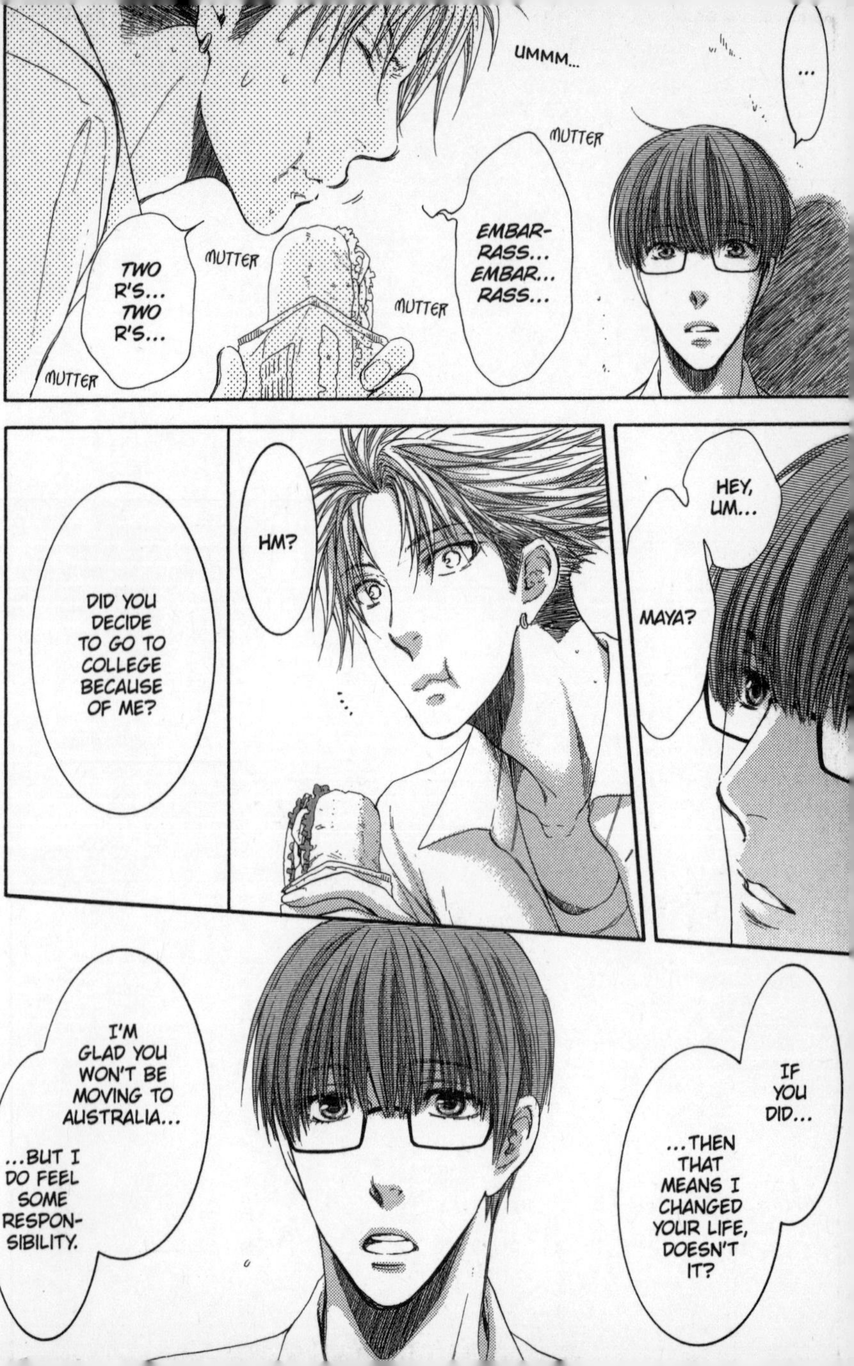
...
UMMM...
MUTTER
EMBAR-RASS... EMBAR... RASS...
MUTTER
MUTTER
TWO R'S... TWO R'S...
MUTTER
HEY, UM...
MAYA?
HM?
...
DID YOU DECIDE TO GO TO COLLEGE BECAUSE OF ME?
IF YOU DID...
...THEN THAT MEANS I CHANGED YOUR LIFE, DOESN'T IT?
I'M GLAD YOU WON'T BE MOVING TO AUSTRALIA...
...BUT I DO FEEL SOME RESPONSIBILITY.

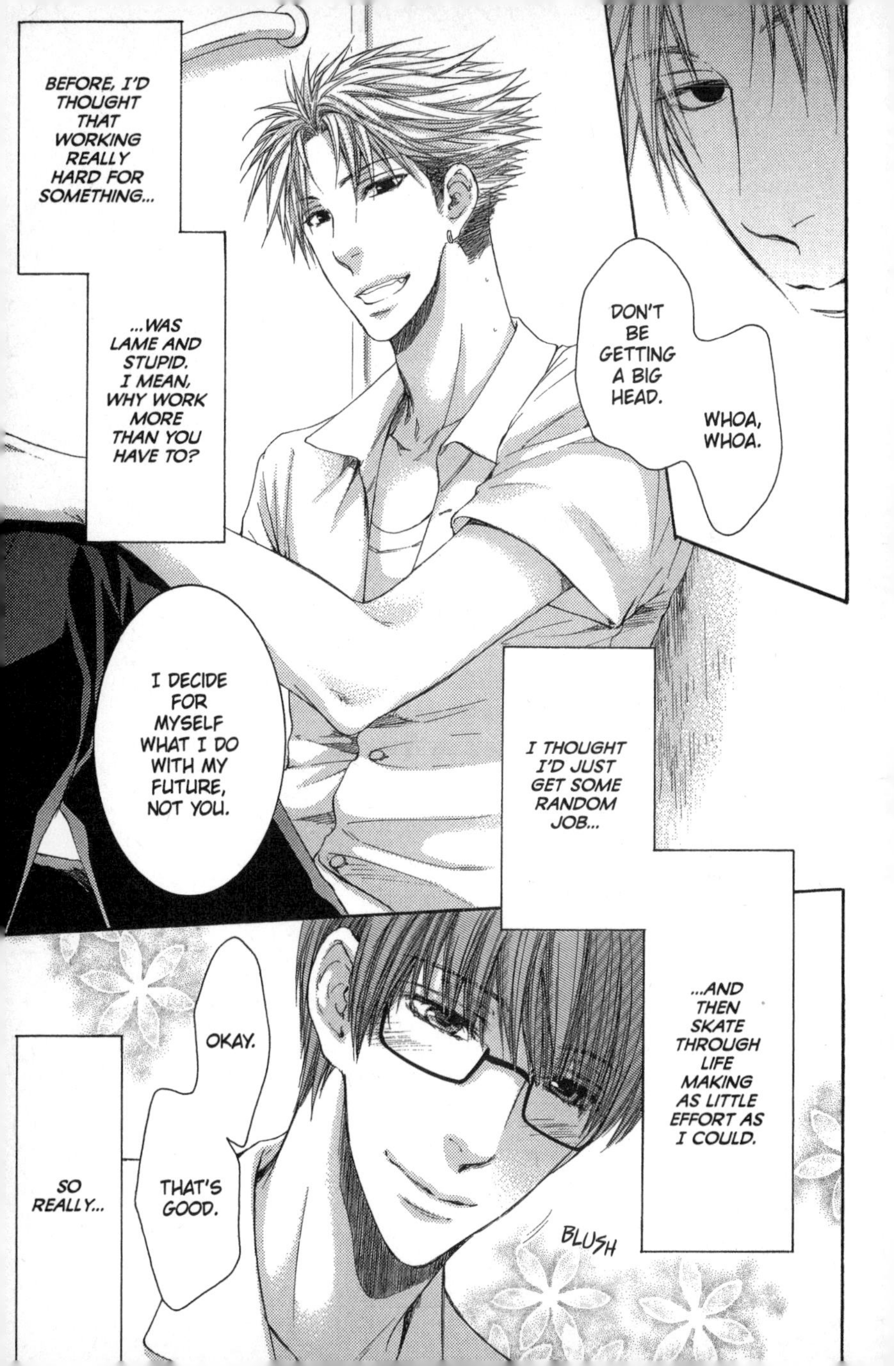
WHOA, WHOA.
DON'T BE GETTING A BIG HEAD.
BEFORE, I'D THOUGHT THAT WORKING REALLY HARD FOR SOMETHING...
...WAS LAME AND STUPID. I MEAN, WHY WORK MORE THAN YOU HAVE TO?
I DECIDE FOR MYSELF WHAT I DO WITH MY FUTURE, NOT YOU.
I THOUGHT I'D JUST GET SOME RANDOM JOB...
...AND THEN SKATE THROUGH LIFE MAKING AS LITTLE EFFORT AS I COULD.
OKAY.
THAT'S GOOD.
BLUSH
SO REALLY...

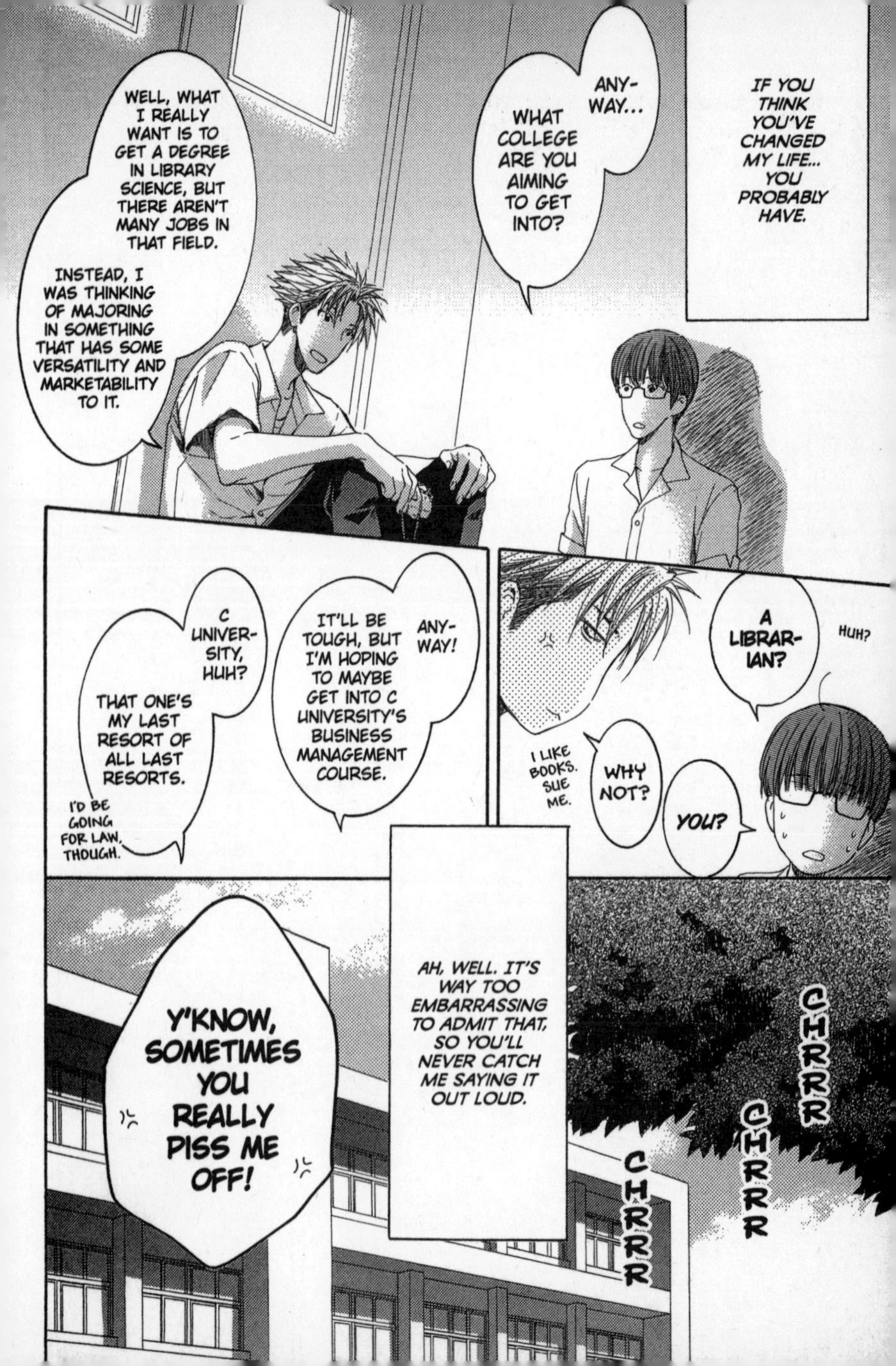
IF YOU THINK YOU'VE CHANGED MY LIFE... YOU PROBABLY HAVE.
ANY-WAY...
WHAT COLLEGE ARE YOU AIMING TO GET INTO?
WELL, WHAT I REALLY WANT IS TO GET A DEGREE IN LIBRARY SCIENCE, BUT THERE AREN'T MANY JOBS IN THAT FIELD.
INSTEAD, I WAS THINKING OF MAJORING IN SOMETHING THAT HAS SOME VERSATILITY AND MARKETABILITY TO IT.
A LIBRAR-IAN?
HUH?
YOU?
WHY NOT?
I LIKE BOOKS. SUE ME.
ANY-WAY!
IT'LL BE TOUGH, BUT I'M HOPING TO MAYBE GET INTO C UNIVERSITY'S BUSINESS MANAGEMENT COURSE.
C UNIVER-SITY, HUH?
THAT ONE'S MY LAST RESORT OF ALL LAST RESORTS.
I'D BE GOING FOR LAW, THOUGH.
CHRRR
CHRRR
CHRRR
AH, WELL. IT'S WAY TOO EMBARRASSING TO ADMIT THAT, SO YOU'LL NEVER CATCH ME SAYING IT OUT LOUD.
Y'KNOW, SOMETIMES YOU REALLY PISS ME OFF!

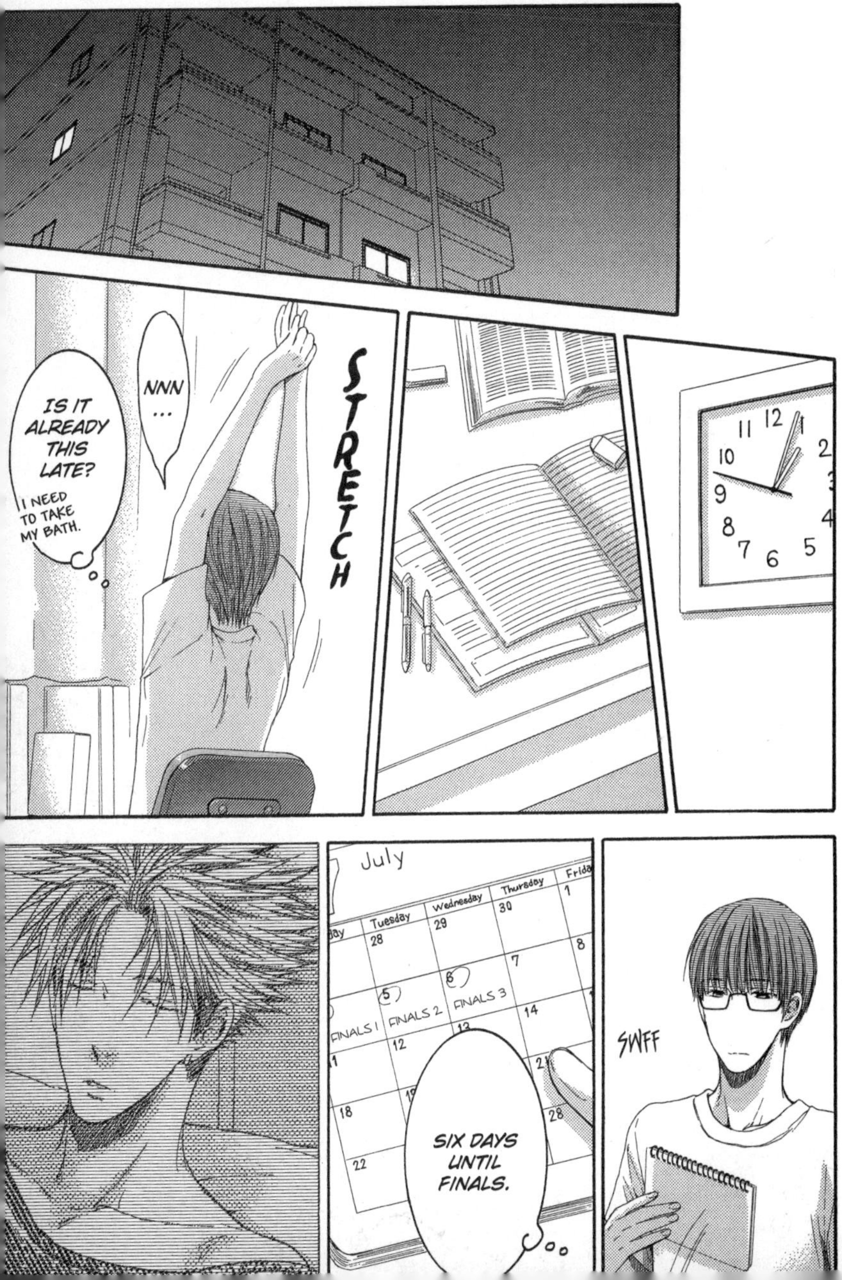
STRETCH
NNN ...
IS IT ALREADY THIS LATE?
I NEED TO TAKE MY BATH.
SWFF
July
Tuesday
Wednesday
Thursday
FINALS 1
FINALS 2
FINALS 3
SIX DAYS UNTIL FINALS.

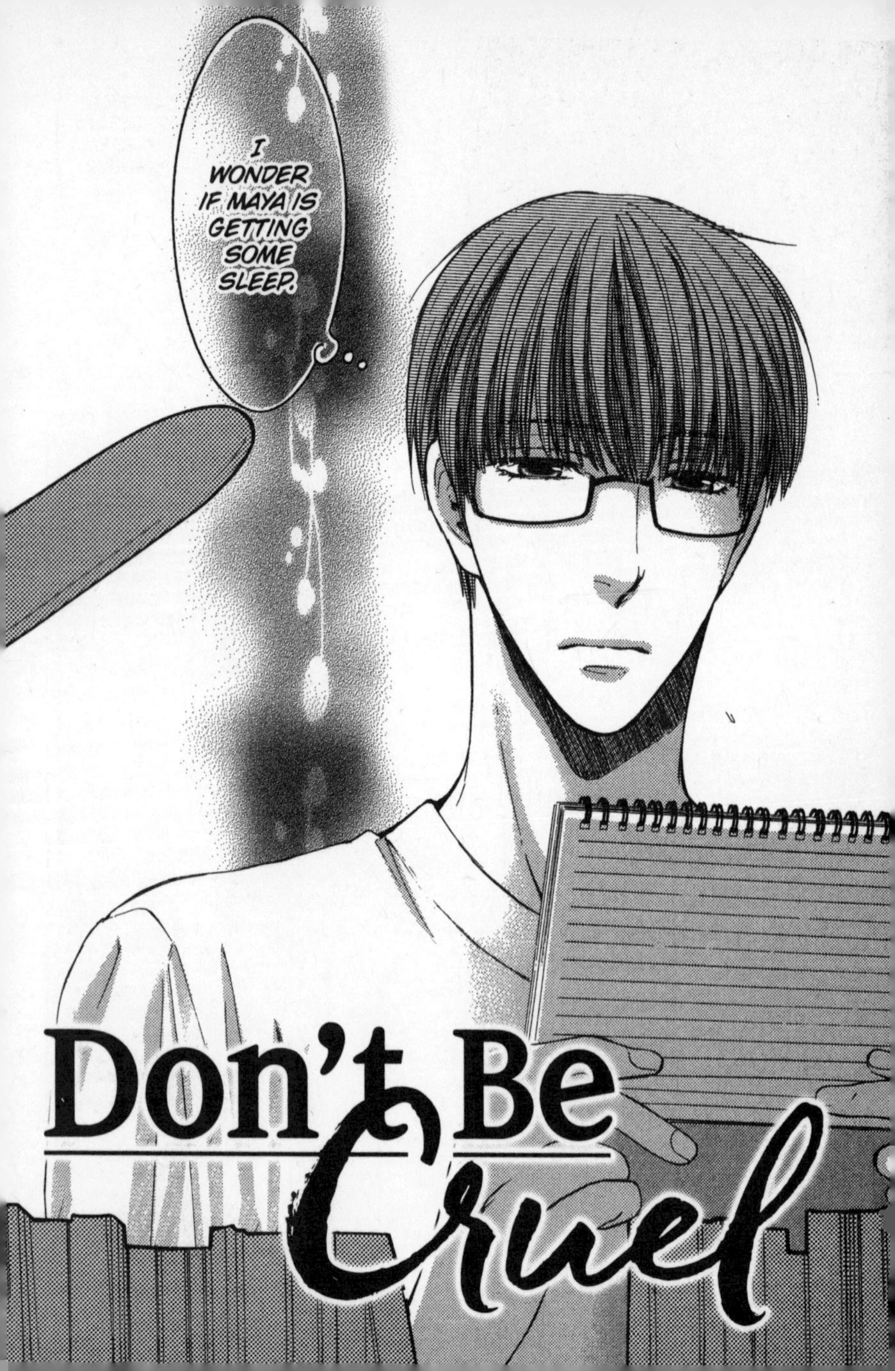
I WONDER IF MAYA IS GETTING SOME SLEEP.
Don't Be Cruel

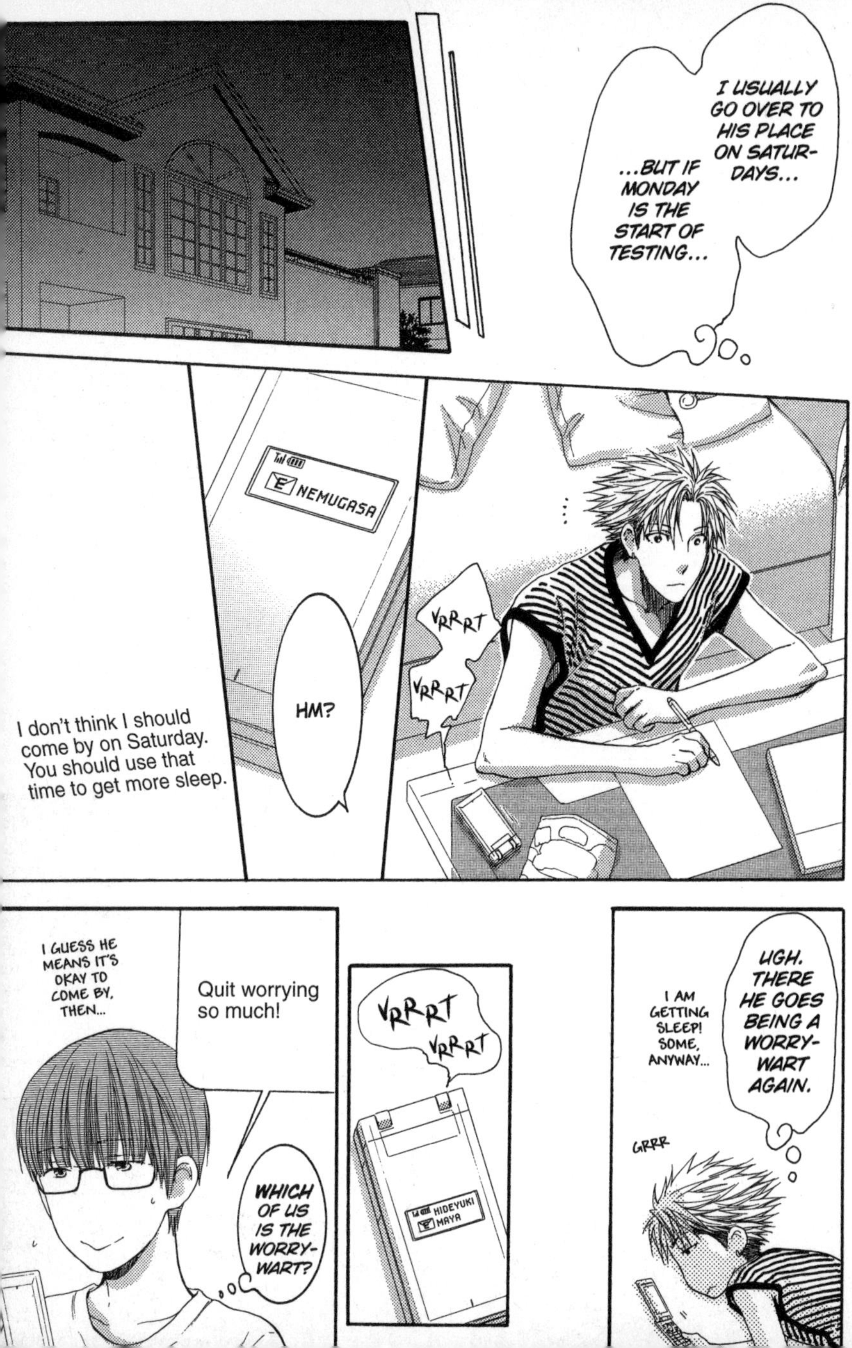
I USUALLY GO OVER TO HIS PLACE ON SATURDAYS...
...BUT IF MONDAY IS THE START OF TESTING...
...
VRRRT
VRRRT
NEMUGASA
HM?
I don't think I should come by on Saturday. You should use that time to get more sleep.
UGH. THERE HE GOES BEING A WORRYWART AGAIN.
I AM GETTING SLEEP! SOME, ANYWAY...
GRRR
VRRRT
VRRRT
HIDEYUKI MAYA
Quit worrying so much!
I GUESS HE MEANS IT'S OKAY TO COME BY, THEN...
WHICH OF US IS THE WORRYWART?

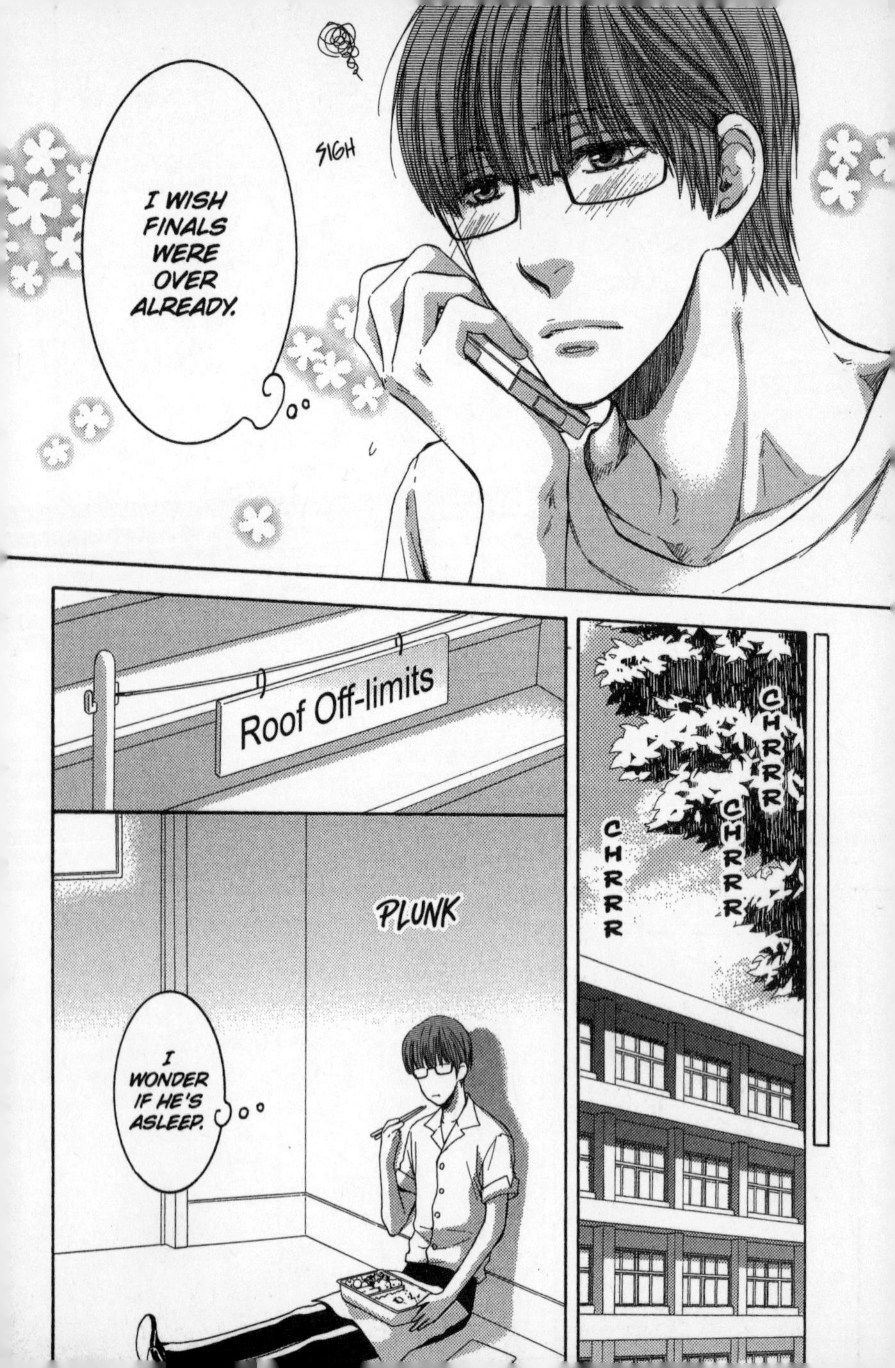
SIGH
I WISH FINALS WERE OVER ALREADY.
CHRRR
CHRRR
CHRRR
Roof Off-limits
PLUNK
I WONDER IF HE'S ASLEEP.

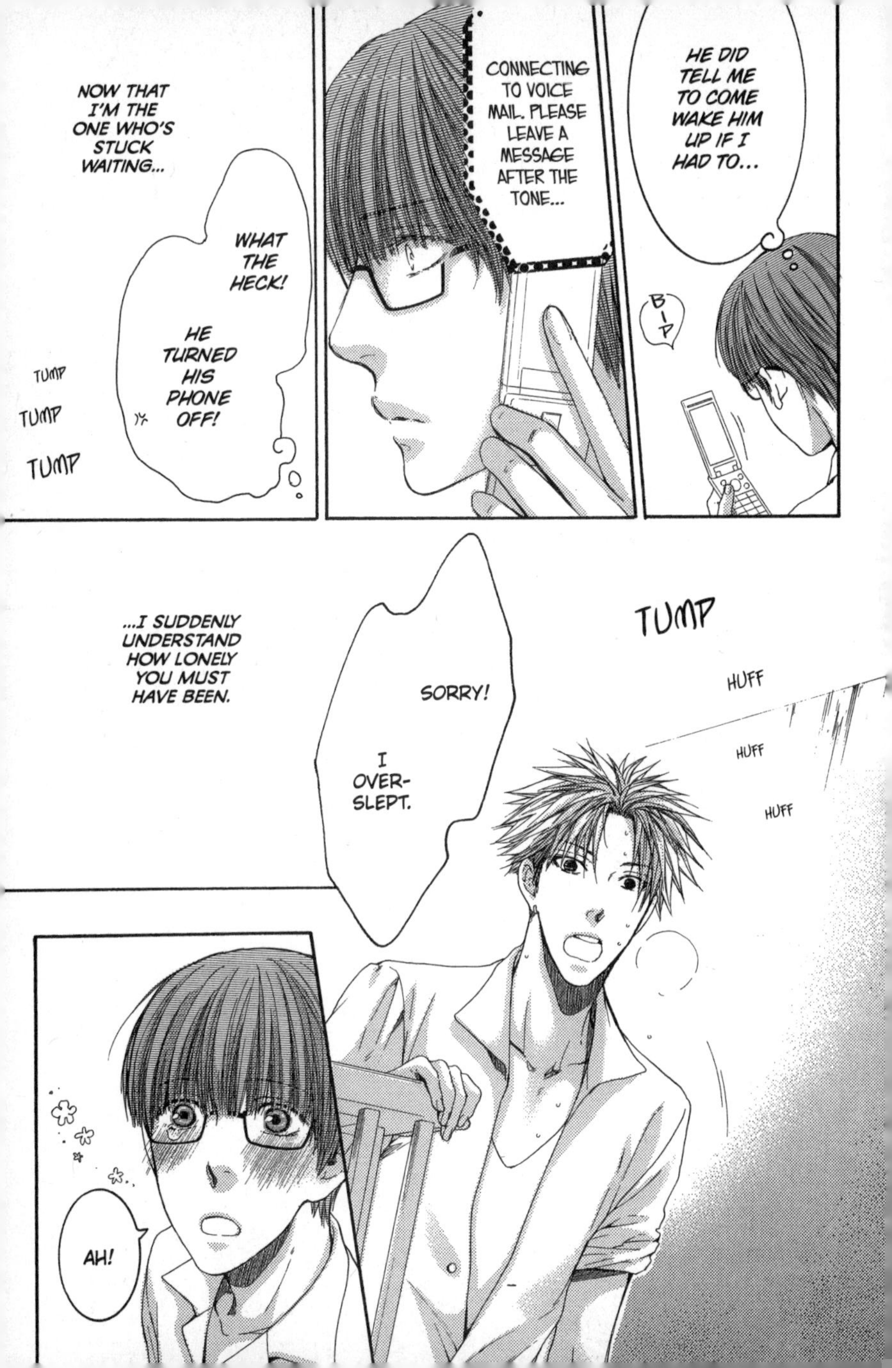
HE DID TELL ME TO COME WAKE HIM UP IF I HAD TO…
BIP
CONNECTING TO VOICE MAIL. PLEASE LEAVE A MESSAGE AFTER THE TONE…
NOW THAT I'M THE ONE WHO'S STUCK WAITING...
WHAT THE HECK!
HE TURNED HIS PHONE OFF!
TUMP
TUMP
TUMP
TUMP
HUFF
HUFF
HUFF
SORRY!
I OVER-SLEPT.
...I SUDDENLY UNDERSTAND HOW LONELY YOU MUST HAVE BEEN.
AH!

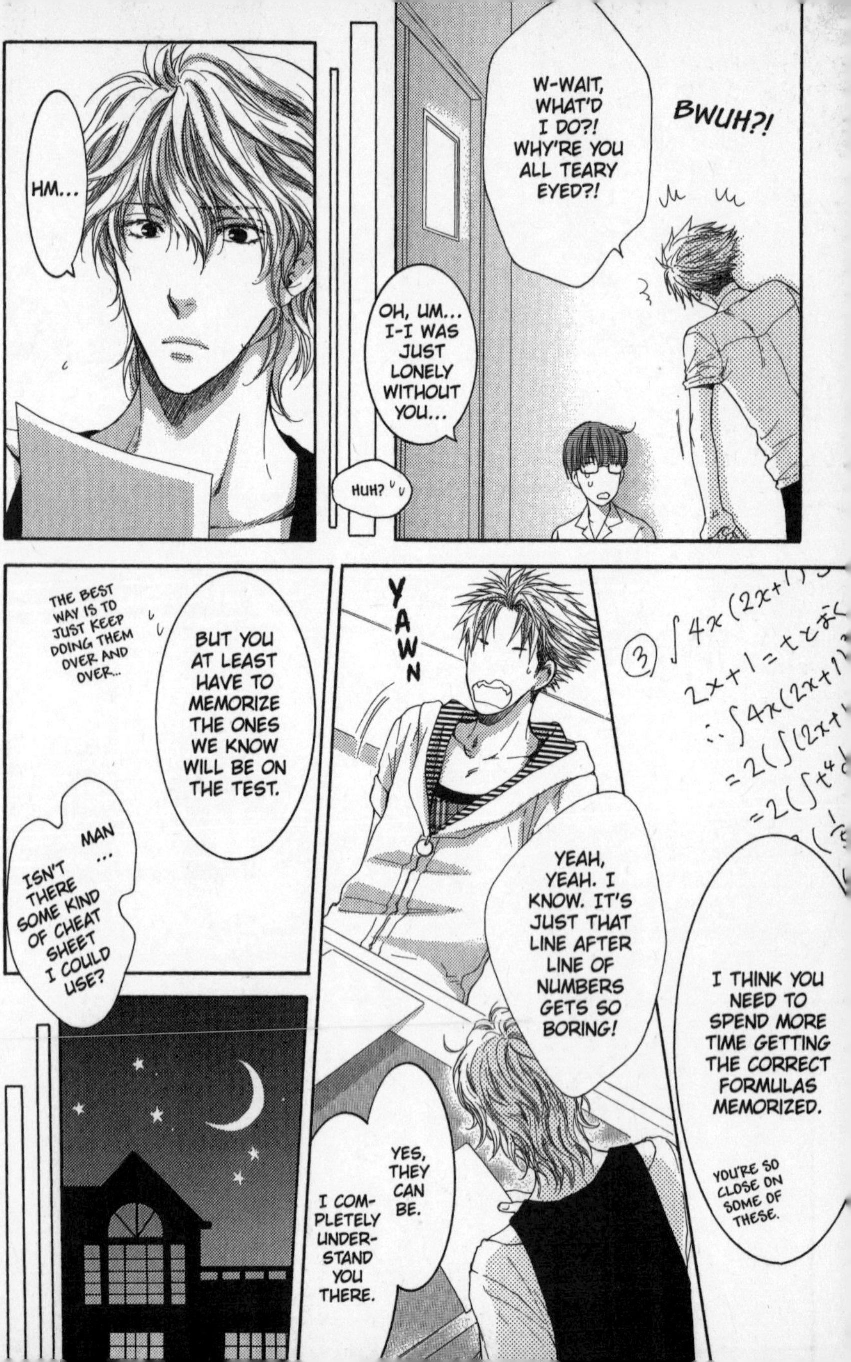
BWUH?!
W-WAIT, WHAT'D I DO?! WHY'RE YOU ALL TEARY EYED?!
OH, UM... I-I WAS JUST LONELY WITHOUT YOU...
HUH?
HM...
I THINK YOU NEED TO SPEND MORE TIME GETTING THE CORRECT FORMULAS MEMORIZED.
YOU'RE SO CLOSE ON SOME OF THESE.
YAWN
YEAH, YEAH. I KNOW. IT'S JUST THAT LINE AFTER LINE OF NUMBERS GETS SO BORING!
YES, THEY CAN BE.
I COM-PLETELY UNDER-STAND YOU THERE.
BUT YOU AT LEAST HAVE TO MEMORIZE THE ONES WE KNOW WILL BE ON THE TEST.
THE BEST WAY IS TO JUST KEEP DOING THEM OVER AND OVER...
MAN...
ISN'T THERE SOME KIND OF CHEAT SHEET I COULD USE?

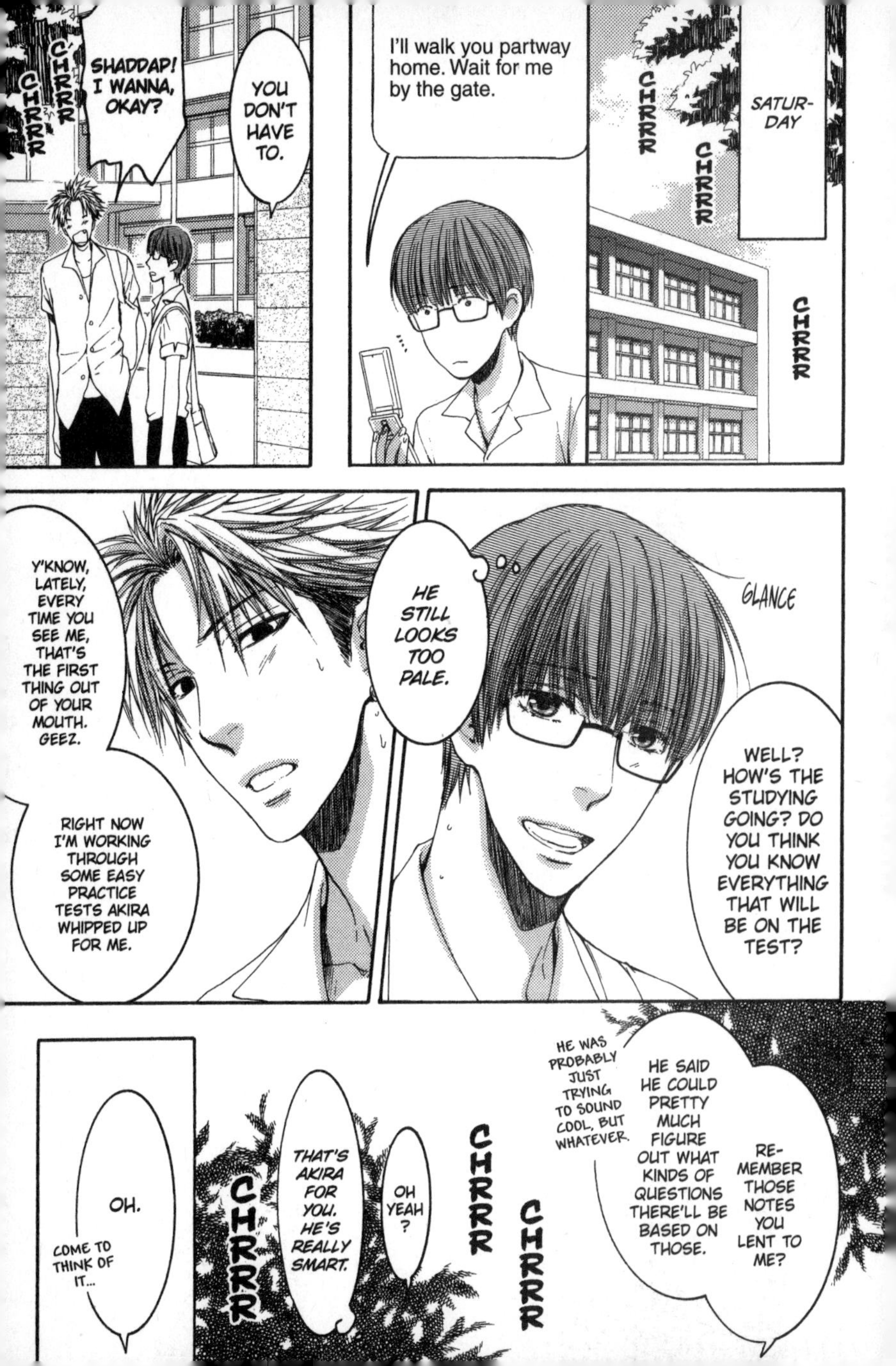
SATUR-DAY
CHRRR
CHRRR
CHRRR
I'll walk you partway home. Wait for me by the gate.
YOU DON'T HAVE TO.
SHADDAP! I WANNA, OKAY?
CHRRR
CHRRR
GLANCE
HE STILL LOOKS TOO PALE.
WELL? HOW'S THE STUDYING GOING? DO YOU THINK YOU KNOW EVERYTHING THAT WILL BE ON THE TEST?
Y'KNOW, LATELY, EVERY TIME YOU SEE ME, THAT'S THE FIRST THING OUT OF YOUR MOUTH. GEEZ.
RIGHT NOW I'M WORKING THROUGH SOME EASY PRACTICE TESTS AKIRA WHIPPED UP FOR ME.
RE-MEMBER THOSE NOTES YOU LENT TO ME?
HE SAID HE COULD PRETTY MUCH FIGURE OUT WHAT KINDS OF QUESTIONS THERE'LL BE BASED ON THOSE.
HE WAS PROBABLY JUST TRYING TO SOUND COOL, BUT WHATEVER.
CHRRR
CHRRR
OH YEAH?
THAT'S AKIRA FOR YOU. HE'S REALLY SMART.
CHRRR
OH.
COME TO THINK OF IT...

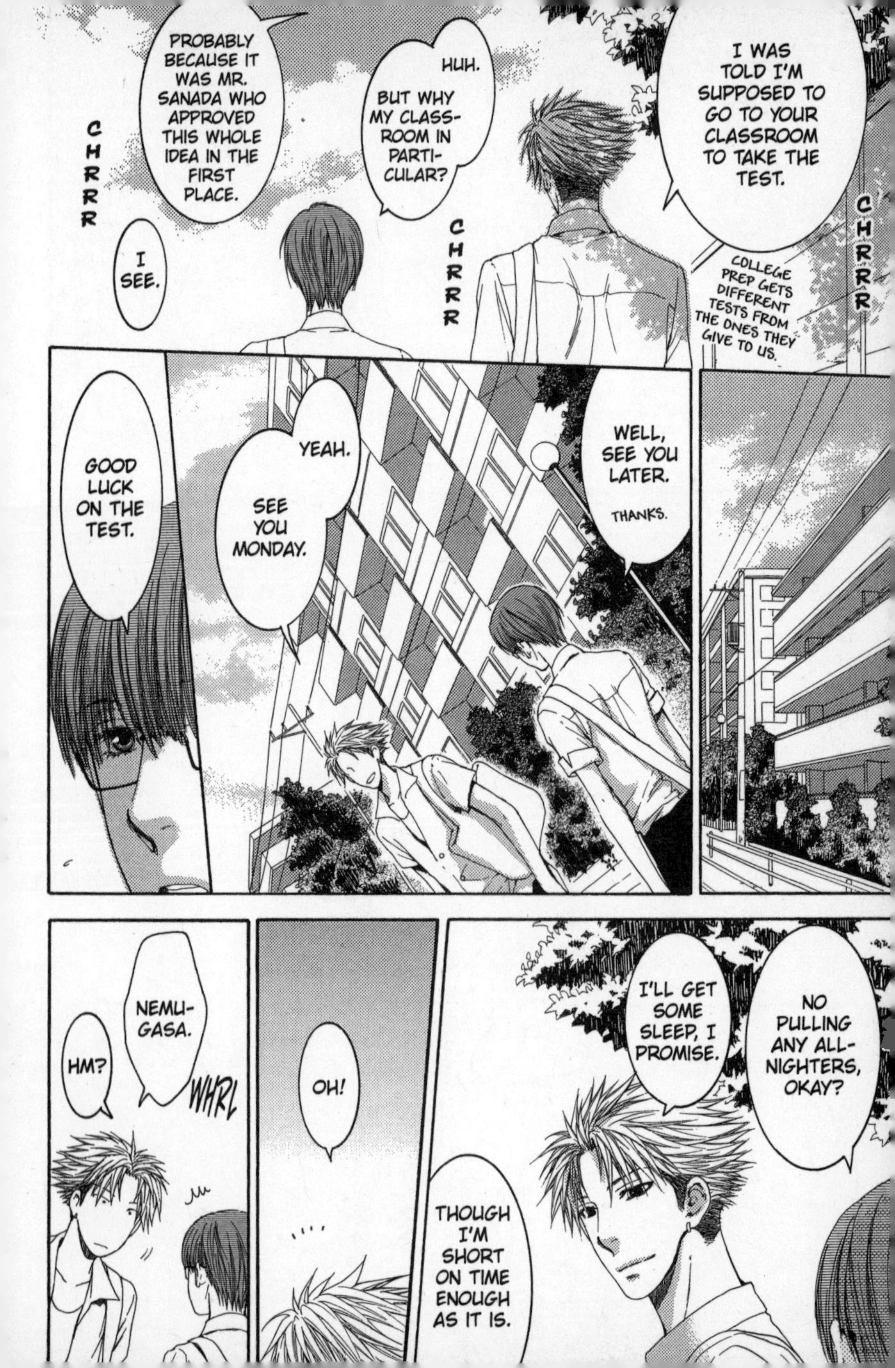

I WAS TOLD I'M SUPPOSED TO GO TO YOUR CLASSROOM TO TAKE THE TEST.
CHRRR
COLLEGE PREP GETS DIFFERENT TESTS FROM THE ONES THEY GIVE TO US.
HUH.
BUT WHY MY CLASS-ROOM IN PARTI-CULAR?
CHRRR
PROBABLY BECAUSE IT WAS MR. SANADA WHO APPROVED THIS WHOLE IDEA IN THE FIRST PLACE.
CHRRR
I SEE.
WELL, SEE YOU LATER.
THANKS.
YEAH.
SEE YOU MONDAY.
GOOD LUCK ON THE TEST.
NO PULLING ANY ALL-NIGHTERS, OKAY?
I'LL GET SOME SLEEP, I PROMISE.
THOUGH I'M SHORT ON TIME ENOUGH AS IT IS.
...
OH!
NEMU-GASA.
WHRL
HM?

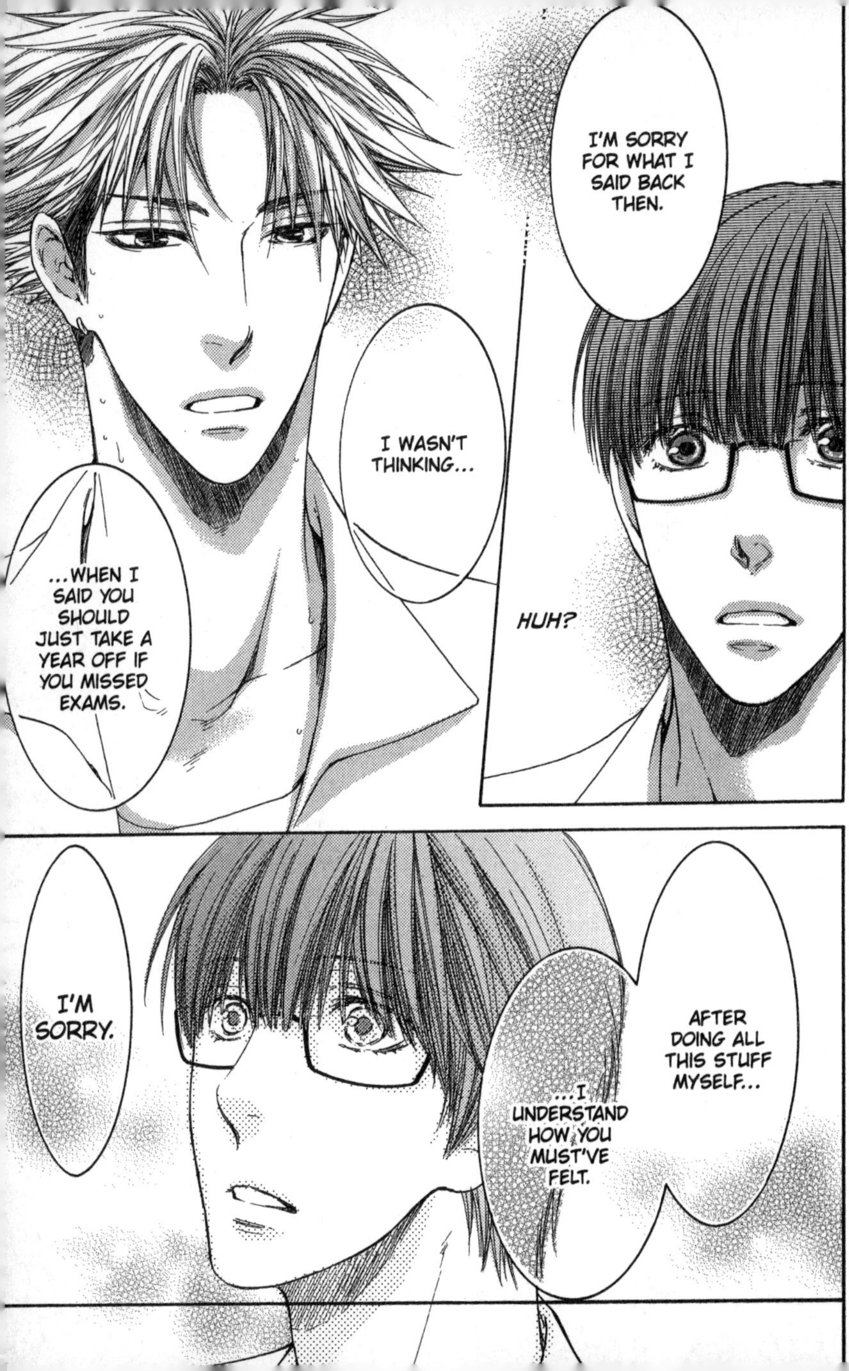
I'M SORRY FOR WHAT I SAID BACK THEN.
HUH?
I WASN'T THINKING...
...WHEN I SAID YOU SHOULD JUST TAKE A YEAR OFF IF YOU MISSED EXAMS.
AFTER DOING ALL THIS STUFF MYSELF...
...I UNDERSTAND HOW YOU MUST'VE FELT.
I'M SORRY.

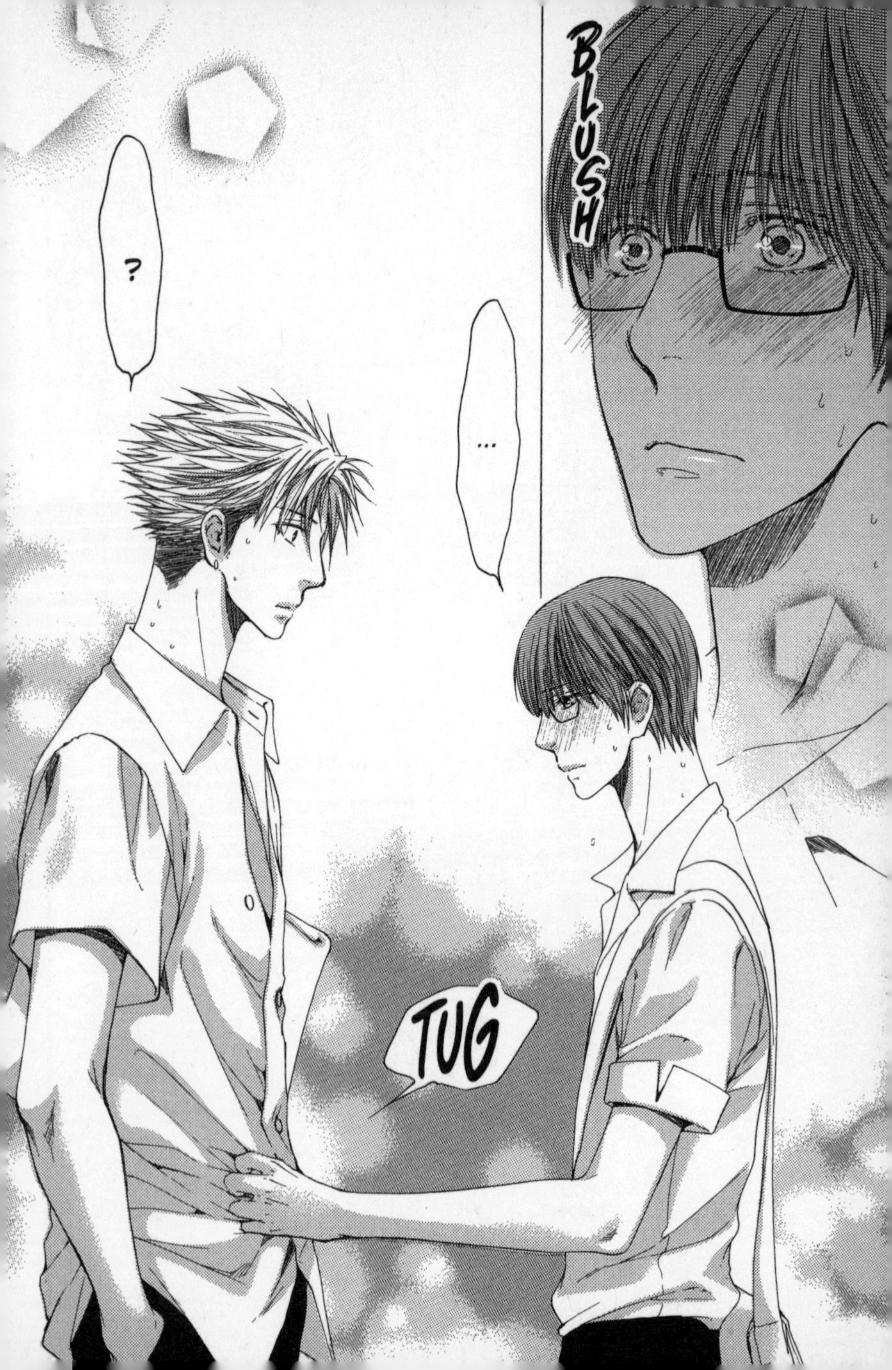
BLUSH
...
?
TUG

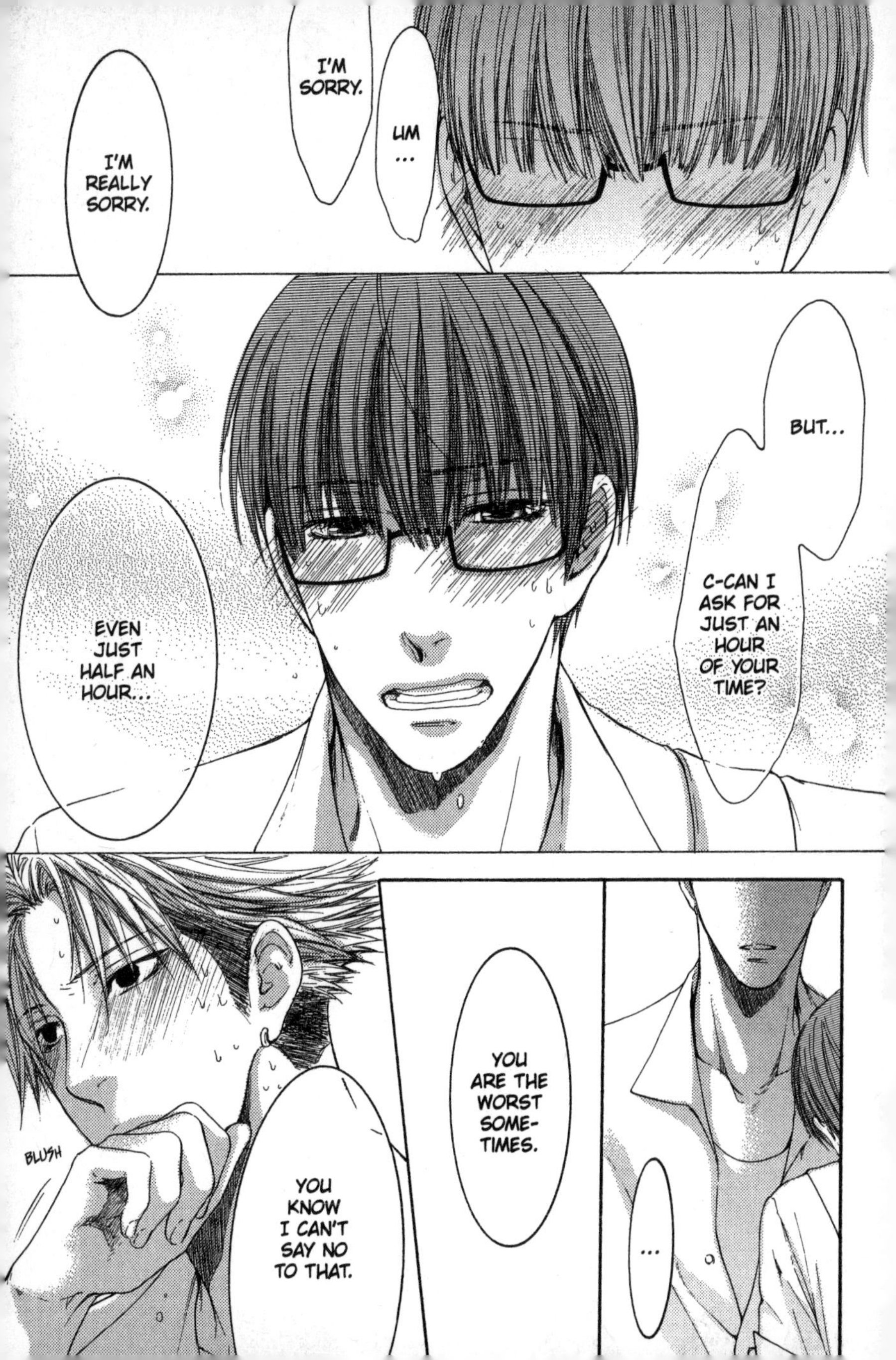
UM...
I'M SORRY.
I'M REALLY SORRY.
BUT...
C-CAN I ASK FOR JUST AN HOUR OF YOUR TIME?
EVEN JUST HALF AN HOUR...
...
YOU ARE THE WORST SOME-TIMES.
YOU KNOW I CAN'T SAY NO TO THAT.
BLUSH

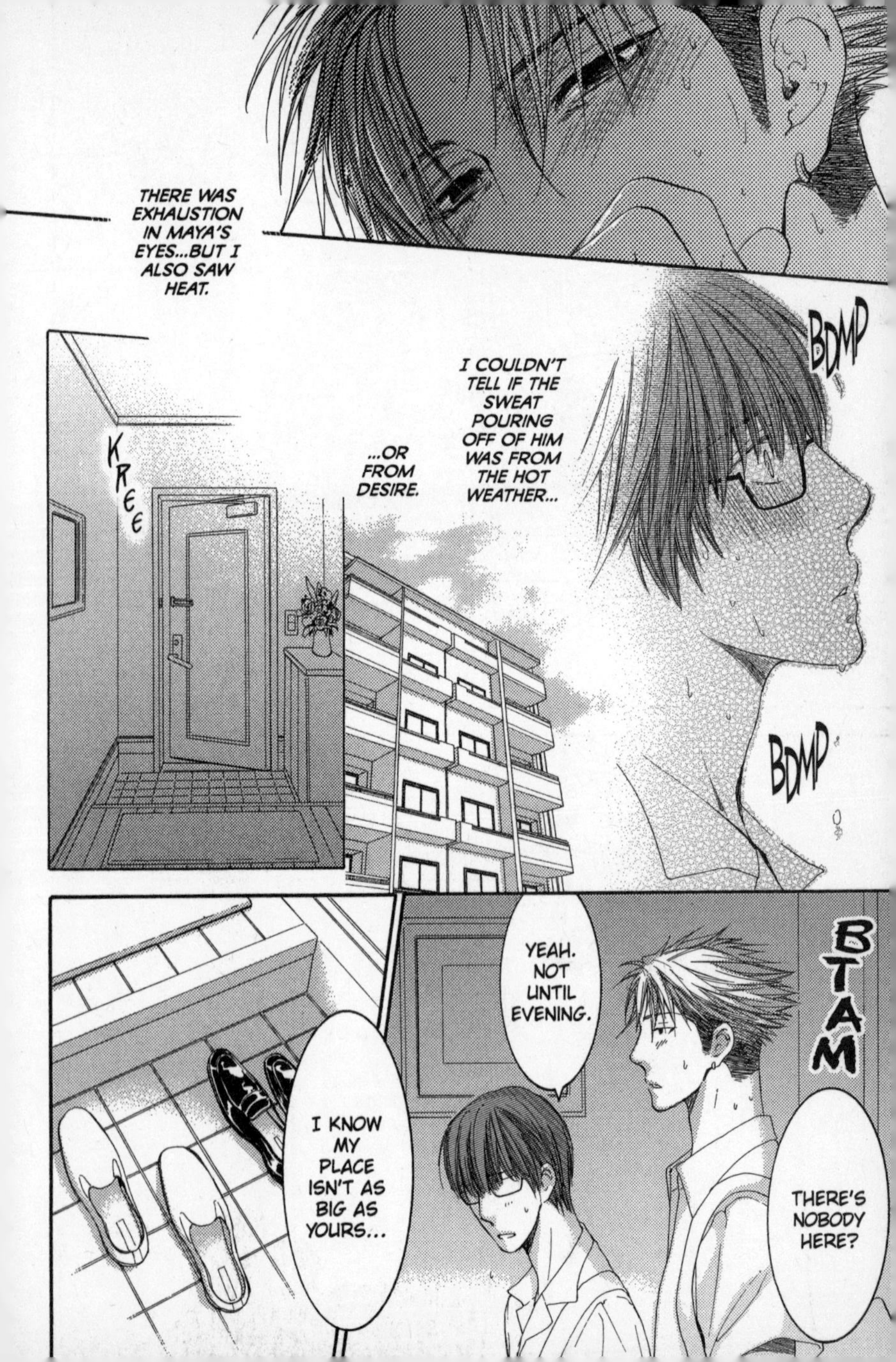
THERE WAS EXHAUSTION IN MAYA'S EYES...BUT I ALSO SAW HEAT.
BDMP
I COULDN'T TELL IF THE SWEAT POURING OFF OF HIM WAS FROM THE HOT WEATHER...
...OR FROM DESIRE.
BDMP
KREE
BTAM
THERE'S NOBODY HERE?
YEAH. NOT UNTIL EVENING.
I KNOW MY PLACE ISN'T AS BIG AS YOURS...

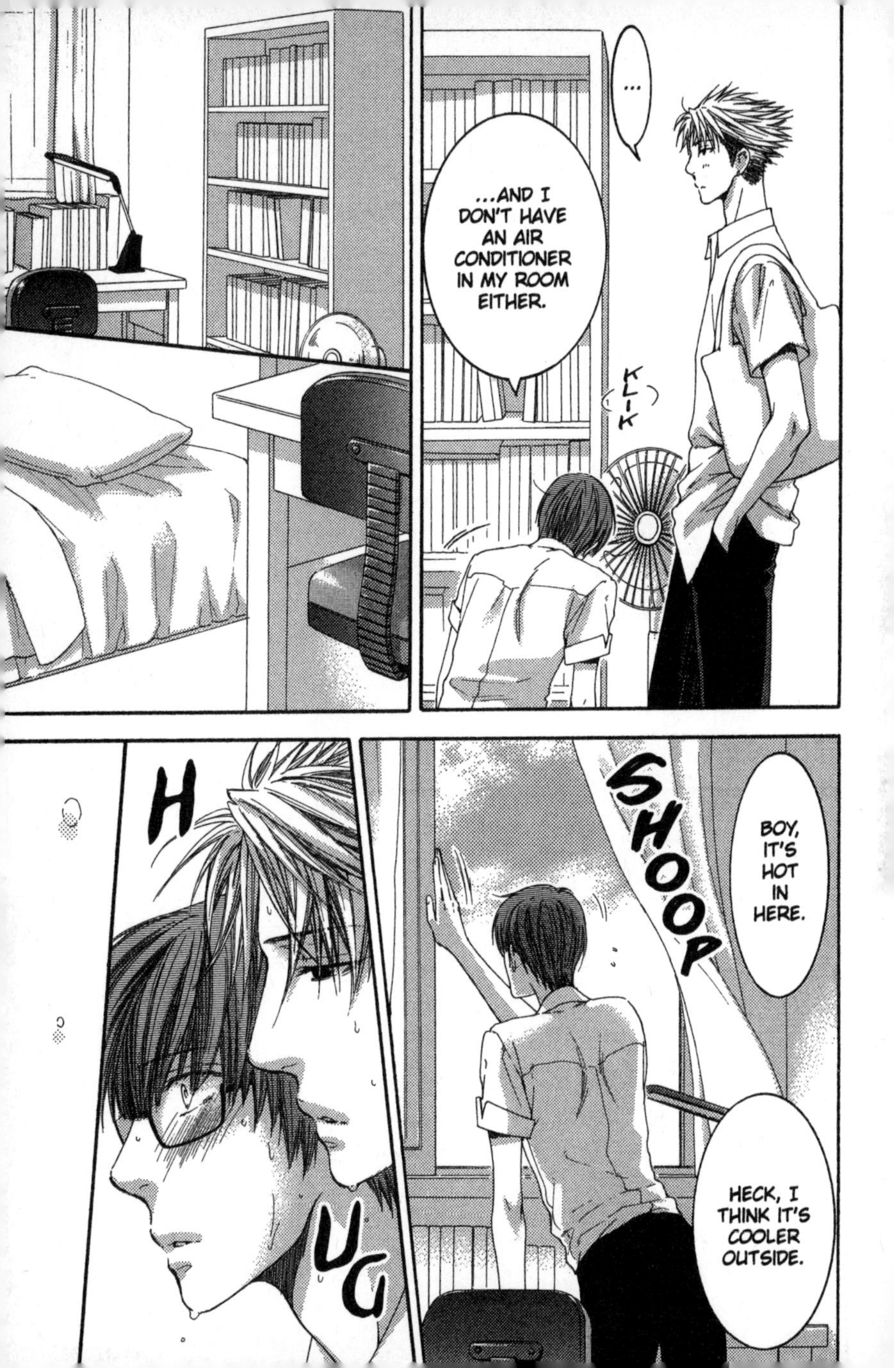
...
...AND I DON'T HAVE AN AIR CONDITIONER IN MY ROOM EITHER.
KLIK
SHOOP
BOY, IT'S HOT IN HERE.
HECK, I THINK IT'S COOLER OUTSIDE.
H
UG

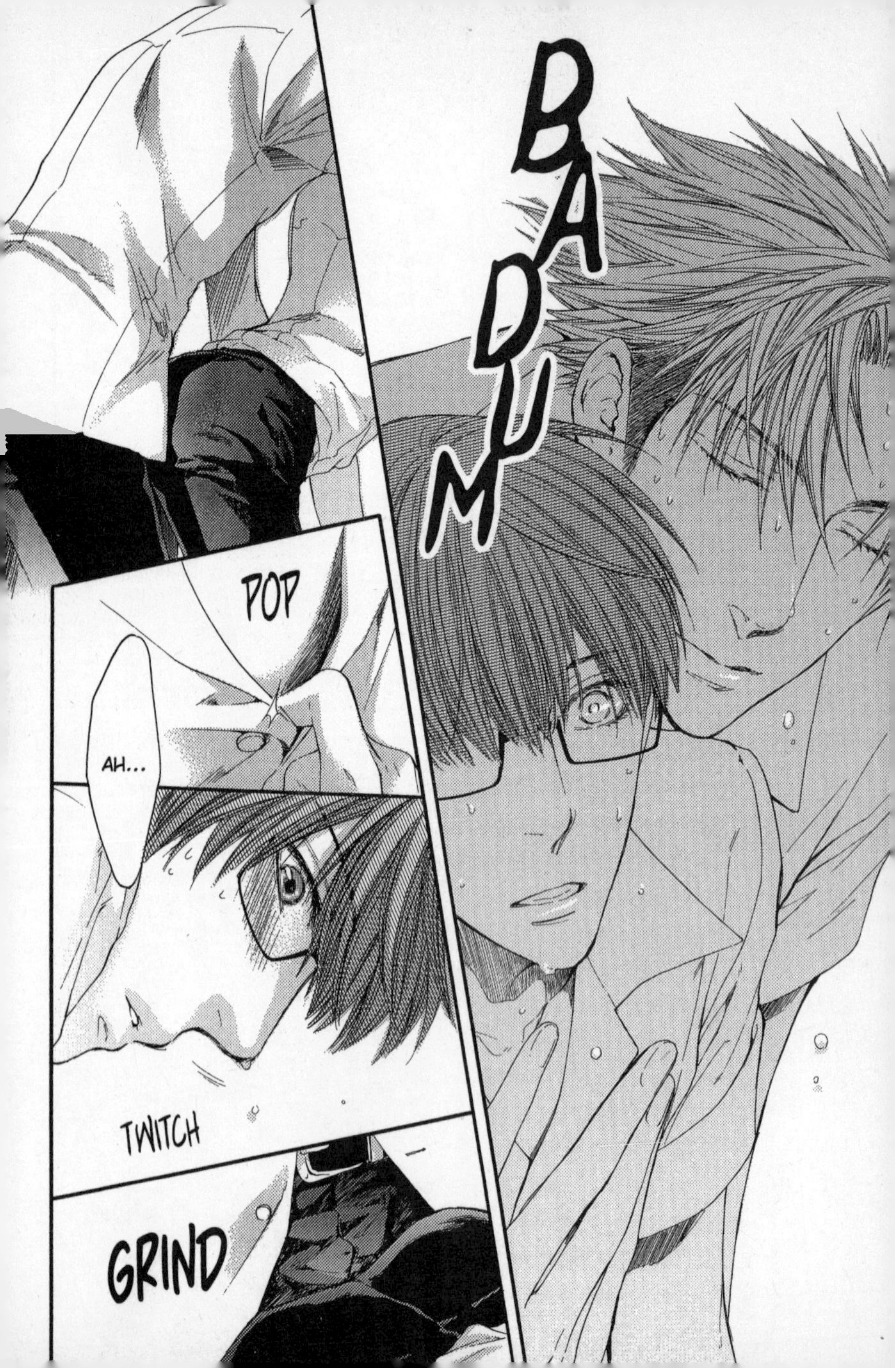
BADUM
POP
AH...
TWITCH
GRIND

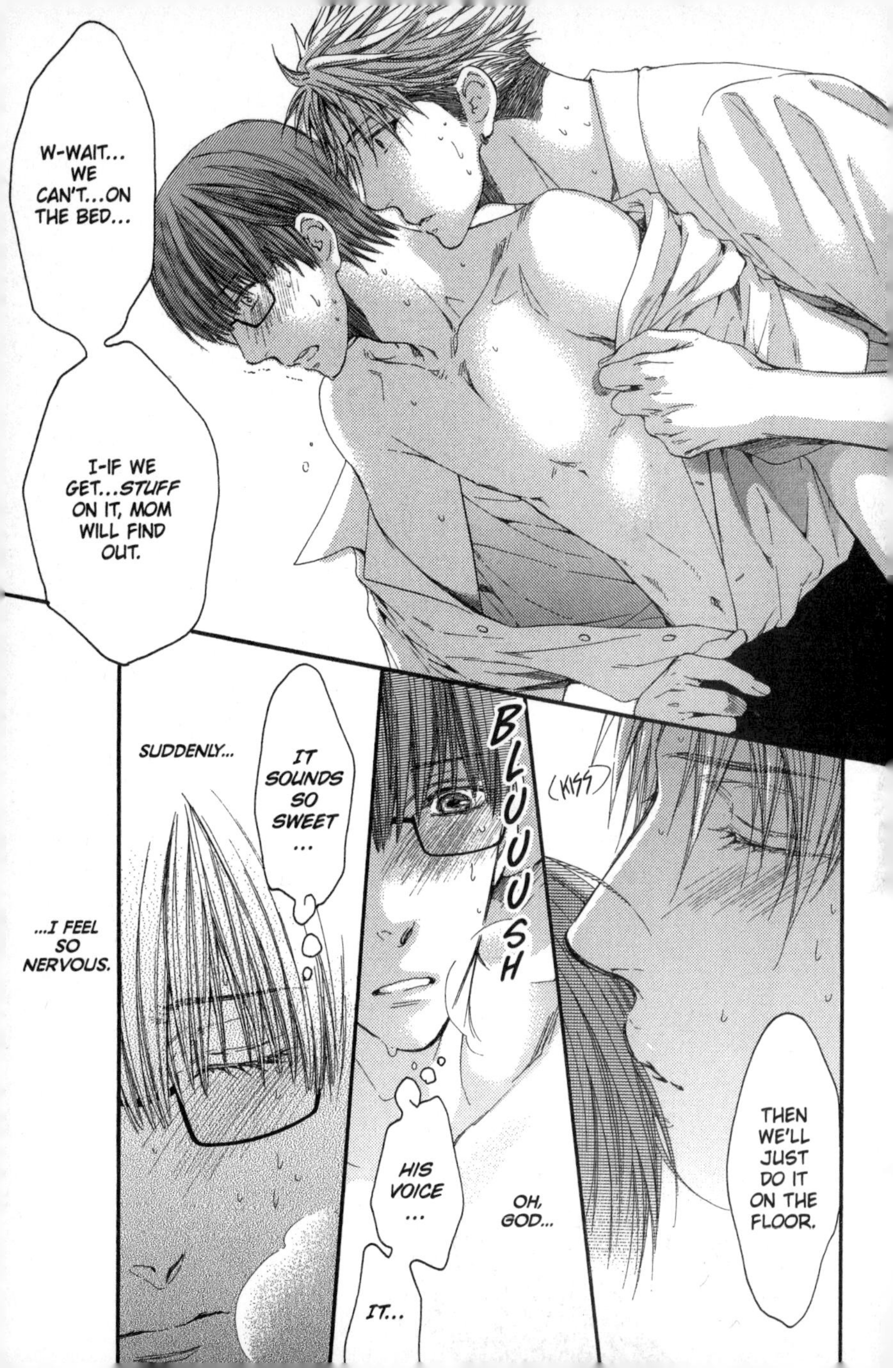
W-WAIT... WE CAN'T...ON THE BED...
I-IF WE GET...STUFF ON IT, MOM WILL FIND OUT.
(KISS)
THEN WE'LL JUST DO IT ON THE FLOOR.
BLUUUUSH
OH, GOD...
HIS VOICE...
IT...
SUDDENLY...
IT SOUNDS SO SWEET...
...I FEEL SO NERVOUS.

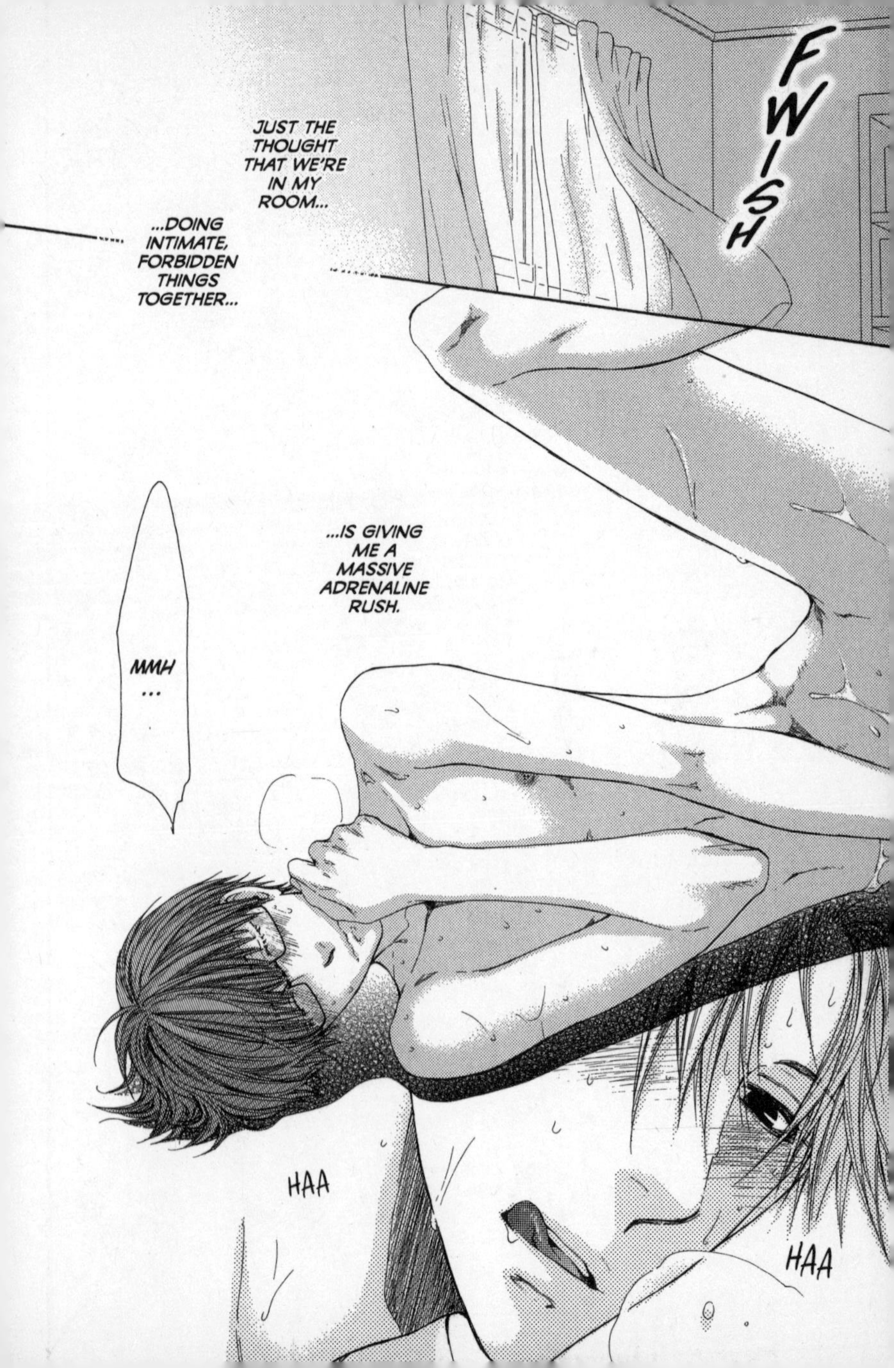
FWISH
JUST THE THOUGHT THAT WE'RE IN MY ROOM...
...DOING INTIMATE, FORBIDDEN THINGS TOGETHER...
...IS GIVING ME A MASSIVE ADRENALINE RUSH.
MMH ...
HAA
HAA

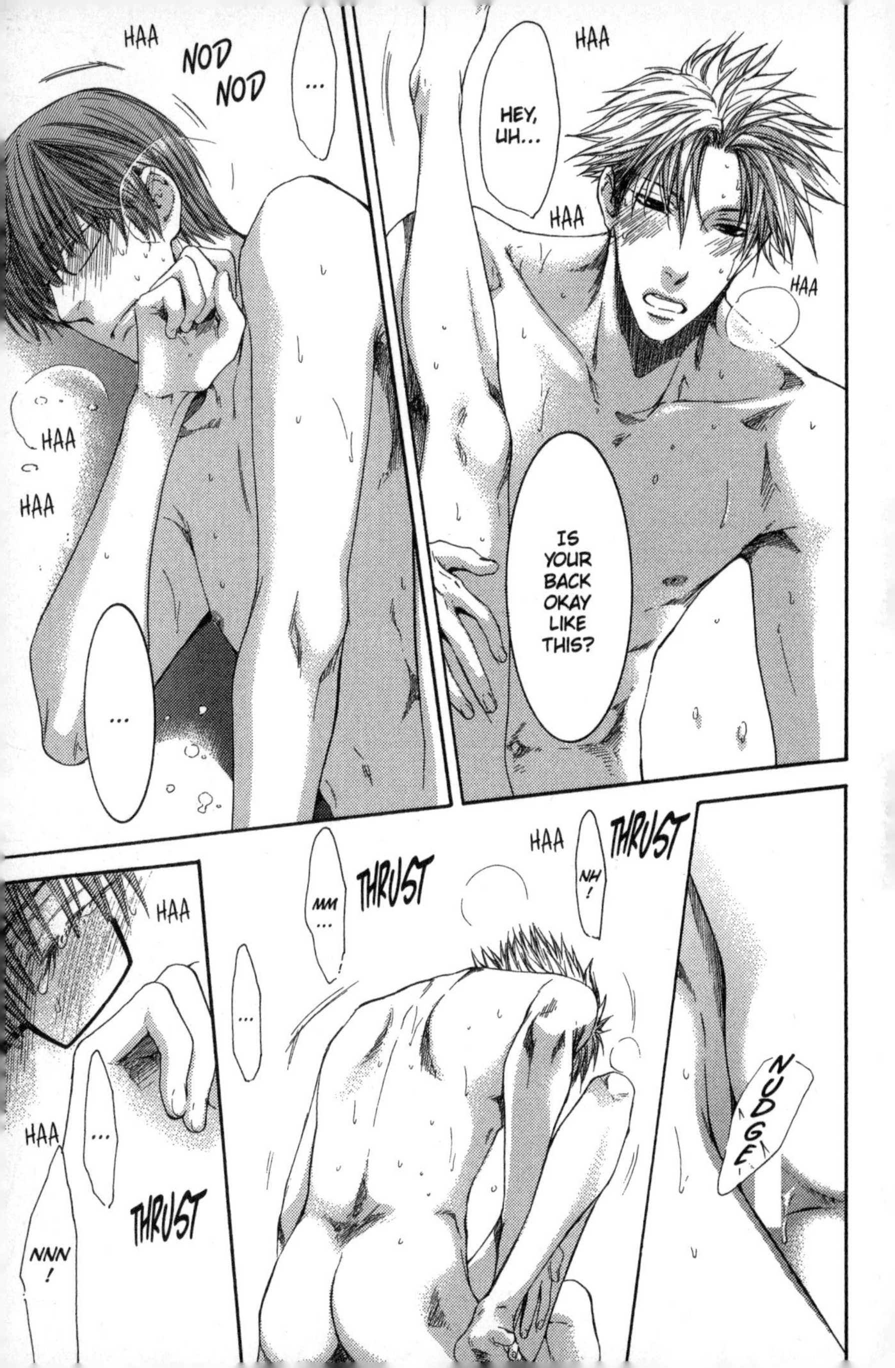
HAA
HEY, UH...
HAA
HAA
IS YOUR BACK OKAY LIKE THIS?
...
HAA
NOD NOD
HAA
HAA
...
THRUST
HAA
NH!
MM...
THRUST
...
NUDGE
HAA
...
HAA
THRUST
NNN!

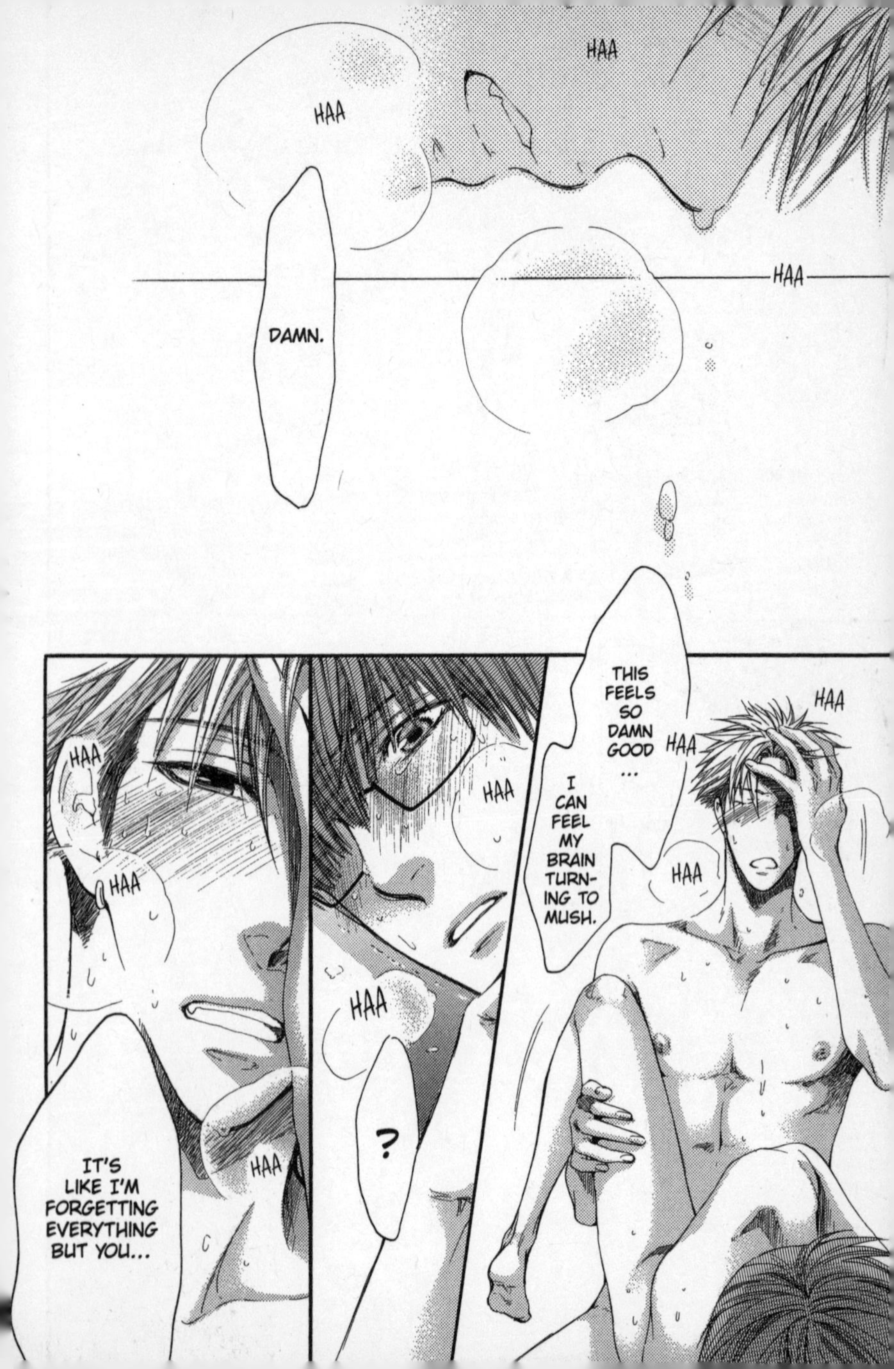
HAA
HAA
HAA
DAMN.
HAA
THIS FEELS SO DAMN GOOD...
HAA
I CAN FEEL MY BRAIN TURNING TO MUSH.
HAA
HAA
HAA
?
HAA
HAA
HAA
IT'S LIKE I'M FORGETTING EVERYTHING BUT YOU...

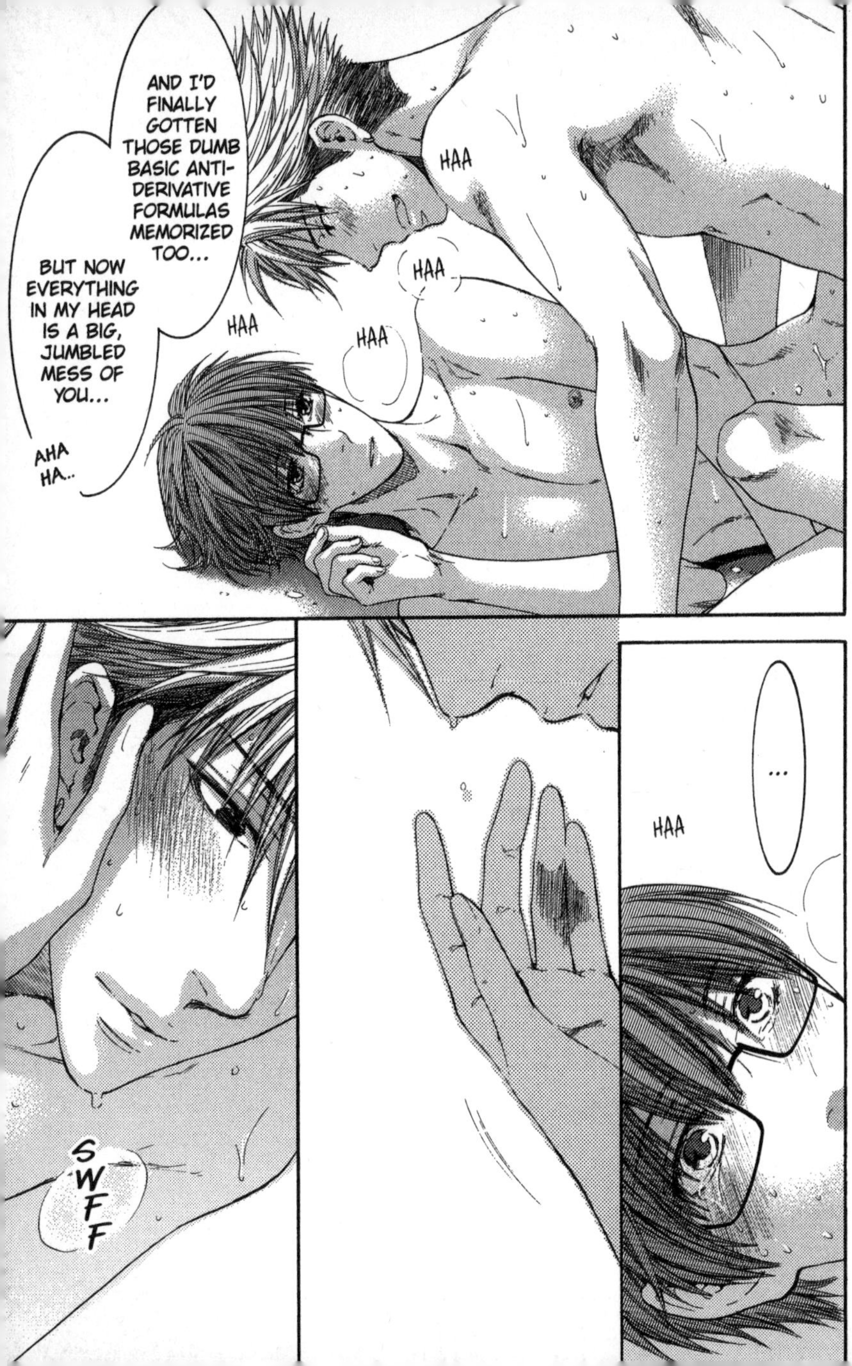
HAA
AND I'D FINALLY GOTTEN THOSE DUMB BASIC ANTI-DERIVATIVE FORMULAS MEMORIZED TOO...
BUT NOW EVERYTHING IN MY HEAD IS A BIG, JUMBLED MESS OF YOU...
AHA HA..
HAA
HAA
HAA
...
HAA
SWFF

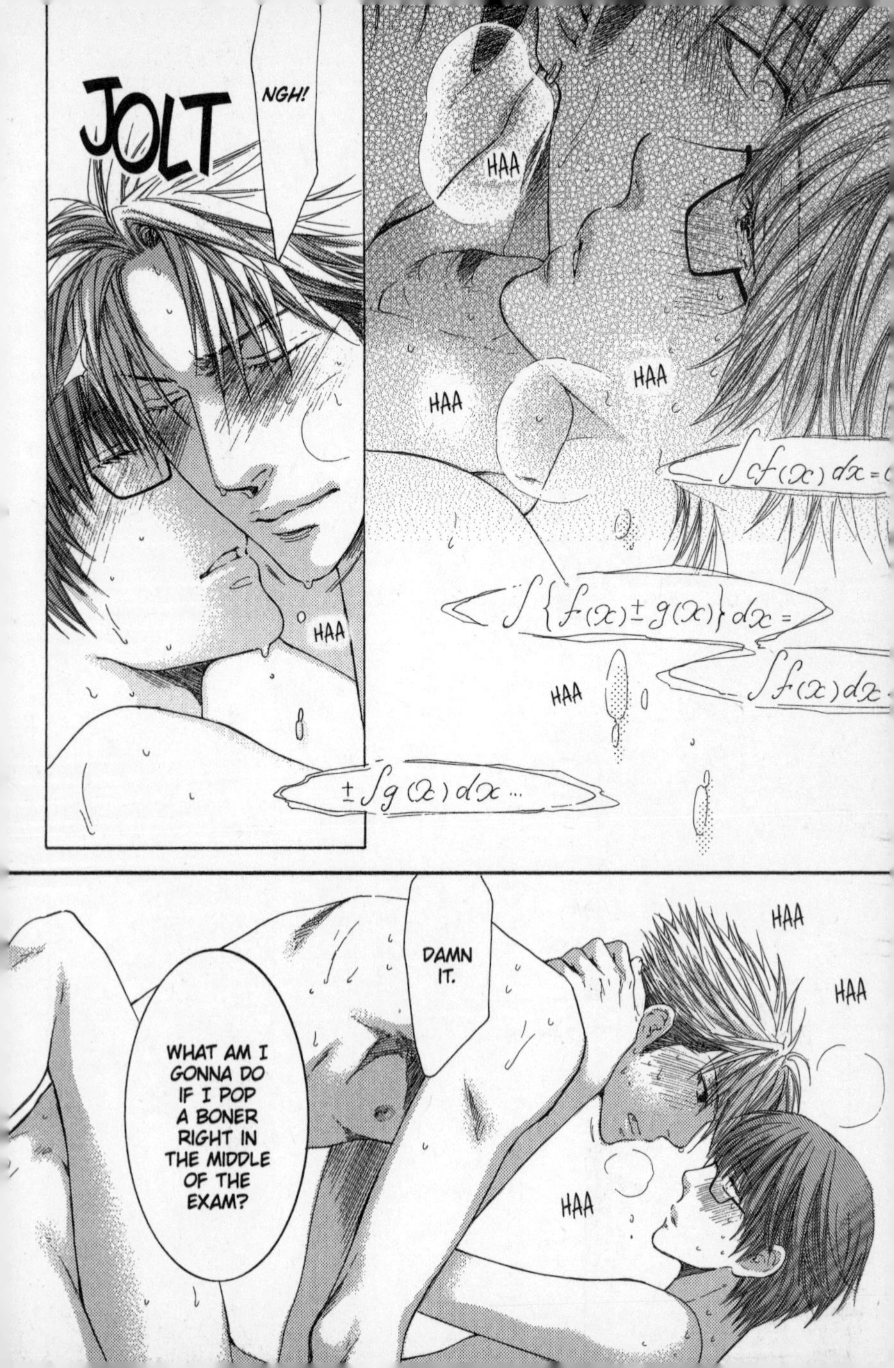
HAA
HAA
HAA
∫cf(x)dx = c
∫{f(x) ± g(x)}dx =
∫f(x)dx
HAA
± ∫g(x)dx...
JOLT
NGH!
HAA
HAA
HAA
DAMN IT.
WHAT AM I GONNA DO IF I POP A BONER RIGHT IN THE MIDDLE OF THE EXAM?
HAA

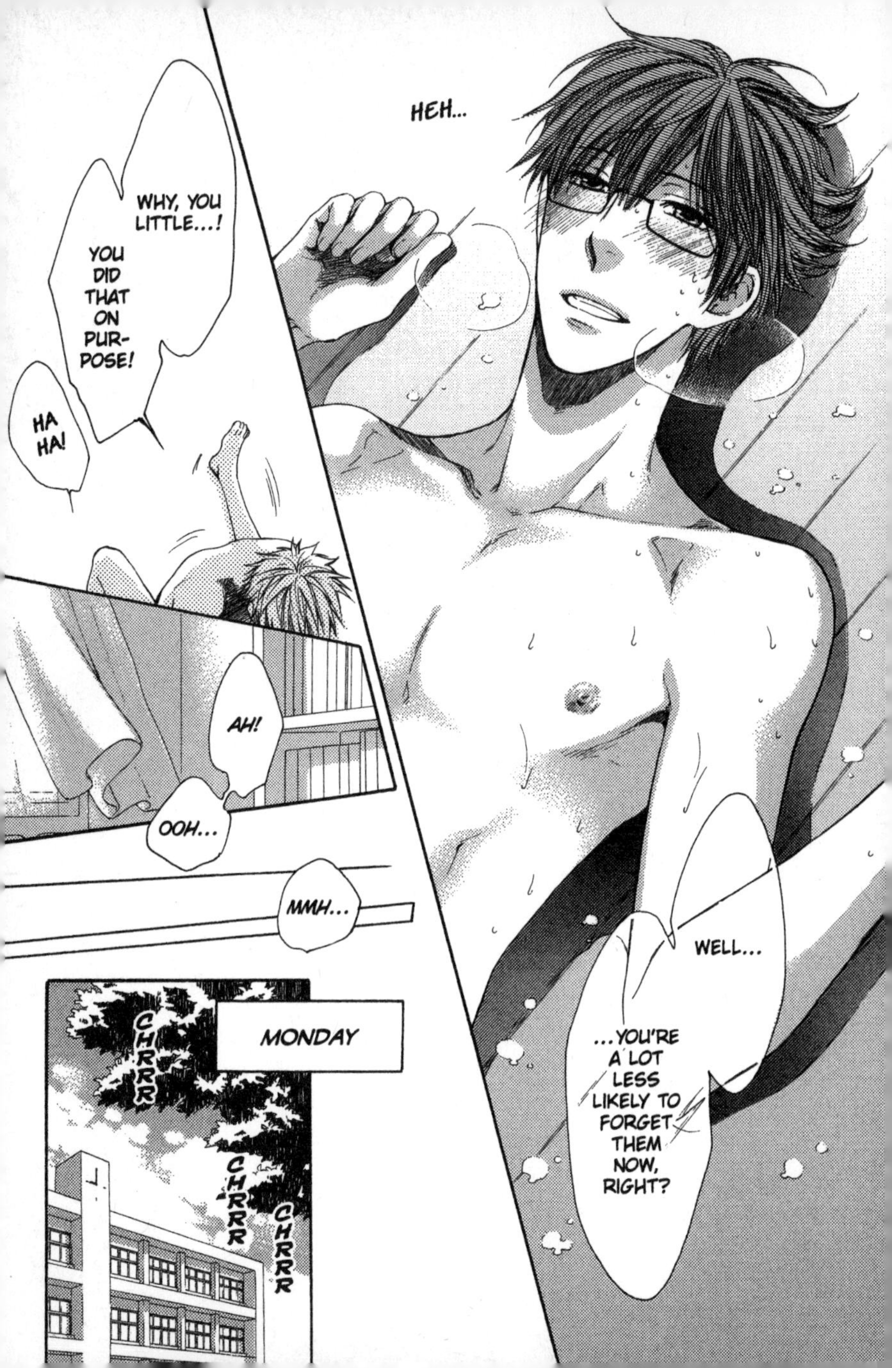
HEH...
WELL...
...YOU'RE A LOT LESS LIKELY TO FORGET THEM NOW, RIGHT?
WHY, YOU LITTLE...!
YOU DID THAT ON PUR-POSE!
HA HA!
AH!
OOH...
MMH...
MONDAY
CHRRR
CHRRR
CHRRR

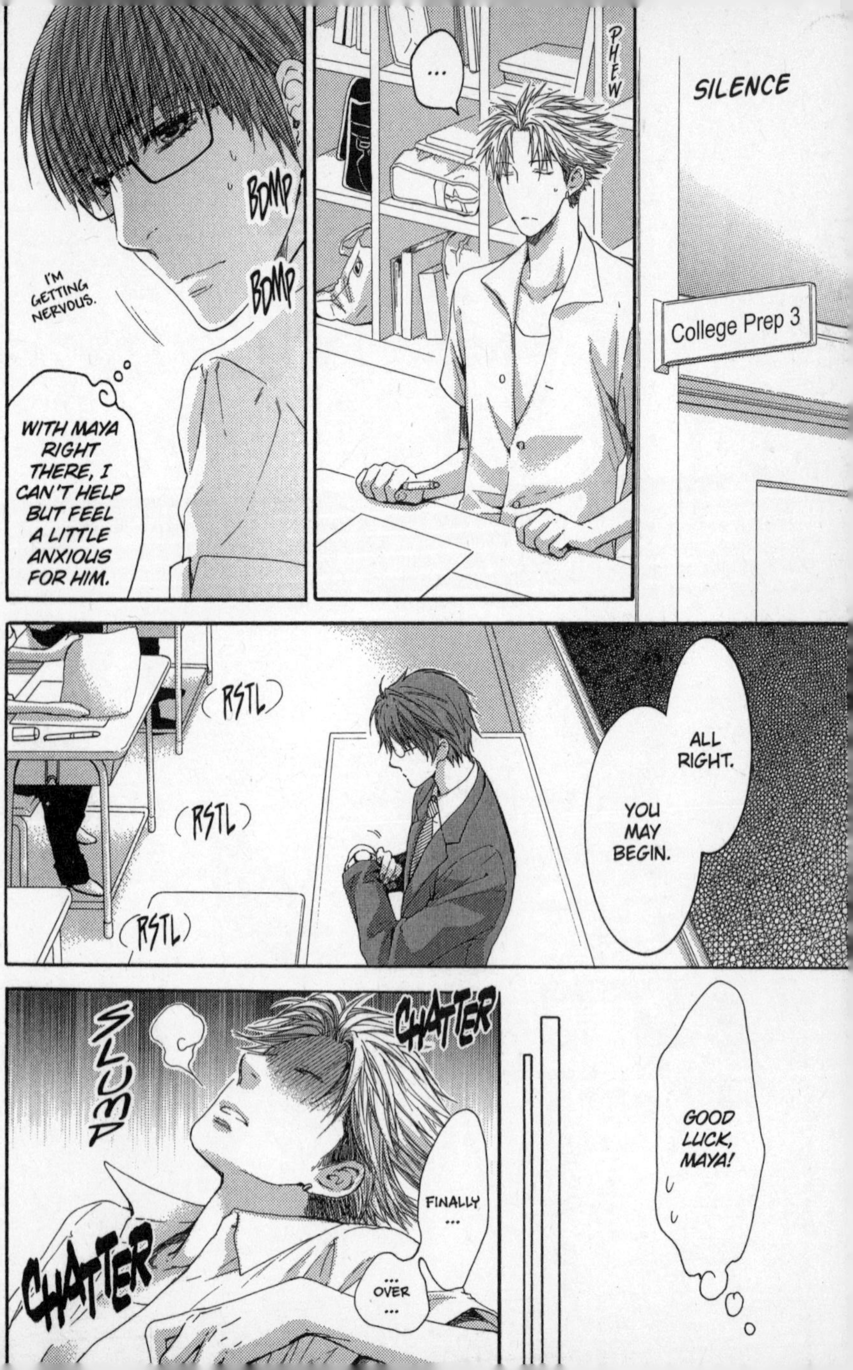
SILENCE
College Prep 3
PHEW
...
BDMP
BDMP
I'M GETTING NERVOUS.
WITH MAYA RIGHT THERE, I CAN'T HELP BUT FEEL A LITTLE ANXIOUS FOR HIM.
ALL RIGHT.
YOU MAY BEGIN.
(RSTL)
(RSTL)
(RSTL)
GOOD LUCK, MAYA!
CHATTER
SLUMP
FINALLY ...
... OVER ...
CHATTER

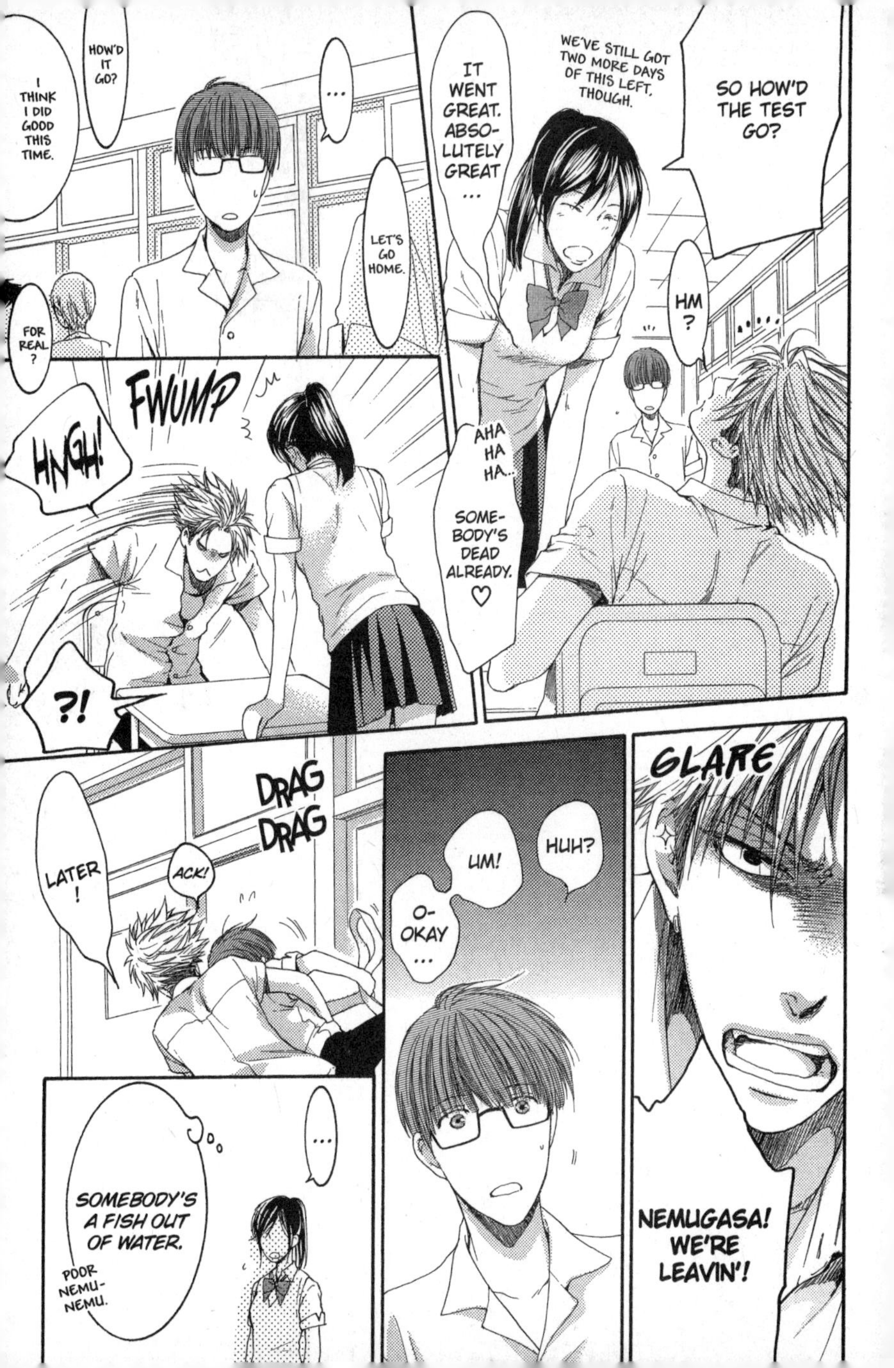
SO HOW'D THE TEST GO?
HM?
...
WE'VE STILL GOT TWO MORE DAYS OF THIS LEFT, THOUGH.
IT WENT GREAT. ABSOLUTELY GREAT...
AHA HA HA...
SOMEBODY'S DEAD ALREADY. ♡
...
HOW'D IT GO?
I THINK I DID GOOD THIS TIME.
LET'S GO HOME.
FOR REAL?
FWUMP
HNGH!
?!
GLARE
NEMUGASA! WE'RE LEAVIN'!
HUH?
UM!
O-OKAY...
DRAG
DRAG
LATER!
ACK!
...
SOMEBODY'S A FISH OUT OF WATER.
POOR NEMU-NEMU.

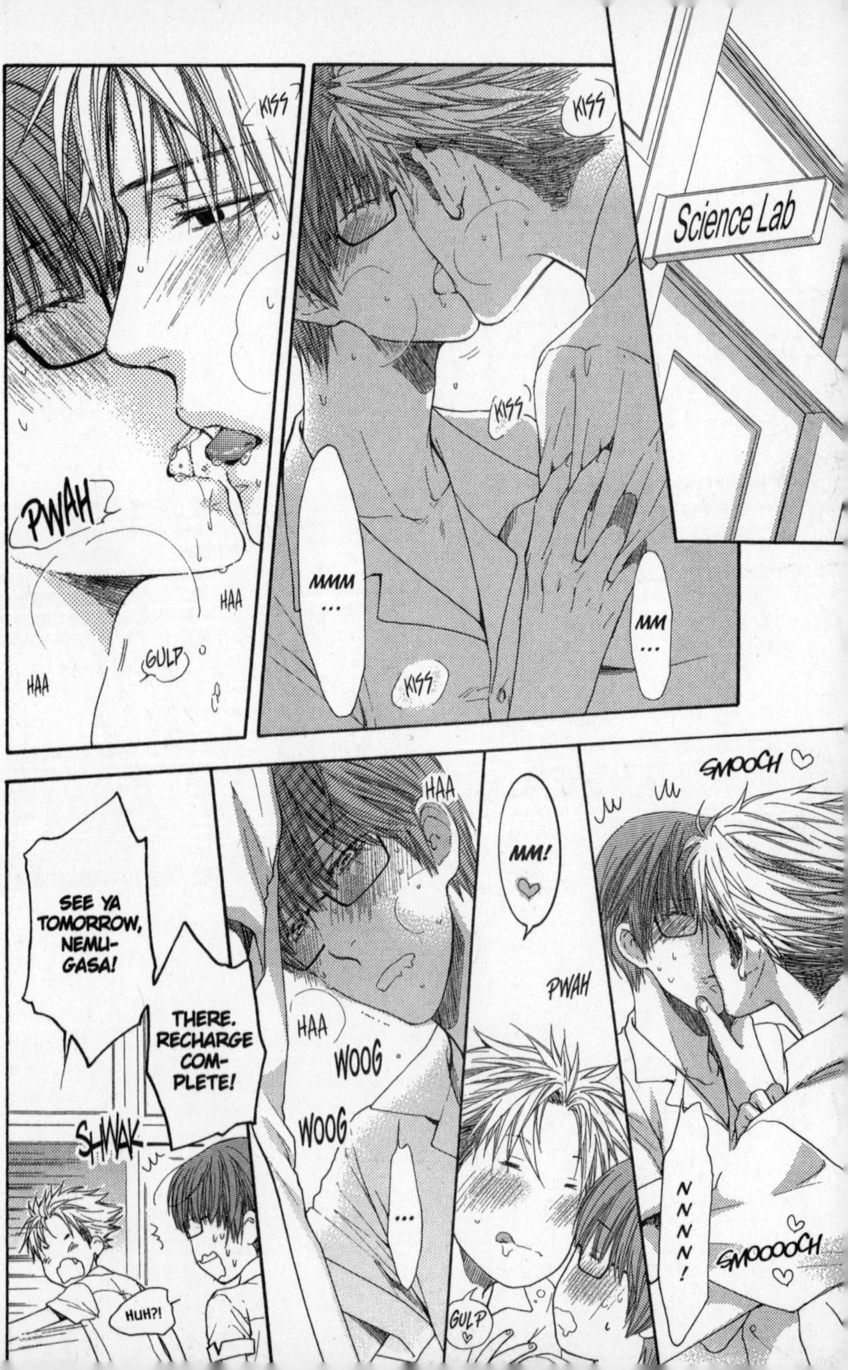
Science Lab
KISS
KISS
MM...
MMM...
KISS
KISS
PWAH
HAA
GULP
HAA
SMOOCH ♡
NNNN!
SMOOOOCH ♡
MM! ♡
PWAH
GULP ♡
HAA
HAA
WOOG
WOOG
...
THERE. RECHARGE COMPLETE!
SEE YA TOMORROW, NEMUGASA!
SHWAK
HUH?!

Hideyuki Maya			
Modern Lit. 92	W T	85	Class Rank / 72ND
assical Lit. 90	L D	86	Math III 89

WOOG

WOOG

WOOG

...

...

...

SO CLOSE, SO CLOSE! BUT TO RANK EVEN THAT HIGH IN A CLASS FULL OF ADVANCED-PLACEMENT KIDS IS REALLY QUITE IMPRESSIVE!

THANKS...

...

YOU SURPRISED ME!

PAFF PAFF

FSS

THIS... THIS IS MY FAULT.

DOOOM

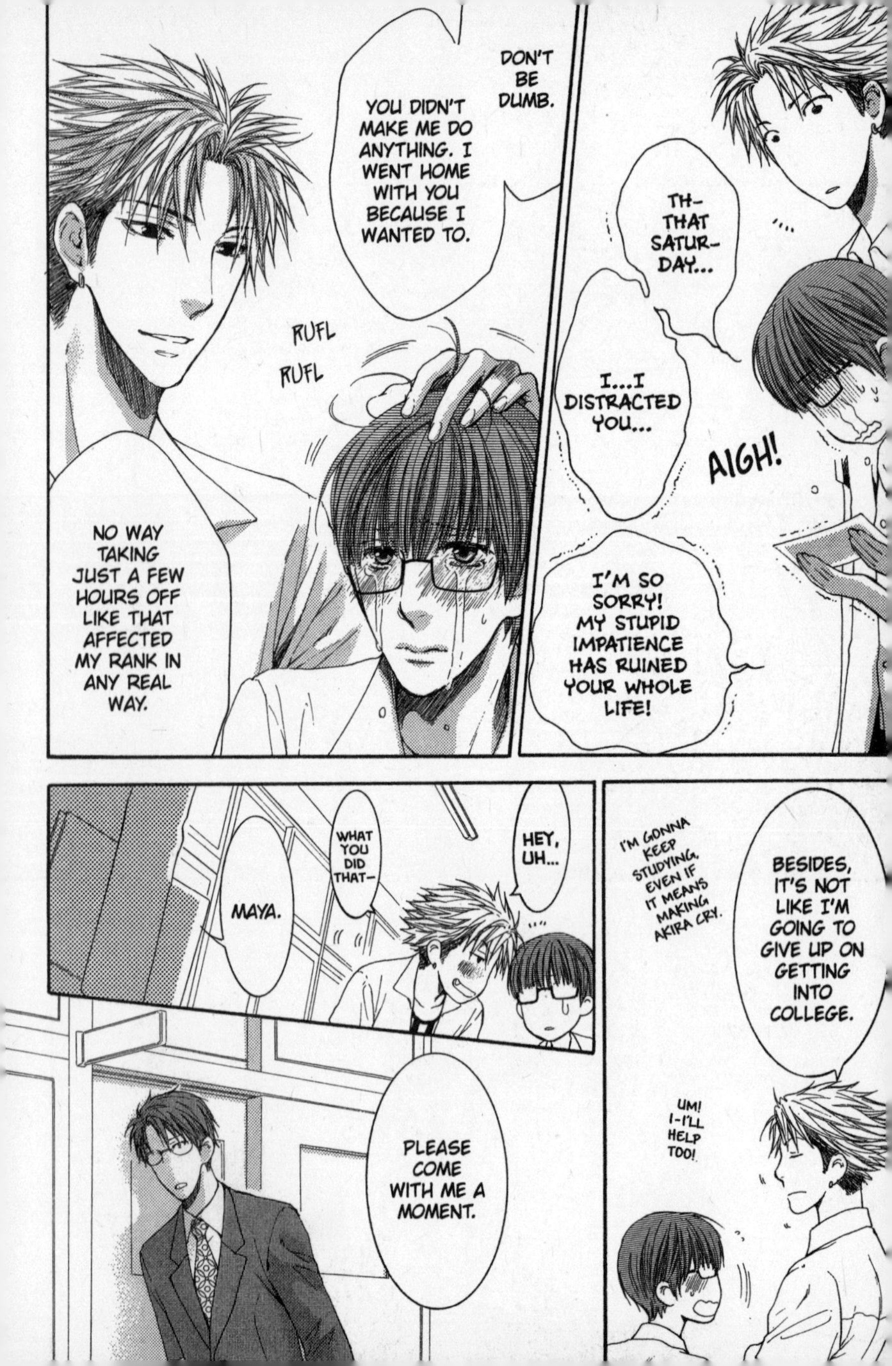
TH-THAT SATUR-DAY...
I...I DISTRACTED YOU...
AIGH!
I'M SO SORRY! MY STUPID IMPATIENCE HAS RUINED YOUR WHOLE LIFE!
DON'T BE DUMB.
YOU DIDN'T MAKE ME DO ANYTHING. I WENT HOME WITH YOU BECAUSE I WANTED TO.
RUFL
RUFL
NO WAY TAKING JUST A FEW HOURS OFF LIKE THAT AFFECTED MY RANK IN ANY REAL WAY.
BESIDES, IT'S NOT LIKE I'M GOING TO GIVE UP ON GETTING INTO COLLEGE.
I'M GONNA KEEP STUDYING, EVEN IF IT MEANS MAKING AKIRA CRY.
UM! I-I'LL HELP TOO!
HEY, UH...
WHAT YOU DID THAT—
MAYA.
PLEASE COME WITH ME A MOMENT.

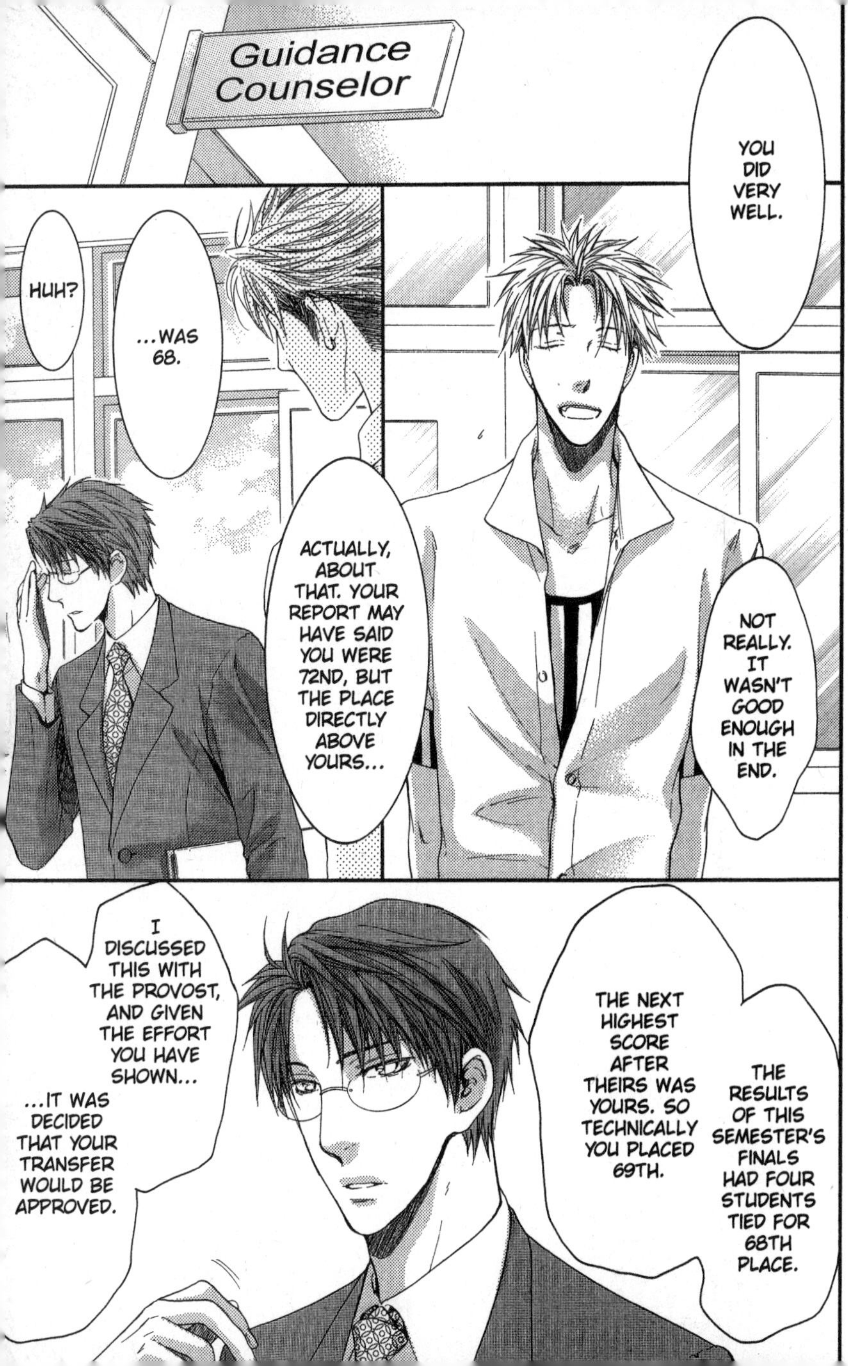
Guidance Counselor
YOU DID VERY WELL.
NOT REALLY. IT WASN'T GOOD ENOUGH IN THE END.
ACTUALLY, ABOUT THAT. YOUR REPORT MAY HAVE SAID YOU WERE 72ND, BUT THE PLACE DIRECTLY ABOVE YOURS...
...WAS 68.
HUH?
THE RESULTS OF THIS SEMESTER'S FINALS HAD FOUR STUDENTS TIED FOR 68TH PLACE.
THE NEXT HIGHEST SCORE AFTER THEIRS WAS YOURS. SO TECHNICALLY YOU PLACED 69TH.
I DISCUSSED THIS WITH THE PROVOST, AND GIVEN THE EFFORT YOU HAVE SHOWN...
...IT WAS DECIDED THAT YOUR TRANSFER WOULD BE APPROVED.

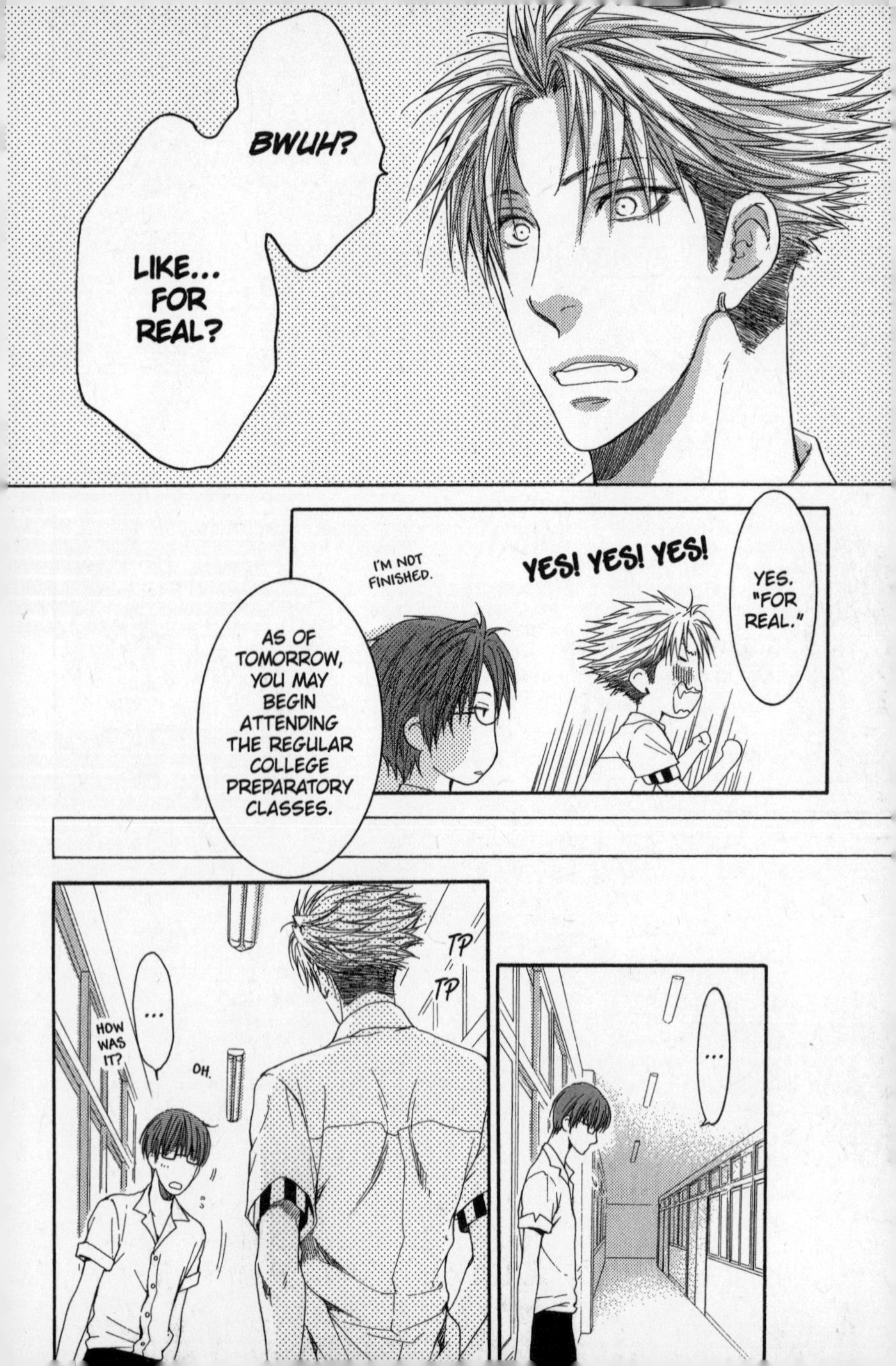
BWUH?
LIKE... FOR REAL?
YES. "FOR REAL."
YES! YES! YES!
I'M NOT FINISHED.
AS OF TOMORROW, YOU MAY BEGIN ATTENDING THE REGULAR COLLEGE PREPARATORY CLASSES.
...
TP TP
...
HOW WAS IT?
OH.

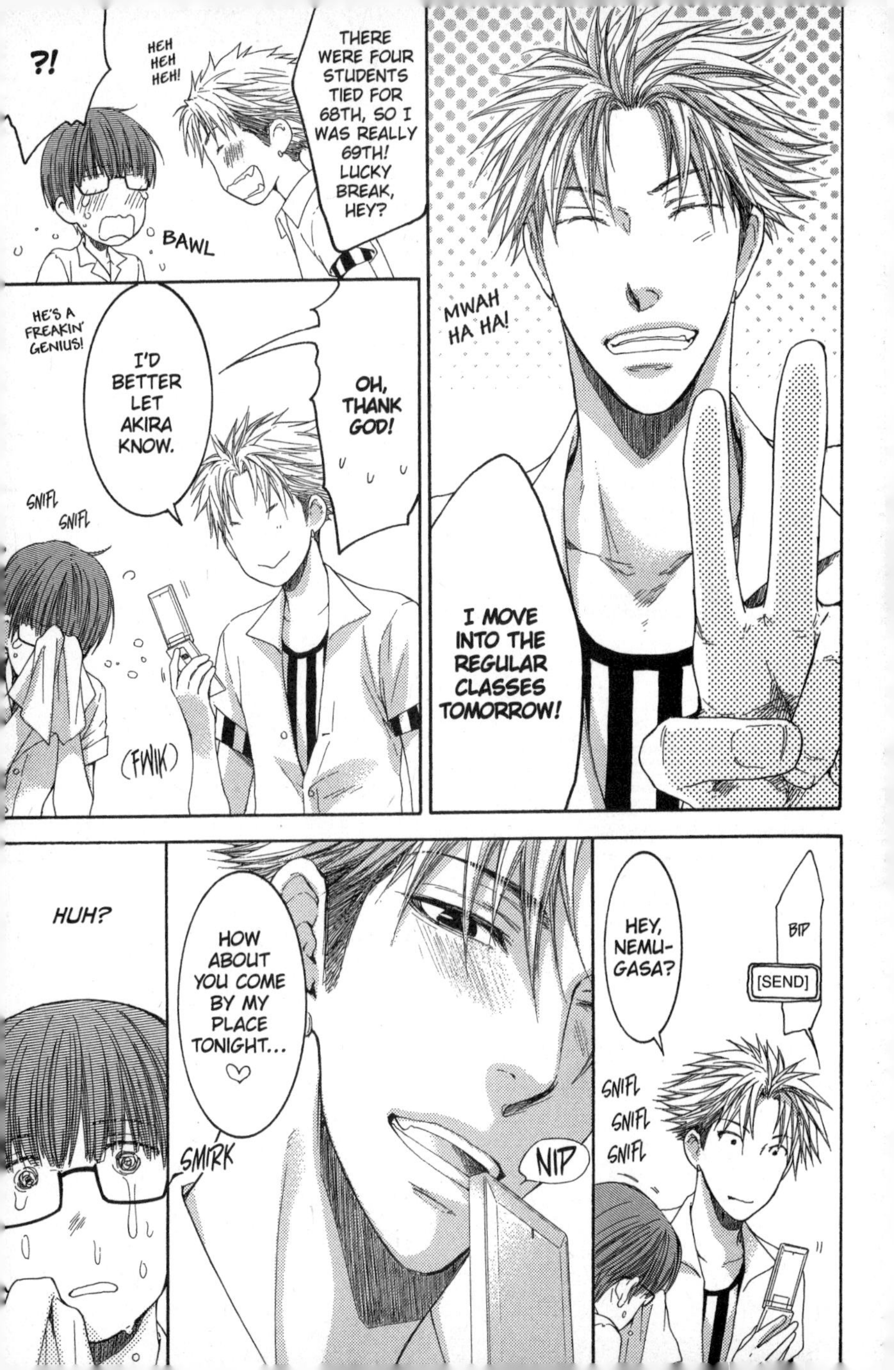
MWAH HA HA!
I MOVE INTO THE REGULAR CLASSES TOMORROW!
THERE WERE FOUR STUDENTS TIED FOR 68TH, SO I WAS REALLY 69TH! LUCKY BREAK, HEY?
HEH HEH HEH!
?!
BAWL
OH, THANK GOD!
I'D BETTER LET AKIRA KNOW.
HE'S A FREAKIN' GENIUS!
SNIFL SNIFL
(FWIK)
BIP
[SEND]
HEY, NEMU-GASA?
SNIFL SNIFL SNIFL
HOW ABOUT YOU COME BY MY PLACE TONIGHT... ♡
NIP
SMIRK
HUH?

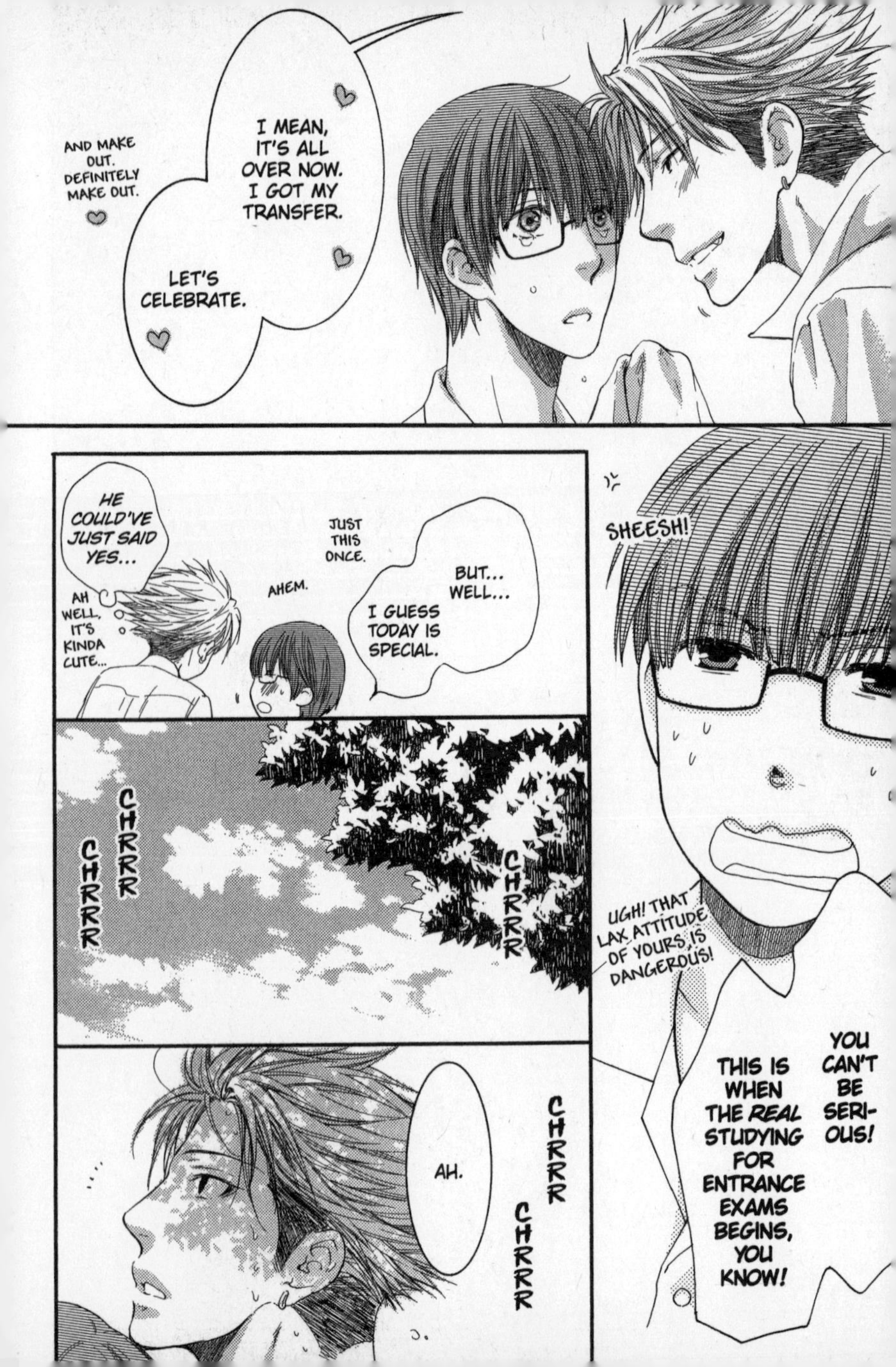

I MEAN, IT'S ALL OVER NOW. I GOT MY TRANSFER.
LET'S CELEBRATE.
AND MAKE OUT. DEFINITELY MAKE OUT.
SHEESH!
YOU CAN'T BE SERI-OUS!
THIS IS WHEN THE *REAL* STUDYING FOR ENTRANCE EXAMS BEGINS, YOU KNOW!
UGH! THAT LAX ATTITUDE OF YOURS IS DANGEROUS!
JUST THIS ONCE.
AHEM.
BUT... WELL...
I GUESS TODAY IS SPECIAL.
HE COULD'VE JUST SAID YES...
AH WELL, IT'S KINDA CUTE...
CHRRR
CHRRR
CHRRR
CHRRR
CHRRR
AH.

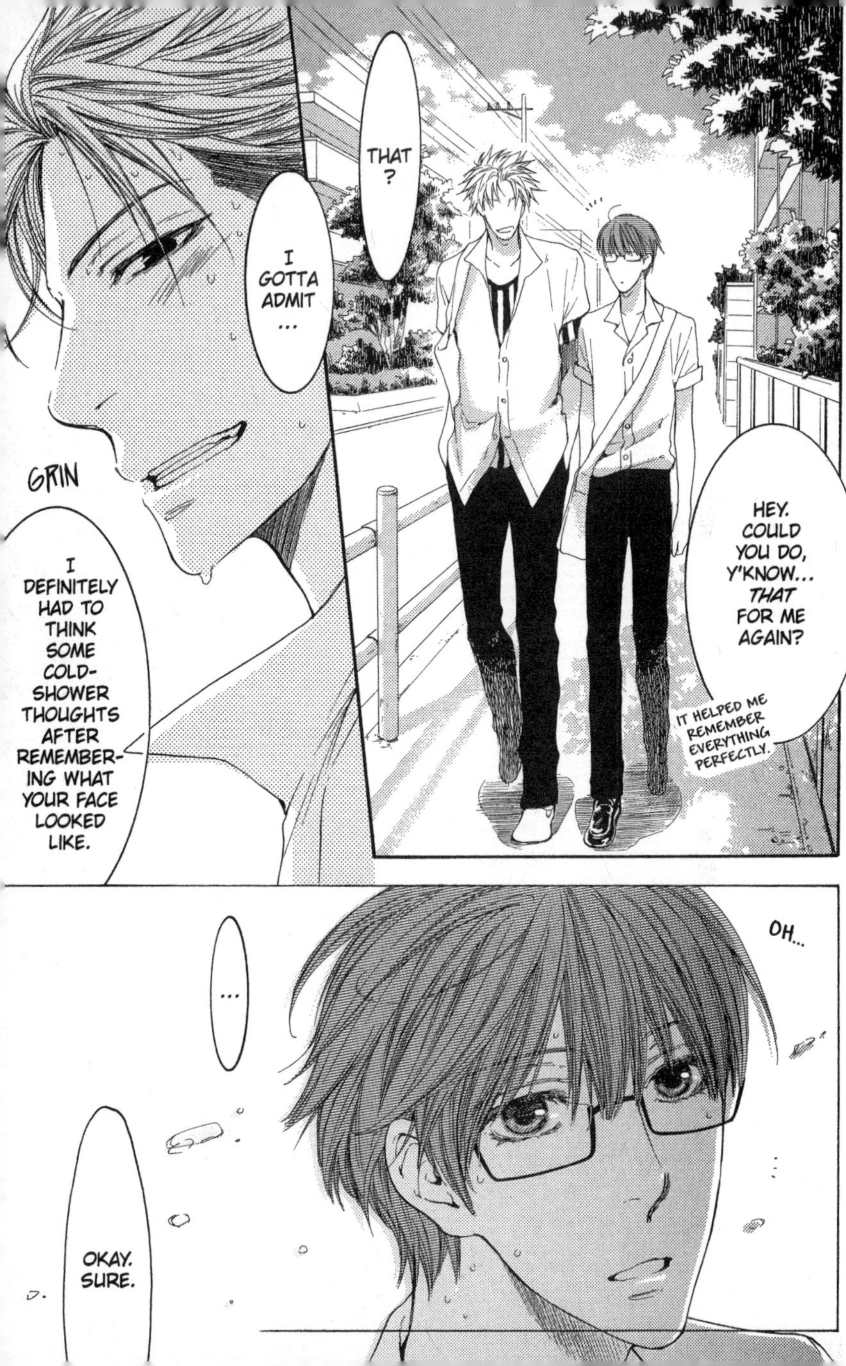
HEY. COULD YOU DO, Y'KNOW... *THAT* FOR ME AGAIN?
IT HELPED ME REMEMBER EVERYTHING PERFECTLY.
THAT ?
I GOTTA ADMIT ...
GRIN
I DEFINITELY HAD TO THINK SOME COLD-SHOWER THOUGHTS AFTER REMEMBER-ING WHAT YOUR FACE LOOKED LIKE.
OH...
...
OKAY. SURE.

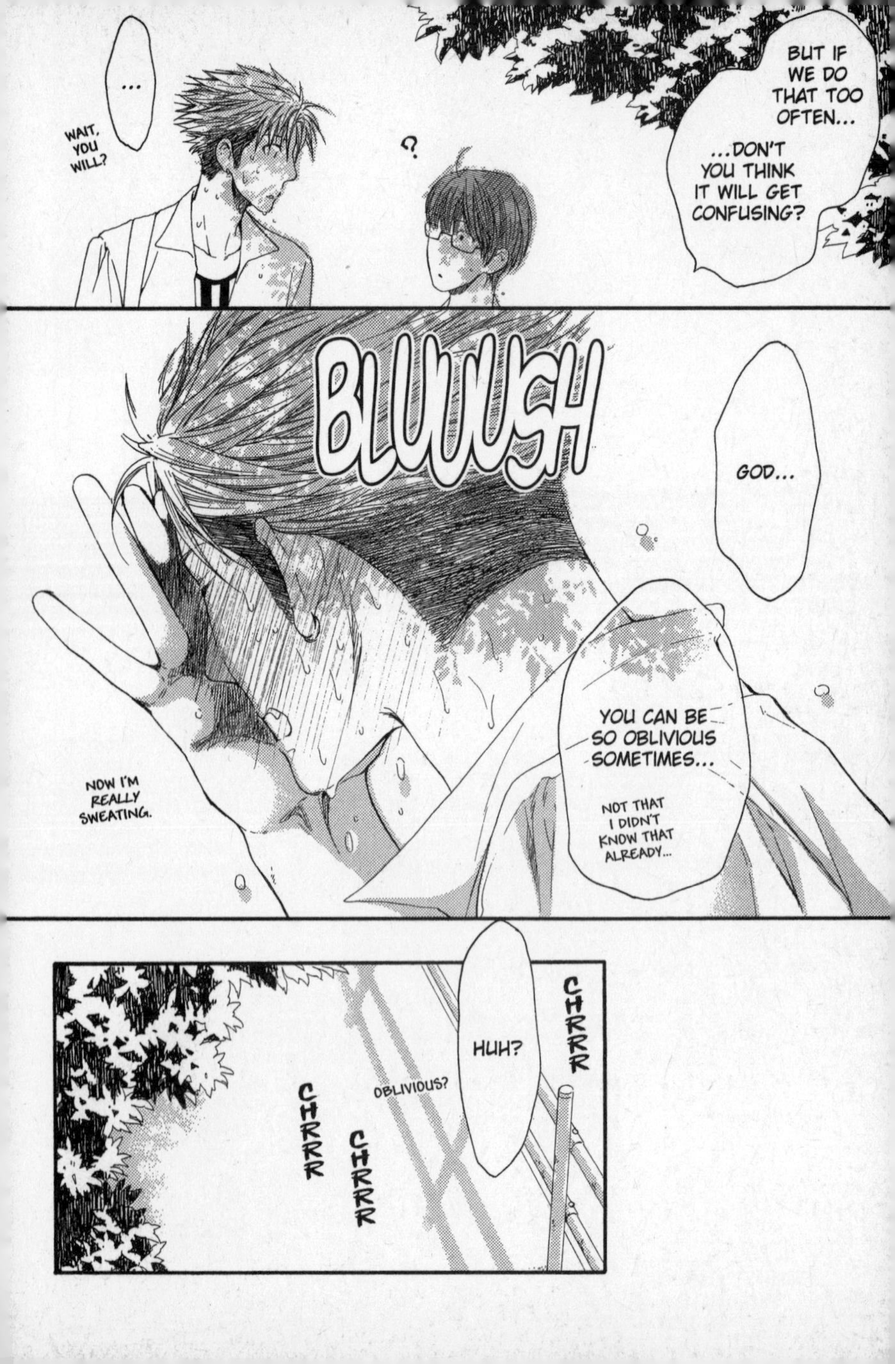
BUT IF WE DO THAT TOO OFTEN...
...DON'T YOU THINK IT WILL GET CONFUSING?
?
...
WAIT, YOU WILL?
BLUUUSH
GOD...
YOU CAN BE SO OBLIVIOUS SOMETIMES...
NOT THAT I DIDN'T KNOW THAT ALREADY...
NOW I'M REALLY SWEATING.
CHRRR
HUH?
OBLIVIOUS?
CHRRR
CHRRR

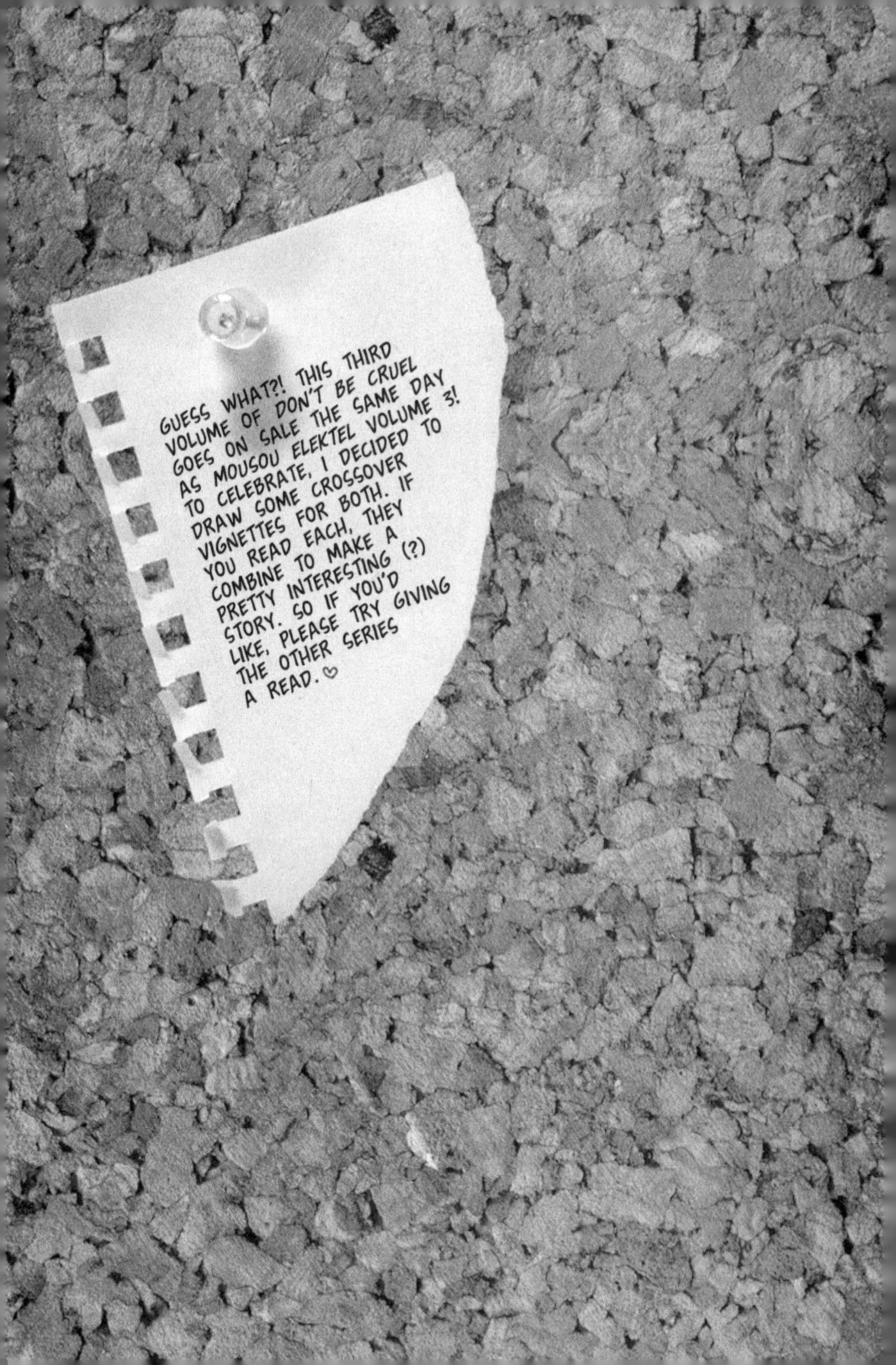
GUESS WHAT?! THIS THIRD VOLUME OF DON'T BE CRUEL GOES ON SALE THE SAME DAY AS MOUSOU ELEKTEL VOLUME 3! TO CELEBRATE, I DECIDED TO DRAW SOME CROSSOVER VIGNETTES FOR BOTH. IF YOU READ EACH, THEY COMBINE TO MAKE A PRETTY INTERESTING (?) STORY. SO IF YOU'D LIKE, PLEASE TRY GIVING THE OTHER SERIES A READ. ♡

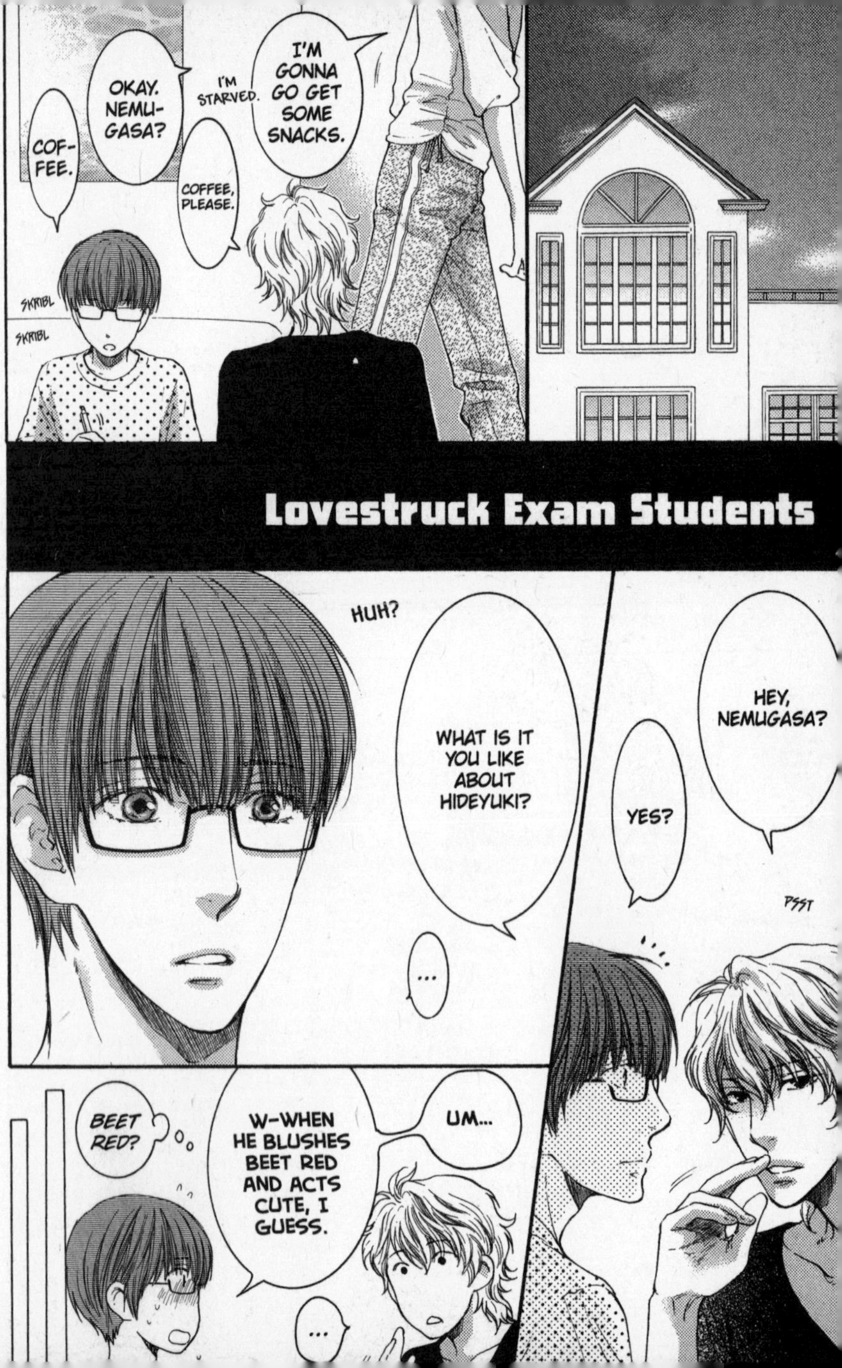
I'M GONNA GO GET SOME SNACKS.
I'M STARVED.
OKAY. NEMUGASA?
COFFEE, PLEASE.
COFFEE.
SKRIBL
SKRIBL
Lovestruck Exam Students
HEY, NEMUGASA?
YES?
PSST
WHAT IS IT YOU LIKE ABOUT HIDEYUKI?
HUH?
...
UM...
W-WHEN HE BLUSHES BEET RED AND ACTS CUTE, I GUESS.
BEET RED?
...

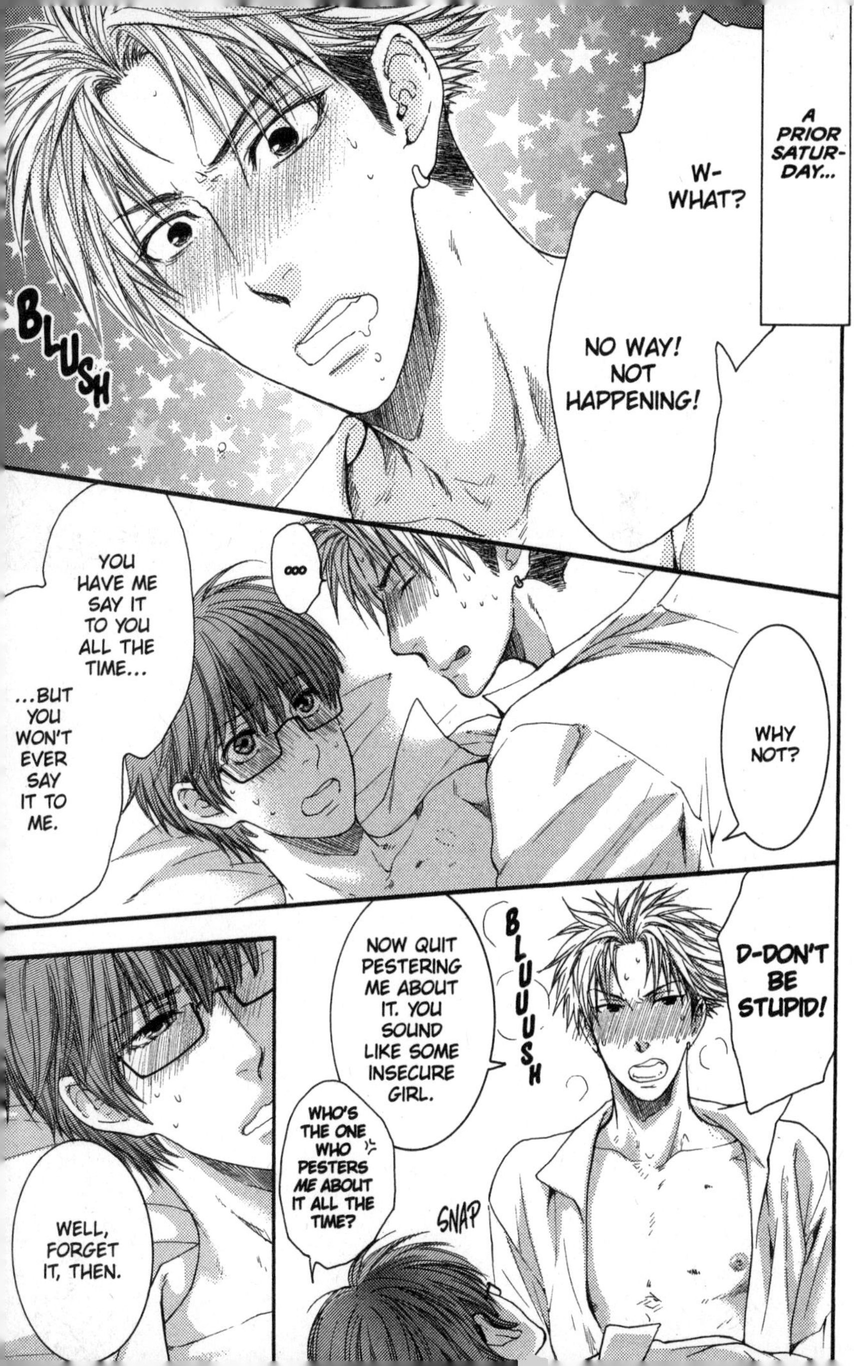
A PRIOR SATURDAY...
W-WHAT?
NO WAY! NOT HAPPENING!
BLUSH
WHY NOT?
...
YOU HAVE ME SAY IT TO YOU ALL THE TIME...
...BUT YOU WON'T EVER SAY IT TO ME.
D-DON'T BE STUPID!
BLUUUSH
NOW QUIT PESTERING ME ABOUT IT. YOU SOUND LIKE SOME INSECURE GIRL.
WHO'S THE ONE WHO PESTERS ME ABOUT IT ALL THE TIME?
SNAP
WELL, FORGET IT, THEN.

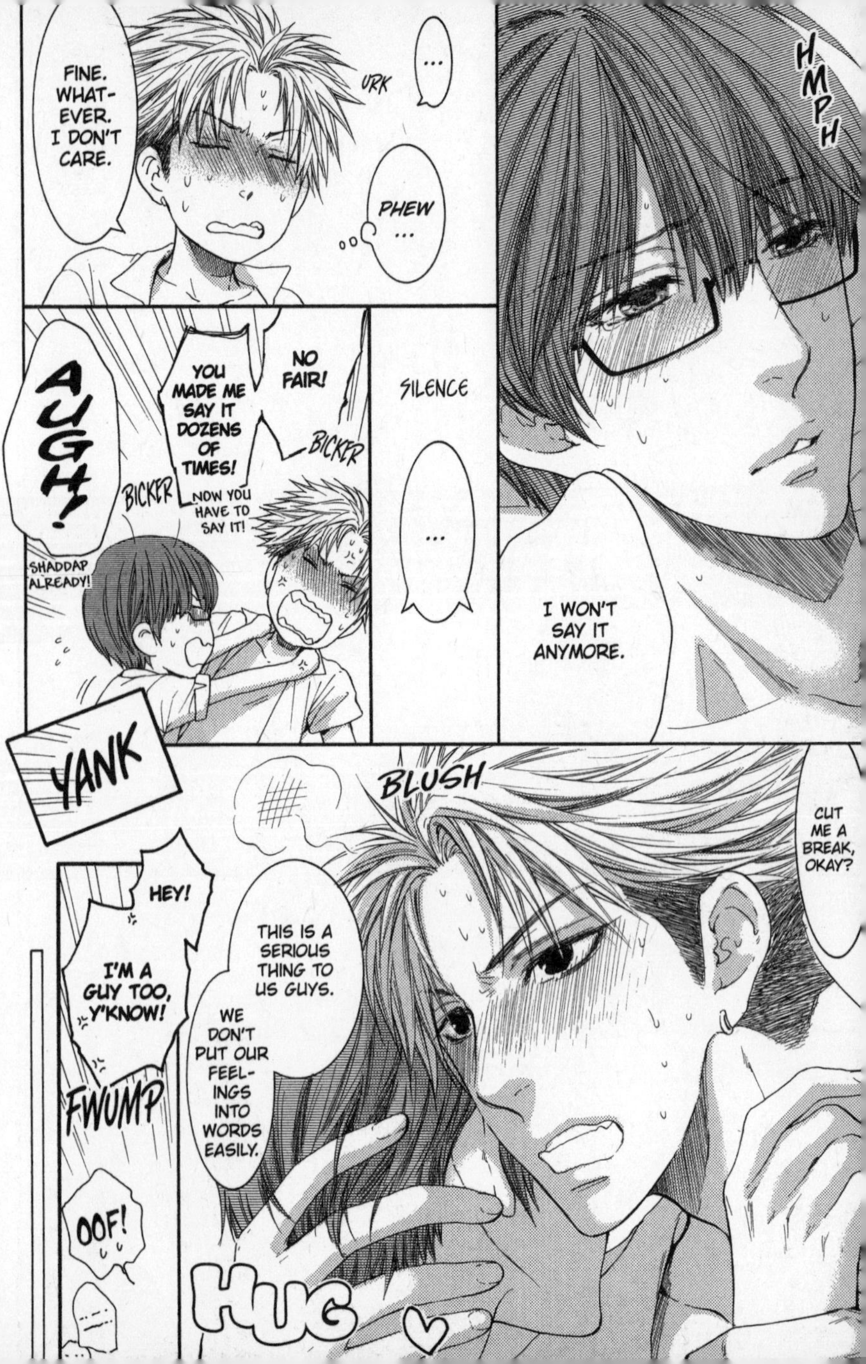
HMPH
I WON'T SAY IT ANYMORE.
...
URK
PHEW ...
FINE. WHATEVER. I DON'T CARE.
SILENCE
...
NO FAIR!
BICKER
YOU MADE ME SAY IT DOZENS OF TIMES!
NOW YOU HAVE TO SAY IT!
BICKER
AUGH!
SHADDAP ALREADY!
YANK
CUT ME A BREAK, OKAY?
BLUSH
THIS IS A SERIOUS THING TO US GUYS.
WE DON'T PUT OUR FEEL-INGS INTO WORDS EASILY.
HUG
HEY!
I'M A GUY TOO, Y'KNOW!
FWUMP
OOF!

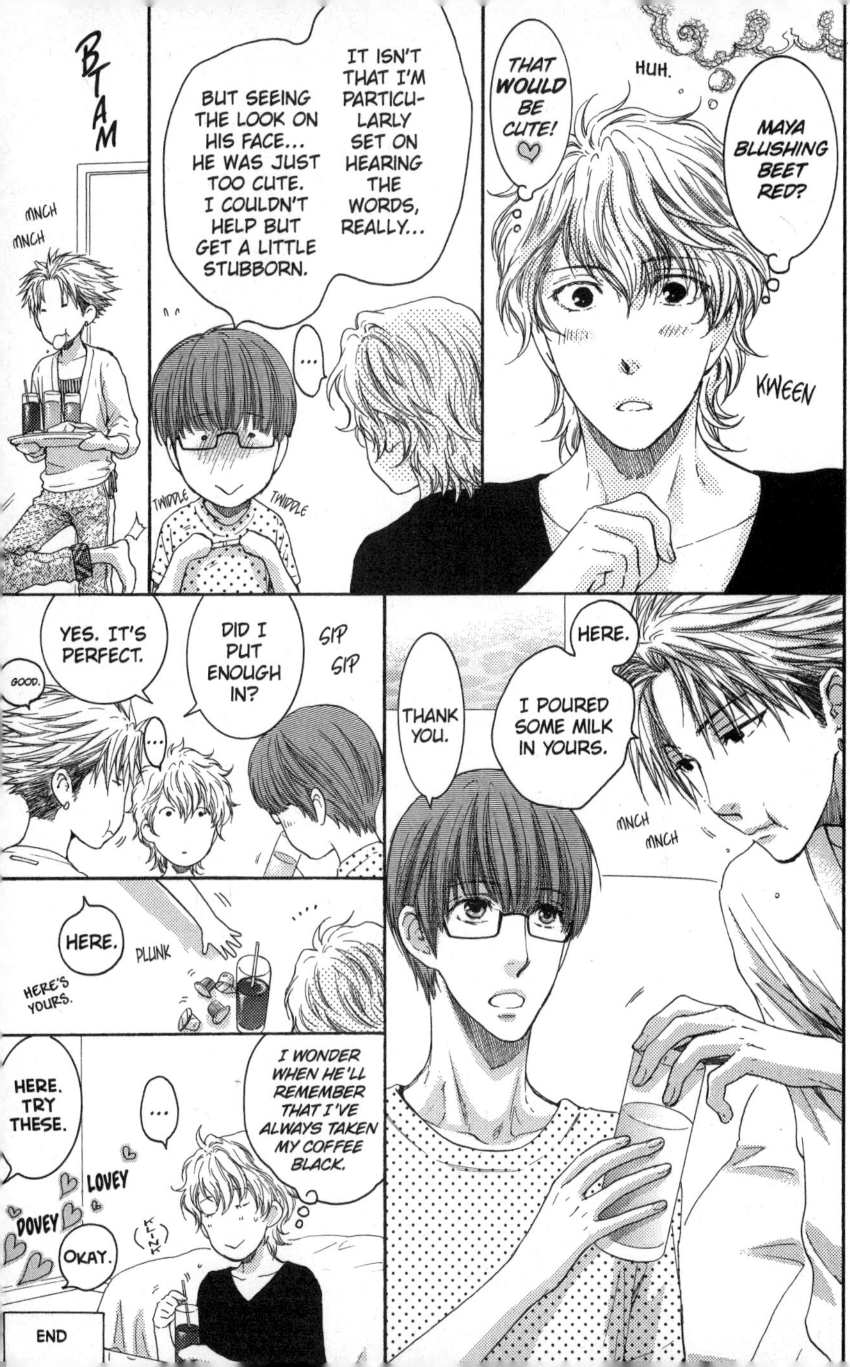
MAYA BLUSHING BEET RED?
HUH.
THAT WOULD BE CUTE! ♥
KWEEN
IT ISN'T THAT I'M PARTICU-LARLY SET ON HEARING THE WORDS, REALLY...
BUT SEEING THE LOOK ON HIS FACE... HE WAS JUST TOO CUTE. I COULDN'T HELP BUT GET A LITTLE STUBBORN.
...
TWIDDLE
TWIDDLE
BTAM
MNCH
MNCH
HERE.
I POURED SOME MILK IN YOURS.
THANK YOU.
MNCH
MNCH
SIP
SIP
DID I PUT ENOUGH IN?
YES. IT'S PERFECT.
GOOD.
...
....
PLUNK
HERE.
HERE'S YOURS.
I WONDER WHEN HE'LL REMEMBER THAT I'VE ALWAYS TAKEN MY COFFEE BLACK.
...
HERE. TRY THESE.
LOVEY
DOVEY
KLINK
OKAY.
END

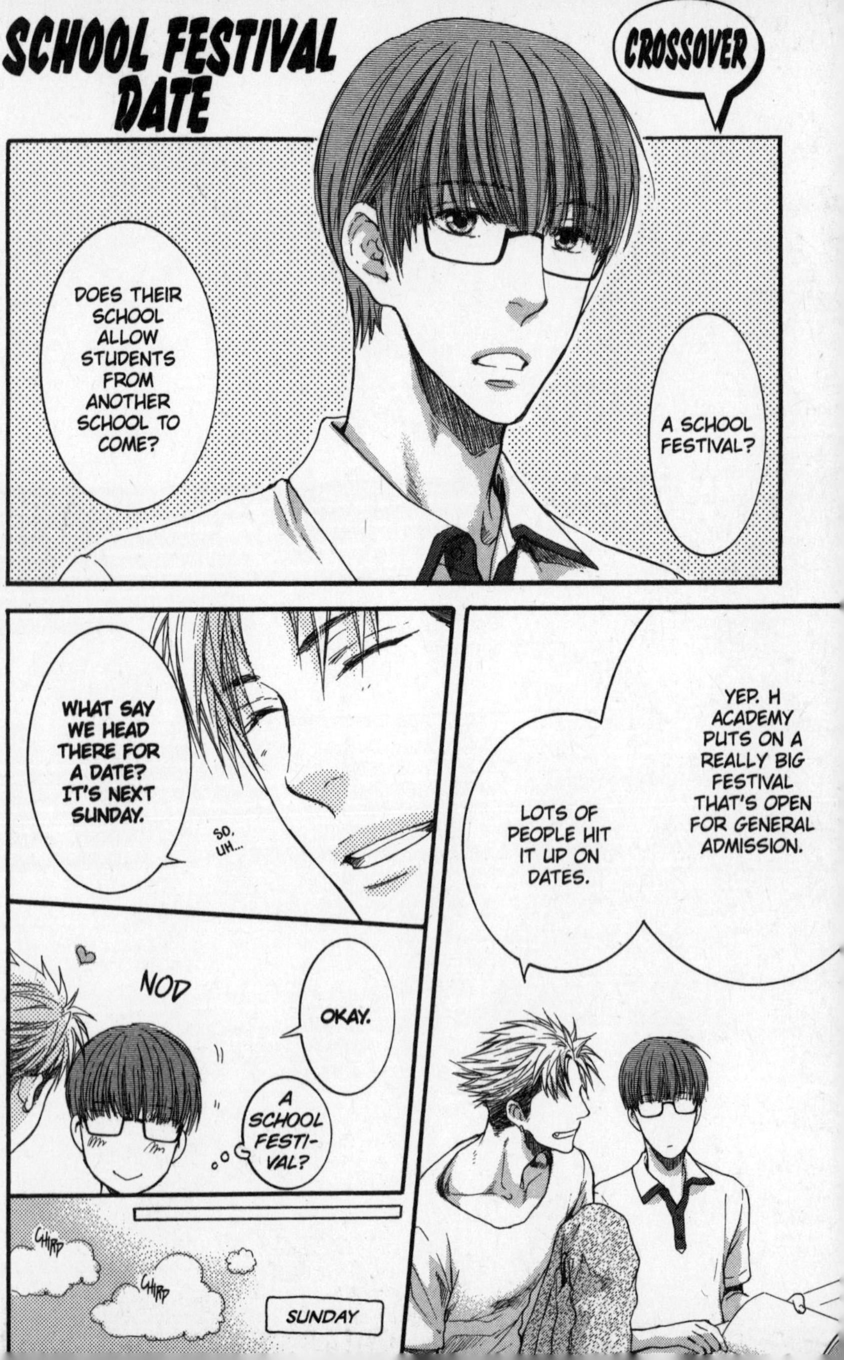
SCHOOL FESTIVAL DATE
CROSSOVER
A SCHOOL FESTIVAL?
DOES THEIR SCHOOL ALLOW STUDENTS FROM ANOTHER SCHOOL TO COME?
YEP. H ACADEMY PUTS ON A REALLY BIG FESTIVAL THAT'S OPEN FOR GENERAL ADMISSION.
LOTS OF PEOPLE HIT IT UP ON DATES.
SO, UH...
WHAT SAY WE HEAD THERE FOR A DATE? IT'S NEXT SUNDAY.
OKAY.
NOD
A SCHOOL FESTI-VAL?
CHIRP
CHIRP
SUNDAY

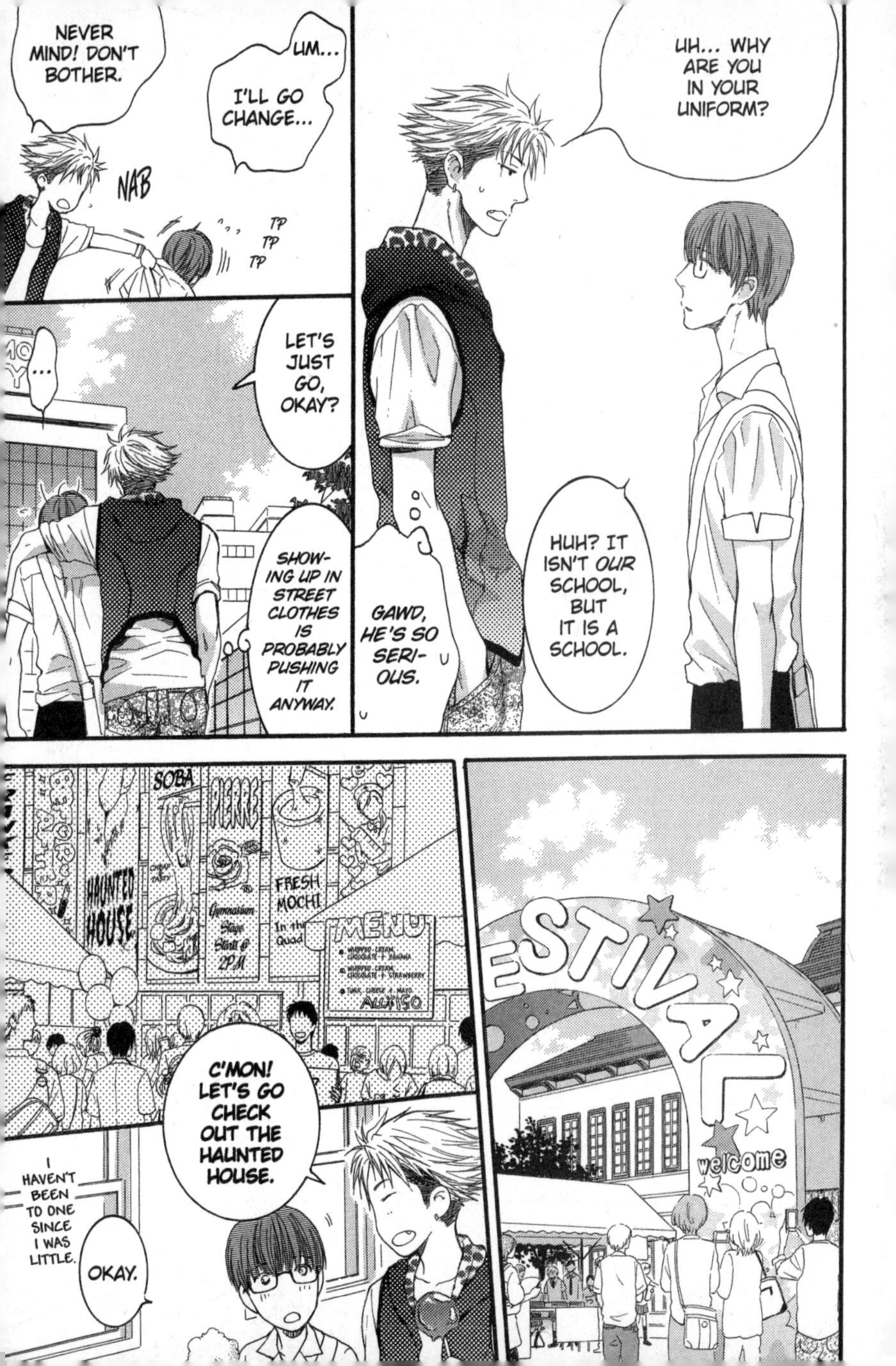

UH... WHY ARE YOU IN YOUR UNIFORM?
HUH? IT ISN'T OUR SCHOOL, BUT IT IS A SCHOOL.
GAWD, HE'S SO SERI-OUS.
UM...
I'LL GO CHANGE...
NEVER MIND! DON'T BOTHER.
NAB
TP TP TP
LET'S JUST GO, OKAY?
...
SHOW-ING UP IN STREET CLOTHES IS PROBABLY PUSHING IT ANYWAY.
ESTIVAL
welcome
SOBA
PIERRE
HAUNTED HOUSE
FRESH MOCHI
In the Quad
Gymnasium Stage Starts @ 2PM
MENU
C'MON! LET'S GO CHECK OUT THE HAUNTED HOUSE.
I HAVEN'T BEEN TO ONE SINCE I WAS LITTLE.
OKAY.

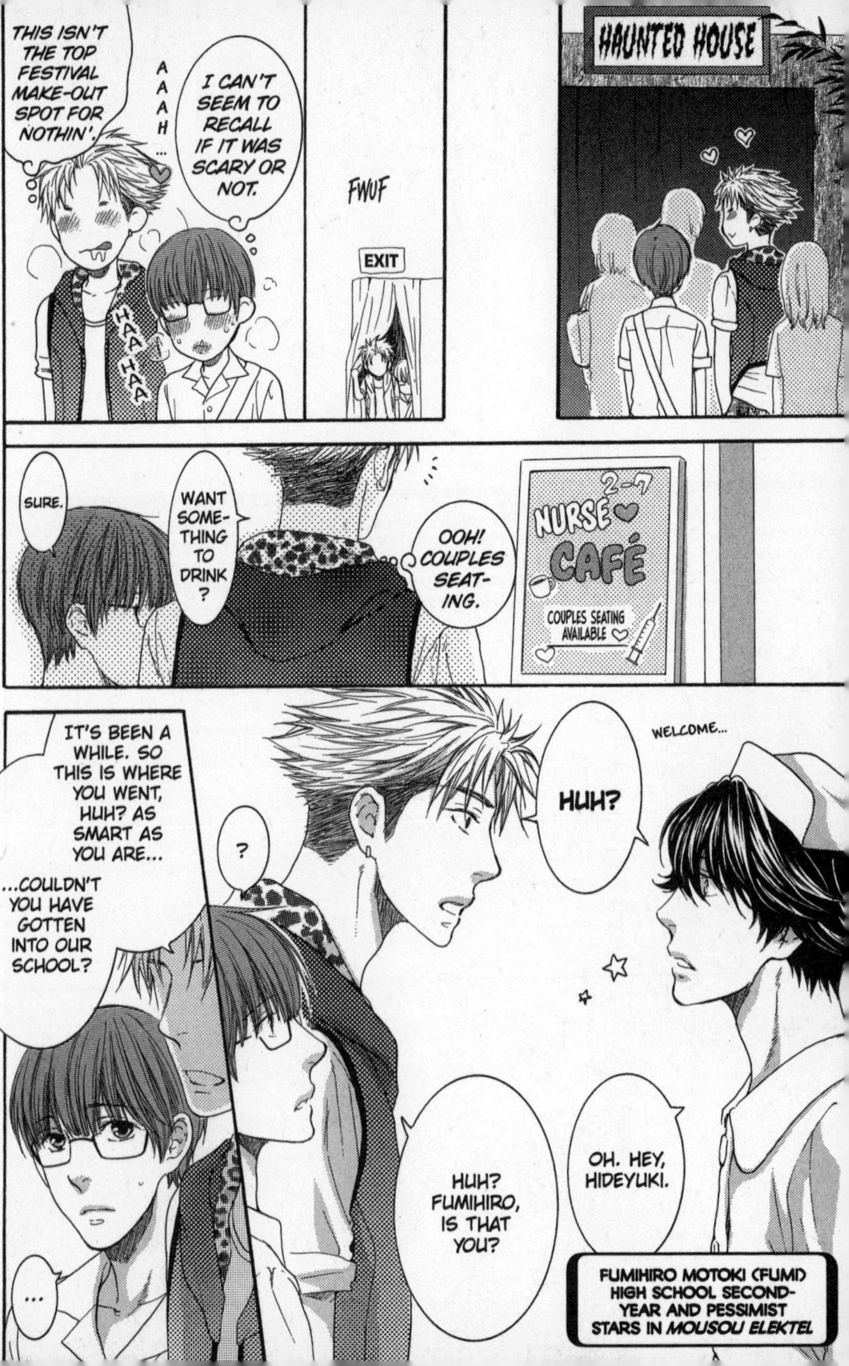
HAUNTED HOUSE
EXIT
FWUF
I CAN'T SEEM TO RECALL IF IT WAS SCARY OR NOT.
AAAAH...
THIS ISN'T THE TOP FESTIVAL MAKE-OUT SPOT FOR NOTHIN'.
HAA HAA
2-7
NURSE CAFÉ
COUPLES SEATING AVAILABLE
OOH! COUPLES SEATING.
WANT SOMETHING TO DRINK?
SURE.
WELCOME...
HUH?
?
OH. HEY, HIDEYUKI.
HUH? FUMIHIRO, IS THAT YOU?
FUMIHIRO MOTOKI (FUMI)
HIGH SCHOOL SECOND-YEAR AND PESSIMIST
STARS IN *MOUSOU ELEKTEL*
IT'S BEEN A WHILE. SO THIS IS WHERE YOU WENT, HUH? AS SMART AS YOU ARE...
...COULDN'T YOU HAVE GOTTEN INTO OUR SCHOOL?
...

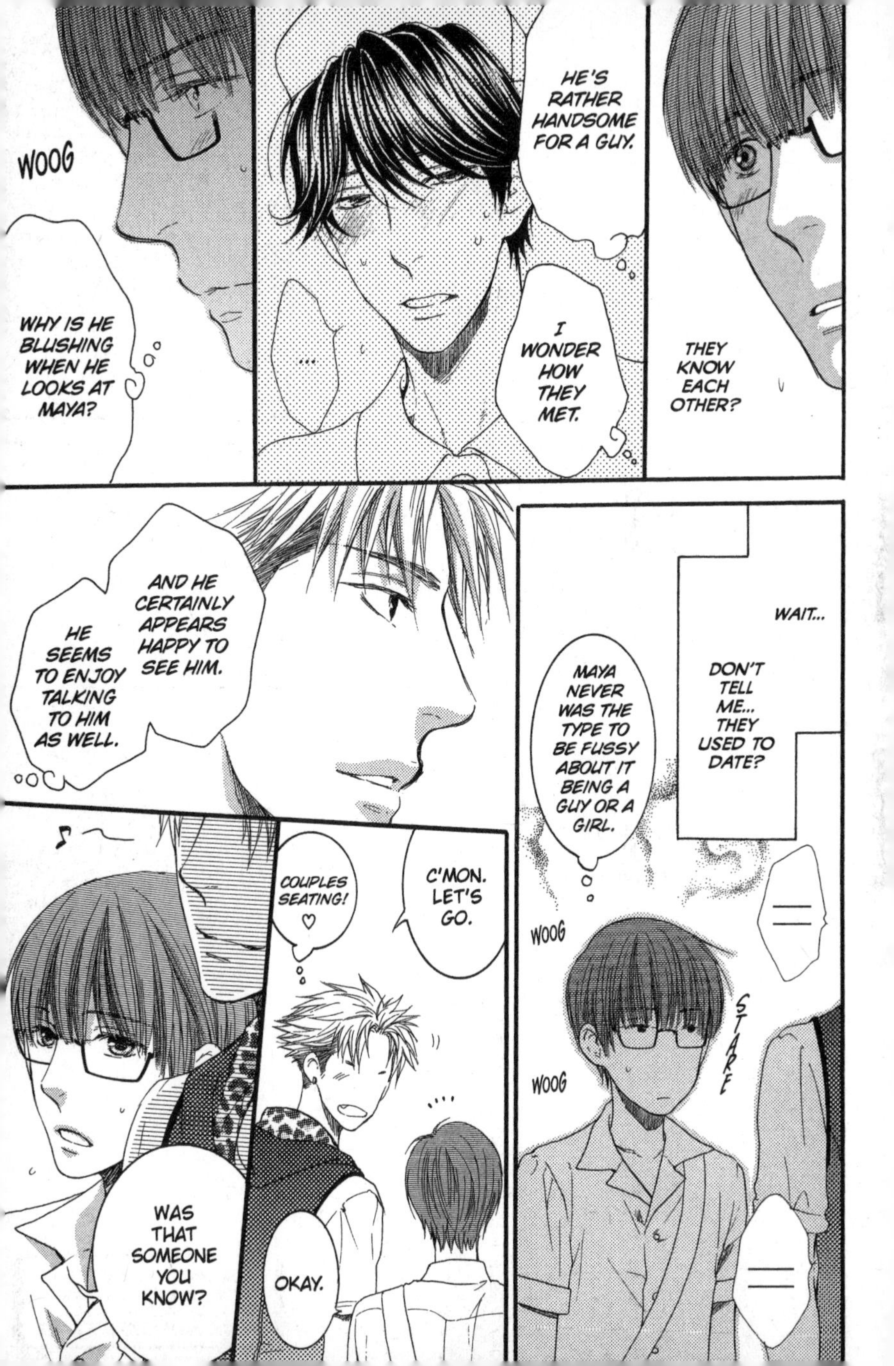

THEY KNOW EACH OTHER?
HE'S RATHER HANDSOME FOR A GUY.
I WONDER HOW THEY MET.
...
WOOG
WHY IS HE BLUSHING WHEN HE LOOKS AT MAYA?
WAIT...
DON'T TELL ME... THEY USED TO DATE?
MAYA NEVER WAS THE TYPE TO BE FUSSY ABOUT IT BEING A GUY OR A GIRL.
——
WOOG
STARE
WOOG
——
AND HE CERTAINLY APPEARS HAPPY TO SEE HIM.
HE SEEMS TO ENJOY TALKING TO HIM AS WELL.
C'MON. LET'S GO.
COUPLES SEATING! ♡
....
OKAY.
WAS THAT SOMEONE YOU KNOW?

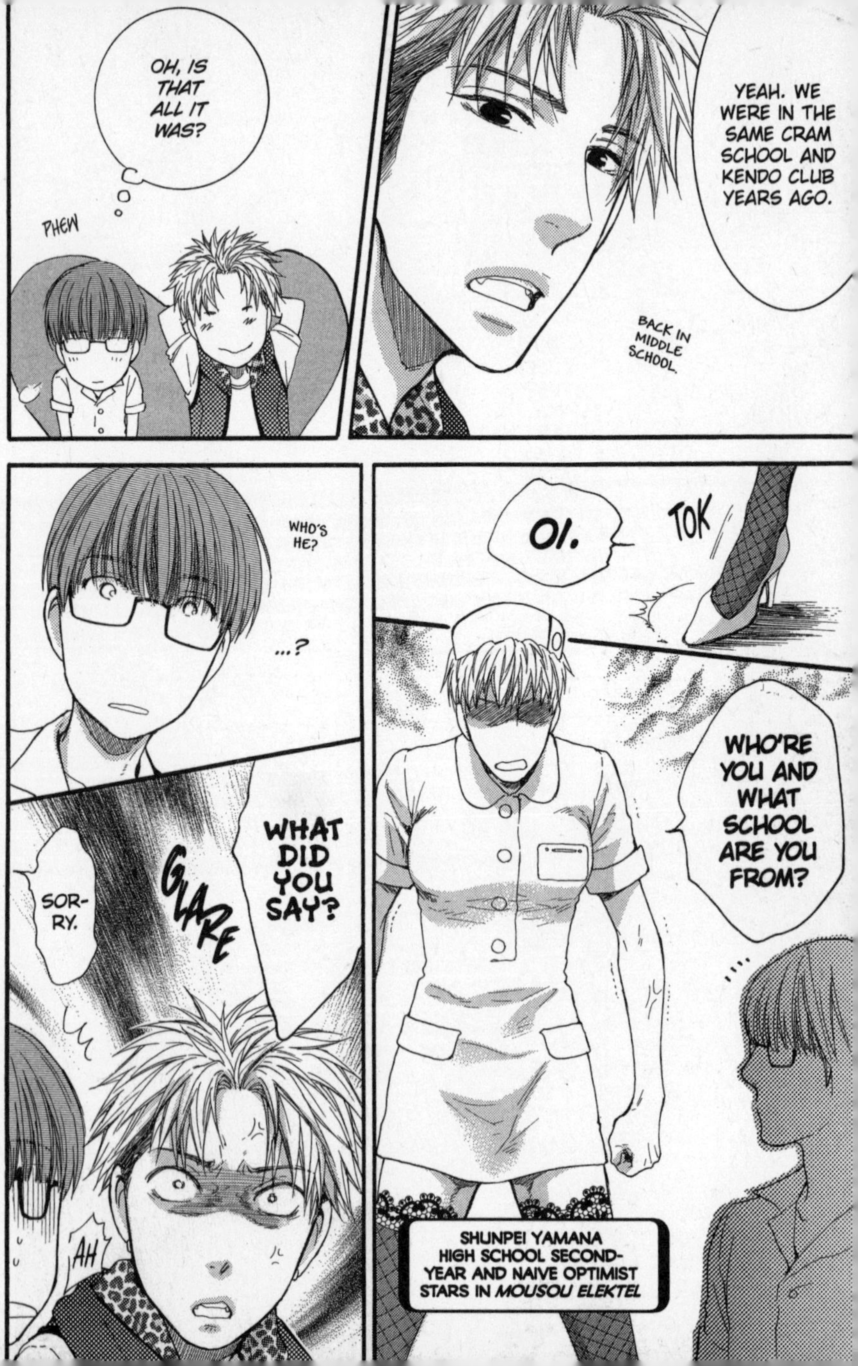
YEAH. WE WERE IN THE SAME CRAM SCHOOL AND KENDO CLUB YEARS AGO.
BACK IN MIDDLE SCHOOL.
OH, IS THAT ALL IT WAS?
PHEW
OI.
TOK
WHO'RE YOU AND WHAT SCHOOL ARE YOU FROM?
....
SHUNPEI YAMANA HIGH SCHOOL SECOND-YEAR AND NAIVE OPTIMIST STARS IN *MOUSOU ELEKTEL*
WHO'S HE?
...?
WHAT DID YOU SAY?
GLARE
SORRY.
AH

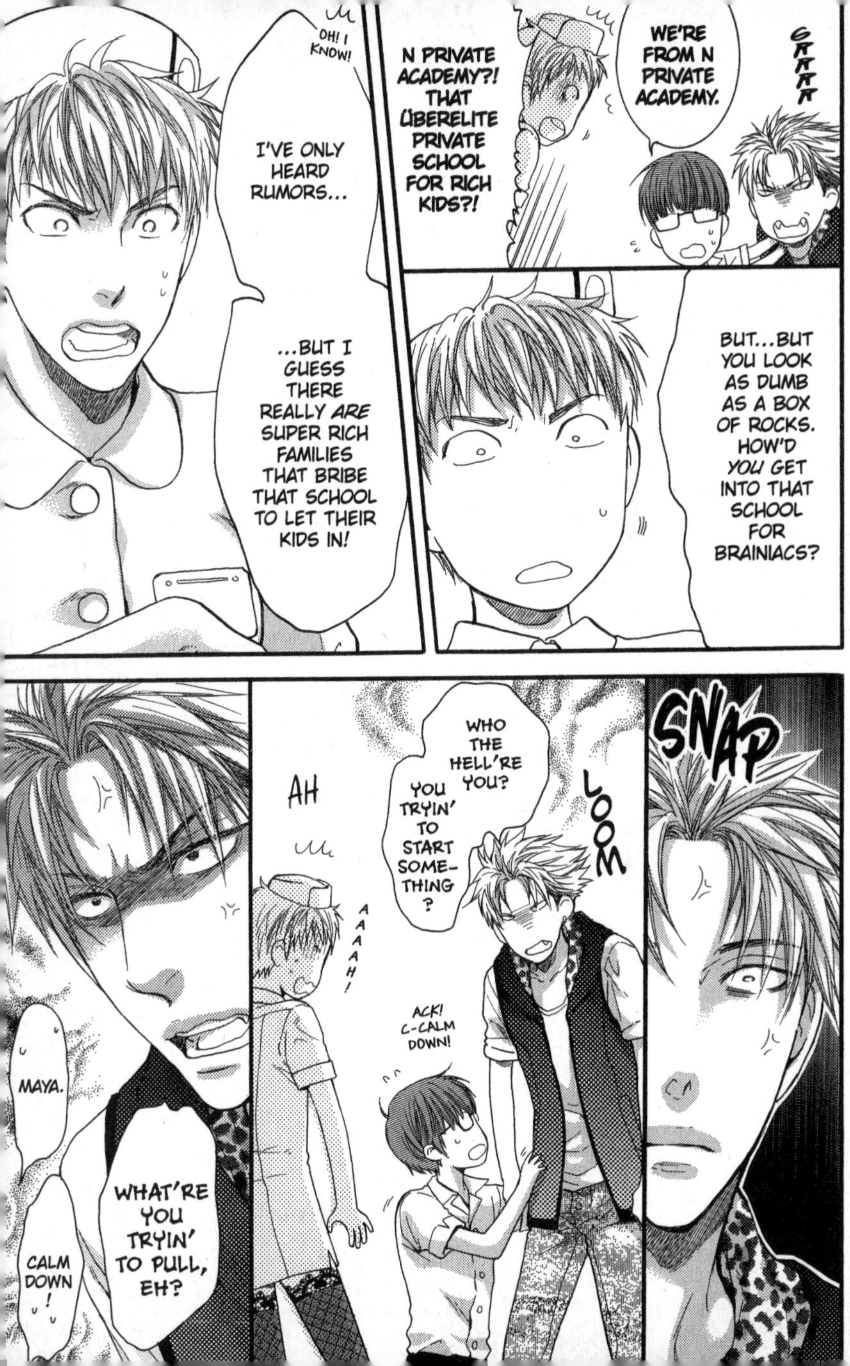
GRRRR
WE'RE FROM N PRIVATE ACADEMY.
N PRIVATE ACADEMY?! THAT ÜBERELITE PRIVATE SCHOOL FOR RICH KIDS?!
BUT...BUT YOU LOOK AS DUMB AS A BOX OF ROCKS. HOW'D *YOU* GET INTO THAT SCHOOL FOR BRAINIACS?
OH! I KNOW!
I'VE ONLY HEARD RUMORS...
...BUT I GUESS THERE REALLY *ARE* SUPER RICH FAMILIES THAT BRIBE THAT SCHOOL TO LET THEIR KIDS IN!
SNAP
WHO THE HELL'RE YOU?
YOU TRYIN' TO START SOMETHING?
LOOM
AH
AAAAAH!
ACK! C-CALM DOWN!
WHAT'RE YOU TRYIN' TO PULL, EH?
MAYA.
CALM DOWN!

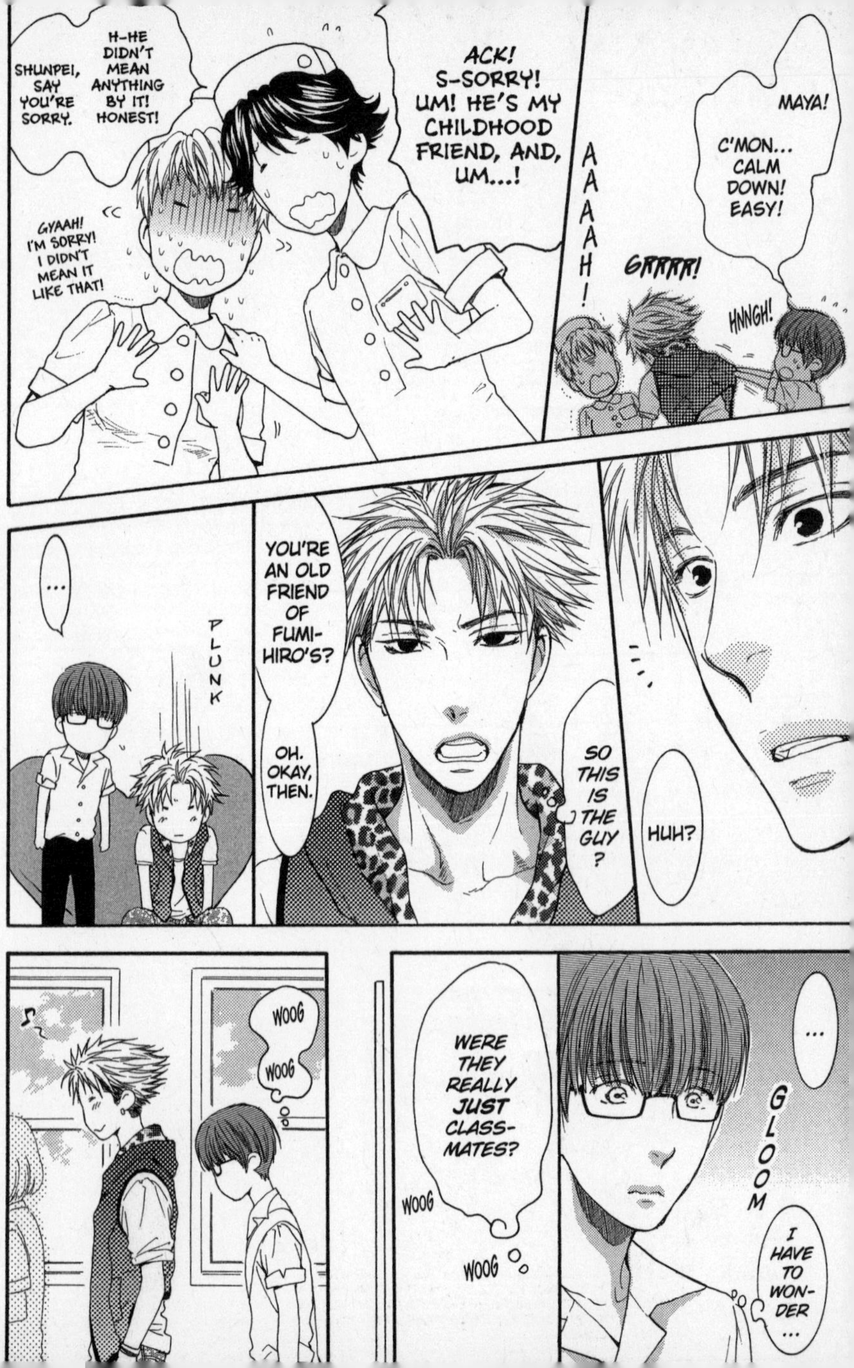
MAYA!
C'MON... CALM DOWN! EASY!
AAAAH!
GRRRR!
HNNGH!
ACK! S-SORRY! UM! HE'S MY CHILDHOOD FRIEND, AND, UM...!
H-HE DIDN'T MEAN ANYTHING BY IT! HONEST!
SHUNPEI, SAY YOU'RE SORRY.
GYAAH! I'M SORRY! I DIDN'T MEAN IT LIKE THAT!
HUH?
SO THIS IS THE GUY?
YOU'RE AN OLD FRIEND OF FUMI-HIRO'S?
OH. OKAY, THEN.
...
PLUNK
...
GLOOM
I HAVE TO WONDER...
WERE THEY REALLY JUST CLASSMATES?
WOOG
WOOG
WOOG
WOOG

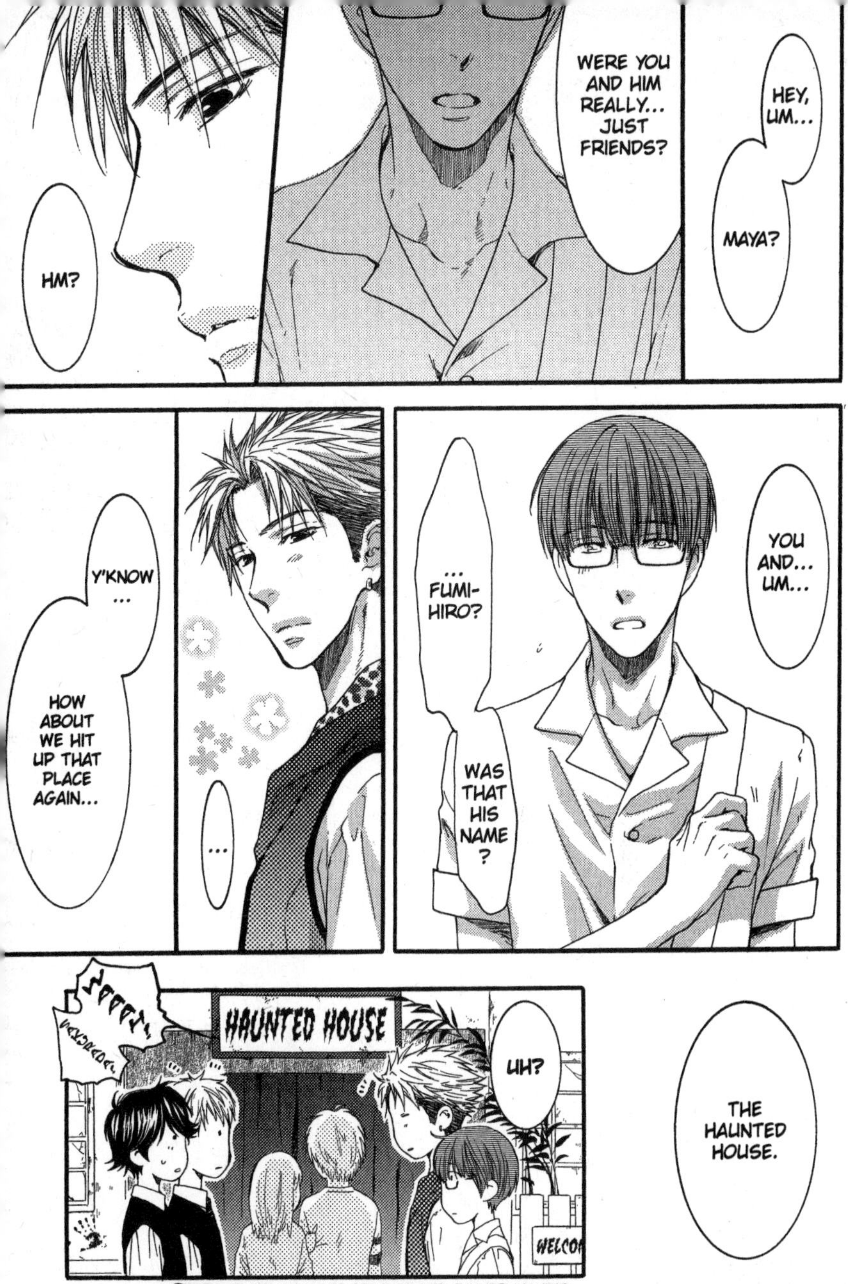
HEY, UM...
MAYA?
WERE YOU AND HIM REALLY... JUST FRIENDS?
HM?
YOU AND... UM...
... FUMI-HIRO?
WAS THAT HIS NAME?
...
Y'KNOW...
HOW ABOUT WE HIT UP THAT PLACE AGAIN...
THE HAUNTED HOUSE.
UH?
HAUNTED HOUSE
WELCO

END

PLUG IF YOU WANT TO SEE FUMI AND SHUNPEI MAKING OUT IN THEIR NURSES' OUTFITS, CHECK OUT THE COMPANION CROSSOVER IN *MOUSOU ELEKTEL* VOLUME 3!

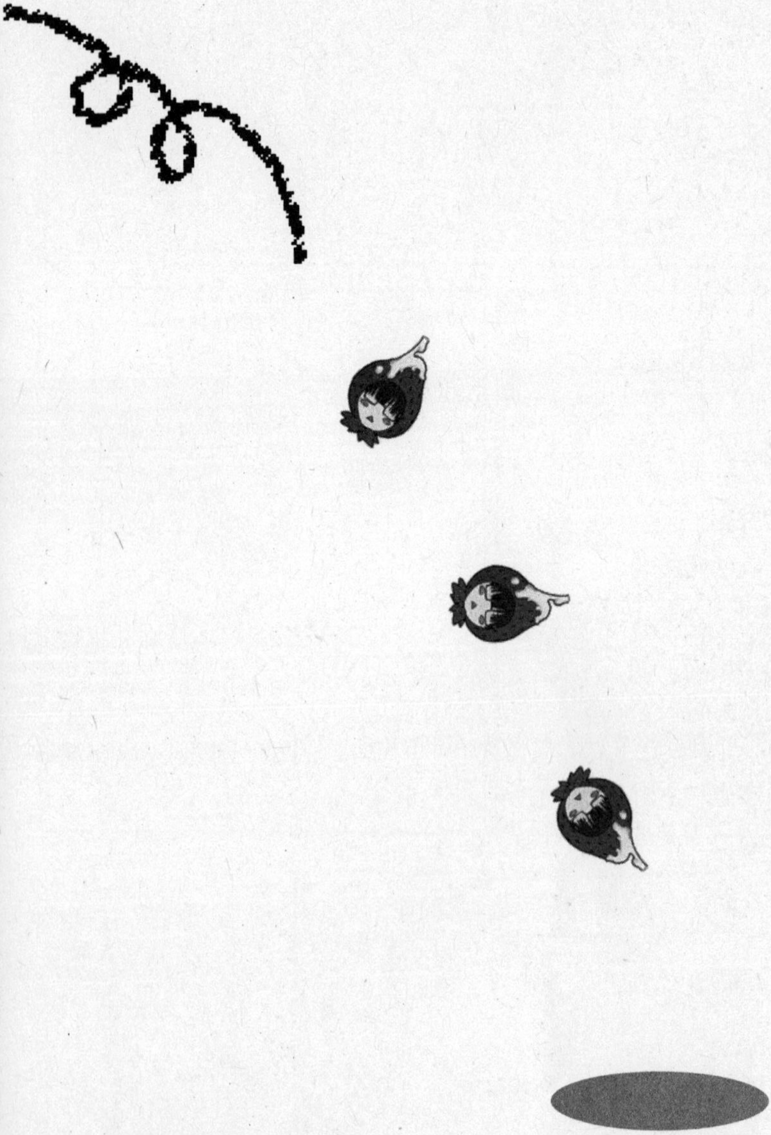

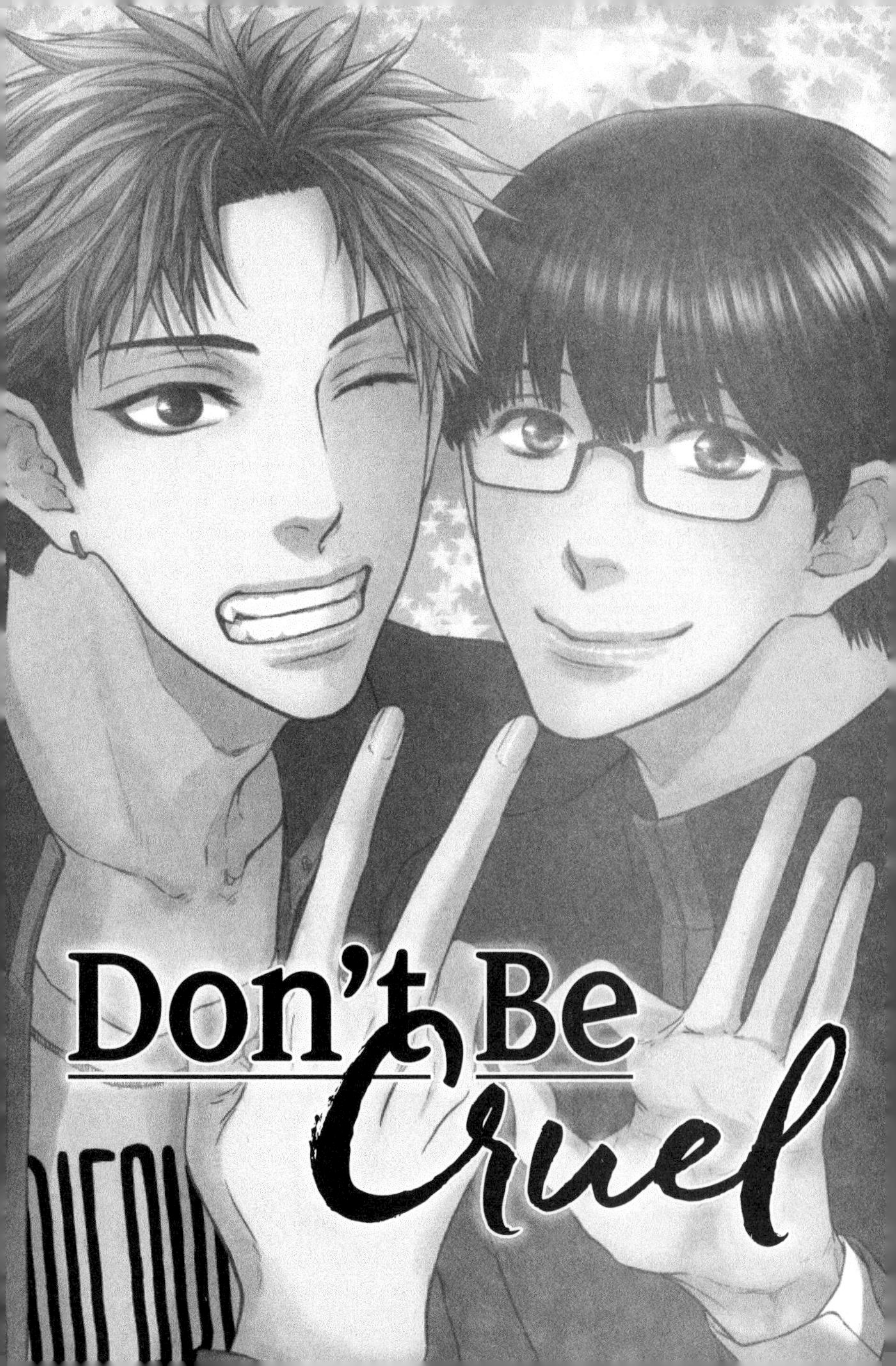
Don't Be
Cruel

Don't Be Cruel

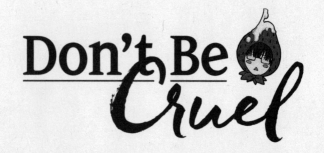

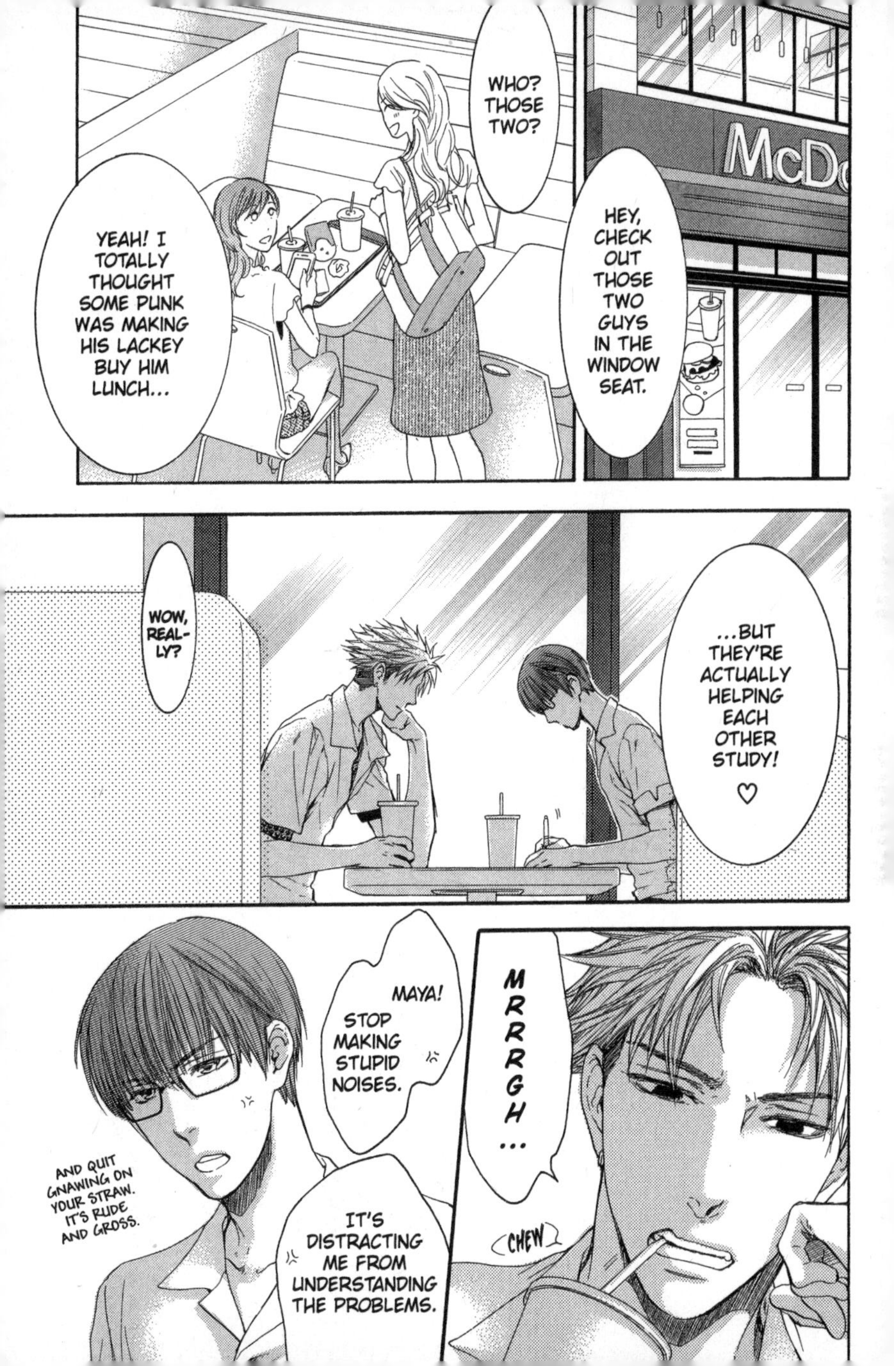
McDo
HEY, CHECK OUT THOSE TWO GUYS IN THE WINDOW SEAT.
WHO? THOSE TWO?
YEAH! I TOTALLY THOUGHT SOME PUNK WAS MAKING HIS LACKEY BUY HIM LUNCH...
...BUT THEY'RE ACTUALLY HELPING EACH OTHER STUDY! ♡
WOW, REAL-LY?
MRRRGH...
CHEW
MAYA! STOP MAKING STUPID NOISES.
IT'S DISTRACTING ME FROM UNDERSTANDING THE PROBLEMS.
AND QUIT GNAWING ON YOUR STRAW. IT'S RUDE AND GROSS.

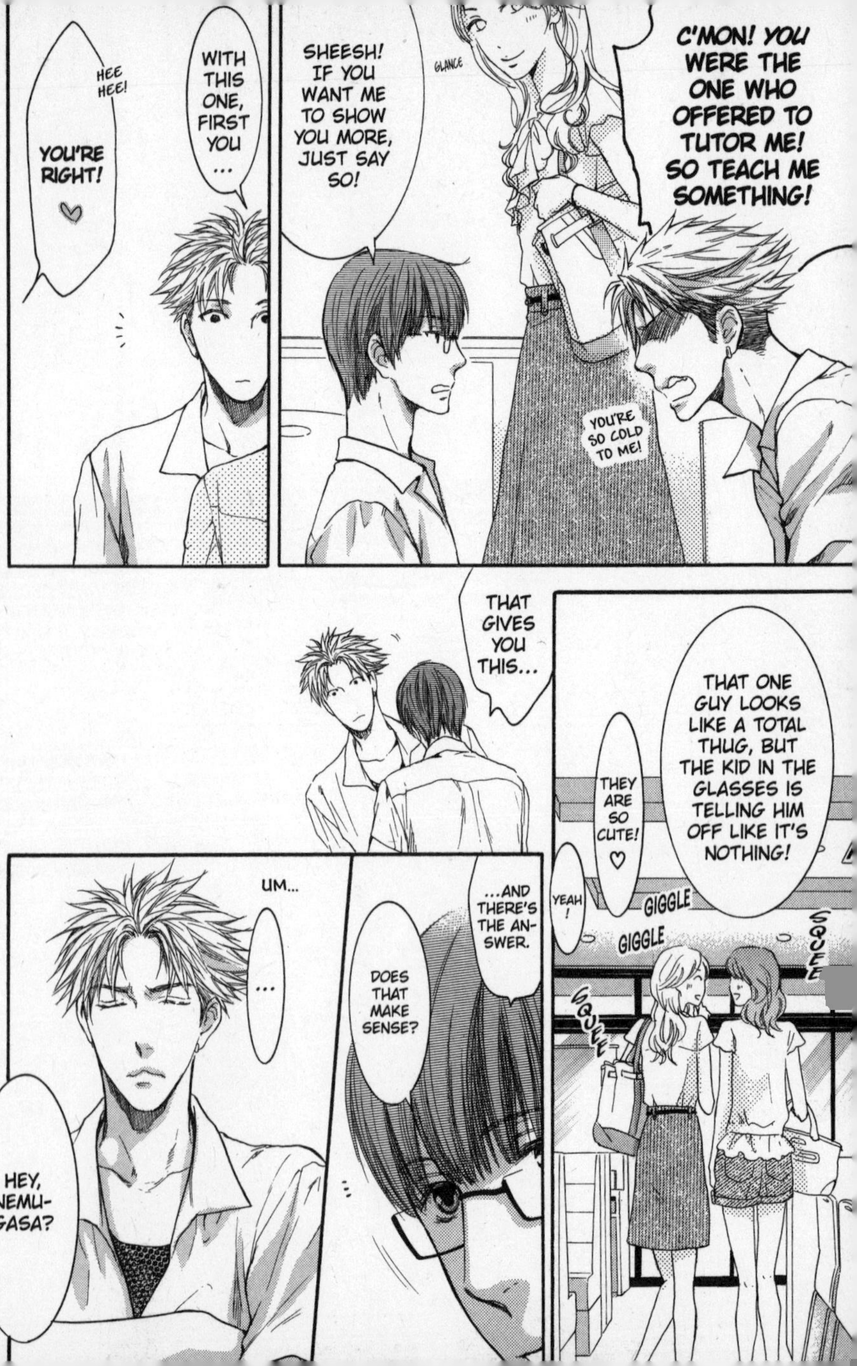

C'MON! YOU WERE THE ONE WHO OFFERED TO TUTOR ME! SO TEACH ME SOMETHING!
GLANCE
YOU'RE SO COLD TO ME!
SHEESH! IF YOU WANT ME TO SHOW YOU MORE, JUST SAY SO!
WITH THIS ONE, FIRST YOU ...
HEE HEE!
YOU'RE RIGHT!
THAT ONE GUY LOOKS LIKE A TOTAL THUG, BUT THE KID IN THE GLASSES IS TELLING HIM OFF LIKE IT'S NOTHING!
THEY ARE SO CUTE!
YEAH!
GIGGLE
GIGGLE
SQUEE
SQUEE
THAT GIVES YOU THIS...
...AND THERE'S THE AN-SWER.
DOES THAT MAKE SENSE?
UM...
...
HEY, NEMU-GASA?

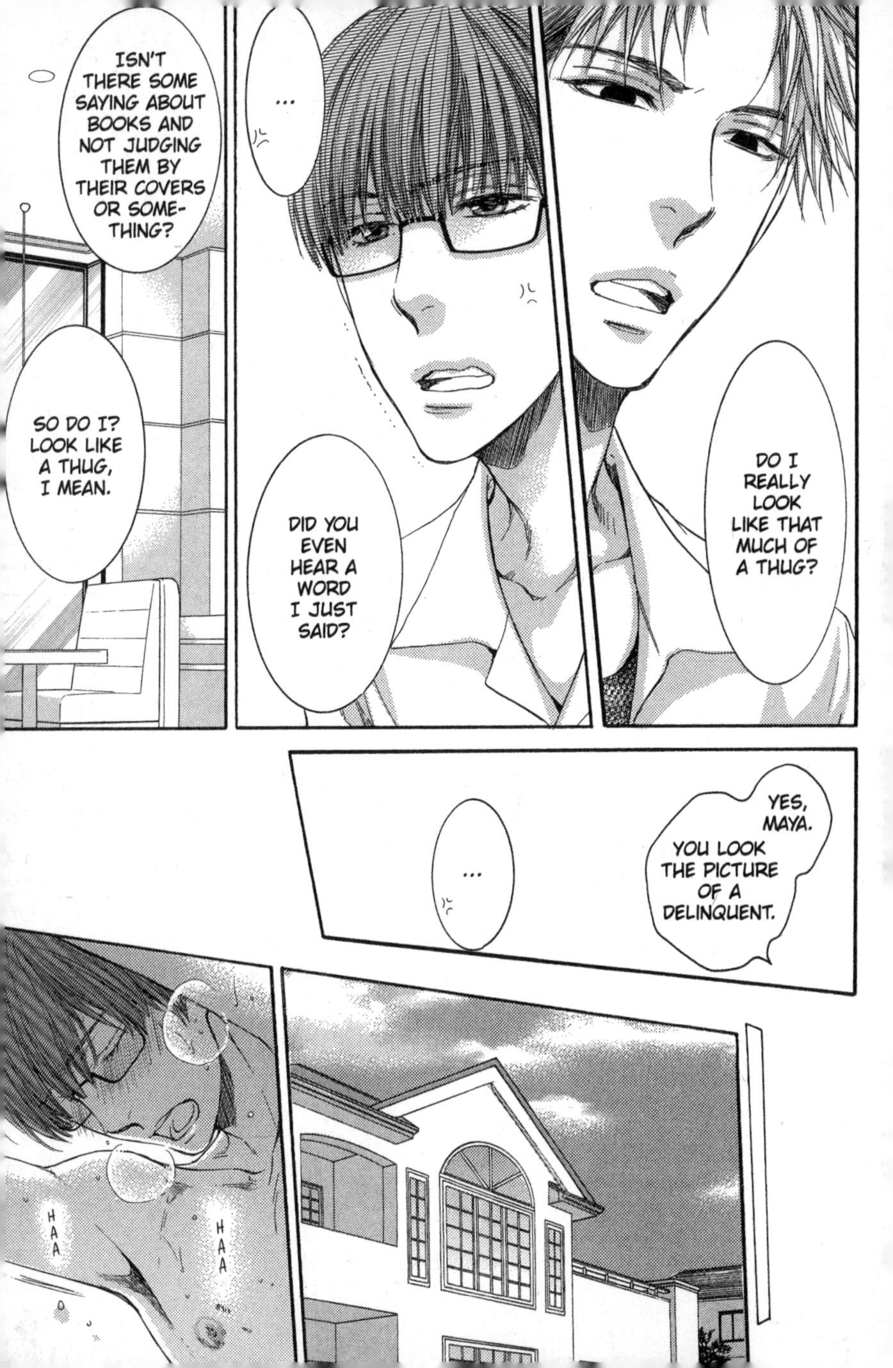
DO I REALLY LOOK LIKE THAT MUCH OF A THUG?
...
DID YOU EVEN HEAR A WORD I JUST SAID?
ISN'T THERE SOME SAYING ABOUT BOOKS AND NOT JUDGING THEM BY THEIR COVERS OR SOME-THING?
SO DO I? LOOK LIKE A THUG, I MEAN.
YES, MAYA. YOU LOOK THE PICTURE OF A DELINQUENT.
...
HAA
HAA

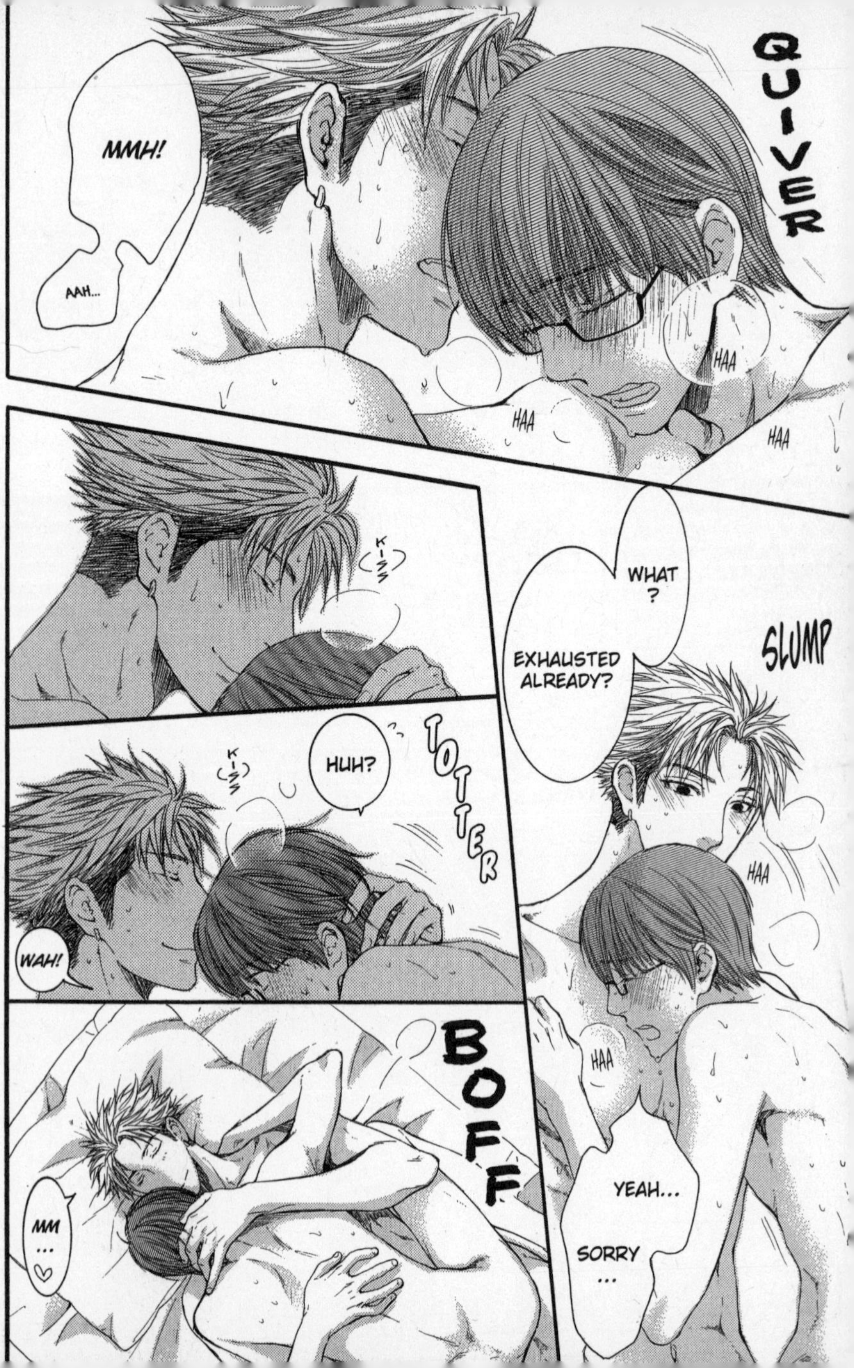
QUIVER
MMH!
AAH...
HAA
HAA
HAA
WHAT? EXHAUSTED ALREADY?
SLUMP
HAA
HAA
YEAH... SORRY...
KISS
TOTTER
HUH?
KISS
WAH!
BOFF
MM... ♥

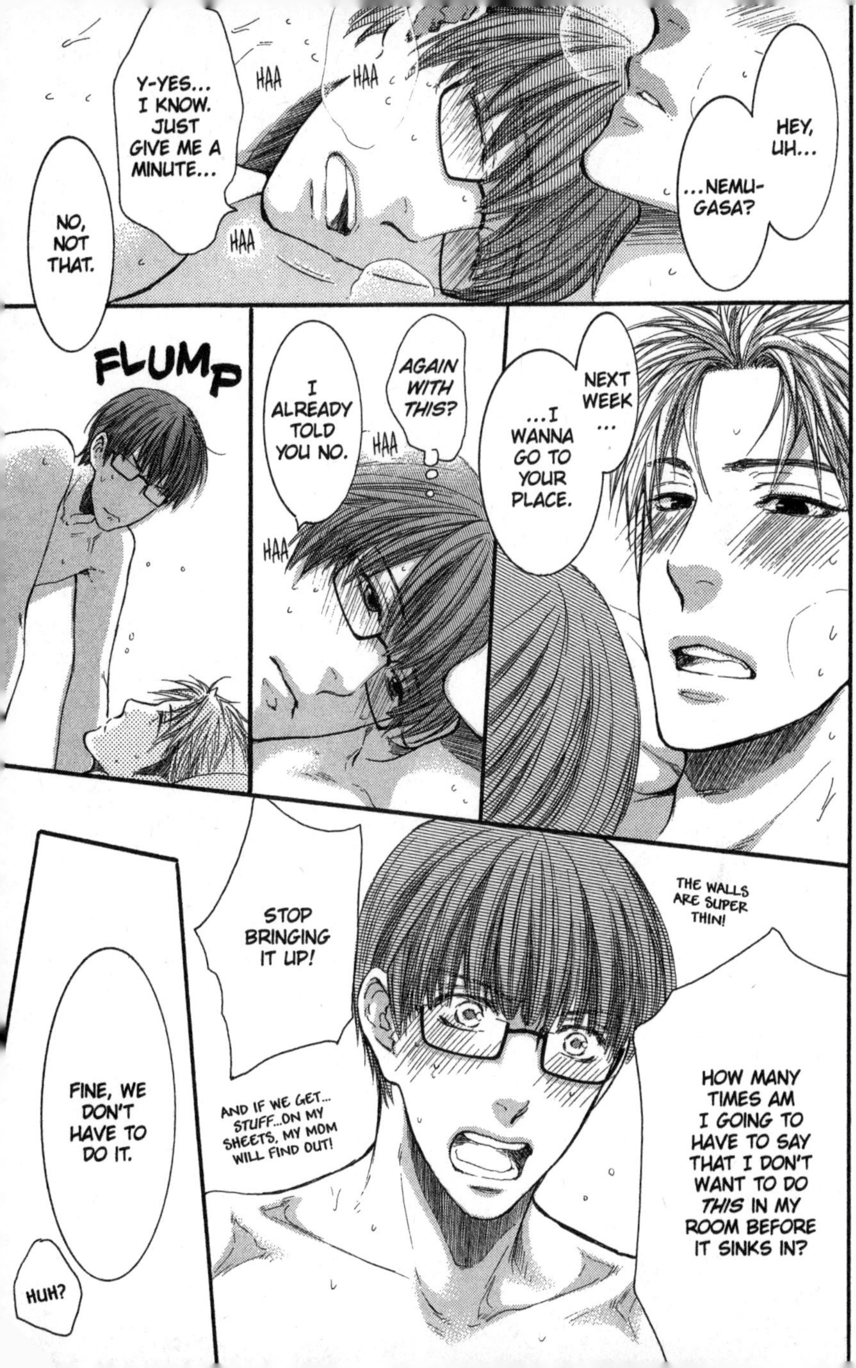

HEY, UH... ...NEMU-GASA?
HAA
HAA
Y-YES... I KNOW. JUST GIVE ME A MINUTE...
HAA
NO, NOT THAT.
NEXT WEEK...
...I WANNA GO TO YOUR PLACE.
AGAIN WITH THIS?
HAA
I ALREADY TOLD YOU NO.
HAA
FLUMP
THE WALLS ARE SUPER THIN!
STOP BRINGING IT UP!
HOW MANY TIMES AM I GOING TO HAVE TO SAY THAT I DON'T WANT TO DO *THIS* IN MY ROOM BEFORE IT SINKS IN?
AND IF WE GET... STUFF...ON MY SHEETS, MY MOM WILL FIND OUT!
FINE, WE DON'T HAVE TO DO IT.
HUH?

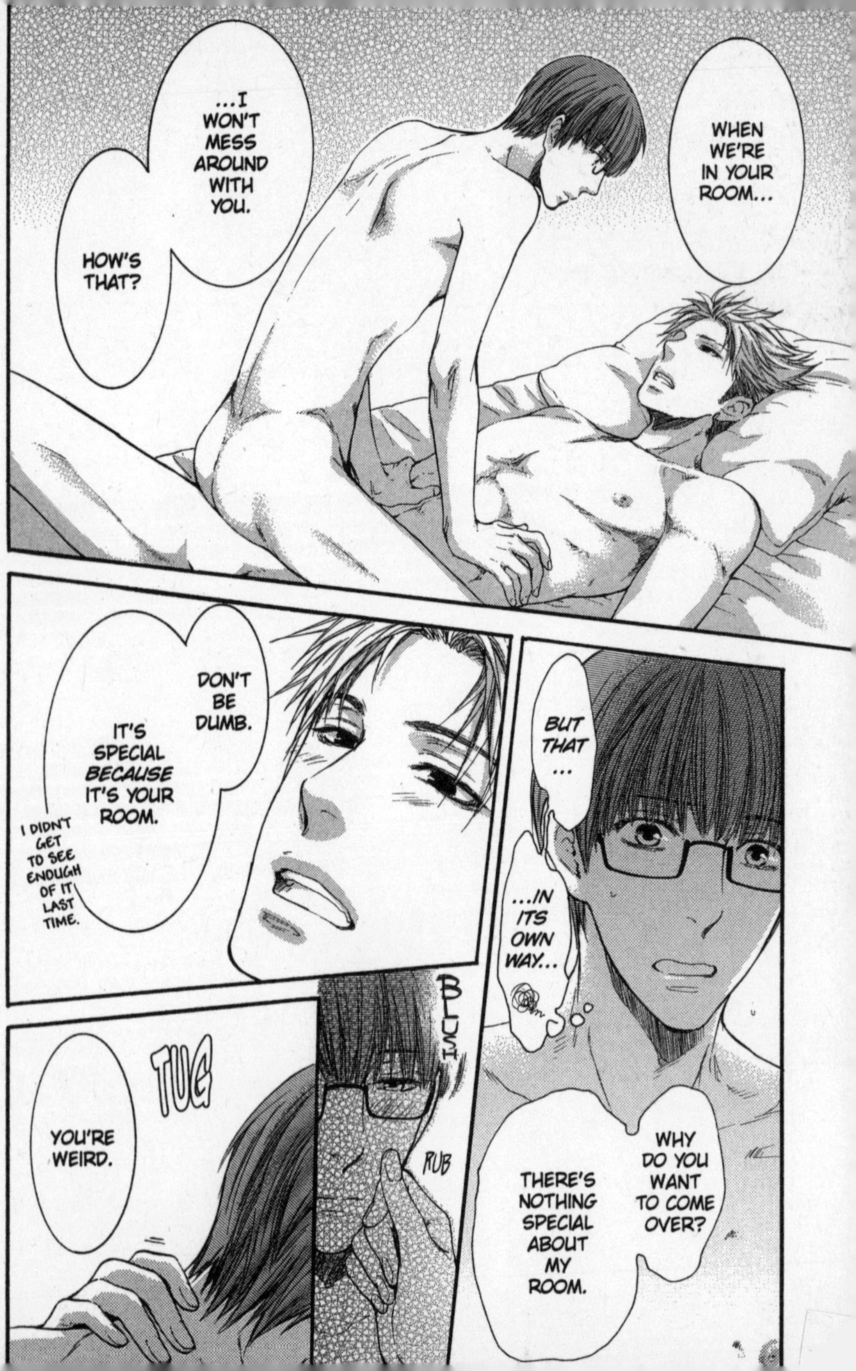
WHEN WE'RE IN YOUR ROOM...
...I WON'T MESS AROUND WITH YOU.
HOW'S THAT?
BUT THAT...
...IN ITS OWN WAY...
WHY DO YOU WANT TO COME OVER?
THERE'S NOTHING SPECIAL ABOUT MY ROOM.
DON'T BE DUMB.
IT'S SPECIAL *BECAUSE* IT'S YOUR ROOM.
I DIDN'T GET TO SEE ENOUGH OF IT LAST TIME.
BLUSH
RUB
TUG
YOU'RE WEIRD.

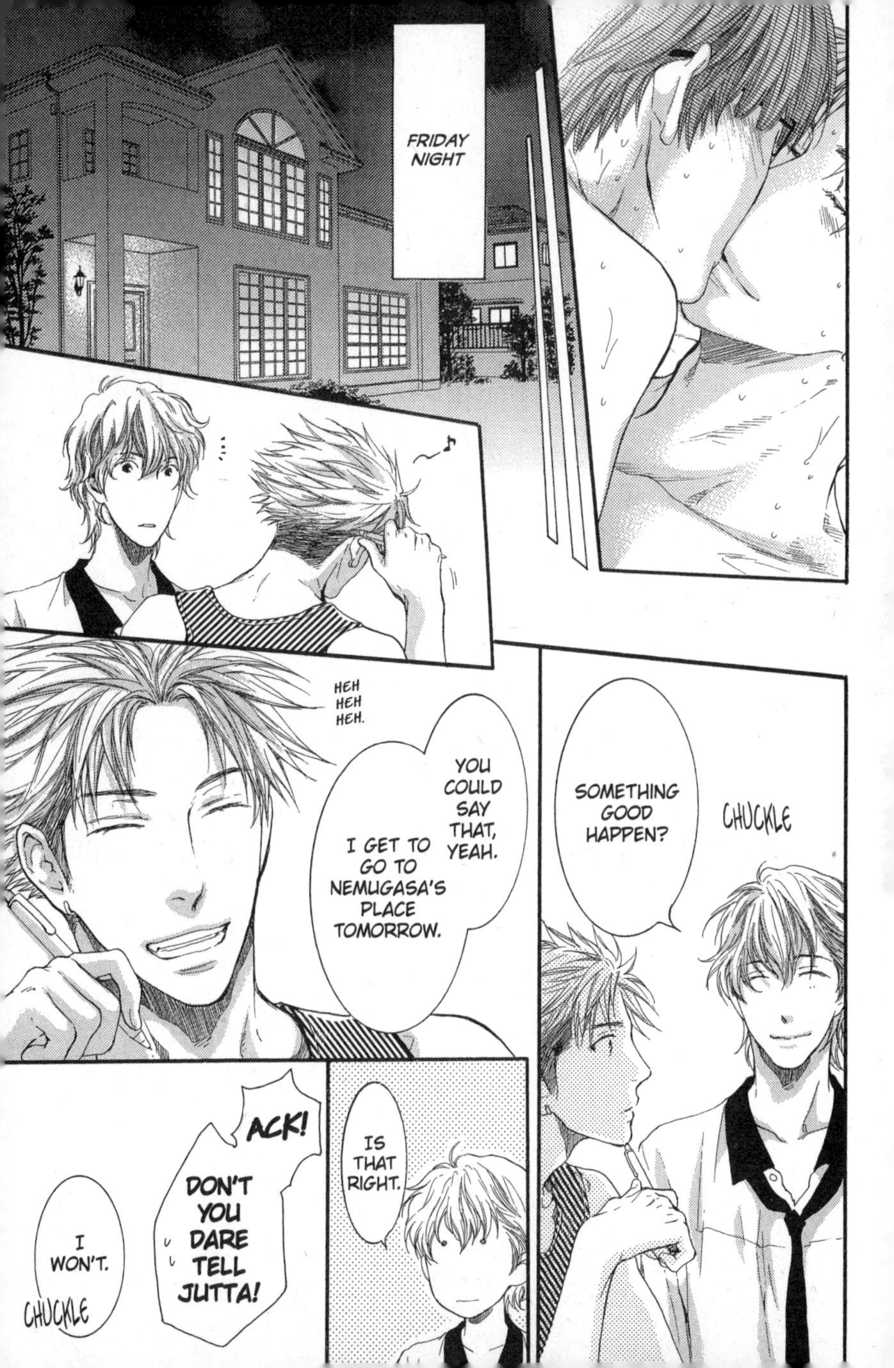
FRIDAY NIGHT
SOMETHING GOOD HAPPEN?
CHUCKLE
HEH HEH HEH.
YOU COULD SAY THAT, YEAH.
I GET TO GO TO NEMUGASA'S PLACE TOMORROW.
IS THAT RIGHT.
ACK!
DON'T YOU DARE TELL JUTTA!
I WON'T.
CHUCKLE

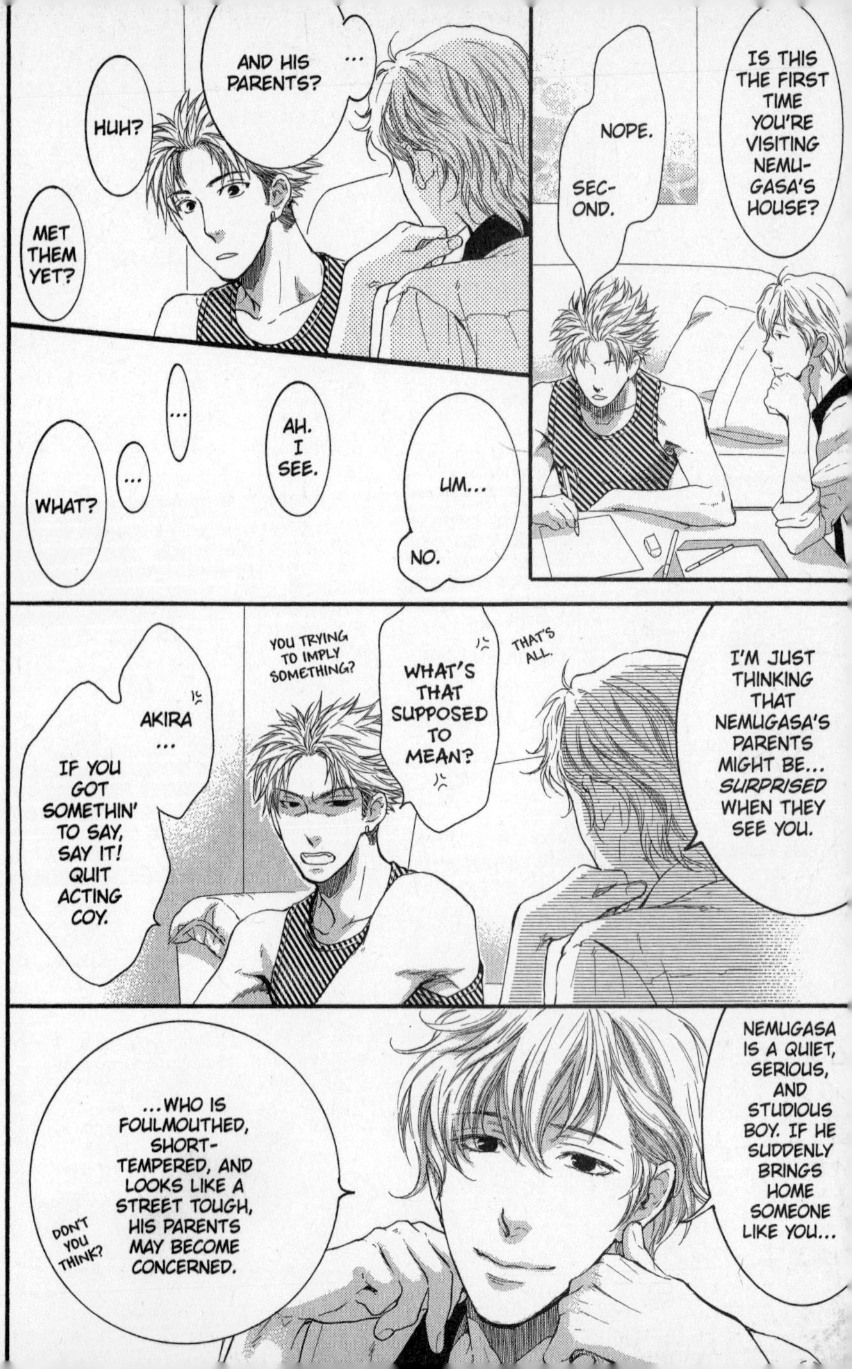
IS THIS THE FIRST TIME YOU'RE VISITING NEMUGASA'S HOUSE?
NOPE.
SEC-OND.
...
AND HIS PARENTS?
HUH?
MET THEM YET?
UM...
NO.
AH. I SEE.
...
...
WHAT?
I'M JUST THINKING THAT NEMUGASA'S PARENTS MIGHT BE... *SURPRISED* WHEN THEY SEE YOU.
THAT'S ALL.
WHAT'S THAT SUPPOSED TO MEAN?
YOU TRYING TO IMPLY SOMETHING?
AKIRA...
IF YOU GOT SOMETHIN' TO SAY, SAY IT! QUIT ACTING COY.
NEMUGASA IS A QUIET, SERIOUS, AND STUDIOUS BOY. IF HE SUDDENLY BRINGS HOME SOMEONE LIKE YOU...
...WHO IS FOULMOUTHED, SHORT-TEMPERED, AND LOOKS LIKE A STREET TOUGH, HIS PARENTS MAY BECOME CONCERNED.
DON'T YOU THINK?

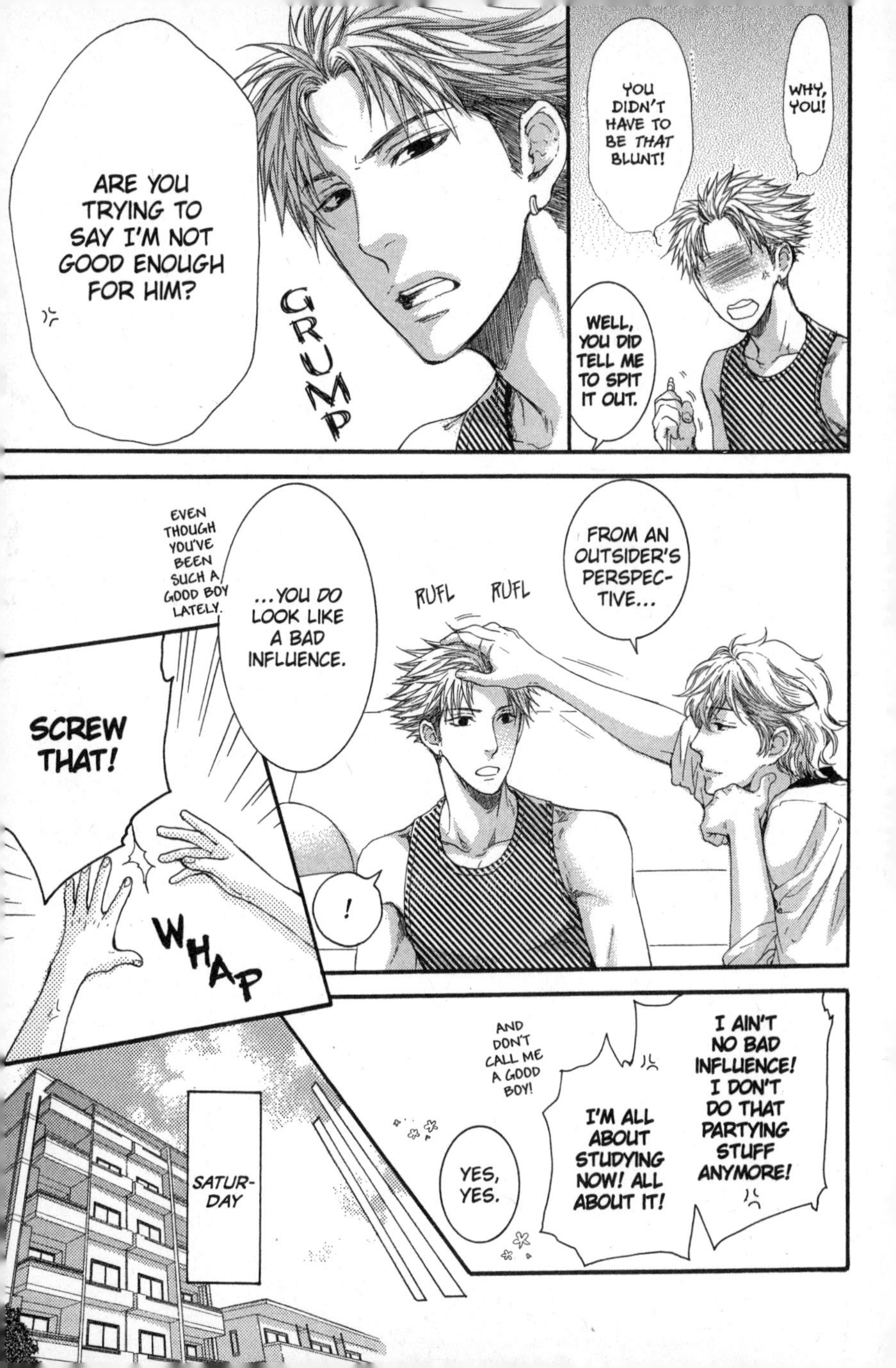
WHY, YOU!
YOU DIDN'T HAVE TO BE *THAT* BLUNT!
WELL, YOU DID TELL ME TO SPIT IT OUT.
GRUMP
ARE YOU TRYING TO SAY I'M NOT GOOD ENOUGH FOR HIM?
FROM AN OUTSIDER'S PERSPEC-TIVE...
RUFL RUFL
...YOU DO LOOK LIKE A BAD INFLUENCE.
EVEN THOUGH YOU'VE BEEN SUCH A GOOD BOY LATELY.
!
SCREW THAT!
WHAP
I AIN'T NO BAD INFLUENCE! I DON'T DO THAT PARTYING STUFF ANYMORE!
AND DON'T CALL ME A GOOD BOY!
I'M ALL ABOUT STUDYING NOW! ALL ABOUT IT!
YES, YES.
SATUR-DAY

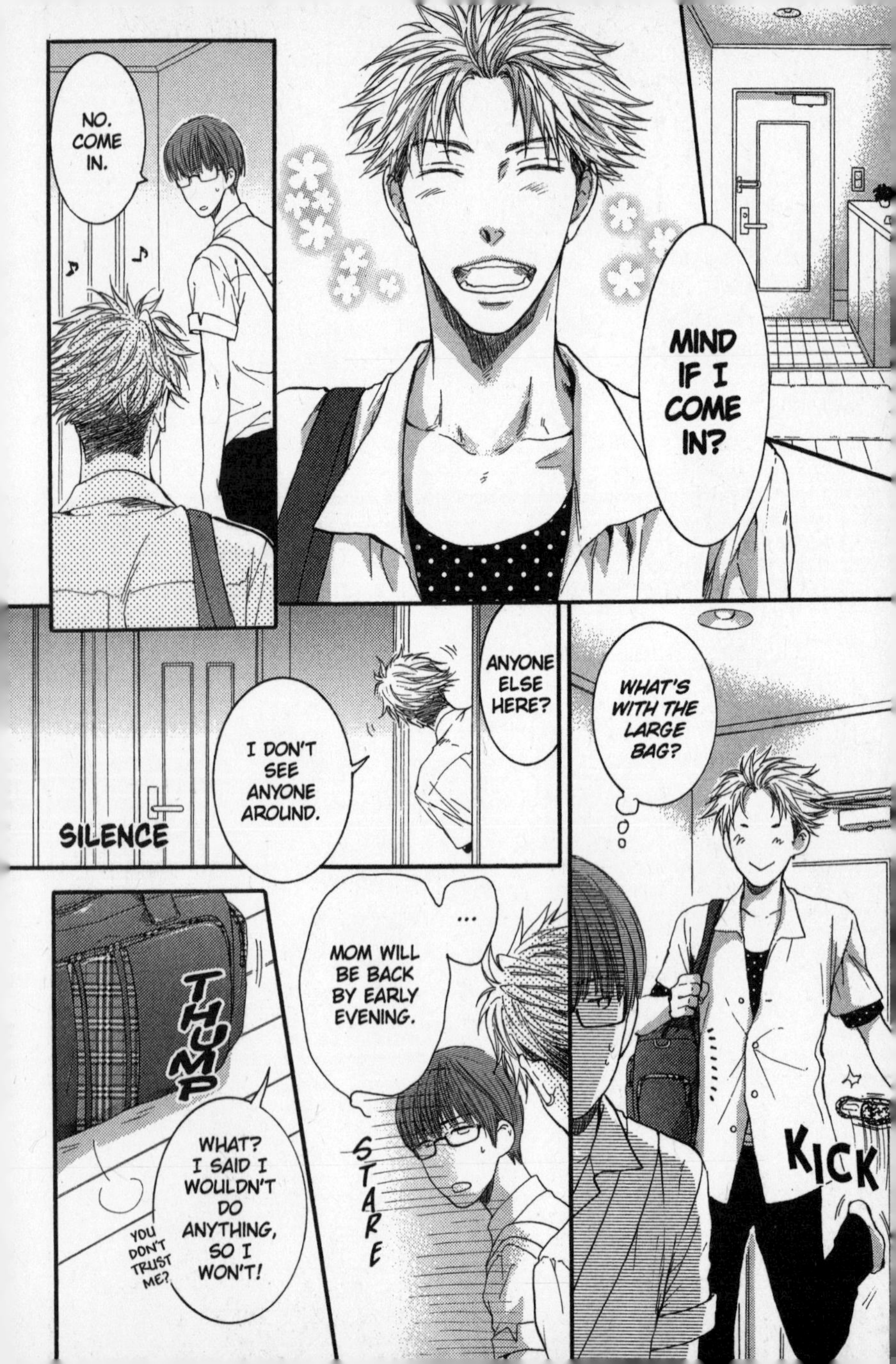
MIND IF I COME IN?
NO. COME IN.
WHAT'S WITH THE LARGE BAG?
KICK
ANYONE ELSE HERE?
I DON'T SEE ANYONE AROUND.
SILENCE
...
MOM WILL BE BACK BY EARLY EVENING.
STARE
THUMP
WHAT? I SAID I WOULDN'T DO ANYTHING, SO I WON'T!
YOU DON'T TRUST ME?

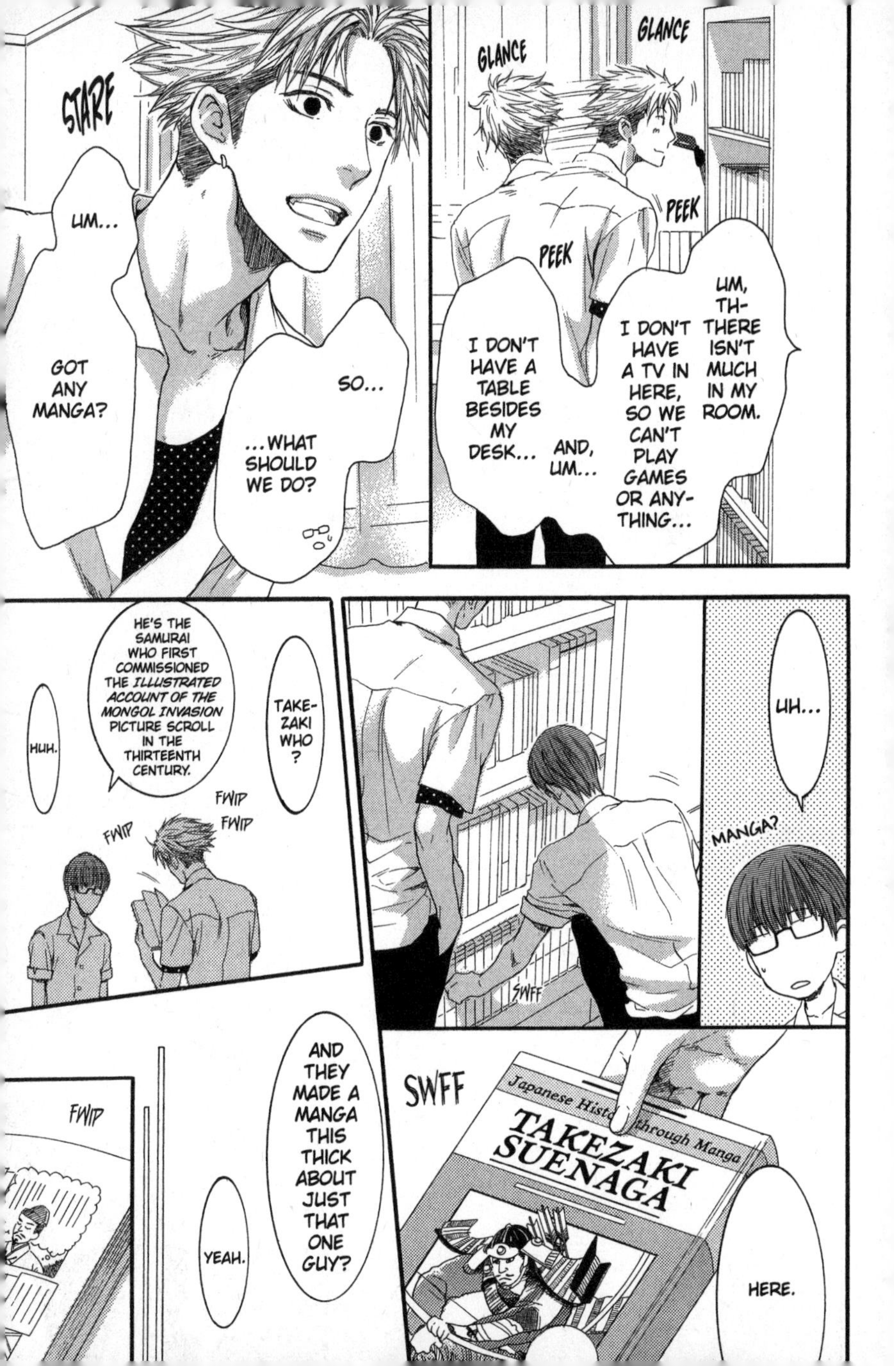
GLANCE
GLANCE
PEEK
PEEK
UM, TH-THERE ISN'T MUCH IN MY ROOM.
I DON'T HAVE A TV IN HERE, SO WE CAN'T PLAY GAMES OR ANY-THING...
I DON'T HAVE A TABLE BESIDES MY DESK...
AND, UM...
STARE
SO...
...WHAT SHOULD WE DO?
UM...
GOT ANY MANGA?
UH...
MANGA?
SWFF
TAKE-ZAKI WHO?
HE'S THE SAMURAI WHO FIRST COMMISSIONED THE *ILLUSTRATED ACCOUNT OF THE MONGOL INVASION PICTURE SCROLL* IN THE THIRTEENTH CENTURY.
HUH.
FWIP
FWIP
FWIP
SWFF
Japanese Histo through Manga
TAKEZAKI SUENAGA
HERE.
AND THEY MADE A MANGA THIS THICK ABOUT JUST THAT ONE GUY?
YEAH.
FWIP

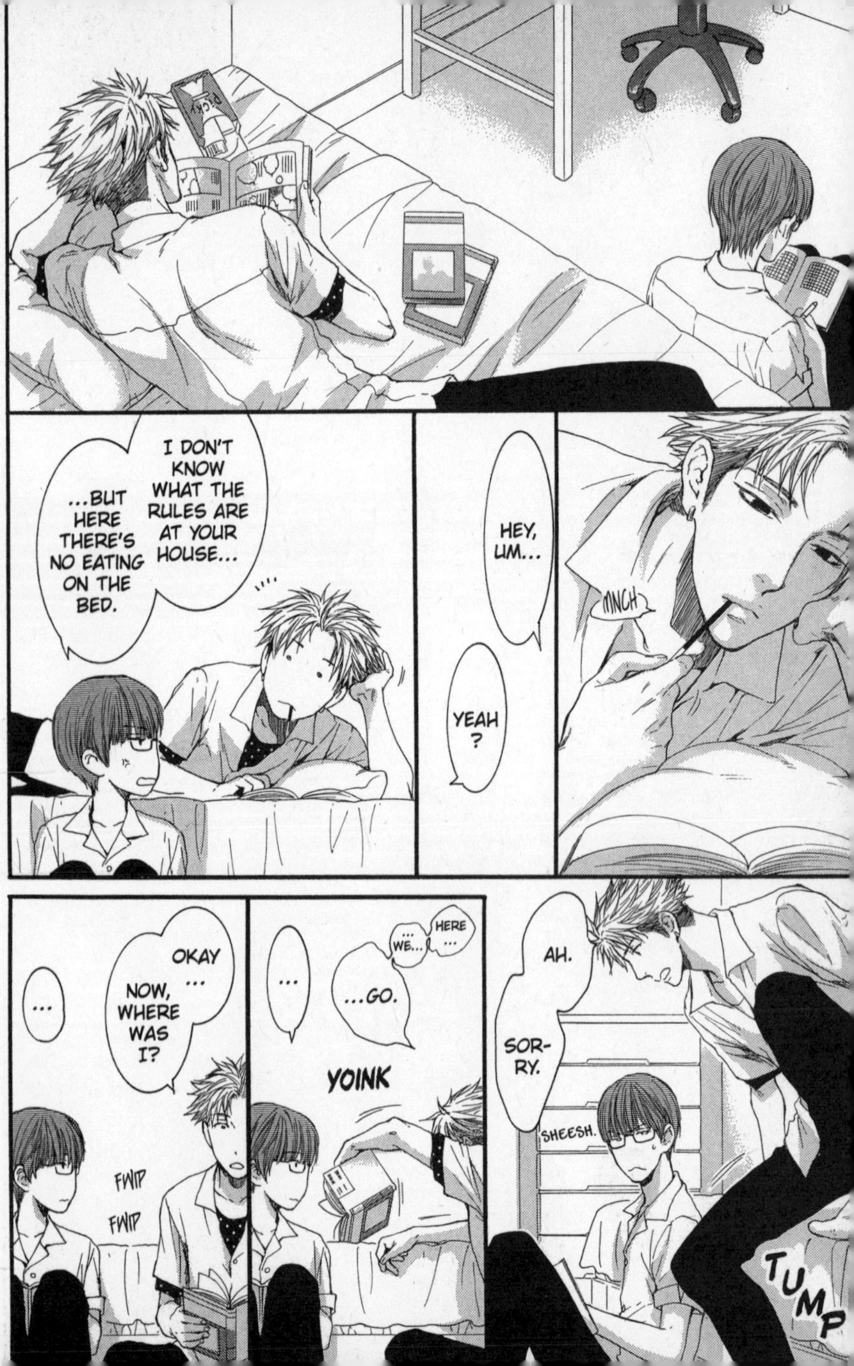
MNCH
HEY, UM...
YEAH?
I DON'T KNOW WHAT THE RULES ARE AT YOUR HOUSE...
...BUT HERE THERE'S NO EATING ON THE BED.
AH.
SORRY.
SHEESH.
TUMP
HERE ...
... WE...
...GO.
...
YOINK
OKAY ... NOW, WHERE WAS I?
...
FWIP
FWIP

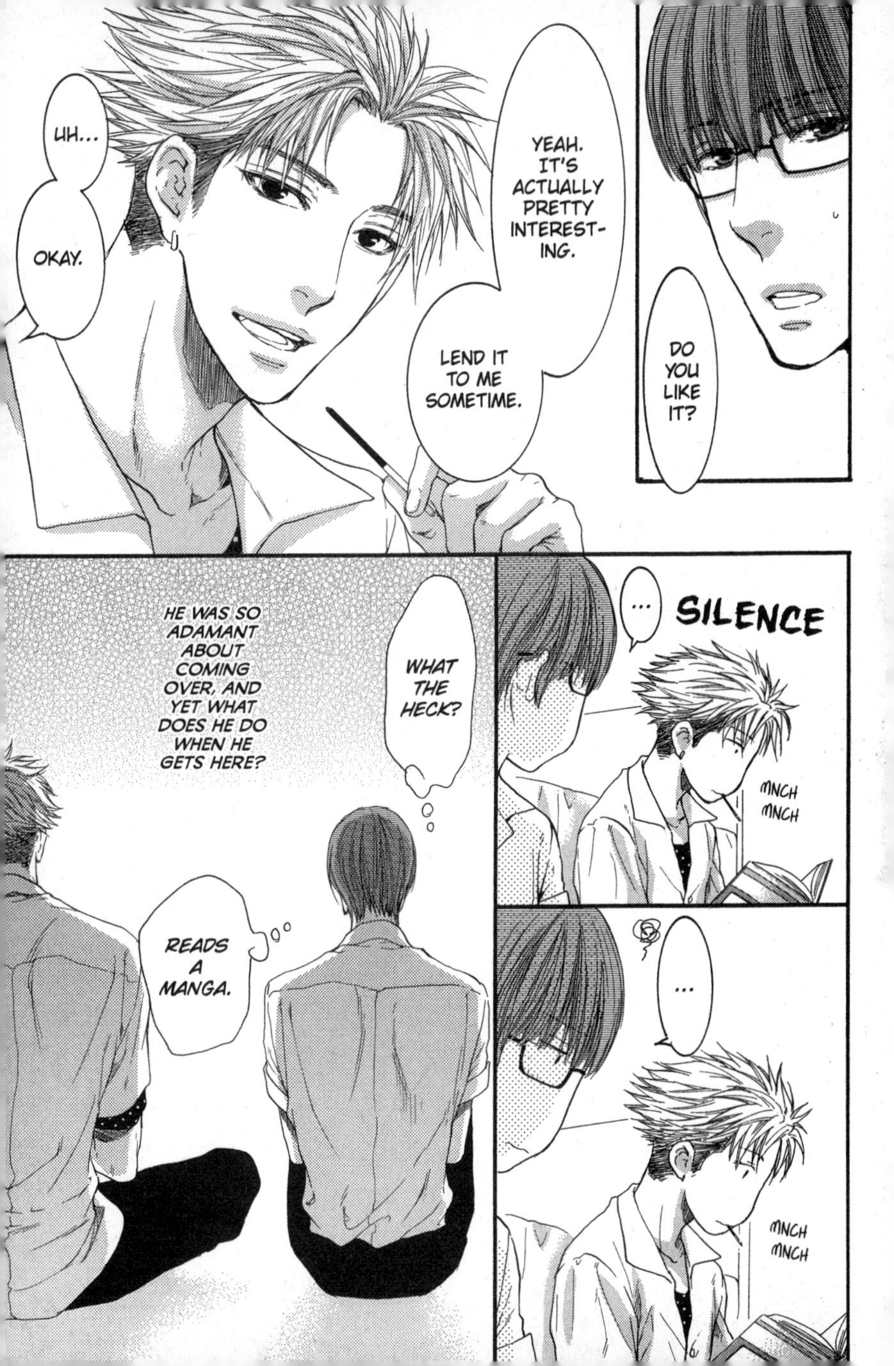
DO YOU LIKE IT?
YEAH. IT'S ACTUALLY PRETTY INTEREST-ING.
LEND IT TO ME SOMETIME.
UH...
OKAY.
...
SILENCE
MNCH MNCH
...
MNCH MNCH
WHAT THE HECK?
HE WAS SO ADAMANT ABOUT COMING OVER, AND YET WHAT DOES HE DO WHEN HE GETS HERE?
READS A MANGA.

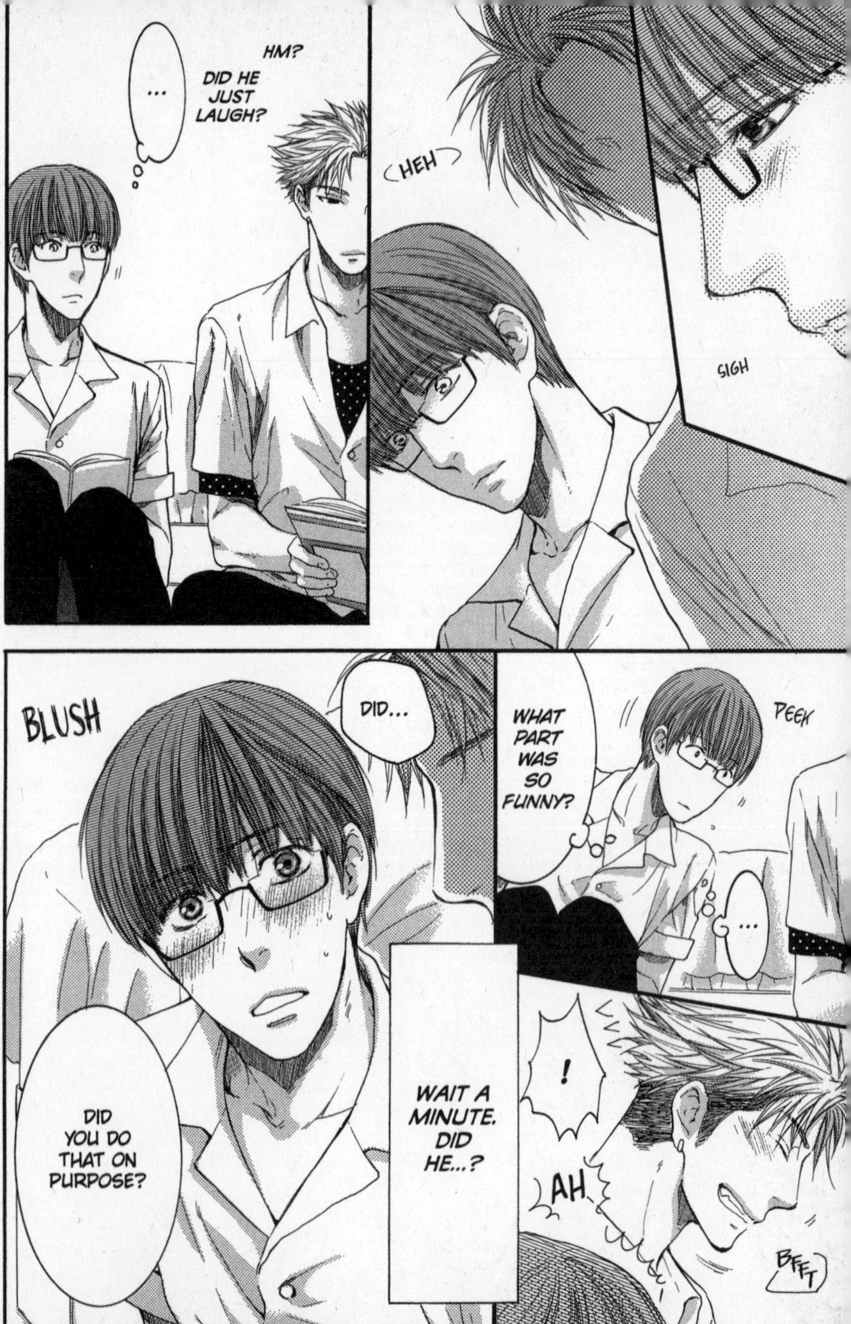

SIGH
HEH
HM?
DID HE JUST LAUGH?
...
PEEK
WHAT PART WAS SO FUNNY?
...
!
AH
BFFT
DID...
BLUSH
WAIT A MINUTE. DID HE...?
DID YOU DO THAT ON PURPOSE?

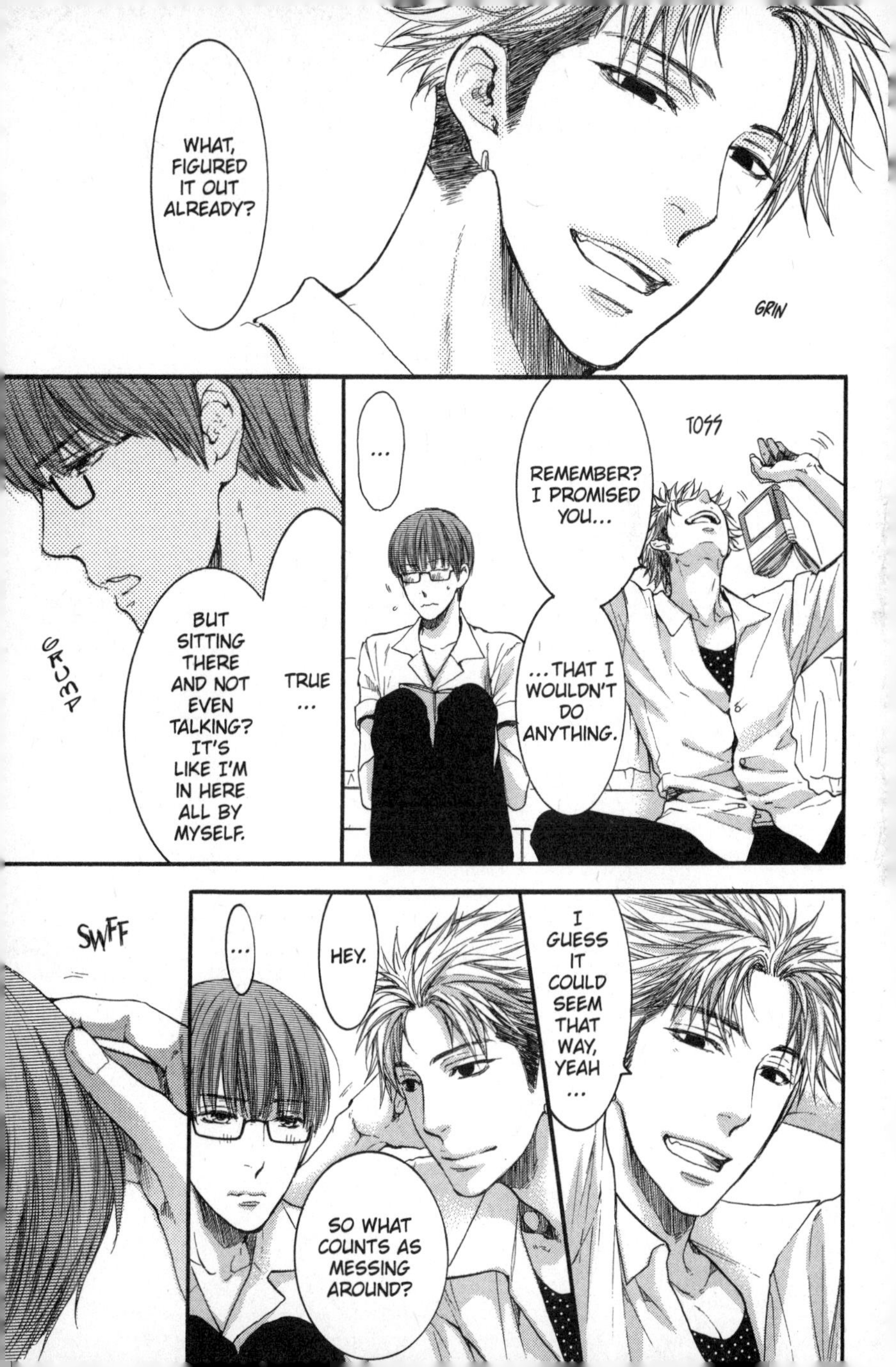
WHAT, FIGURED IT OUT ALREADY?
GRIN
TOSS
REMEMBER? I PROMISED YOU...
...THAT I WOULDN'T DO ANYTHING.
...
TRUE ...
BUT SITTING THERE AND NOT EVEN TALKING? IT'S LIKE I'M IN HERE ALL BY MYSELF.
I GUESS IT COULD SEEM THAT WAY, YEAH ...
HEY.
...
SO WHAT COUNTS AS MESSING AROUND?
SWFF

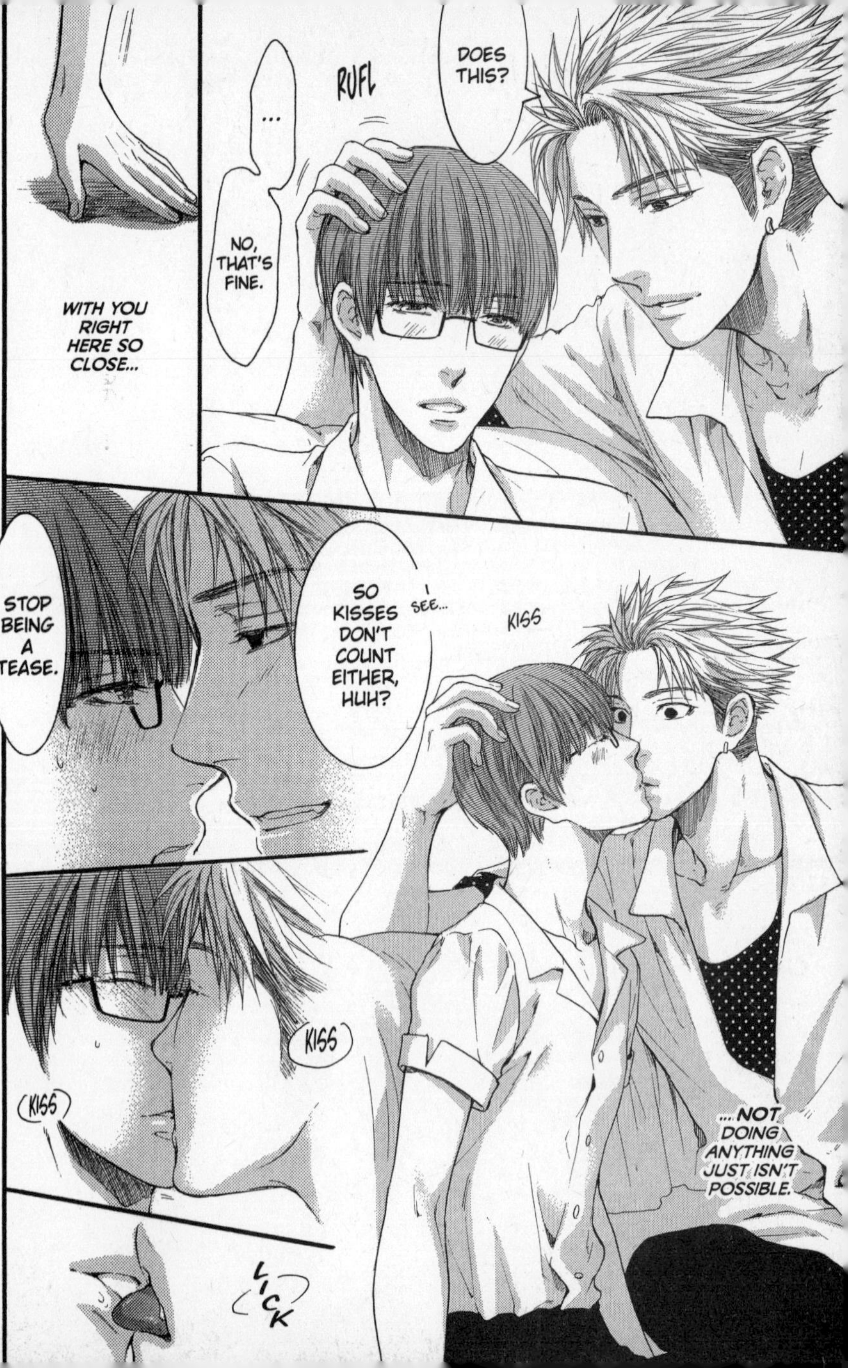
DOES THIS?
RUFL
...
NO, THAT'S FINE.
WITH YOU RIGHT HERE SO CLOSE...
KISS
I SEE...
SO KISSES DON'T COUNT EITHER, HUH?
...NOT DOING ANYTHING JUST ISN'T POSSIBLE.
STOP BEING A TEASE.
KISS
KISS
LICK

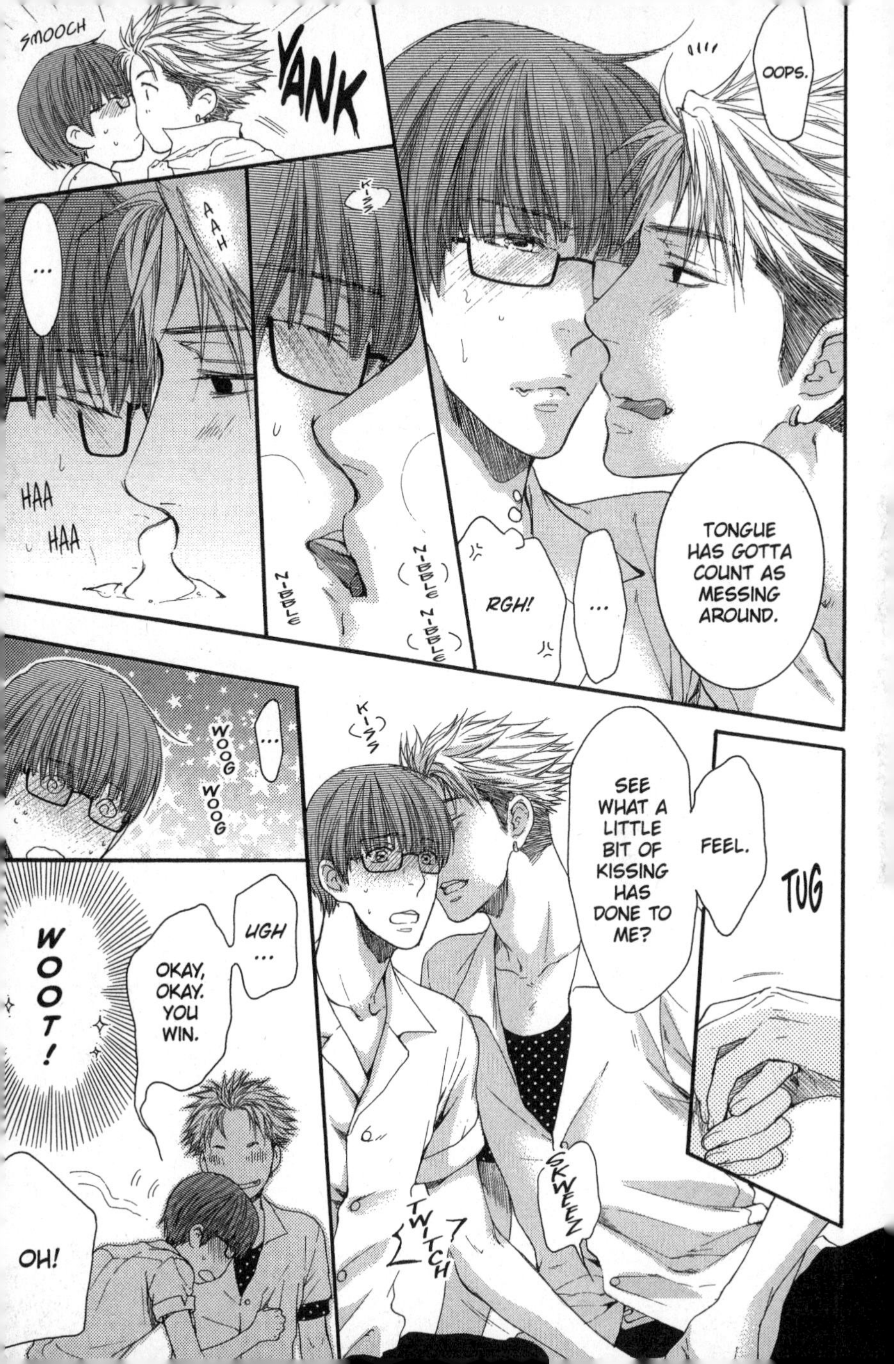
OOPS.
TONGUE HAS GOTTA COUNT AS MESSING AROUND.
RGH!
...
SMOOCH
YANK
KISS
NIBBLE
NIBBLE NIBBLE
AAH
...
HAA HAA
TUG
KISS
SEE WHAT A LITTLE BIT OF KISSING HAS DONE TO ME?
FEEL.
SKWEEZ
TWITCH
...
WOOG WOOG
WOOT!
UGH ...
OKAY, OKAY. YOU WIN.
OH!

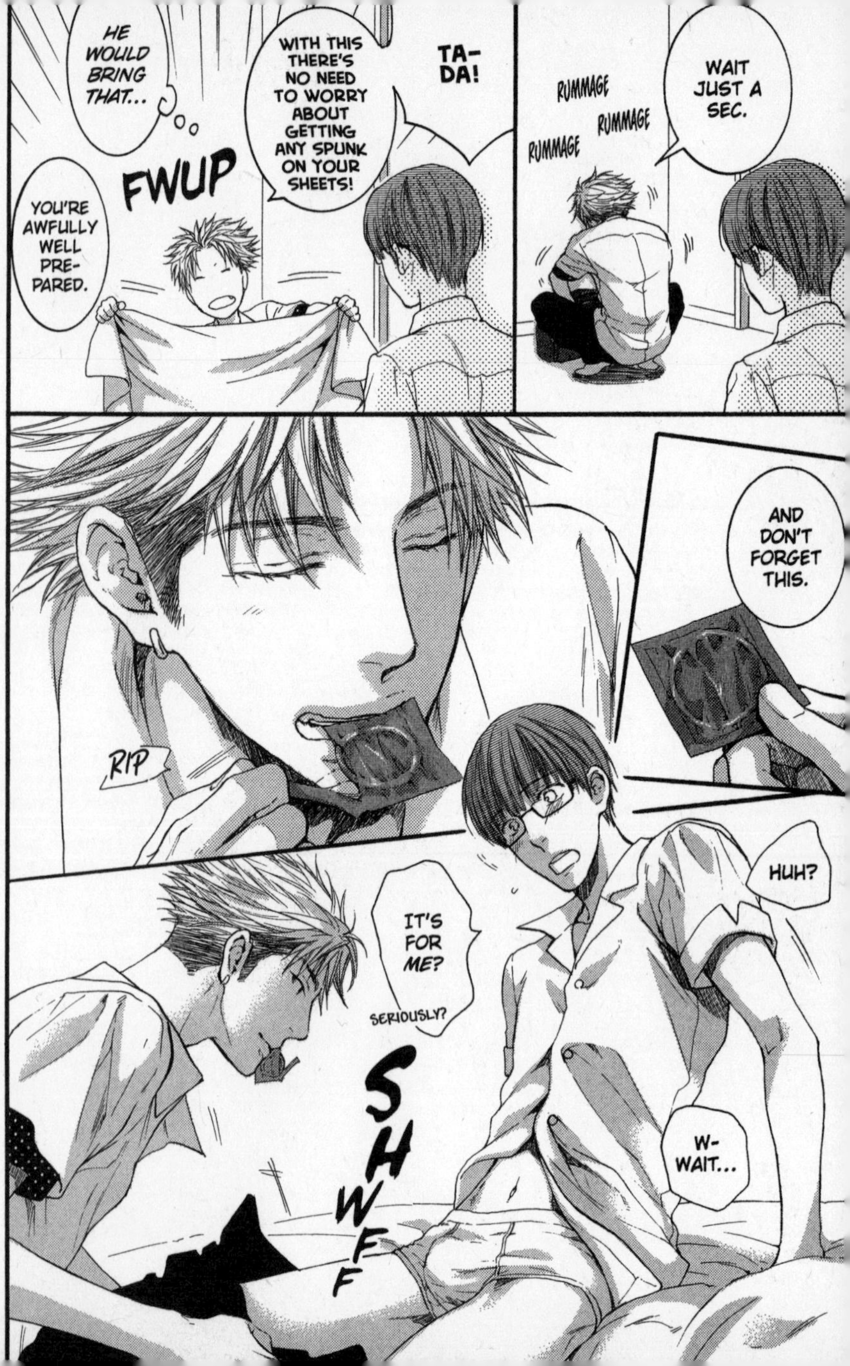
WAIT JUST A SEC.
RUMMAGE
RUMMAGE
RUMMAGE
TA-DA!
WITH THIS THERE'S NO NEED TO WORRY ABOUT GETTING ANY SPUNK ON YOUR SHEETS!
HE WOULD BRING THAT...
FWUP
YOU'RE AWFULLY WELL PRE-PARED.
AND DON'T FORGET THIS.
RIP
HUH?
IT'S FOR ME?
SERIOUSLY?
SHWFF
W-WAIT...

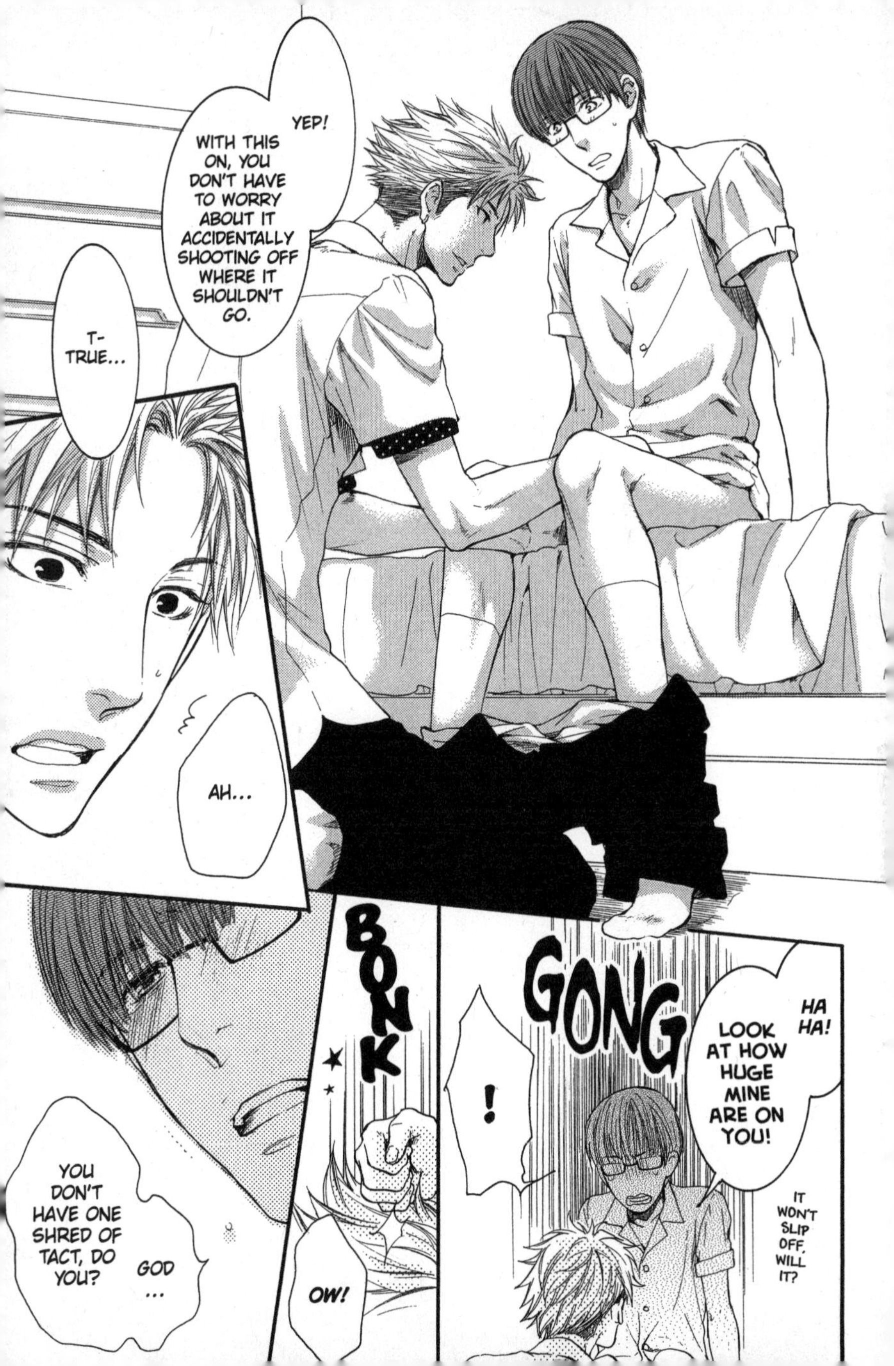
YEP! WITH THIS ON, YOU DON'T HAVE TO WORRY ABOUT IT ACCIDENTALLY SHOOTING OFF WHERE IT SHOULDN'T GO.
T-TRUE...
AH...
HA HA! LOOK AT HOW HUGE MINE ARE ON YOU!
GONG
!
IT WON'T SLIP OFF, WILL IT?
BONK
OW!
YOU DON'T HAVE ONE SHRED OF TACT, DO YOU?
GOD ...

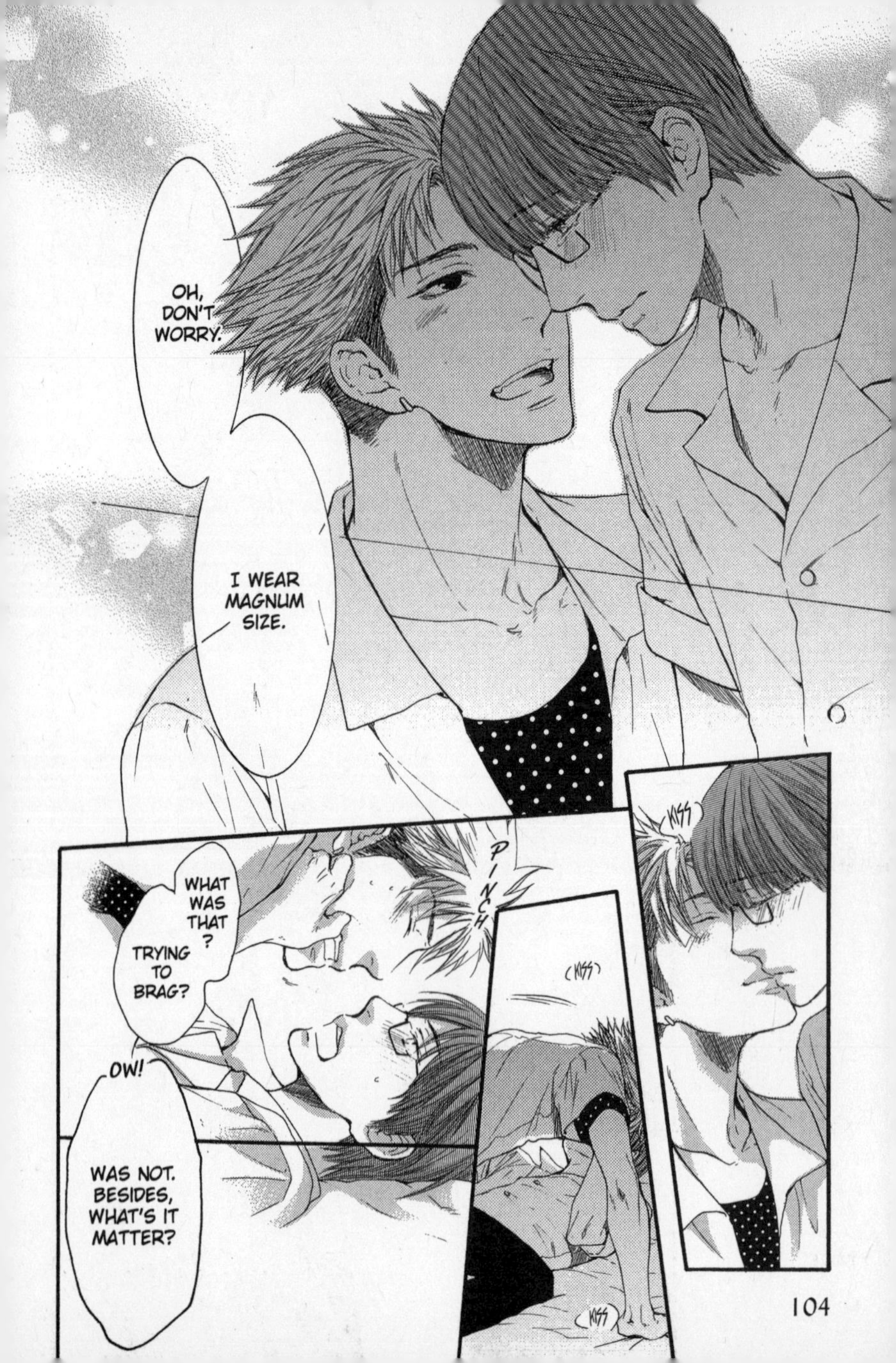

OH, DON'T WORRY.
I WEAR MAGNUM SIZE.
KISS
KISS
KISS
PINCH
WHAT WAS THAT?
TRYING TO BRAG?
OW!
WAS NOT. BESIDES, WHAT'S IT MATTER?

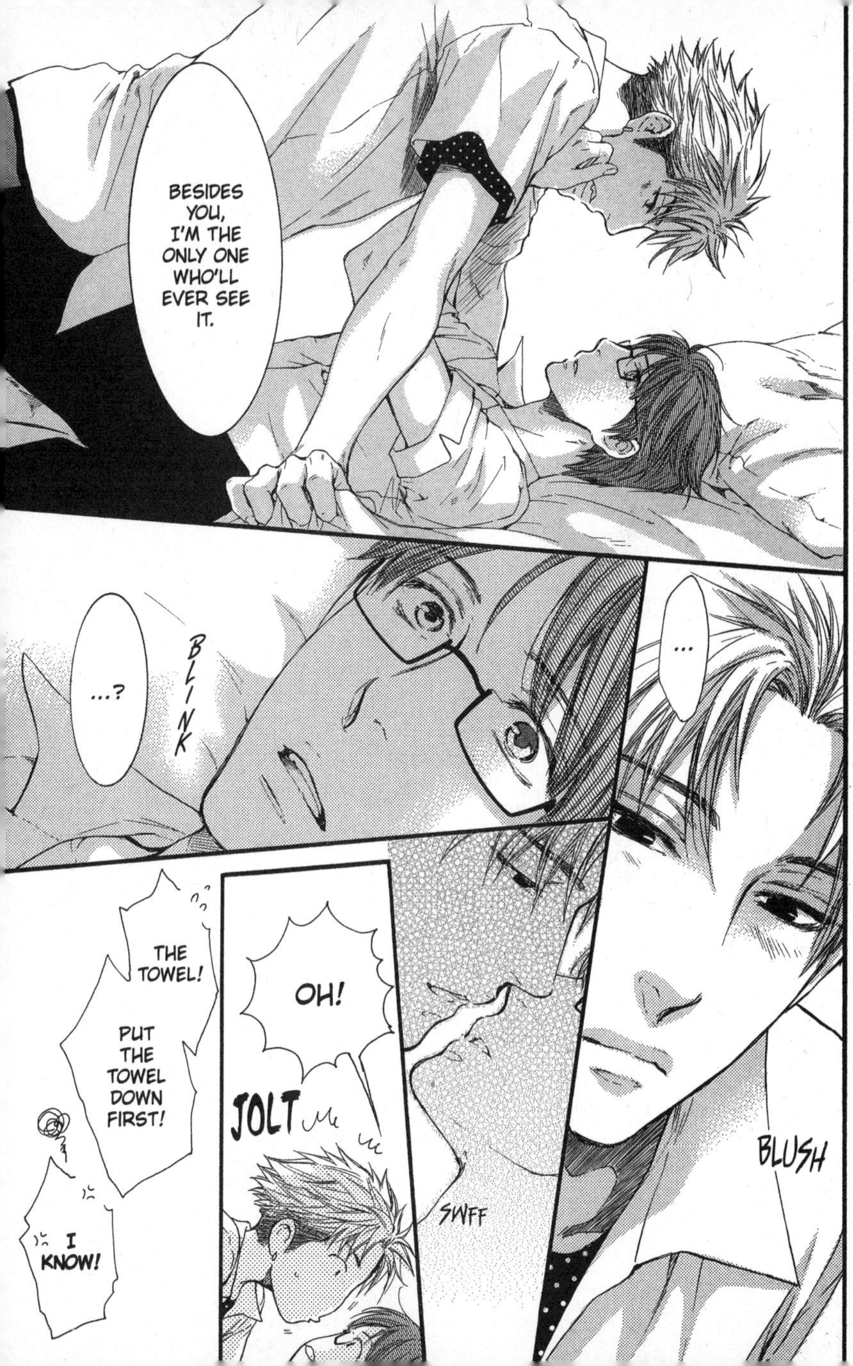
BESIDES YOU, I'M THE ONLY ONE WHO'LL EVER SEE IT.
...
BLUSH
BLINK
...?
OH!
JOLT
SWFF
THE TOWEL!
PUT THE TOWEL DOWN FIRST!
I KNOW!

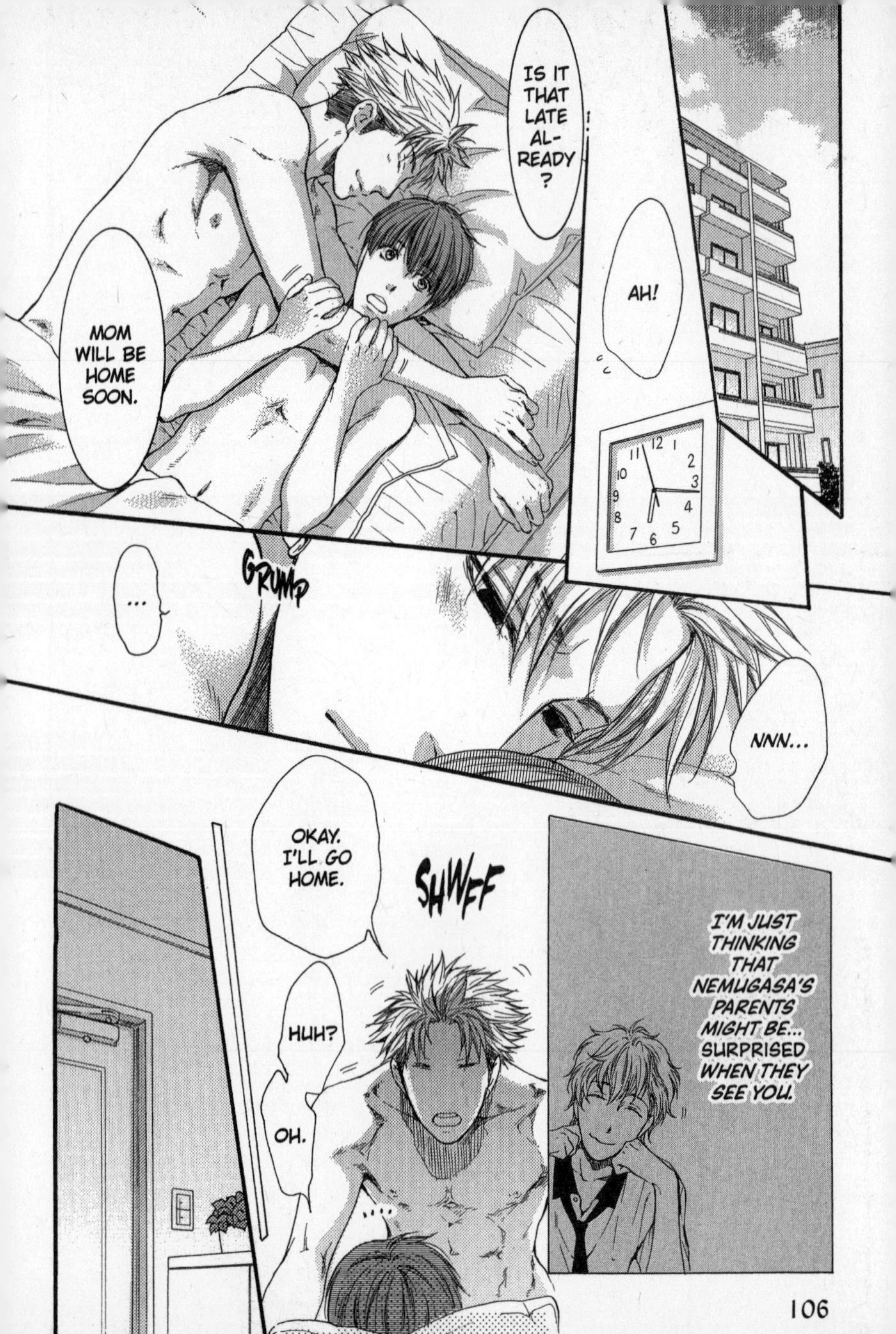
AH!
IS IT THAT LATE AL-READY?
MOM WILL BE HOME SOON.
NNN...
GRUMP
...
I'M JUST THINKING THAT NEMUGASA'S PARENTS MIGHT BE... SURPRISED WHEN THEY SEE YOU.
SHWFF
OKAY. I'LL GO HOME.
HUH?
OH.
....

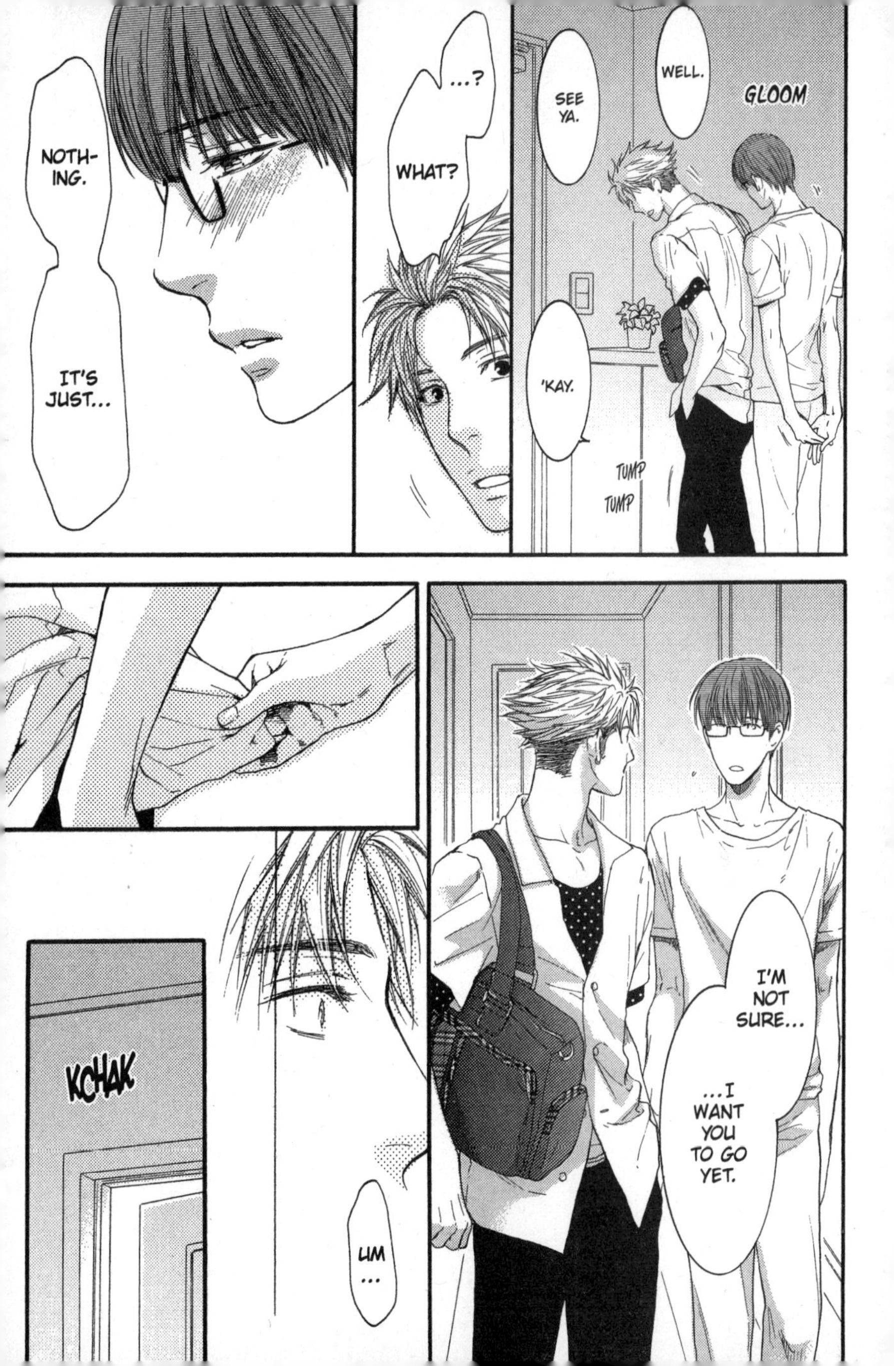
WELL.
GLOOM
SEE YA.
'KAY.
TUMP
TUMP
...?
WHAT?
NOTHING.
IT'S JUST...
I'M NOT SURE...
...I WANT YOU TO GO YET.
UM...
KCHAK

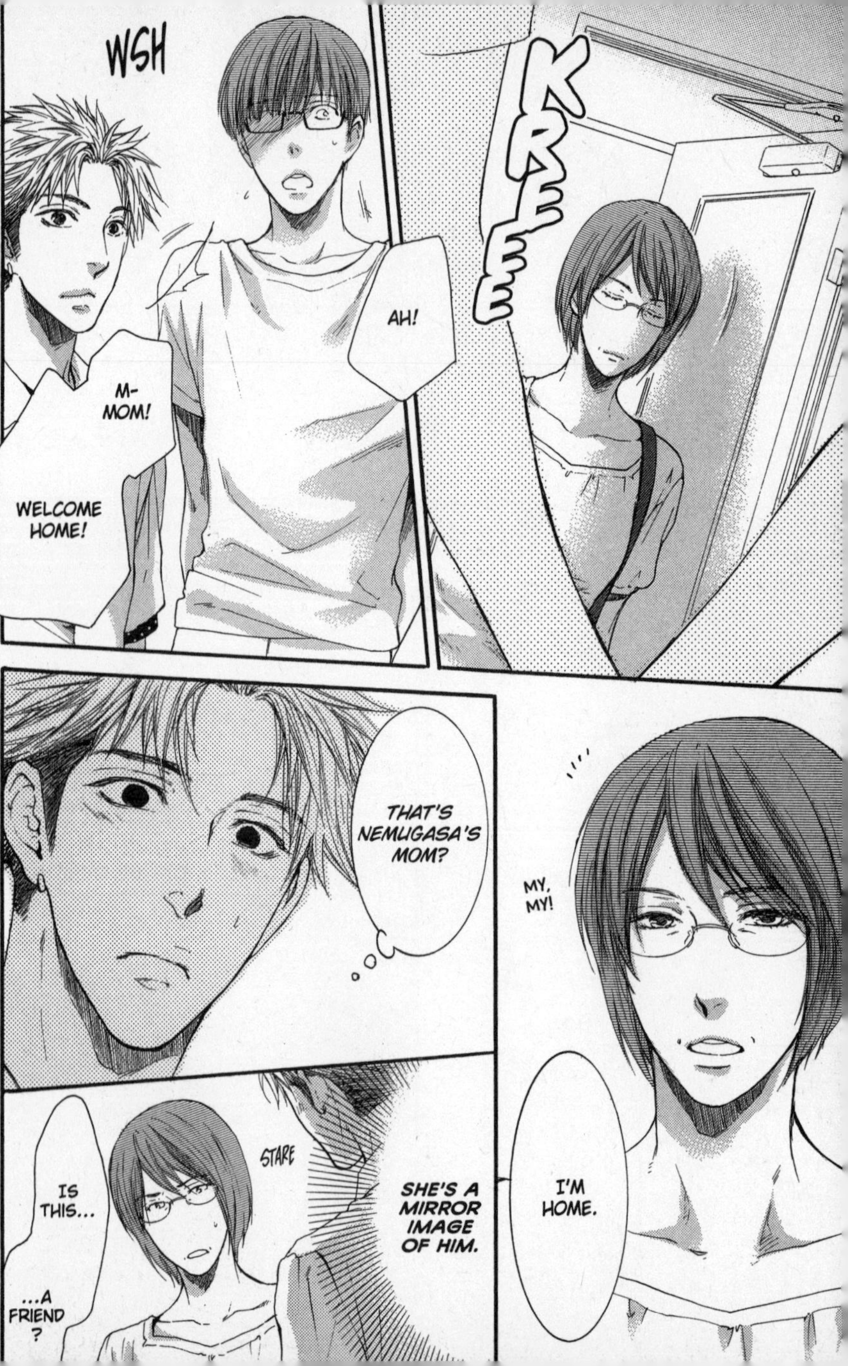
KREEE
WSH
AH!
M-MOM!
WELCOME HOME!
MY, MY!
I'M HOME.
THAT'S NEMUGASA'S MOM?
STARE
SHE'S A MIRROR IMAGE OF HIM.
IS THIS...
...A FRIEND?

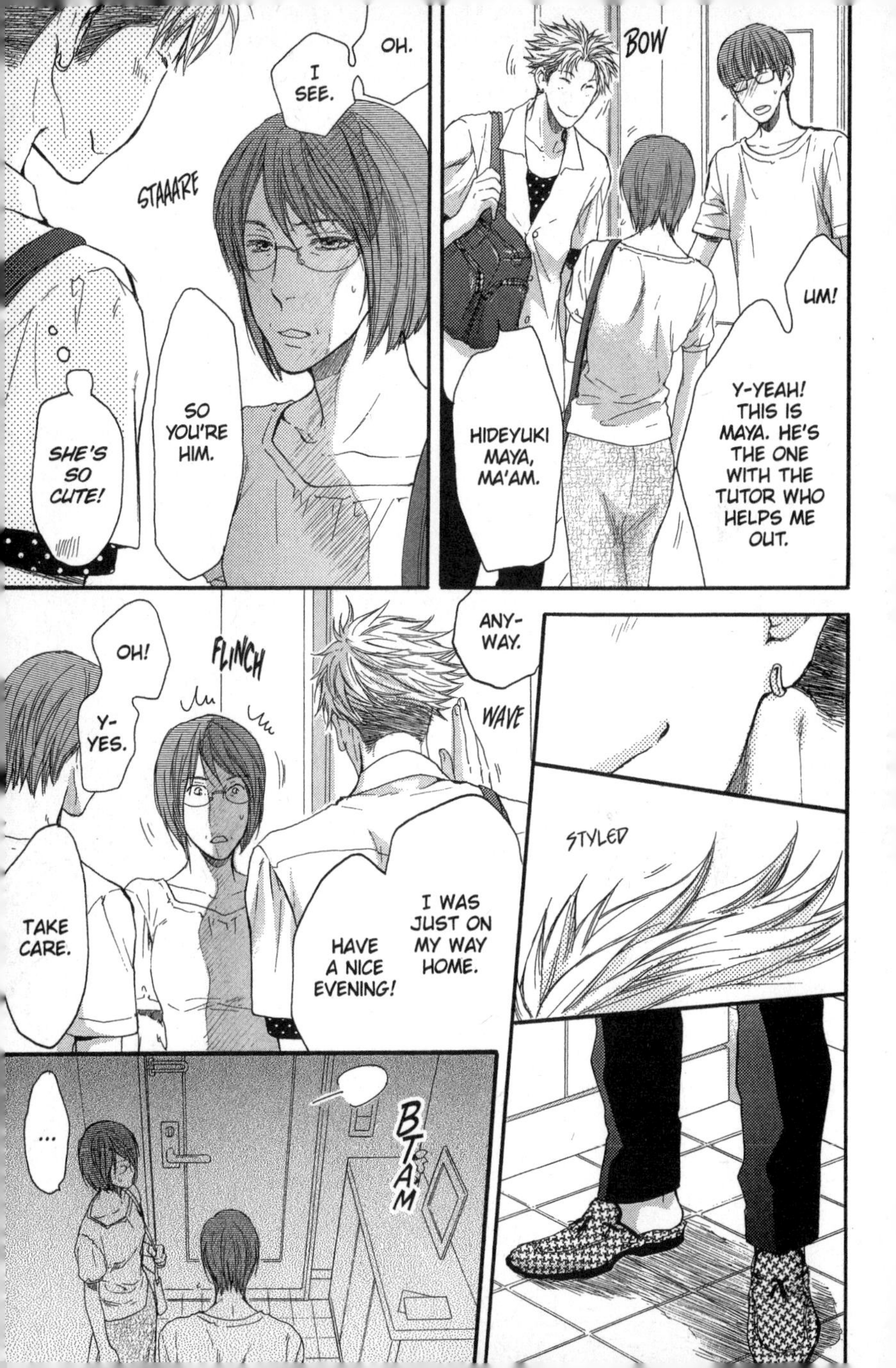
UM!
Y-YEAH! THIS IS MAYA. HE'S THE ONE WITH THE TUTOR WHO HELPS ME OUT.
BOW
HIDEYUKI MAYA, MA'AM.
OH.
I SEE.
STAAARE
SO YOU'RE HIM.
SHE'S SO CUTE!
ANY-WAY.
WAVE
I WAS JUST ON MY WAY HOME.
HAVE A NICE EVENING!
FLINCH
OH!
Y-YES.
TAKE CARE.
STYLED
BTAM
...

HEH HEH!

THEY HAVE THE EXACT SAME FACE! THAT'S SO CUTE!

GUESS NEMUGASA REALLY TAKES AFTER HIS MOM.

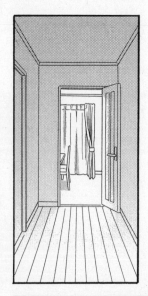

SHHH

KLINK

KLINK

SO THAT WAS MAYA, HM?

SHHH

I HAD EXPECTED HIM TO BE A BIT MORE... NORMAL.

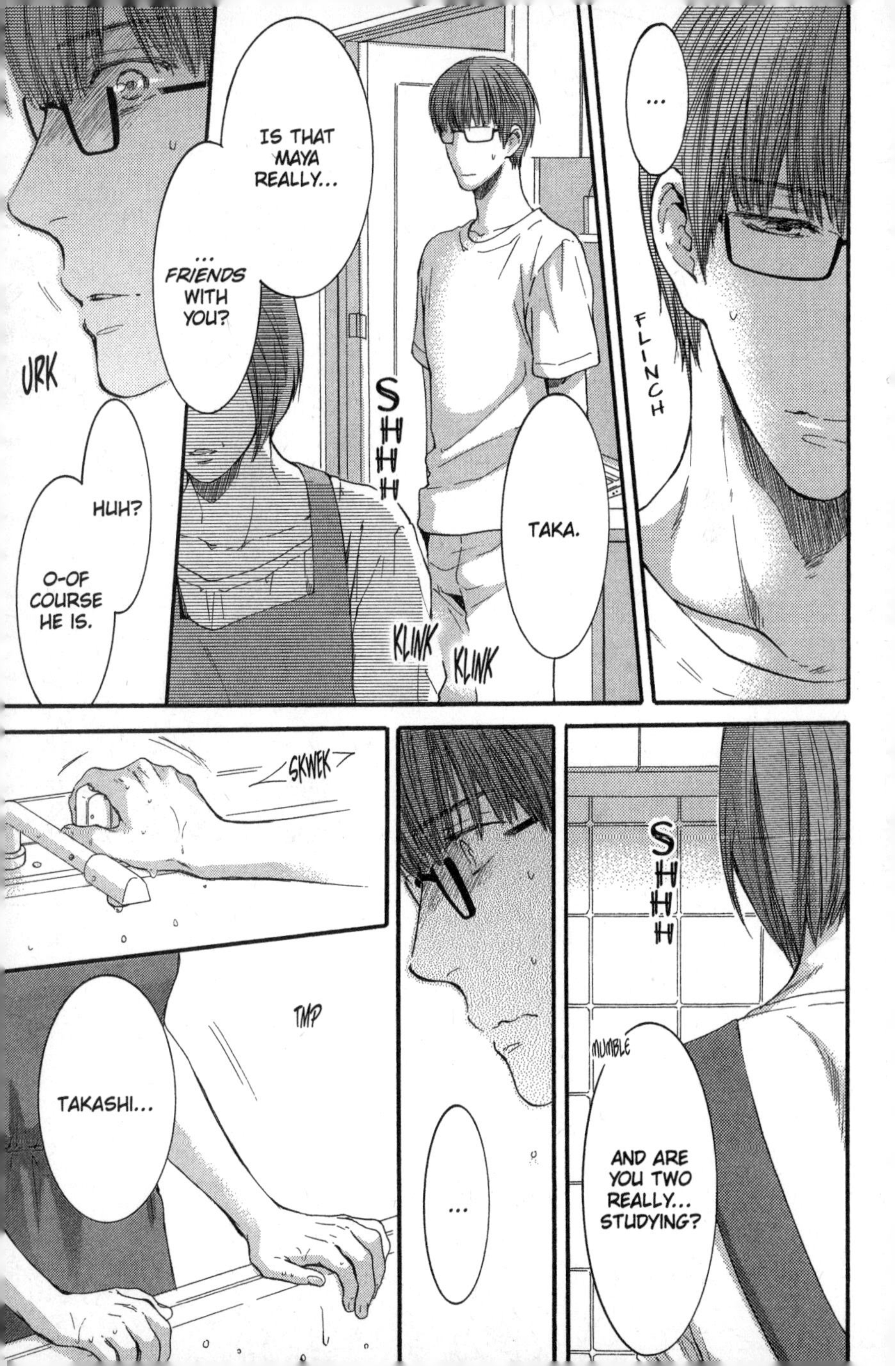
...
FLINCH
TAKA.
SHHH
KLINK
KLINK
IS THAT MAYA REALLY...
... FRIENDS WITH YOU?
URK
HUH?
O-OF COURSE HE IS.
SHHH
MUMBLE
AND ARE YOU TWO REALLY... STUDYING?
...
SKWEK
TMP
TAKASHI...

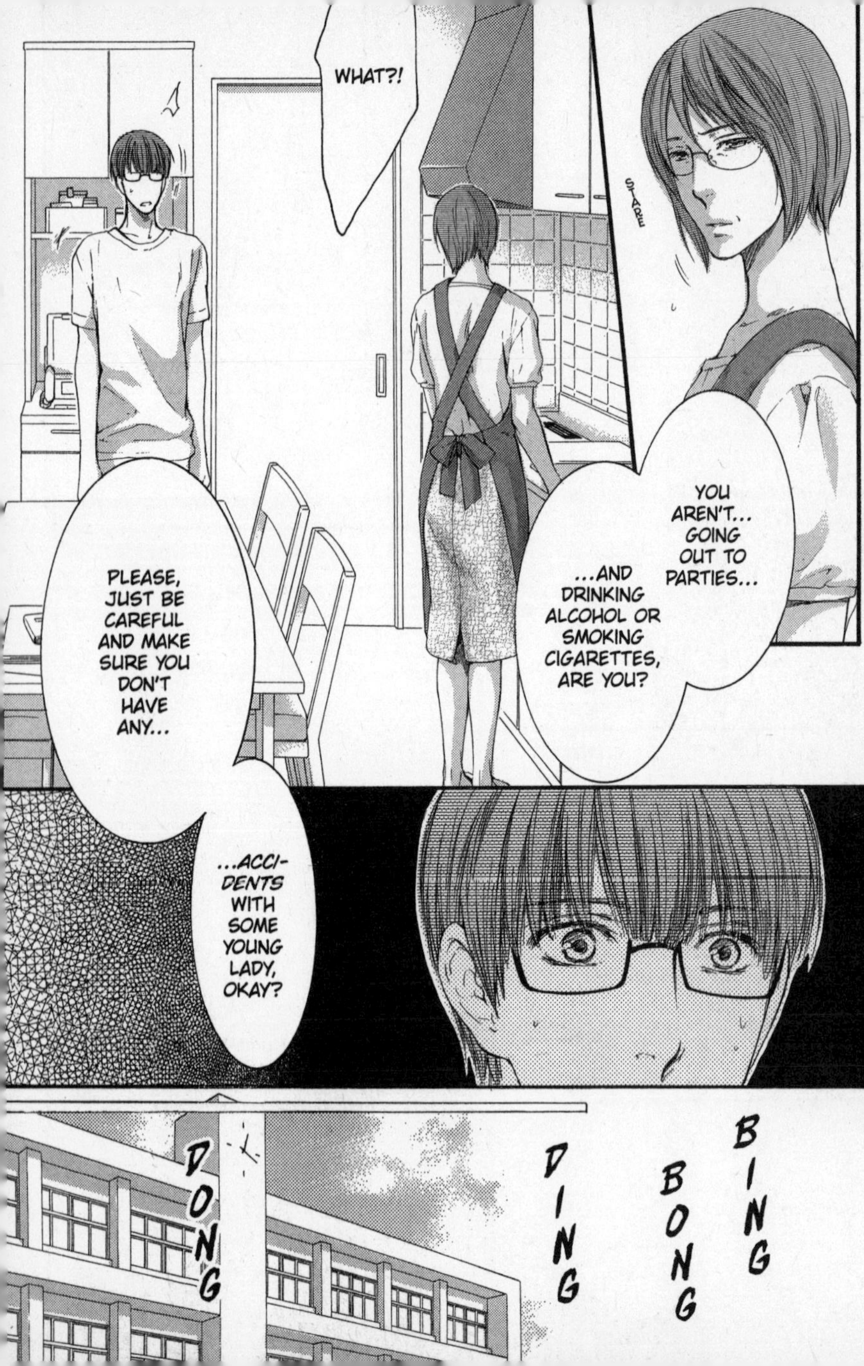
STARE
YOU AREN'T... GOING OUT TO PARTIES...
...AND DRINKING ALCOHOL OR SMOKING CIGARETTES, ARE YOU?
WHAT?!
PLEASE, JUST BE CAREFUL AND MAKE SURE YOU DON'T HAVE ANY...
...ACCI-DENTS WITH SOME YOUNG LADY, OKAY?
BING
BONG
DING
DONG

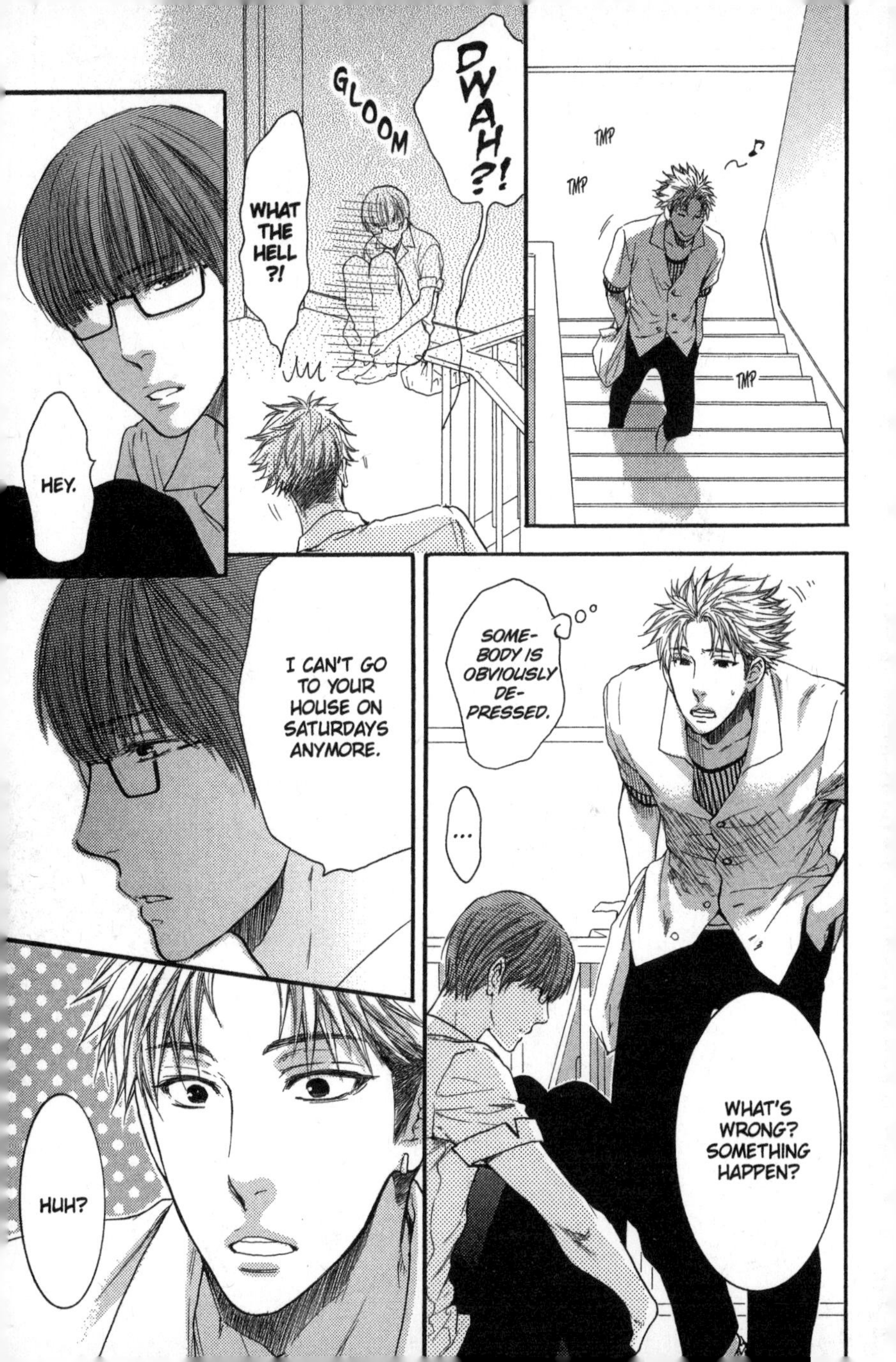
TMP
TMP
~♪
TMP
DWAH?!
GLOOM
WHAT THE HELL ?!
HEY.
SOME-BODY IS OBVIOUSLY DE-PRESSED.
...
WHAT'S WRONG? SOMETHING HAPPEN?
I CAN'T GO TO YOUR HOUSE ON SATURDAYS ANYMORE.
HUH?

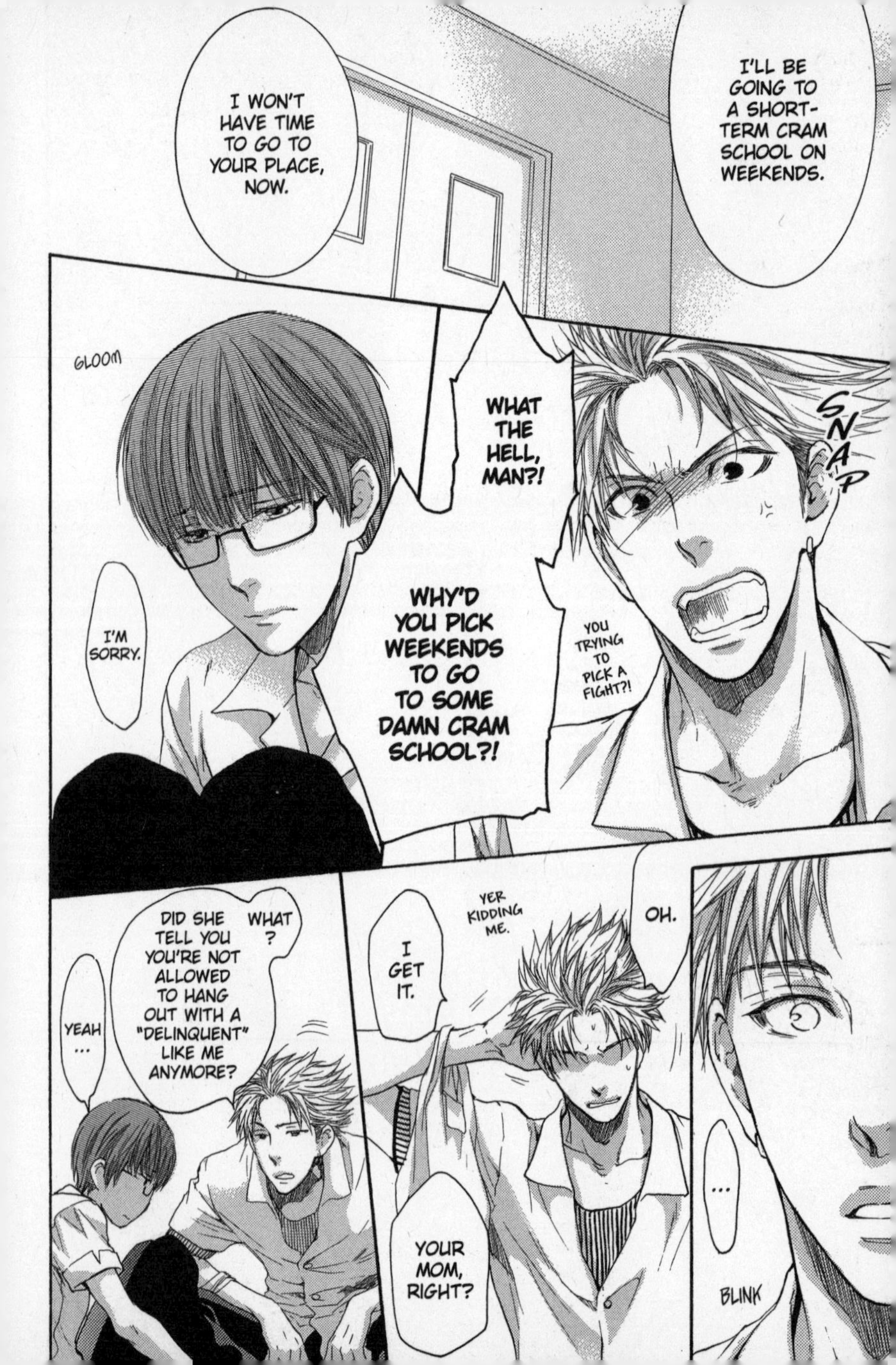
I'LL BE GOING TO A SHORT-TERM CRAM SCHOOL ON WEEKENDS.
I WON'T HAVE TIME TO GO TO YOUR PLACE, NOW.
SNAP
WHAT THE HELL, MAN?!
YOU TRYING TO PICK A FIGHT?!
WHY'D YOU PICK WEEKENDS TO GO TO SOME DAMN CRAM SCHOOL?!
GLOOM
I'M SORRY.
OH.
...
BLINK
YER KIDDING ME.
I GET IT.
YOUR MOM, RIGHT?
WHAT?
DID SHE TELL YOU YOU'RE NOT ALLOWED TO HANG OUT WITH A "DELINQUENT" LIKE ME ANYMORE?
YEAH...

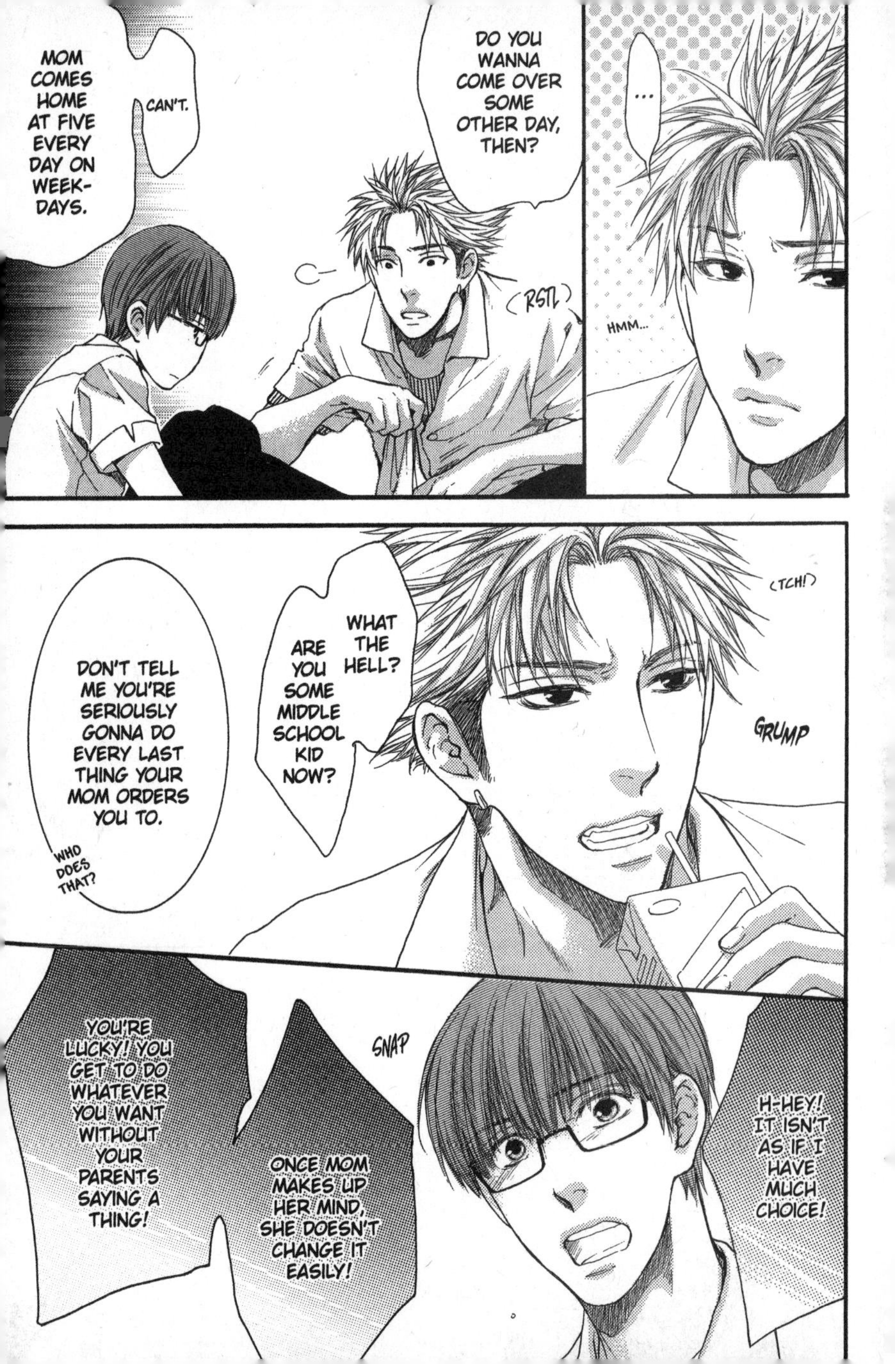
...
HMM...
DO YOU WANNA COME OVER SOME OTHER DAY, THEN?
(RSTL)
CAN'T.
MOM COMES HOME AT FIVE EVERY DAY ON WEEK-DAYS.
(TCH!)
WHAT THE HELL? ARE YOU SOME MIDDLE SCHOOL KID NOW?
GRUMP
DON'T TELL ME YOU'RE SERIOUSLY GONNA DO EVERY LAST THING YOUR MOM ORDERS YOU TO.
WHO DOES THAT?
H-HEY! IT ISN'T AS IF I HAVE MUCH CHOICE!
SNAP
ONCE MOM MAKES UP HER MIND, SHE DOESN'T CHANGE IT EASILY!
YOU'RE LUCKY! YOU GET TO DO WHATEVER YOU WANT WITHOUT YOUR PARENTS SAYING A THING!

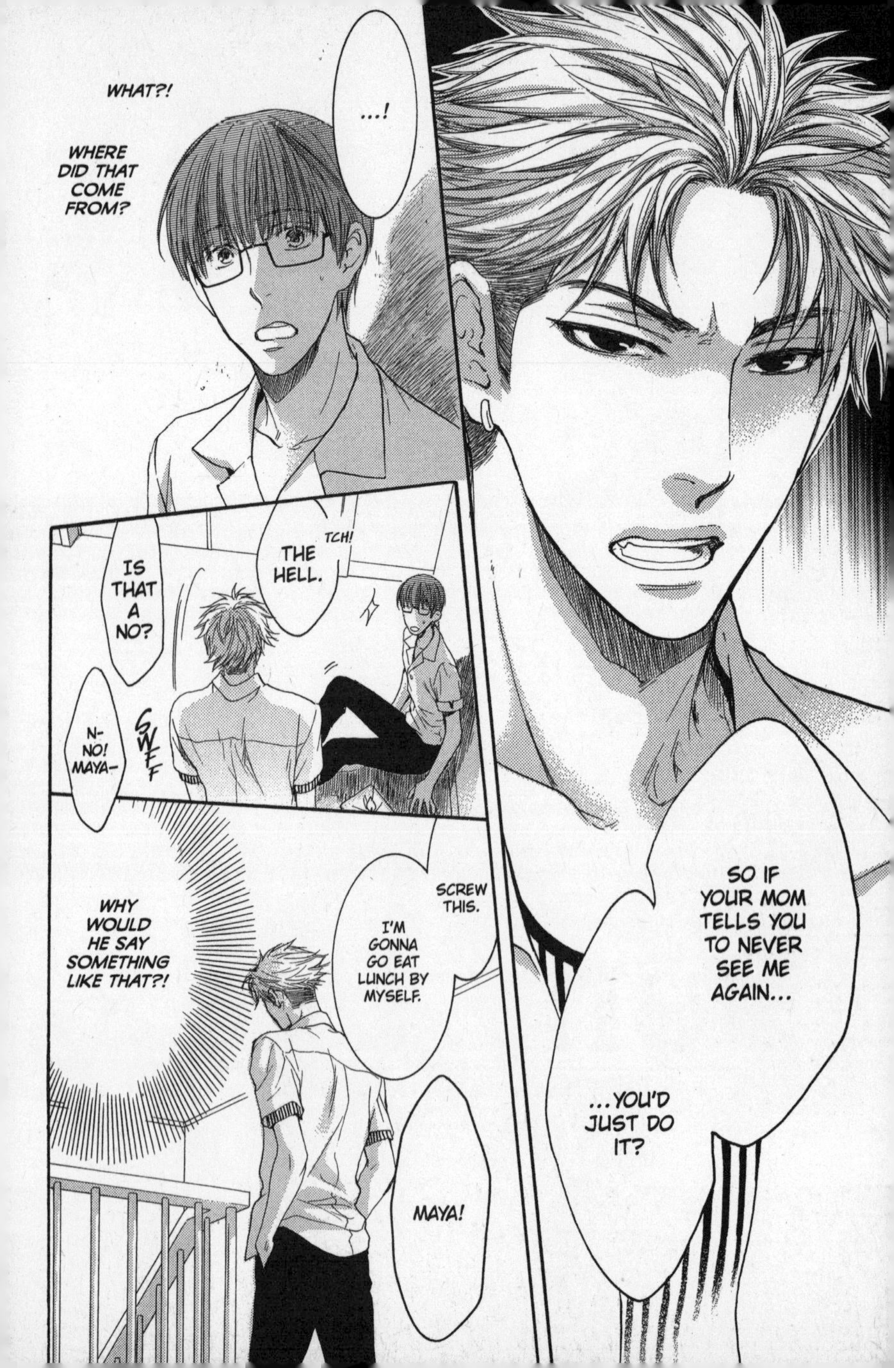
SO IF YOUR MOM TELLS YOU TO NEVER SEE ME AGAIN...
...YOU'D JUST DO IT?
...!
WHAT?!
WHERE DID THAT COME FROM?
TCH!
THE HELL.
IS THAT A NO?
SWFF
N-NO! MAYA-
SCREW THIS.
I'M GONNA GO EAT LUNCH BY MYSELF.
WHY WOULD HE SAY SOMETHING LIKE THAT?!
MAYA!

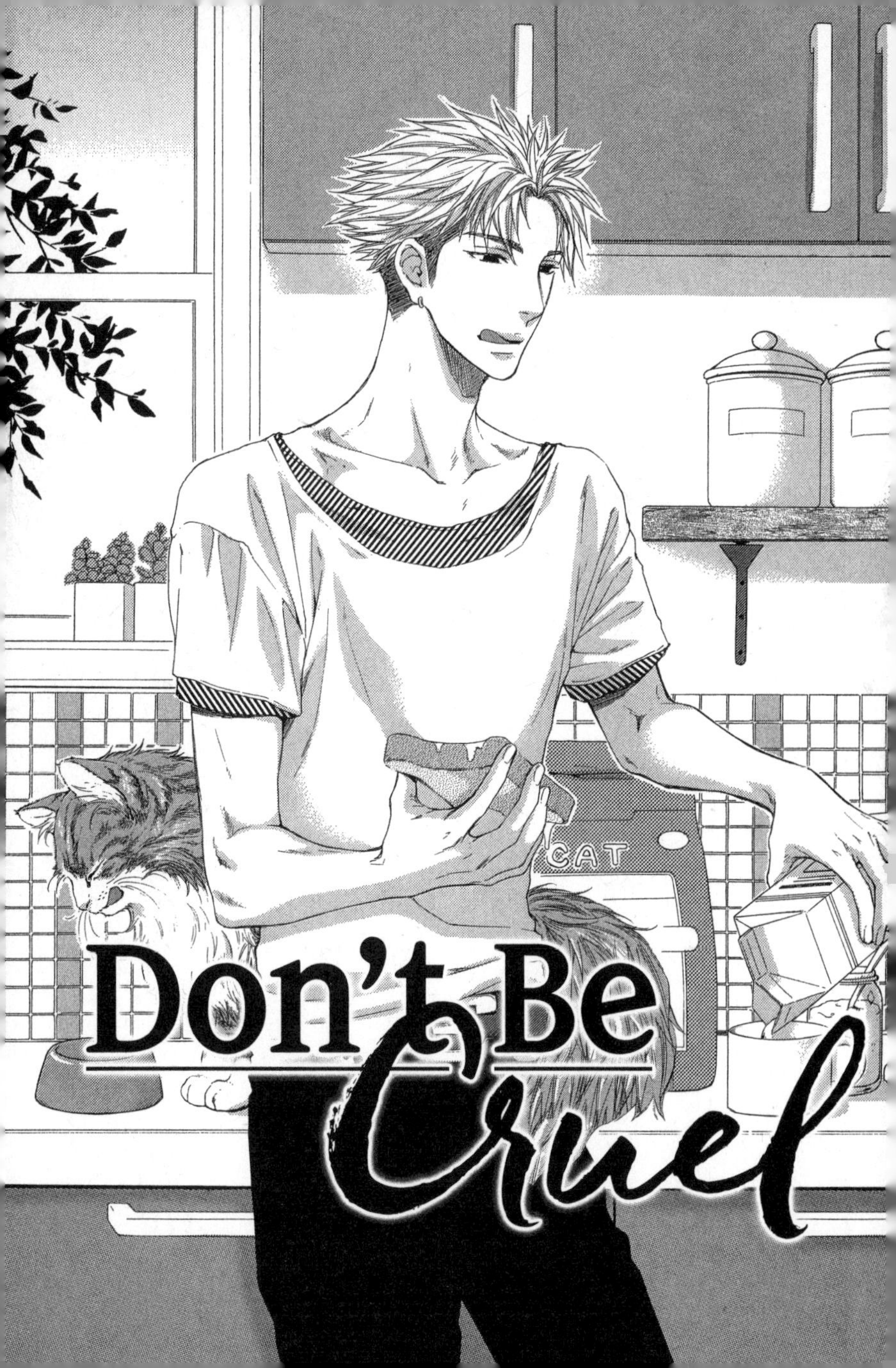
CAT
Don't Be Cruel

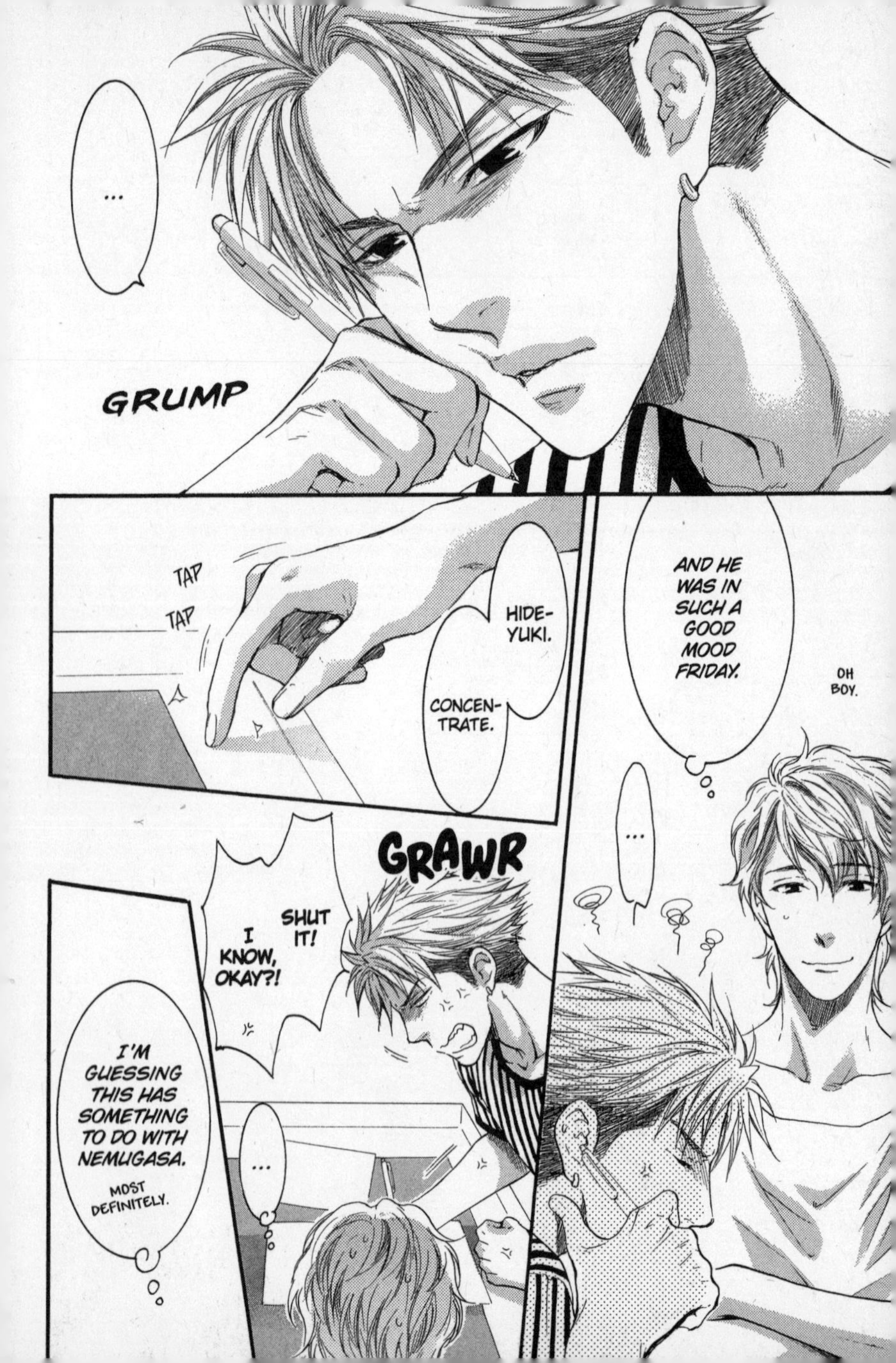
...
GRUMP
AND HE WAS IN SUCH A GOOD MOOD FRIDAY.
OH BOY.
...
TAP
TAP
HIDE-YUKI.
CONCENTRATE.
GRAWR
SHUT IT!
I KNOW, OKAY?!
...
I'M GUESSING THIS HAS SOMETHING TO DO WITH NEMUGASA.
MOST DEFINITELY.

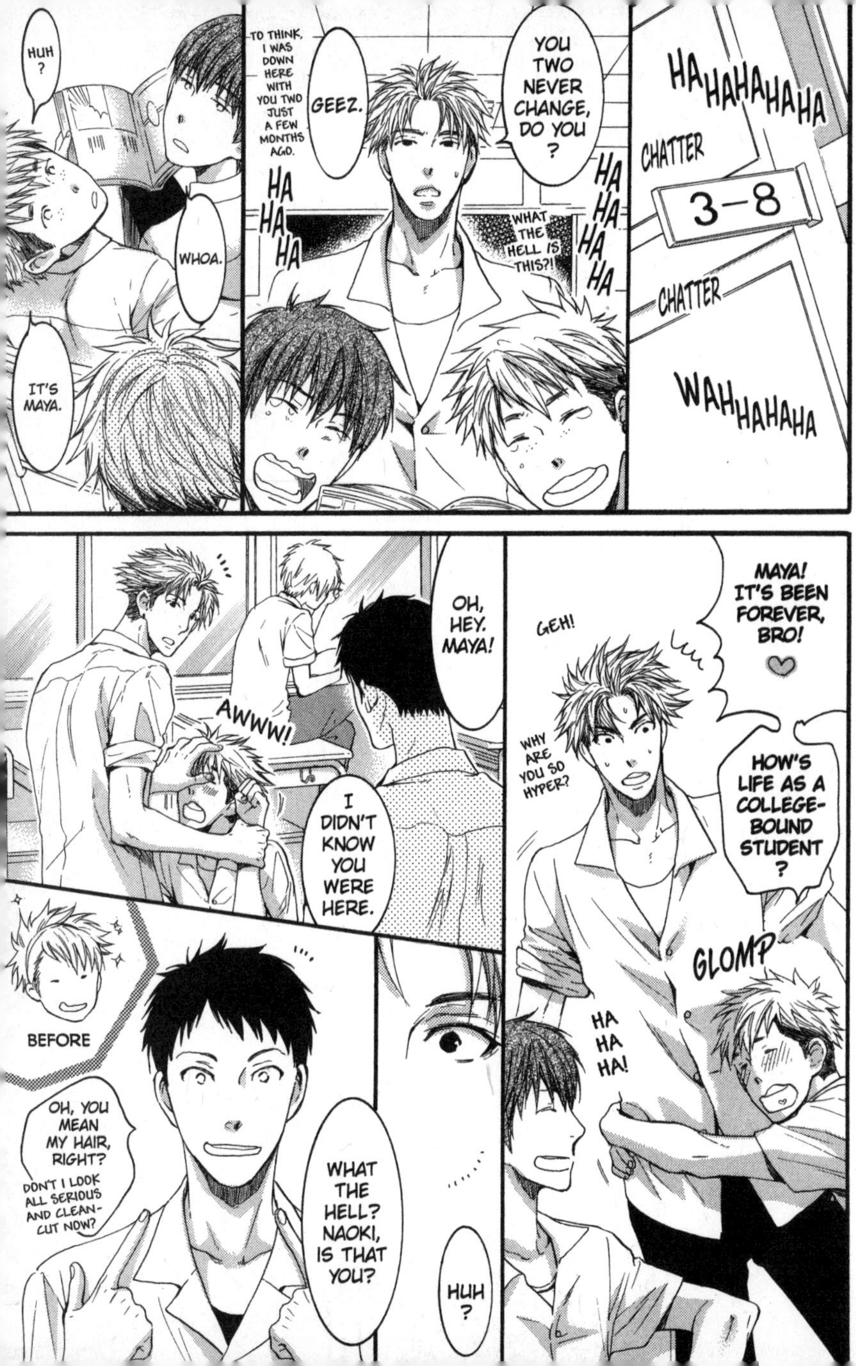
HAHAHAHAHA
CHATTER
3-8
CHATTER
WAHHAHAHA
YOU TWO NEVER CHANGE, DO YOU?
HA HA HA HA HA
GEEZ.
TO THINK, I WAS DOWN HERE WITH YOU TWO JUST A FEW MONTHS AGO.
WHAT THE HELL IS THIS?!
HA HA HA
HUH?
WHOA.
IT'S MAYA.
MAYA! IT'S BEEN FOREVER, BRO!
GEH!
HOW'S LIFE AS A COLLEGE-BOUND STUDENT?
WHY ARE YOU SO HYPER?
GLOMP
HA HA HA!
OH, HEY. MAYA!
I DIDN'T KNOW YOU WERE HERE.
AWWW!
WHAT THE HELL? NAOKI, IS THAT YOU?
HUH?
BEFORE
OH, YOU MEAN MY HAIR, RIGHT?
DON'T I LOOK ALL SERIOUS AND CLEAN-CUT NOW?

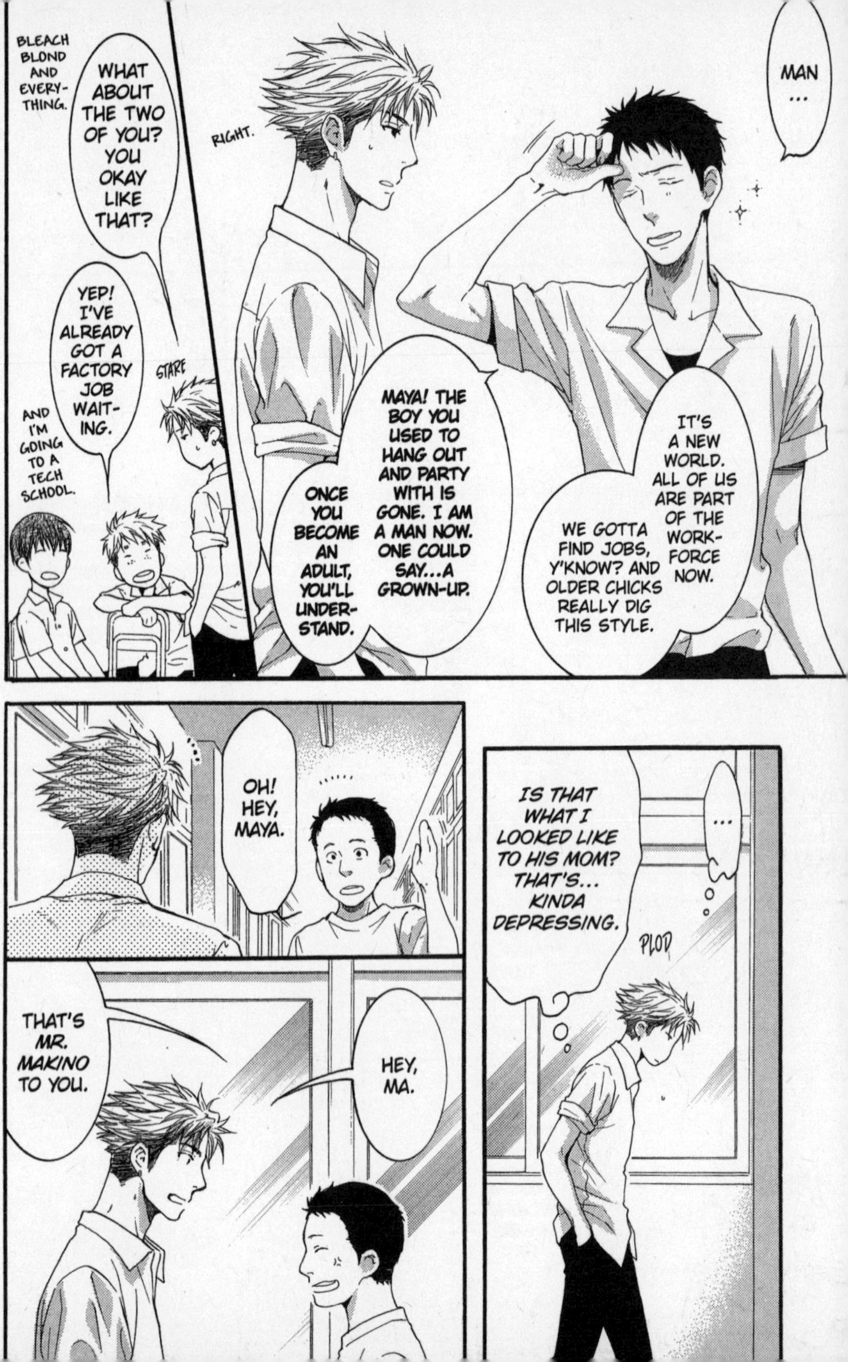
MAN ...
IT'S A NEW WORLD. ALL OF US ARE PART OF THE WORK-FORCE NOW.
WE GOTTA FIND JOBS, Y'KNOW? AND OLDER CHICKS REALLY DIG THIS STYLE.
MAYA! THE BOY YOU USED TO HANG OUT AND PARTY WITH IS GONE. I AM A MAN NOW. ONE COULD SAY...A GROWN-UP.
ONCE YOU BECOME AN ADULT, YOU'LL UNDER-STAND.
RIGHT.
WHAT ABOUT THE TWO OF YOU? YOU OKAY LIKE THAT?
BLEACH BLOND AND EVERY-THING.
STARE
YEP! I'VE ALREADY GOT A FACTORY JOB WAIT-ING.
AND I'M GOING TO A TECH SCHOOL.
...
IS THAT WHAT I LOOKED LIKE TO HIS MOM? THAT'S... KINDA DEPRESSING.
PLOD
OH! HEY, MAYA.
......
HEY, MA.
THAT'S MR. MAKINO TO YOU.

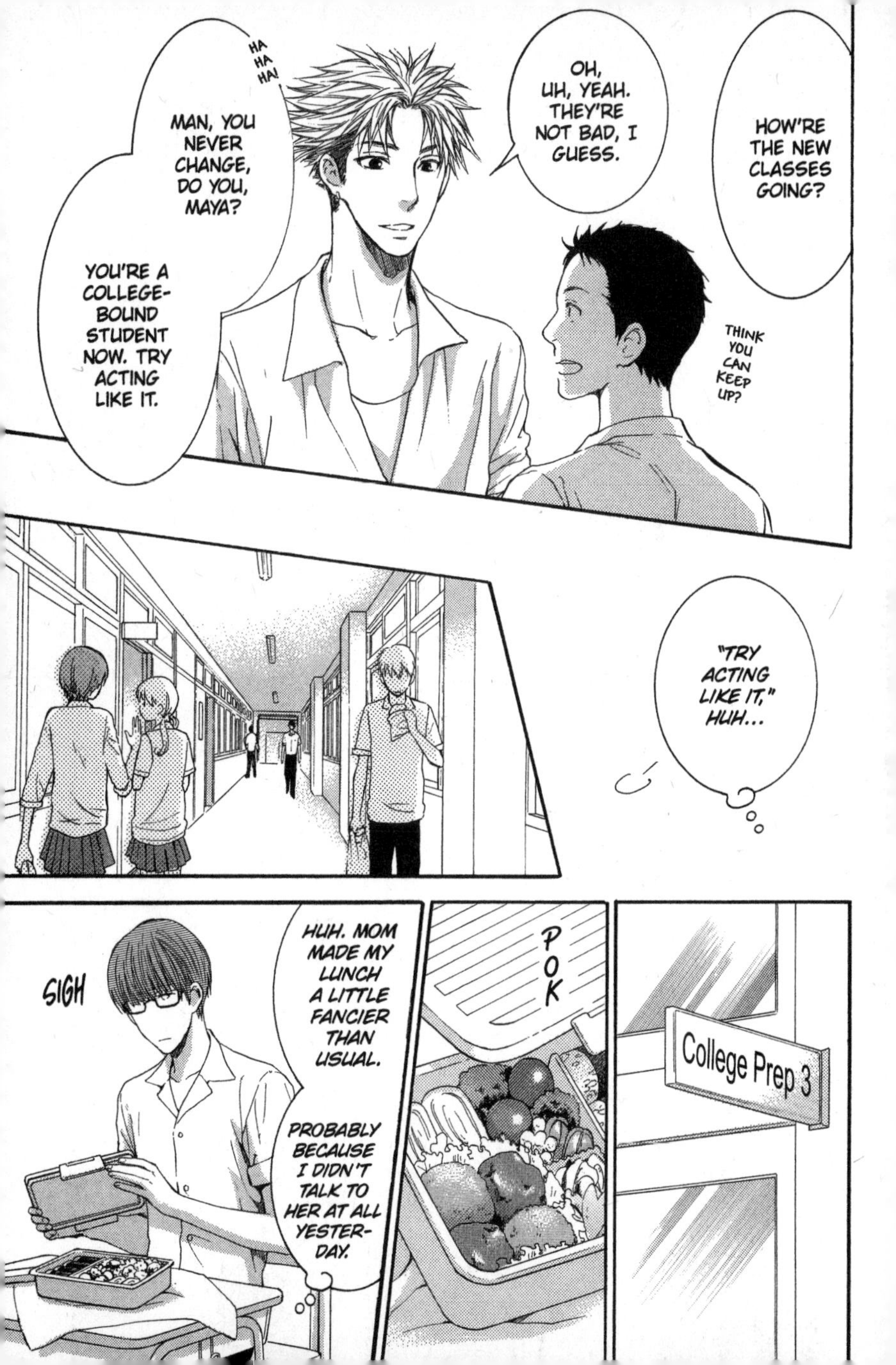
HOW'RE THE NEW CLASSES GOING?
THINK YOU CAN KEEP UP?
OH, UH, YEAH. THEY'RE NOT BAD, I GUESS.
HA HA HA!
MAN, YOU NEVER CHANGE, DO YOU, MAYA?
YOU'RE A COLLEGE-BOUND STUDENT NOW. TRY ACTING LIKE IT.
"TRY ACTING LIKE IT," HUH...
College Prep 3
POK
HUH. MOM MADE MY LUNCH A LITTLE FANCIER THAN USUAL.
PROBABLY BECAUSE I DIDN'T TALK TO HER AT ALL YESTER-DAY.
SIGH

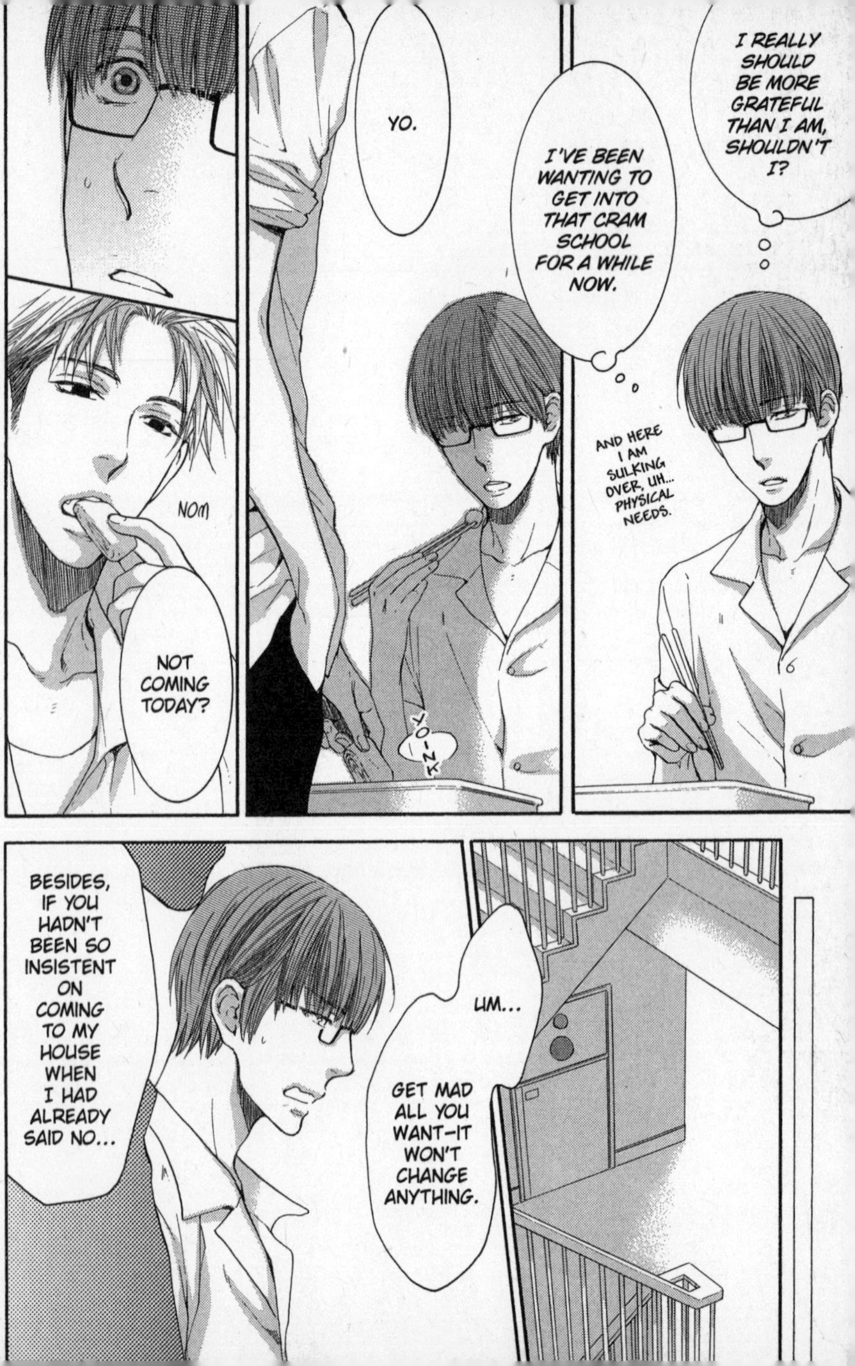
I REALLY SHOULD BE MORE GRATEFUL THAN I AM, SHOULDN'T I?
AND HERE I AM SULKING OVER, UH... PHYSICAL NEEDS.
I'VE BEEN WANTING TO GET INTO THAT CRAM SCHOOL FOR A WHILE NOW.
YO.
YO-NK
NOM
NOT COMING TODAY?
UM...
GET MAD ALL YOU WANT—IT WON'T CHANGE ANYTHING.
BESIDES, IF YOU HADN'T BEEN SO INSISTENT ON COMING TO MY HOUSE WHEN I HAD ALREADY SAID NO...

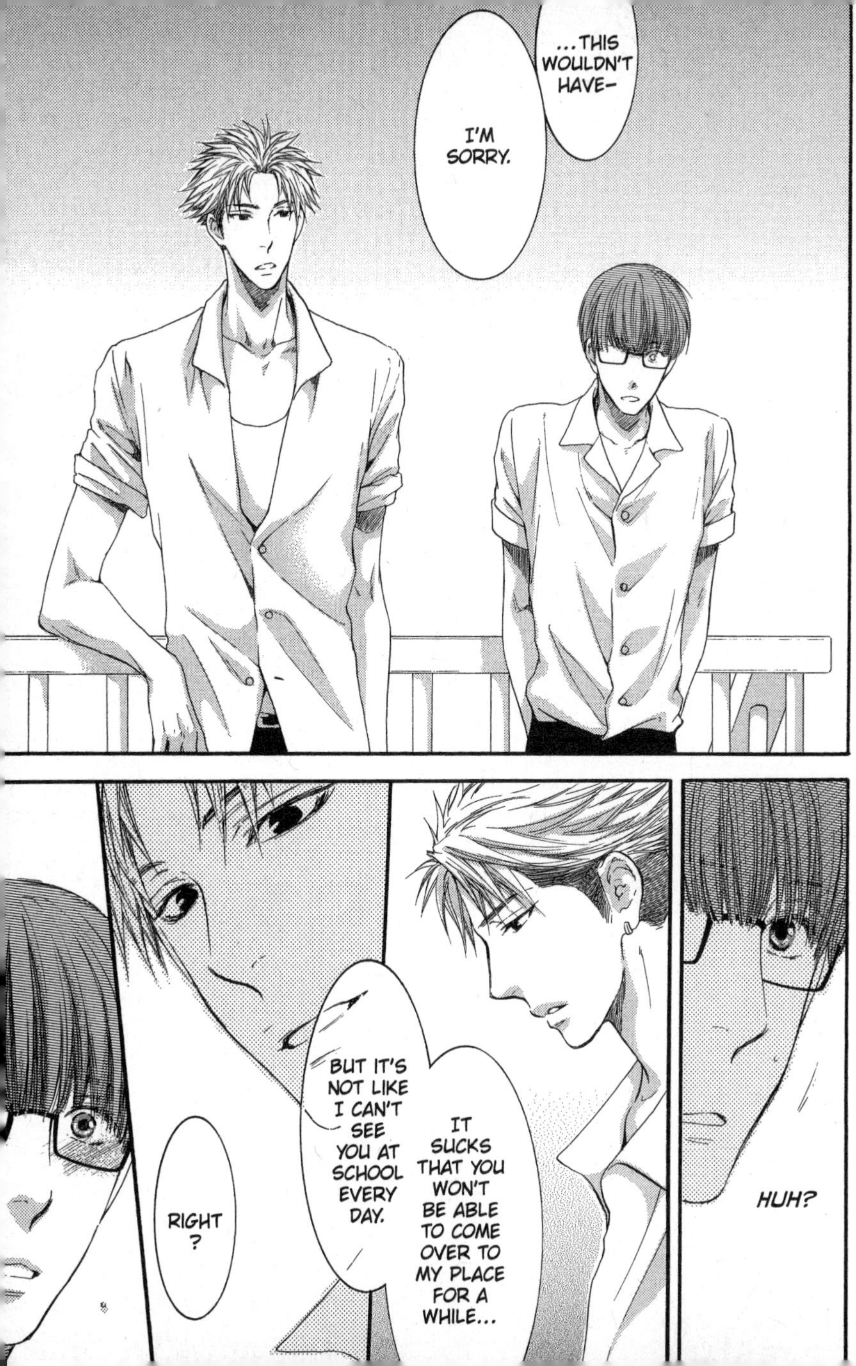
...THIS WOULDN'T HAVE—
I'M SORRY.
HUH?
IT SUCKS THAT YOU WON'T BE ABLE TO COME OVER TO MY PLACE FOR A WHILE...
BUT IT'S NOT LIKE I CAN'T SEE YOU AT SCHOOL EVERY DAY.
RIGHT?

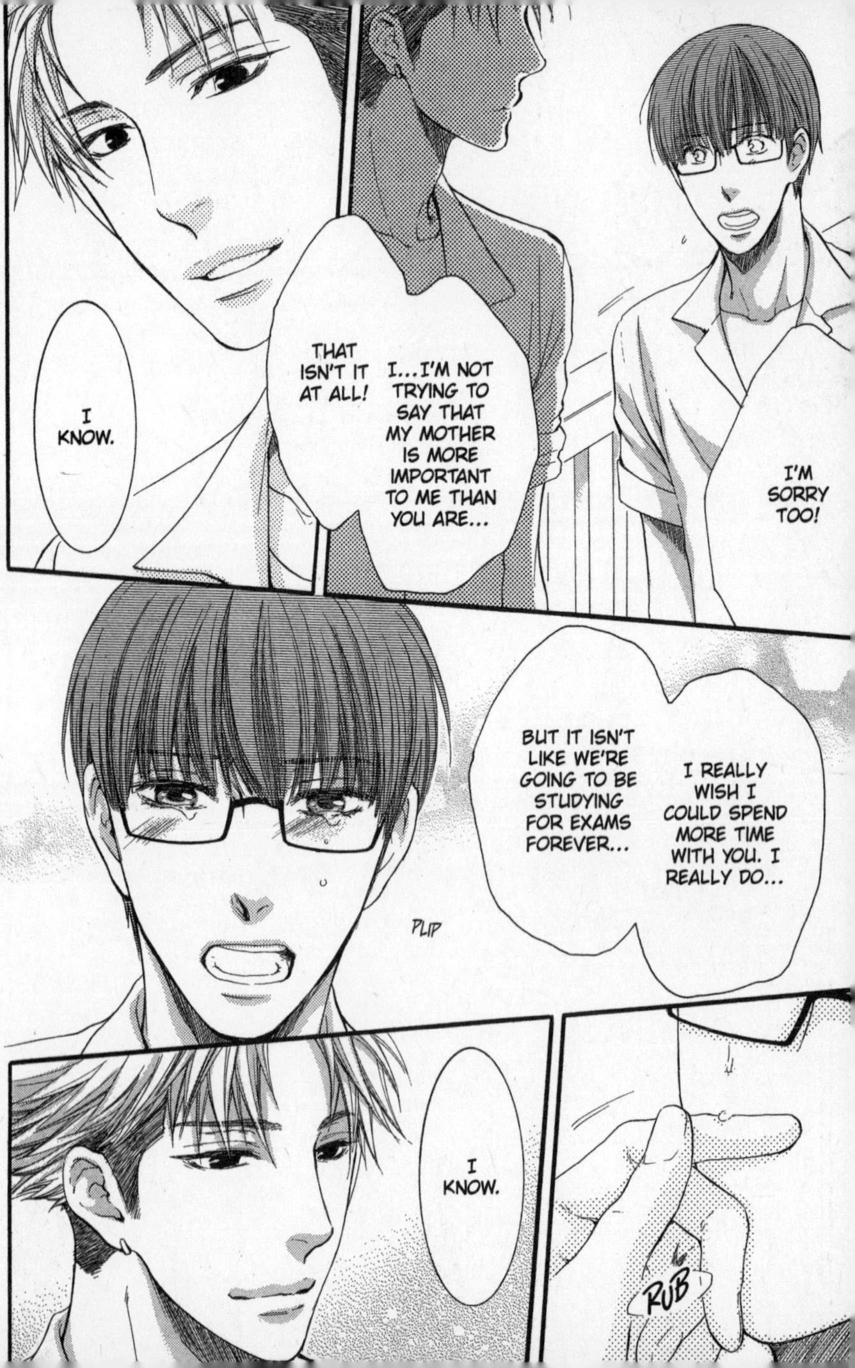
I'M SORRY TOO!
I...I'M NOT TRYING TO SAY THAT MY MOTHER IS MORE IMPORTANT TO ME THAN YOU ARE...
THAT ISN'T IT AT ALL!
I KNOW.
I REALLY WISH I COULD SPEND MORE TIME WITH YOU. I REALLY DO...
BUT IT ISN'T LIKE WE'RE GOING TO BE STUDYING FOR EXAMS FOREVER...
PLIP
RUB
I KNOW.

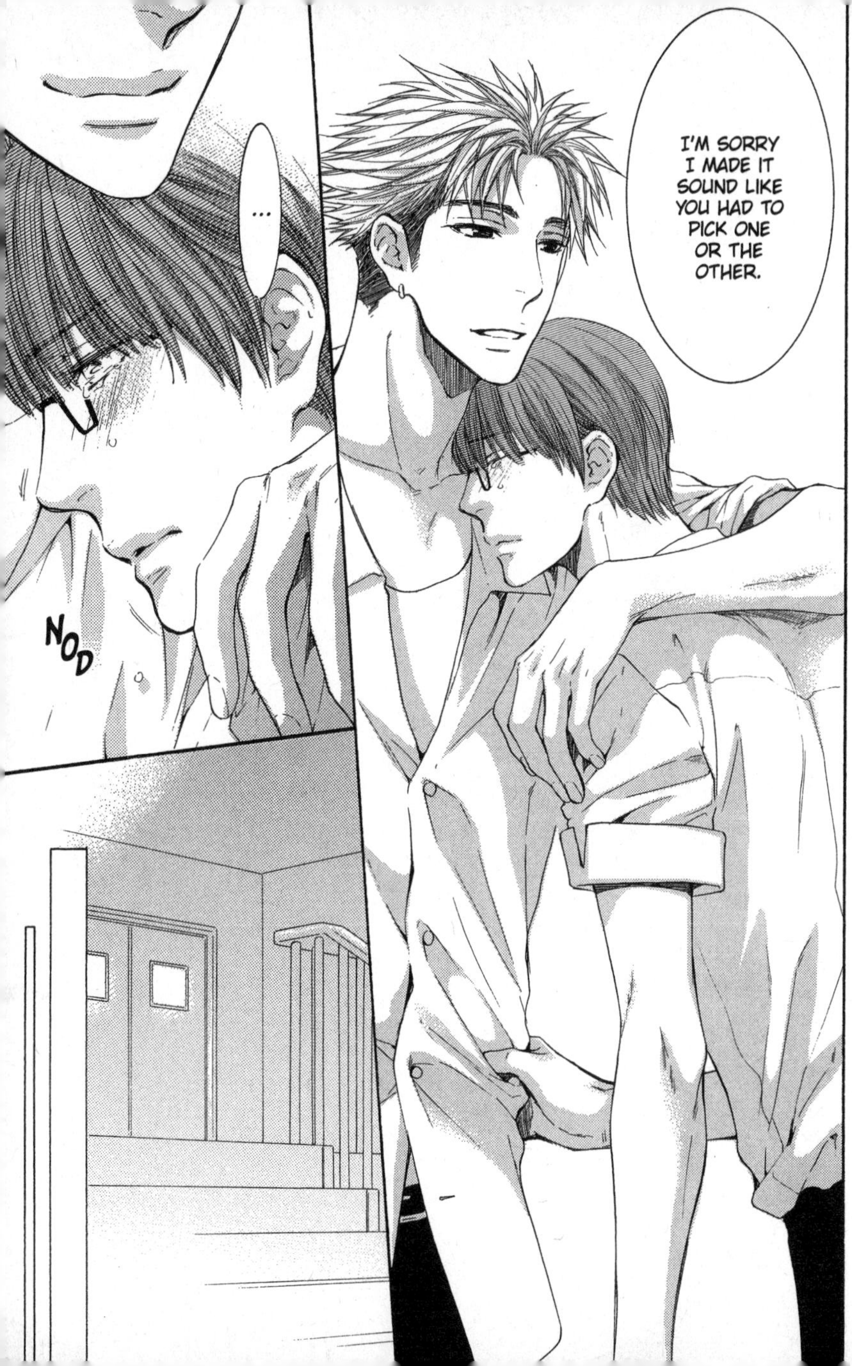
I'M SORRY I MADE IT SOUND LIKE YOU HAD TO PICK ONE OR THE OTHER.
...
NOD

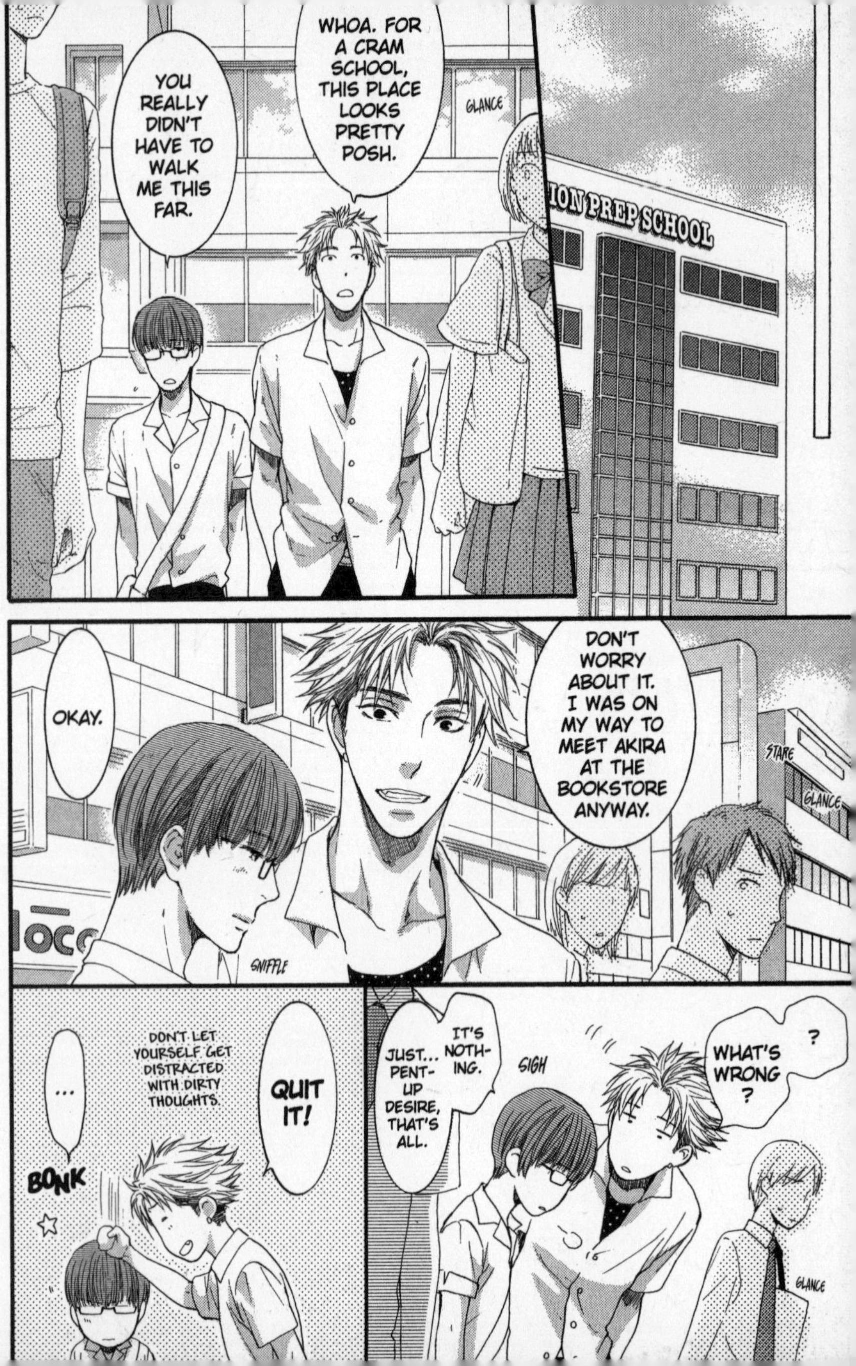
ION PREP SCHOOL
GLANCE
WHOA. FOR A CRAM SCHOOL, THIS PLACE LOOKS PRETTY POSH.
YOU REALLY DIDN'T HAVE TO WALK ME THIS FAR.
DON'T WORRY ABOUT IT. I WAS ON MY WAY TO MEET AKIRA AT THE BOOKSTORE ANYWAY.
STARE
GLANCE
OKAY.
SNIFFLE
?
WHAT'S WRONG?
SIGH
IT'S NOTHING.
JUST... PENT-UP DESIRE, THAT'S ALL.
GLANCE
QUIT IT!
DON'T LET YOURSELF GET DISTRACTED WITH DIRTY THOUGHTS.
...
BONK

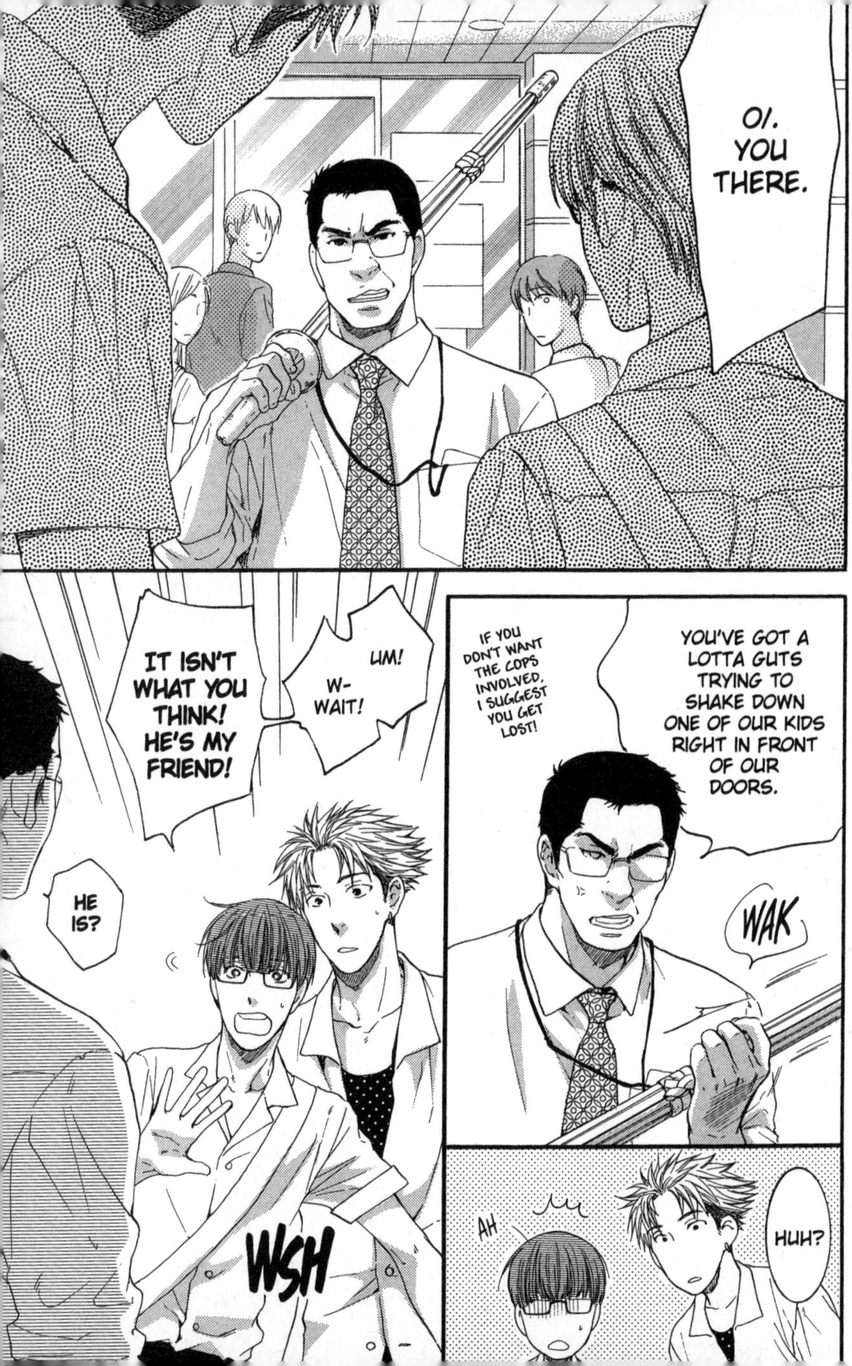
O/. YOU THERE.
YOU'VE GOT A LOTTA GUTS TRYING TO SHAKE DOWN ONE OF OUR KIDS RIGHT IN FRONT OF OUR DOORS.
IF YOU DON'T WANT THE COPS INVOLVED, I SUGGEST YOU GET LOST!
WAK
HUH?
AH
UM!
W-WAIT!
IT ISN'T WHAT YOU THINK! HE'S MY FRIEND!
HE IS?
WSH

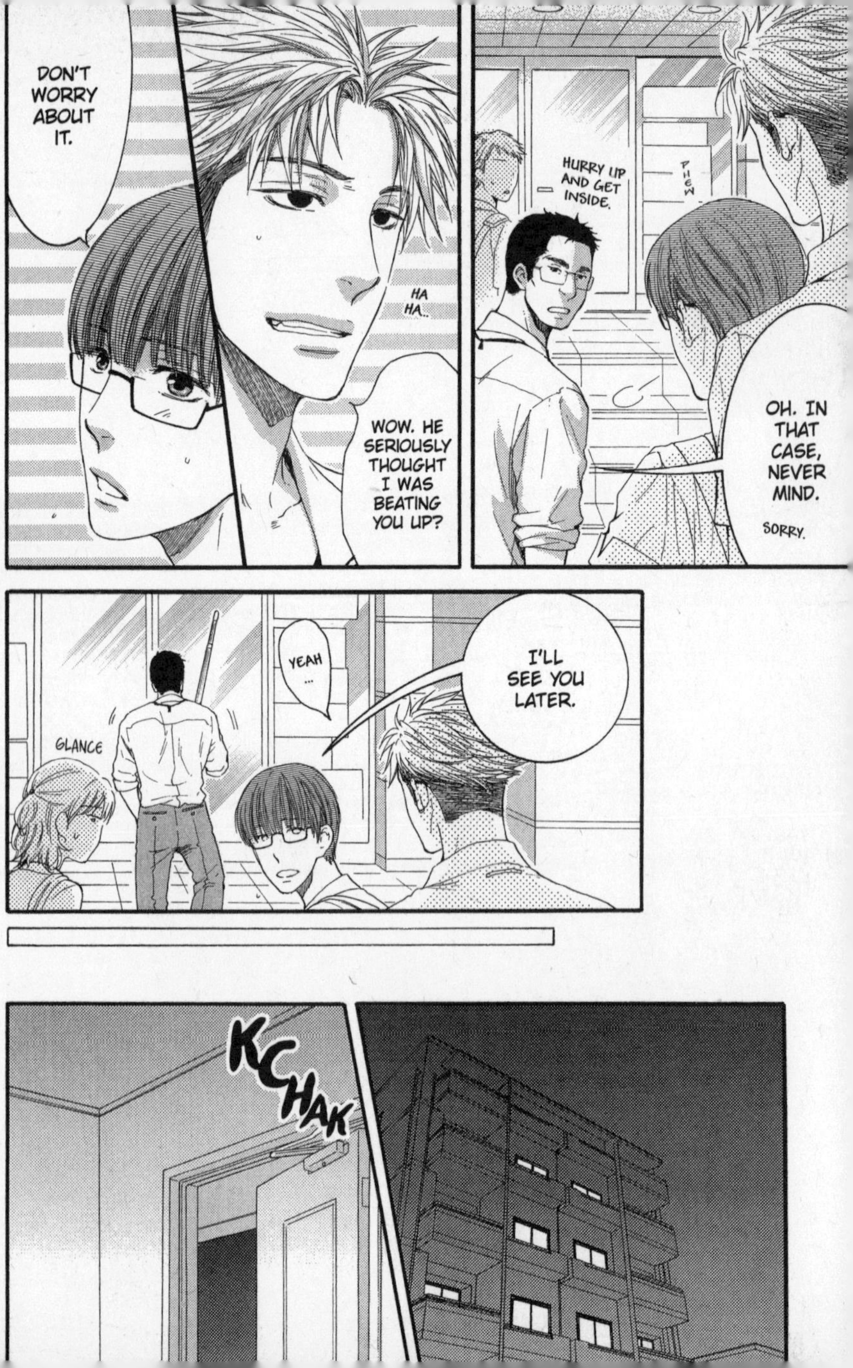
PHEW
HURRY UP AND GET INSIDE.
OH. IN THAT CASE, NEVER MIND.
SORRY.
DON'T WORRY ABOUT IT.
HA HA..
WOW. HE SERIOUSLY THOUGHT I WAS BEATING YOU UP?
I'LL SEE YOU LATER.
YEAH ...
GLANCE
KCHAK

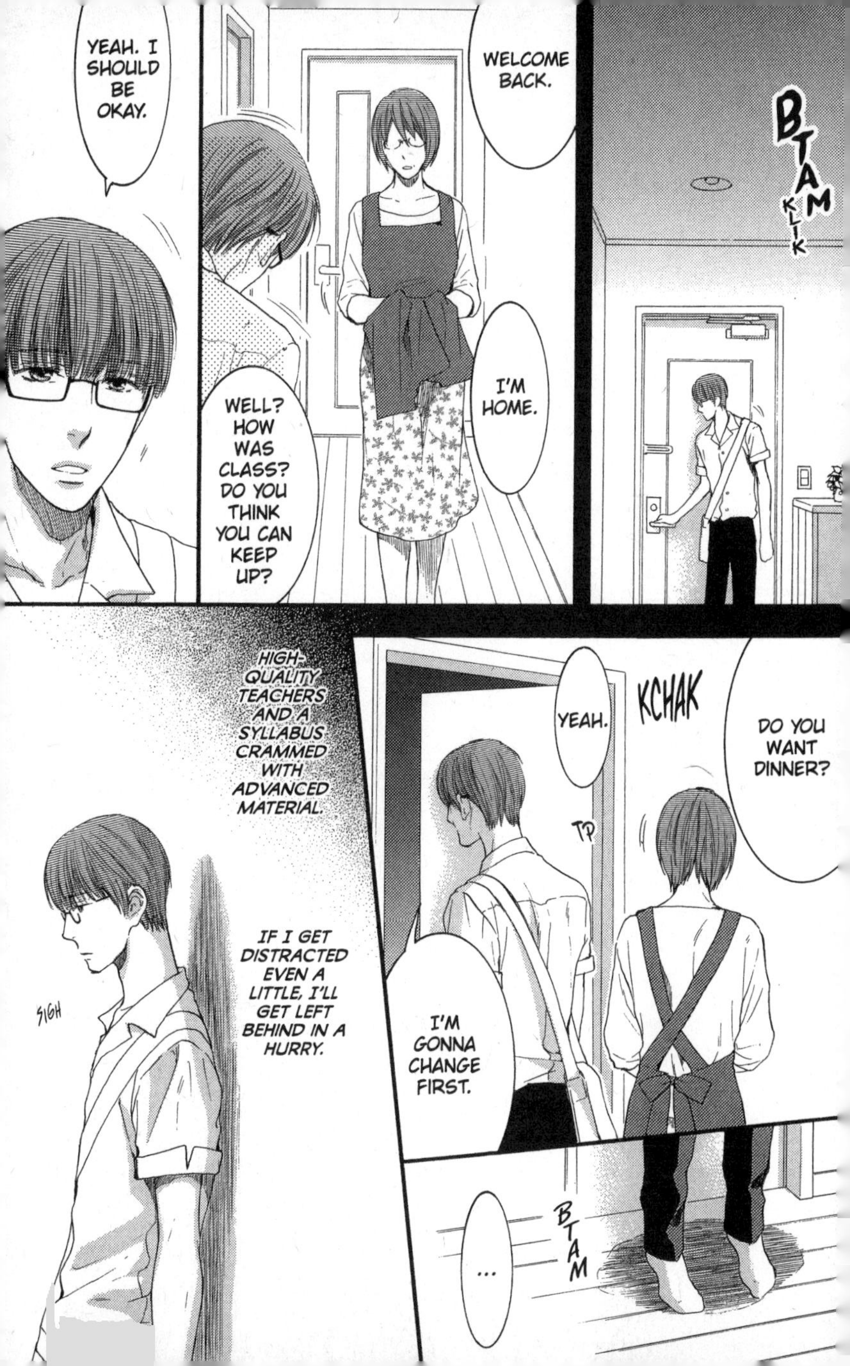

BTAM
KLIK
WELCOME BACK.
I'M HOME.
WELL? HOW WAS CLASS? DO YOU THINK YOU CAN KEEP UP?
YEAH. I SHOULD BE OKAY.
DO YOU WANT DINNER?
KCHAK
YEAH.
TP
I'M GONNA CHANGE FIRST.
BTAM
...
HIGH-QUALITY TEACHERS AND A SYLLABUS CRAMMED WITH ADVANCED MATERIAL.
IF I GET DISTRACTED EVEN A LITTLE, I'LL GET LEFT BEHIND IN A HURRY.
SIGH

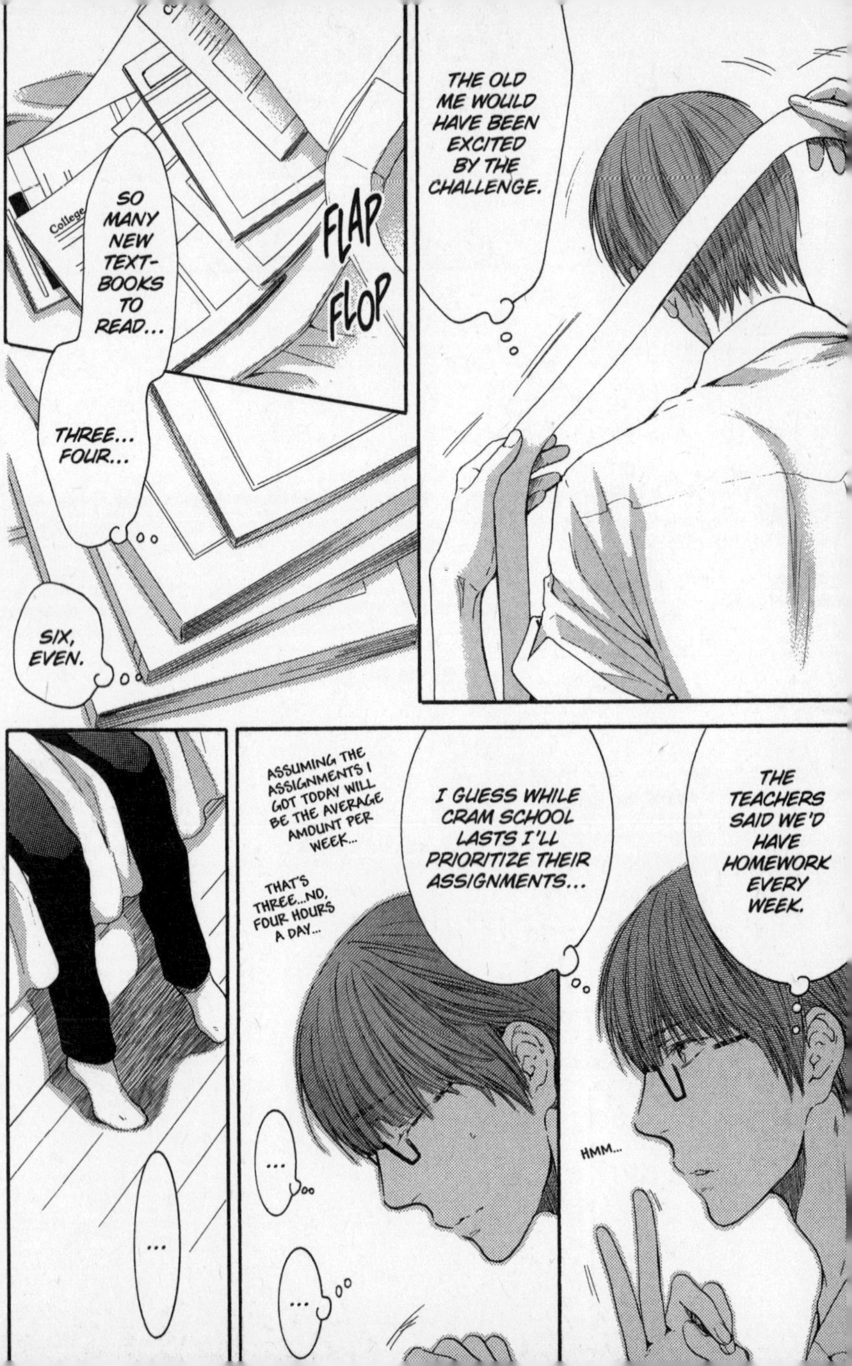
THE OLD ME WOULD HAVE BEEN EXCITED BY THE CHALLENGE.
SO MANY NEW TEXT-BOOKS TO READ...
FLAP
FLOP
THREE... FOUR...
SIX, EVEN.
THE TEACHERS SAID WE'D HAVE HOMEWORK EVERY WEEK.
HMM...
I GUESS WHILE CRAM SCHOOL LASTS I'LL PRIORITIZE THEIR ASSIGNMENTS...
ASSUMING THE ASSIGNMENTS I GOT TODAY WILL BE THE AVERAGE AMOUNT PER WEEK...
THAT'S THREE...NO, FOUR HOURS A DAY...
...
...
...

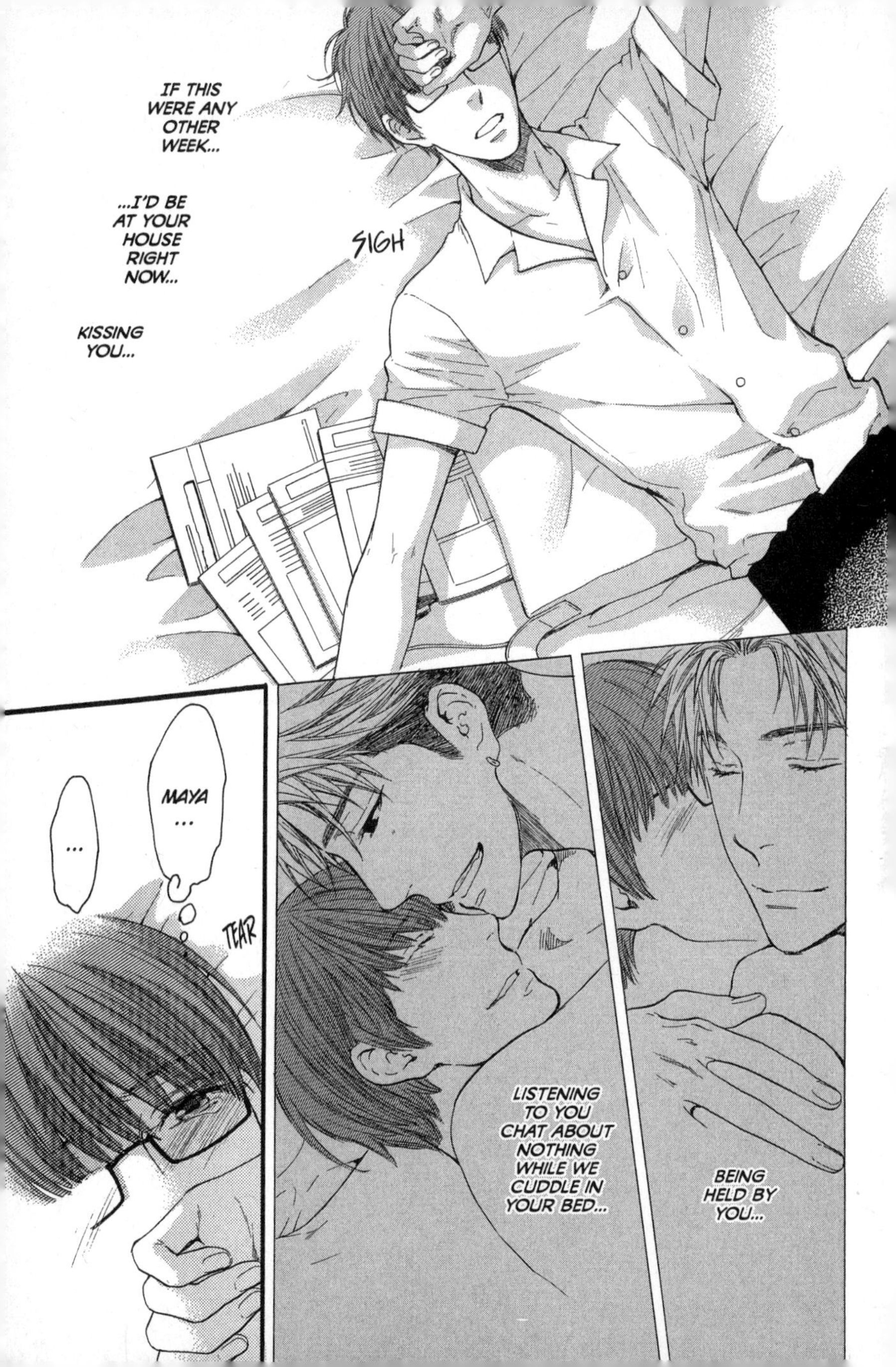
IF THIS WERE ANY OTHER WEEK...
...I'D BE AT YOUR HOUSE RIGHT NOW...
SIGH
KISSING YOU...
BEING HELD BY YOU...
LISTENING TO YOU CHAT ABOUT NOTHING WHILE WE CUDDLE IN YOUR BED...
MAYA ...
...
TEAR

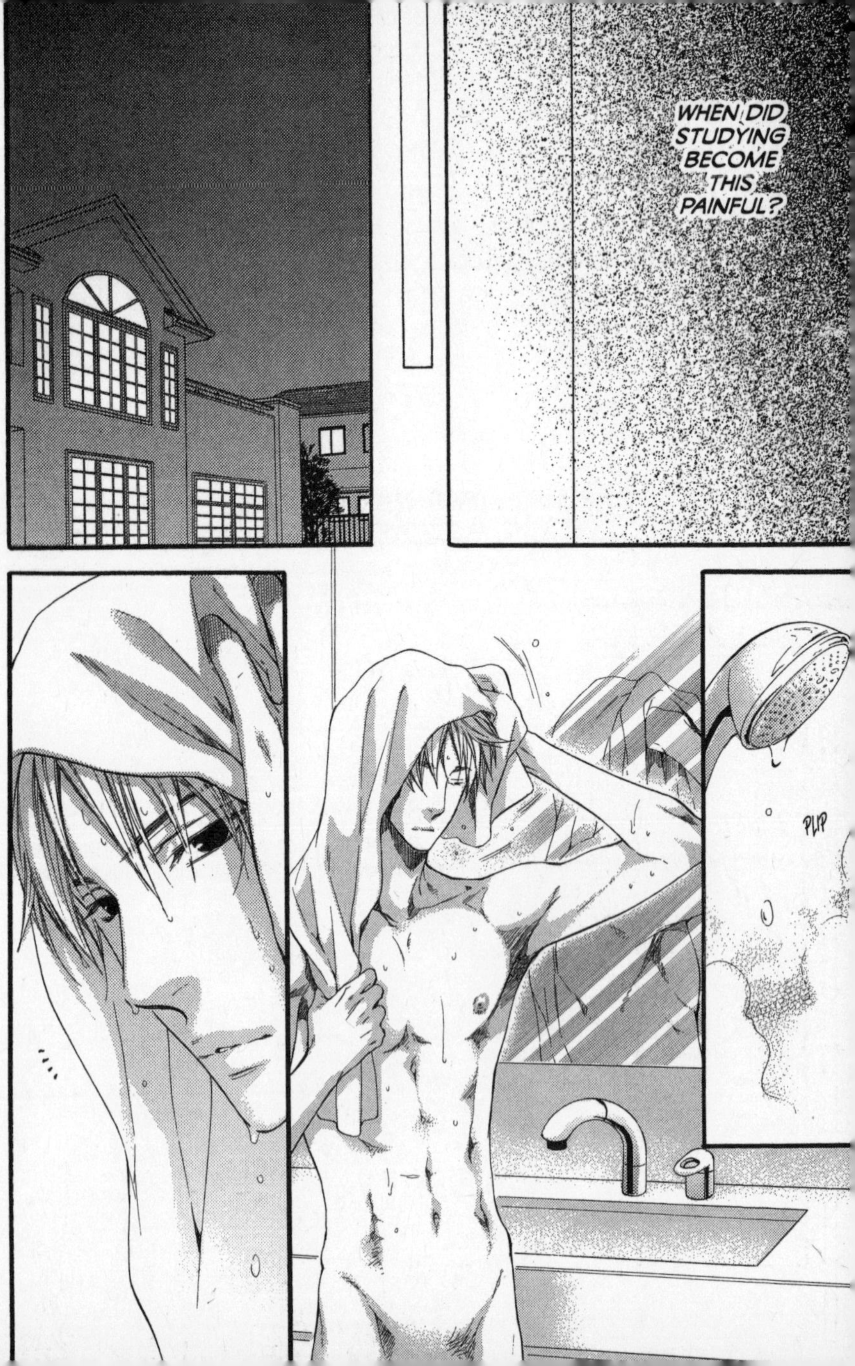
WHEN DID STUDYING BECOME THIS PAINFUL?
PLIP
...

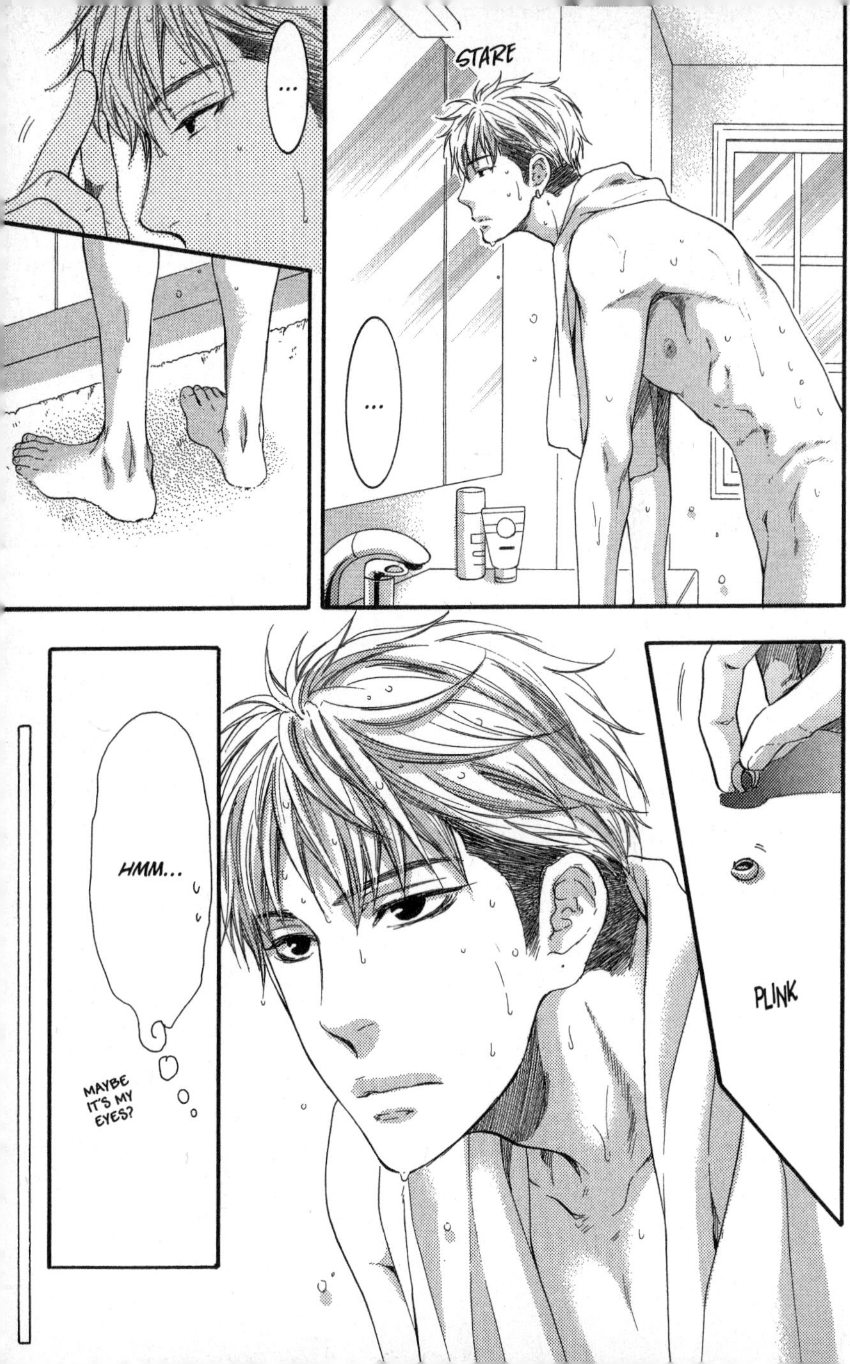
STARE
...
...
PLINK
HMM...
MAYBE IT'S MY EYES?

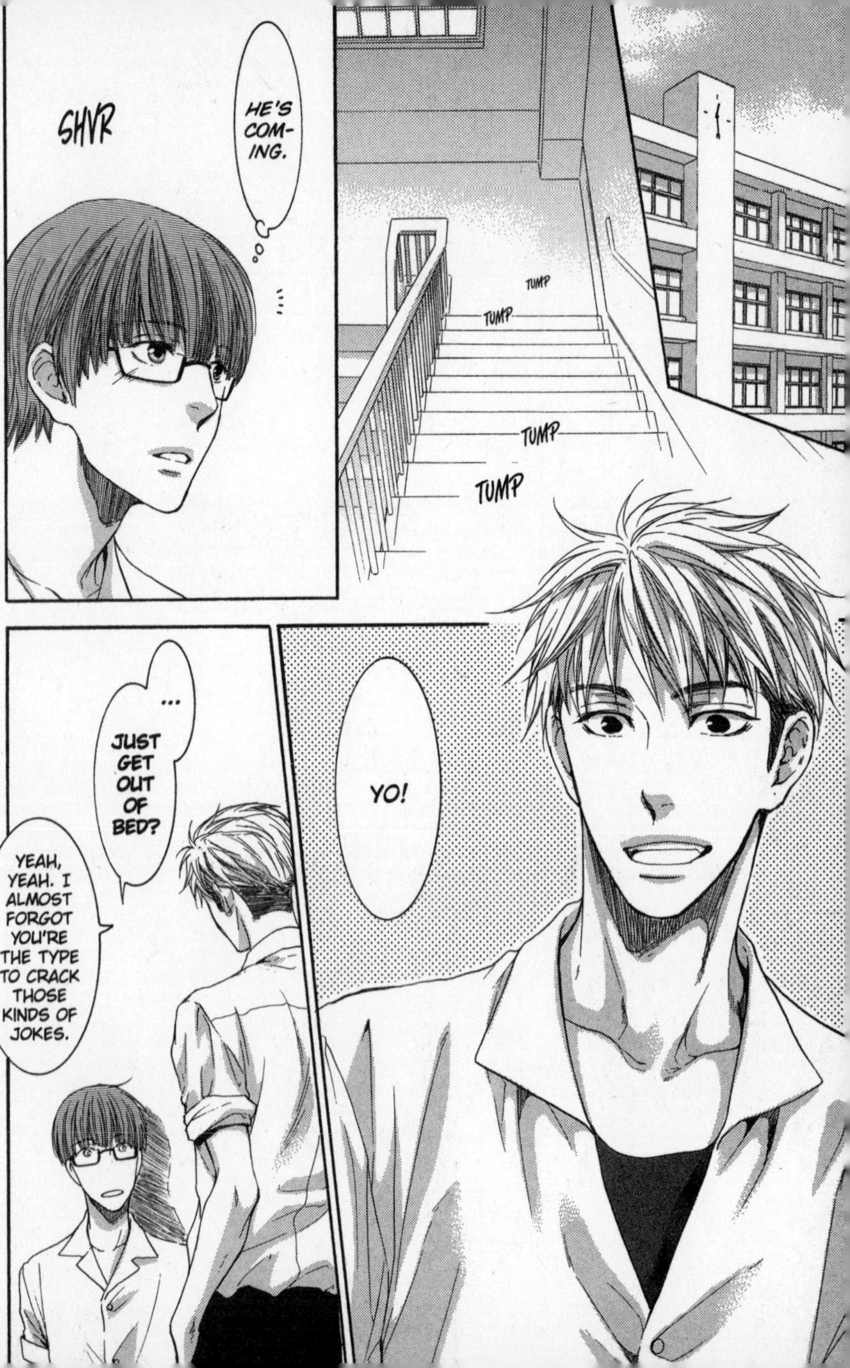
TUMP
TUMP
TUMP
TUMP
HE'S COM-ING.
SHVR
YO!
... JUST GET OUT OF BED?
YEAH, YEAH. I ALMOST FORGOT YOU'RE THE TYPE TO CRACK THOSE KINDS OF JOKES.

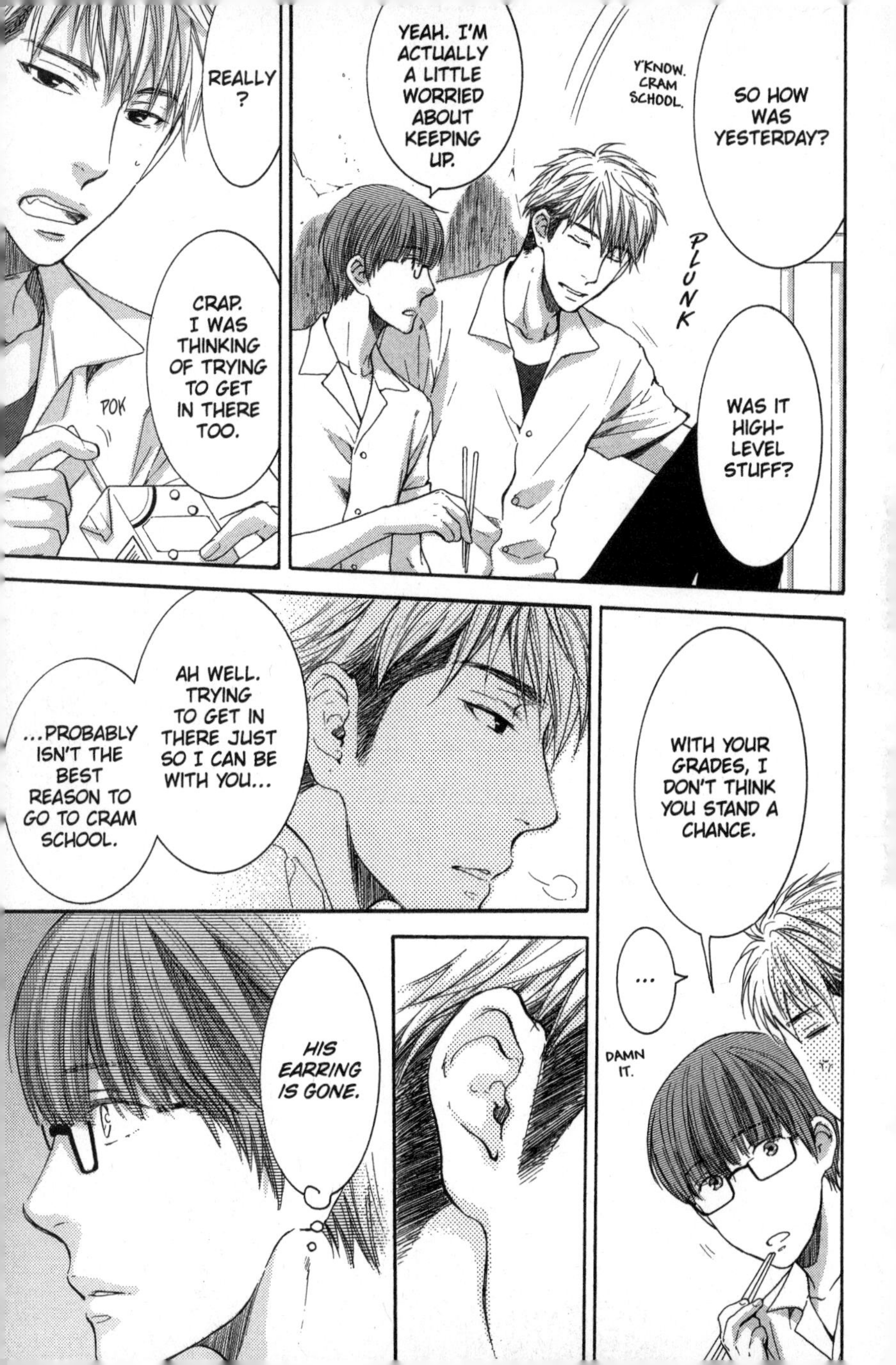
SO HOW WAS YESTERDAY?
Y'KNOW. CRAM SCHOOL.
PLUNK
WAS IT HIGH-LEVEL STUFF?
YEAH. I'M ACTUALLY A LITTLE WORRIED ABOUT KEEPING UP.
REALLY?
CRAP. I WAS THINKING OF TRYING TO GET IN THERE TOO.
POK
WITH YOUR GRADES, I DON'T THINK YOU STAND A CHANCE.
...
DAMN IT.
AH WELL. TRYING TO GET IN THERE JUST SO I CAN BE WITH YOU...
...PROBABLY ISN'T THE BEST REASON TO GO TO CRAM SCHOOL.
HIS EARRING IS GONE.

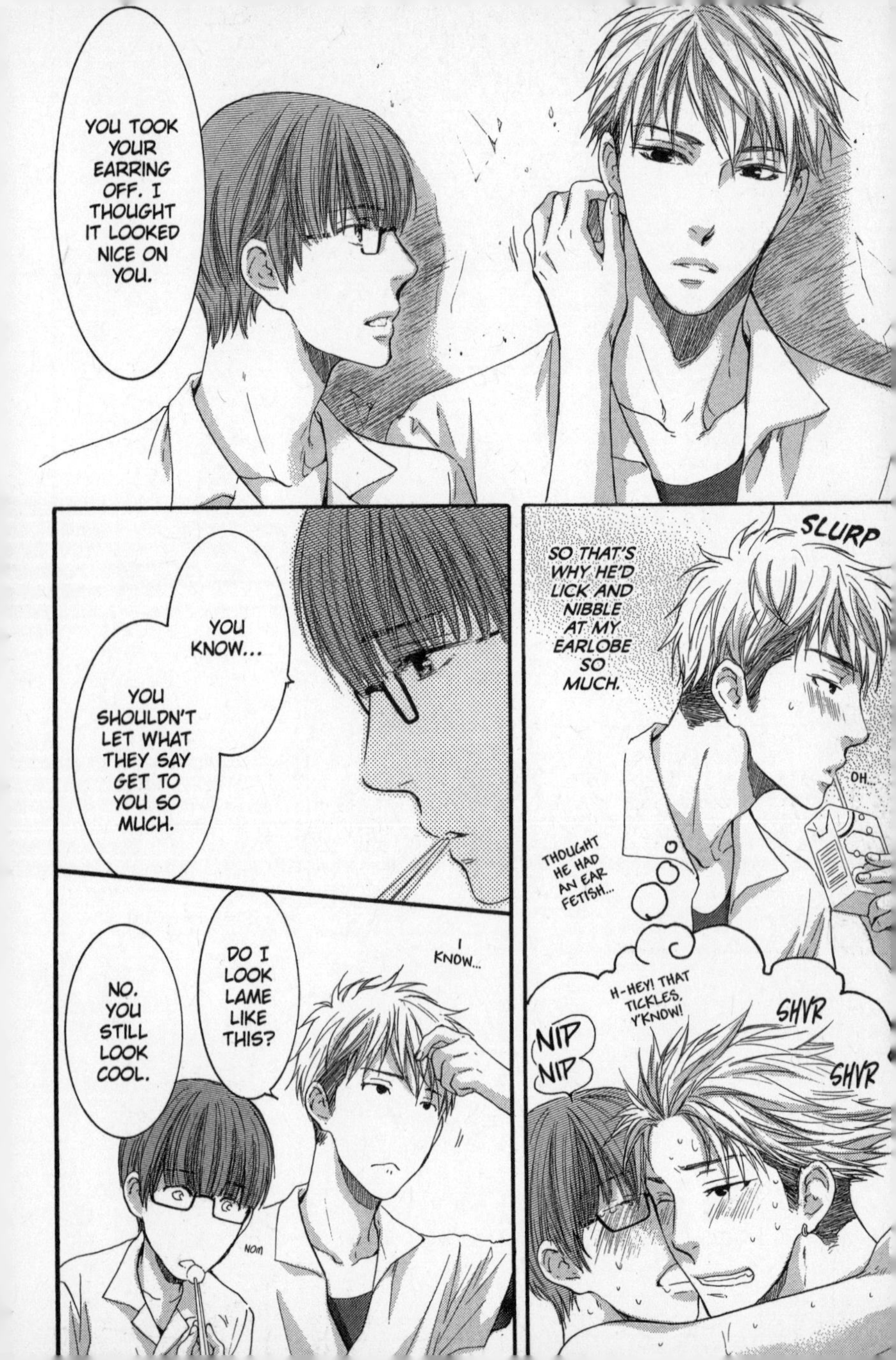
YOU TOOK YOUR EARRING OFF. I THOUGHT IT LOOKED NICE ON YOU.
SLURP
SO THAT'S WHY HE'D LICK AND NIBBLE AT MY EARLOBE SO MUCH.
OH...
THOUGHT HE HAD AN EAR FETISH...
H-HEY! THAT TICKLES, Y'KNOW!
SHVR
SHVR
NIP NIP
YOU KNOW...
YOU SHOULDN'T LET WHAT THEY SAY GET TO YOU SO MUCH.
I KNOW...
DO I LOOK LAME LIKE THIS?
NO. YOU STILL LOOK COOL.
NOM

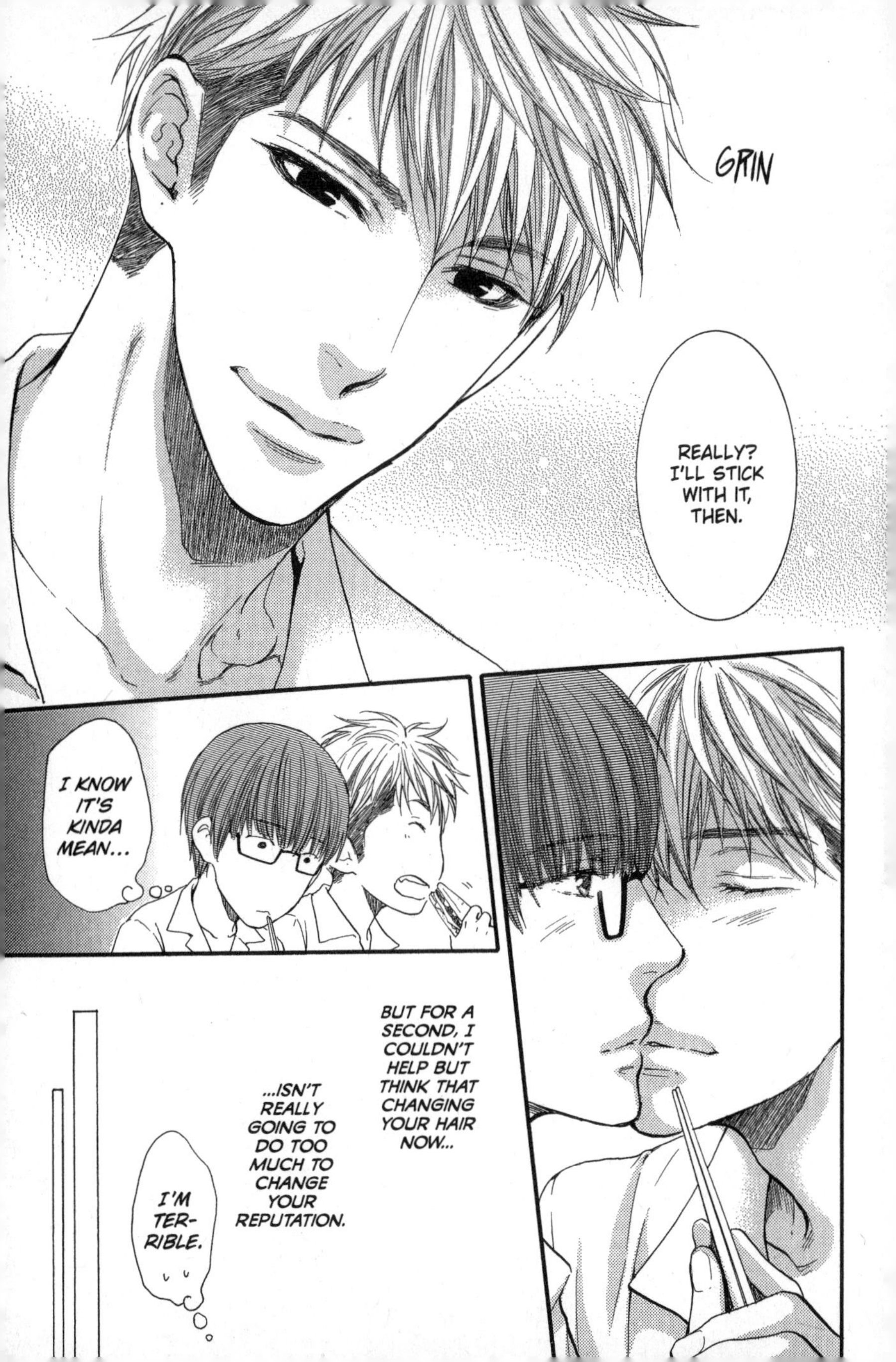
GRIN
REALLY? I'LL STICK WITH IT, THEN.
I KNOW IT'S KINDA MEAN...
BUT FOR A SECOND, I COULDN'T HELP BUT THINK THAT CHANGING YOUR HAIR NOW...
...ISN'T REALLY GOING TO DO TOO MUCH TO CHANGE YOUR REPUTATION.
I'M TER-RIBLE.

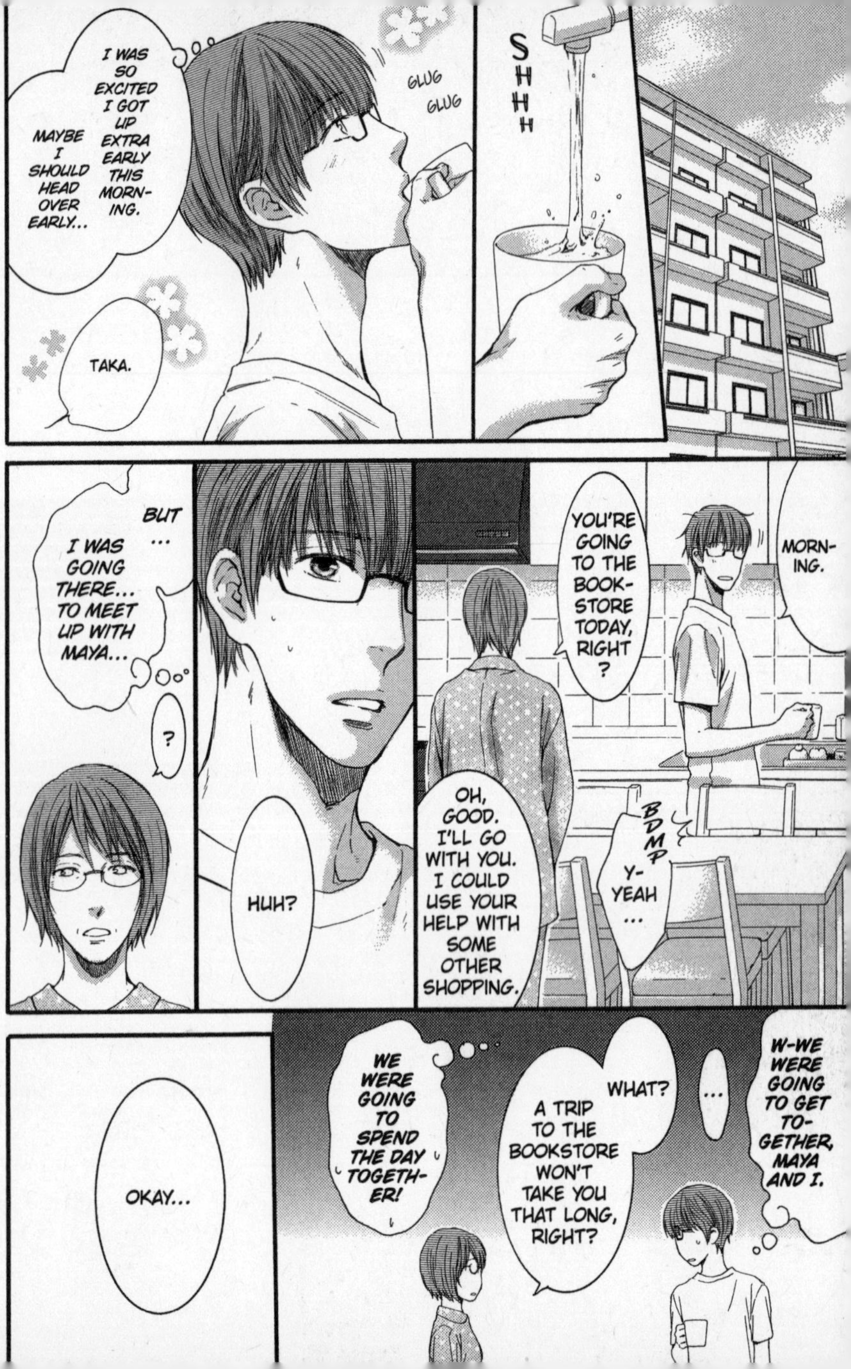
SHHHH
GLUG GLUG
I WAS SO EXCITED I GOT UP EXTRA EARLY THIS MORNING.
MAYBE I SHOULD HEAD OVER EARLY...
TAKA.
MORNING.
YOU'RE GOING TO THE BOOKSTORE TODAY, RIGHT?
BDMP
Y-YEAH...
OH, GOOD. I'LL GO WITH YOU. I COULD USE YOUR HELP WITH SOME OTHER SHOPPING.
HUH?
BUT... I WAS GOING THERE... TO MEET UP WITH MAYA...
?
W-WE WERE GOING TO GET TOGETHER, MAYA AND I.
...
WHAT? A TRIP TO THE BOOKSTORE WON'T TAKE YOU THAT LONG, RIGHT?
WE WERE GOING TO SPEND THE DAY TOGETHER!
OKAY...

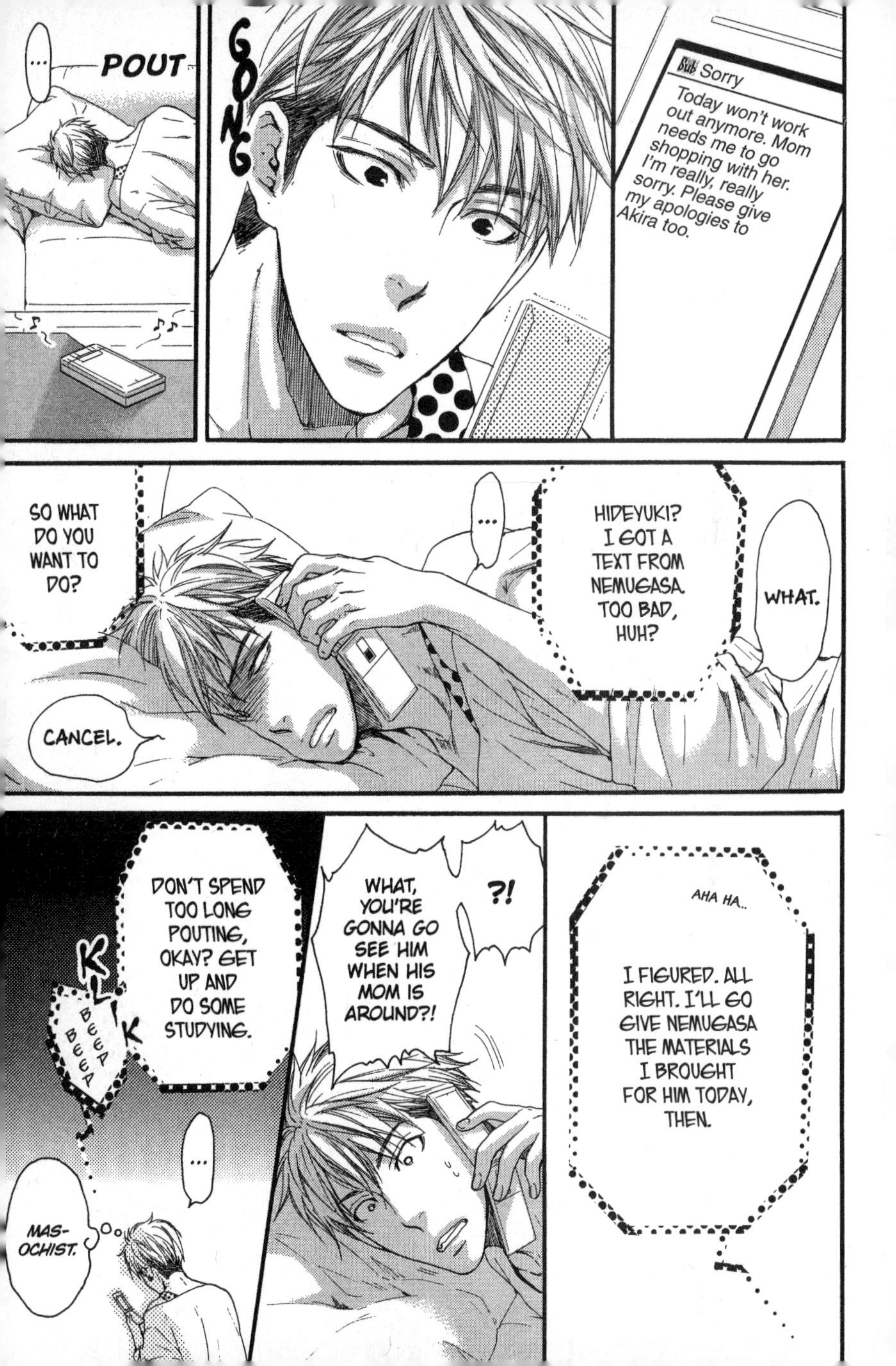
Sub Sorry
Today won't work out anymore. Mom needs me to go shopping with her. I'm really, really sorry. Please give my apologies to Akira too.
GONG
...
POUT
WHAT.
HIDEYUKI? I GOT A TEXT FROM NEMUGASA. TOO BAD, HUH?
...
SO WHAT DO YOU WANT TO DO?
CANCEL.
AHA HA..
I FIGURED. ALL RIGHT. I'LL GO GIVE NEMUGASA THE MATERIALS I BROUGHT FOR HIM TODAY, THEN.
?!
WHAT, YOU'RE GONNA GO SEE HIM WHEN HIS MOM IS AROUND?!
DON'T SPEND TOO LONG POUTING, OKAY? GET UP AND DO SOME STUDYING.
KLIK
BEEP BEEP
...
MAS-OCHIST.

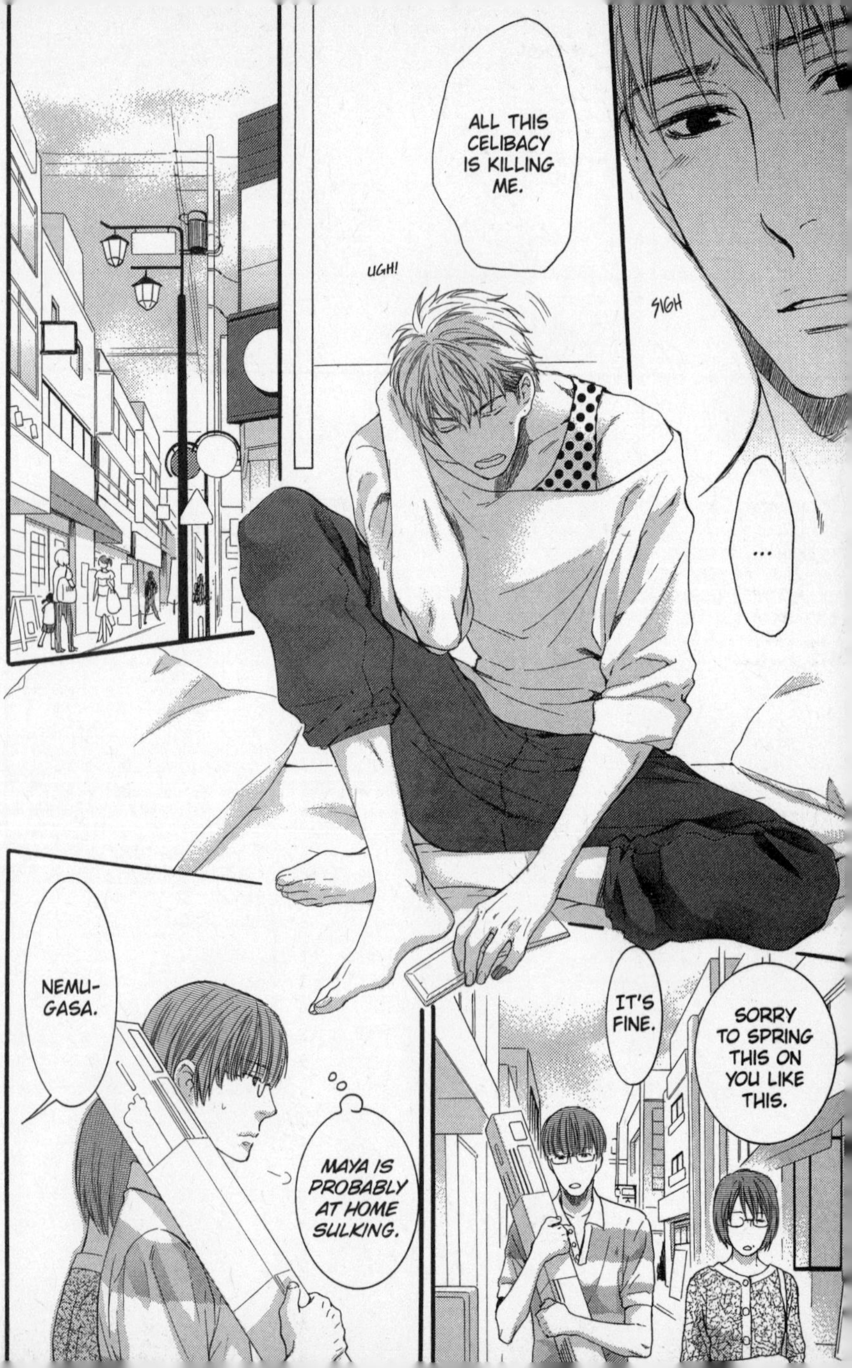
SIGH
...
ALL THIS CELIBACY IS KILLING ME.
UGH!
SORRY TO SPRING THIS ON YOU LIKE THIS.
IT'S FINE.
NEMU-GASA.
MAYA IS PROBABLY AT HOME SULKING.

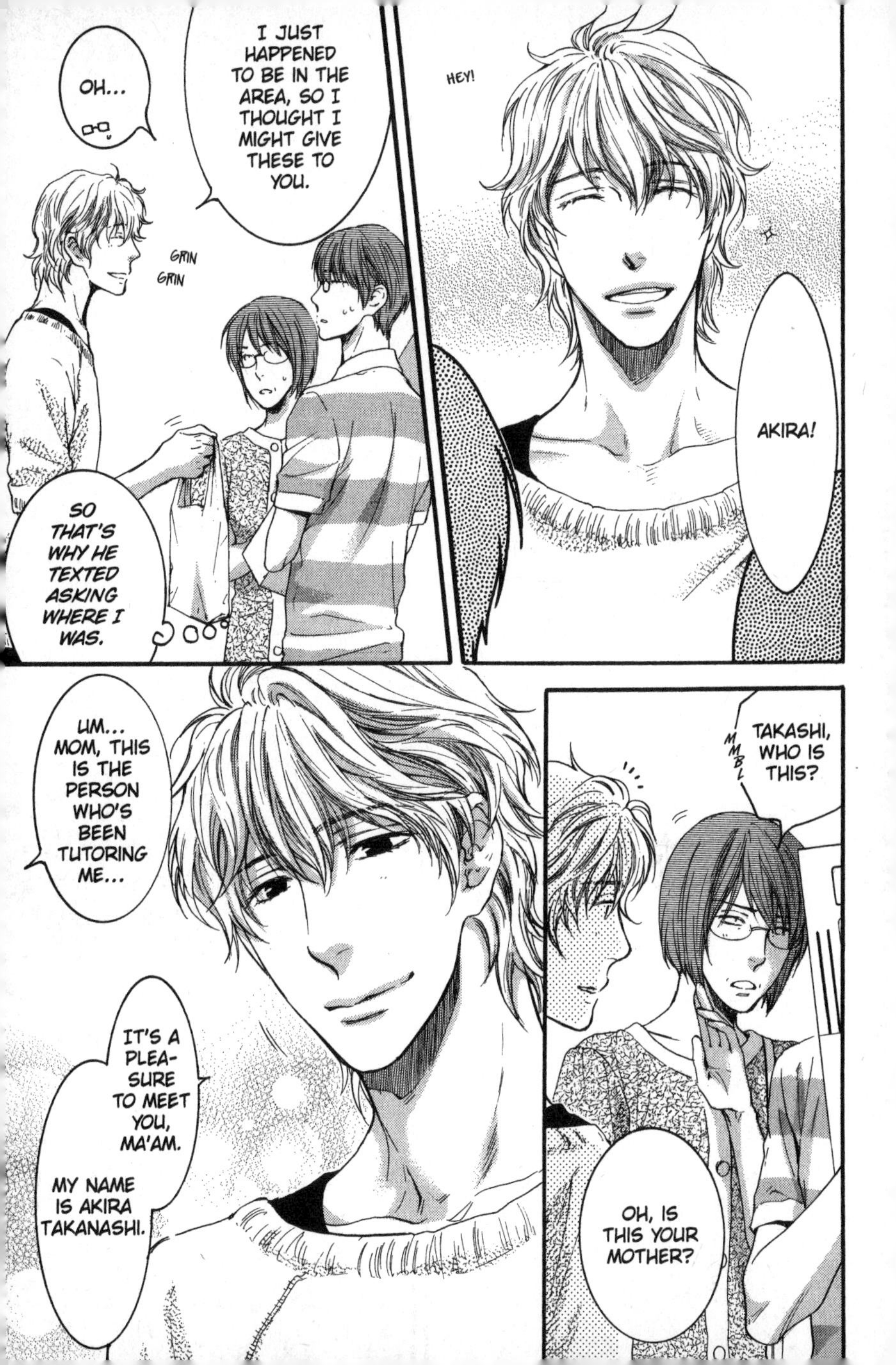
AKIRA!
HEY!
I JUST HAPPENED TO BE IN THE AREA, SO I THOUGHT I MIGHT GIVE THESE TO YOU.
OH...
GRIN
GRIN
SO THAT'S WHY HE TEXTED ASKING WHERE I WAS.
TAKASHI, WHO IS THIS?
MMBL
OH, IS THIS YOUR MOTHER?
UM... MOM, THIS IS THE PERSON WHO'S BEEN TUTORING ME...
IT'S A PLEASURE TO MEET YOU, MA'AM.
MY NAME IS AKIRA TAKANASHI.

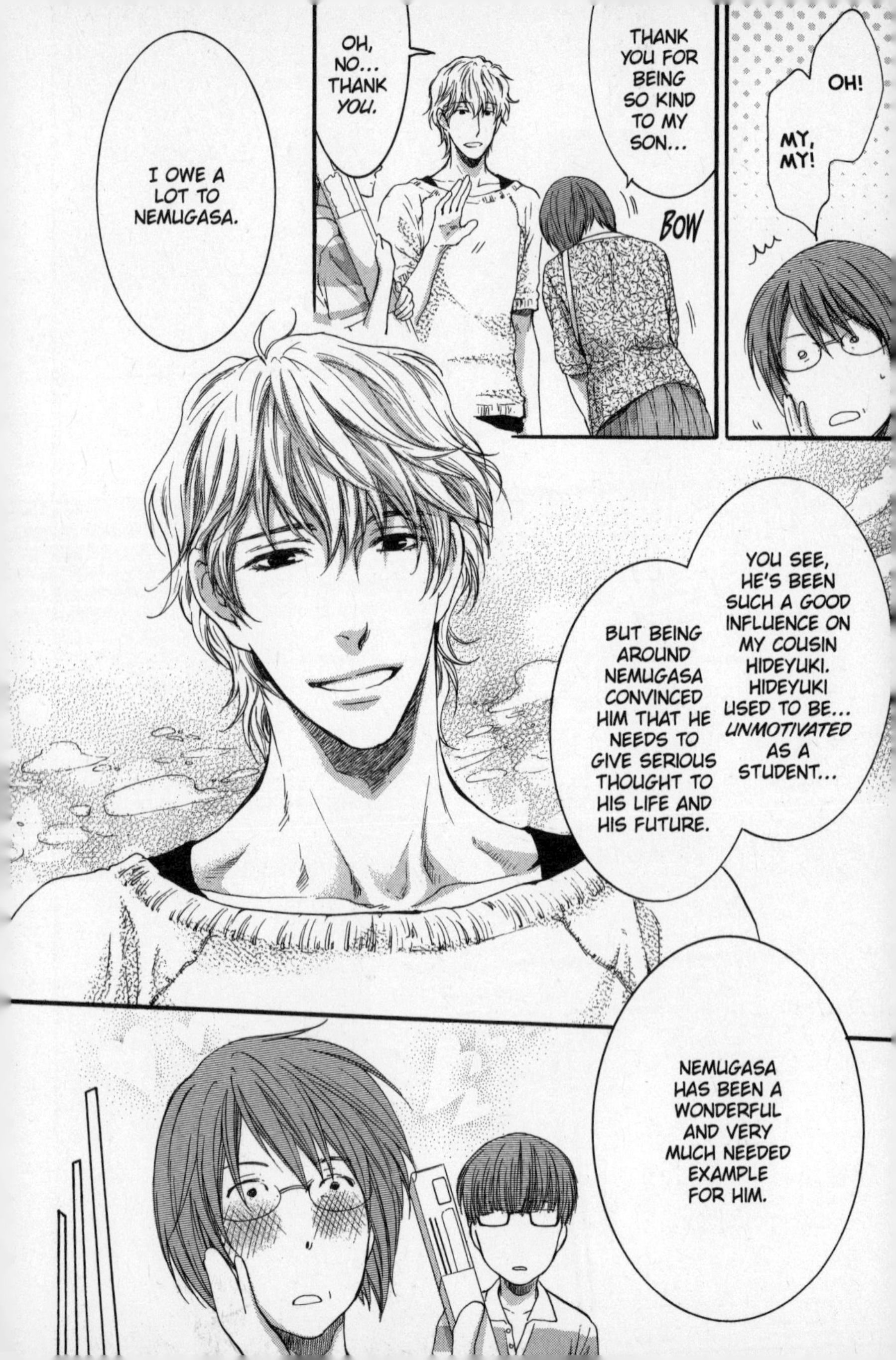
OH!
MY, MY!
THANK YOU FOR BEING SO KIND TO MY SON...
BOW
OH, NO... THANK *YOU.*
I OWE A LOT TO NEMUGASA.
YOU SEE, HE'S BEEN SUCH A GOOD INFLUENCE ON MY COUSIN HIDEYUKI. HIDEYUKI USED TO BE... *UNMOTIVATED* AS A STUDENT...
BUT BEING AROUND NEMUGASA CONVINCED HIM THAT HE NEEDS TO GIVE SERIOUS THOUGHT TO HIS LIFE AND HIS FUTURE.
NEMUGASA HAS BEEN A WONDERFUL AND VERY MUCH NEEDED EXAMPLE FOR HIM.

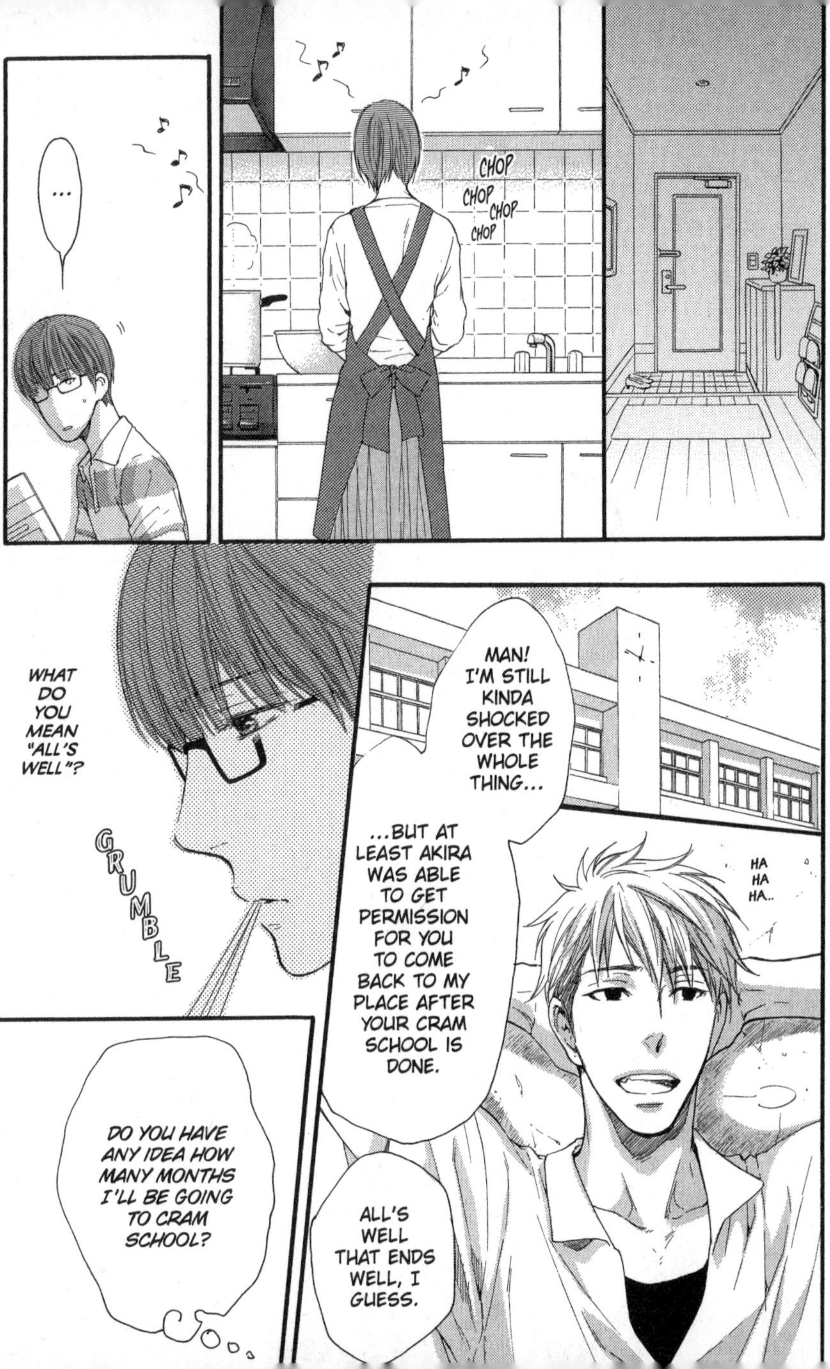
CHOP
CHOP
CHOP
CHOP
...
MAN! I'M STILL KINDA SHOCKED OVER THE WHOLE THING...
...BUT AT LEAST AKIRA WAS ABLE TO GET PERMISSION FOR YOU TO COME BACK TO MY PLACE AFTER YOUR CRAM SCHOOL IS DONE.
HA HA HA..
ALL'S WELL THAT ENDS WELL, I GUESS.
WHAT DO YOU MEAN "ALL'S WELL"?
GRUMBLE
DO YOU HAVE ANY IDEA HOW MANY MONTHS I'LL BE GOING TO CRAM SCHOOL?

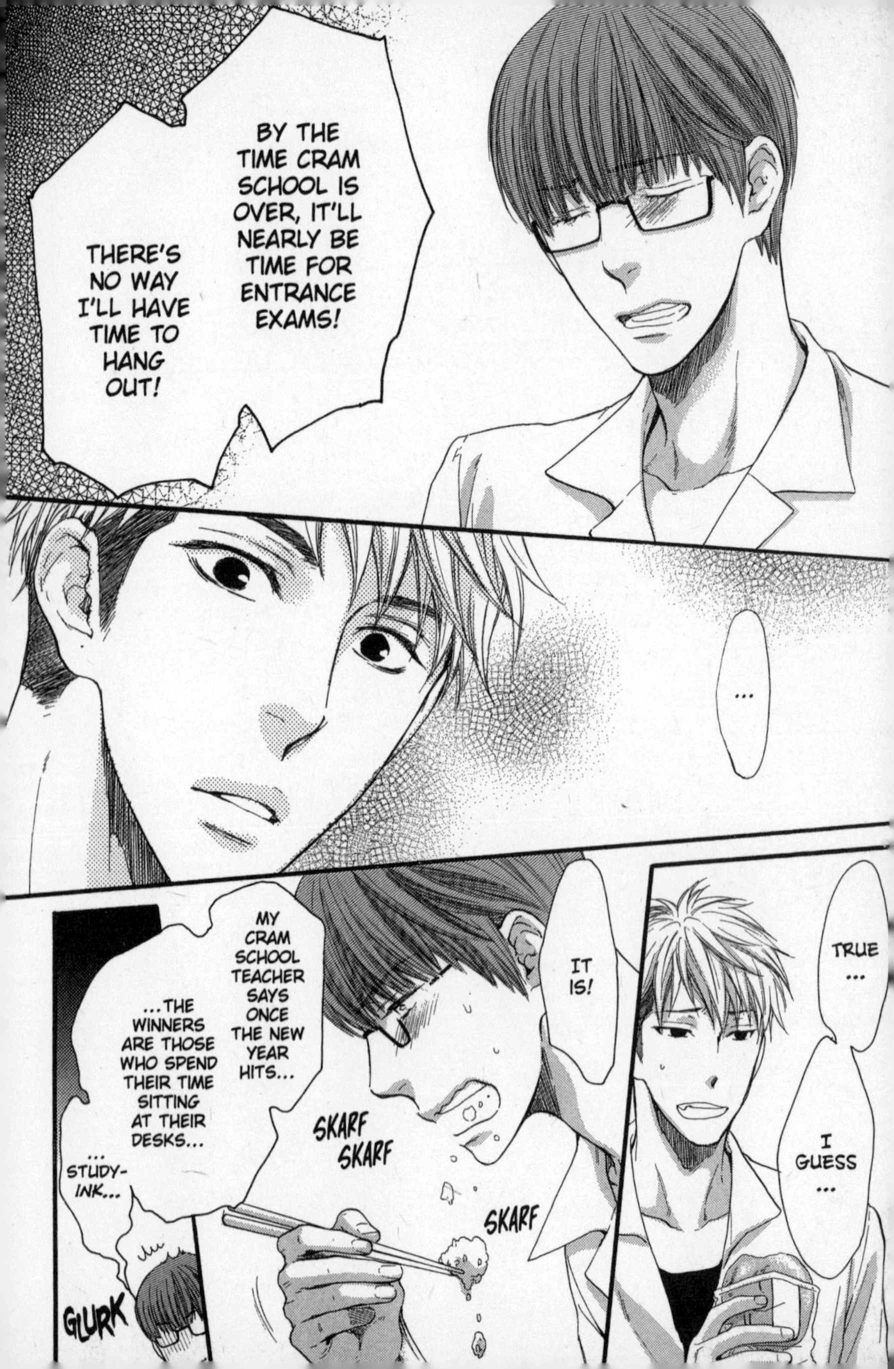
BY THE TIME CRAM SCHOOL IS OVER, IT'LL NEARLY BE TIME FOR ENTRANCE EXAMS!
THERE'S NO WAY I'LL HAVE TIME TO HANG OUT!
...
TRUE ...
I GUESS ...
IT IS!
MY CRAM SCHOOL TEACHER SAYS ONCE THE NEW YEAR HITS...
...THE WINNERS ARE THOSE WHO SPEND THEIR TIME SITTING AT THEIR DESKS...
SKARF SKARF
SKARF
... STUDY-INK...
GLURK

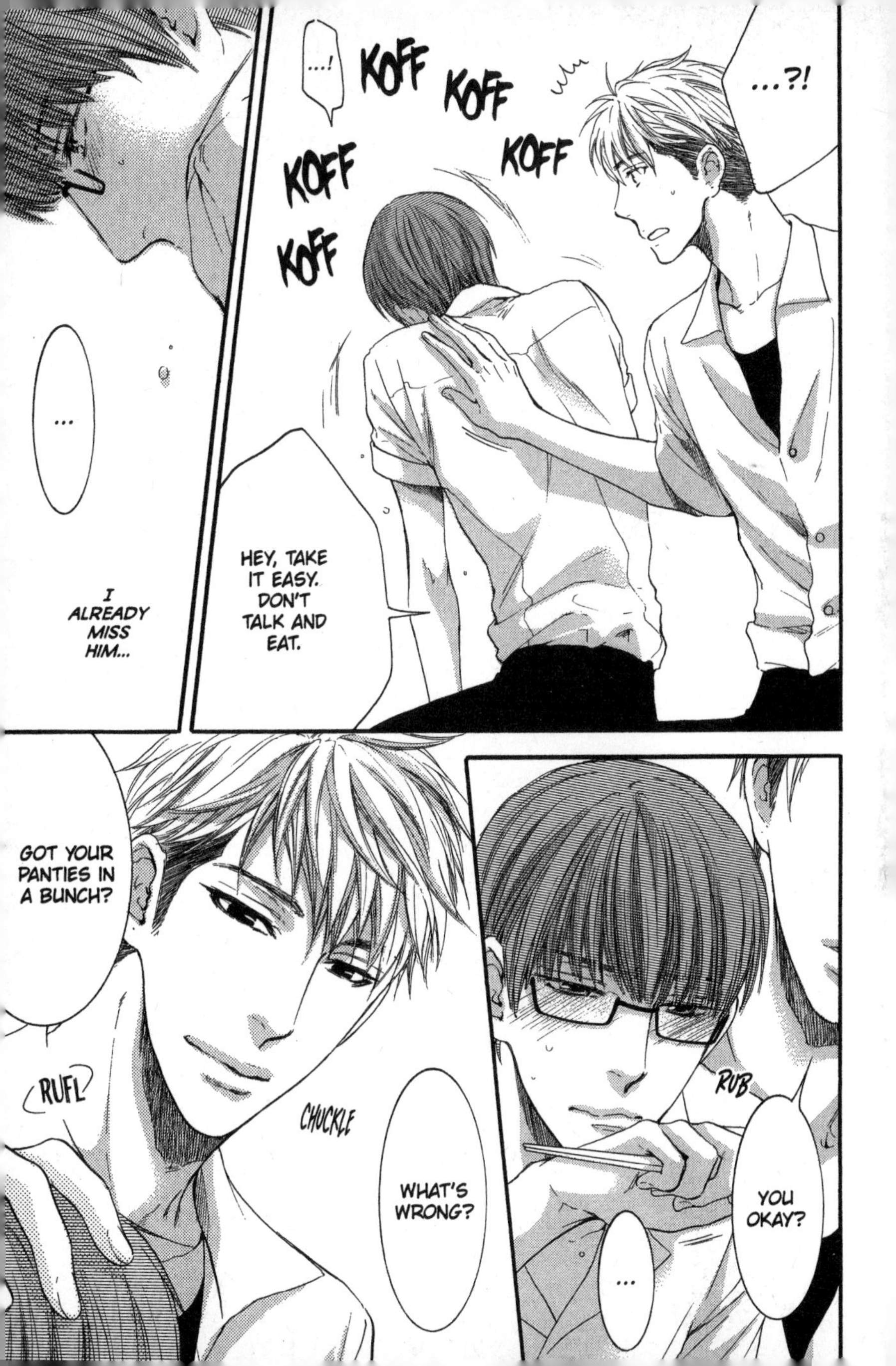
...?!
...!
KOFF
KOFF
KOFF
KOFF
KOFF
HEY, TAKE IT EASY. DON'T TALK AND EAT.
...
I ALREADY MISS HIM...
RUB
YOU OKAY?
...
WHAT'S WRONG?
CHUCKLE
GOT YOUR PANTIES IN A BUNCH?
RUFL

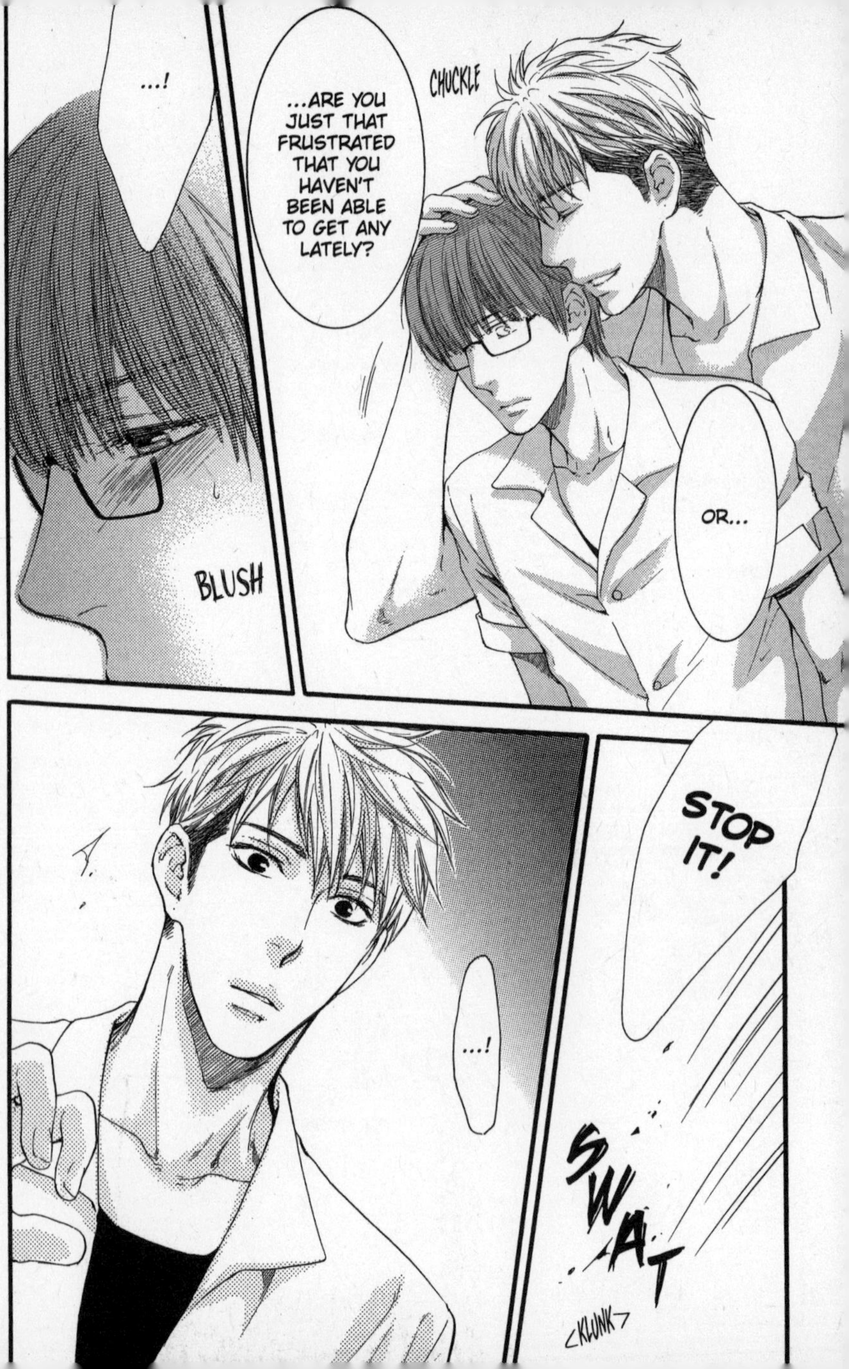
CHUCKLE
...ARE YOU JUST THAT FRUSTRATED THAT YOU HAVEN'T BEEN ABLE TO GET ANY LATELY?
OR...
...!
BLUSH
STOP IT!
SWAT
<KLUNK>
...!

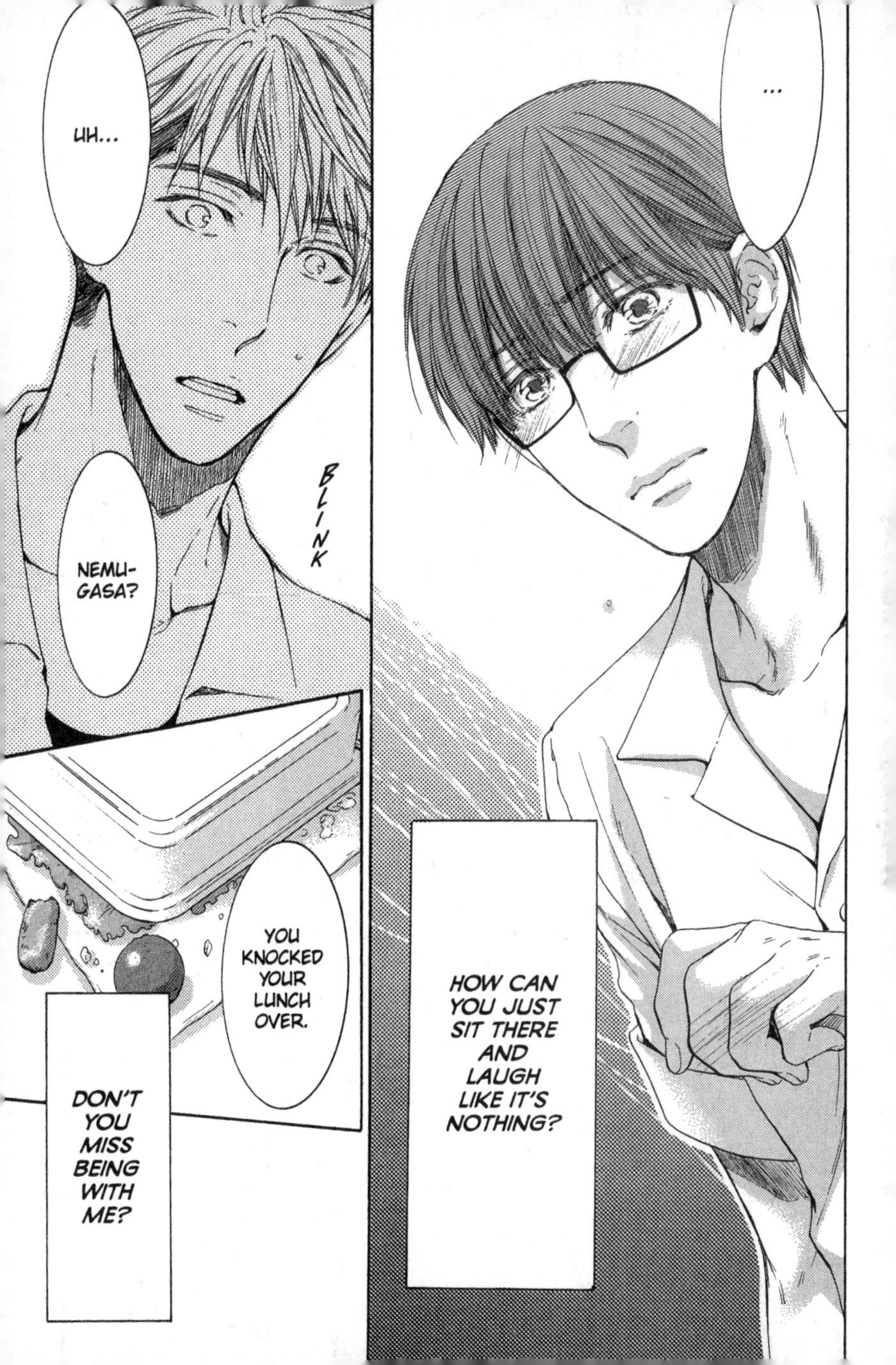
...
HOW CAN YOU JUST SIT THERE AND LAUGH LIKE IT'S NOTHING?
UH...
BLINK
NEMU-GASA?
YOU KNOCKED YOUR LUNCH OVER.
DON'T YOU MISS BEING WITH ME?

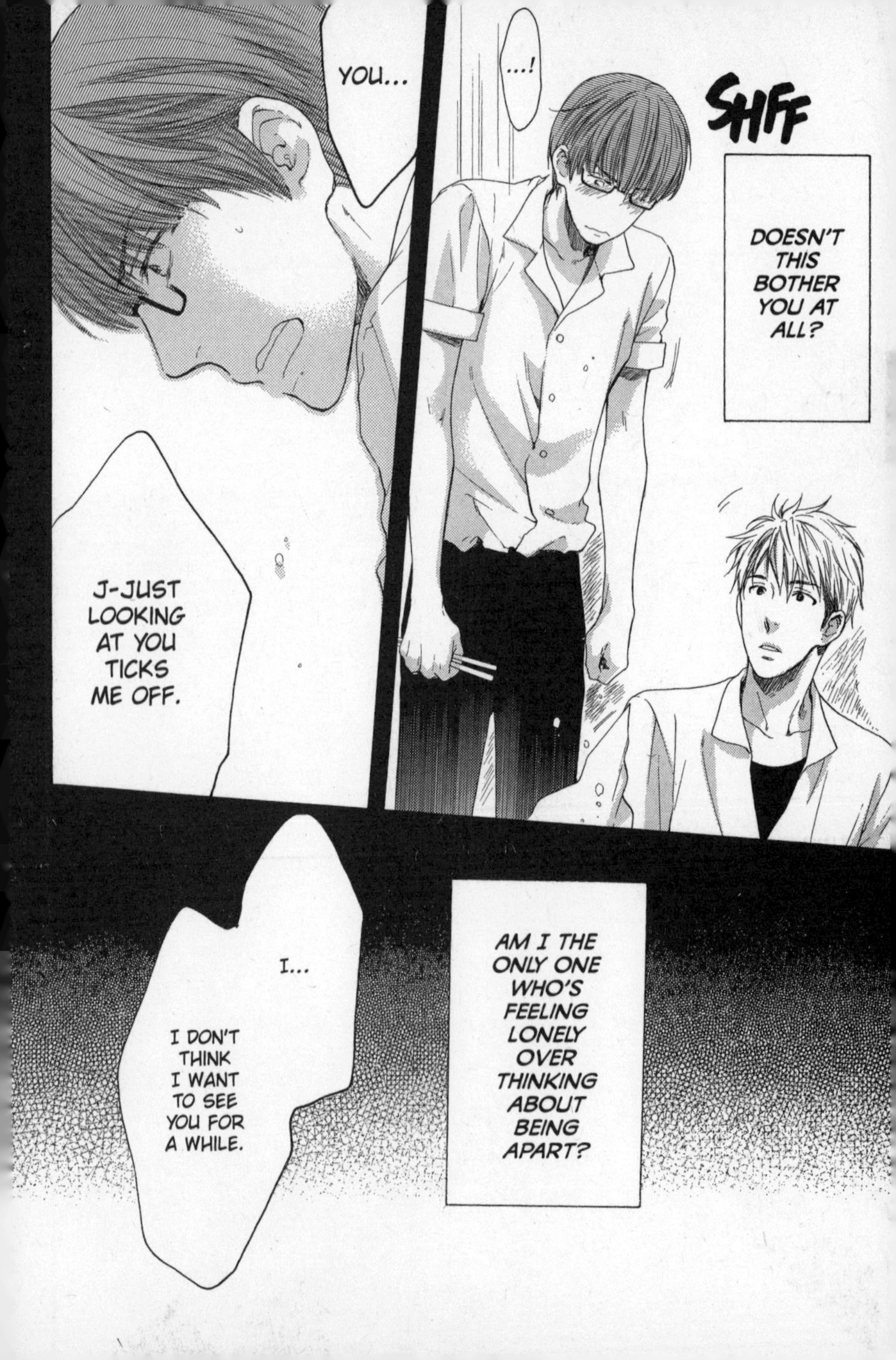
...!
SHFF
DOESN'T THIS BOTHER YOU AT ALL?
YOU...
J-JUST LOOKING AT YOU TICKS ME OFF.
AM I THE ONLY ONE WHO'S FEELING LONELY OVER THINKING ABOUT BEING APART?
I...
I DON'T THINK I WANT TO SEE YOU FOR A WHILE.

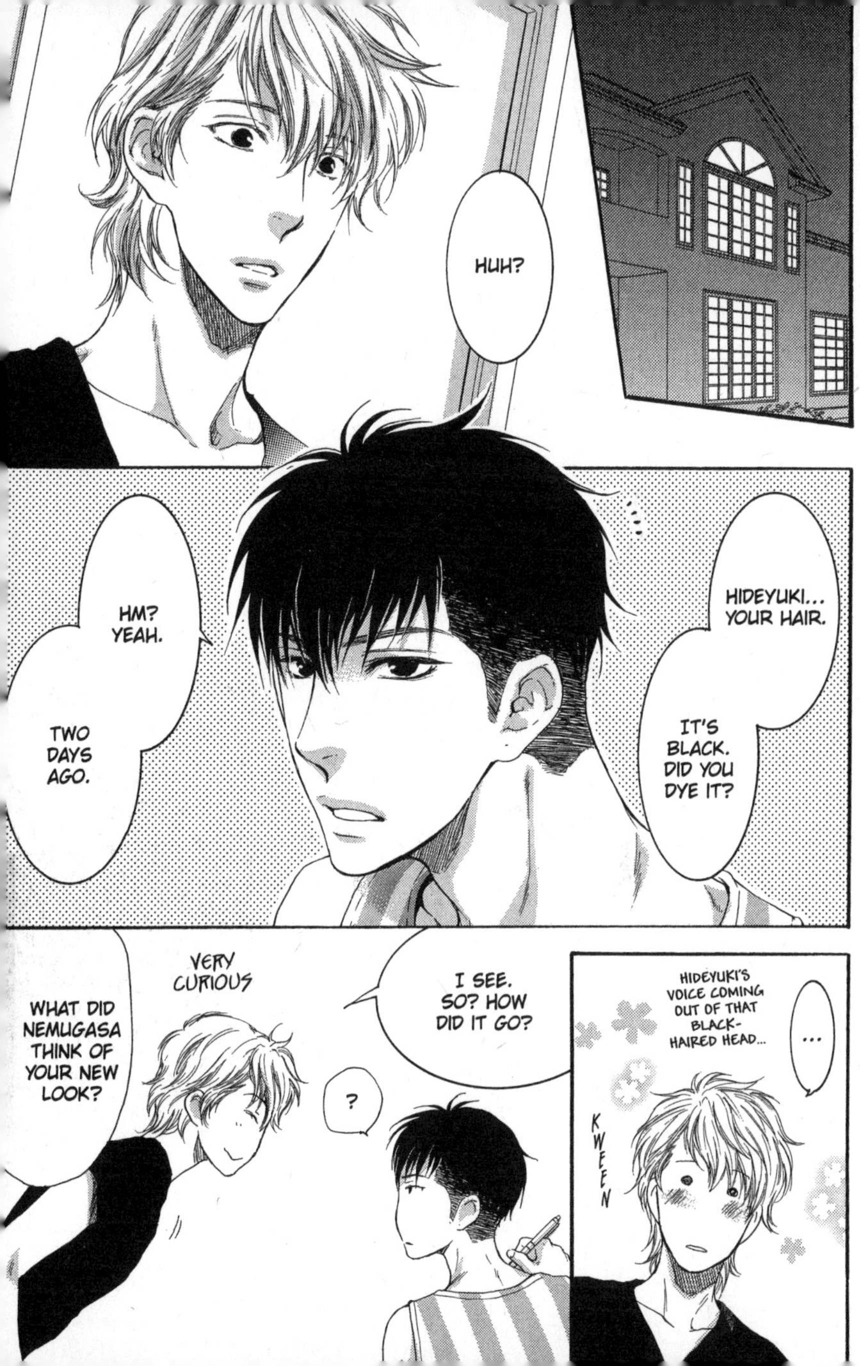
HUH?
.....
HIDEYUKI... YOUR HAIR.
IT'S BLACK. DID YOU DYE IT?
HM? YEAH.
TWO DAYS AGO.
...
HIDEYUKI'S VOICE COMING OUT OF THAT BLACK-HAIRED HEAD...
KWEEN
I SEE. SO? HOW DID IT GO?
?
VERY CURIOUS
WHAT DID NEMUGASA THINK OF YOUR NEW LOOK?

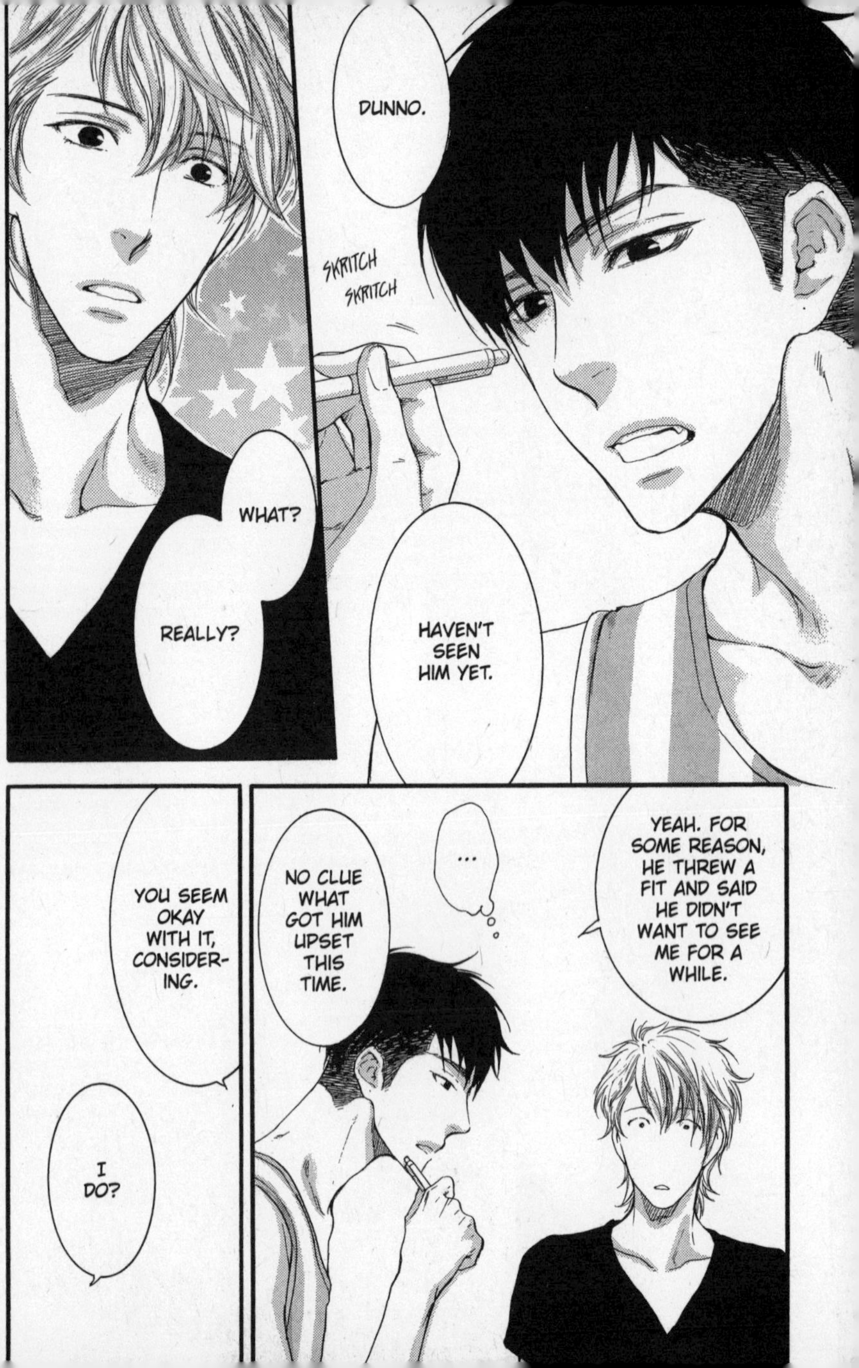
DUNNO.
SKRITCH SKRITCH
HAVEN'T SEEN HIM YET.
WHAT?
REALLY?
YEAH. FOR SOME REASON, HE THREW A FIT AND SAID HE DIDN'T WANT TO SEE ME FOR A WHILE.
...
NO CLUE WHAT GOT HIM UPSET THIS TIME.
YOU SEEM OKAY WITH IT, CONSIDER-ING.
I DO?

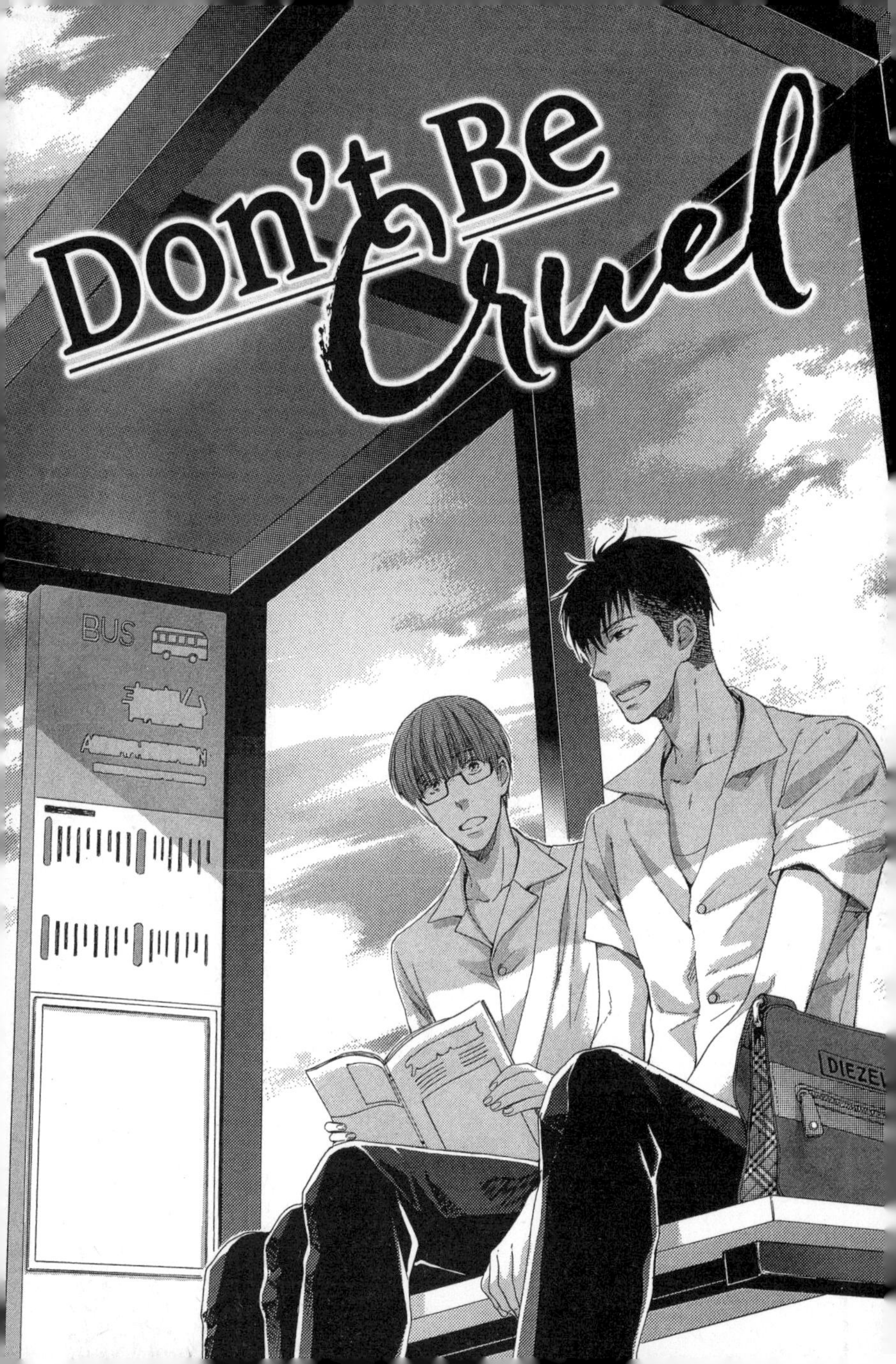
Don't Be Cruel
BUS

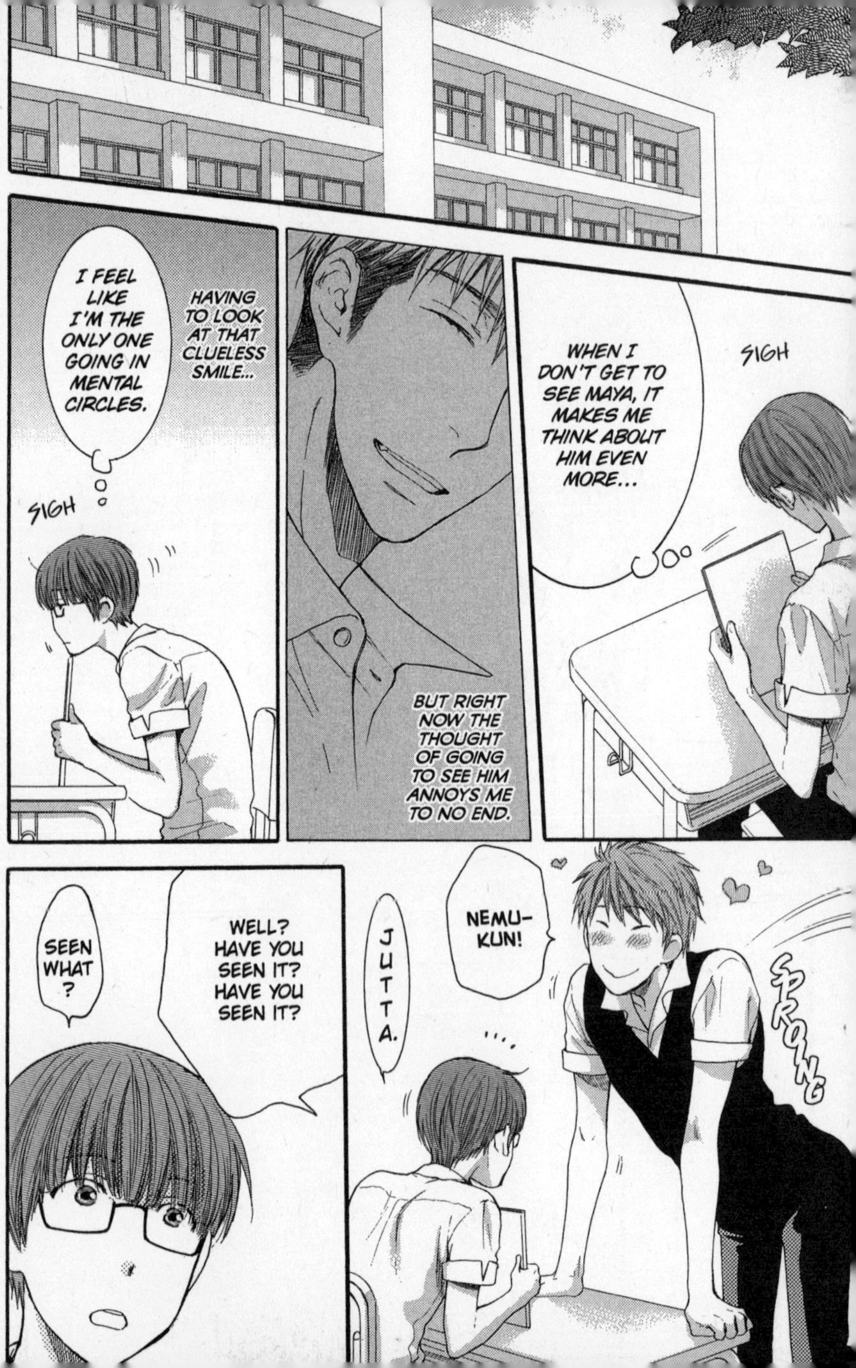
SIGH
WHEN I DON'T GET TO SEE MAYA, IT MAKES ME THINK ABOUT HIM EVEN MORE...
BUT RIGHT NOW THE THOUGHT OF GOING TO SEE HIM ANNOYS ME TO NO END.
HAVING TO LOOK AT THAT CLUELESS SMILE...
I FEEL LIKE I'M THE ONLY ONE GOING IN MENTAL CIRCLES.
SIGH
SPROING
NEMU-KUN!
JUTTA.
...
WELL? HAVE YOU SEEN IT? HAVE YOU SEEN IT?
SEEN WHAT?

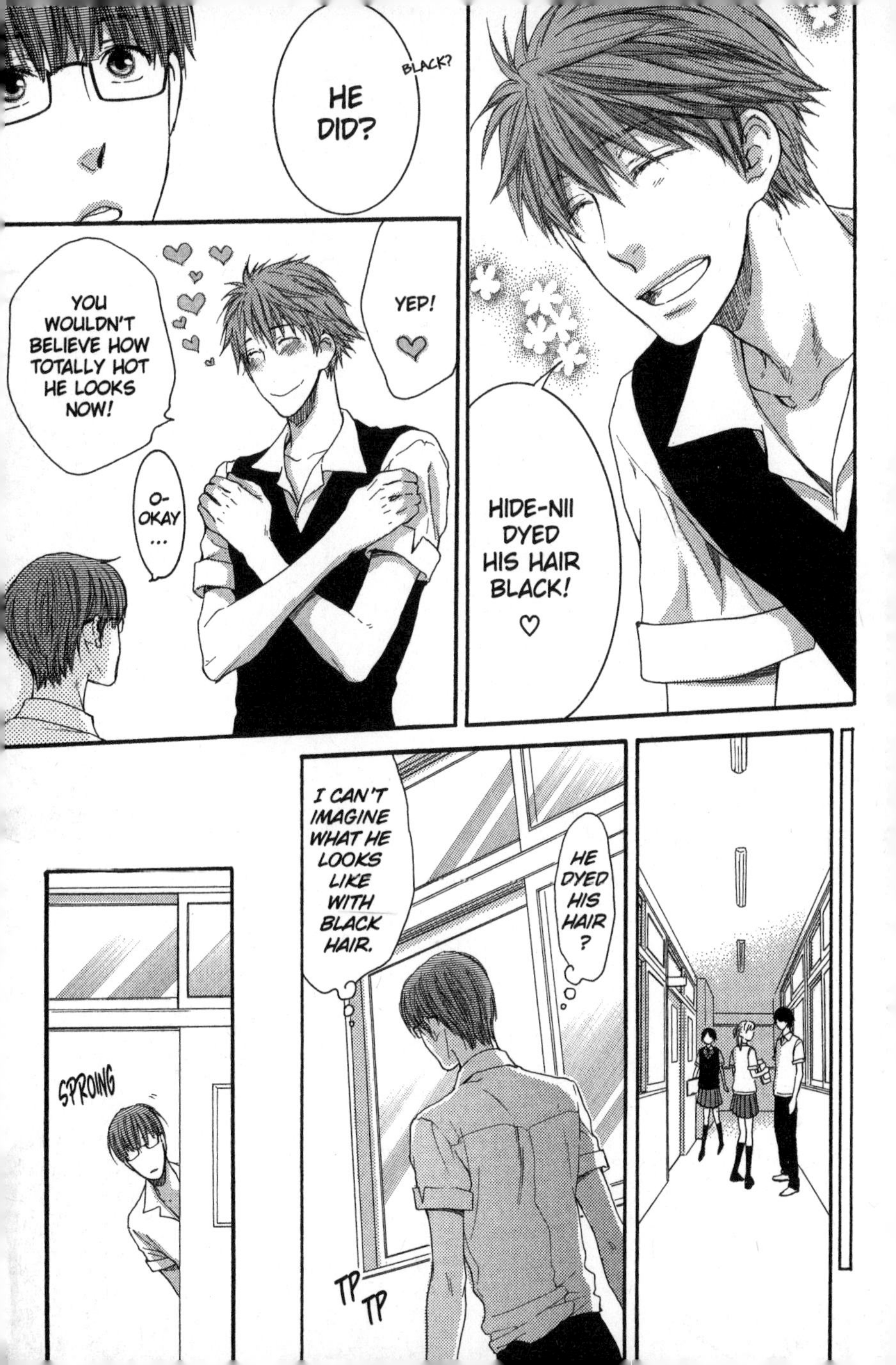
HIDE-NII DYED HIS HAIR BLACK! ♡
HE DID?
BLACK?
YEP! ♡
YOU WOULDN'T BELIEVE HOW TOTALLY HOT HE LOOKS NOW!
O-OKAY...
HE DYED HIS HAIR?
I CAN'T IMAGINE WHAT HE LOOKS LIKE WITH BLACK HAIR.
TP TP
SPROING

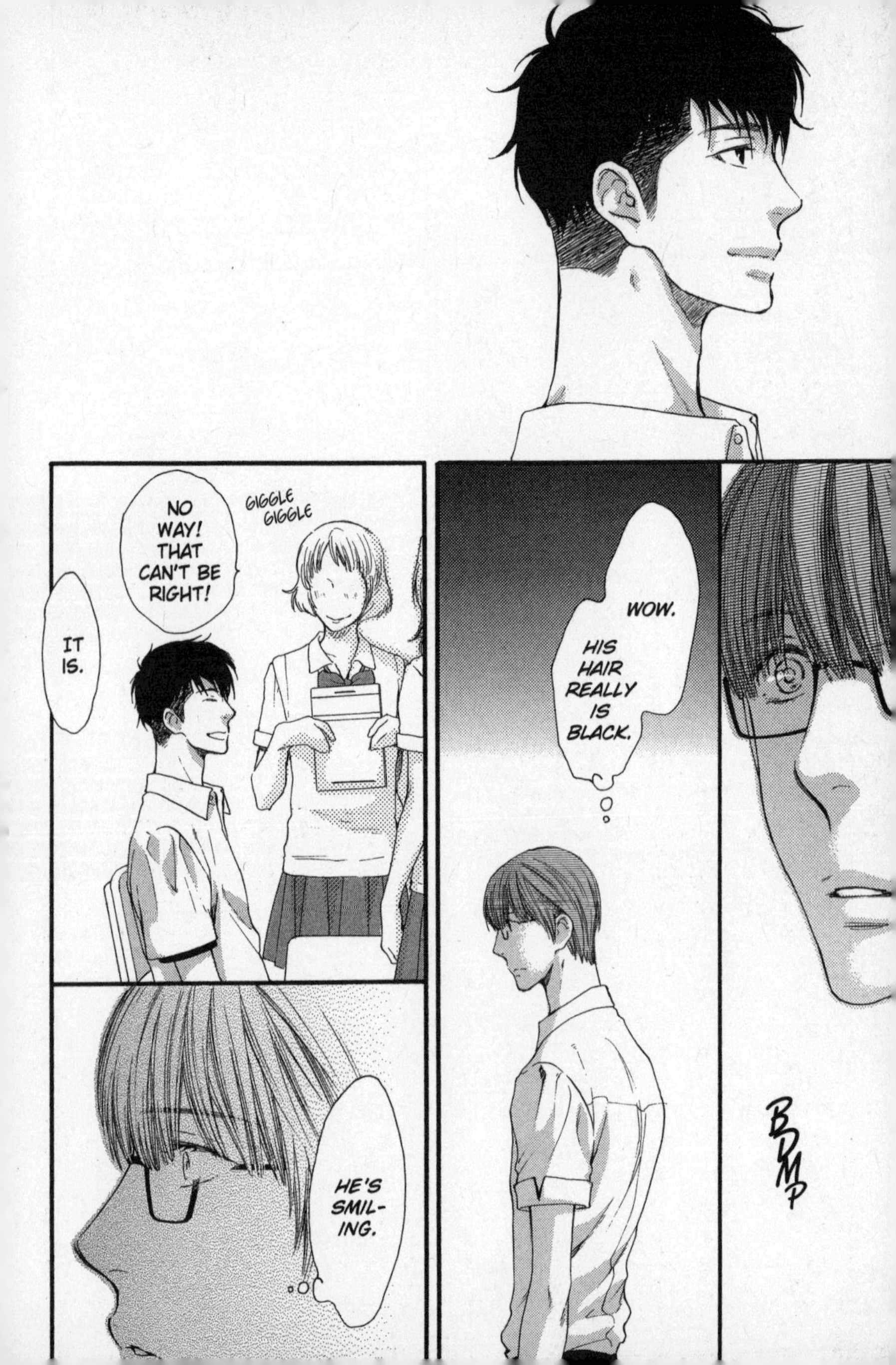
BDMP
WOW.
HIS HAIR REALLY IS BLACK.
GIGGLE GIGGLE
NO WAY! THAT CAN'T BE RIGHT!
IT IS.
HE'S SMIL-ING.

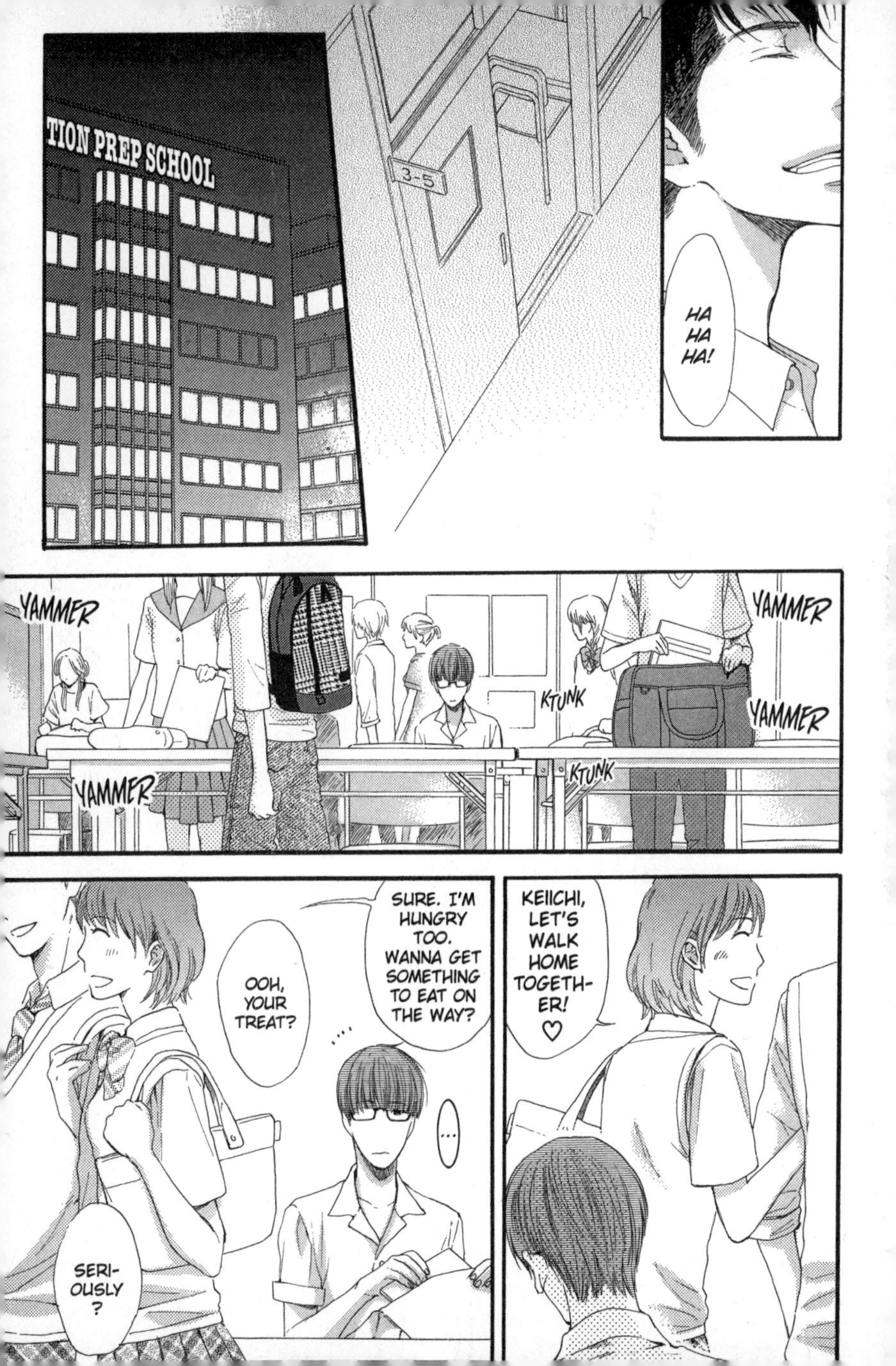
HA HA HA!
3-5
TION PREP SCHOOL
YAMMER
KTUNK
YAMMER
KTUNK
YAMMER
YAMMER
KEIICHI, LET'S WALK HOME TOGETH-ER! ♡
SURE. I'M HUNGRY TOO. WANNA GET SOMETHING TO EAT ON THE WAY?
OOH, YOUR TREAT?
....
...
SERI-OUSLY?

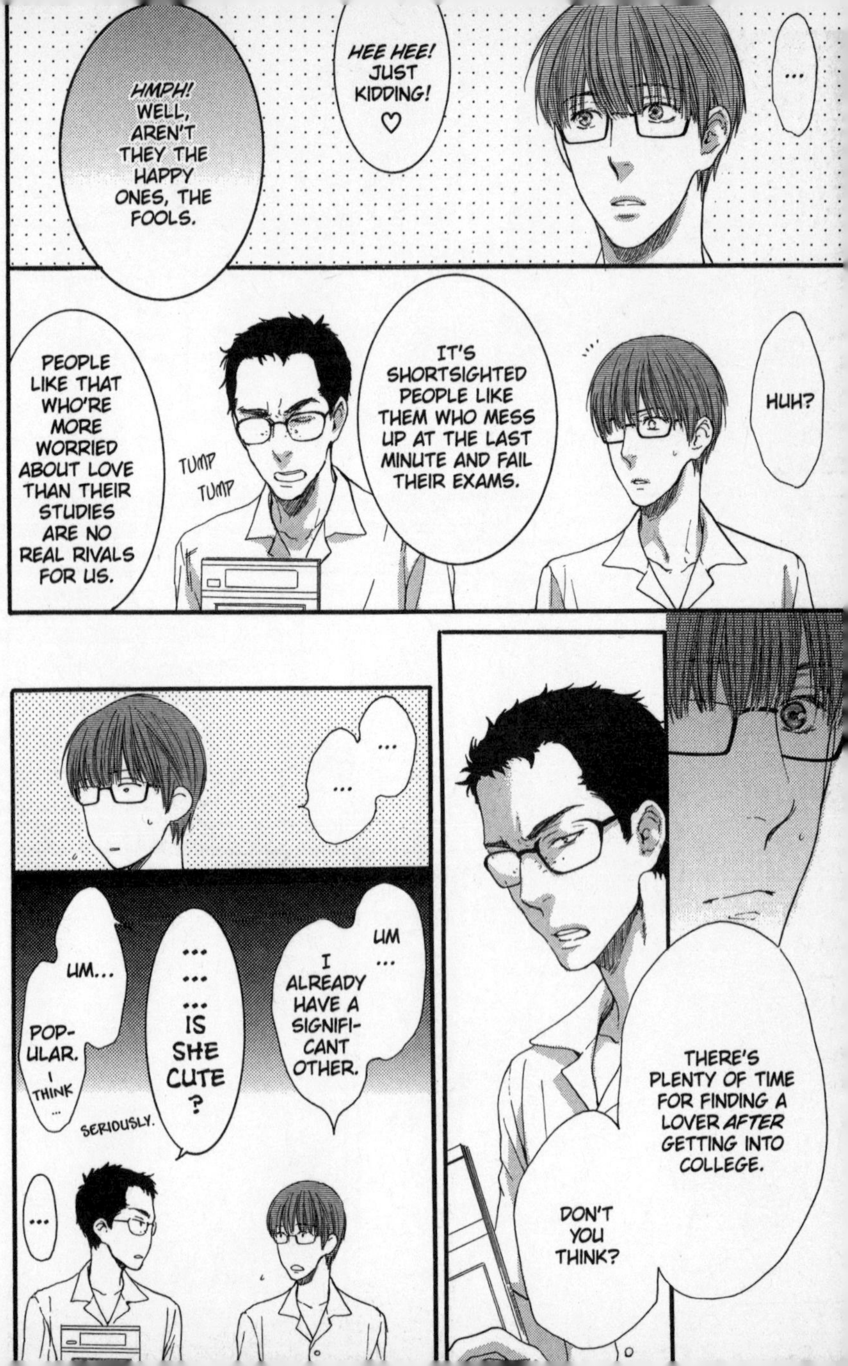
...
HEE HEE! JUST KIDDING! ♡
HMPH! WELL, AREN'T THEY THE HAPPY ONES, THE FOOLS.
HUH?
IT'S SHORTSIGHTED PEOPLE LIKE THEM WHO MESS UP AT THE LAST MINUTE AND FAIL THEIR EXAMS.
TUMP TUMP
PEOPLE LIKE THAT WHO'RE MORE WORRIED ABOUT LOVE THAN THEIR STUDIES ARE NO REAL RIVALS FOR US.
THERE'S PLENTY OF TIME FOR FINDING A LOVER *AFTER* GETTING INTO COLLEGE.
DON'T YOU THINK?
...
...
UM ...
I ALREADY HAVE A SIGNIFICANT OTHER.
... ... IS SHE CUTE?
UM...
POPULAR.
I THINK ...
SERIOUSLY.
...

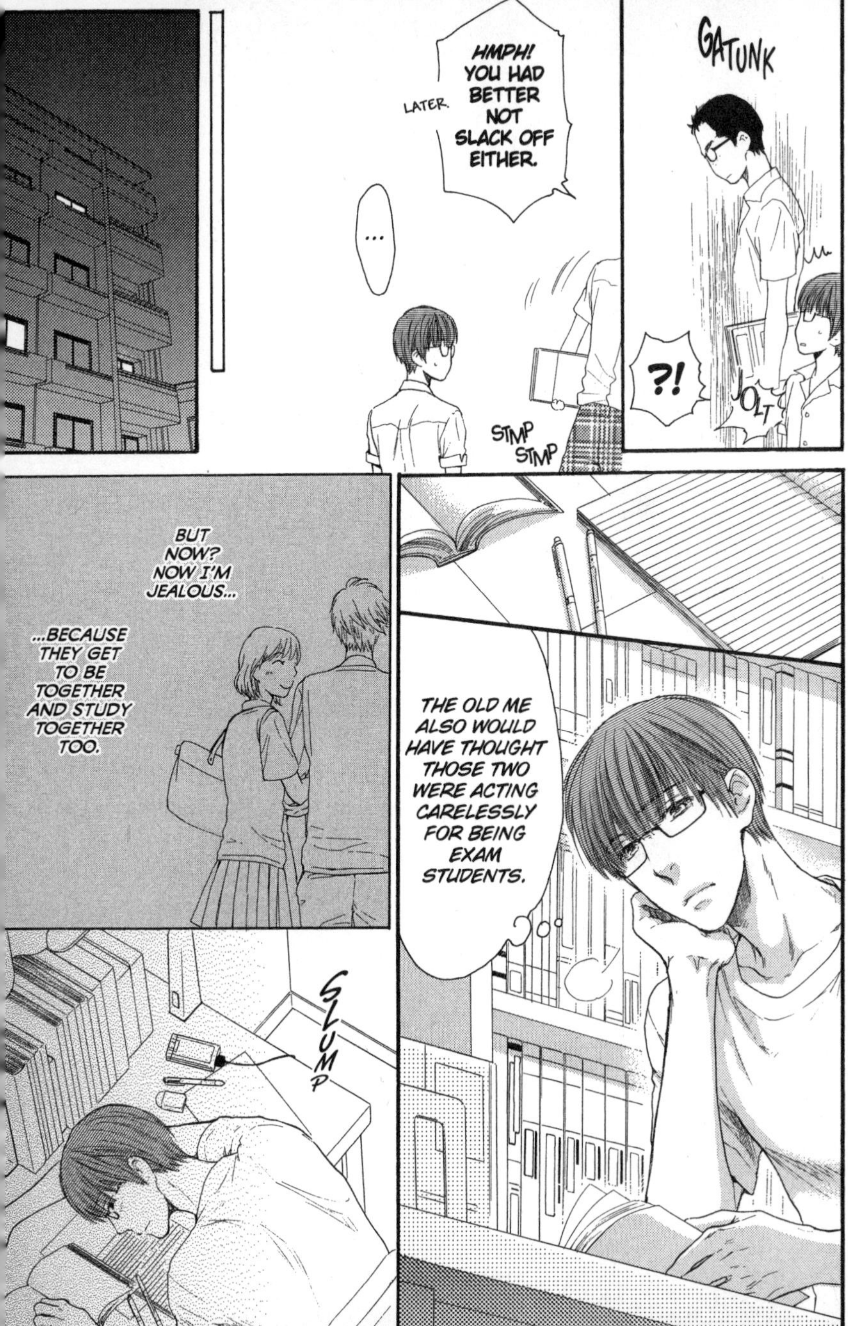
GATUNK
?!
JOLT
HMPH! YOU HAD BETTER NOT SLACK OFF EITHER.
LATER.
...
STMP STMP
THE OLD ME ALSO WOULD HAVE THOUGHT THOSE TWO WERE ACTING CARELESSLY FOR BEING EXAM STUDENTS.
BUT NOW? NOW I'M JEALOUS...
...BECAUSE THEY GET TO BE TOGETHER AND STUDY TOGETHER TOO.
SLUMP

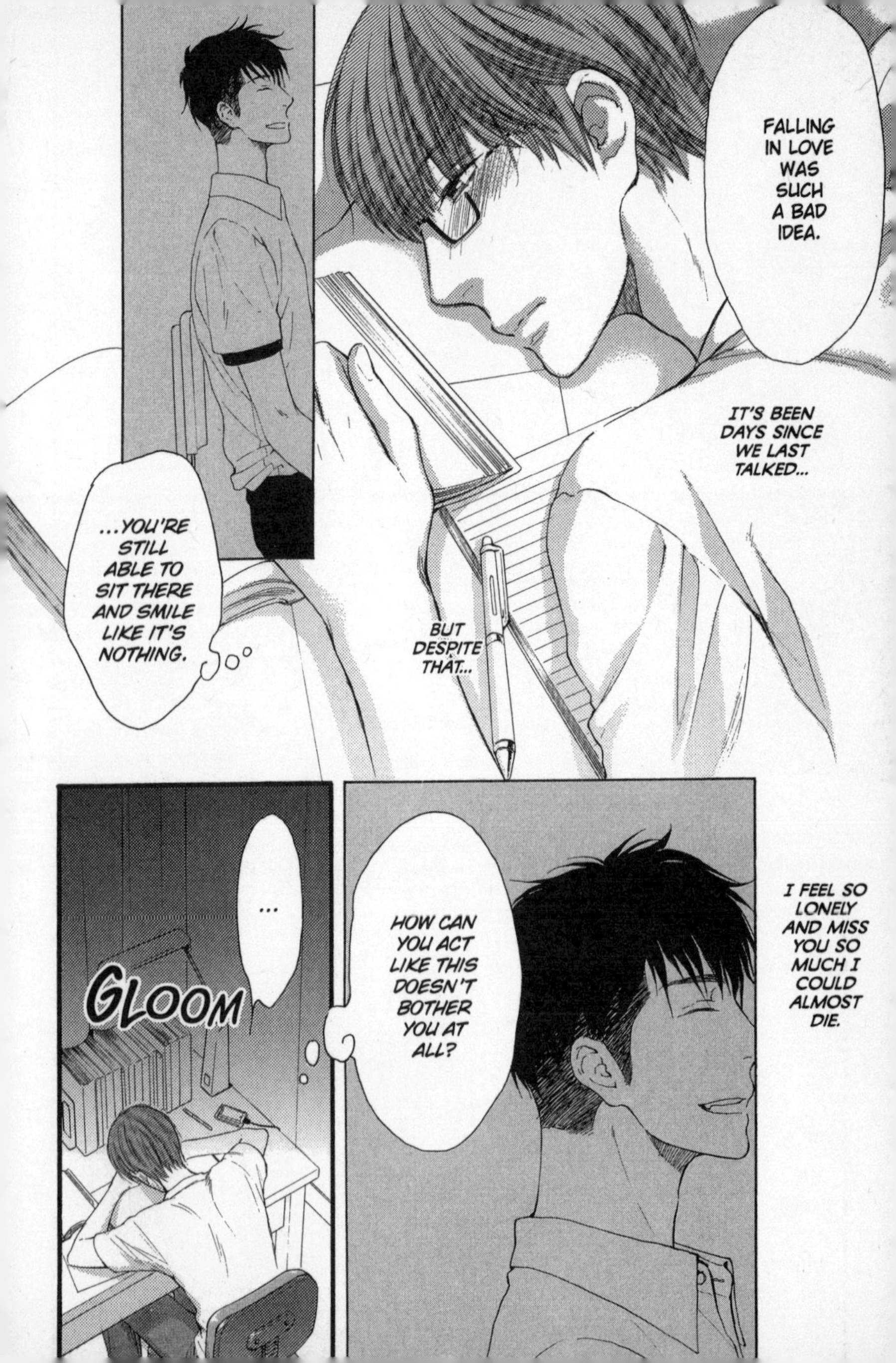
FALLING IN LOVE WAS SUCH A BAD IDEA.
IT'S BEEN DAYS SINCE WE LAST TALKED...
BUT DESPITE THAT...
...YOU'RE STILL ABLE TO SIT THERE AND SMILE LIKE IT'S NOTHING.
I FEEL SO LONELY AND MISS YOU SO MUCH I COULD ALMOST DIE.
HOW CAN YOU ACT LIKE THIS DOESN'T BOTHER YOU AT ALL?
...
GLOOM

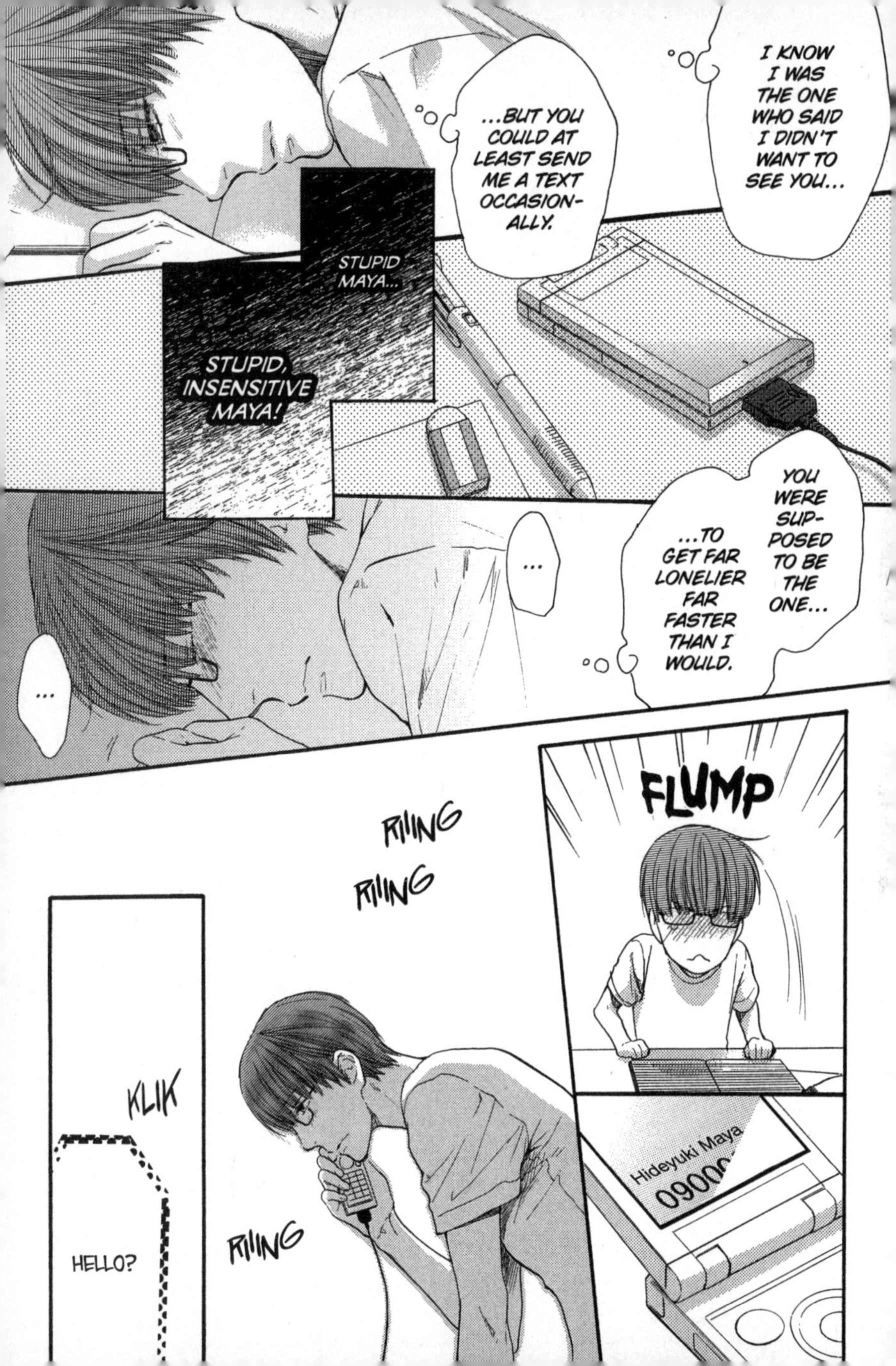
I KNOW I WAS THE ONE WHO SAID I DIDN'T WANT TO SEE YOU...
...BUT YOU COULD AT LEAST SEND ME A TEXT OCCASION-ALLY.
STUPID MAYA...
STUPID, INSENSITIVE MAYA!
YOU WERE SUP-POSED TO BE THE ONE...
...TO GET FAR LONELIER FAR FASTER THAN I WOULD.
...
...
FLUMP
Hideyuki Maya
RIIING
RIIING
KLIK
RIIING
HELLO?

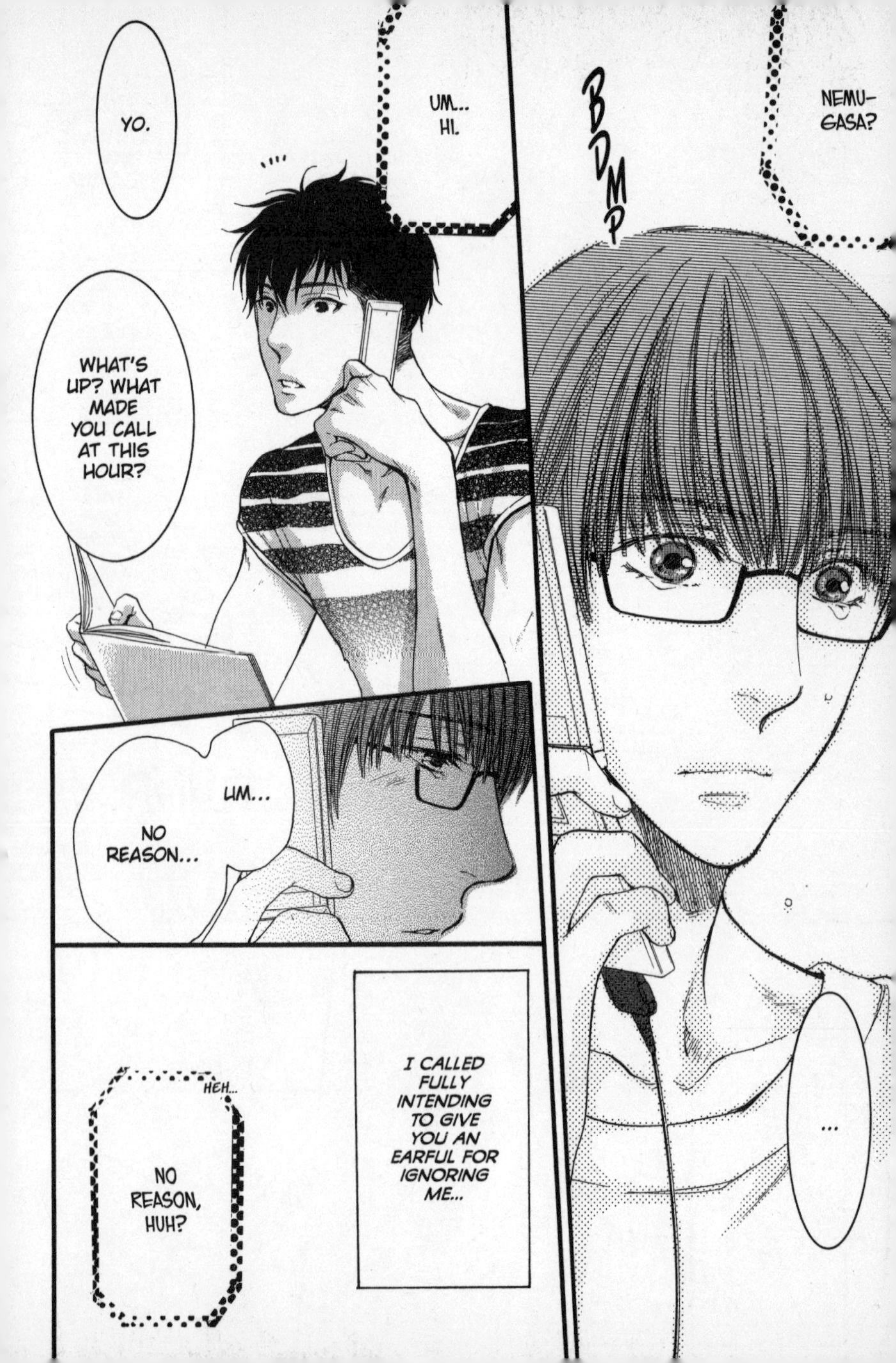
NEMU-GASA?
BDMP
...
UM... HI.
'''
YO.
WHAT'S UP? WHAT MADE YOU CALL AT THIS HOUR?
UM...
NO REASON...
I CALLED FULLY INTENDING TO GIVE YOU AN EARFUL FOR IGNORING ME...
HEH...
NO REASON, HUH?

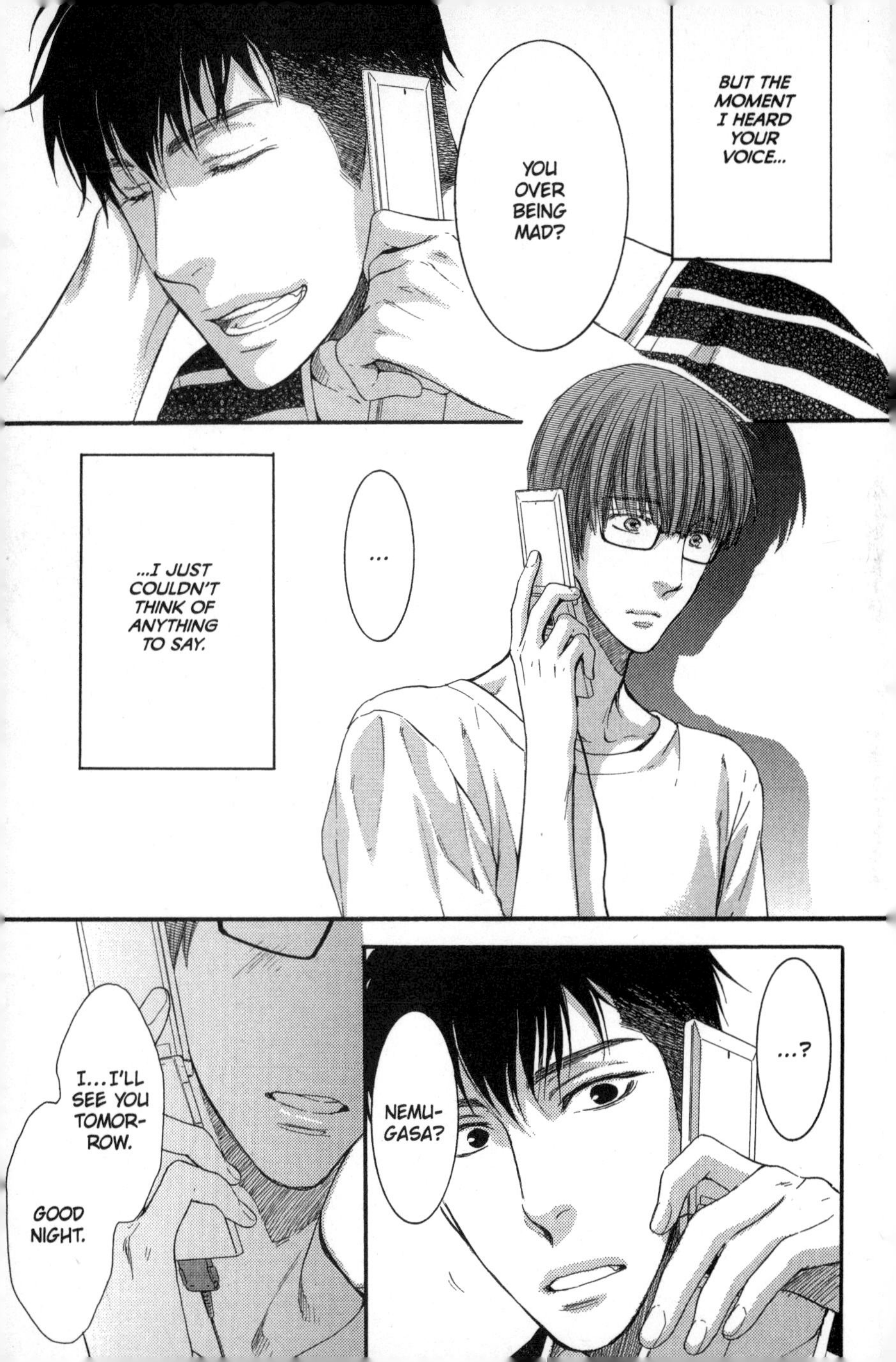
BUT THE MOMENT I HEARD YOUR VOICE...
YOU OVER BEING MAD?
...
...I JUST COULDN'T THINK OF ANYTHING TO SAY.
...?
NEMU-GASA?
I...I'LL SEE YOU TOMOR-ROW.
GOOD NIGHT.

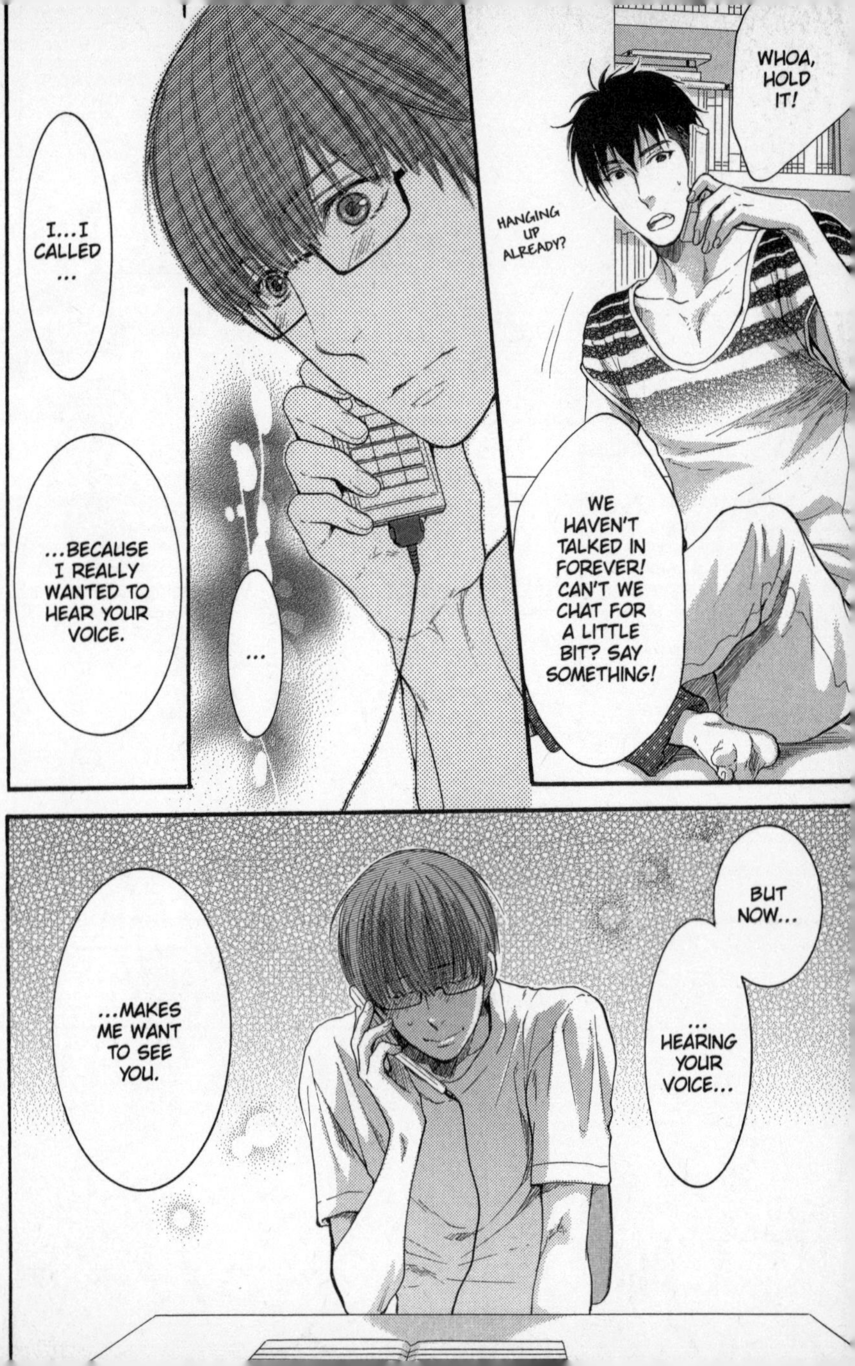
WHOA, HOLD IT!
HANGING UP ALREADY?
WE HAVEN'T TALKED IN FOREVER! CAN'T WE CHAT FOR A LITTLE BIT? SAY SOMETHING!
...
I...I CALLED ...
...BECAUSE I REALLY WANTED TO HEAR YOUR VOICE.
BUT NOW...
...HEARING YOUR VOICE...
...MAKES ME WANT TO SEE YOU.

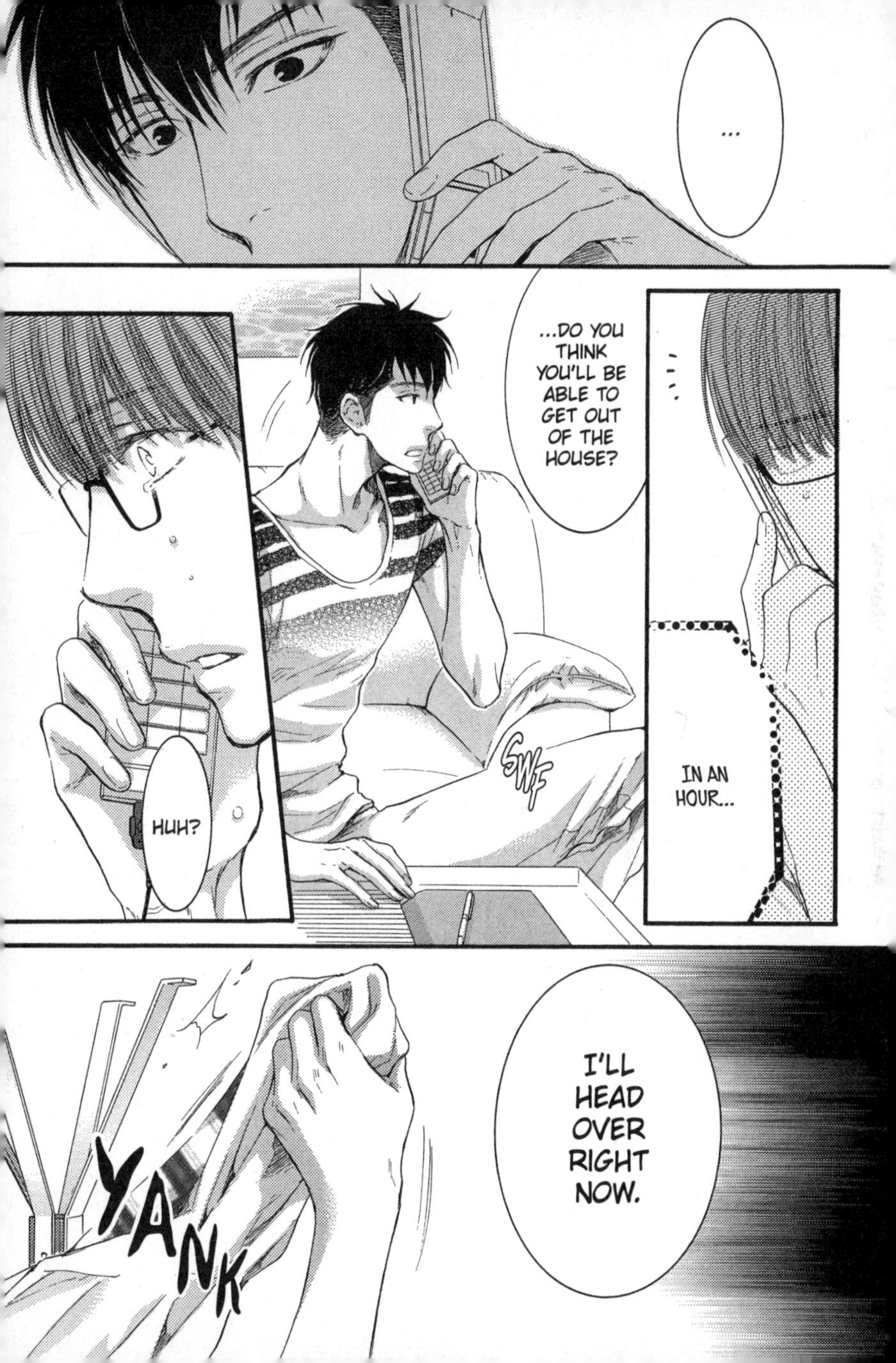
...
...
IN AN HOUR...
...DO YOU THINK YOU'LL BE ABLE TO GET OUT OF THE HOUSE?
SWF
HUH?
I'LL HEAD OVER RIGHT NOW.
YANK

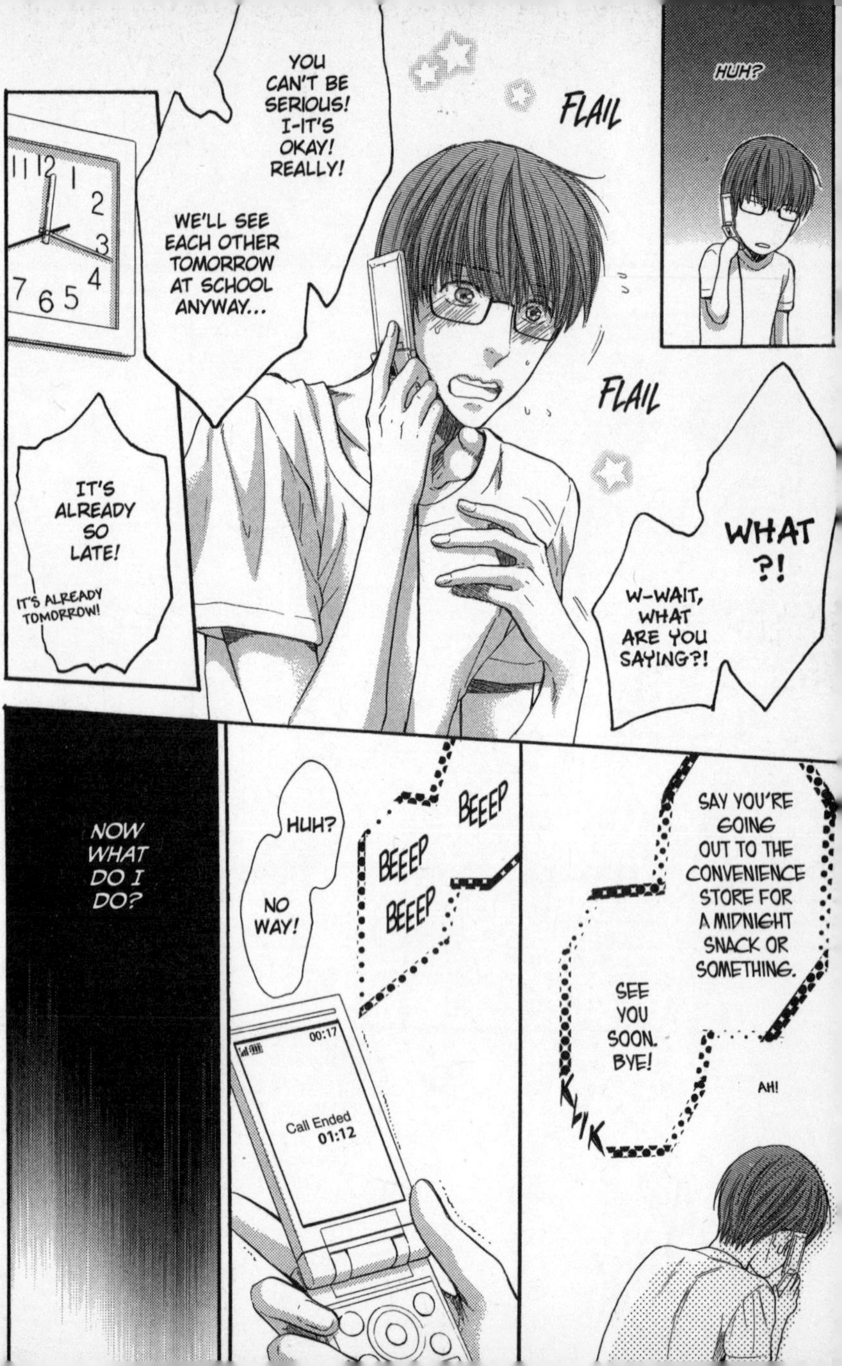
HUH?
WHAT?!
W-WAIT, WHAT ARE YOU SAYING?!
FLAIL
FLAIL
YOU CAN'T BE SERIOUS! I-IT'S OKAY! REALLY!
WE'LL SEE EACH OTHER TOMORROW AT SCHOOL ANYWAY...
IT'S ALREADY SO LATE!
IT'S ALREADY TOMORROW!
SAY YOU'RE GOING OUT TO THE CONVENIENCE STORE FOR A MIDNIGHT SNACK OR SOMETHING.
SEE YOU SOON. BYE!
KLIK
AH!
BEEEP
BEEEP
BEEEP
HUH?
NO WAY!
00:17
Call Ended
01:12
NOW WHAT DO I DO?

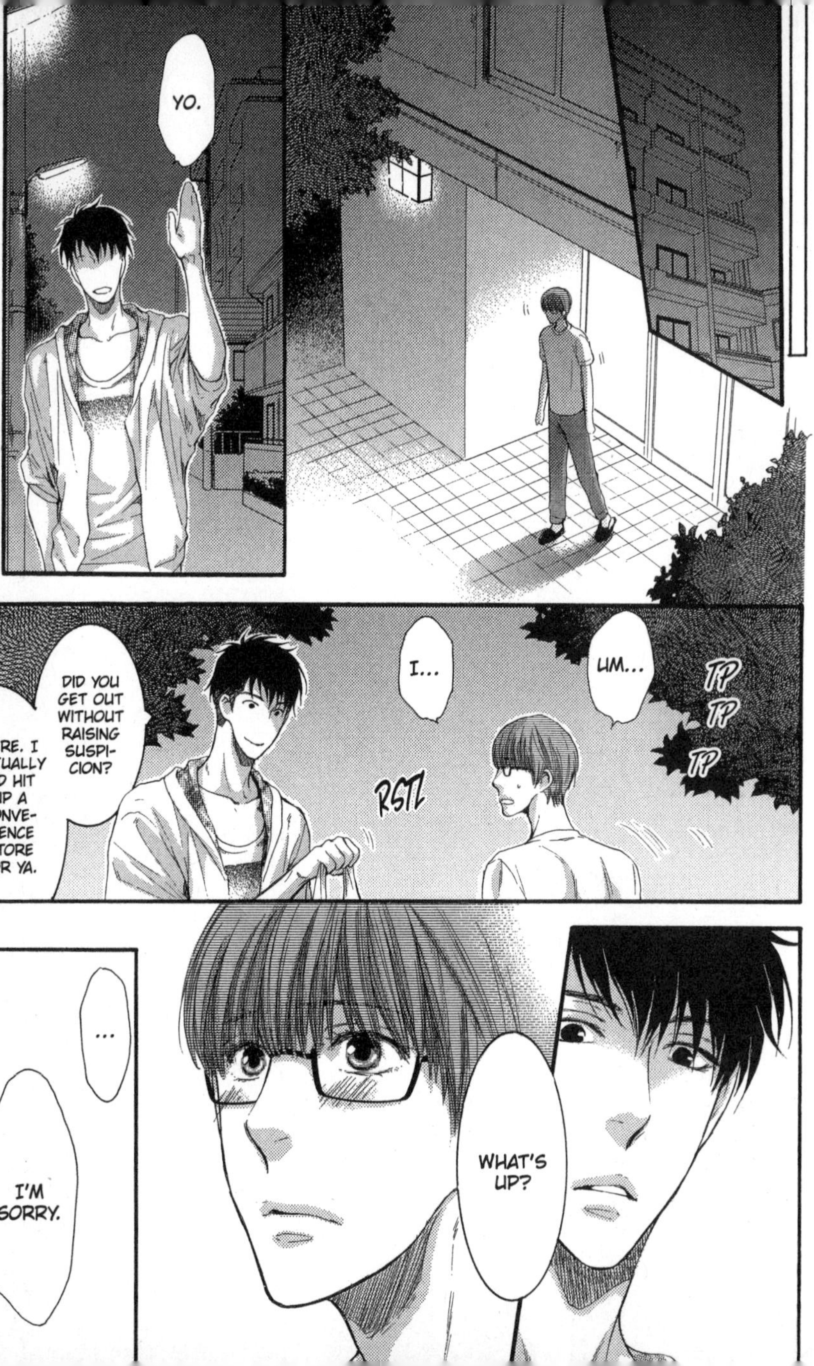
YO.
TP
TP
TP
UM...
I...
RSTL
DID YOU GET OUT WITHOUT RAISING SUSPICION?
HERE. I ACTUALLY DID HIT UP A CONVENIENCE STORE FOR YA.
WHAT'S UP?
...
I'M SORRY.

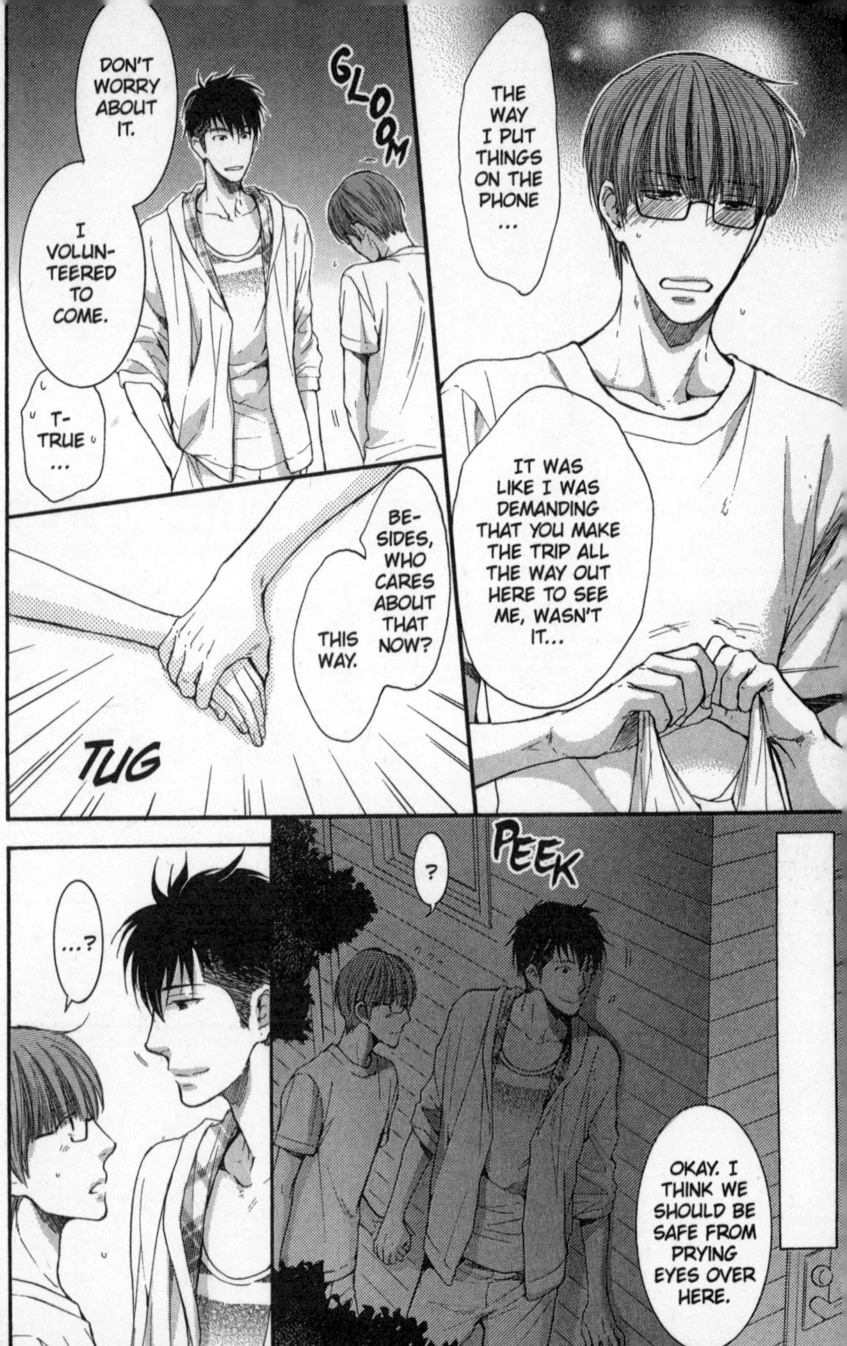
THE WAY I PUT THINGS ON THE PHONE...
IT WAS LIKE I WAS DEMANDING THAT YOU MAKE THE TRIP ALL THE WAY OUT HERE TO SEE ME, WASN'T IT...
GLOOM
DON'T WORRY ABOUT IT.
I VOLUNTEERED TO COME.
T-TRUE...
BESIDES, WHO CARES ABOUT THAT NOW?
THIS WAY.
TUG
PEEK
?
OKAY. I THINK WE SHOULD BE SAFE FROM PRYING EYES OVER HERE.
...?

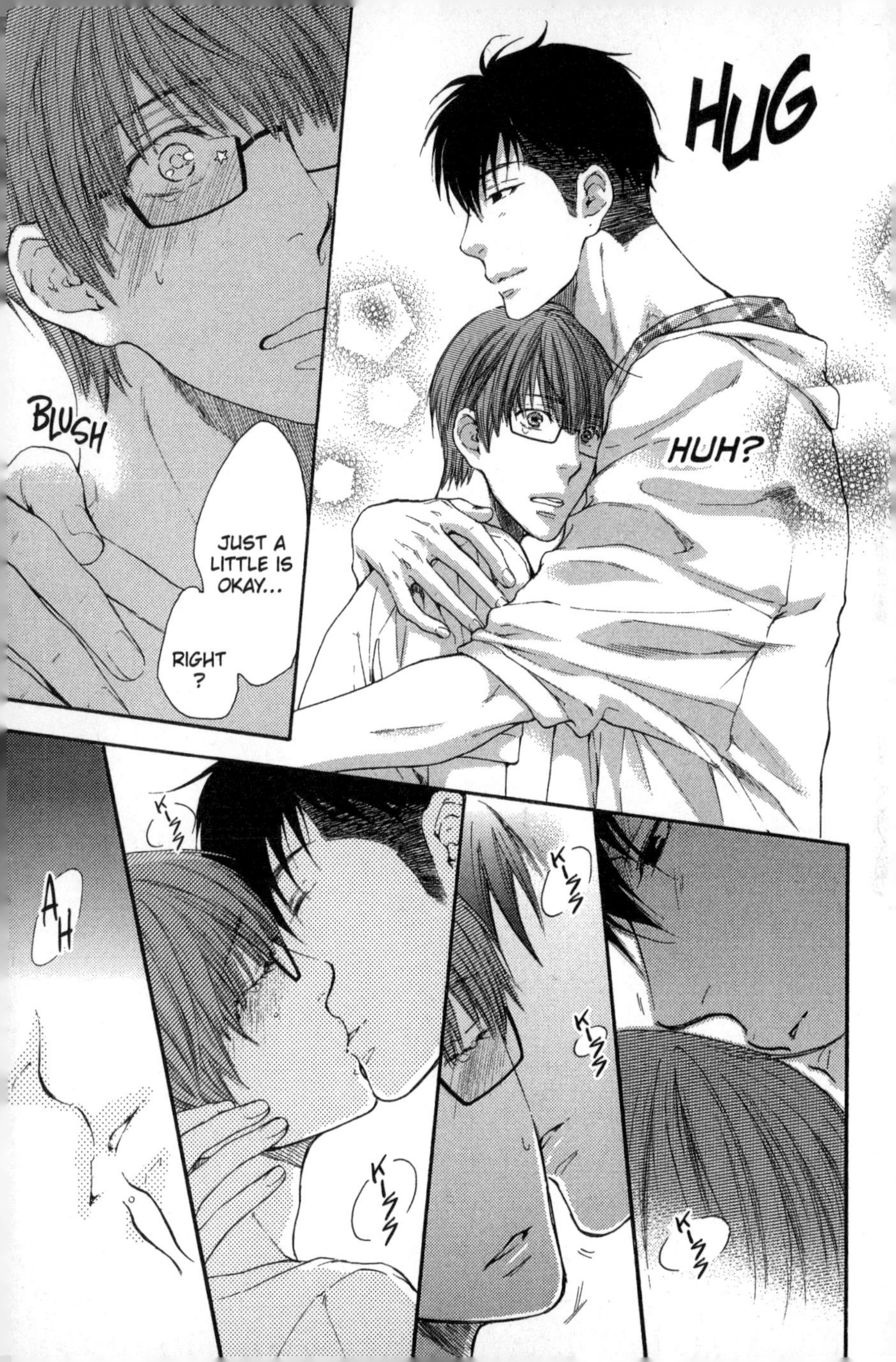
HUG
HUH?
BLUSH
JUST A LITTLE IS OKAY...
RIGHT?
KISS
KISS
KISS
KISS
KISS
AH

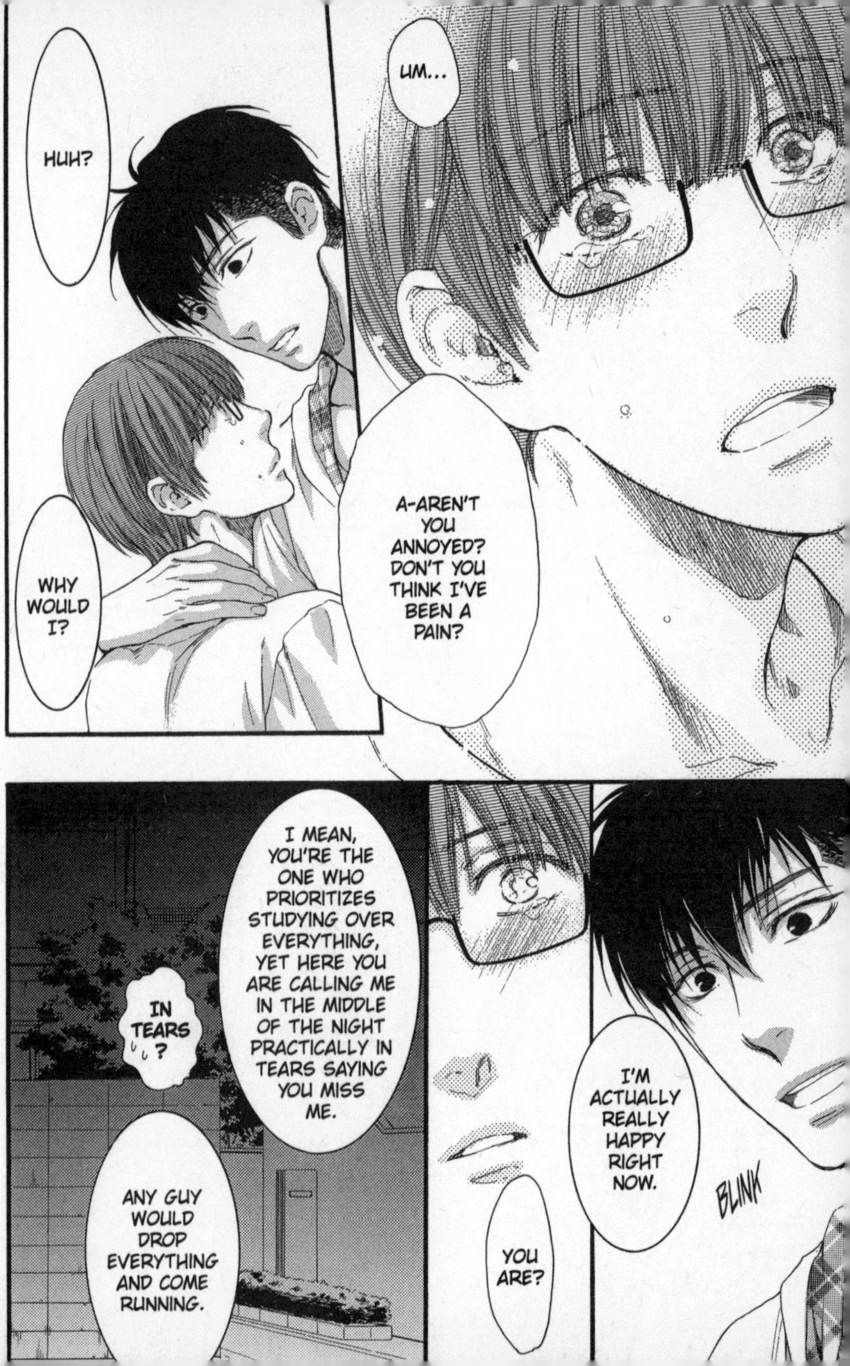
UM...
A-AREN'T YOU ANNOYED? DON'T YOU THINK I'VE BEEN A PAIN?
HUH?
WHY WOULD I?
I'M ACTUALLY REALLY HAPPY RIGHT NOW.
BLINK
YOU ARE?
I MEAN, YOU'RE THE ONE WHO PRIORITIZES STUDYING OVER EVERYTHING, YET HERE YOU ARE CALLING ME IN THE MIDDLE OF THE NIGHT PRACTICALLY IN TEARS SAYING YOU MISS ME.
IN TEARS?
ANY GUY WOULD DROP EVERYTHING AND COME RUNNING.

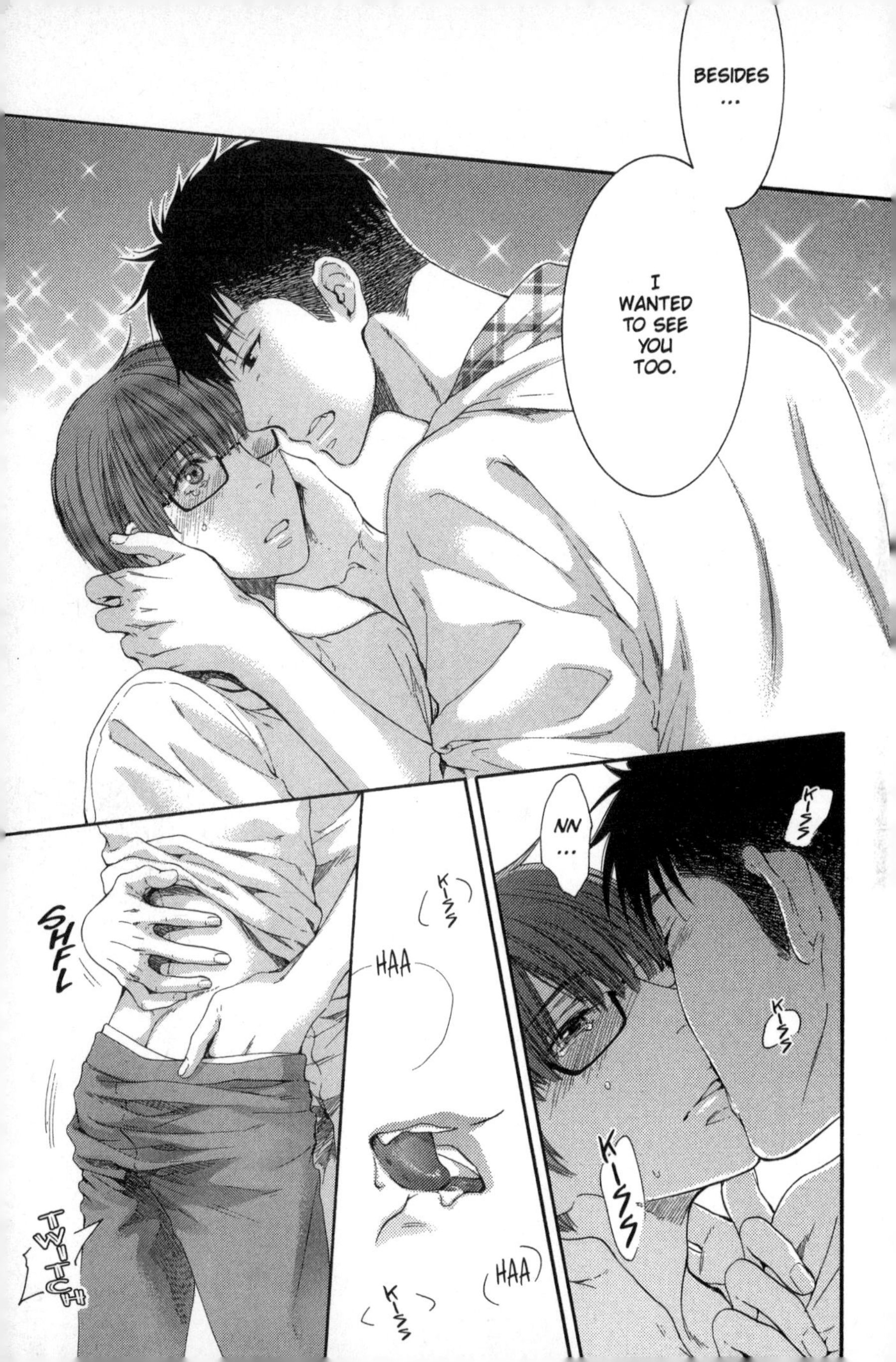
BESIDES ...
I WANTED TO SEE YOU TOO.
KISS
NN ...
KISS
KISS
KISS
HAA
HAA
KISS
SHFL
TWITCH

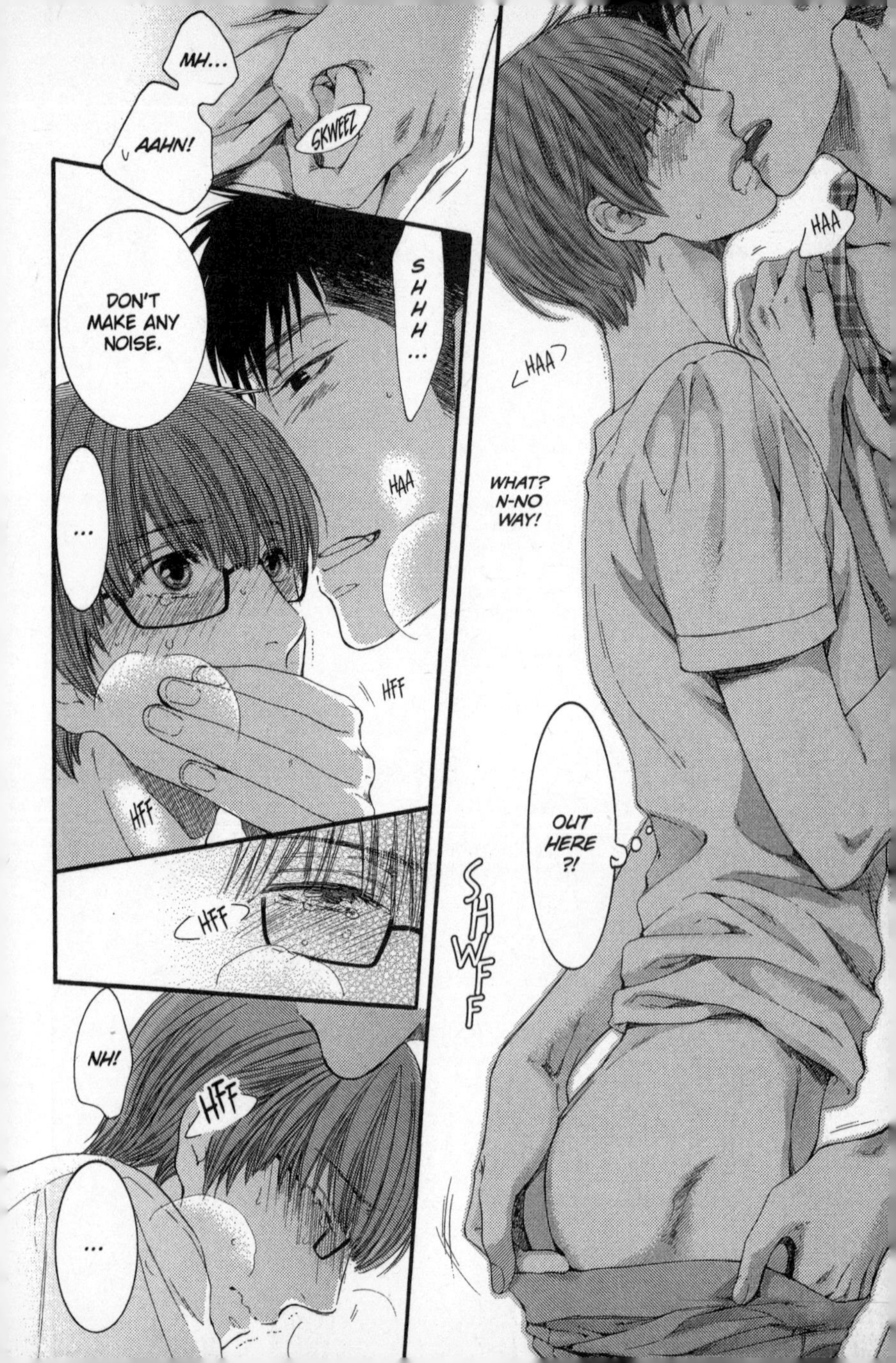
HAA
HAA
WHAT? N-NO WAY!
OUT HERE ?!
SHWFF
MH...
SKWEEZ
AAHN!
SHHH...
DON'T MAKE ANY NOISE.
HAA
...
HFF
HFF
HFF
NH!
HFF
...

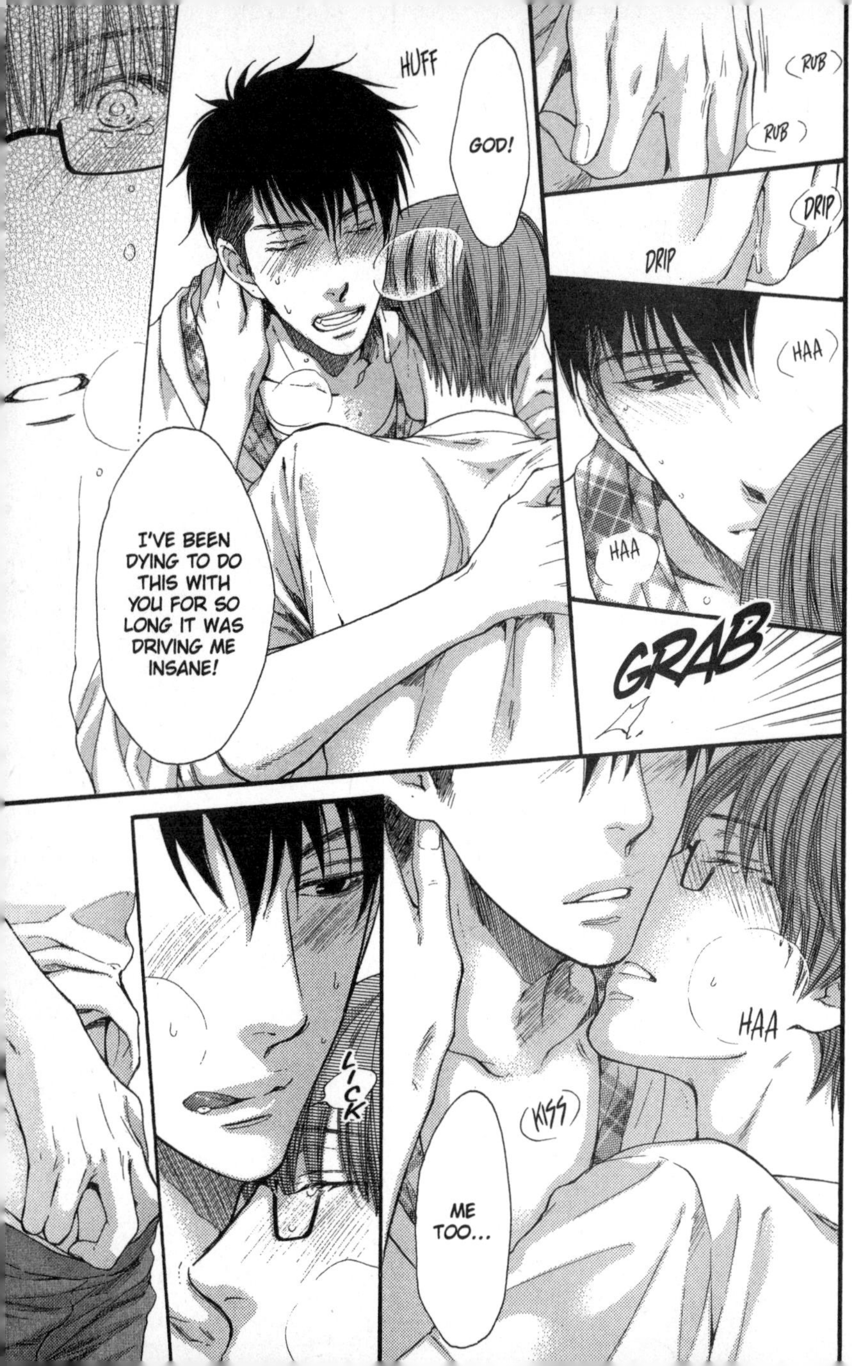
RUB
RUB
DRIP
DRIP
HAA
HAA
GRAB
HUFF
GOD!
I'VE BEEN DYING TO DO THIS WITH YOU FOR SO LONG IT WAS DRIVING ME INSANE!
HAA
KISS
ME TOO...
LICK

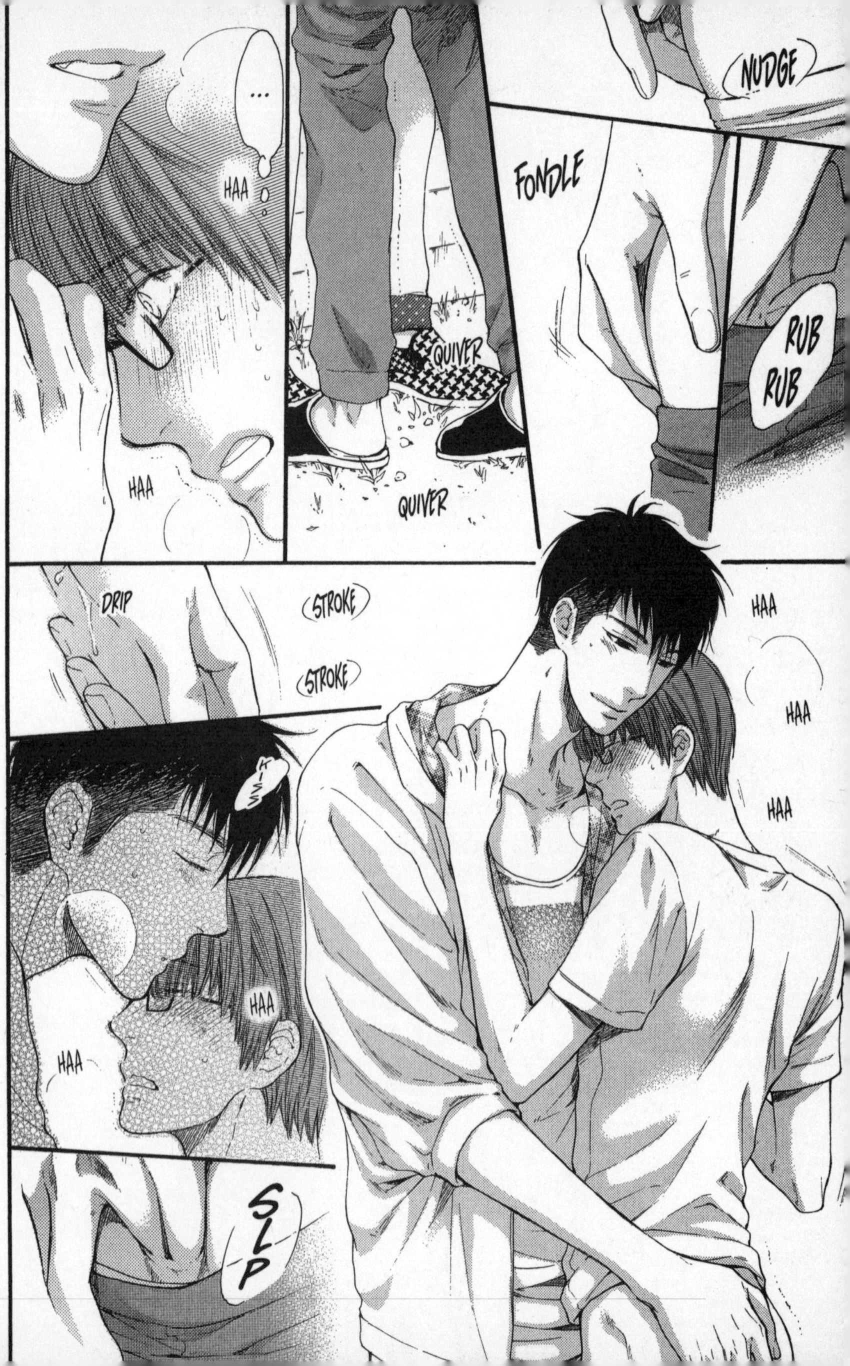
NUDGE
FONDLE
RUB RUB
QUIVER
QUIVER
...
HAA
HAA
HAA
HAA
HAA
STROKE
STROKE
DRIP
KISS
HAA
HAA
SLP

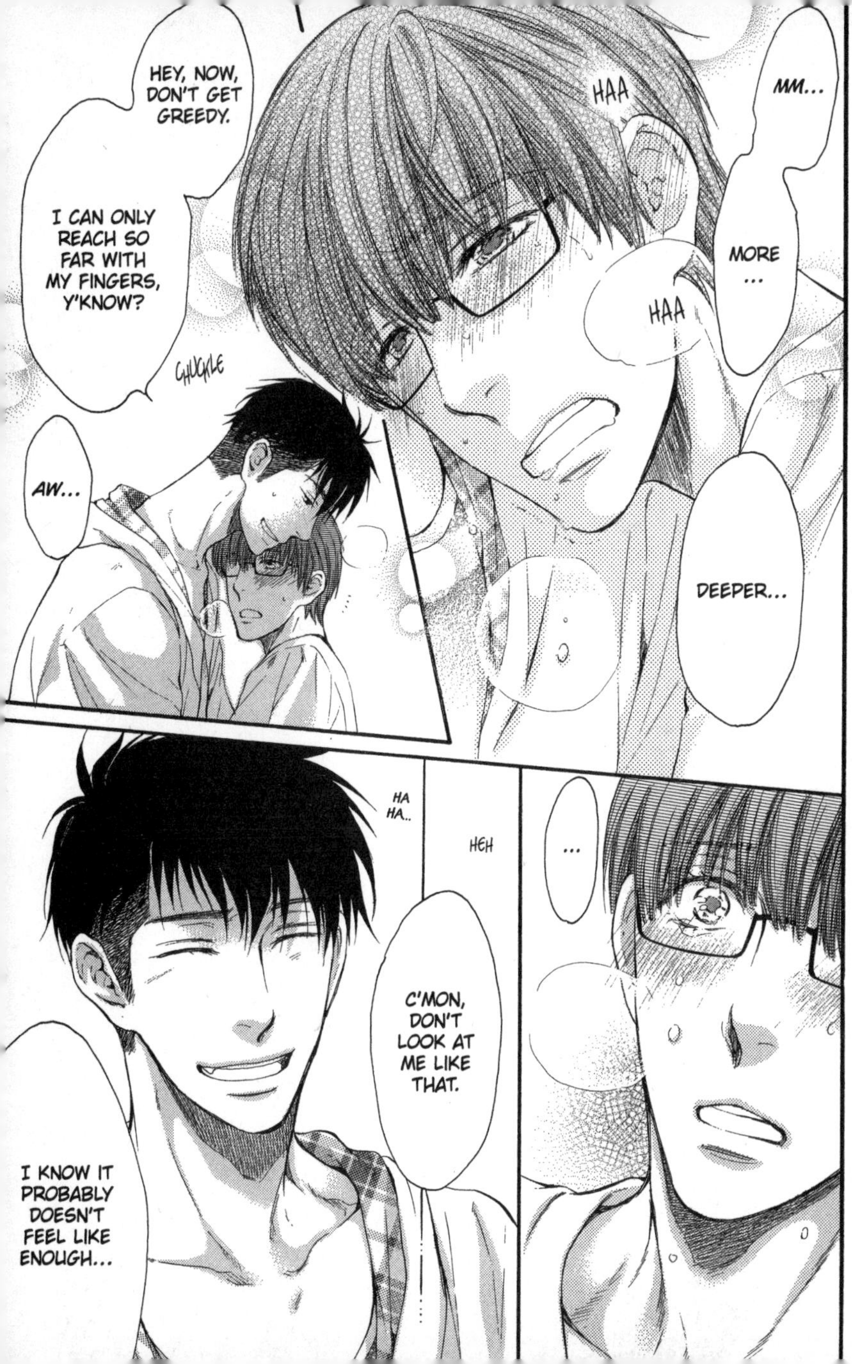
MM...
HAA
MORE ...
HAA
DEEPER...
HEY, NOW, DON'T GET GREEDY.
I CAN ONLY REACH SO FAR WITH MY FINGERS, Y'KNOW?
CHUCKLE
AW...
...
HEH
HA HA..
C'MON, DON'T LOOK AT ME LIKE THAT.
I KNOW IT PROBABLY DOESN'T FEEL LIKE ENOUGH...

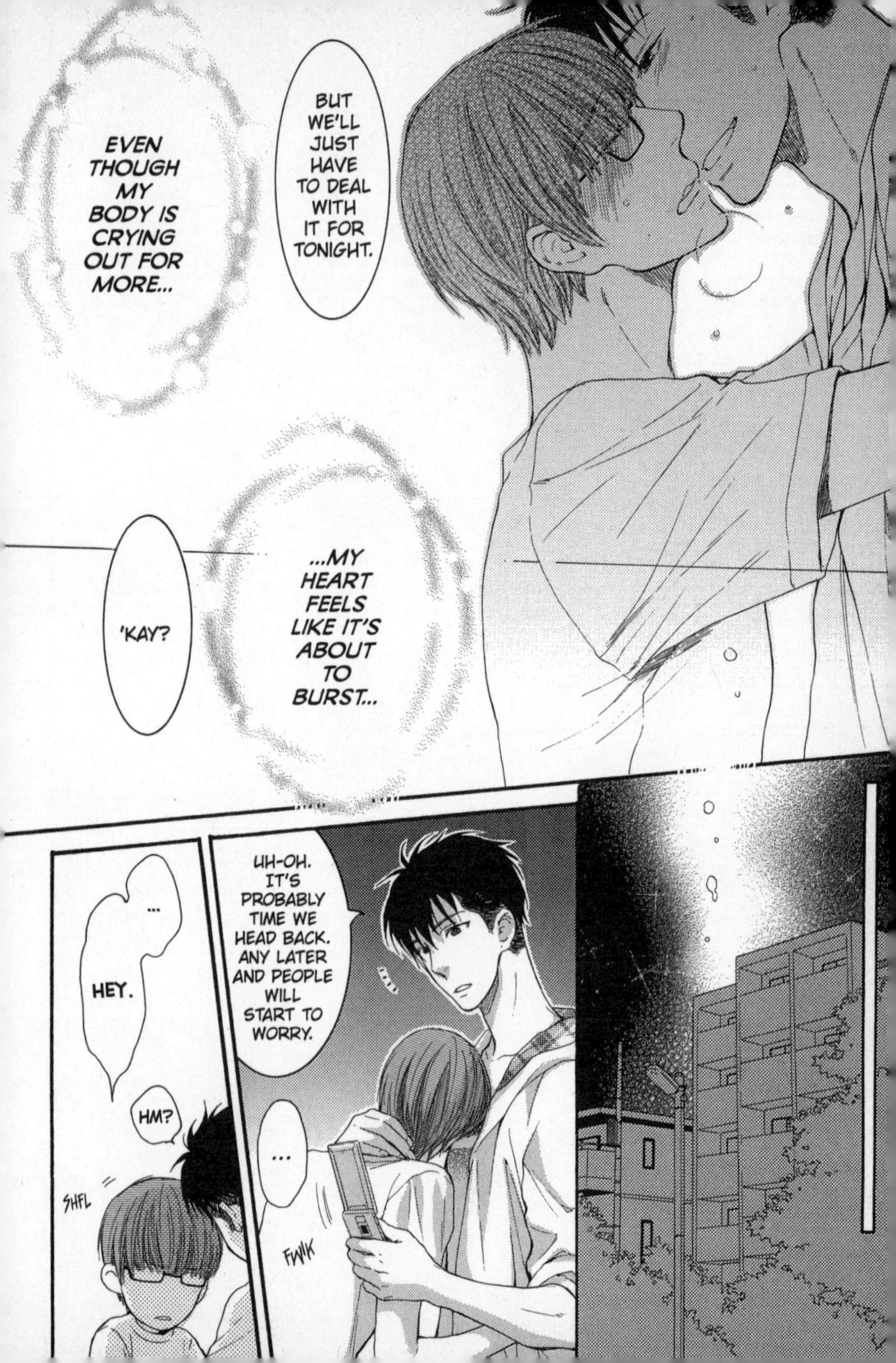
BUT WE'LL JUST HAVE TO DEAL WITH IT FOR TONIGHT.
EVEN THOUGH MY BODY IS CRYING OUT FOR MORE...
...MY HEART FEELS LIKE IT'S ABOUT TO BURST...
'KAY?
UH-OH. IT'S PROBABLY TIME WE HEAD BACK. ANY LATER AND PEOPLE WILL START TO WORRY.
...
FWIK
...
... HEY.
HM?
SHFL

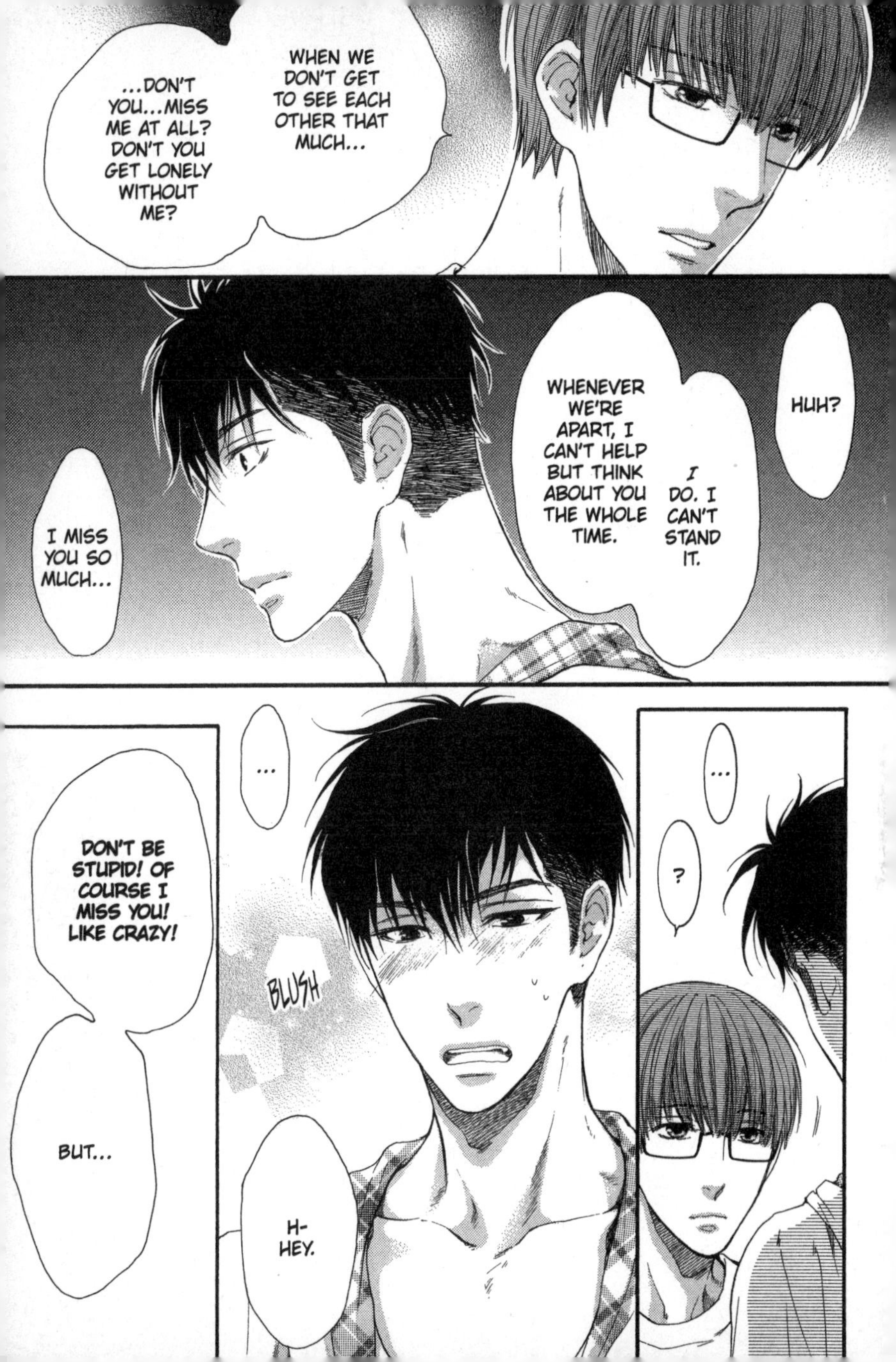
WHEN WE DON'T GET TO SEE EACH OTHER THAT MUCH...
...DON'T YOU...MISS ME AT ALL? DON'T YOU GET LONELY WITHOUT ME?
HUH?
I DO. I CAN'T STAND IT.
WHENEVER WE'RE APART, I CAN'T HELP BUT THINK ABOUT YOU THE WHOLE TIME.
I MISS YOU SO MUCH...
...
?
...
BLUSH
H-HEY.
DON'T BE STUPID! OF COURSE I MISS YOU! LIKE CRAZY!
BUT...

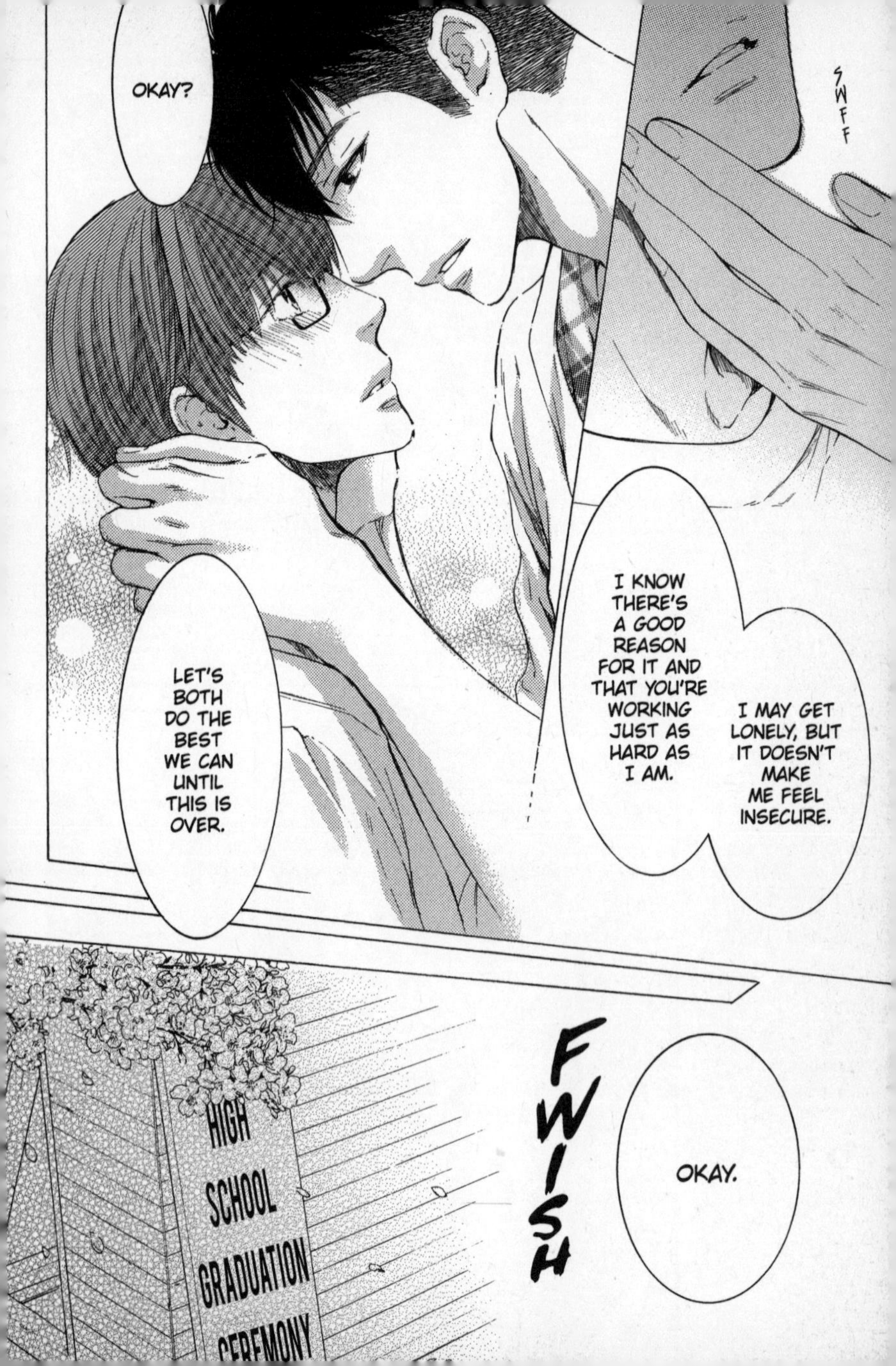
SWFF
I MAY GET LONELY, BUT IT DOESN'T MAKE ME FEEL INSECURE.
I KNOW THERE'S A GOOD REASON FOR IT AND THAT YOU'RE WORKING JUST AS HARD AS I AM.
OKAY?
LET'S BOTH DO THE BEST WE CAN UNTIL THIS IS OVER.
OKAY.
FWISH
HIGH SCHOOL GRADUATION CEREMONY

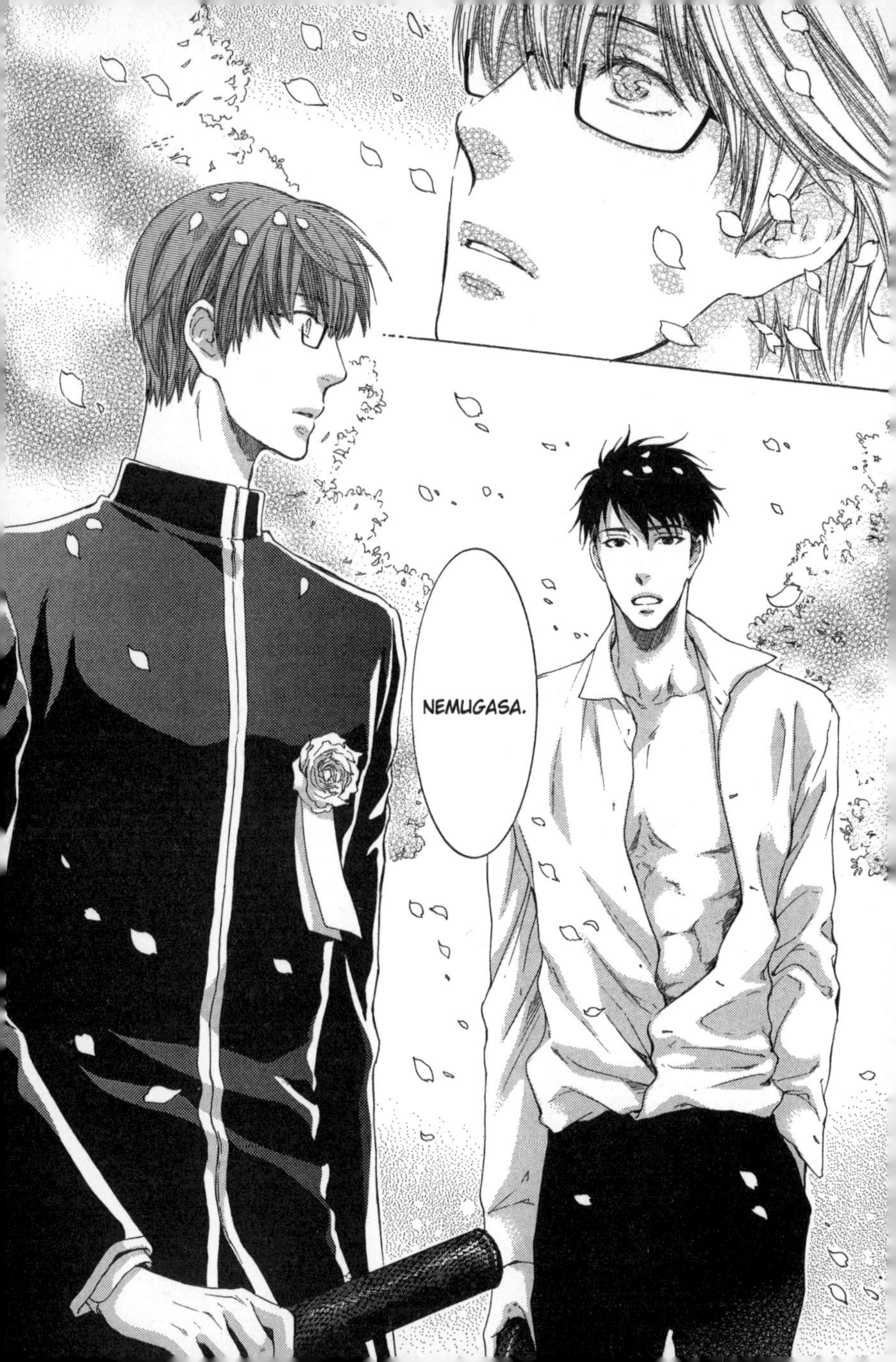
NEMUGASA.

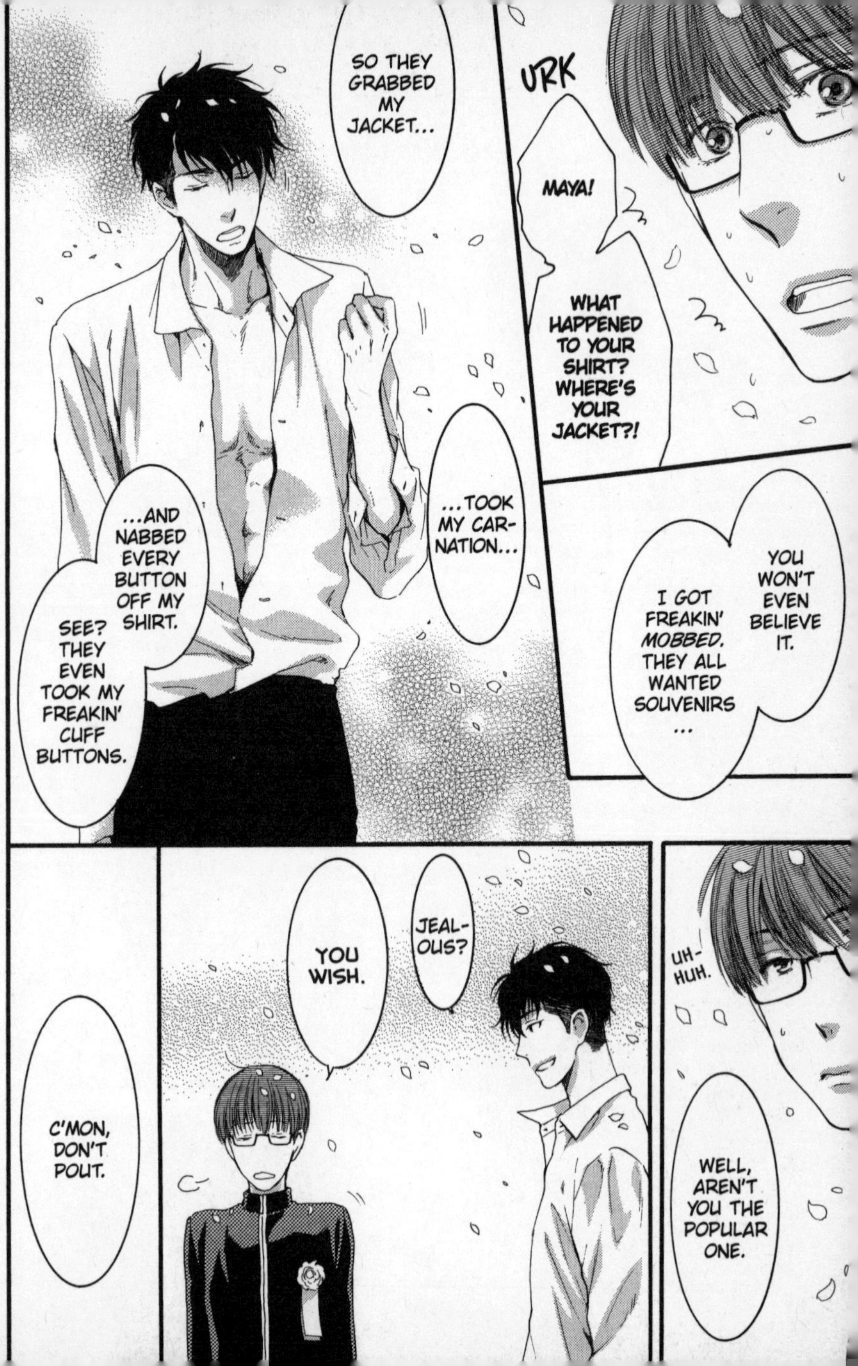
URK
MAYA!
WHAT HAPPENED TO YOUR SHIRT? WHERE'S YOUR JACKET?!
YOU WON'T EVEN BELIEVE IT.
I GOT FREAKIN' *MOBBED*. THEY ALL WANTED SOUVENIRS...
SO THEY GRABBED MY JACKET...
...TOOK MY CAR-NATION...
...AND NABBED EVERY BUTTON OFF MY SHIRT.
SEE? THEY EVEN TOOK MY FREAKIN' CUFF BUTTONS.
UH-HUH.
WELL, AREN'T YOU THE POPULAR ONE.
JEAL-OUS?
YOU WISH.
C'MON, DON'T POUT.

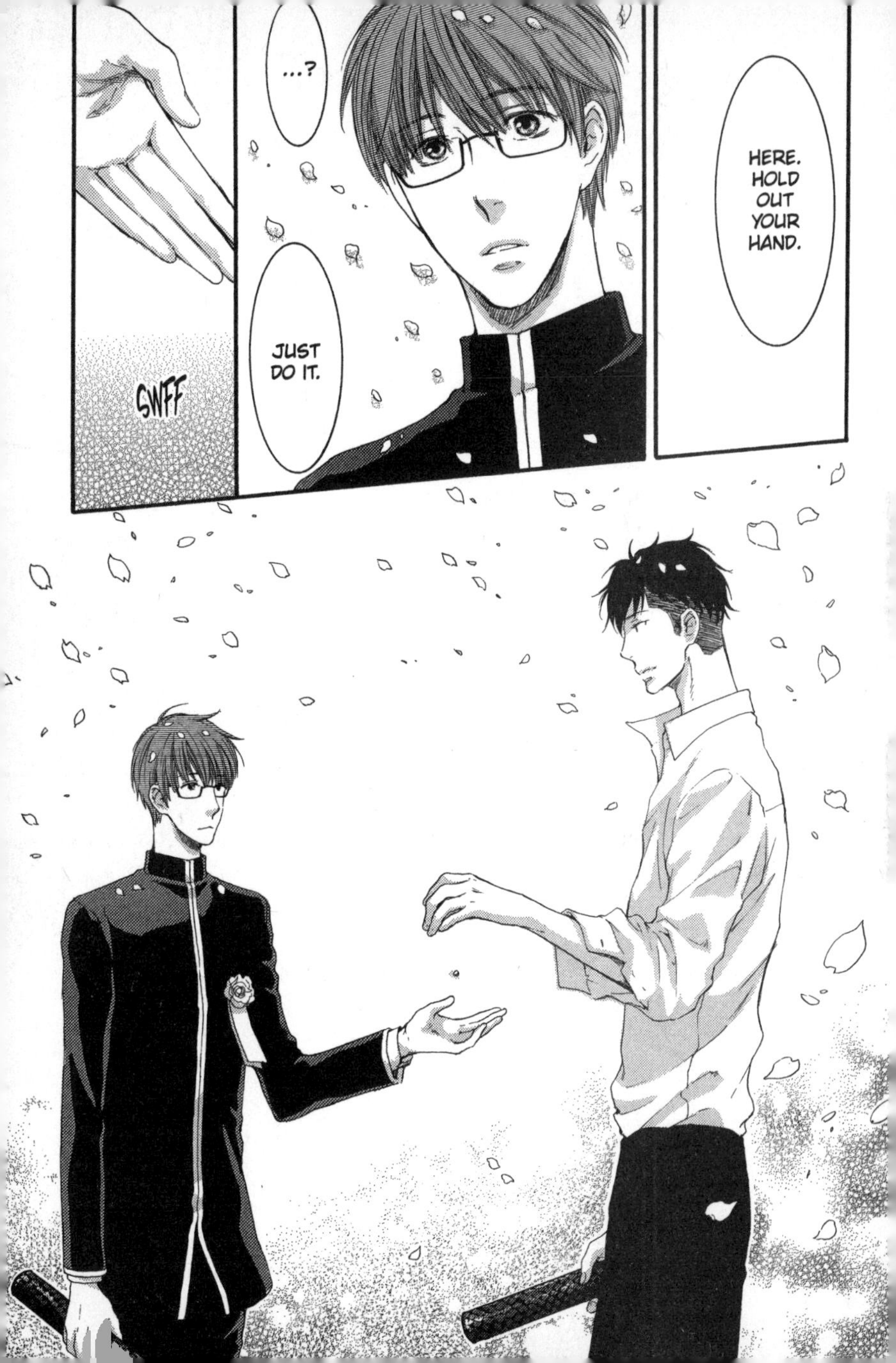
HERE. HOLD OUT YOUR HAND.
...?
JUST DO IT.
SWFF

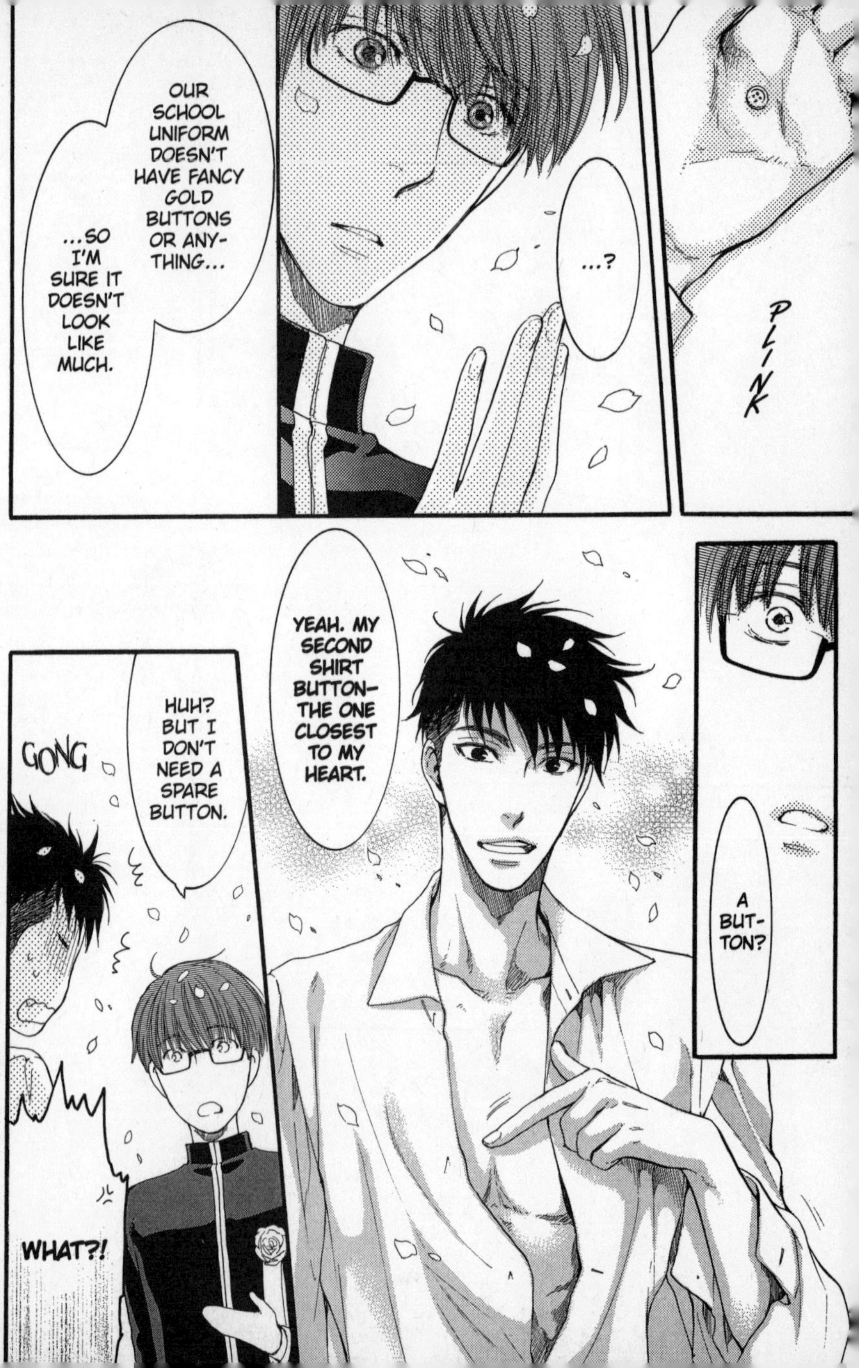
PLINK
...?
OUR SCHOOL UNIFORM DOESN'T HAVE FANCY GOLD BUTTONS OR ANY-THING...
...SO I'M SURE IT DOESN'T LOOK LIKE MUCH.
A BUT-TON?
YEAH. MY SECOND SHIRT BUTTON—THE ONE CLOSEST TO MY HEART.
HUH? BUT I DON'T NEED A SPARE BUTTON.
GONG
WHAT?!

THE SECOND BUTTON IS SAID TO CONTAIN THE EMOTIONS OF ALL THREE HIGH SCHOOL YEARS AND IS GIVEN AS A MEANS OF CONFESSING ONE'S LOVE FOR ANOTHER.

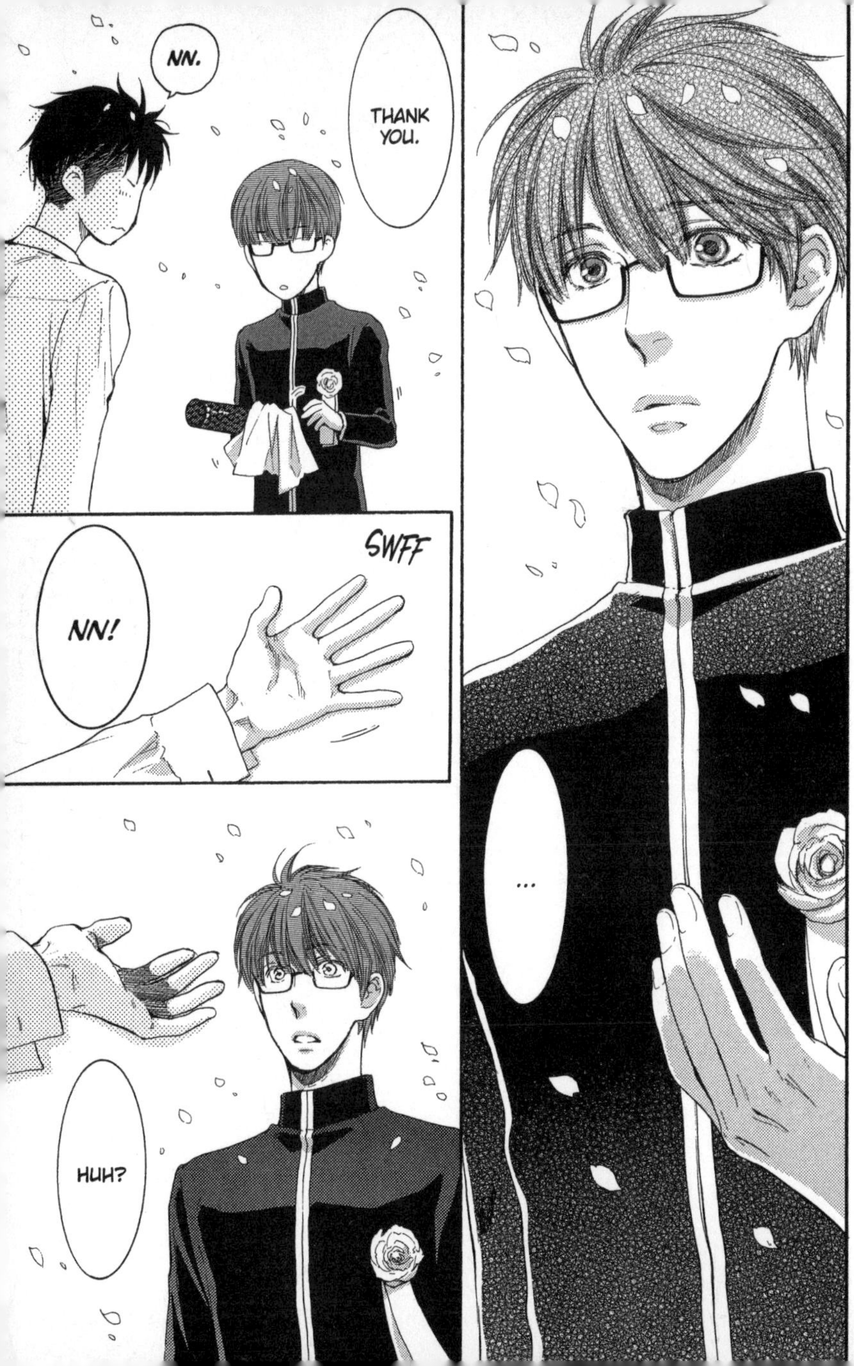
...
THANK YOU.
NN.
SWFF
NN!
HUH?

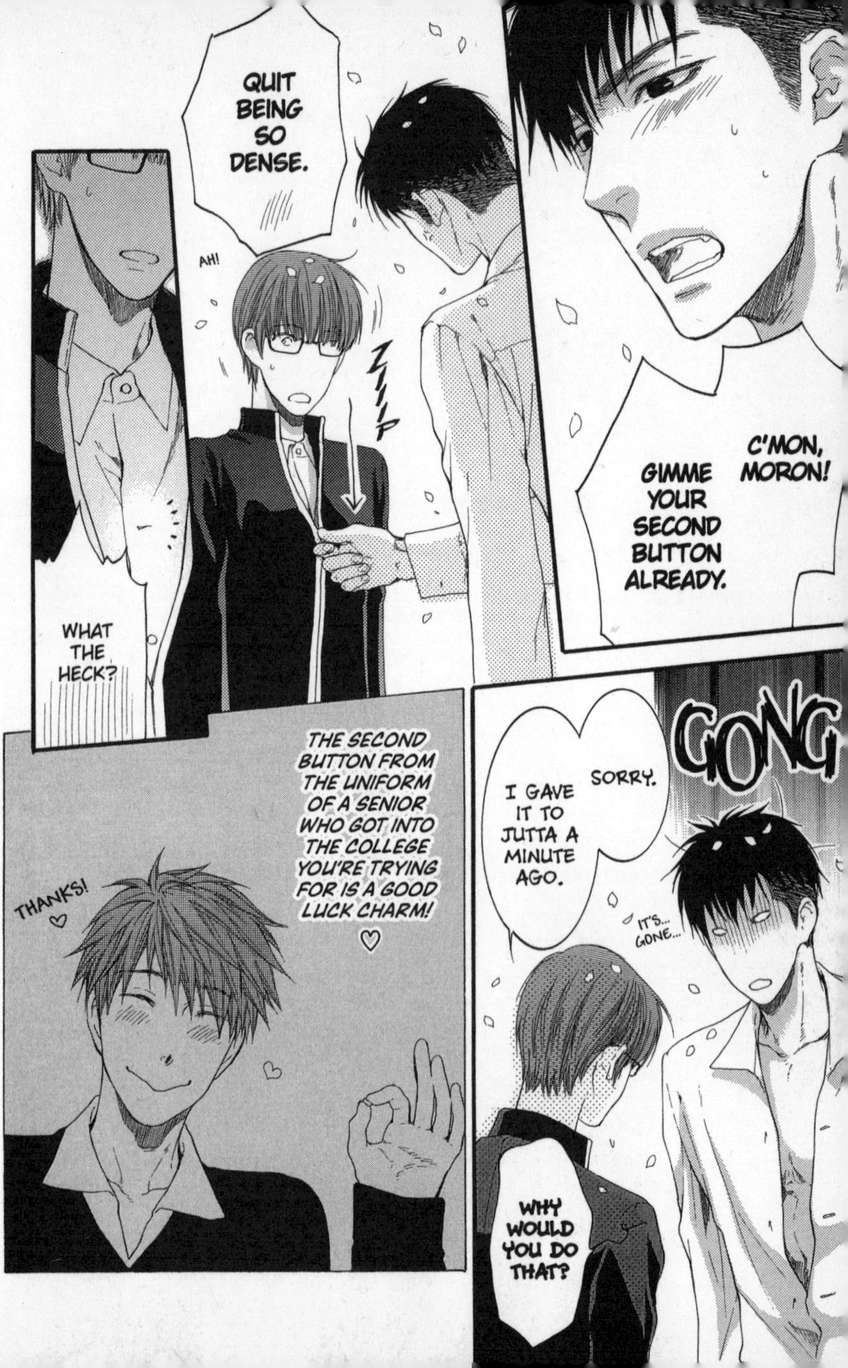
C'MON, MORON!
GIMME YOUR SECOND BUTTON ALREADY.
QUIT BEING SO DENSE.
AH!
ZIIIP
WHAT THE HECK?
GONG
SORRY.
I GAVE IT TO JUTTA A MINUTE AGO.
IT'S... GONE...
WHY WOULD YOU DO THAT?
THE SECOND BUTTON FROM THE UNIFORM OF A SENIOR WHO GOT INTO THE COLLEGE YOU'RE TRYING FOR IS A GOOD LUCK CHARM! ♡
THANKS! ♡

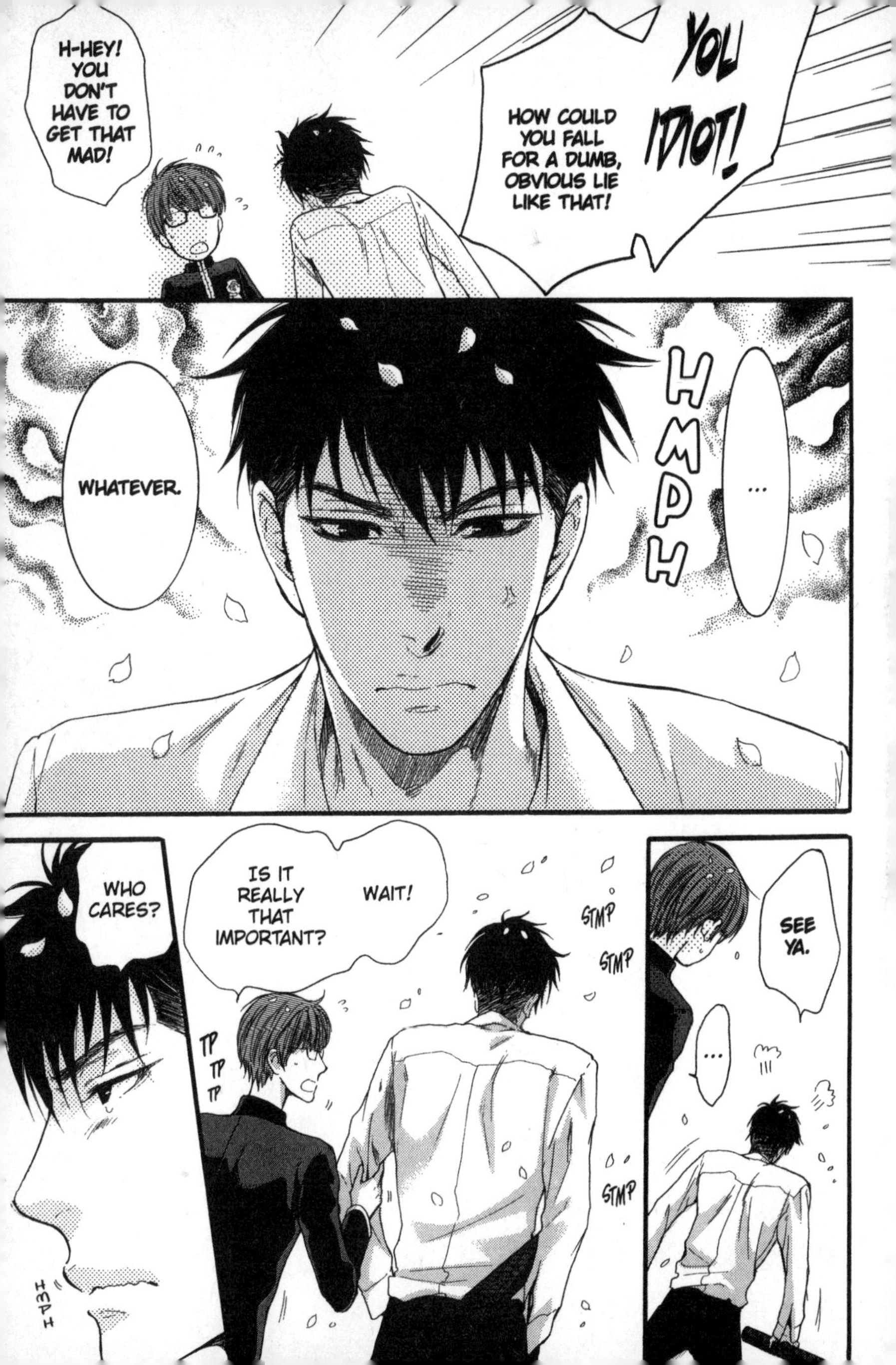
YOU IDIOT!
HOW COULD YOU FALL FOR A DUMB, OBVIOUS LIE LIKE THAT!
H-HEY! YOU DON'T HAVE TO GET THAT MAD!
...
HMPH
WHATEVER.
SEE YA.
...
STMP
STMP
STMP
WAIT!
IS IT REALLY THAT IMPORTANT?
TP TP TP
WHO CARES?
HMPH

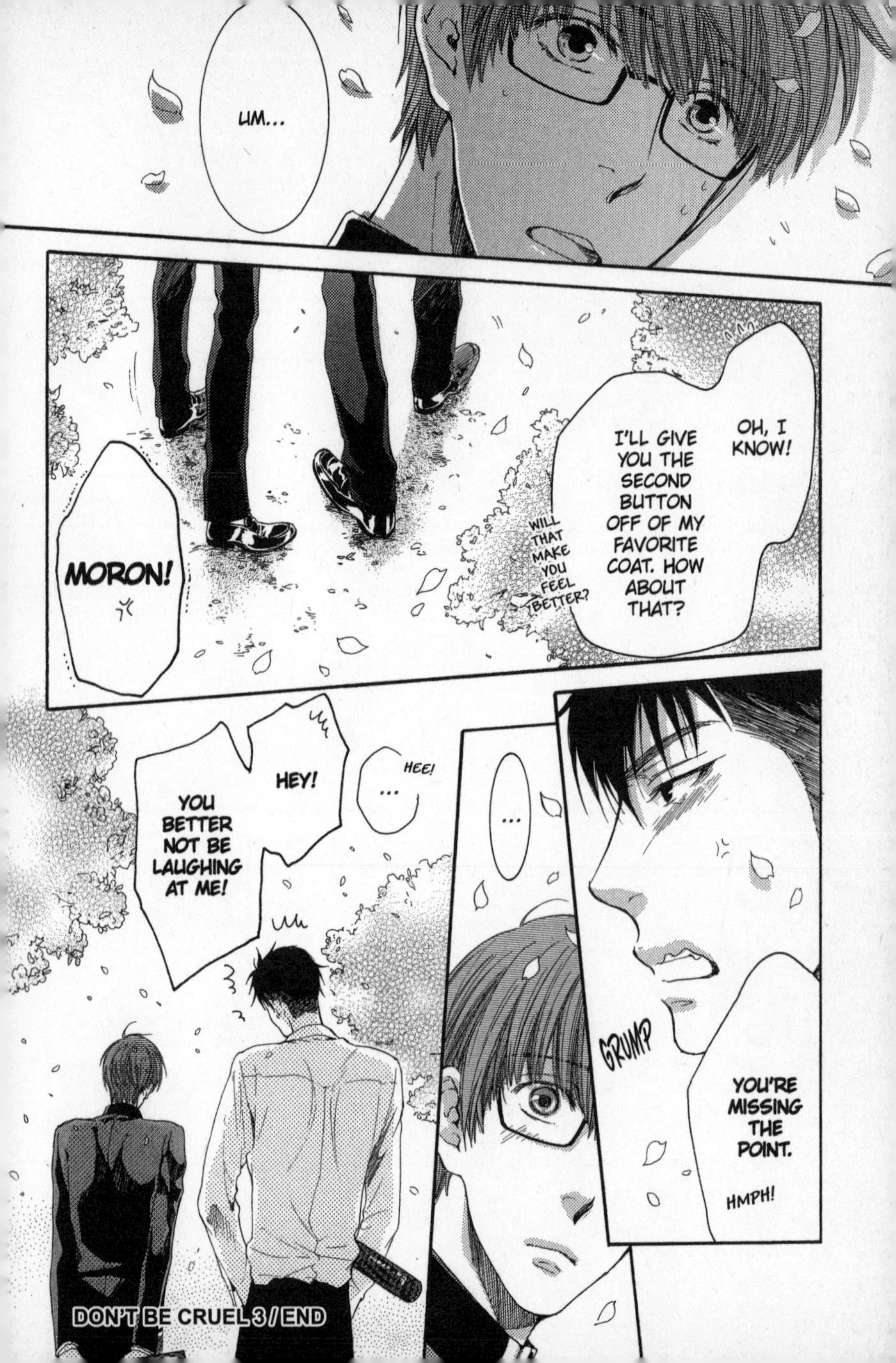
UM...
OH, I KNOW!
I'LL GIVE YOU THE SECOND BUTTON OFF OF MY FAVORITE COAT. HOW ABOUT THAT?
WILL THAT MAKE YOU FEEL BETTER?
MORON!
...
GRUMP
YOU'RE MISSING THE POINT.
HMPH!
...
HEE!
HEY!
YOU BETTER NOT BE LAUGHING AT ME!

DON'T BE CRUEL 3 / END

♥ MAYA'S MAKEOVER

AS YOU NOW KNOW, MAYA DYED HIS HAIR BLACK THIS VOLUME.
I HEAR SOME PEOPLE WERE REALLY SURPRISED BY THAT. WELL,
OKAY, EVERYBODY WAS SURPRISED (GRIMACE). WHEN I TALKED
IT OVER WITH MY EDITOR M-SAN, SHE WAS LIKE, "OH. SURE.
OKAY," GREEN-LIGHTING IT JUST LIKE THAT. I STILL GAVE IT
SOME MORE THOUGHT, BUT I REALLY WANTED TO CHANGE HIS
HAIR, SO I WENT AHEAD AND DID IT. HE HAD BLACK HAIR
FOR ONLY THE VERY LAST CHAPTER OF THIS VOLUME, SO I
DECIDED TO ADD SOME BLACK-HAIRED MAYA BONUS CONTENT
TO HELP PEOPLE GET USED TO THE CHANGE (SMILES). I KNOW
THERE ARE LOTS OF READERS OUT THERE WHO TEND TO READ
JUST THE COLLECTED VOLUMES, SO I CAN'T WAIT TO HEAR WHAT
THEY THINK OF HIS NEW LOOK. IF YOU'D LIKE, PLEASE SEND ME
YOUR COMMENTS AND FEEDBACK.

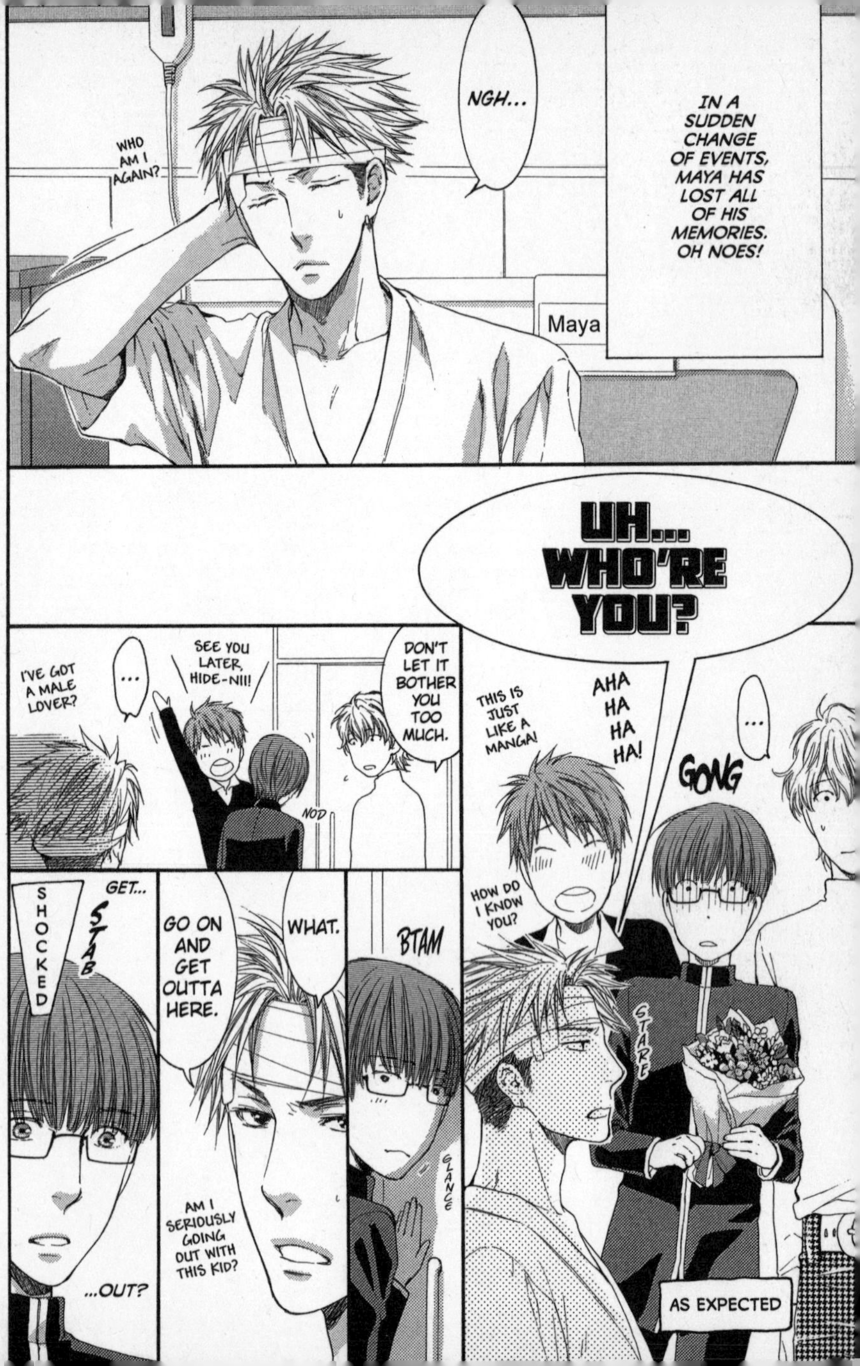
IN A SUDDEN CHANGE OF EVENTS, MAYA HAS LOST ALL OF HIS MEMORIES. OH NOES!
NGH...
WHO AM I AGAIN?
Maya
UH... WHO'RE YOU?
...
GONG
AHA HA HA HA!
THIS IS JUST LIKE A MANGA!
HOW DO I KNOW YOU?
STARE
AS EXPECTED
DON'T LET IT BOTHER YOU TOO MUCH.
NOD
SEE YOU LATER, HIDE-NII!
...
I'VE GOT A MALE LOVER?
BTAM
GLANCE
WHAT.
GO ON AND GET OUTTA HERE.
AM I SERIOUSLY GOING OUT WITH THIS KID?
GET...
STAB
SHOCKED
...OUT?

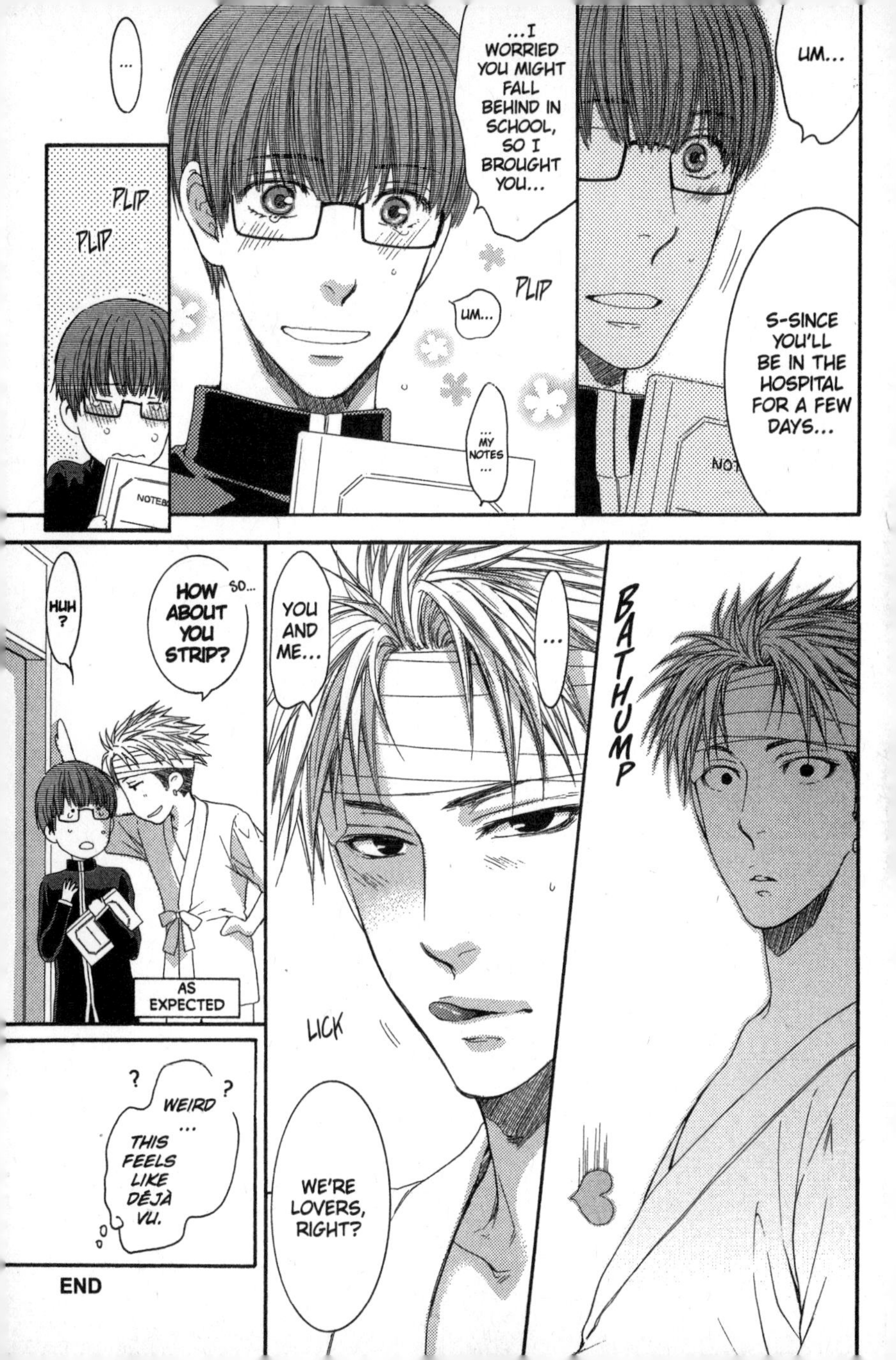
UM...
S-SINCE YOU'LL BE IN THE HOSPITAL FOR A FEW DAYS...
...I WORRIED YOU MIGHT FALL BEHIND IN SCHOOL, SO I BROUGHT YOU...
PLIP
UM...
...MY NOTES...
...
PLIP
PLIP
BATHUMP
...
YOU AND ME...
LICK
WE'RE LOVERS, RIGHT?
SO...
HOW ABOUT YOU STRIP?
HUH?
AS EXPECTED
? ?
WEIRD... THIS FEELS LIKE DÉJÀ VU.
END

WHEN I READ OVER THE CHAPTERS THAT WERE GOING TO BE COLLECTED INTO THIS VOLUME, IT FELT LIKE THERE WAS SOMETHING LACKING. SO I DECIDED TO ADD ANOTHER BONUS CHAPTER TO FIX THAT. YOU SEE...THERE WAS A CRITICAL LACK OF NEMU-NEMU'S TIGHTY-WHITIES. ONLY ONE PANEL IN FIVE CHAPTERS ISN'T ENOUGH! I'M SURE BY THIS POINT I MUST HAVE INFECTED SOME OF YOU WITH MY LOVE OF UNDERWEAR... NO, I KNOW I HAVE! AND NOT ON JUST ANYONE EITHER! IT HAS TO BE ON A CHARACTER THAT IS THE PICTURE OF SERIOUS RESPONSIBILITY! THEY'RE SO SERIOUS, BUT WHEN YOU—OKAY I'LL STOP NOW.

❀ MY MIGHTY HELPERS WHO I AM ALWAYS THANKFUL FOR. ♥
SUPER EDITOR: MIYOSHI-SAN GRAPHIC NOVEL EDITOR: SATO-SAN
EXCELLENT BACKGROUNDS: MUCCHI   AWESOME SCREENTONE: M-IKO
HELP FOR CHAPTER 5 ONLY: MY SISTER   And You!!

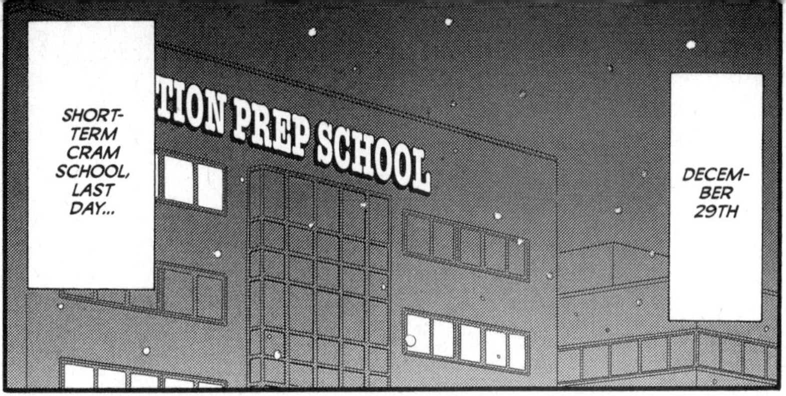
DECEMBER 29TH
TION PREP SCHOOL
SHORT-TERM CRAM SCHOOL, LAST DAY...

FIRST ATTEMPT AT A MIDNIGHT TRYST

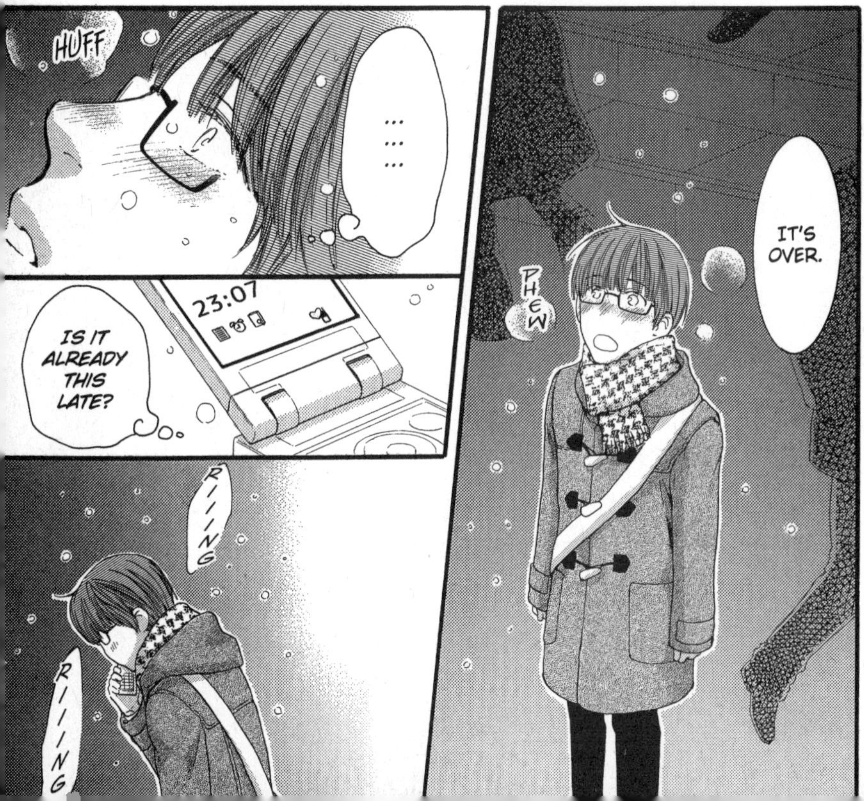
IT'S OVER.
PHEW
......
HUFF
23:07
IS IT ALREADY THIS LATE?
RIIING
RIIING

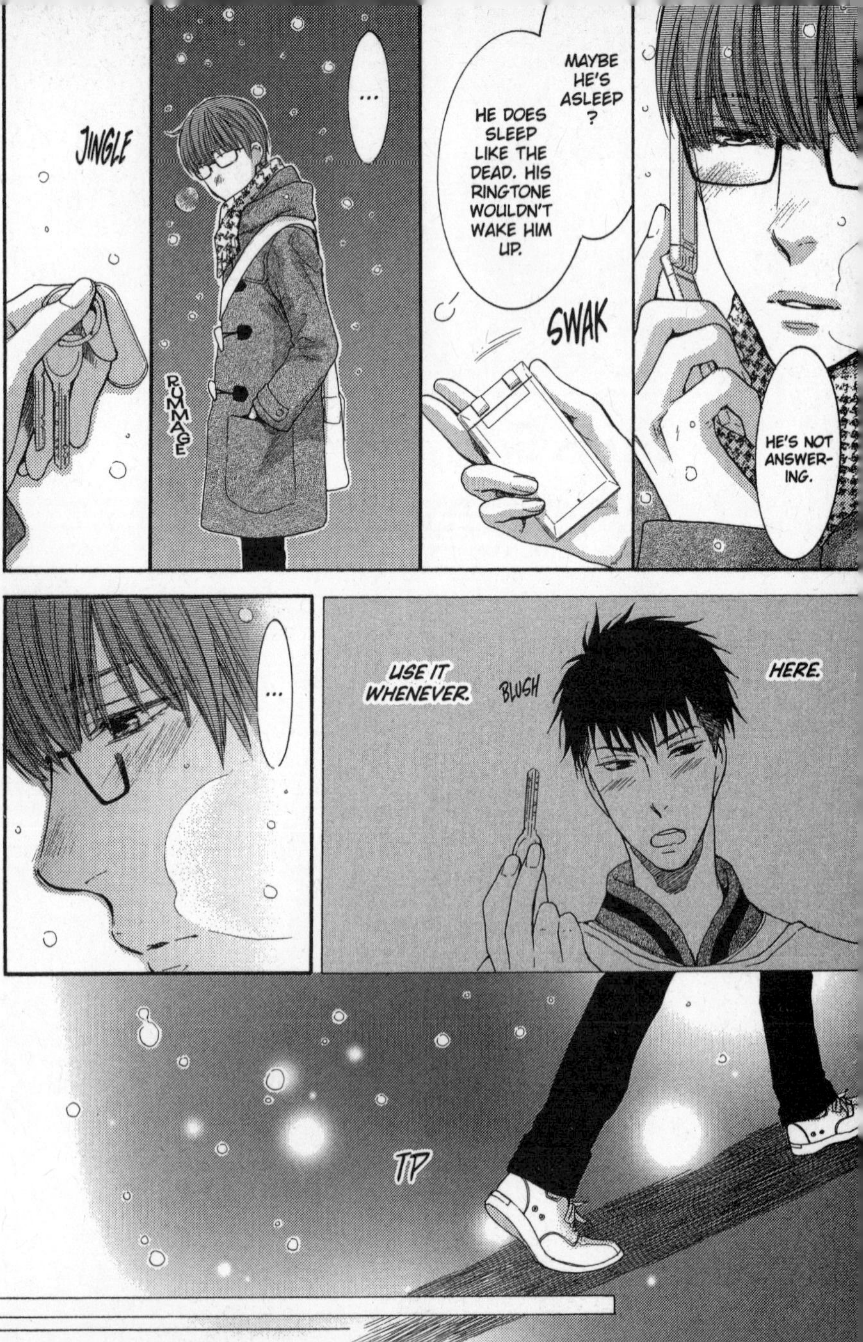
HE'S NOT ANSWER-ING.
MAYBE HE'S ASLEEP?
HE DOES SLEEP LIKE THE DEAD. HIS RINGTONE WOULDN'T WAKE HIM UP.
SWAK
...
RUMMAGE
JINGLE
HERE.
BLUSH
USE IT WHENEVER.
...
TP

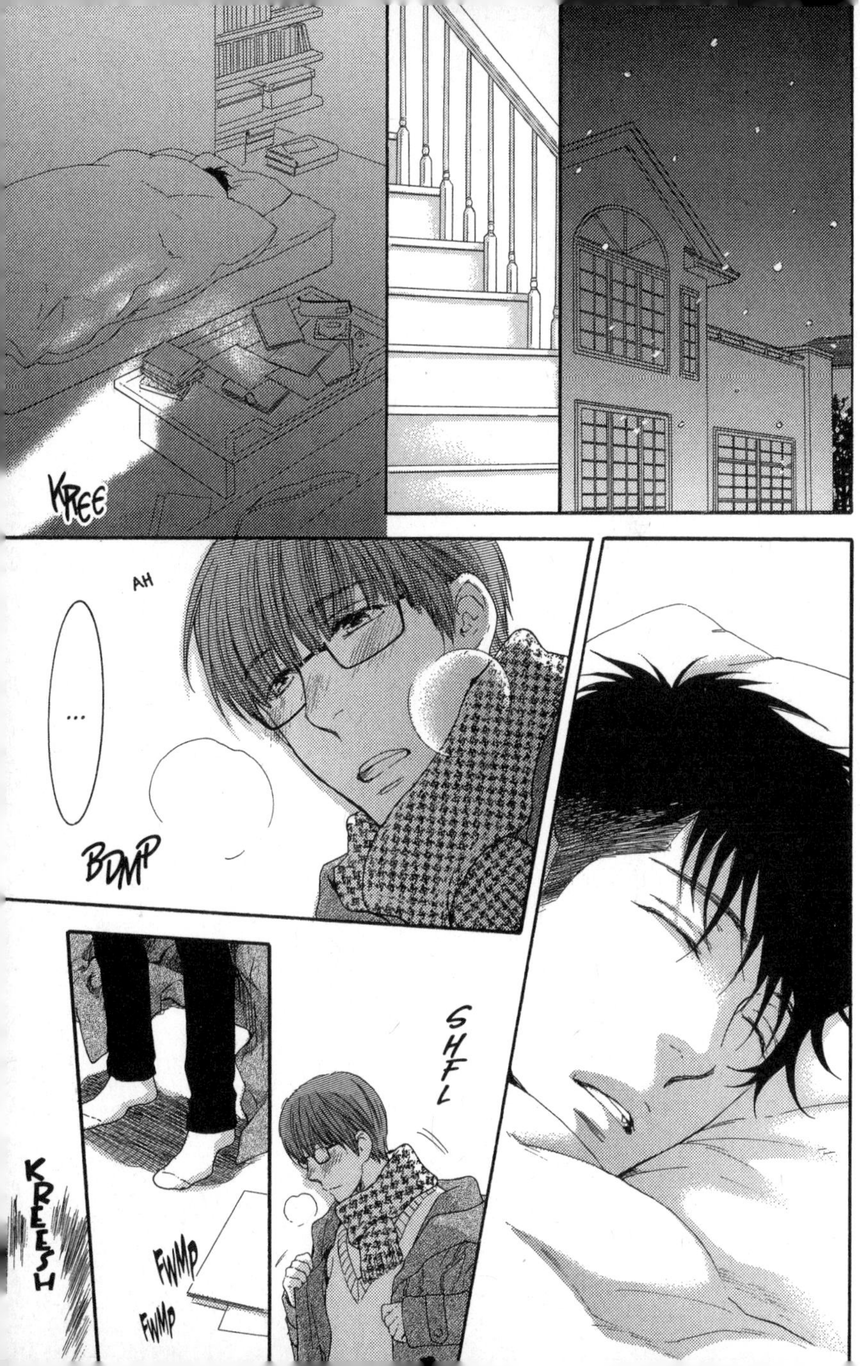

KREE
AH
...
BDMP
SHFL
KREESH
FWMP
FWMP

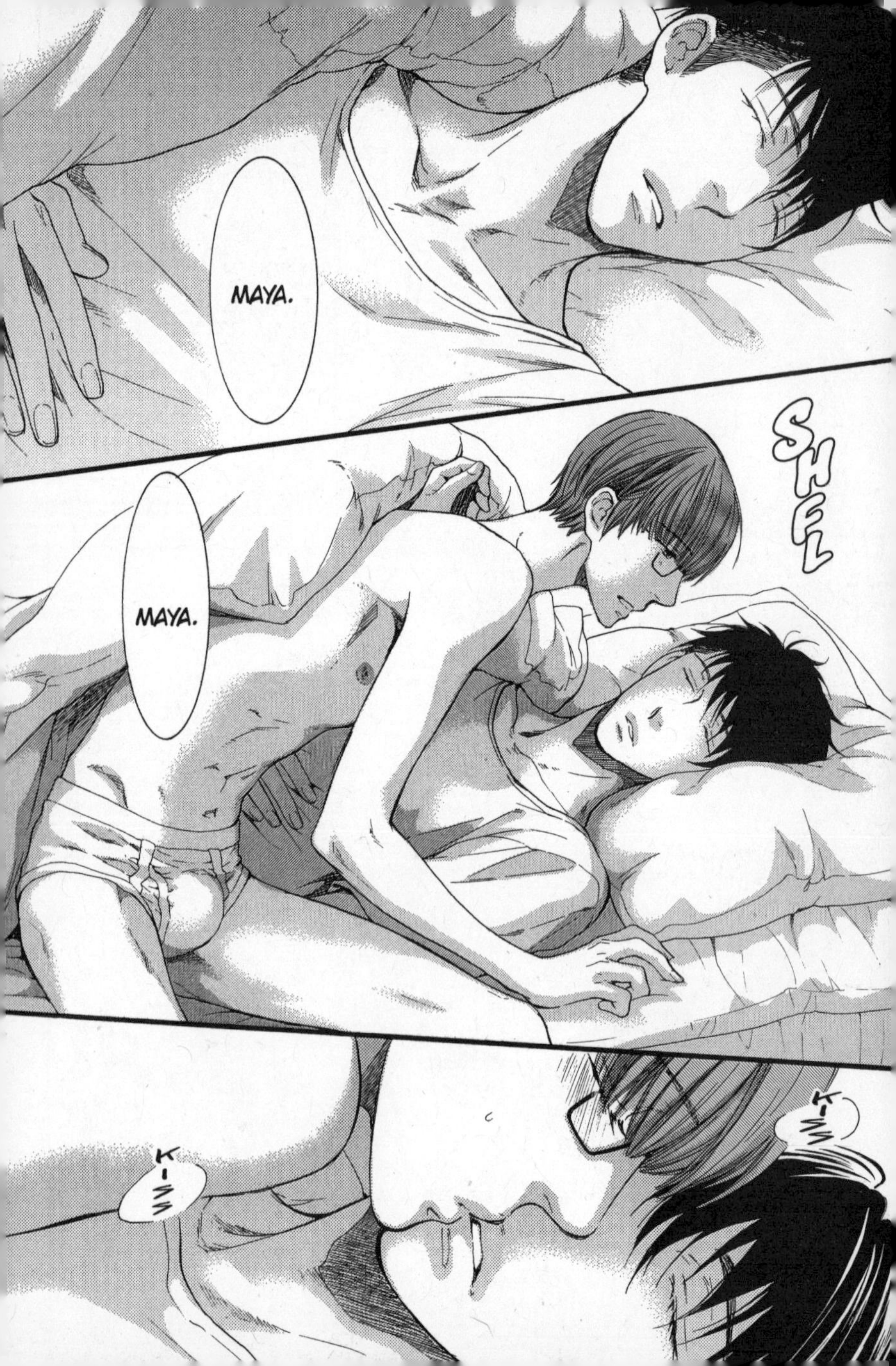
MAYA.
SHFL
MAYA.
KISS
KISS

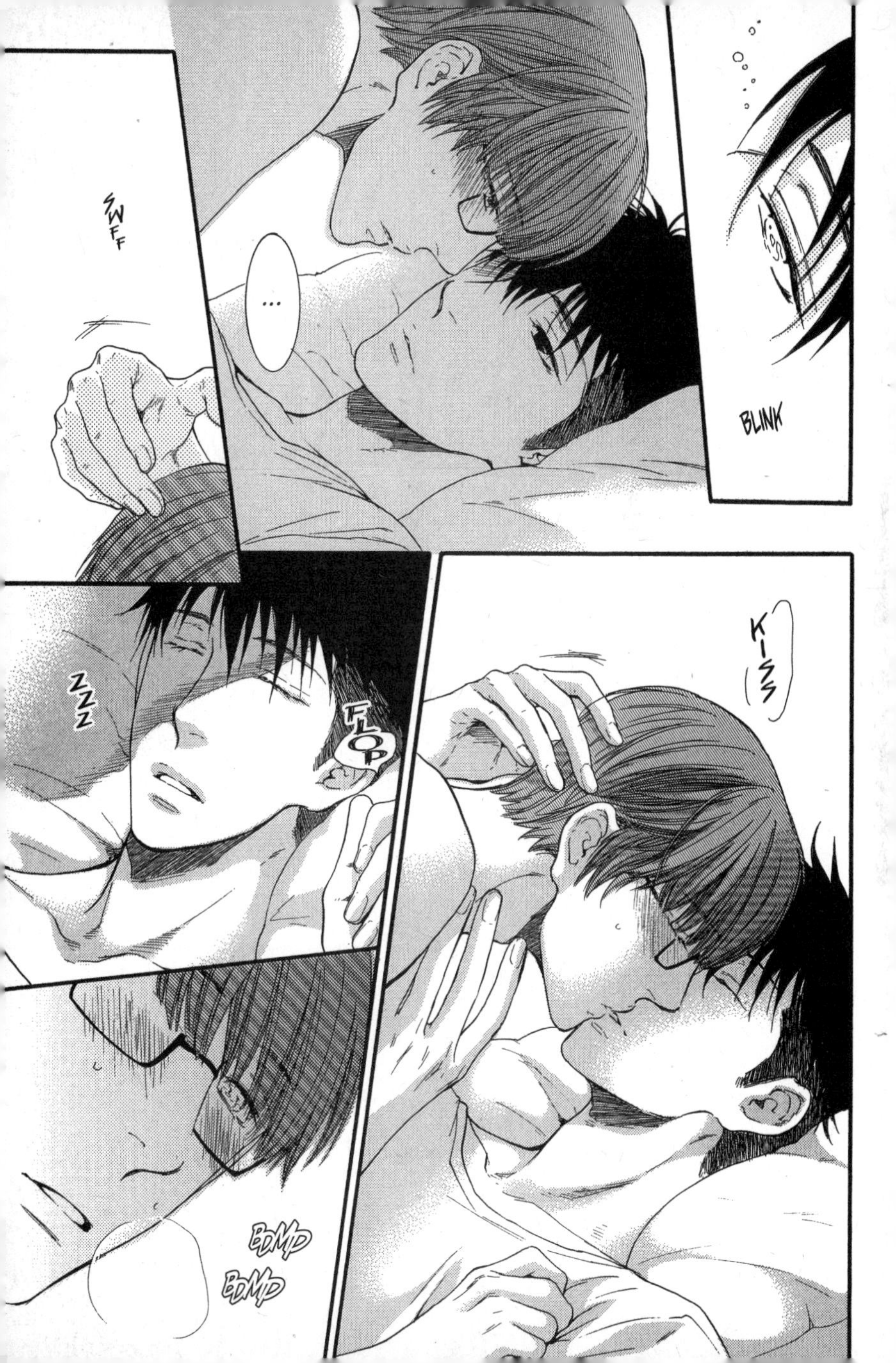
KISS
BLINK
...
SWFF
KISS
FLOP
ZZZ
BDMP
BDMP

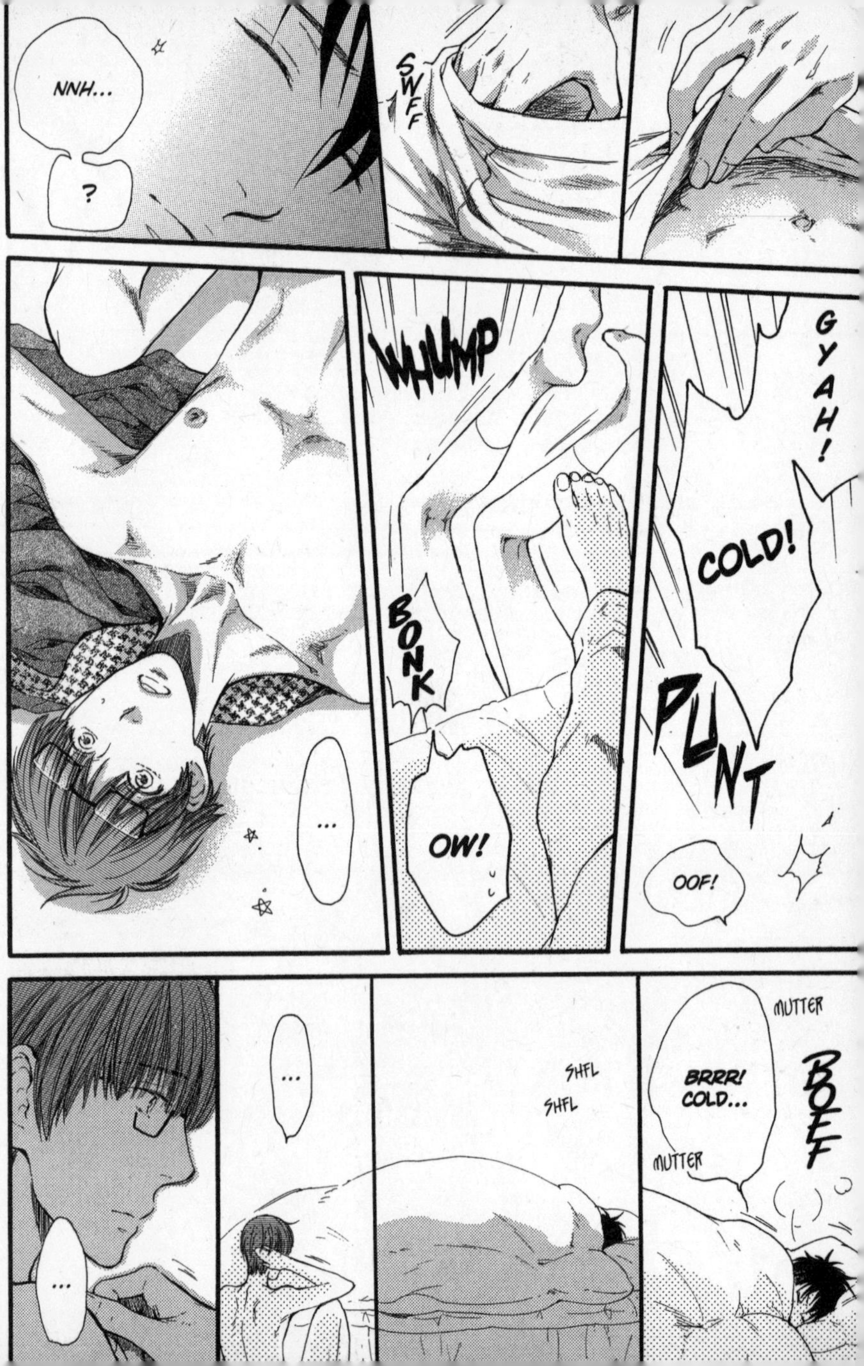
SWFF
NNH...
?
GYAH!
COLD!
PUNT
OOF!
WHUMP
BONK
OW!
...
MUTTER
BRRR! COLD...
BOFF
MUTTER
SHFL
SHFL
...
...

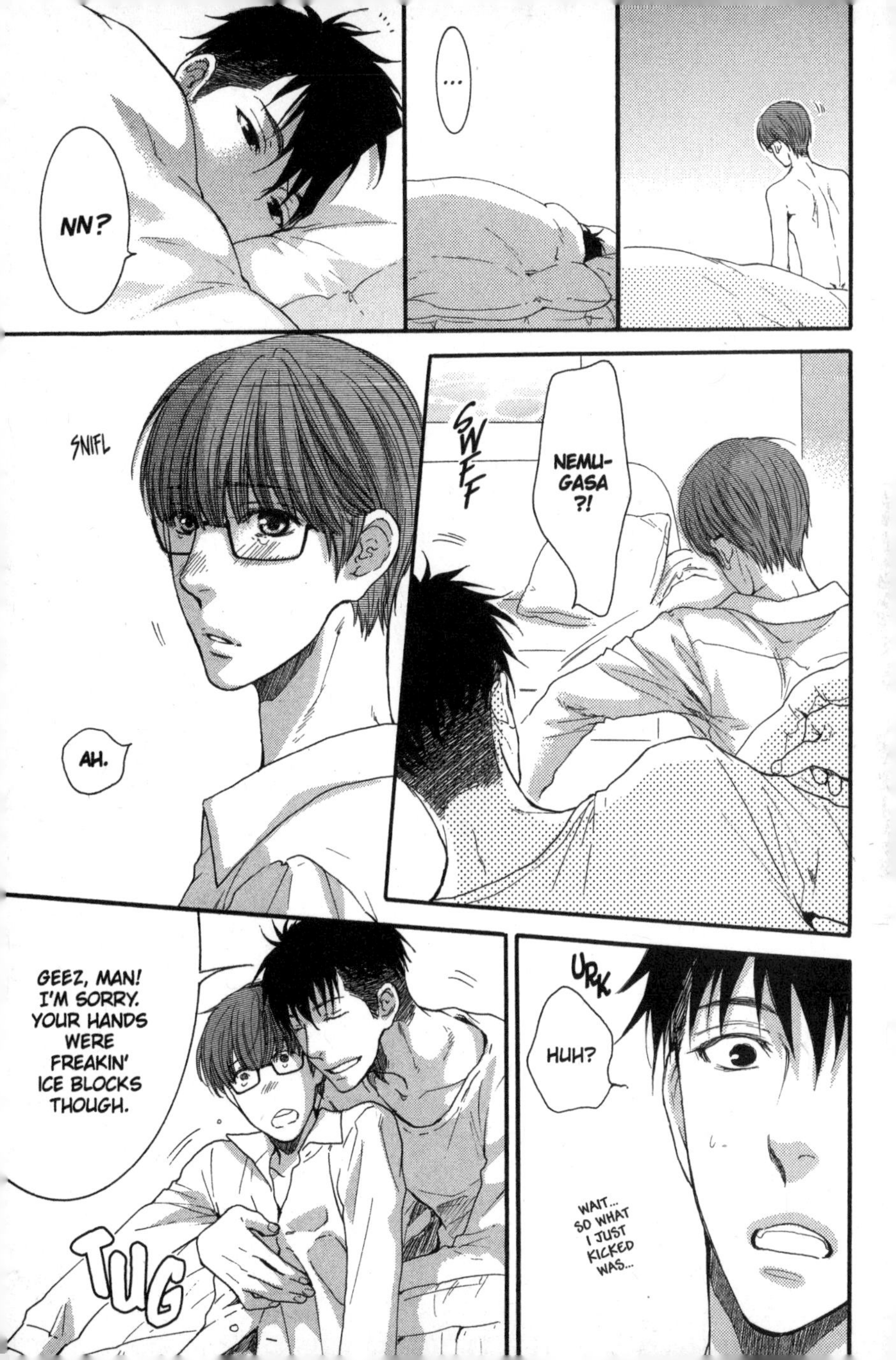
...
NN?
SWFF
NEMU-GASA?!
SNIFL
AH.
URK
HUH?
WAIT... SO WHAT I JUST KICKED WAS...
GEEZ, MAN! I'M SORRY. YOUR HANDS WERE FREAKIN' ICE BLOCKS THOUGH.
TUG

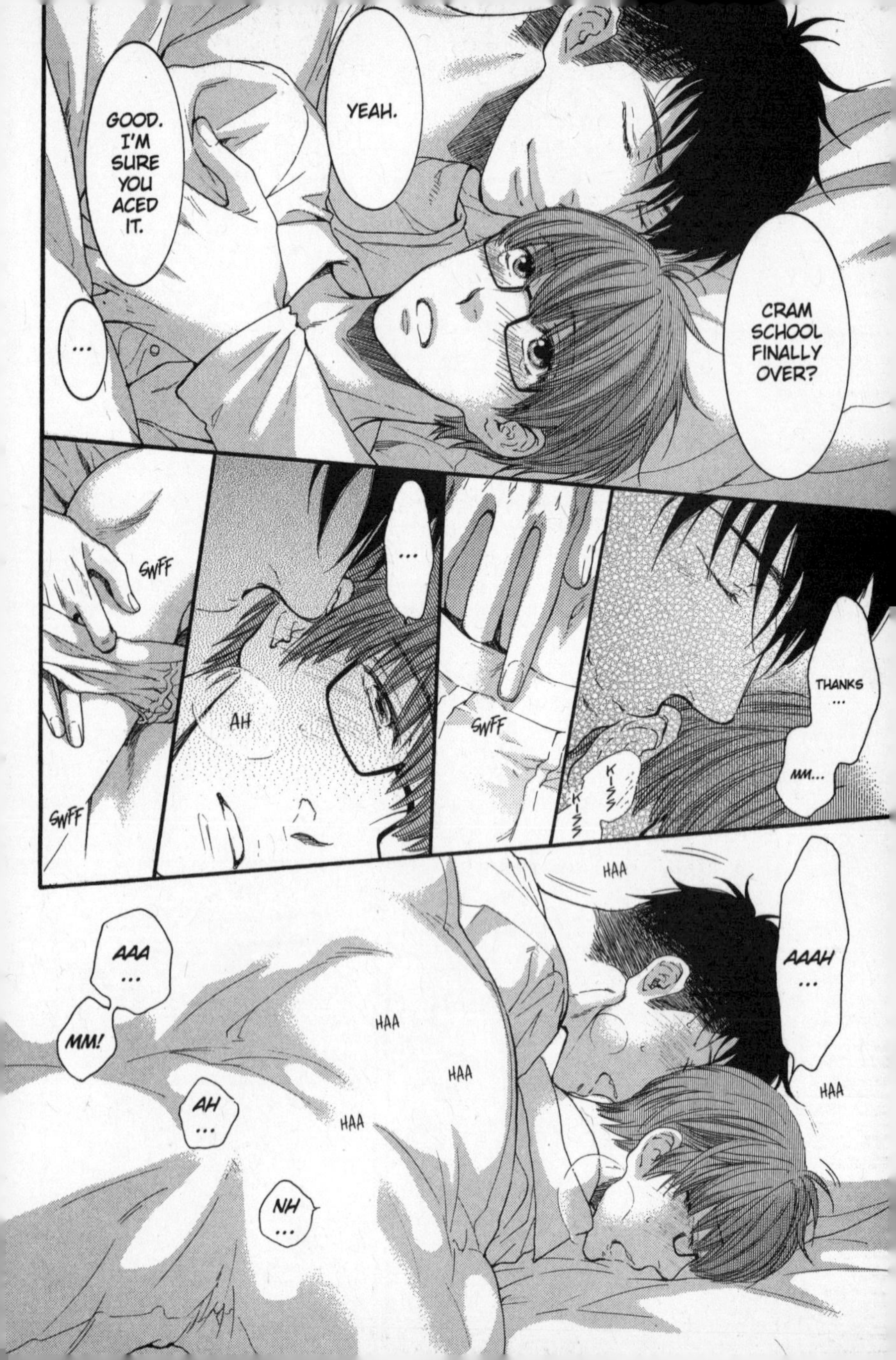
CRAM SCHOOL FINALLY OVER?
YEAH.
GOOD. I'M SURE YOU ACED IT.
...
THANKS ...
MM...
KISS KISS
SWFF
...
AH
SWFF
SWFF
HAA
AAAH ...
HAA
AAA ...
MM!
HAA
HAA
AH ...
HAA
NH ...

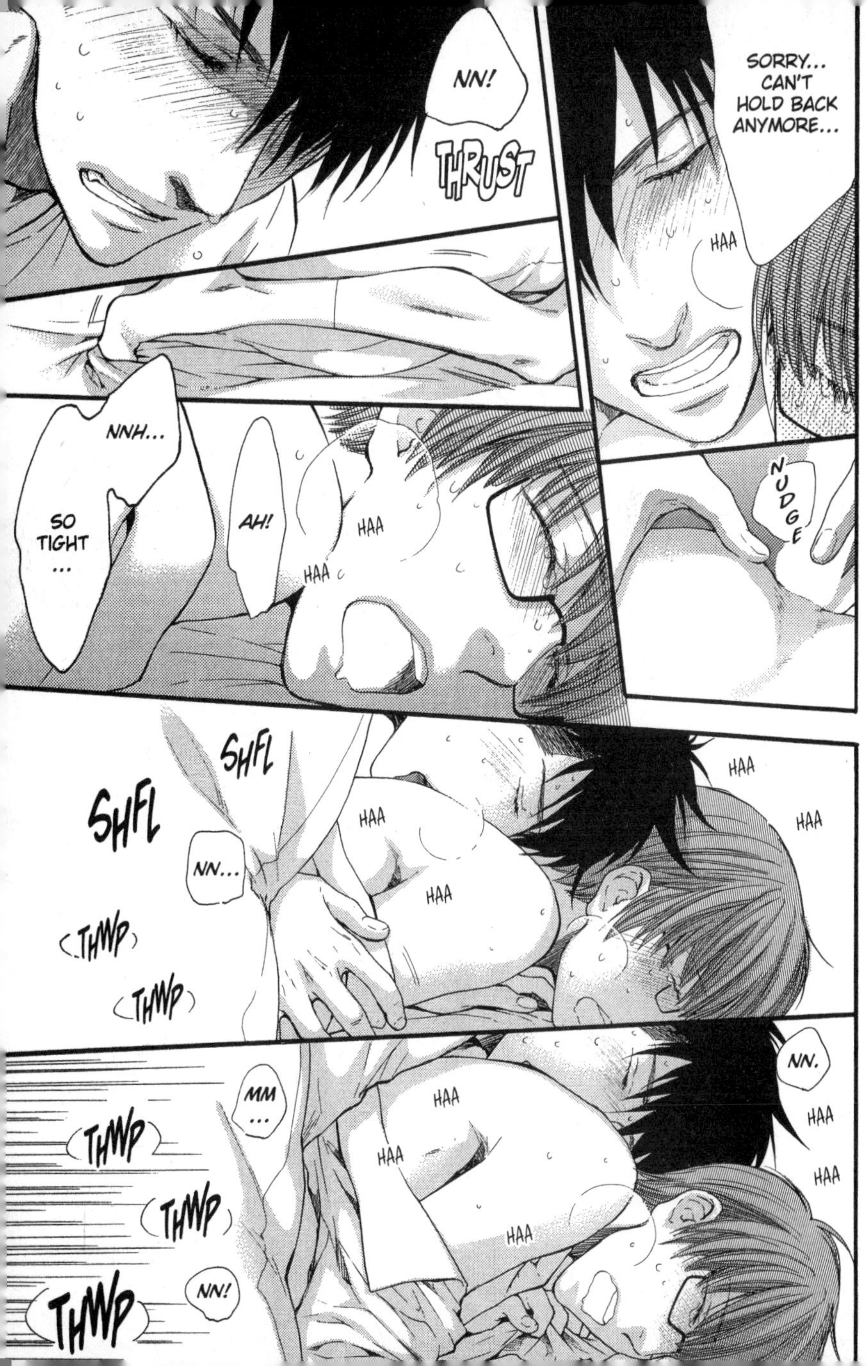
SORRY... CAN'T HOLD BACK ANYMORE...
HAA
NN!
THRUST
NUDGE
AH!
HAA
HAA
NNH...
SO TIGHT ...
HAA
HAA
SHFL
HAA
HAA
SHFL
NN...
THWP
THWP
NN.
HAA
HAA
HAA
MM ...
HAA
HAA
THWP
THWP
NN!
THWP

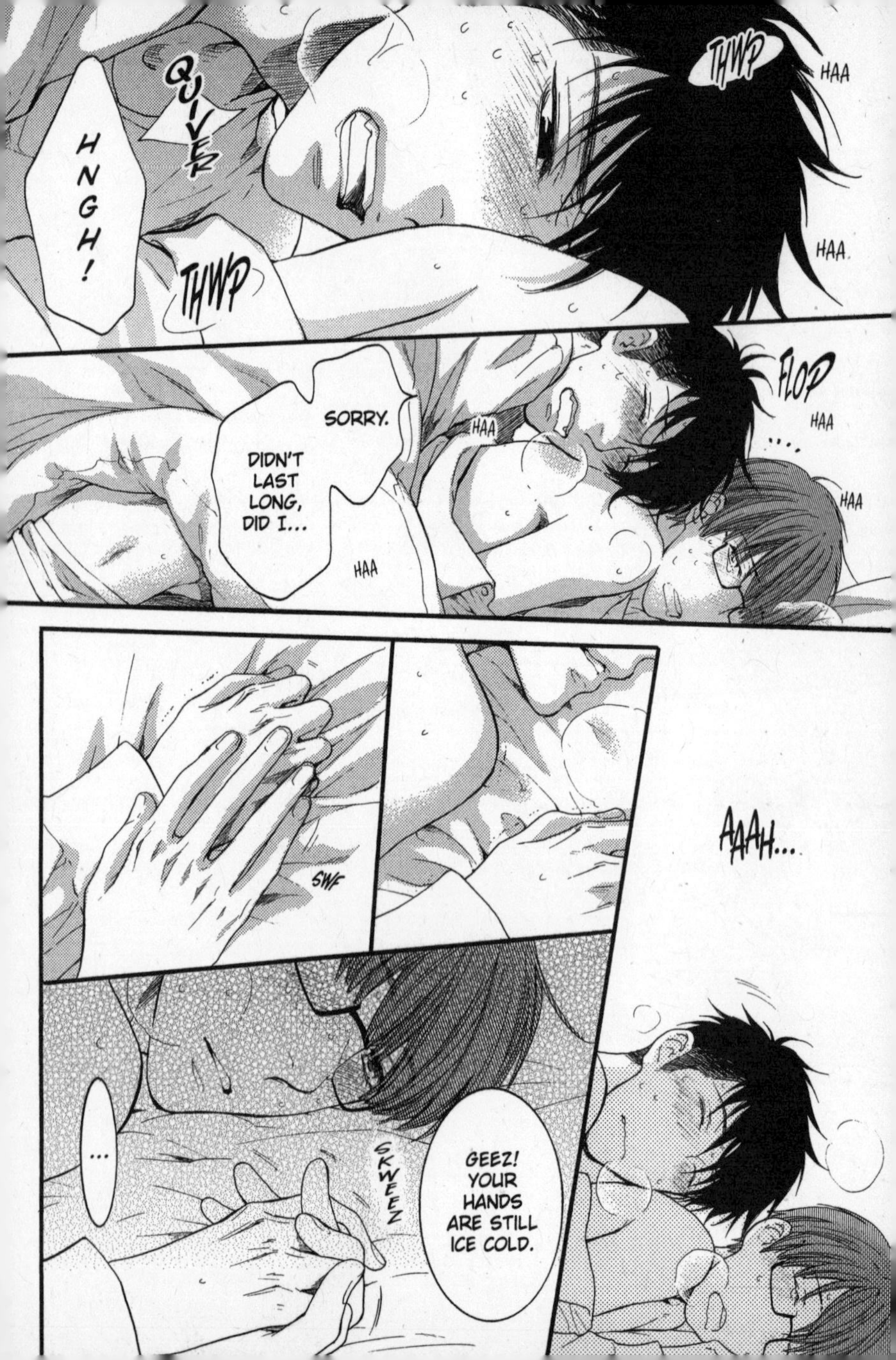
THWP
HAA
QUIVER
HAA
HNGH!
THWP
FLOP
HAA
...
HAA
HAA
SORRY.
DIDN'T LAST LONG, DID I...
HAA
AAAH...
SWF
GEEZ! YOUR HANDS ARE STILL ICE COLD.
SKWEEZ
...

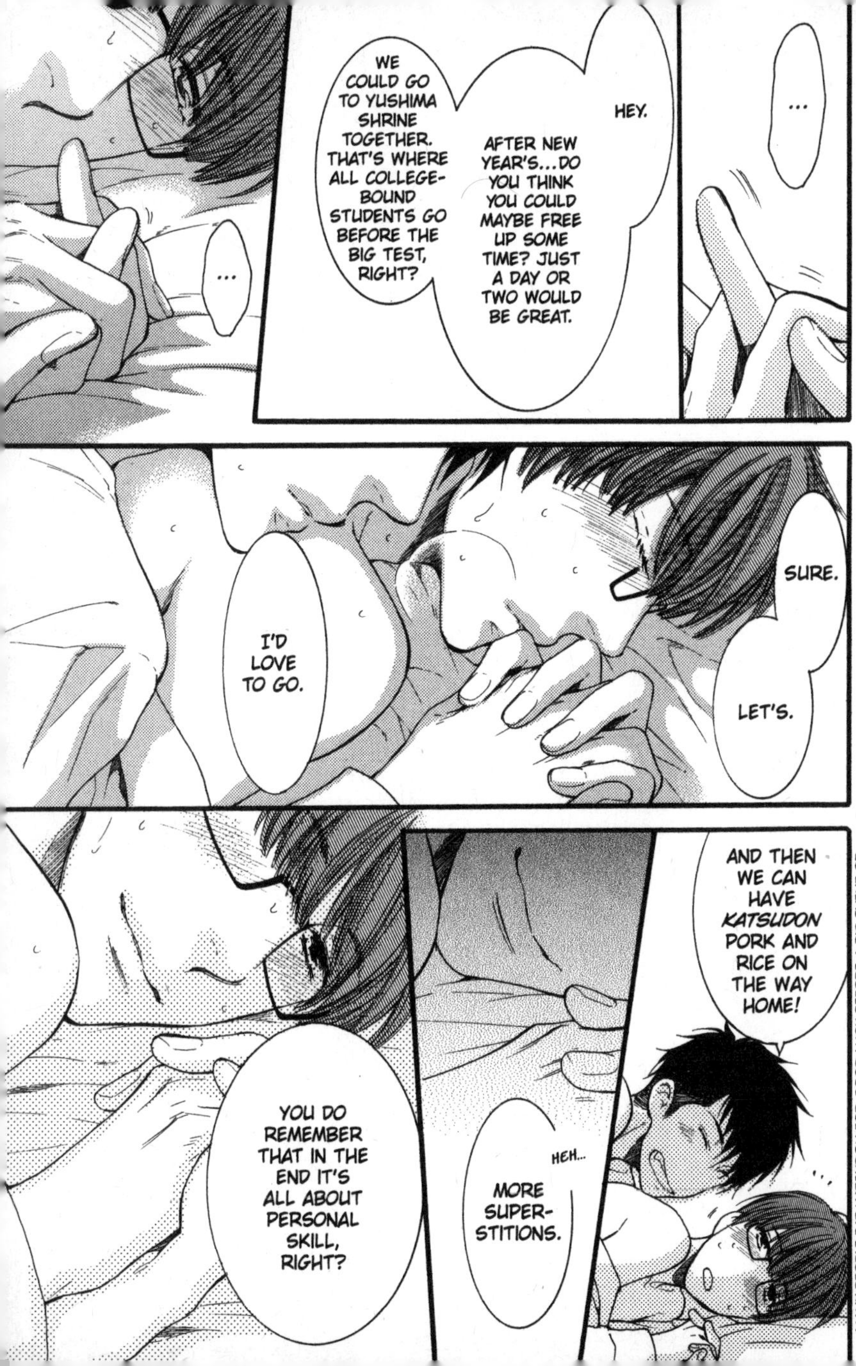
...
HEY.
AFTER NEW YEAR'S...DO YOU THINK YOU COULD MAYBE FREE UP SOME TIME? JUST A DAY OR TWO WOULD BE GREAT.
WE COULD GO TO YUSHIMA SHRINE TOGETHER. THAT'S WHERE ALL COLLEGE-BOUND STUDENTS GO BEFORE THE BIG TEST, RIGHT?
...
SURE.
LET'S.
I'D LOVE TO GO.
AND THEN WE CAN HAVE *KATSUDON* PORK AND RICE ON THE WAY HOME!
HEH...
MORE SUPER-STITIONS.
...
YOU DO REMEMBER THAT IN THE END IT'S ALL ABOUT PERSONAL SKILL, RIGHT?

MANY PEOPLE EAT KATSUDON FOR GOOD LUCK BEFORE A BIG EVENT OR TEST BECAUSE THE *KATSU* IN *KATSUDON* IS A HOMOPHONE FOR "TO WIN."

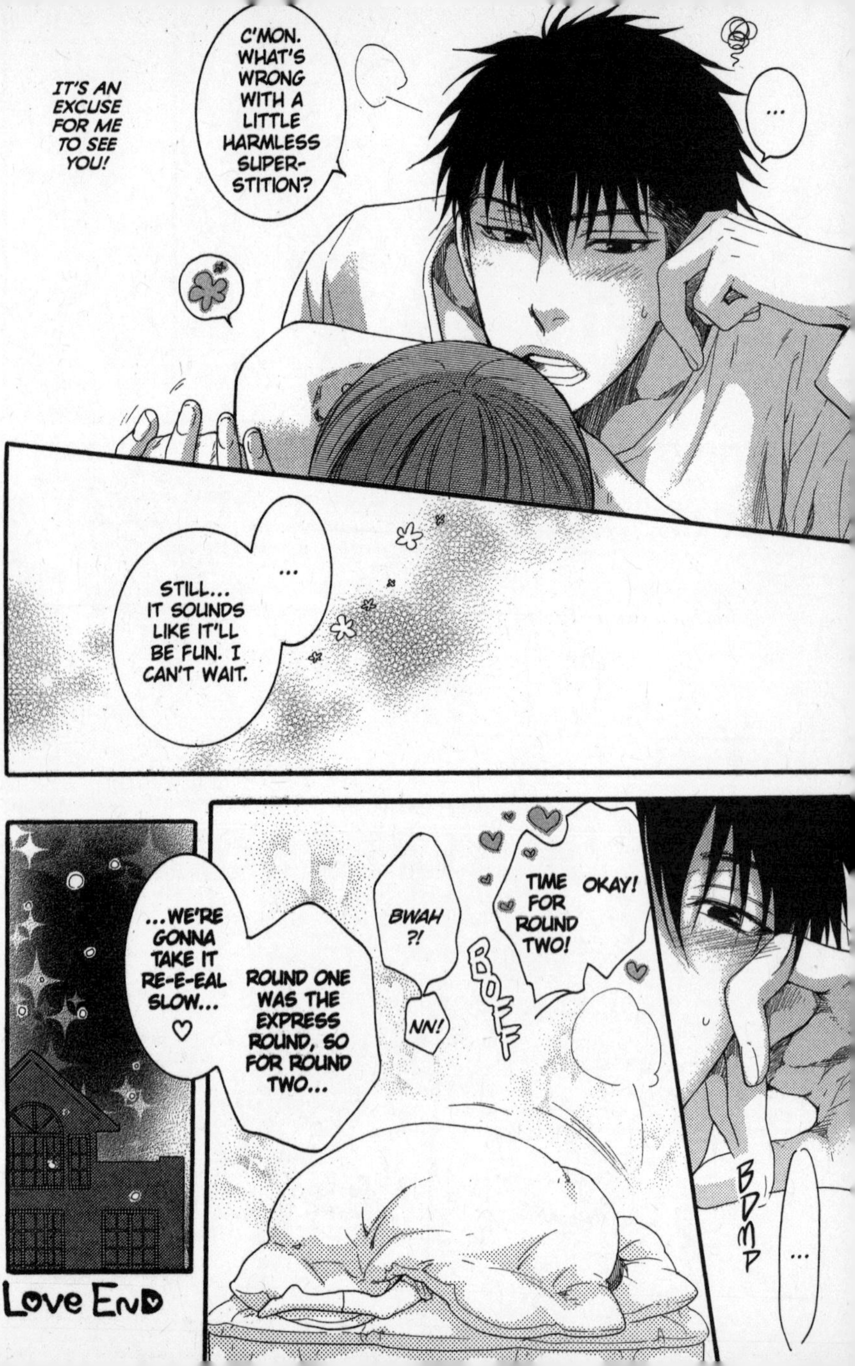
...
C'MON. WHAT'S WRONG WITH A LITTLE HARMLESS SUPER-STITION?
IT'S AN EXCUSE FOR ME TO SEE YOU!
... STILL... IT SOUNDS LIKE IT'LL BE FUN. I CAN'T WAIT.
...
BDMP
OKAY! TIME FOR ROUND TWO!
BOFF
BWAH?!
NN!
ROUND ONE WAS THE EXPRESS ROUND, SO FOR ROUND TWO...
...WE'RE GONNA TAKE IT RE-E-EAL SLOW... ♡
Love End

Don't Be Cruel

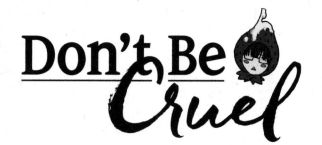

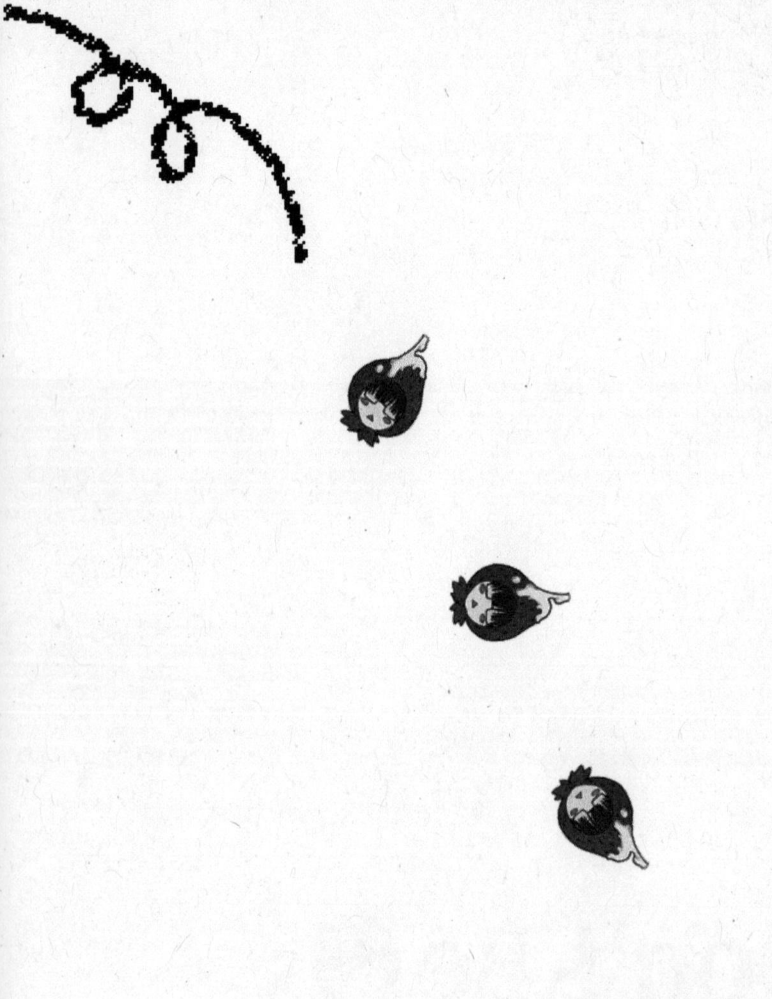

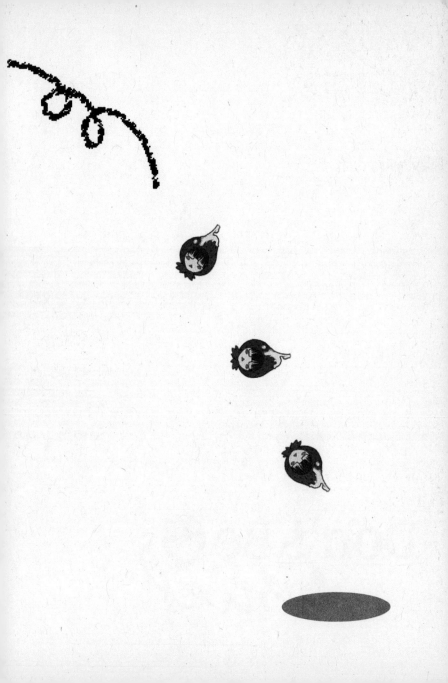

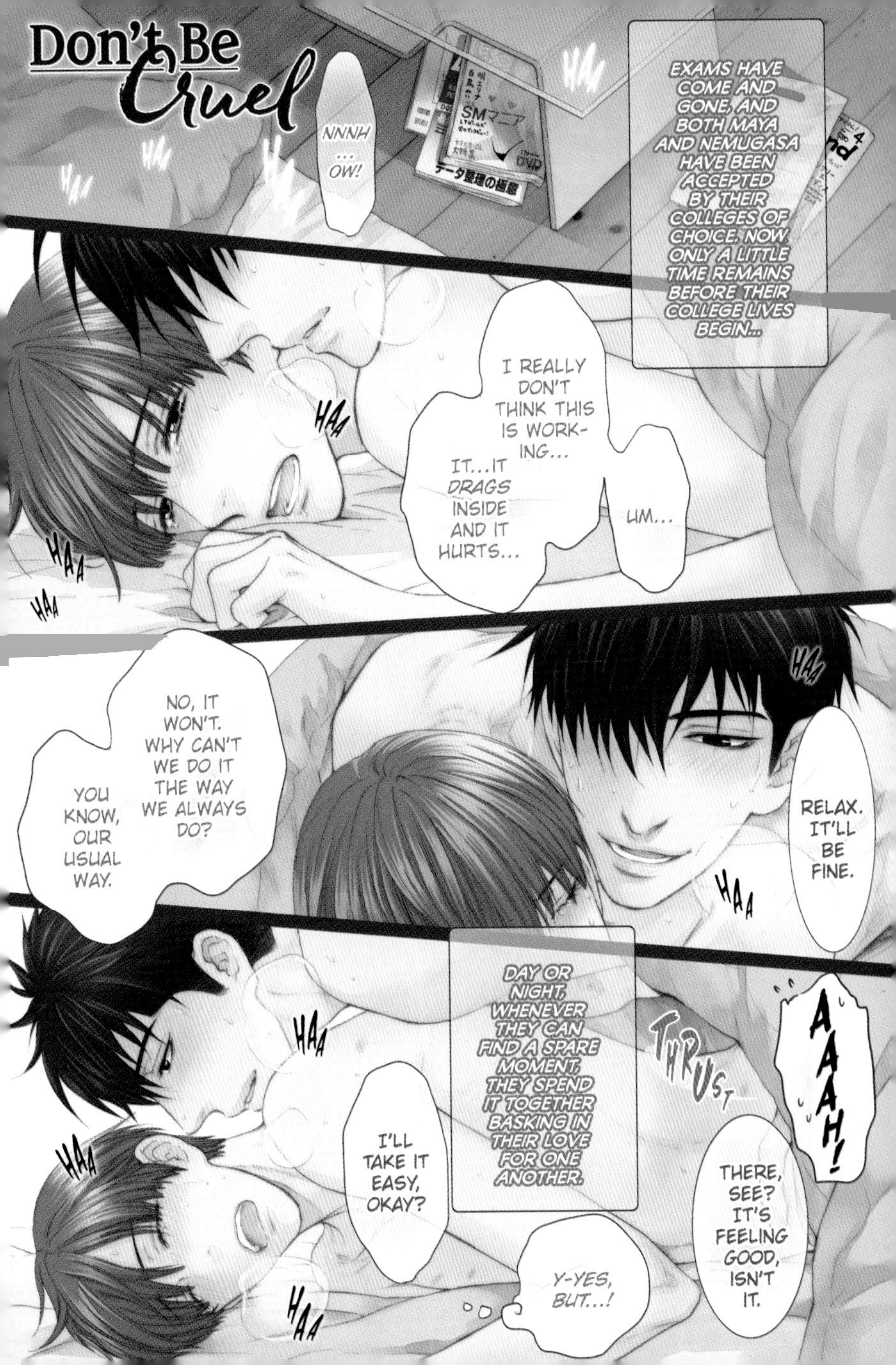
Don't Be Cruel
EXAMS HAVE COME AND GONE, AND BOTH MAYA AND NEMUGASA HAVE BEEN ACCEPTED BY THEIR COLLEGES OF CHOICE. NOW, ONLY A LITTLE TIME REMAINS BEFORE THEIR COLLEGE LIVES BEGIN...
HAA
SMマニア
DVD
データ整理の極意
NNNH ... OW!
HAA
HAA
HAA
I REALLY DON'T THINK THIS IS WORKING...
IT...IT *DRAGS* INSIDE AND IT HURTS...
UM...
HAA
HAA
HAA
HAA
RELAX. IT'LL BE FINE.
NO, IT WON'T. WHY CAN'T WE DO IT THE WAY WE ALWAYS DO?
YOU KNOW, OUR USUAL WAY.
HAA
AAAH!
THRUST
DAY OR NIGHT, WHENEVER THEY CAN FIND A SPARE MOMENT, THEY SPEND IT TOGETHER BASKING IN THEIR LOVE FOR ONE ANOTHER.
HAA
THERE, SEE? IT'S FEELING GOOD, ISN'T IT.
I'LL TAKE IT EASY, OKAY?
Y-YES, BUT...!
HAA
HAA

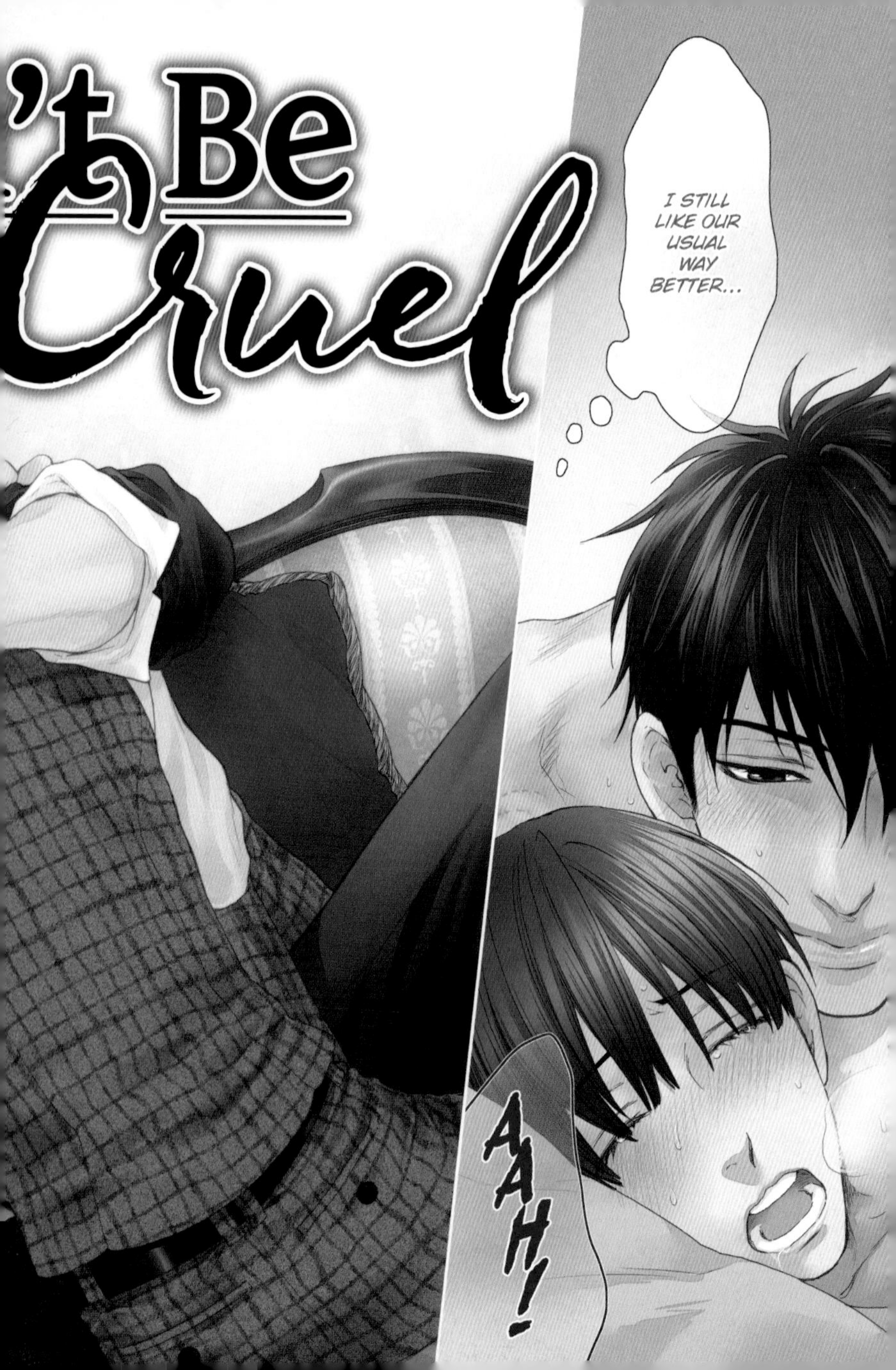
I STILL LIKE OUR USUAL WAY BETTER...
AAH!
't Be Cruel

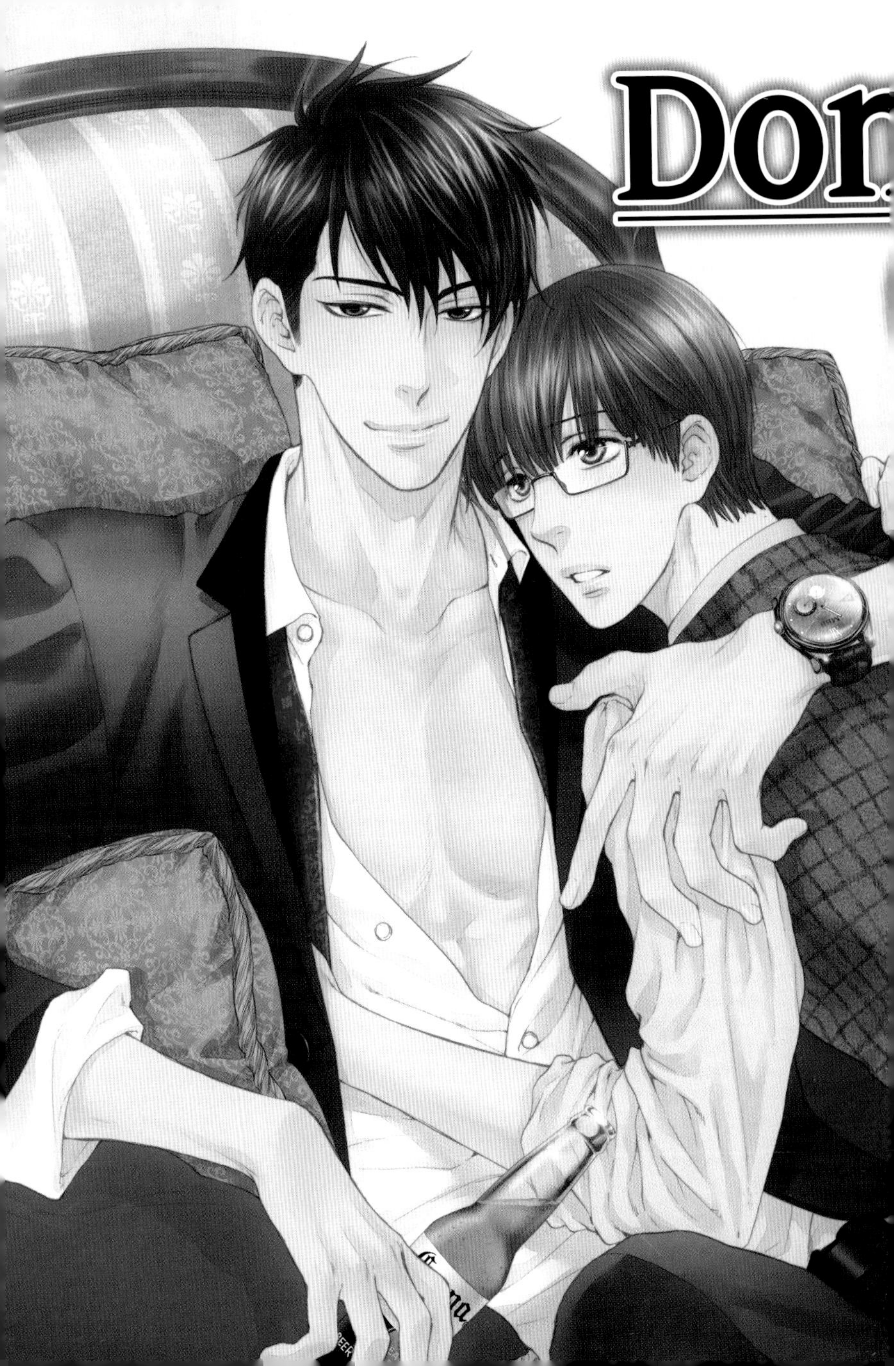
Don

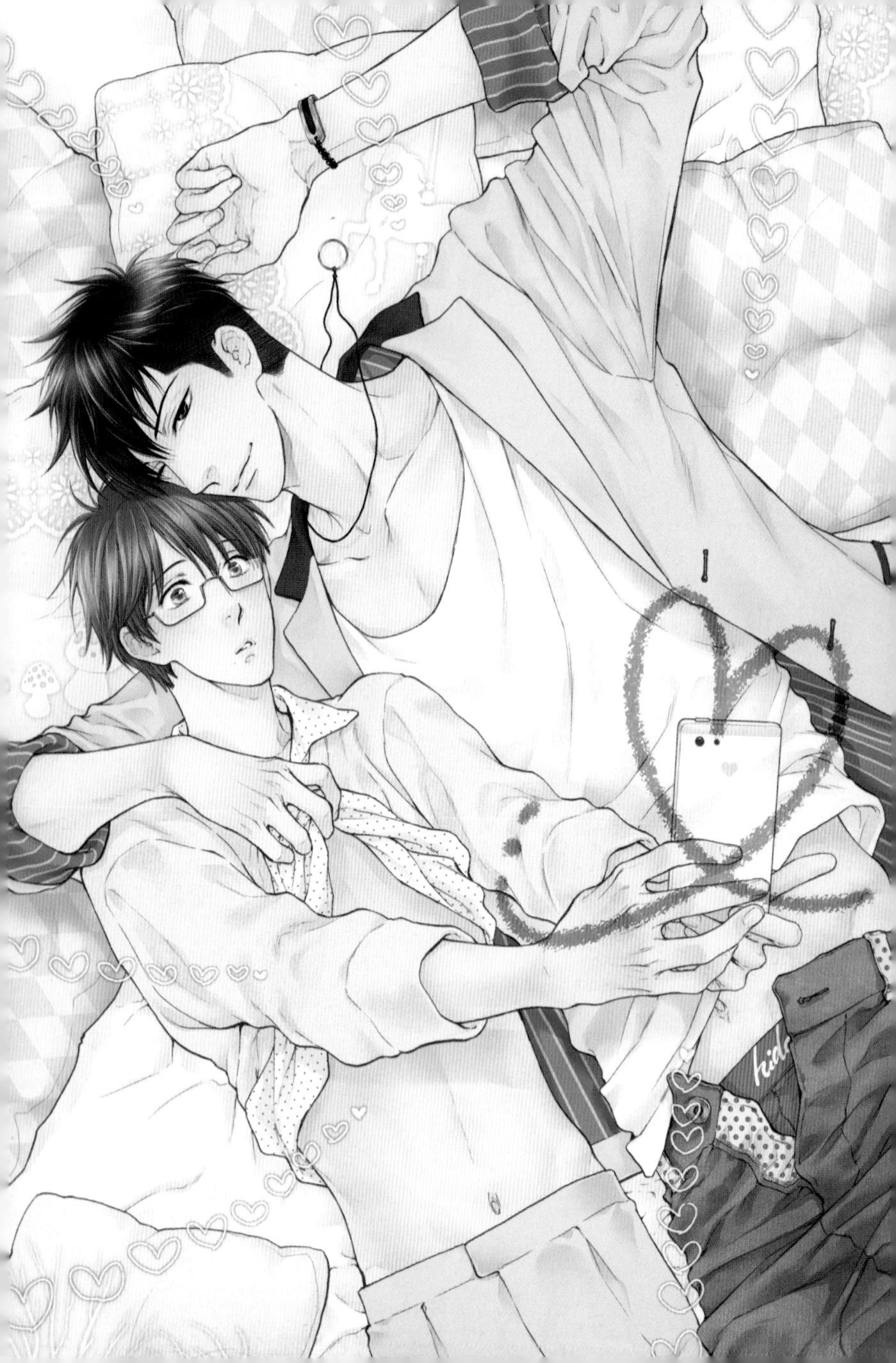

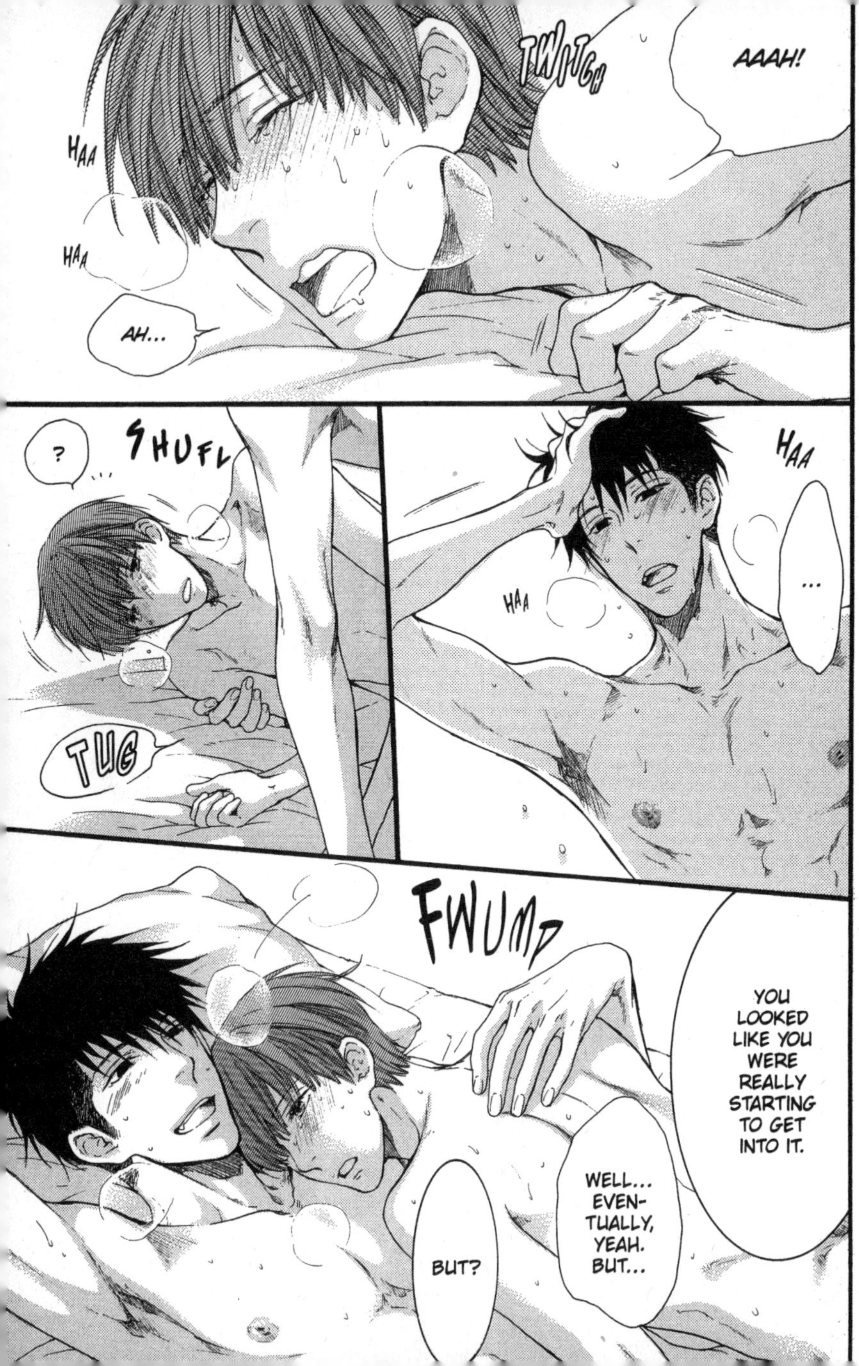
AAAH!
TWITCH
HAA
HAA
AH...
HAA
...
HAA
SHUFL
?
...
TUG
FWUMP
YOU LOOKED LIKE YOU WERE REALLY STARTING TO GET INTO IT.
WELL... EVEN-TUALLY, YEAH. BUT...
BUT?

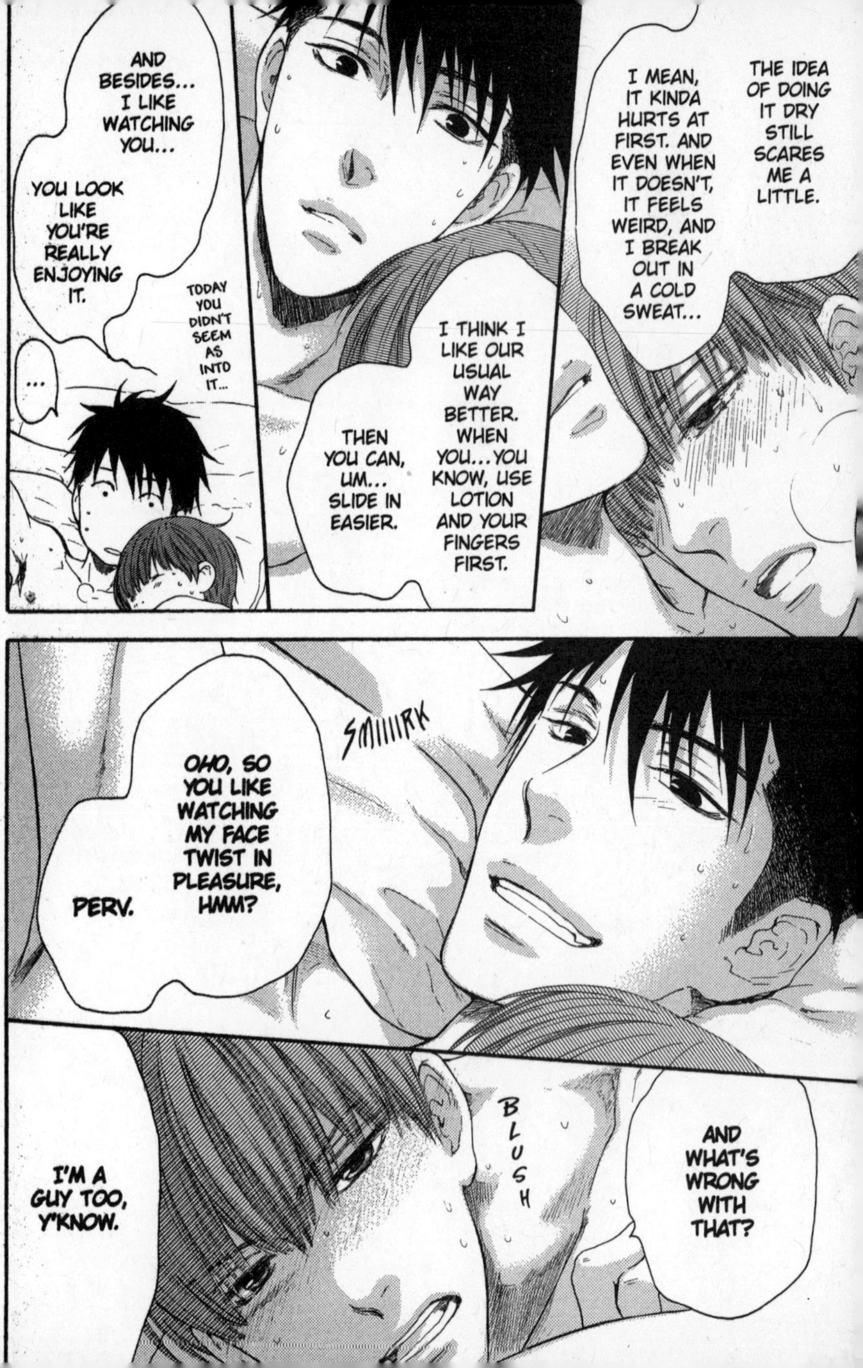
THE IDEA OF DOING IT DRY STILL SCARES ME A LITTLE.
I MEAN, IT KINDA HURTS AT FIRST. AND EVEN WHEN IT DOESN'T, IT FEELS WEIRD, AND I BREAK OUT IN A COLD SWEAT...
I THINK I LIKE OUR USUAL WAY BETTER. WHEN YOU... YOU KNOW, USE LOTION AND YOUR FINGERS FIRST.
THEN YOU CAN, UM... SLIDE IN EASIER.
AND BESIDES... I LIKE WATCHING YOU...
YOU LOOK LIKE YOU'RE REALLY ENJOYING IT.
TODAY YOU DIDN'T SEEM AS INTO IT...
...
SMIIIIRK
OHO, SO YOU LIKE WATCHING MY FACE TWIST IN PLEASURE, HMM?
PERV.
AND WHAT'S WRONG WITH THAT?
BLUSH
I'M A GUY TOO, Y'KNOW.

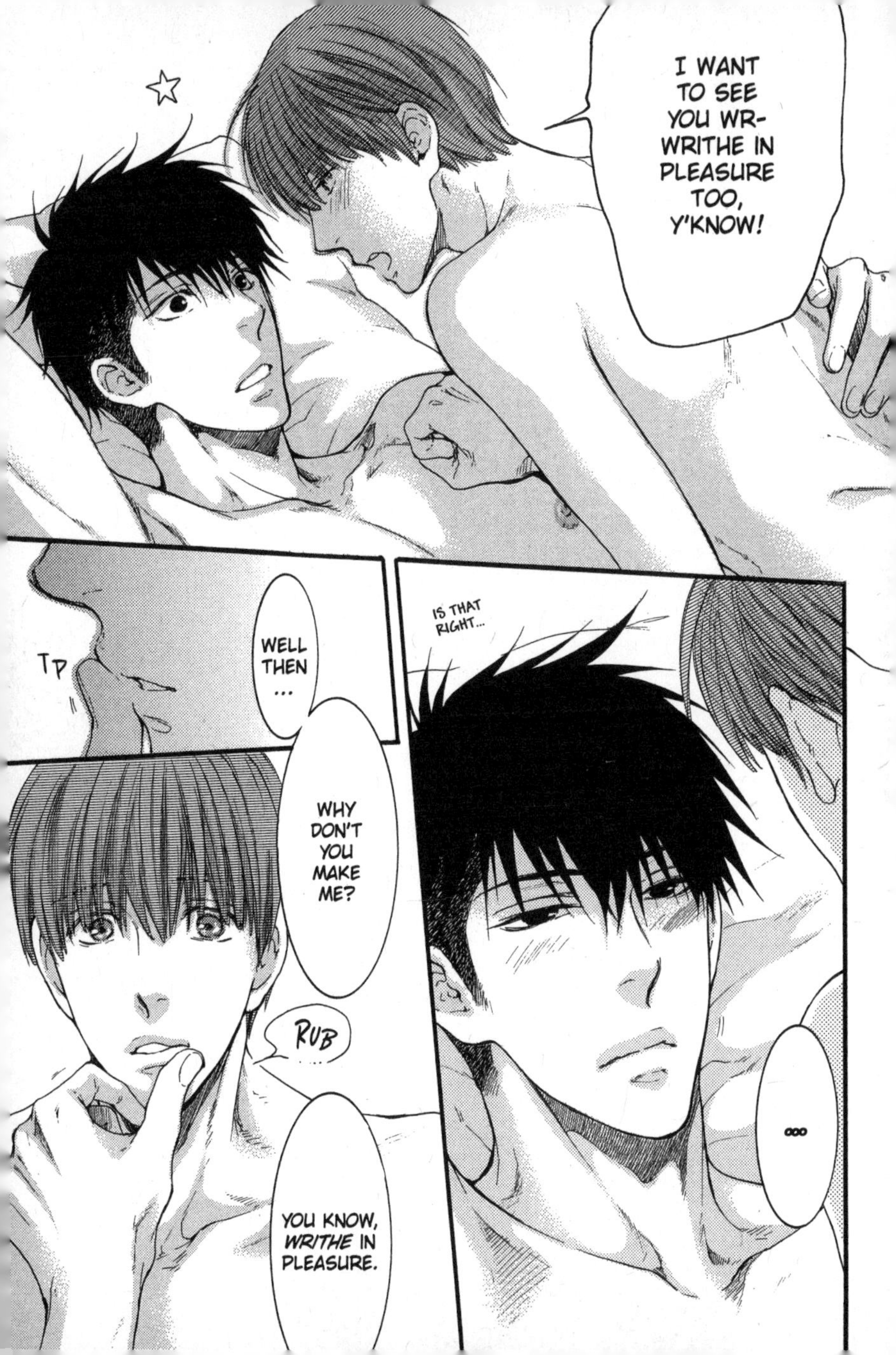
I WANT TO SEE YOU WR- WRITHE IN PLEASURE TOO, Y'KNOW!
IS THAT RIGHT...
...
Tp
WELL THEN ...
WHY DON'T YOU MAKE ME?
RUB
...
YOU KNOW, WRITHE IN PLEASURE.

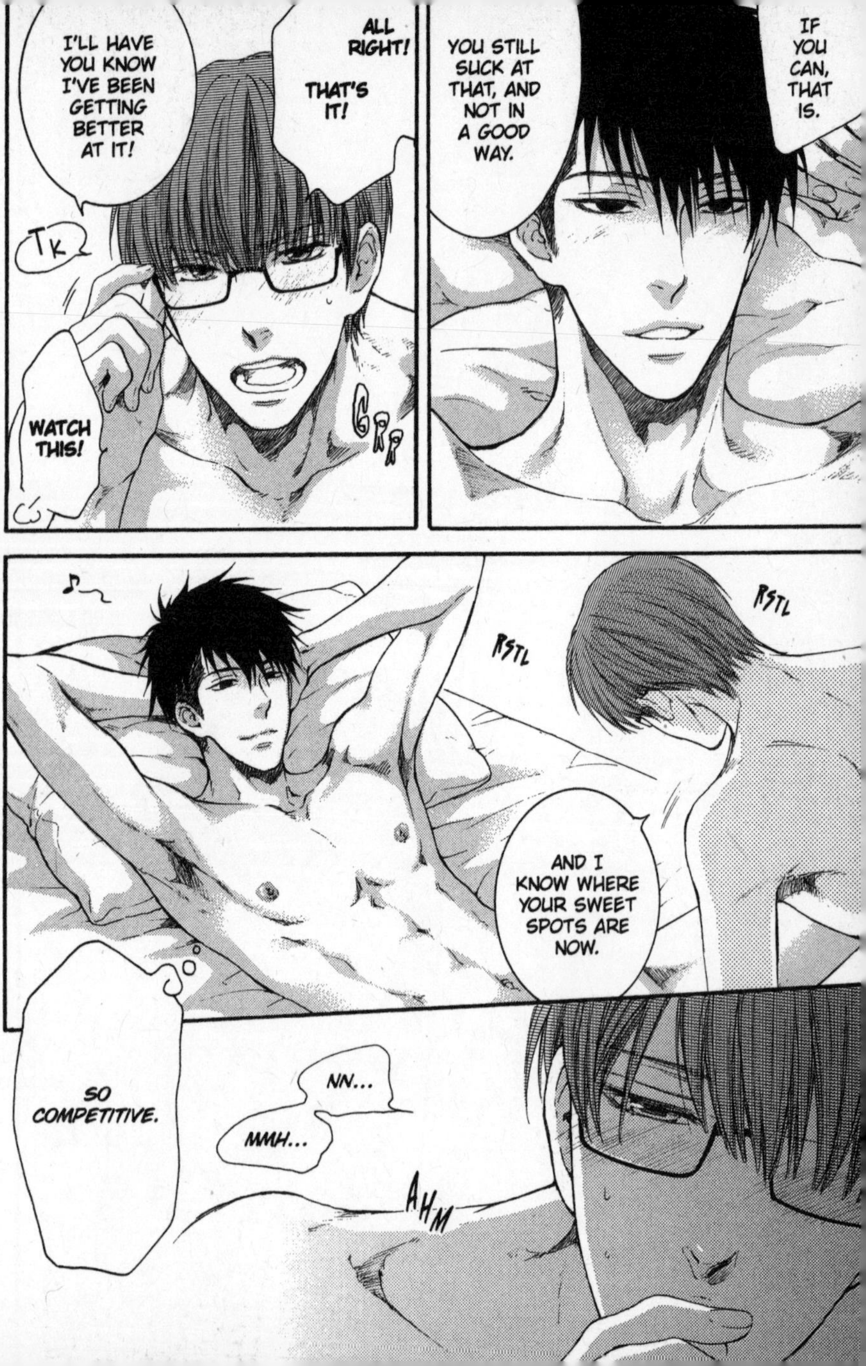
IF YOU CAN, THAT IS.
YOU STILL SUCK AT THAT, AND NOT IN A GOOD WAY.
ALL RIGHT!
THAT'S IT!
I'LL HAVE YOU KNOW I'VE BEEN GETTING BETTER AT IT!
TK
GRR
WATCH THIS!
RSTL
RSTL
♪~
AND I KNOW WHERE YOUR SWEET SPOTS ARE NOW.
AHM
NN...
MMH...
SO COMPETITIVE.

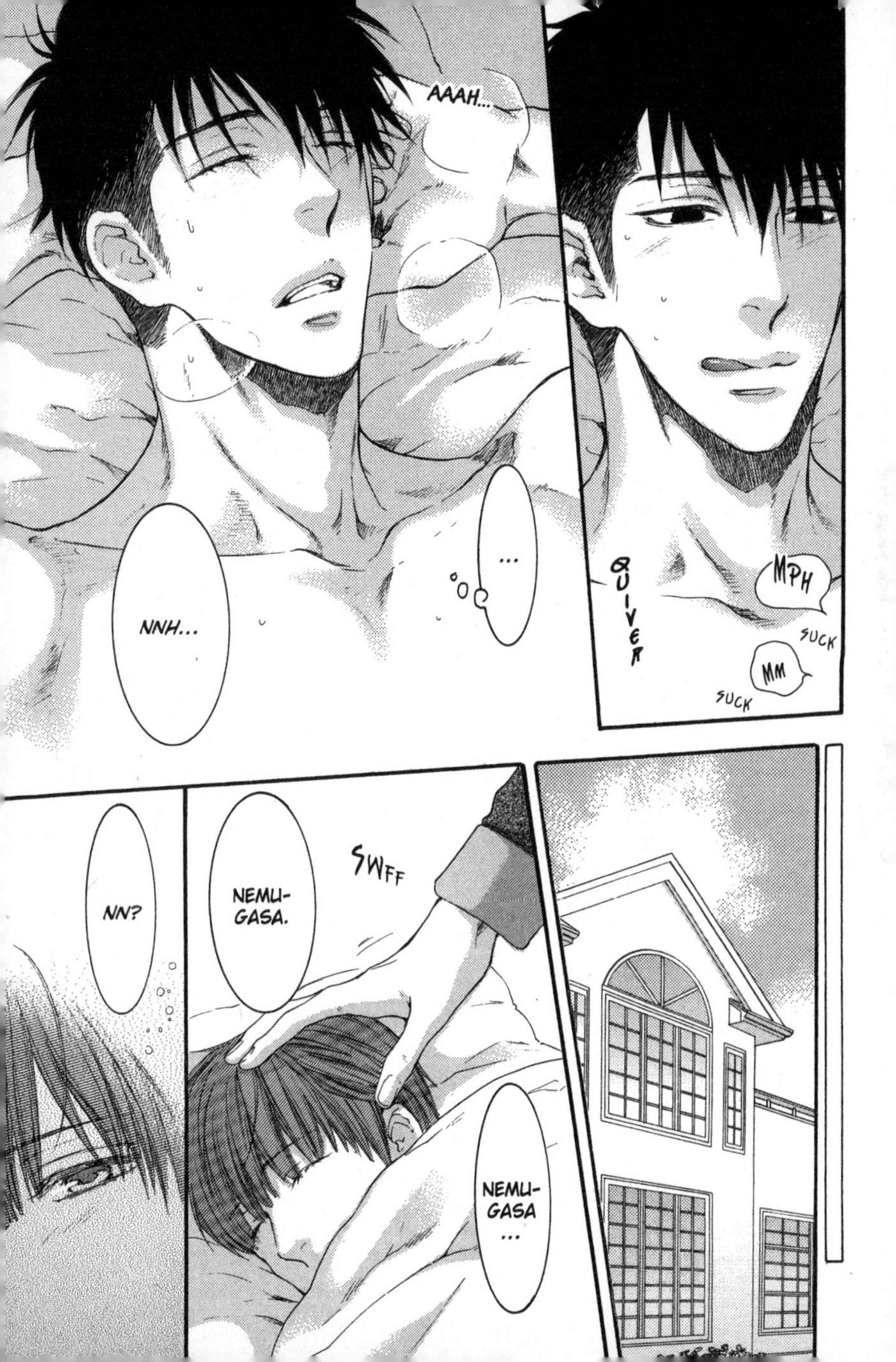
MPH
QUIVER
SUCK
MM
SUCK
AAAH...
...
NNH...
SWFF
NEMU-GASA.
NEMU-GASA...
NN?

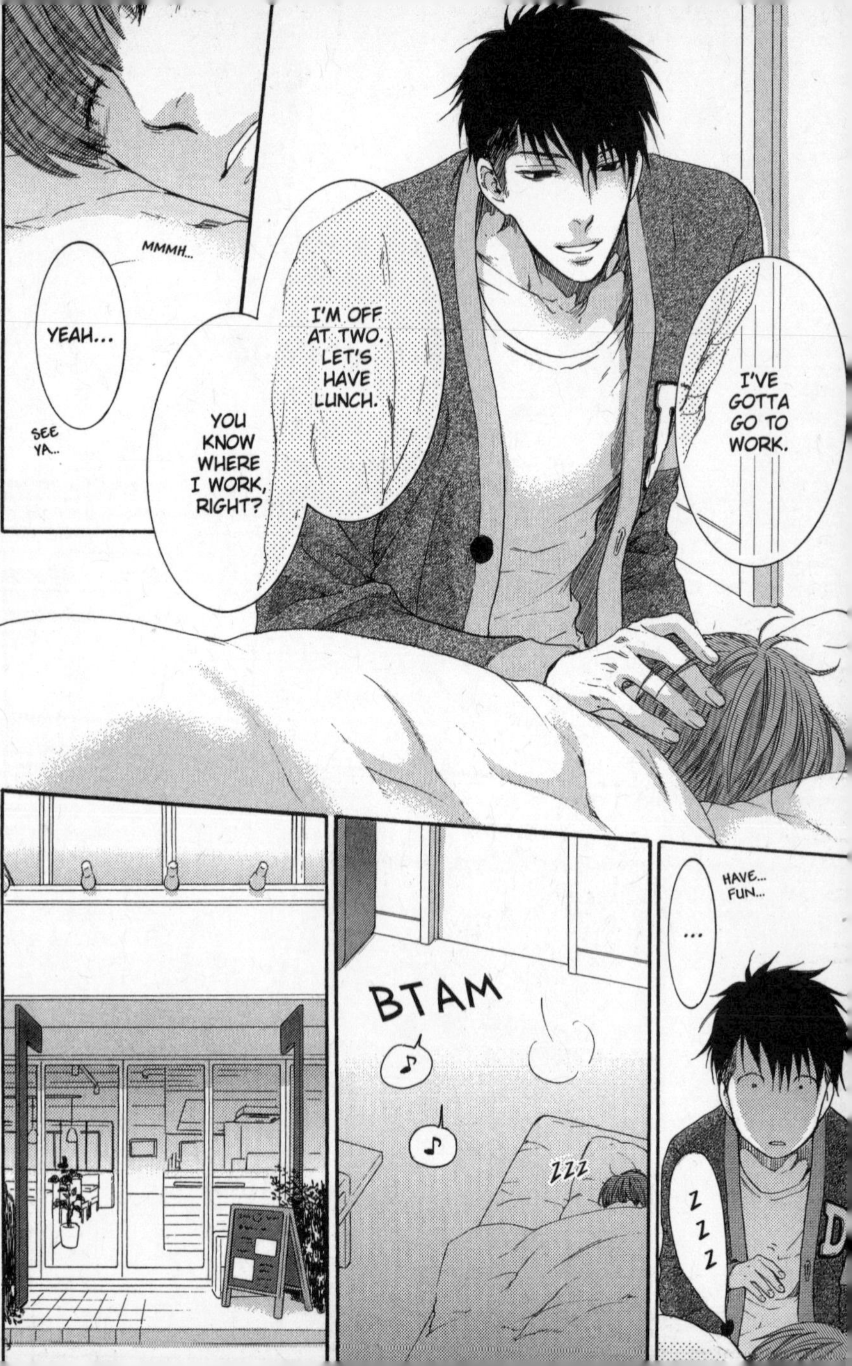
I'VE GOTTA GO TO WORK.
I'M OFF AT TWO. LET'S HAVE LUNCH.
YOU KNOW WHERE I WORK, RIGHT?
MMMH...
YEAH...
SEE YA...
HAVE... FUN...
...
ZZZ
BTAM
♪
♪
ZZZ

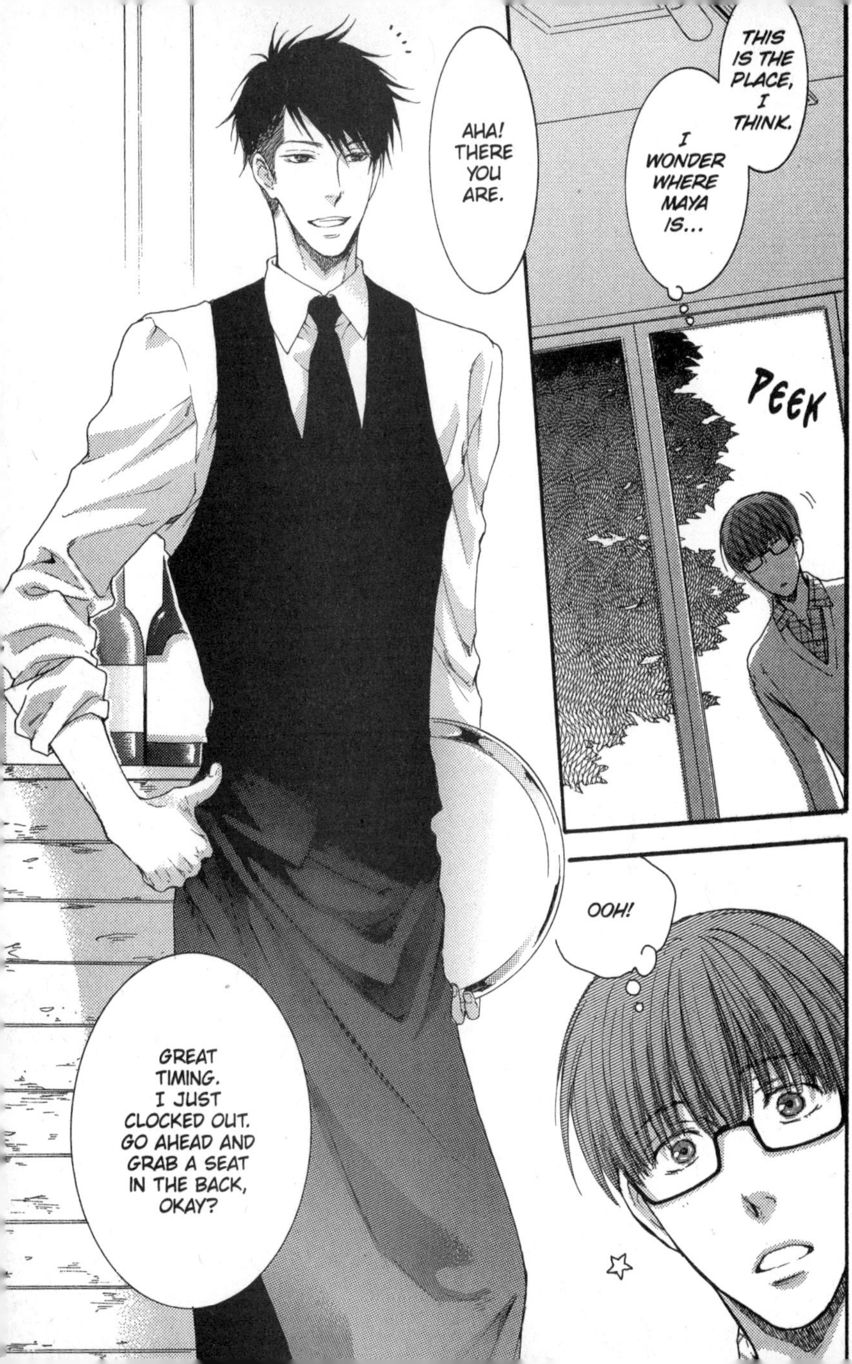
THIS IS THE PLACE, I THINK.
I WONDER WHERE MAYA IS...
PEEK
OOH!
AHA! THERE YOU ARE.
GREAT TIMING. I JUST CLOCKED OUT. GO AHEAD AND GRAB A SEAT IN THE BACK, OKAY?

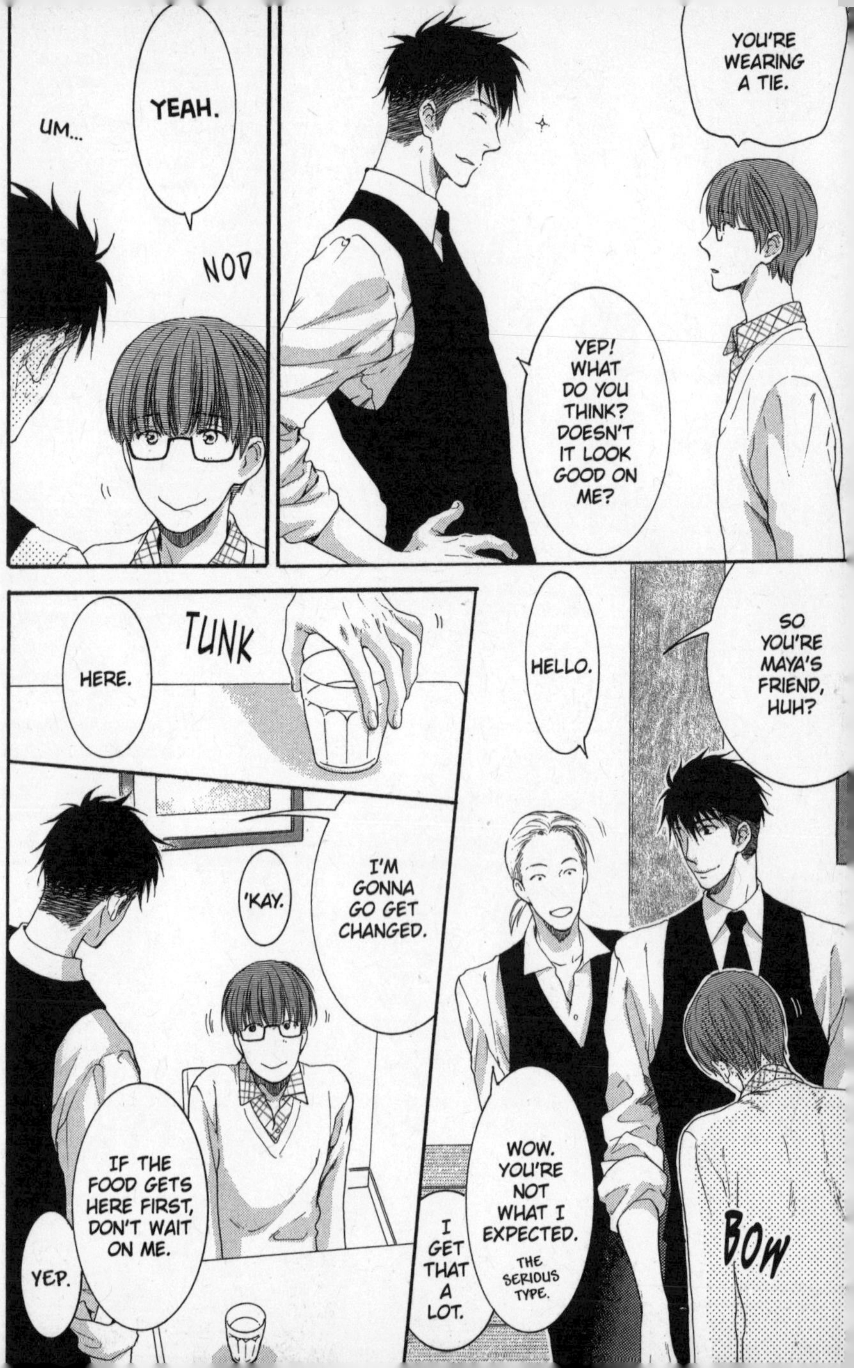
YOU'RE WEARING A TIE.
YEP! WHAT DO YOU THINK? DOESN'T IT LOOK GOOD ON ME?
YEAH.
UM...
NOD
SO YOU'RE MAYA'S FRIEND, HUH?
HELLO.
WOW. YOU'RE NOT WHAT I EXPECTED.
THE SERIOUS TYPE.
I GET THAT A LOT.
BOW
TUNK
HERE.
I'M GONNA GO GET CHANGED.
'KAY.
IF THE FOOD GETS HERE FIRST, DON'T WAIT ON ME.
YEP.

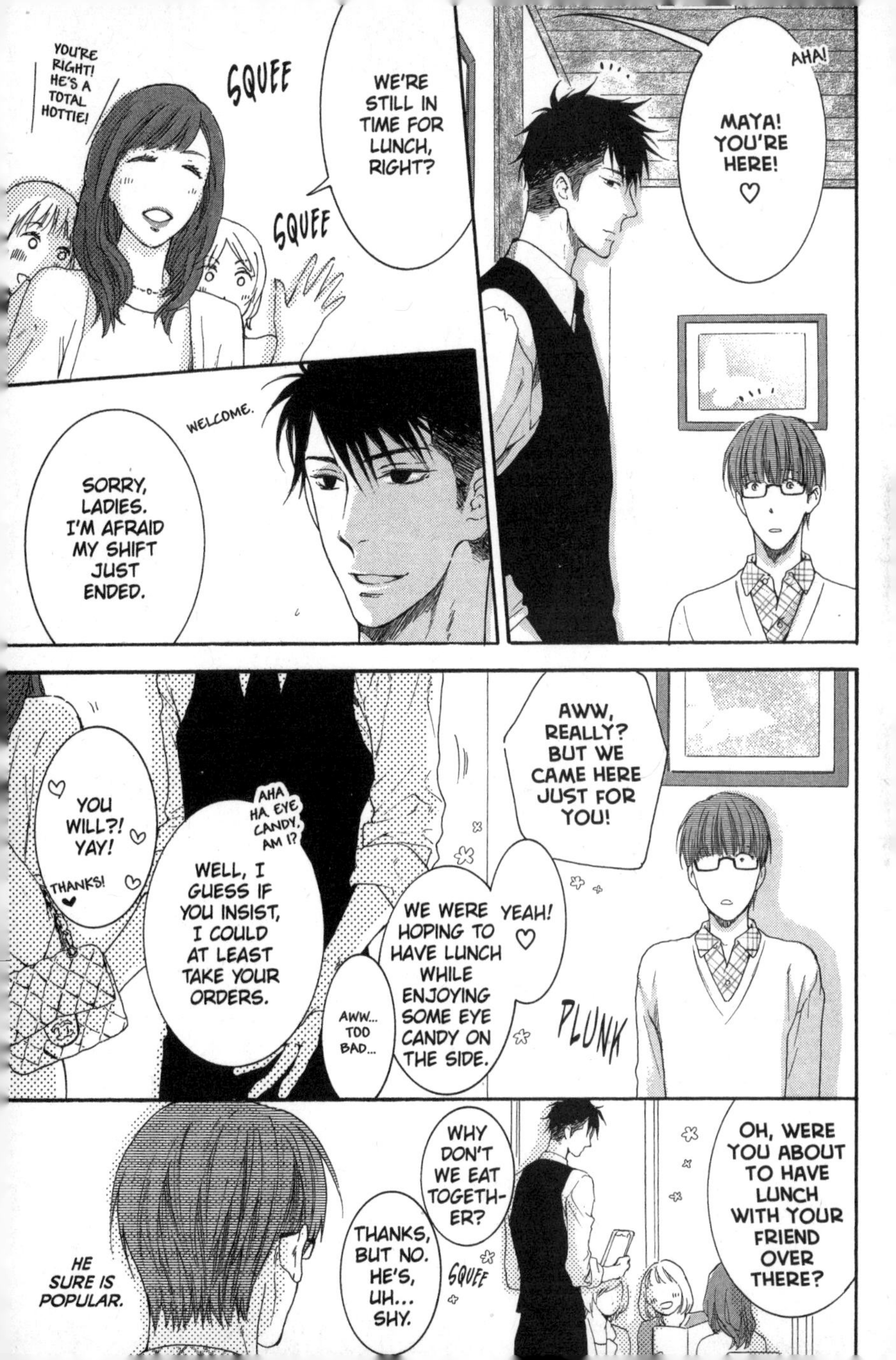
AHA!
MAYA! YOU'RE HERE! ♡
WE'RE STILL IN TIME FOR LUNCH, RIGHT?
SQUEE
SQUEE
YOU'RE RIGHT! HE'S A TOTAL HOTTIE!
WELCOME.
SORRY, LADIES. I'M AFRAID MY SHIFT JUST ENDED.
AWW, REALLY? BUT WE CAME HERE JUST FOR YOU!
YEAH! ♡
WE WERE HOPING TO HAVE LUNCH WHILE ENJOYING SOME EYE CANDY ON THE SIDE.
PLUNK
AWW... TOO BAD...
AHA HA, EYE CANDY, AM I?
WELL, I GUESS IF YOU INSIST, I COULD AT LEAST TAKE YOUR ORDERS.
YOU WILL?! YAY!
THANKS!
OH, WERE YOU ABOUT TO HAVE LUNCH WITH YOUR FRIEND OVER THERE?
WHY DON'T WE EAT TOGETH-ER?
THANKS, BUT NO. HE'S, UH... SHY.
SQUEE
HE SURE IS POPULAR.

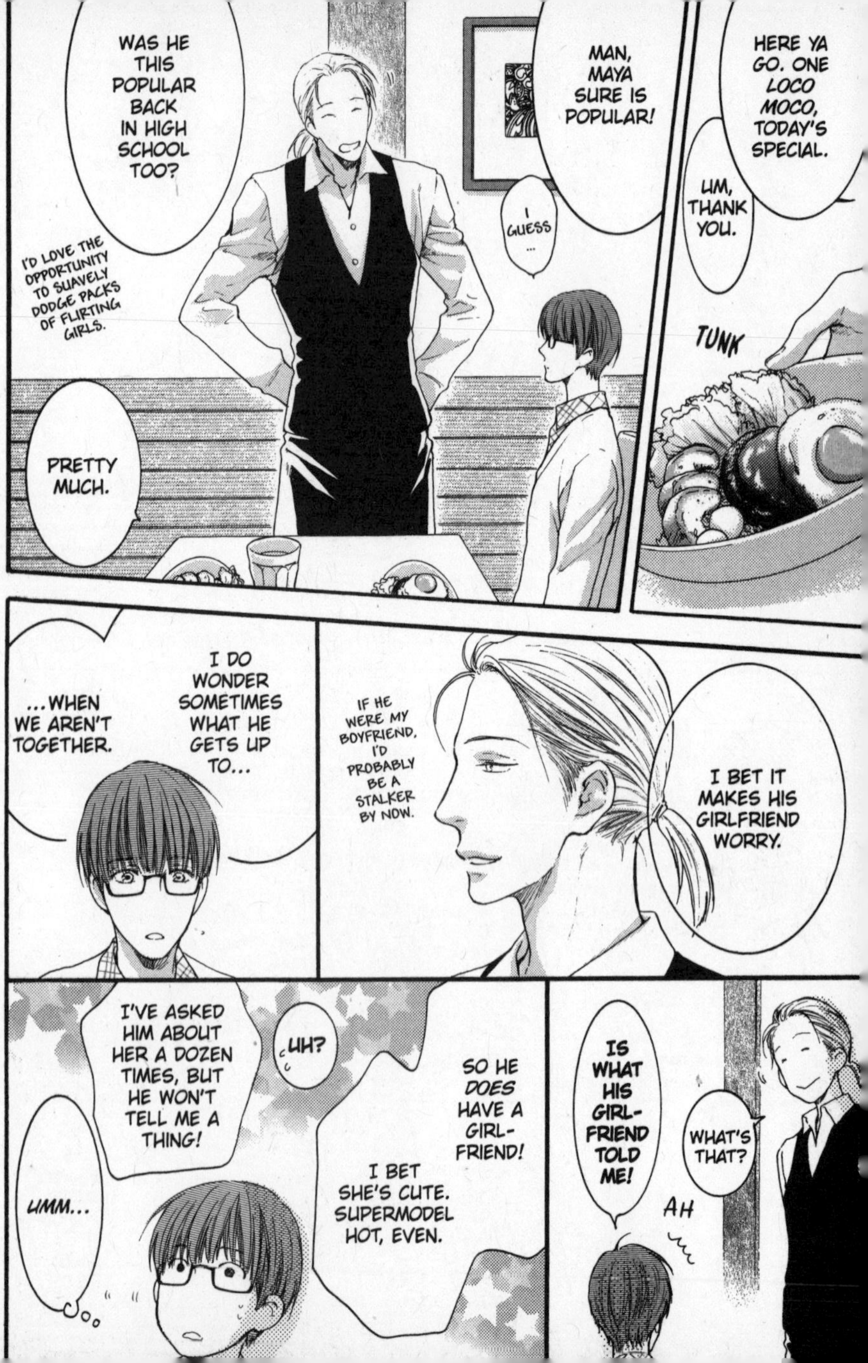
HERE YA GO. ONE *LOCO MOCO,* TODAY'S SPECIAL.
UM, THANK YOU.
TUNK
MAN, MAYA SURE IS POPULAR!
I GUESS ...
WAS HE THIS POPULAR BACK IN HIGH SCHOOL TOO?
I'D LOVE THE OPPORTUNITY TO SUAVELY DODGE PACKS OF FLIRTING GIRLS.
PRETTY MUCH.
I BET IT MAKES HIS GIRLFRIEND WORRY.
IF HE WERE MY BOYFRIEND, I'D PROBABLY BE A STALKER BY NOW.
I DO WONDER SOMETIMES WHAT HE GETS UP TO...
...WHEN WE AREN'T TOGETHER.
IS WHAT HIS GIRL-FRIEND TOLD ME!
WHAT'S THAT?
AH
SO HE *DOES* HAVE A GIRL-FRIEND!
I BET SHE'S CUTE. SUPERMODEL HOT, EVEN.
UH?
I'VE ASKED HIM ABOUT HER A DOZEN TIMES, BUT HE WON'T TELL ME A THING!
UMM...

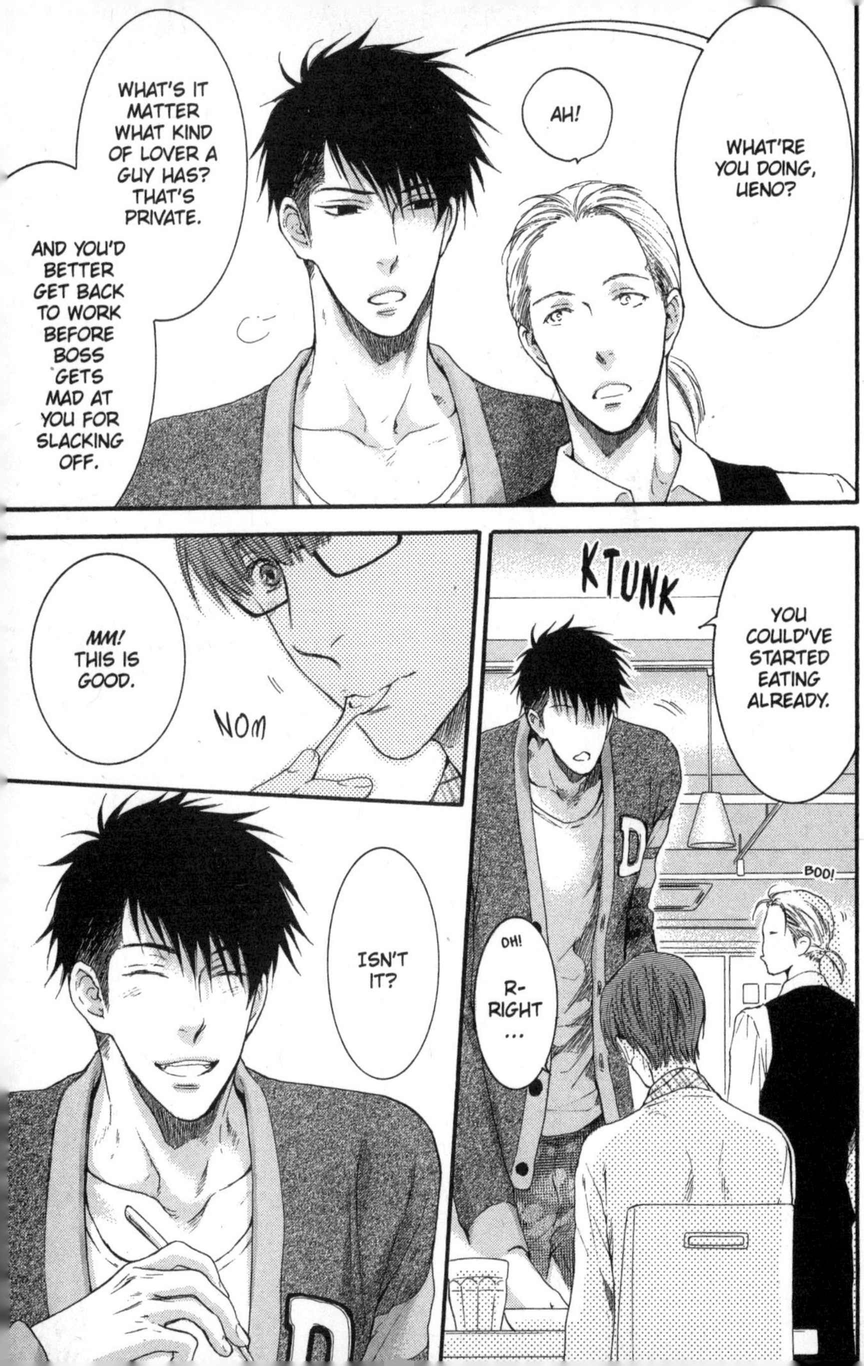
WHAT'RE YOU DOING, UENO?
AH!
WHAT'S IT MATTER WHAT KIND OF LOVER A GUY HAS? THAT'S PRIVATE.
AND YOU'D BETTER GET BACK TO WORK BEFORE BOSS GETS MAD AT YOU FOR SLACKING OFF.
KTUNK
YOU COULD'VE STARTED EATING ALREADY.
BOO!
OH!
R-RIGHT...
MM! THIS IS GOOD.
NOM
ISN'T IT?

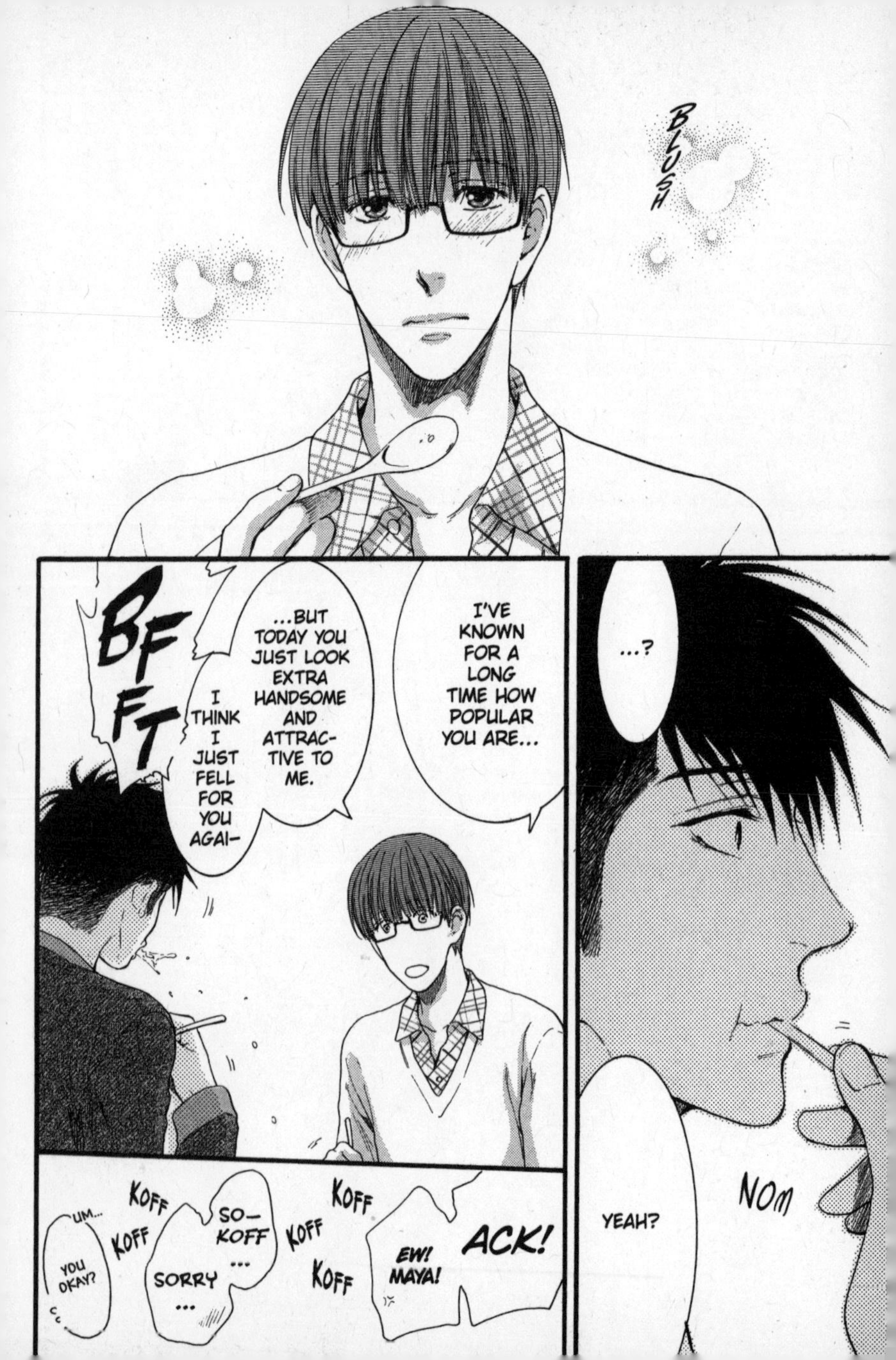
BLUSH
...?
NOM
YEAH?
I'VE KNOWN FOR A LONG TIME HOW POPULAR YOU ARE...
...BUT TODAY YOU JUST LOOK EXTRA HANDSOME AND ATTRACTIVE TO ME.
I THINK I JUST FELL FOR YOU AGAI-
BFFT
ACK!
EW! MAYA!
KOFF
KOFF
KOFF
SO— KOFF ...
SORRY ...
KOFF
KOFF
UM... YOU OKAY?

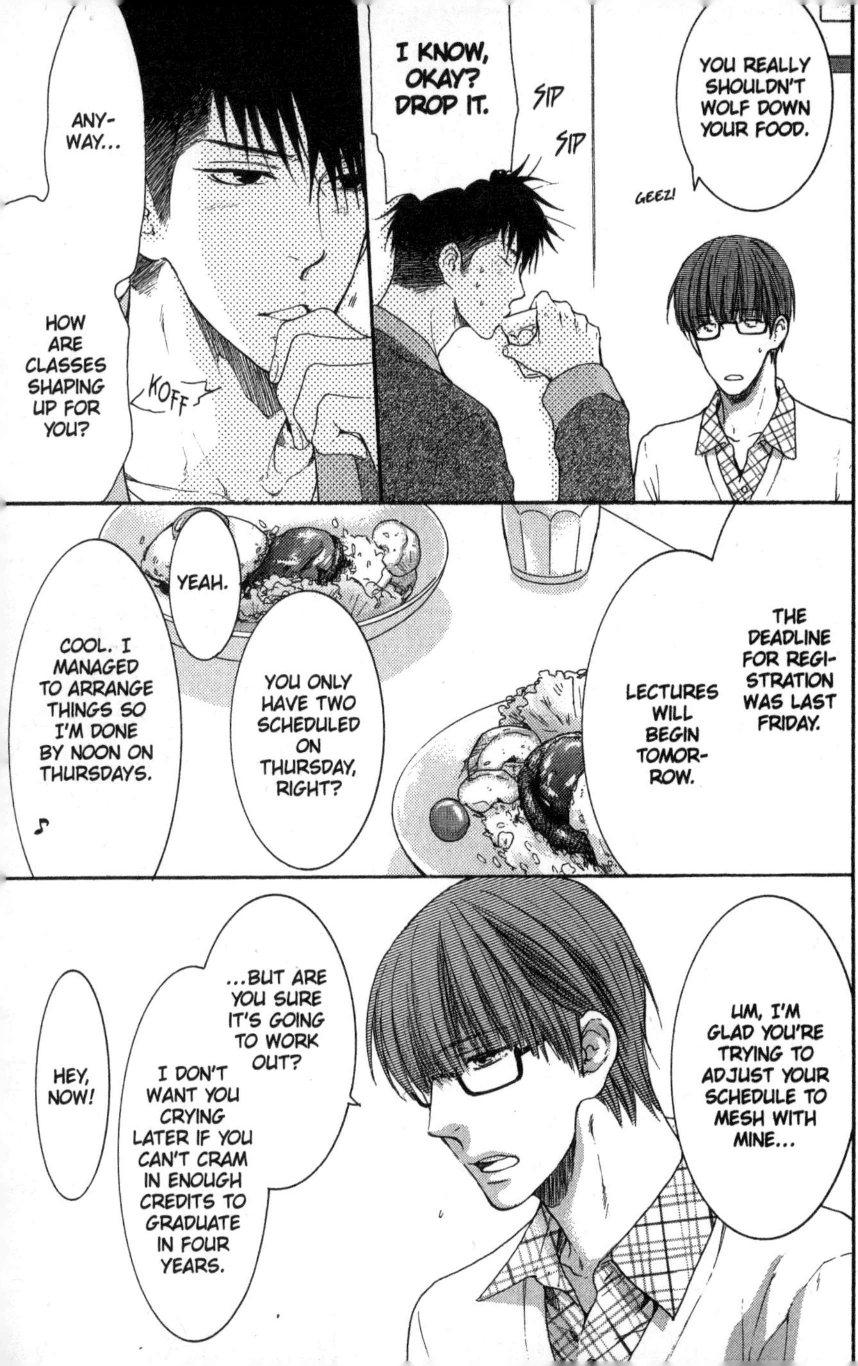
YOU REALLY SHOULDN'T WOLF DOWN YOUR FOOD.
GEEZ!
SIP
SIP
I KNOW, OKAY? DROP IT.
ANYWAY...
KOFF
HOW ARE CLASSES SHAPING UP FOR YOU?
THE DEADLINE FOR REGISTRATION WAS LAST FRIDAY.
LECTURES WILL BEGIN TOMORROW.
YOU ONLY HAVE TWO SCHEDULED ON THURSDAY, RIGHT?
YEAH.
COOL. I MANAGED TO ARRANGE THINGS SO I'M DONE BY NOON ON THURSDAYS. ♪
UM, I'M GLAD YOU'RE TRYING TO ADJUST YOUR SCHEDULE TO MESH WITH MINE...
...BUT ARE YOU SURE IT'S GOING TO WORK OUT?
I DON'T WANT YOU CRYING LATER IF YOU CAN'T CRAM IN ENOUGH CREDITS TO GRADUATE IN FOUR YEARS.
HEY, NOW!

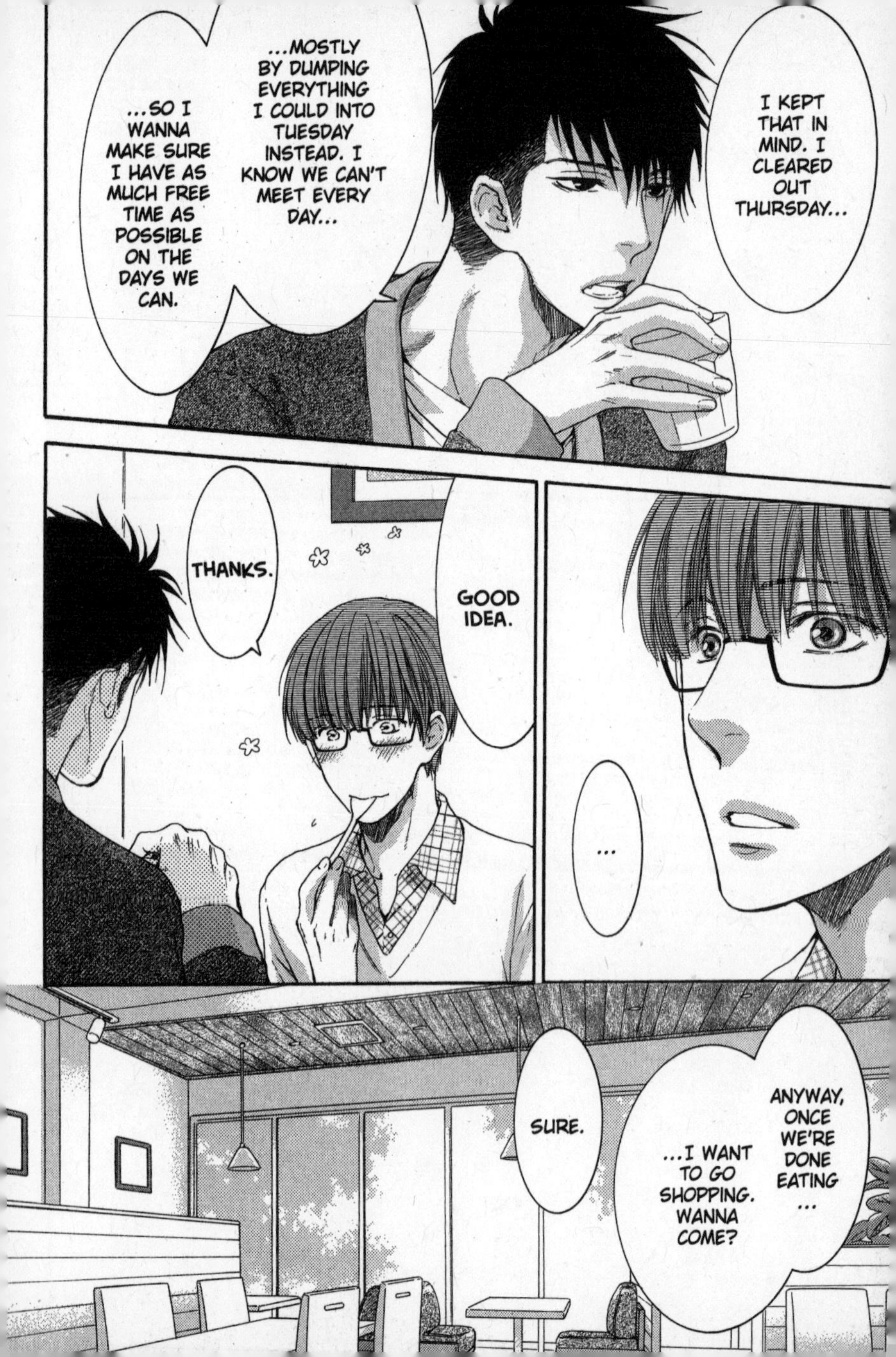
I KEPT THAT IN MIND. I CLEARED OUT THURSDAY...
...MOSTLY BY DUMPING EVERYTHING I COULD INTO TUESDAY INSTEAD. I KNOW WE CAN'T MEET EVERY DAY...
...SO I WANNA MAKE SURE I HAVE AS MUCH FREE TIME AS POSSIBLE ON THE DAYS WE CAN.
...
GOOD IDEA.
THANKS.
ANYWAY, ONCE WE'RE DONE EATING ...
...I WANT TO GO SHOPPING. WANNA COME?
SURE.

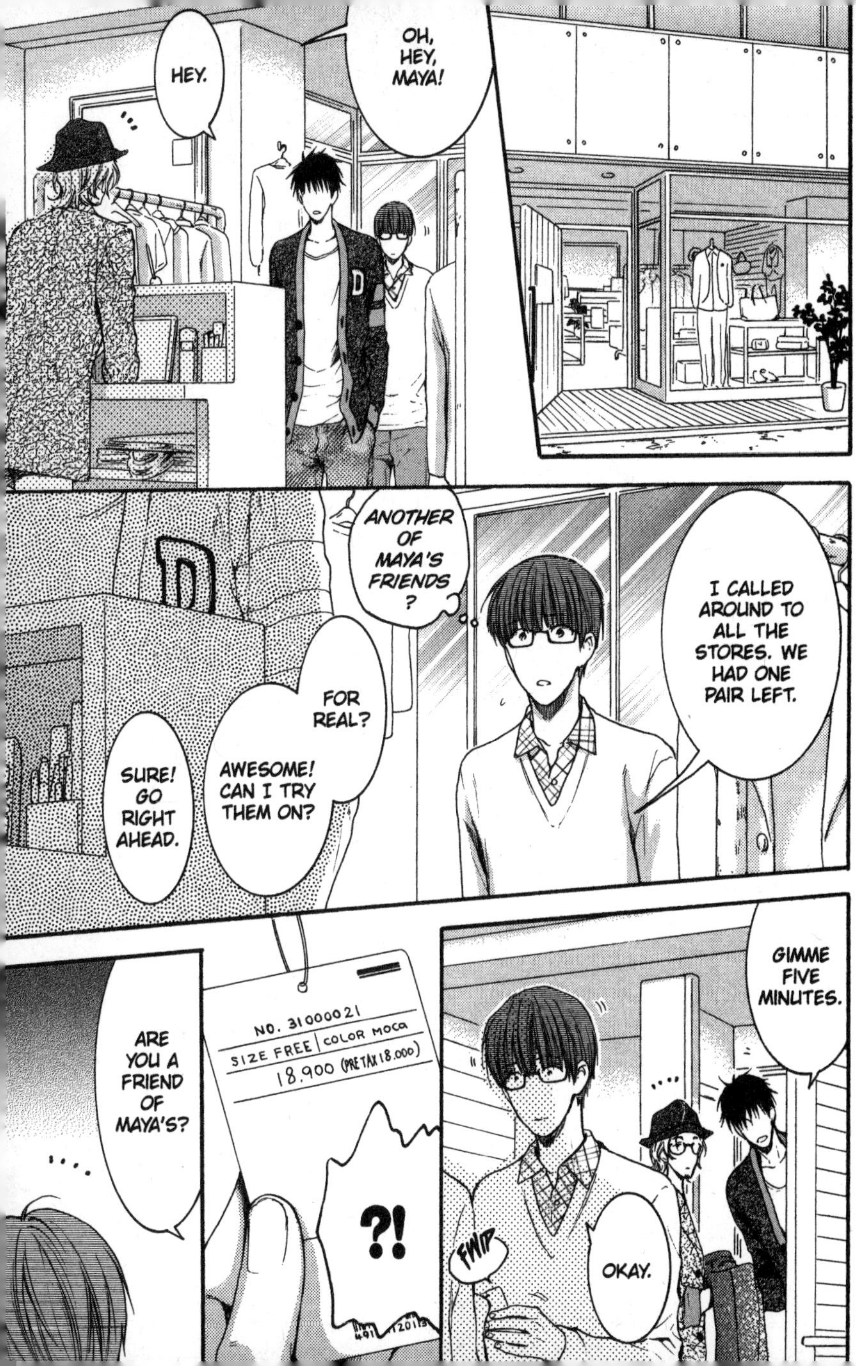
OH, HEY, MAYA!
HEY.
...
I CALLED AROUND TO ALL THE STORES. WE HAD ONE PAIR LEFT.
ANOTHER OF MAYA'S FRIENDS ?
FOR REAL?
AWESOME! CAN I TRY THEM ON?
SURE! GO RIGHT AHEAD.
GIMME FIVE MINUTES.
...
OKAY.
FWIP
NO. 31000021
SIZE FREE | COLOR MOCA
18,900 (PRETAX 18,000)
?!
ARE YOU A FRIEND OF MAYA'S?
...

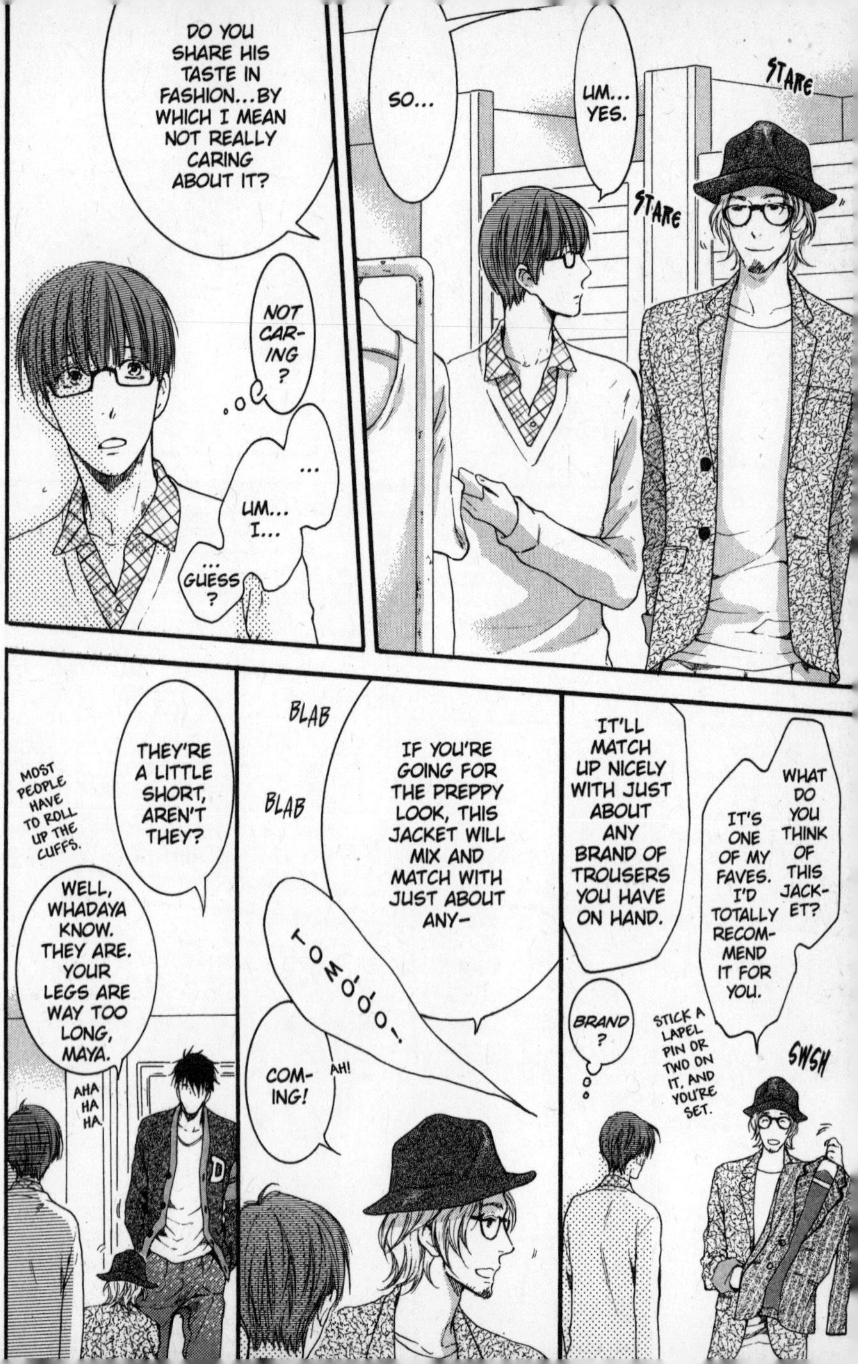
STARE
UM... YES.
STARE
SO...
DO YOU SHARE HIS TASTE IN FASHION...BY WHICH I MEAN NOT REALLY CARING ABOUT IT?
NOT CARING?
... UM... I... ...GUESS?
WHAT DO YOU THINK OF THIS JACKET?
IT'S ONE OF MY FAVES. I'D TOTALLY RECOMMEND IT FOR YOU.
SWSH
STICK A LAPEL PIN OR TWO ON IT, AND YOU'RE SET.
IT'LL MATCH UP NICELY WITH JUST ABOUT ANY BRAND OF TROUSERS YOU HAVE ON HAND.
BRAND?
BLAB
BLAB
IF YOU'RE GOING FOR THE PREPPY LOOK, THIS JACKET WILL MIX AND MATCH WITH JUST ABOUT ANY–
TOMOOOO!
AH!
COMING!
THEY'RE A LITTLE SHORT, AREN'T THEY?
MOST PEOPLE HAVE TO ROLL UP THE CUFFS.
WELL, WHADAYA KNOW. THEY ARE. YOUR LEGS ARE WAY TOO LONG, MAYA.
AHA HA HA

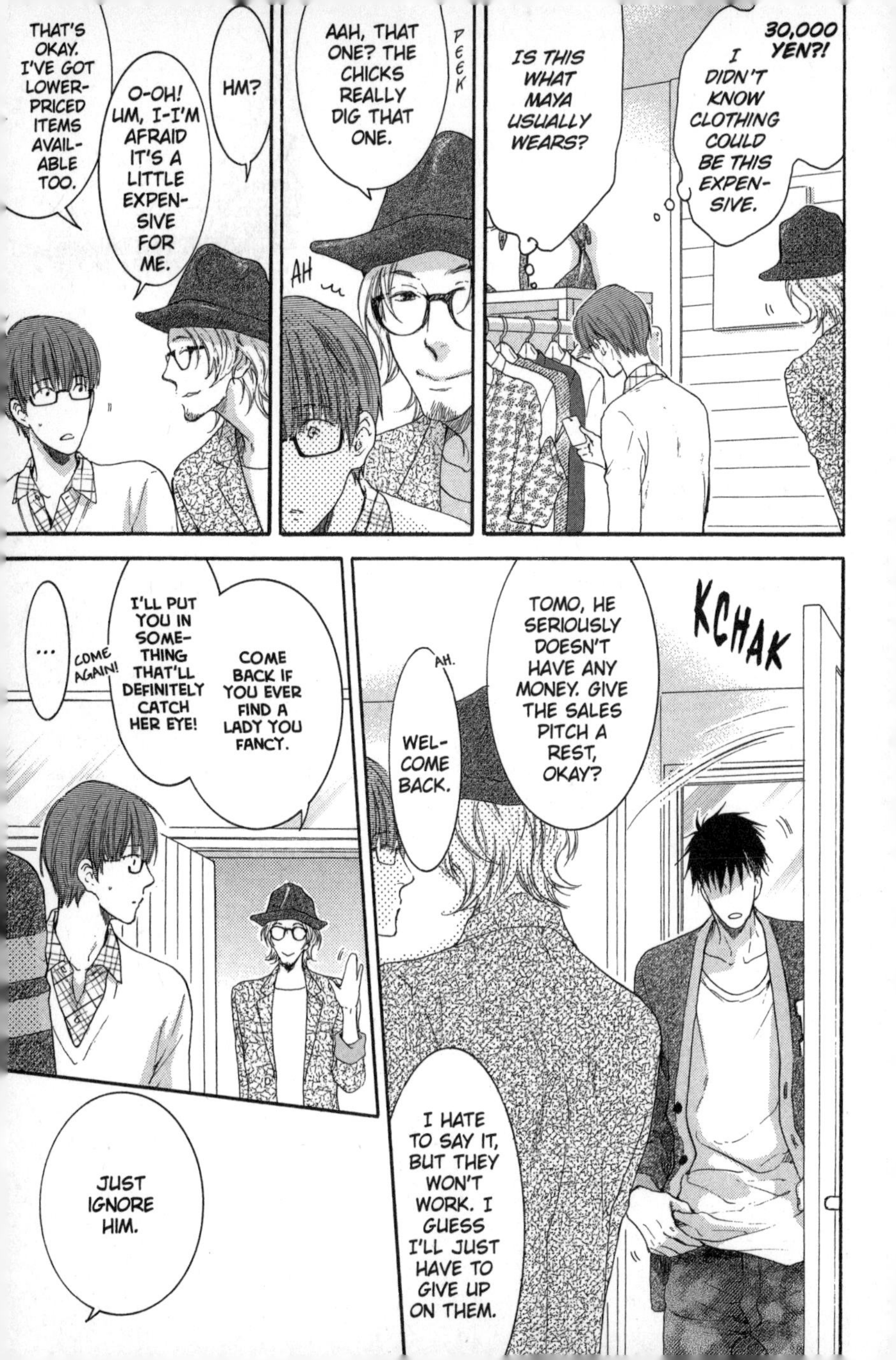
30,000 YEN?!
I DIDN'T KNOW CLOTHING COULD BE THIS EXPENSIVE.
IS THIS WHAT MAYA USUALLY WEARS?
PEEK
AAH, THAT ONE? THE CHICKS REALLY DIG THAT ONE.
AH
HM?
O-OH! UM, I-I'M AFRAID IT'S A LITTLE EXPENSIVE FOR ME.
THAT'S OKAY. I'VE GOT LOWER-PRICED ITEMS AVAILABLE TOO.
KCHAK
TOMO, HE SERIOUSLY DOESN'T HAVE ANY MONEY. GIVE THE SALES PITCH A REST, OKAY?
AH.
WELCOME BACK.
I HATE TO SAY IT, BUT THEY WON'T WORK. I GUESS I'LL JUST HAVE TO GIVE UP ON THEM.
COME BACK IF YOU EVER FIND A LADY YOU FANCY.
I'LL PUT YOU IN SOMETHING THAT'LL DEFINITELY CATCH HER EYE!
COME AGAIN!
...
JUST IGNORE HIM.

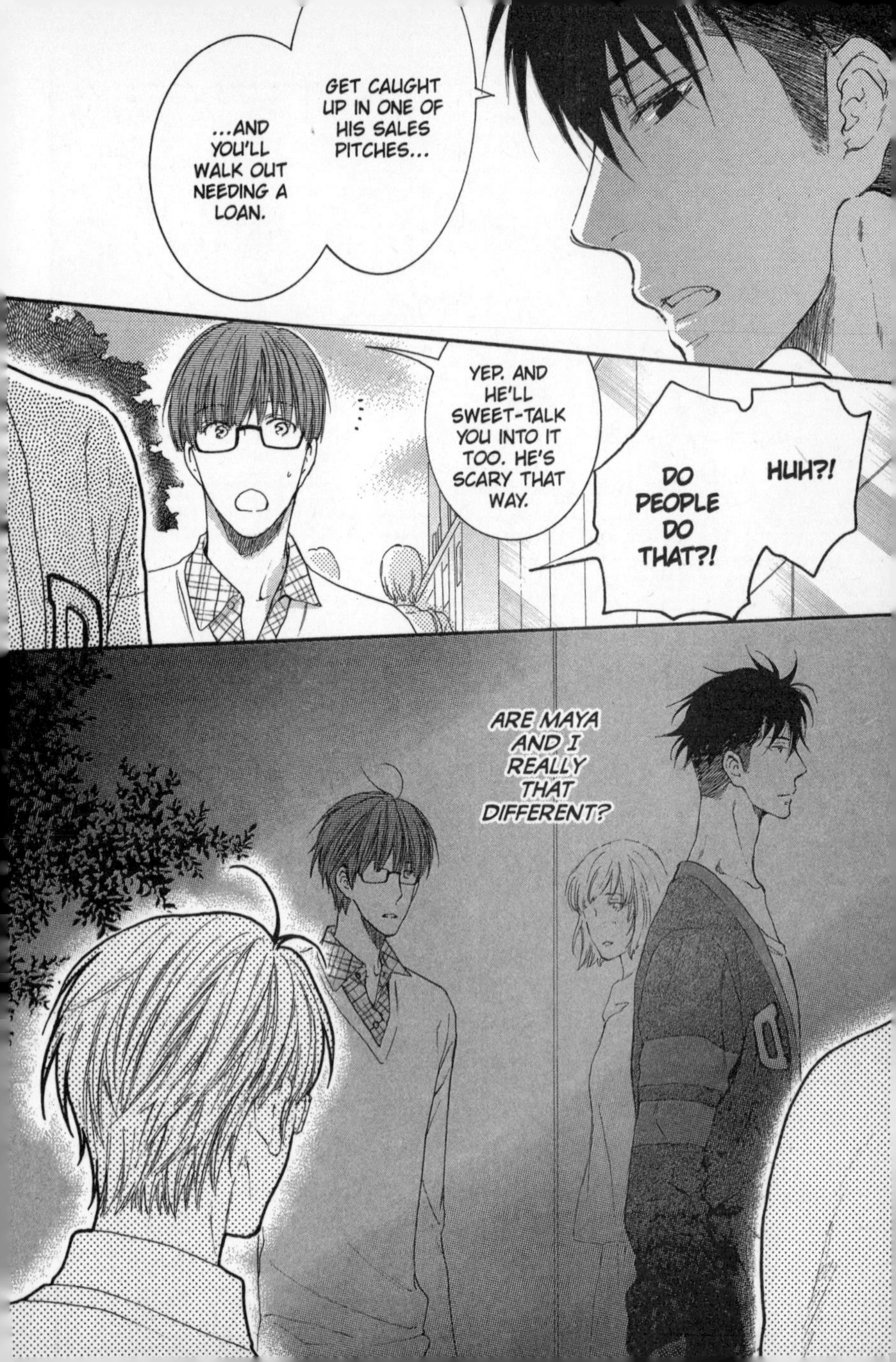
GET CAUGHT UP IN ONE OF HIS SALES PITCHES...
...AND YOU'LL WALK OUT NEEDING A LOAN.
HUH?!
DO PEOPLE DO THAT?!
YEP. AND HE'LL SWEET-TALK YOU INTO IT TOO. HE'S SCARY THAT WAY.
...
ARE MAYA AND I REALLY THAT DIFFERENT?

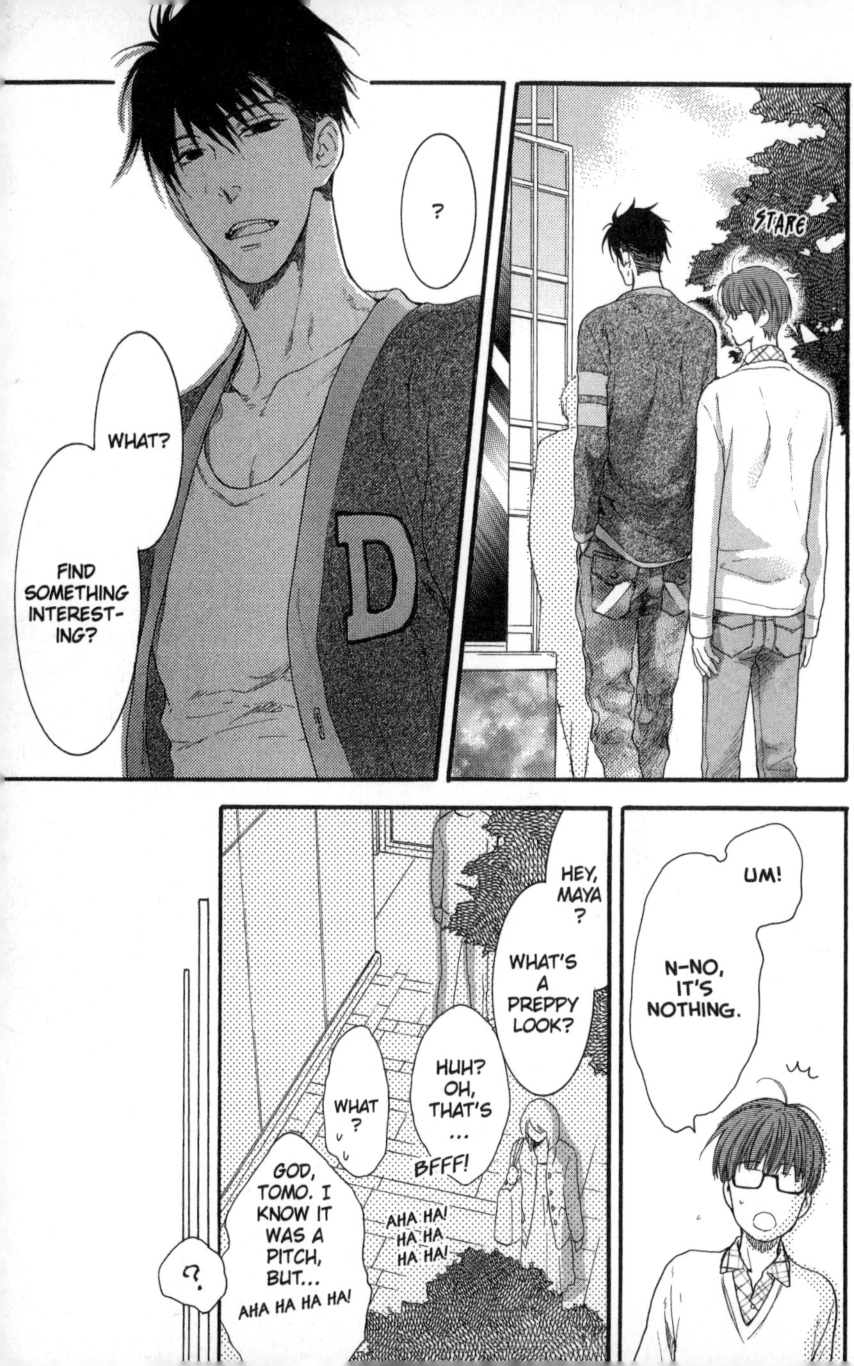
STARE
?
WHAT?
FIND SOMETHING INTERESTING?
UM!
N-NO, IT'S NOTHING.
HEY, MAYA?
WHAT'S A PREPPY LOOK?
HUH? OH, THAT'S...
BFFF!
WHAT?
GOD, TOMO. I KNOW IT WAS A PITCH, BUT...
AHA HA HA HA!
AHA HA! HA HA HA HA!
?

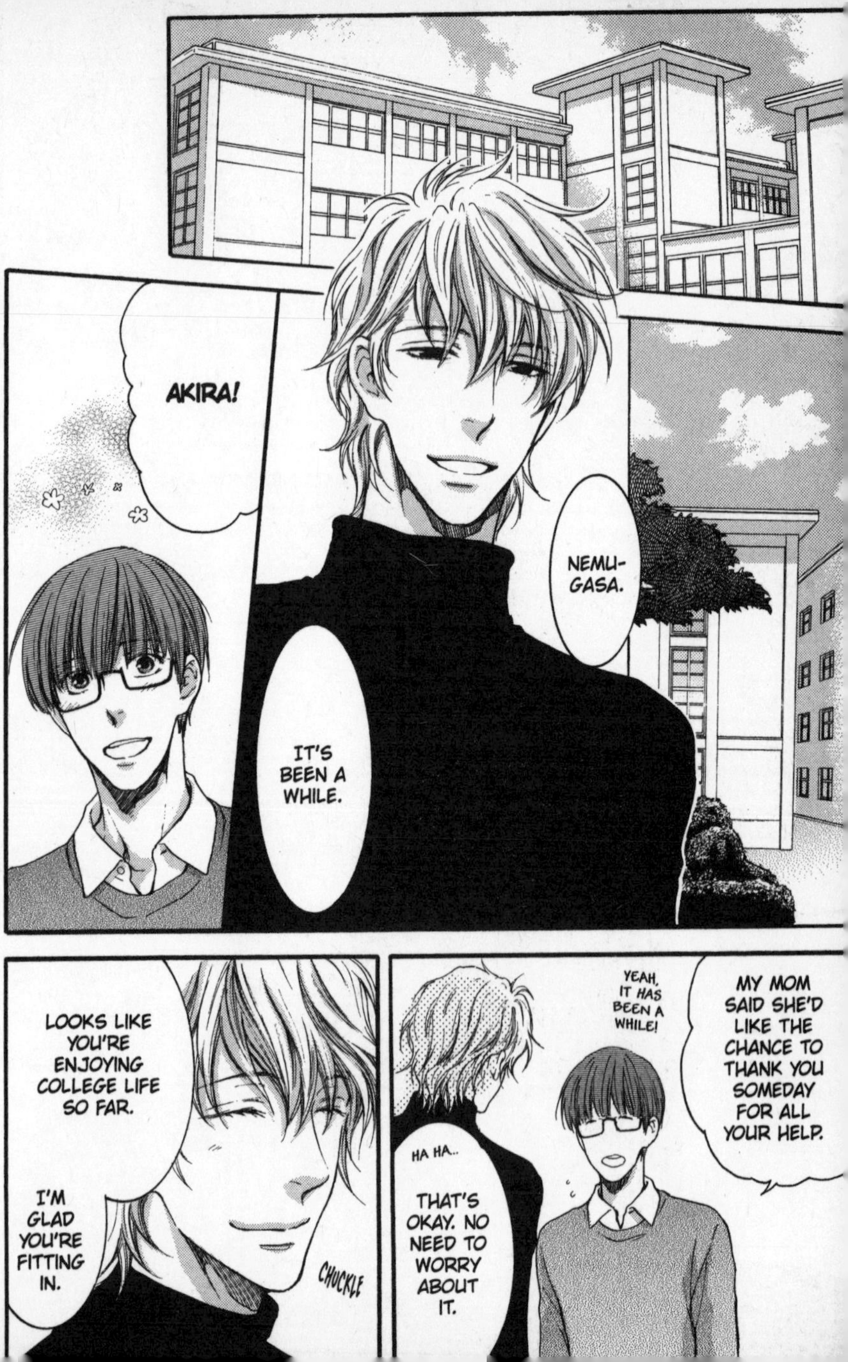
NEMU-GASA.
IT'S BEEN A WHILE.
AKIRA!
MY MOM SAID SHE'D LIKE THE CHANCE TO THANK YOU SOMEDAY FOR ALL YOUR HELP.
YEAH, IT HAS BEEN A WHILE!
HA HA..
THAT'S OKAY. NO NEED TO WORRY ABOUT IT.
LOOKS LIKE YOU'RE ENJOYING COLLEGE LIFE SO FAR.
I'M GLAD YOU'RE FITTING IN.
CHUCKLE

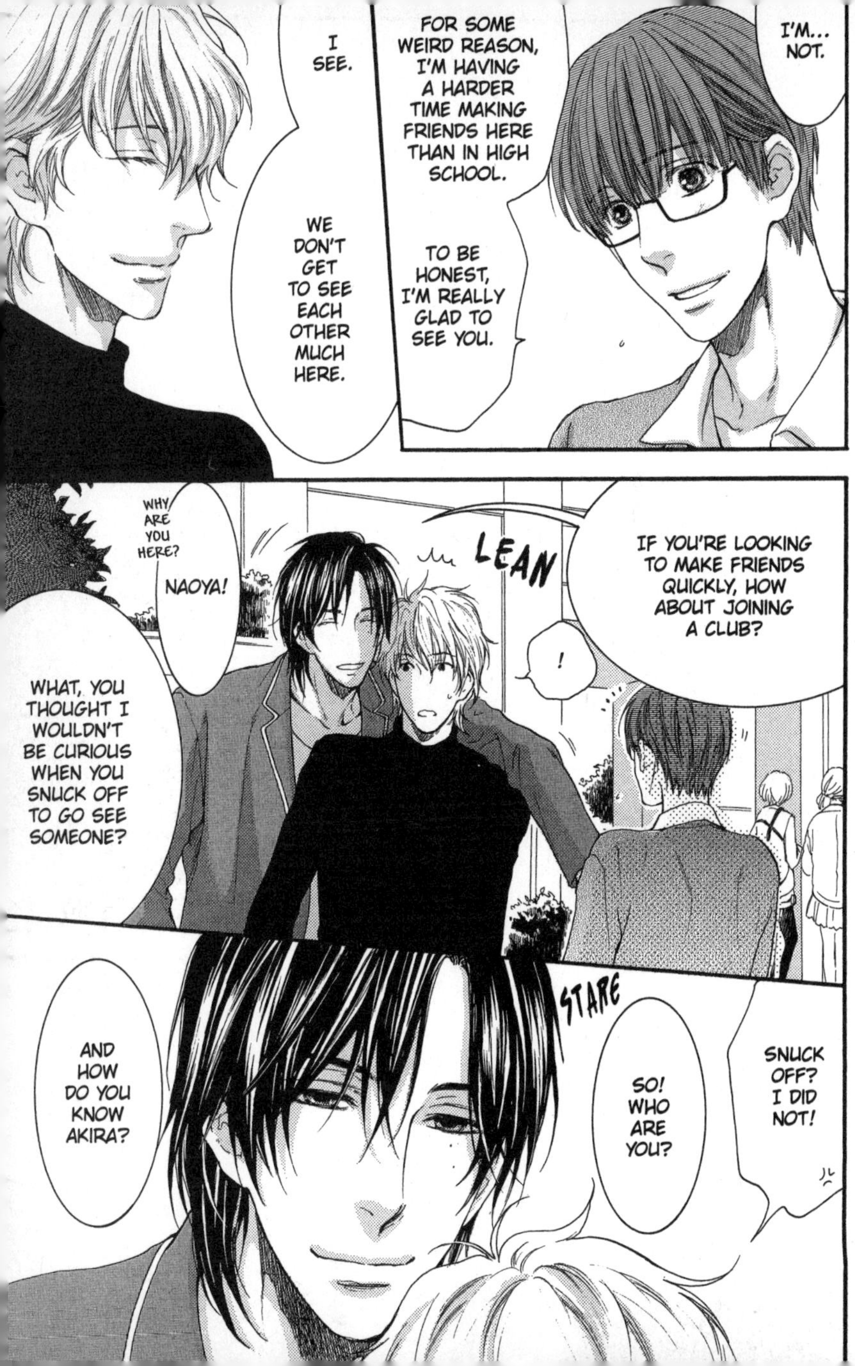
I'M... NOT.
FOR SOME WEIRD REASON, I'M HAVING A HARDER TIME MAKING FRIENDS HERE THAN IN HIGH SCHOOL.
TO BE HONEST, I'M REALLY GLAD TO SEE YOU.
I SEE.
WE DON'T GET TO SEE EACH OTHER MUCH HERE.
IF YOU'RE LOOKING TO MAKE FRIENDS QUICKLY, HOW ABOUT JOINING A CLUB?
!
LEAN
NAOYA!
WHY ARE YOU HERE?
WHAT, YOU THOUGHT I WOULDN'T BE CURIOUS WHEN YOU SNUCK OFF TO GO SEE SOMEONE?
SNUCK OFF? I DID NOT!
STARE
SO! WHO ARE YOU?
AND HOW DO YOU KNOW AKIRA?

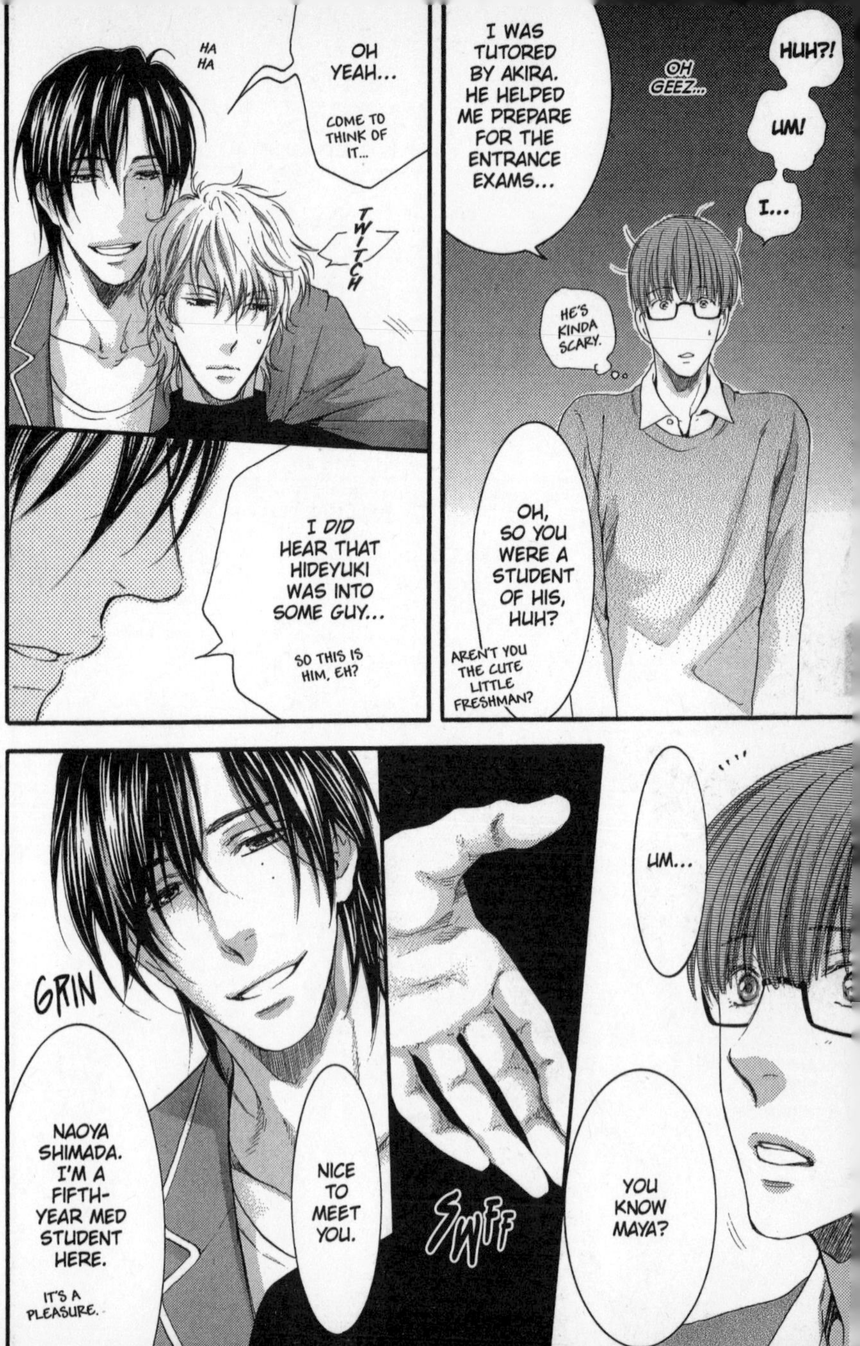
HUH?!
UM!
I...
I WAS TUTORED BY AKIRA. HE HELPED ME PREPARE FOR THE ENTRANCE EXAMS...
OH GEEZ...
HE'S KINDA SCARY.
OH, SO YOU WERE A STUDENT OF HIS, HUH?
AREN'T YOU THE CUTE LITTLE FRESHMAN?
OH YEAH...
COME TO THINK OF IT...
HA HA
TWITCH
I DID HEAR THAT HIDEYUKI WAS INTO SOME GUY...
SO THIS IS HIM, EH?
...
UM...
YOU KNOW MAYA?
NICE TO MEET YOU.
SWFF
NAOYA SHIMADA. I'M A FIFTH-YEAR MED STUDENT HERE.
IT'S A PLEASURE.
GRIN

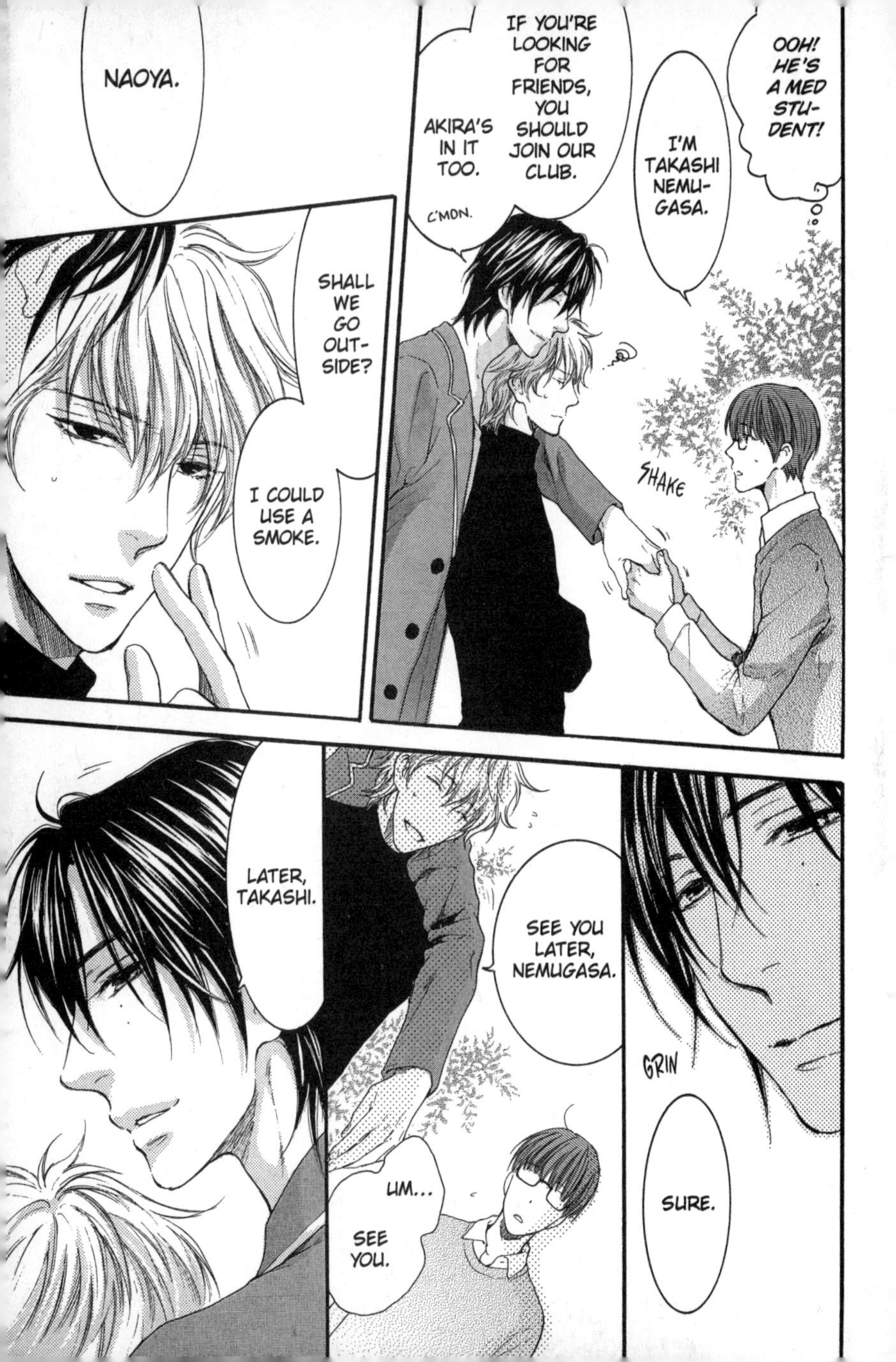
OOH! HE'S A MED STU-DENT!
I'M TAKASHI NEMU-GASA.
IF YOU'RE LOOKING FOR FRIENDS, YOU SHOULD JOIN OUR CLUB.
AKIRA'S IN IT TOO.
C'MON.
SHAKE
NAOYA.
SHALL WE GO OUT-SIDE?
I COULD USE A SMOKE.
GRIN
SURE.
SEE YOU LATER, NEMUGASA.
UM...
SEE YOU.
LATER, TAKASHI.

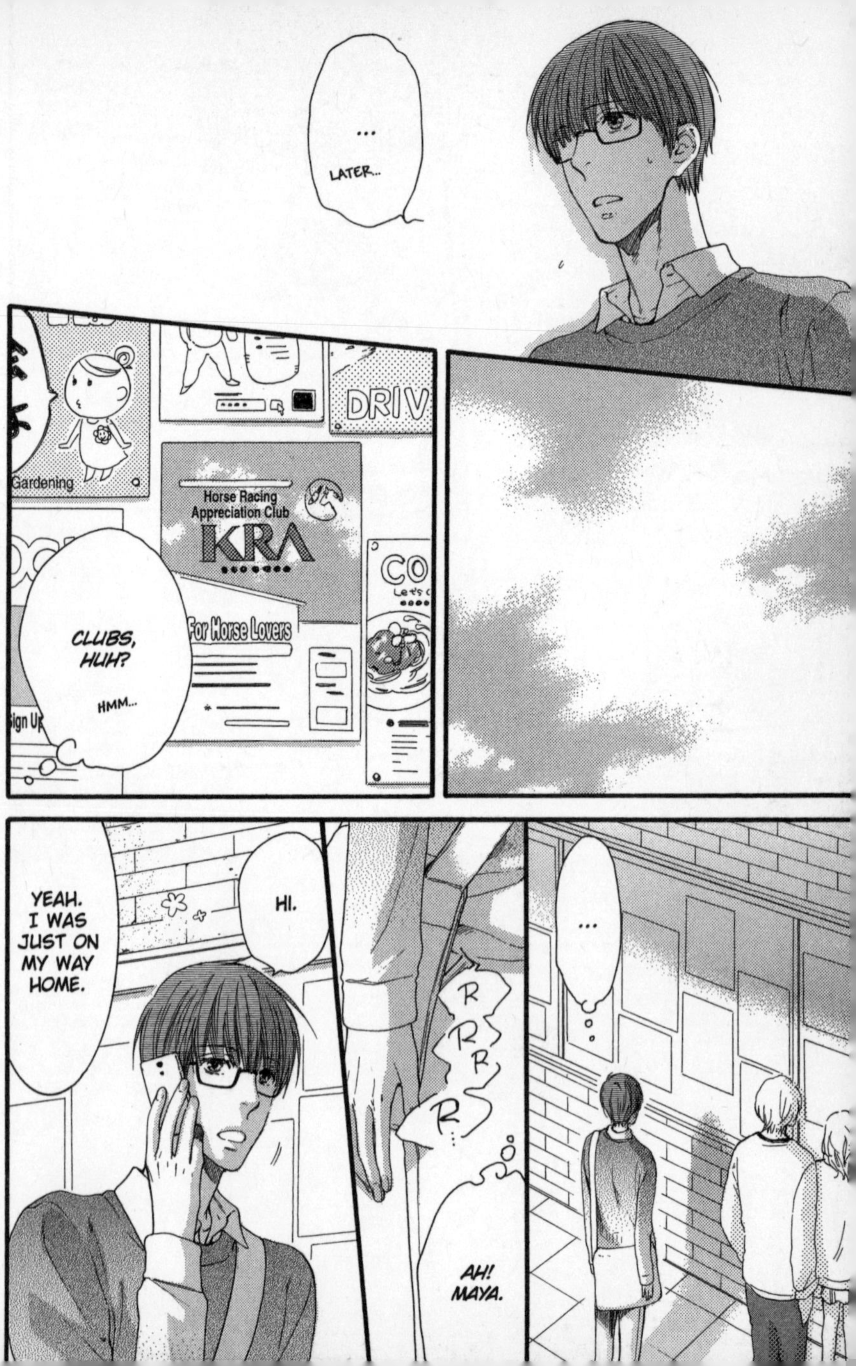
... LATER...
Gardening
Horse Racing Appreciation Club
KRA
For Horse Lovers
CLUBS, HUH? HMM...
...
RRRR...
AH! MAYA.
HI.
YEAH. I WAS JUST ON MY WAY HOME.

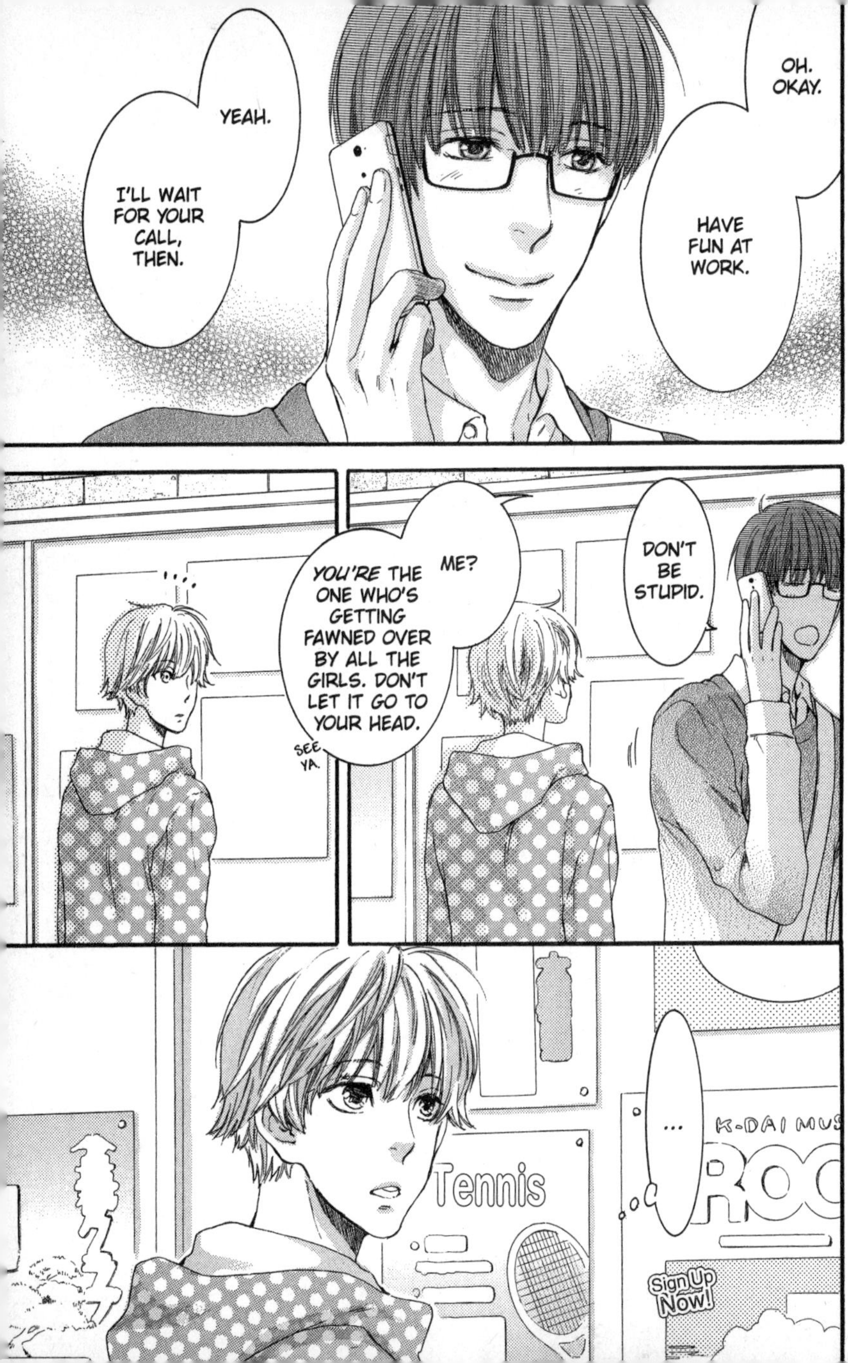

OH. OKAY.
HAVE FUN AT WORK.
YEAH.
I'LL WAIT FOR YOUR CALL, THEN.
DON'T BE STUPID.
ME?
YOU'RE THE ONE WHO'S GETTING FAWNED OVER BY ALL THE GIRLS. DON'T LET IT GO TO YOUR HEAD.
SEE YA.
...
...
K-DAI MUS
Tennis
Sign Up Now!

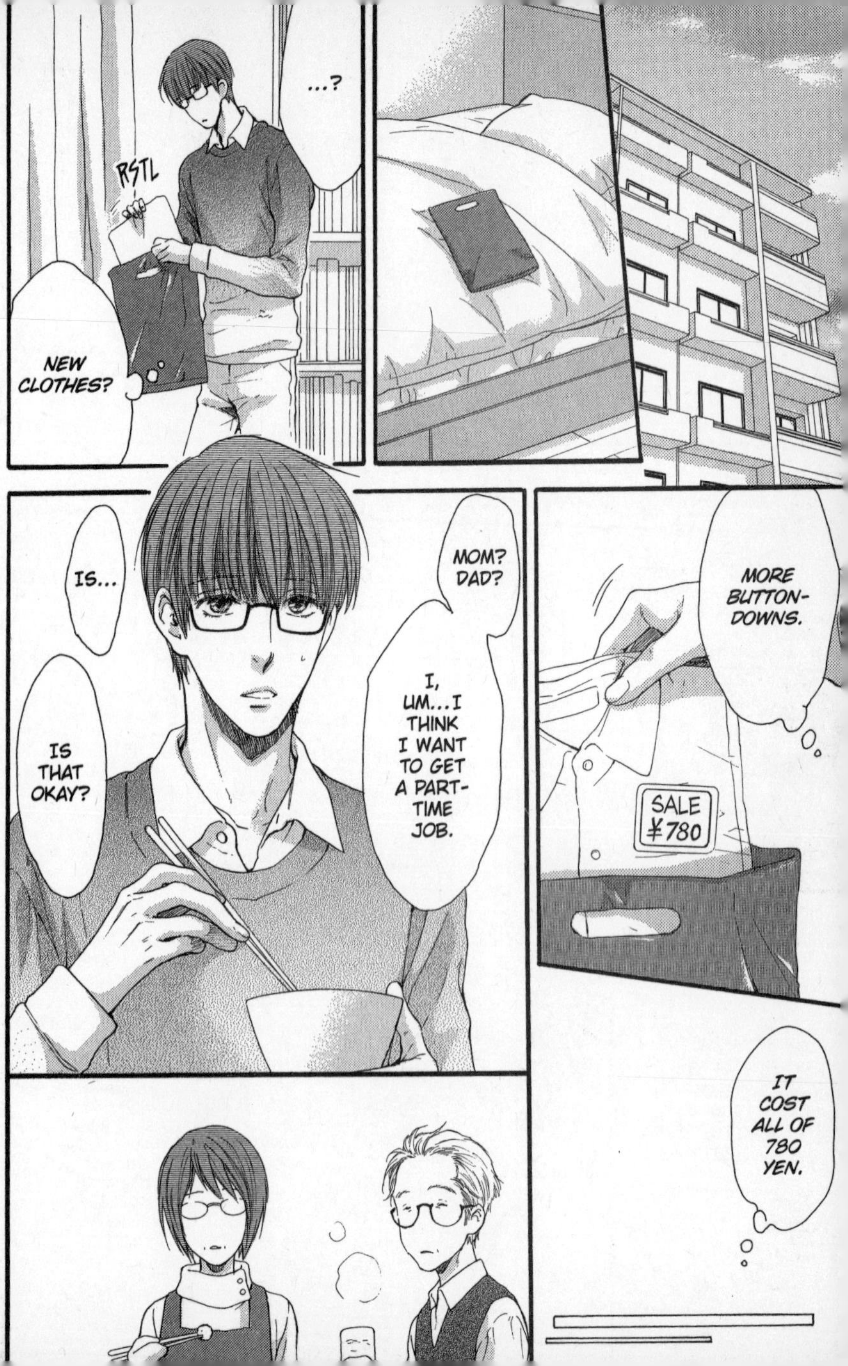

...?
RSTL
NEW CLOTHES?
MORE BUTTON-DOWNS.
SALE ¥780
MOM? DAD?
I, UM...I THINK I WANT TO GET A PART-TIME JOB.
IS...
IS THAT OKAY?
IT COST ALL OF 780 YEN.

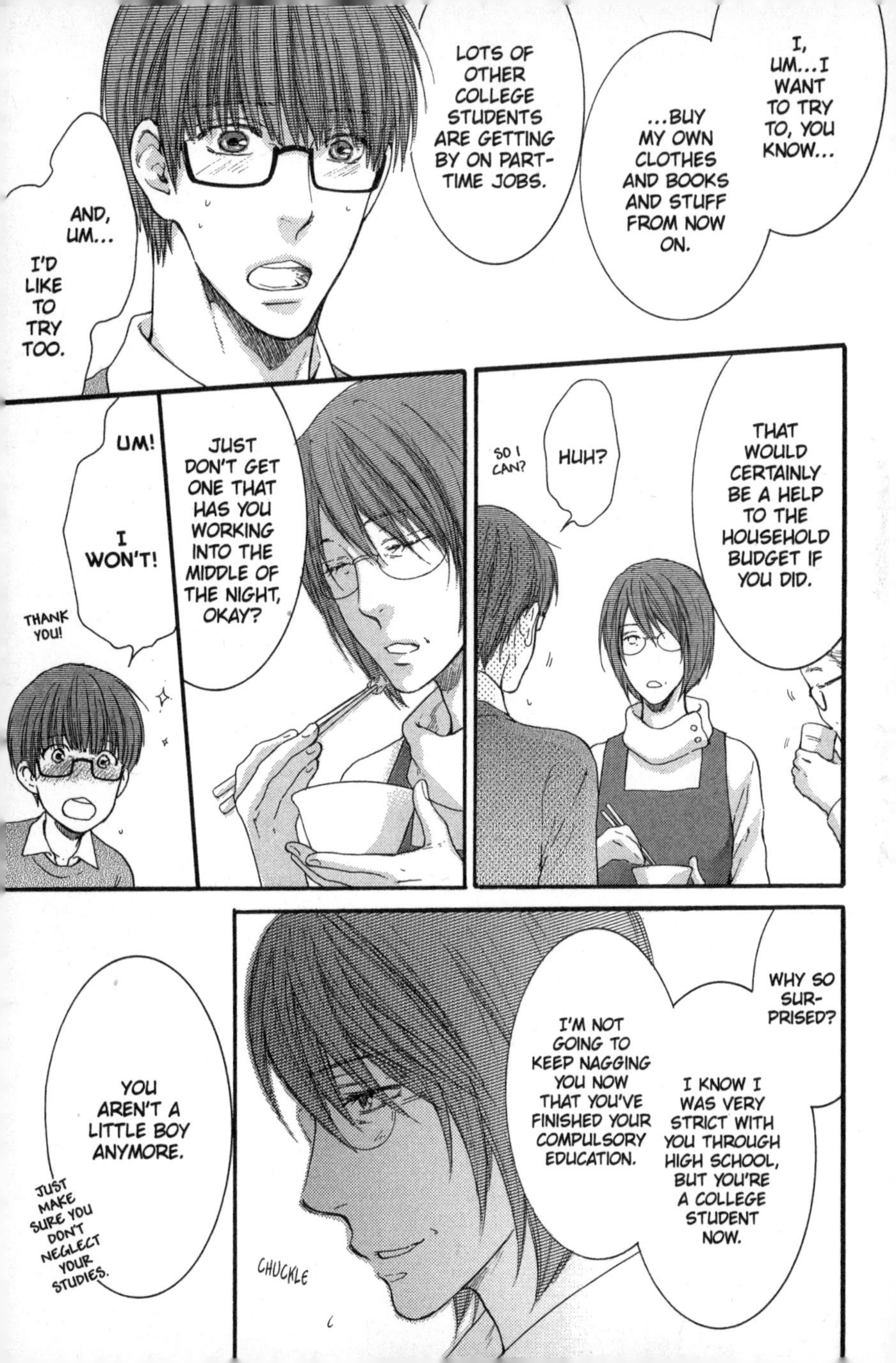
I, UM...I WANT TO TRY TO, YOU KNOW...
...BUY MY OWN CLOTHES AND BOOKS AND STUFF FROM NOW ON.
LOTS OF OTHER COLLEGE STUDENTS ARE GETTING BY ON PART-TIME JOBS.
AND, UM...
I'D LIKE TO TRY TOO.
THAT WOULD CERTAINLY BE A HELP TO THE HOUSEHOLD BUDGET IF YOU DID.
HUH?
SO I CAN?
JUST DON'T GET ONE THAT HAS YOU WORKING INTO THE MIDDLE OF THE NIGHT, OKAY?
UM!
I WON'T!
THANK YOU!
WHY SO SURPRISED?
I KNOW I WAS VERY STRICT WITH YOU THROUGH HIGH SCHOOL, BUT YOU'RE A COLLEGE STUDENT NOW.
I'M NOT GOING TO KEEP NAGGING YOU NOW THAT YOU'VE FINISHED YOUR COMPULSORY EDUCATION.
YOU AREN'T A LITTLE BOY ANYMORE.
CHUCKLE
JUST MAKE SURE YOU DON'T NEGLECT YOUR STUDIES.

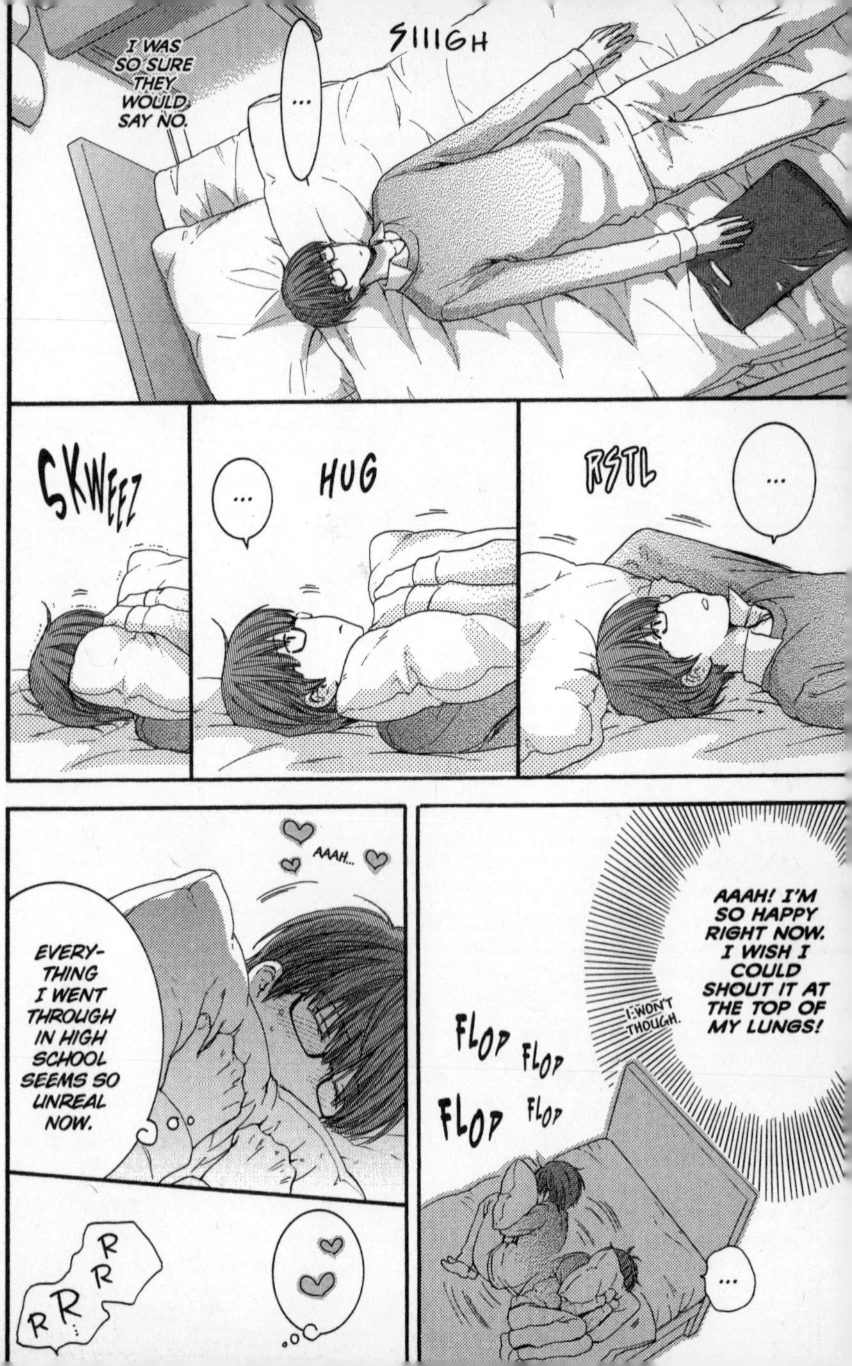
SIIIGH
...
I WAS SO SURE THEY WOULD SAY NO.
RSTL
...
HUG
...
SKWEEZ
AAAH! I'M SO HAPPY RIGHT NOW. I WISH I COULD SHOUT IT AT THE TOP OF MY LUNGS!
I WON'T THOUGH.
FLOP FLOP
FLOP FLOP
...
AAAH..
EVERY-THING I WENT THROUGH IN HIGH SCHOOL SEEMS SO UNREAL NOW.
RRRR...

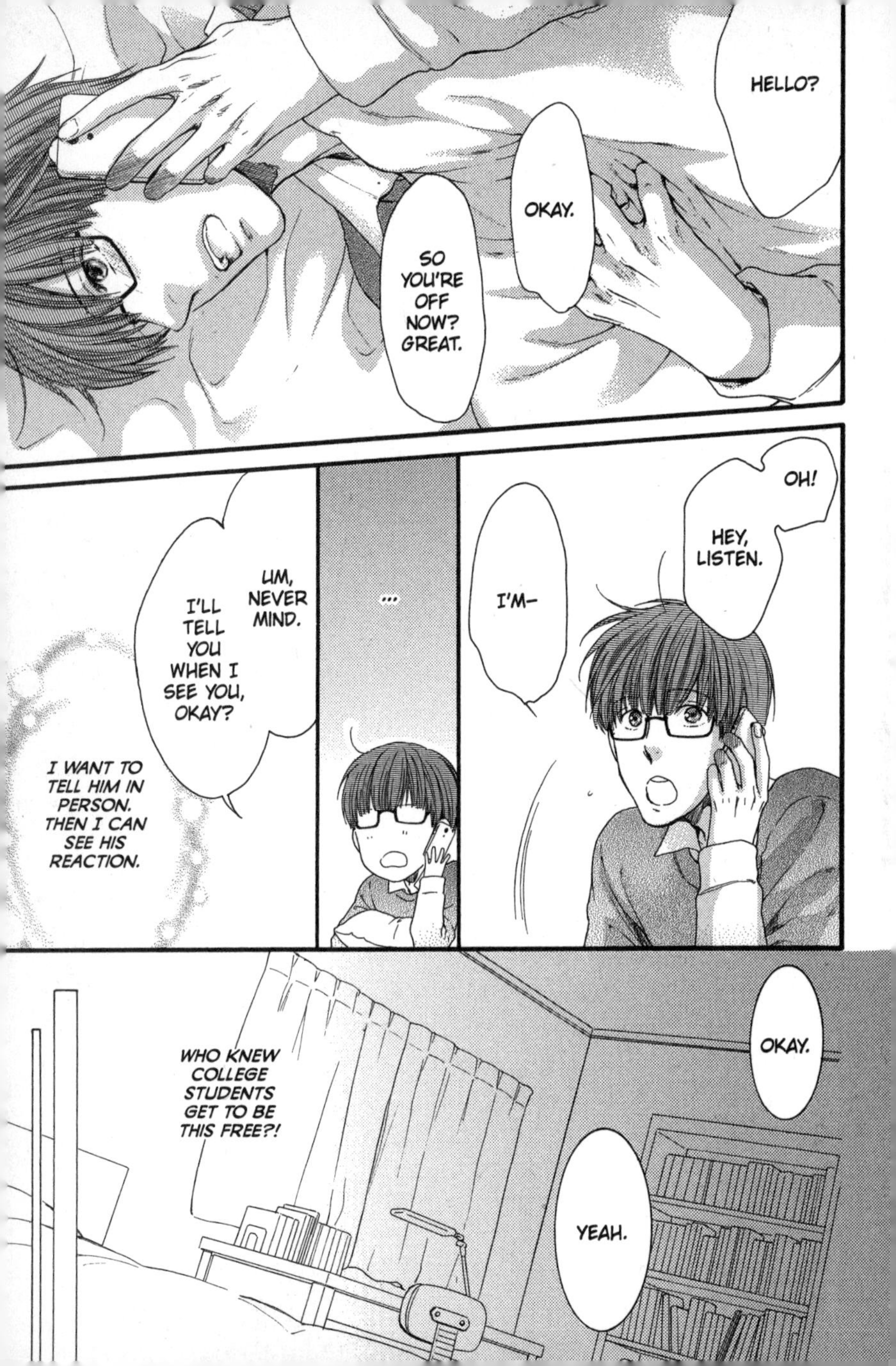
HELLO?
OKAY.
SO YOU'RE OFF NOW? GREAT.
OH!
HEY, LISTEN.
I'M—
...
UM, NEVER MIND.
I'LL TELL YOU WHEN I SEE YOU, OKAY?
I WANT TO TELL HIM IN PERSON. THEN I CAN SEE HIS REACTION.
OKAY.
YEAH.
WHO KNEW COLLEGE STUDENTS GET TO BE THIS FREE?!

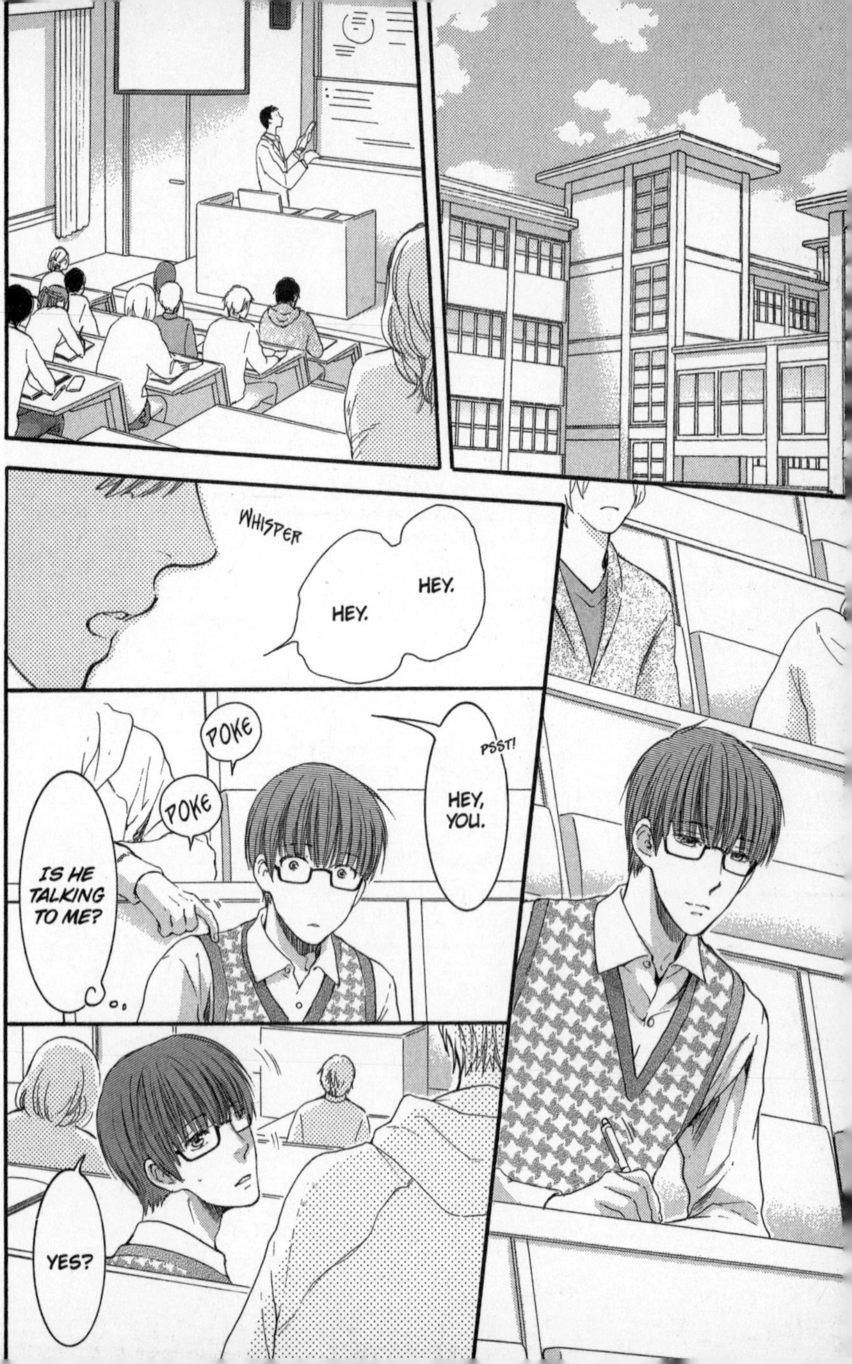

HEY.
HEY.
WHISPER
PSST!
HEY, YOU.
POKE
POKE
IS HE TALKING TO ME?
YES?

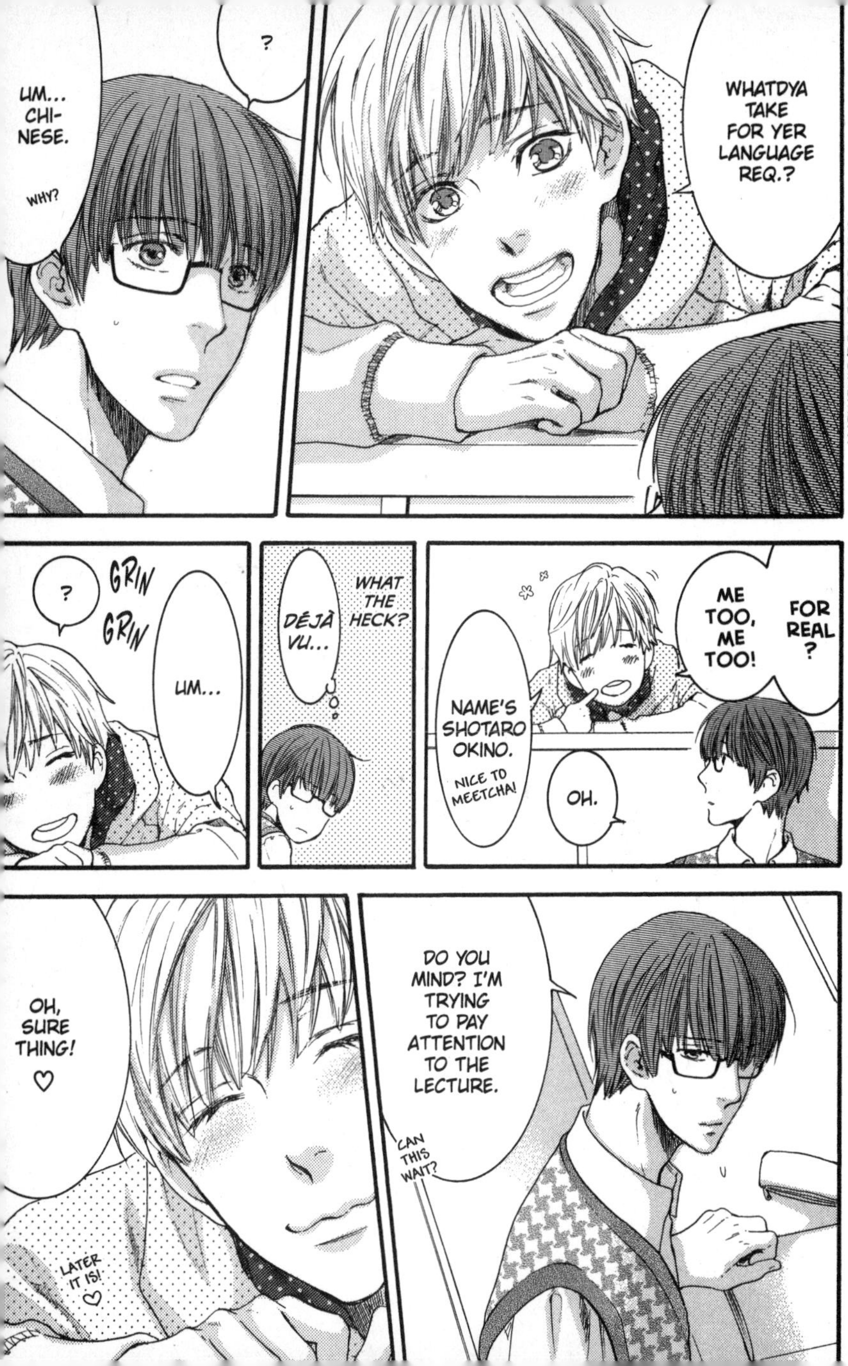
WHATDYA TAKE FOR YER LANGUAGE REQ.?
?
UM... CHI-NESE.
WHY?
FOR REAL?
ME TOO, ME TOO!
NAME'S SHOTARO OKINO.
NICE TO MEETCHA!
OH.
WHAT THE HECK?
DÉJÀ VU...
GRIN GRIN
?
UM...
DO YOU MIND? I'M TRYING TO PAY ATTENTION TO THE LECTURE.
CAN THIS WAIT?
OH, SURE THING! ♡
LATER IT IS! ♡

※ LANGUAGE REQ. = FOREIGN LANGUAGE REQUIREMENT

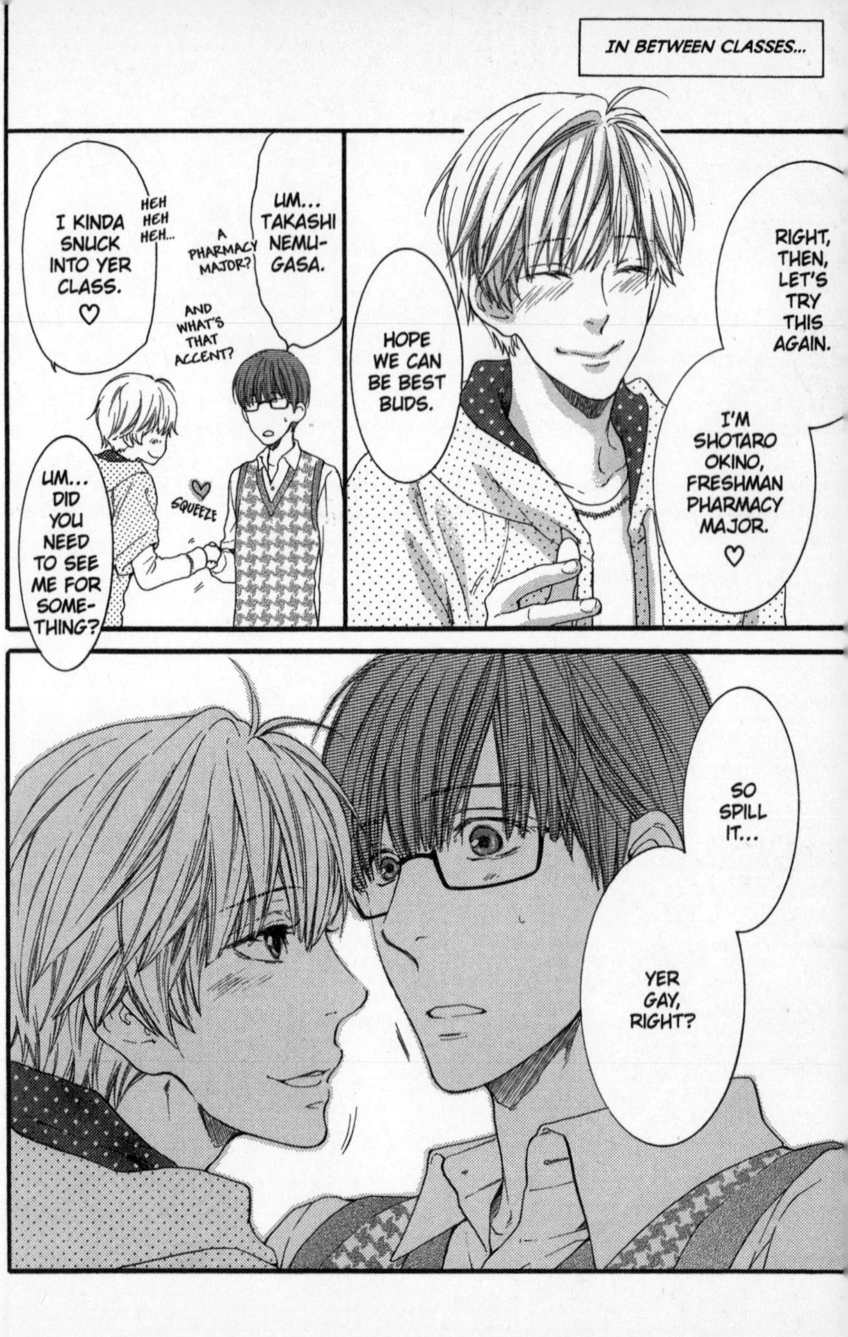
IN BETWEEN CLASSES...
RIGHT, THEN, LET'S TRY THIS AGAIN.
I'M SHOTARO OKINO, FRESHMAN PHARMACY MAJOR. ♡
HOPE WE CAN BE BEST BUDS.
UM... TAKASHI NEMU-GASA.
A PHARMACY MAJOR?
HEH HEH HEH...
I KINDA SNUCK INTO YER CLASS. ♡
AND WHAT'S THAT ACCENT?
♡ SQUEEZE
UM... DID YOU NEED TO SEE ME FOR SOME-THING?
SO SPILL IT...
YER GAY, RIGHT?

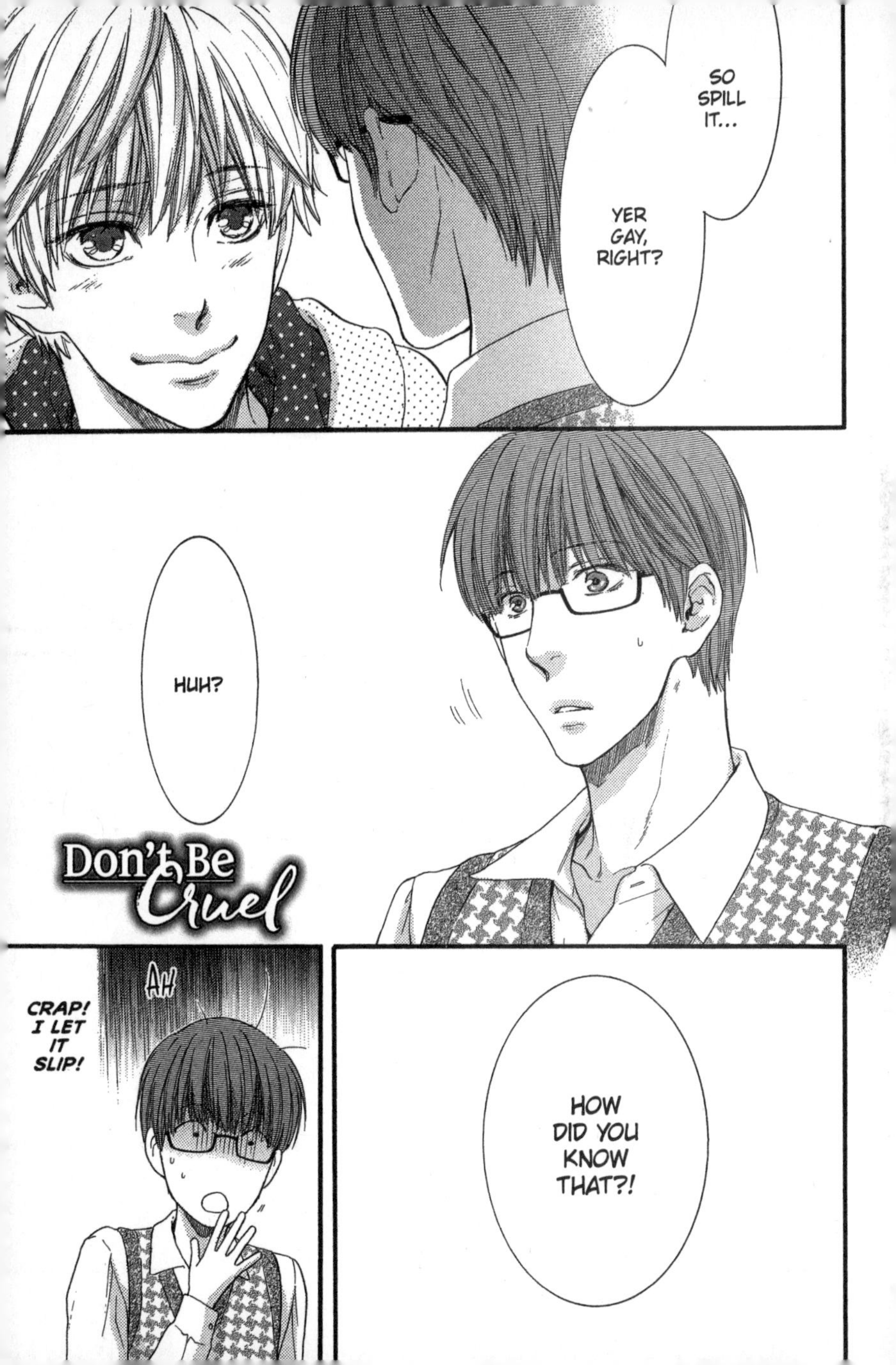
SO SPILL IT...
YER GAY, RIGHT?
HUH?
Don't Be Cruel
HOW DID YOU KNOW THAT?!
AH
CRAP! I LET IT SLIP!

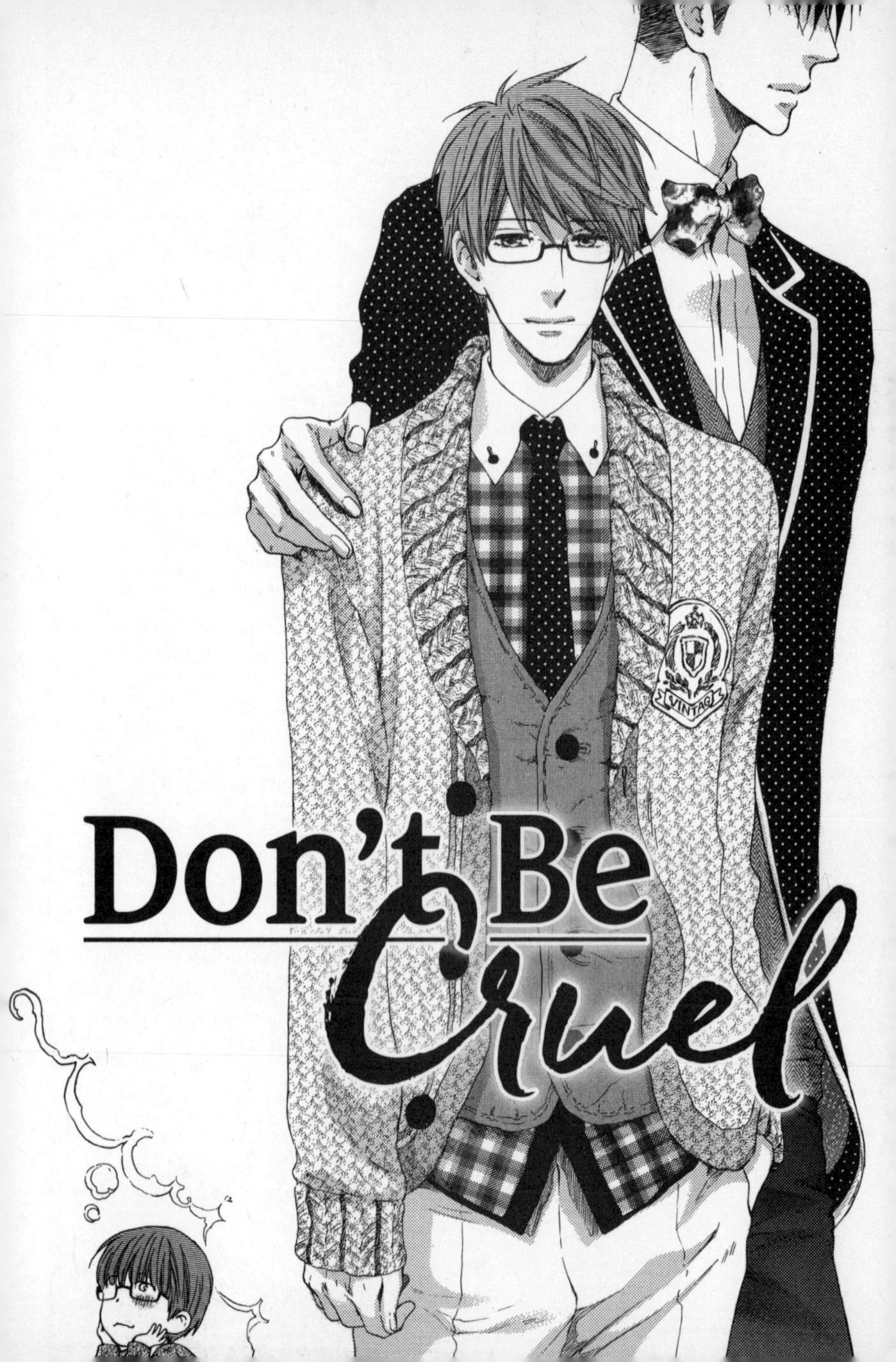
Don't Be Cruel
VINTAG

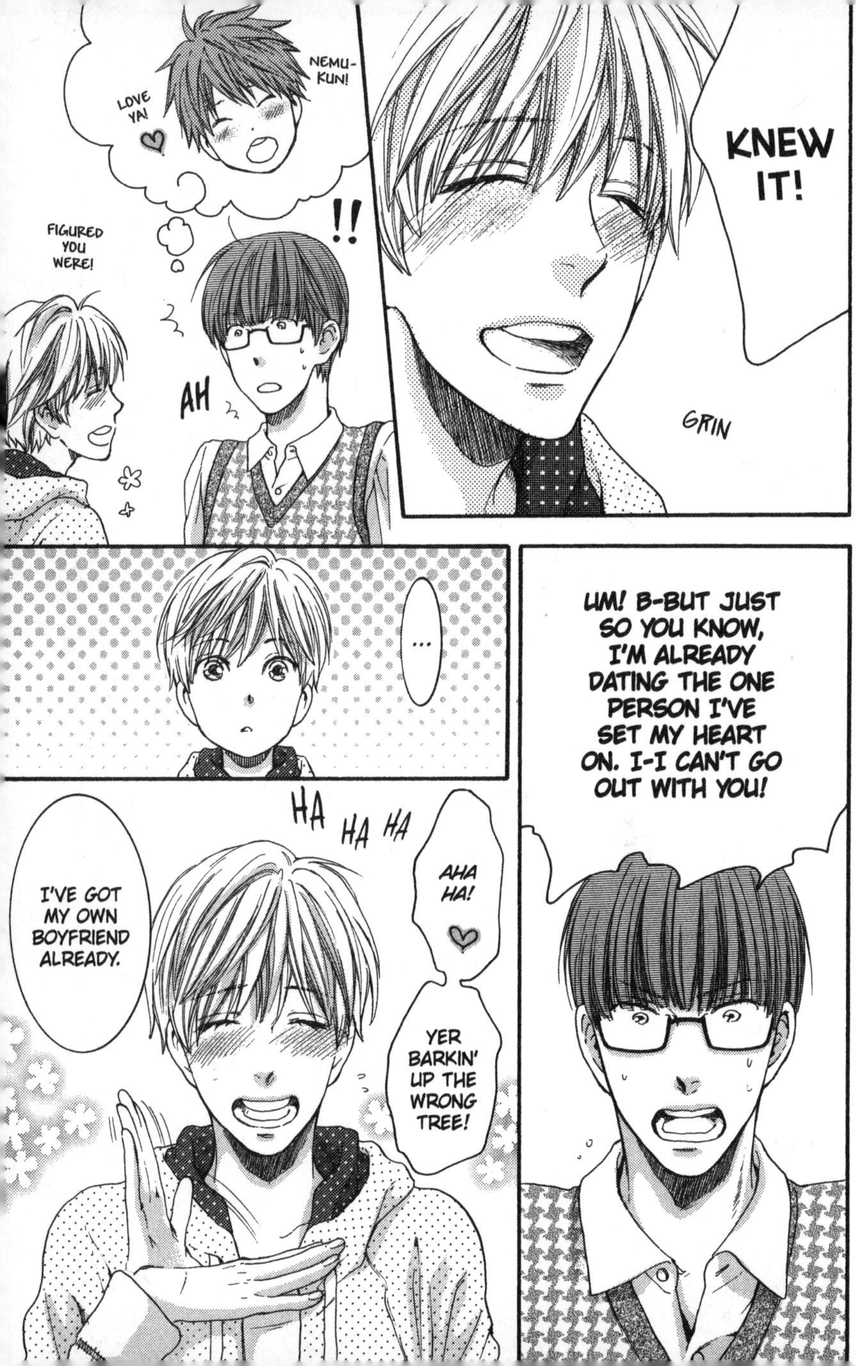
KNEW IT!
GRIN
NEMU-KUN!
LOVE YA!
!!
FIGURED YOU WERE!
AH
UM! B-BUT JUST SO YOU KNOW, I'M ALREADY DATING THE ONE PERSON I'VE SET MY HEART ON. I-I CAN'T GO OUT WITH YOU!
...
HA HA HA
AHA HA!
YER BARKIN' UP THE WRONG TREE!
I'VE GOT MY OWN BOYFRIEND ALREADY.

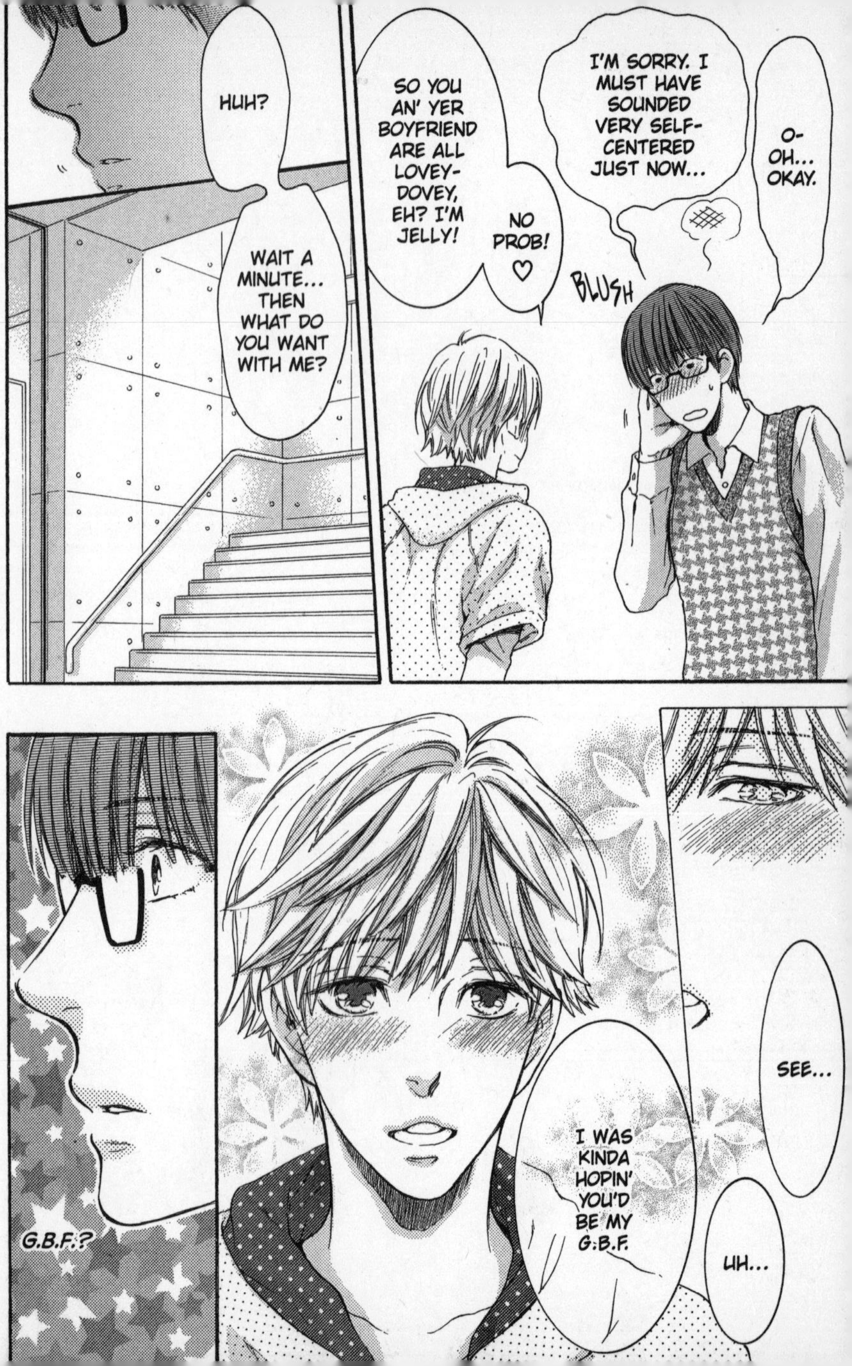
O-OH... OKAY.
I'M SORRY. I MUST HAVE SOUNDED VERY SELF-CENTERED JUST NOW...
BLUSH
NO PROB! ♡
SO YOU AN' YER BOYFRIEND ARE ALL LOVEY-DOVEY, EH? I'M JELLY!
HUH?
WAIT A MINUTE... THEN WHAT DO YOU WANT WITH ME?
SEE...
UH...
I WAS KINDA HOPIN' YOU'D BE MY G.B.F.
G.B.F.?

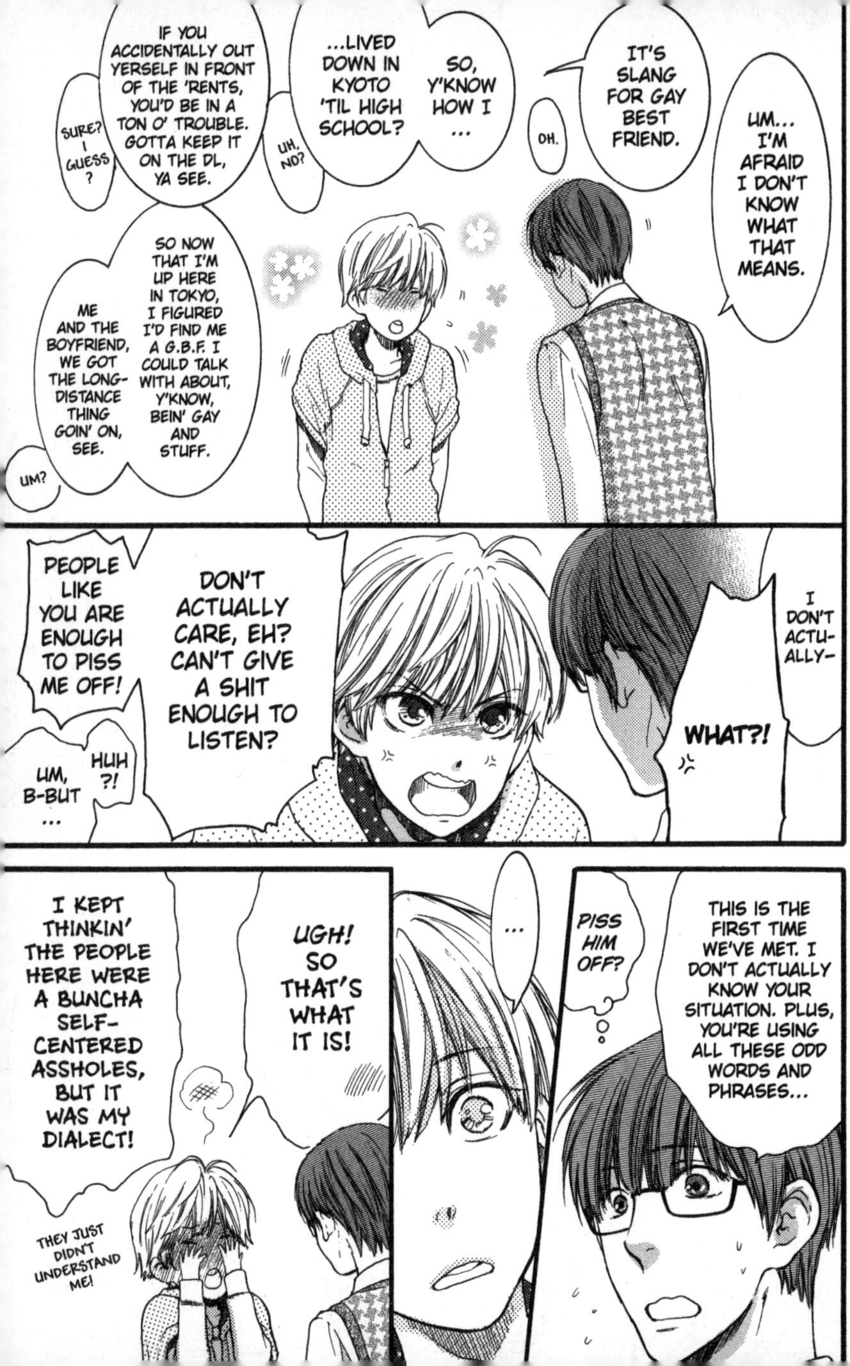
UM... I'M AFRAID I DON'T KNOW WHAT THAT MEANS.
IT'S SLANG FOR GAY BEST FRIEND.
OH.
SO, Y'KNOW HOW I ...
...LIVED DOWN IN KYOTO 'TIL HIGH SCHOOL?
UH, NO?
IF YOU ACCIDENTALLY OUT YERSELF IN FRONT OF THE 'RENTS, YOU'D BE IN A TON O' TROUBLE. GOTTA KEEP IT ON THE DL, YA SEE.
SURE? I GUESS ?
SO NOW THAT I'M UP HERE IN TOKYO, I FIGURED I'D FIND ME A G.B.F. I COULD TALK WITH ABOUT, Y'KNOW, BEIN' GAY AND STUFF.
ME AND THE BOYFRIEND, WE GOT THE LONG-DISTANCE THING GOIN' ON, SEE.
UM?
I DON'T ACTU-ALLY-
WHAT?!
DON'T ACTUALLY CARE, EH? CAN'T GIVE A SHIT ENOUGH TO LISTEN?
PEOPLE LIKE YOU ARE ENOUGH TO PISS ME OFF!
HUH ?!
UM, B-BUT ...
THIS IS THE FIRST TIME WE'VE MET. I DON'T ACTUALLY KNOW YOUR SITUATION. PLUS, YOU'RE USING ALL THESE ODD WORDS AND PHRASES...
PISS HIM OFF?
...
UGH! SO THAT'S WHAT IT IS!
I KEPT THINKIN' THE PEOPLE HERE WERE A BUNCHA SELF-CENTERED ASSHOLES, BUT IT WAS MY DIALECT!
THEY JUST DIDN'T UNDERSTAND ME!

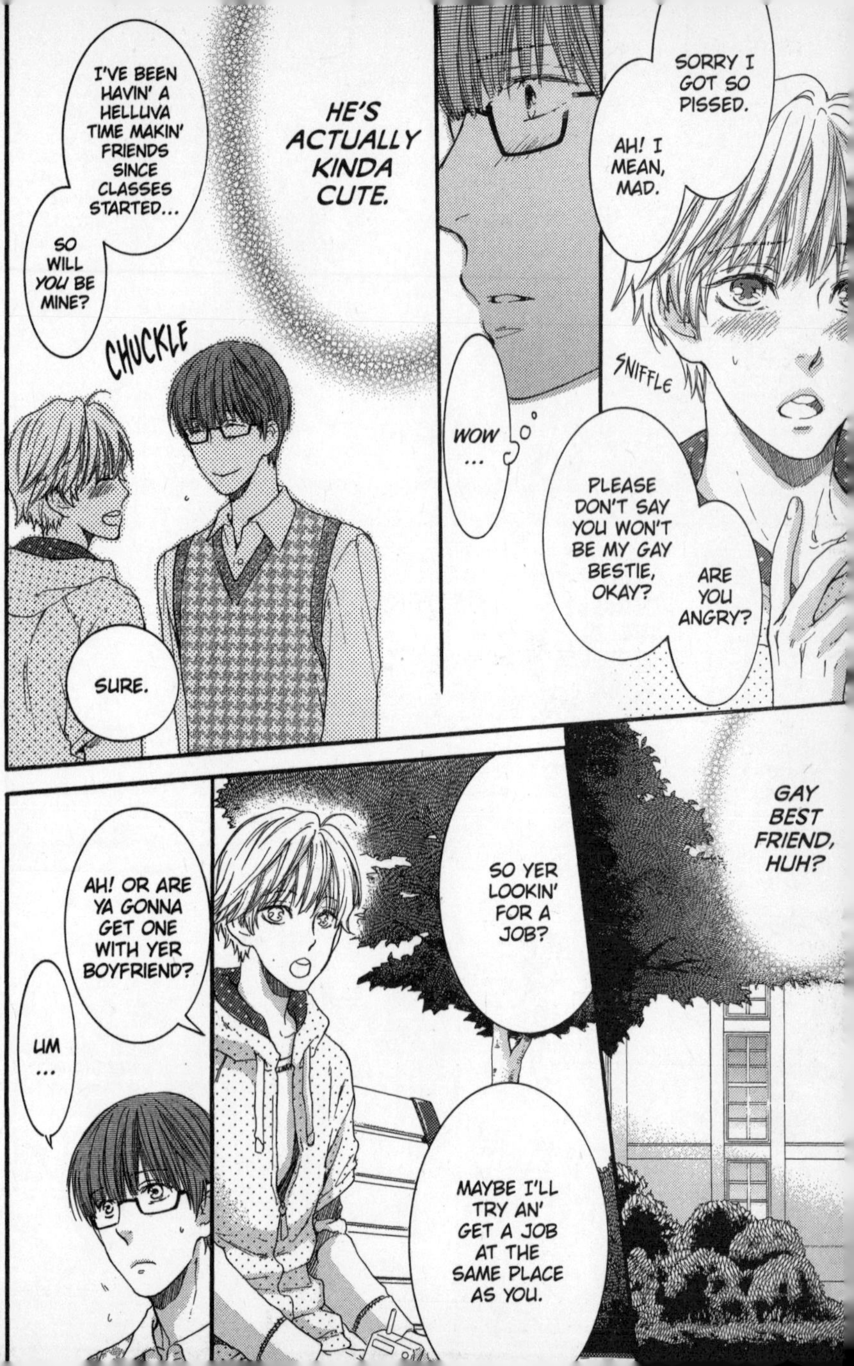
SORRY I GOT SO PISSED.
AH! I MEAN, MAD.
SNIFFLE
ARE YOU ANGRY?
PLEASE DON'T SAY YOU WON'T BE MY GAY BESTIE, OKAY?
WOW ...
HE'S ACTUALLY KINDA CUTE.
I'VE BEEN HAVIN' A HELLUVA TIME MAKIN' FRIENDS SINCE CLASSES STARTED...
SO WILL *YOU* BE MINE?
CHUCKLE
SURE.
GAY BEST FRIEND, HUH?
SO YER LOOKIN' FOR A JOB?
MAYBE I'LL TRY AN' GET A JOB AT THE SAME PLACE AS YOU.
AH! OR ARE YA GONNA GET ONE WITH YER BOYFRIEND?
UM ...

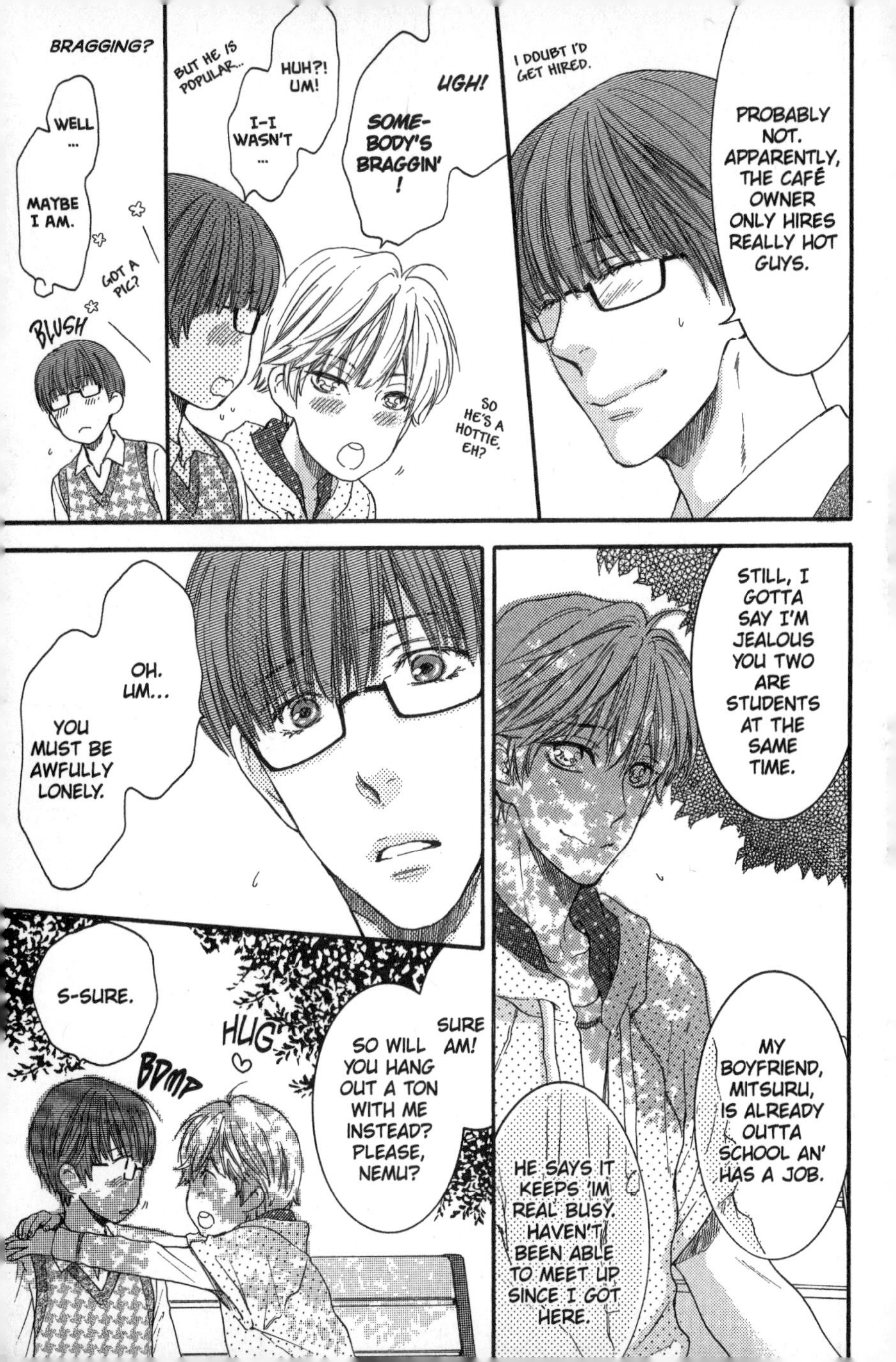
PROBABLY NOT. APPARENTLY, THE CAFÉ OWNER ONLY HIRES REALLY HOT GUYS.
I DOUBT I'D GET HIRED.
UGH!
SOME-BODY'S BRAGGIN'!
HUH?! UM!
I-I WASN'T...
BUT HE IS POPULAR...
SO HE'S A HOTTIE, EH?
BRAGGING?
WELL... MAYBE I AM.
GOT A PIC?
BLUSH
STILL, I GOTTA SAY I'M JEALOUS YOU TWO ARE STUDENTS AT THE SAME TIME.
MY BOYFRIEND, MITSURU, IS ALREADY OUTTA SCHOOL AN' HAS A JOB.
HE SAYS IT KEEPS 'IM REAL BUSY. HAVEN'T BEEN ABLE TO MEET UP SINCE I GOT HERE.
OH. UM... YOU MUST BE AWFULLY LONELY.
SURE AM!
SO WILL YOU HANG OUT A TON WITH ME INSTEAD? PLEASE, NEMU?
HUG
BDMP
S-SURE.

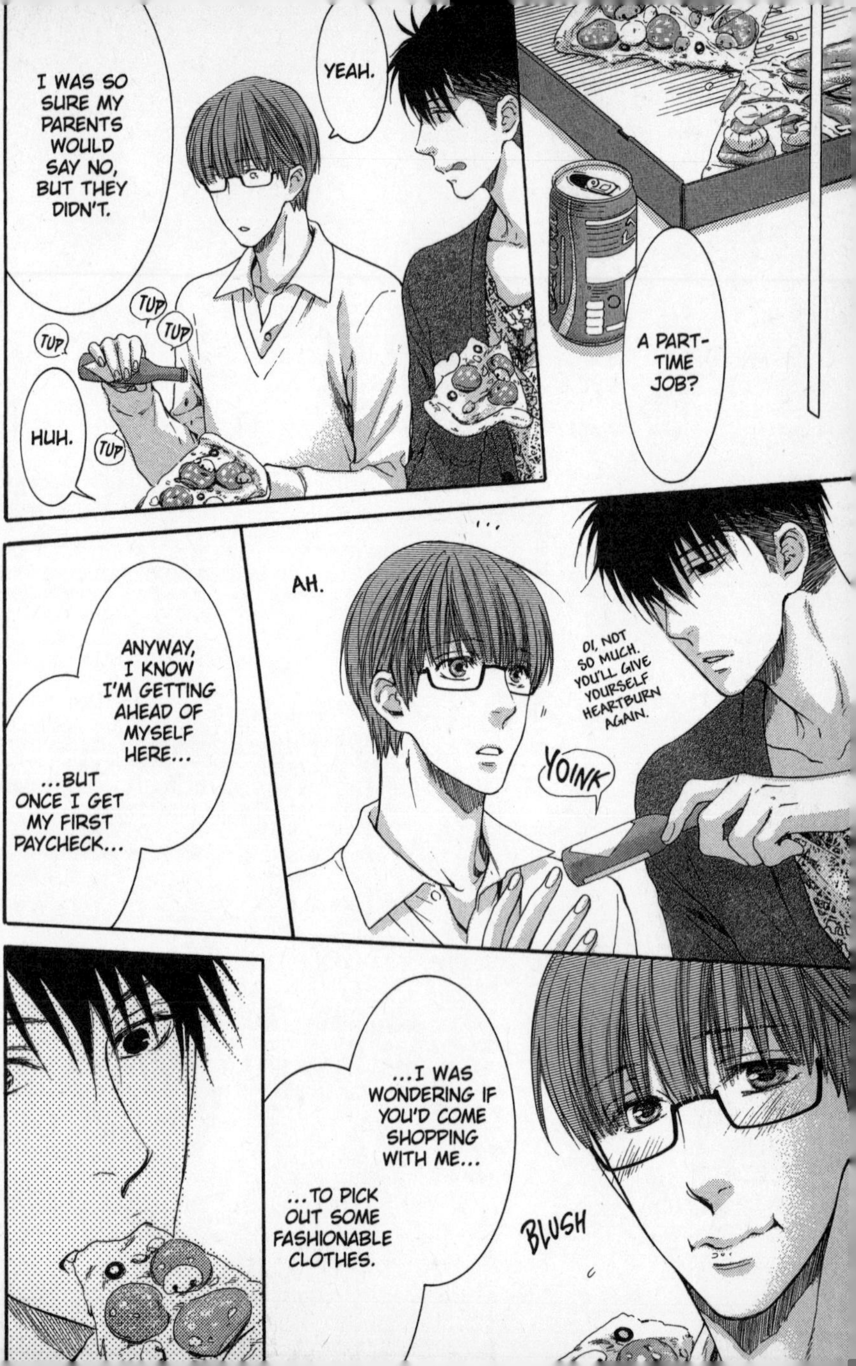
A PART-TIME JOB?
YEAH.
I WAS SO SURE MY PARENTS WOULD SAY NO, BUT THEY DIDN'T.
TUP
TUP
TUP
TUP
HUH.
...
AH.
OI, NOT SO MUCH. YOU'LL GIVE YOURSELF HEARTBURN AGAIN.
YOINK
ANYWAY, I KNOW I'M GETTING AHEAD OF MYSELF HERE...
...BUT ONCE I GET MY FIRST PAYCHECK...
...I WAS WONDERING IF YOU'D COME SHOPPING WITH ME...
...TO PICK OUT SOME FASHIONABLE CLOTHES.
BLUSH

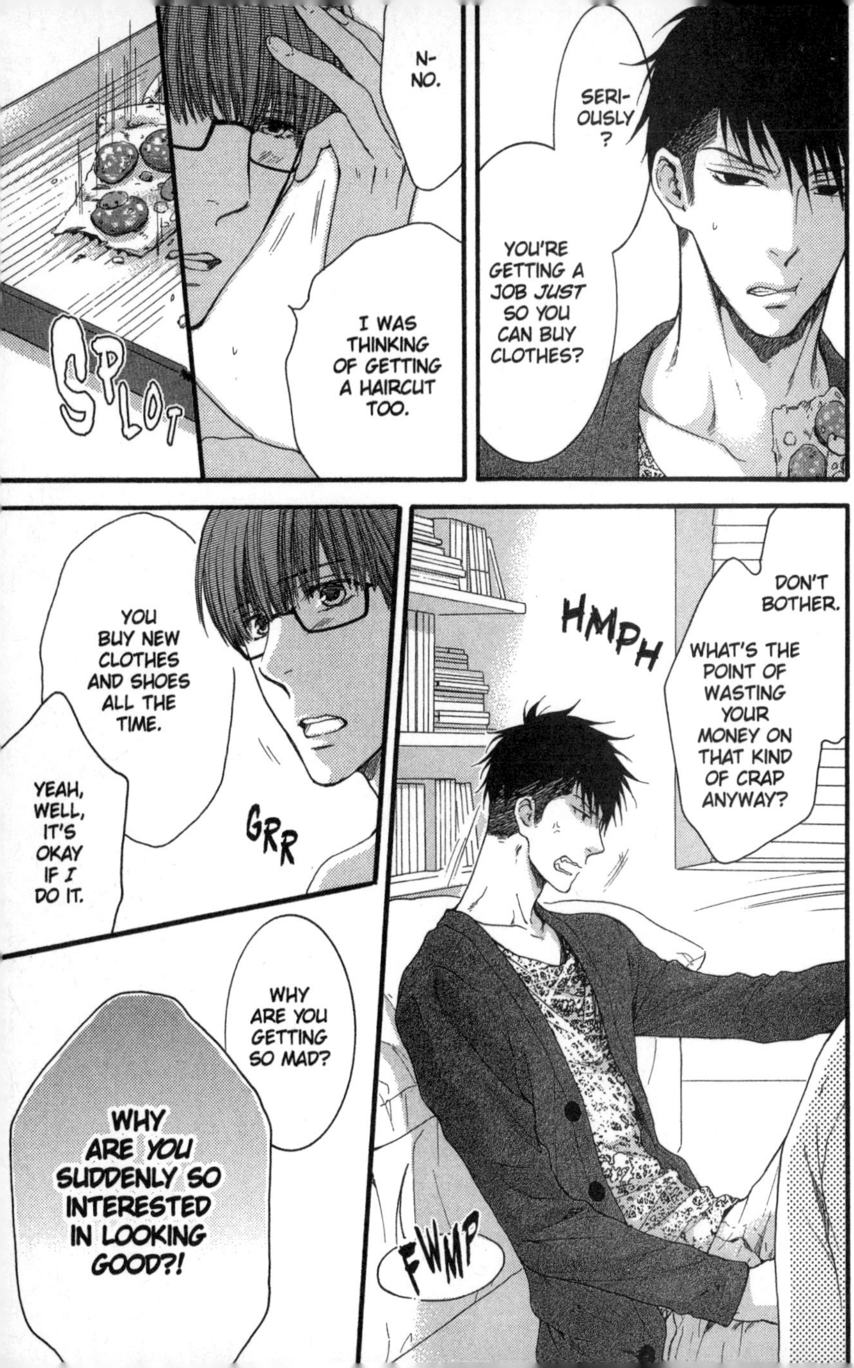

SERI-OUSLY?
YOU'RE GETTING A JOB JUST SO YOU CAN BUY CLOTHES?
N-NO.
I WAS THINKING OF GETTING A HAIRCUT TOO.
SPLOT
DON'T BOTHER.
WHAT'S THE POINT OF WASTING YOUR MONEY ON THAT KIND OF CRAP ANYWAY?
HMPH
YOU BUY NEW CLOTHES AND SHOES ALL THE TIME.
YEAH, WELL, IT'S OKAY IF I DO IT.
GRR
WHY ARE YOU GETTING SO MAD?
WHY ARE YOU SUDDENLY SO INTERESTED IN LOOKING GOOD?!
FWMP

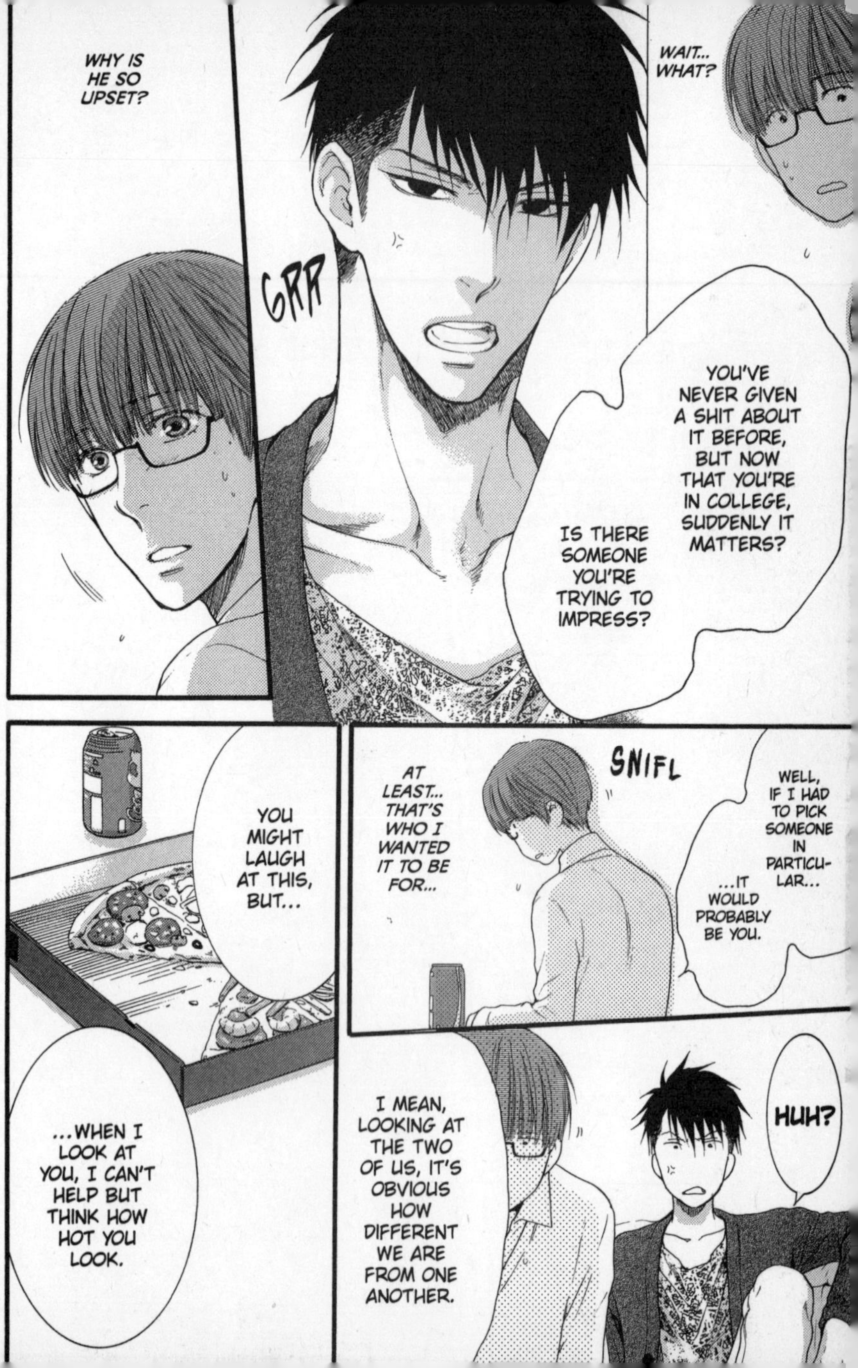

WAIT... WHAT?
YOU'VE NEVER GIVEN A SHIT ABOUT IT BEFORE, BUT NOW THAT YOU'RE IN COLLEGE, SUDDENLY IT MATTERS?
IS THERE SOMEONE YOU'RE TRYING TO IMPRESS?
GRR
WHY IS HE SO UPSET?
WELL, IF I HAD TO PICK SOMEONE IN PARTICULAR...
...IT WOULD PROBABLY BE YOU.
SNIFL
AT LEAST... THAT'S WHO I WANTED IT TO BE FOR...
HUH?
I MEAN, LOOKING AT THE TWO OF US, IT'S OBVIOUS HOW DIFFERENT WE ARE FROM ONE ANOTHER.
YOU MIGHT LAUGH AT THIS, BUT...
...WHEN I LOOK AT YOU, I CAN'T HELP BUT THINK HOW HOT YOU LOOK.

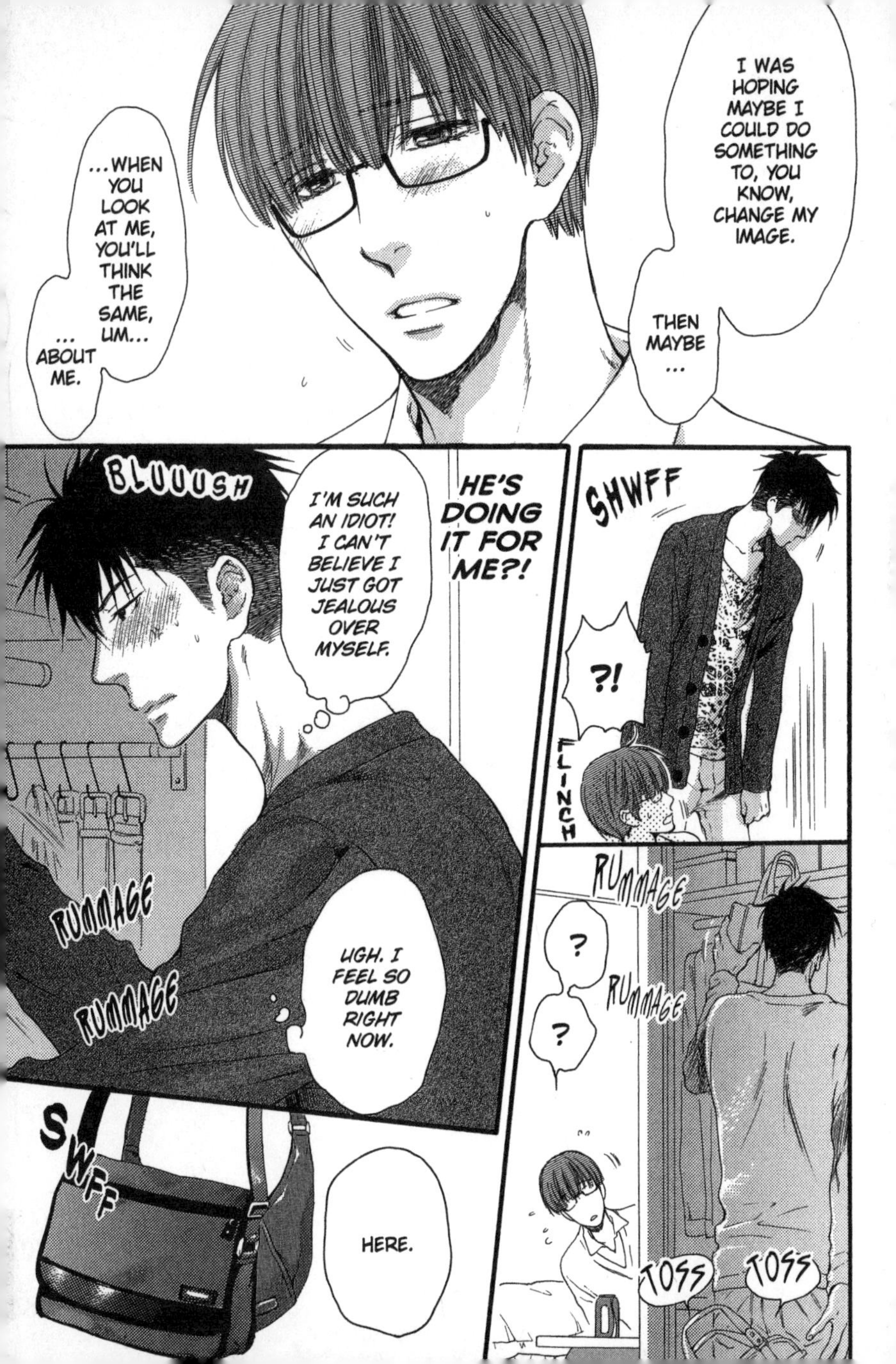
I WAS HOPING MAYBE I COULD DO SOMETHING TO, YOU KNOW, CHANGE MY IMAGE.
THEN MAYBE ...
...WHEN YOU LOOK AT ME, YOU'LL THINK THE SAME, UM...
... ABOUT ME.
SHWFF
?!
FLINCH
RUMMAGE
?
?
RUMMAGE
TOSS
TOSS
HE'S DOING IT FOR ME?!
BLUUUSH
I'M SUCH AN IDIOT! I CAN'T BELIEVE I JUST GOT JEALOUS OVER MYSELF.
RUMMAGE
RUMMAGE
UGH. I FEEL SO DUMB RIGHT NOW.
HERE.
SWFF

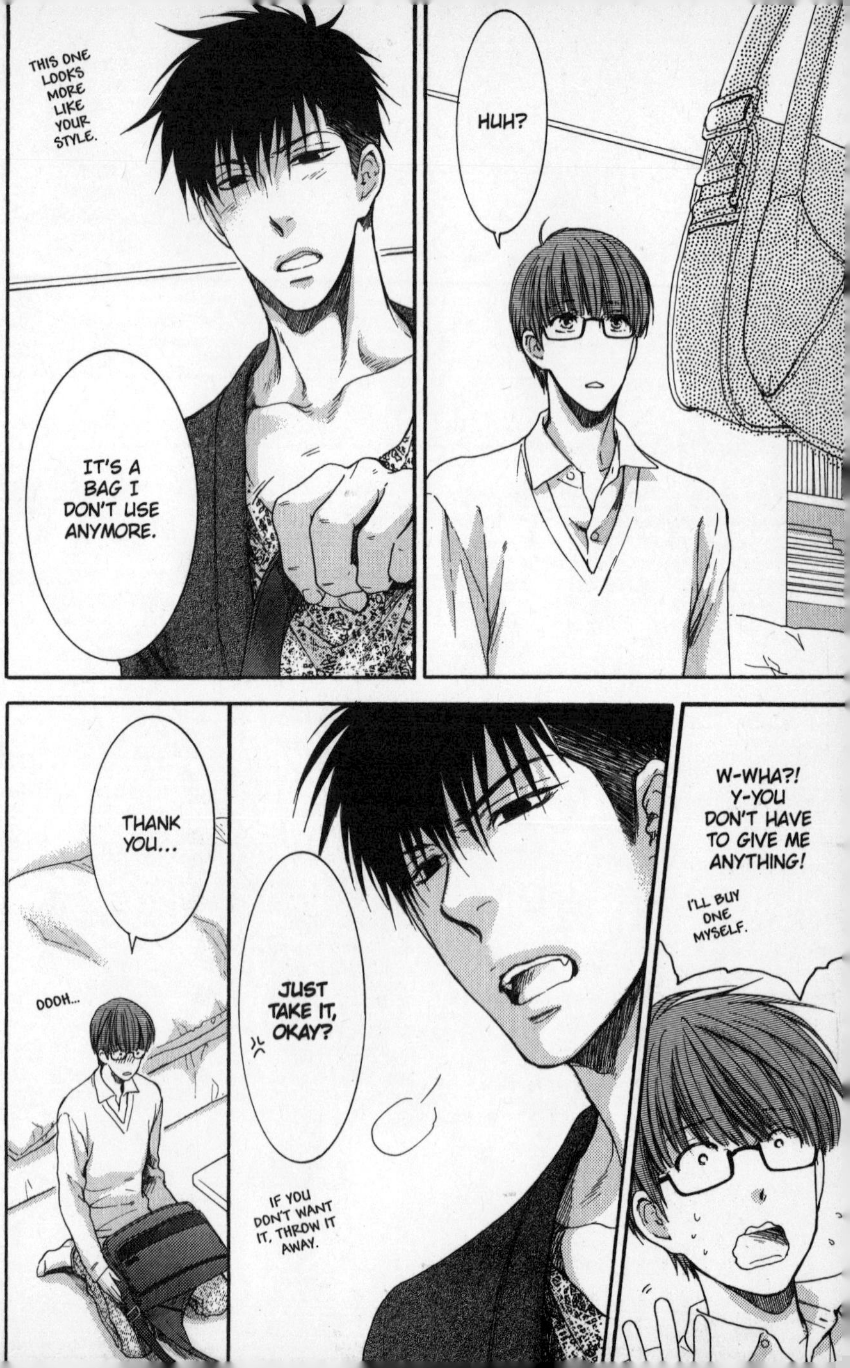
HUH?
THIS ONE LOOKS MORE LIKE YOUR STYLE.
IT'S A BAG I DON'T USE ANYMORE.
W-WHA?! Y-YOU DON'T HAVE TO GIVE ME ANYTHING!
I'LL BUY ONE MYSELF.
JUST TAKE IT, OKAY?
IF YOU DON'T WANT IT, THROW IT AWAY.
THANK YOU...
OOOH...

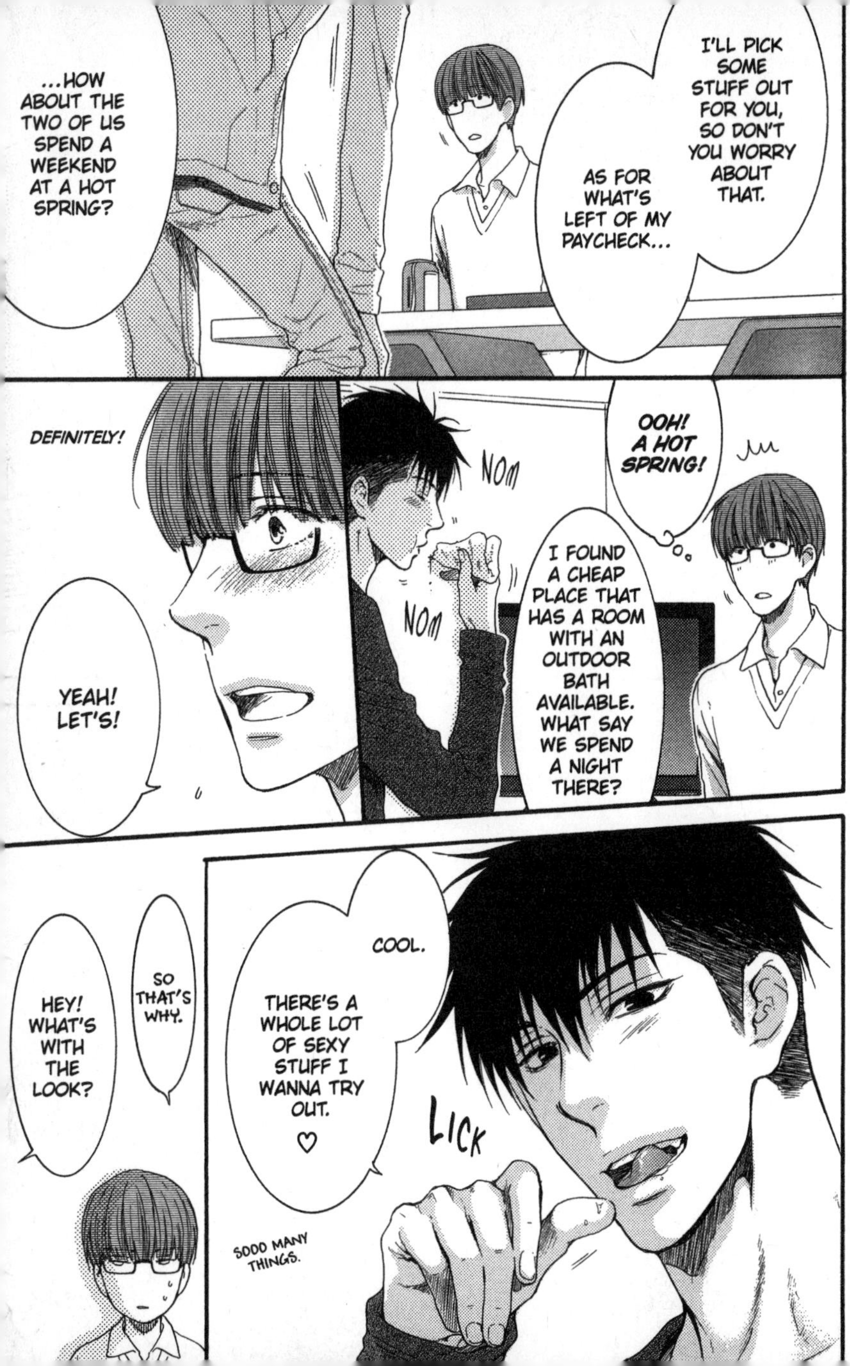
I'LL PICK SOME STUFF OUT FOR YOU, SO DON'T YOU WORRY ABOUT THAT.
AS FOR WHAT'S LEFT OF MY PAYCHECK...
...HOW ABOUT THE TWO OF US SPEND A WEEKEND AT A HOT SPRING?
OOH! A HOT SPRING!
I FOUND A CHEAP PLACE THAT HAS A ROOM WITH AN OUTDOOR BATH AVAILABLE. WHAT SAY WE SPEND A NIGHT THERE?
NOM
NOM
DEFINITELY!
YEAH! LET'S!
COOL.
THERE'S A WHOLE LOT OF SEXY STUFF I WANNA TRY OUT. ♡
LICK
SOOO MANY THINGS.
SO THAT'S WHY.
HEY! WHAT'S WITH THE LOOK?

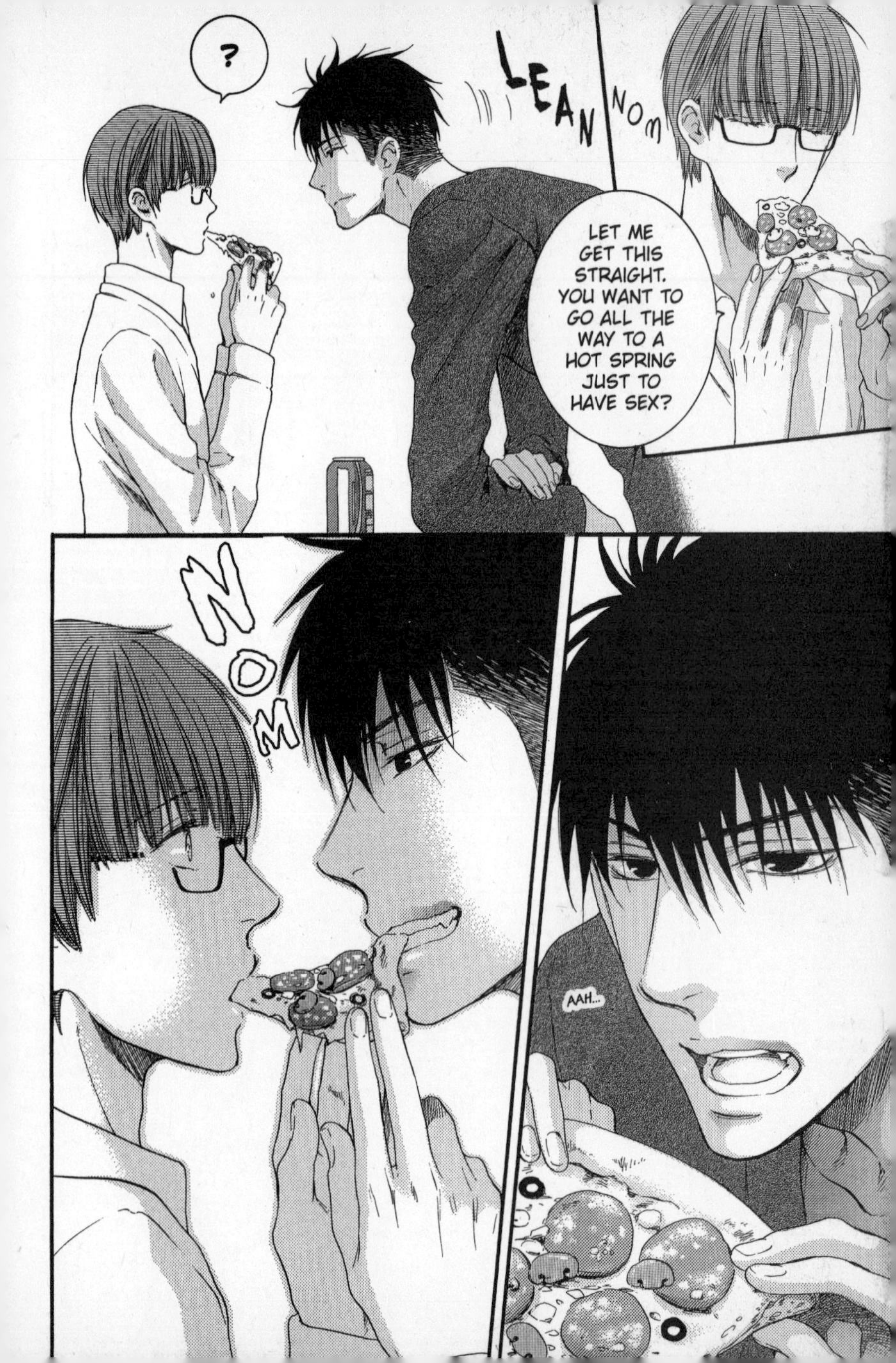
NOM
LET ME GET THIS STRAIGHT. YOU WANT TO GO ALL THE WAY TO A HOT SPRING JUST TO HAVE SEX?
LEAN
?
AAH...
NOM

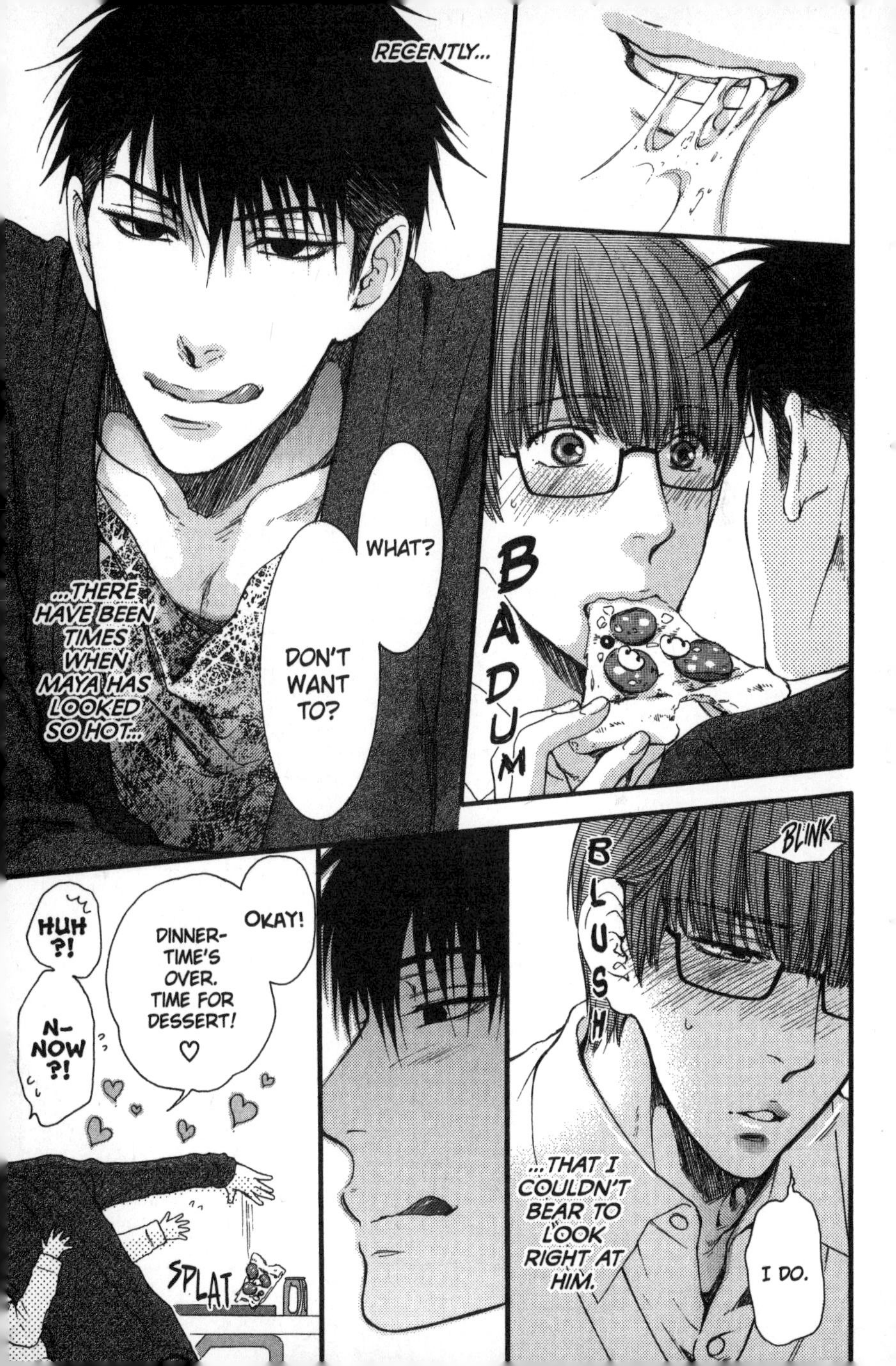
BADUM
RECENTLY...
WHAT?
DON'T WANT TO?
...THERE HAVE BEEN TIMES WHEN MAYA HAS LOOKED SO HOT...
BLINK
BLUSH
...THAT I COULDN'T BEAR TO LOOK RIGHT AT HIM.
I DO.
OKAY!
DINNER-TIME'S OVER. TIME FOR DESSERT! ♡
HUH?!
N-NOW?!
SPLAT

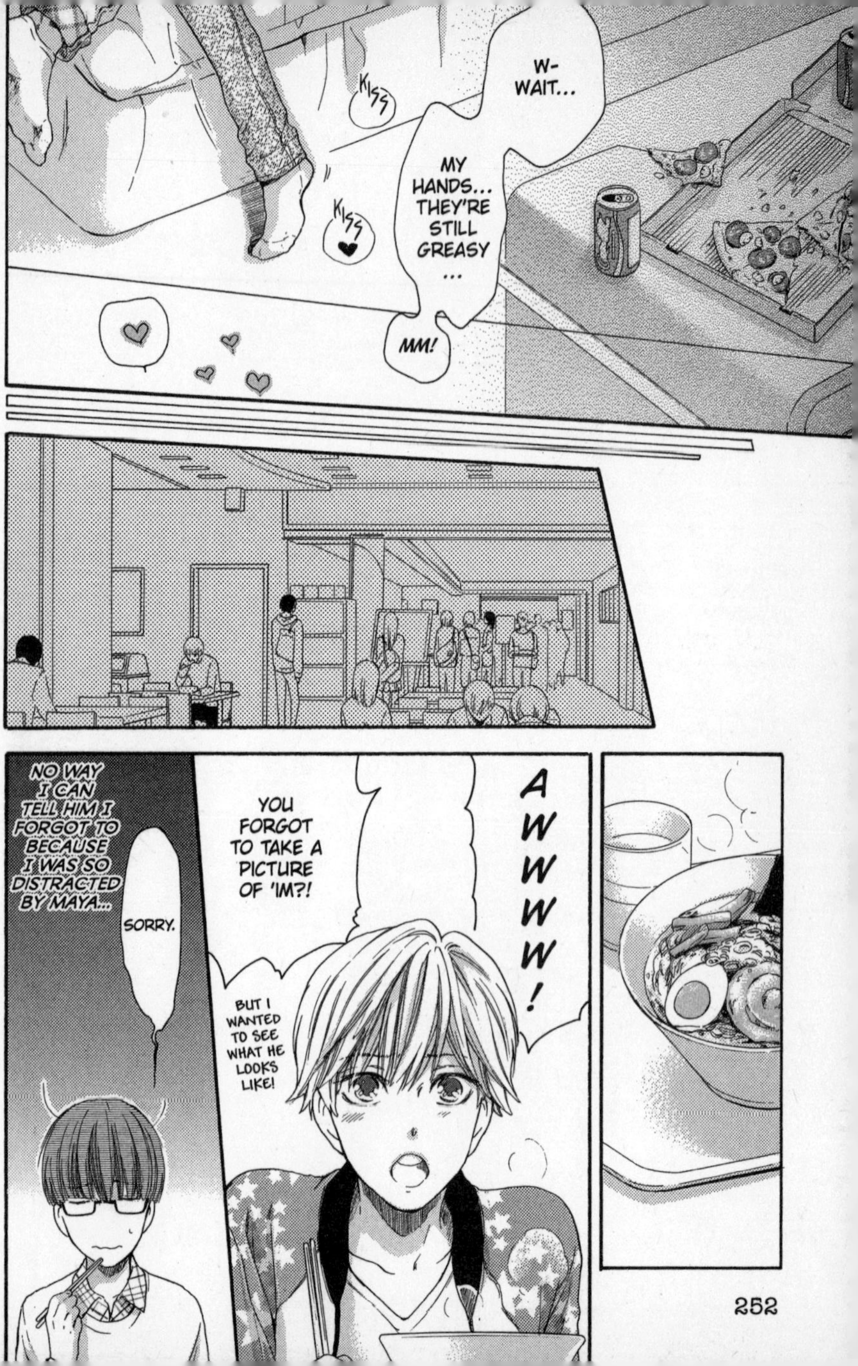

W- WAIT...
MY HANDS... THEY'RE STILL GREASY ...
KISS
KISS
MM!
AWWWWW!
YOU FORGOT TO TAKE A PICTURE OF 'IM?!
BUT I WANTED TO SEE WHAT HE LOOKS LIKE!
SORRY.
NO WAY I CAN TELL HIM I FORGOT TO BECAUSE I WAS SO DISTRACTED BY MAYA...

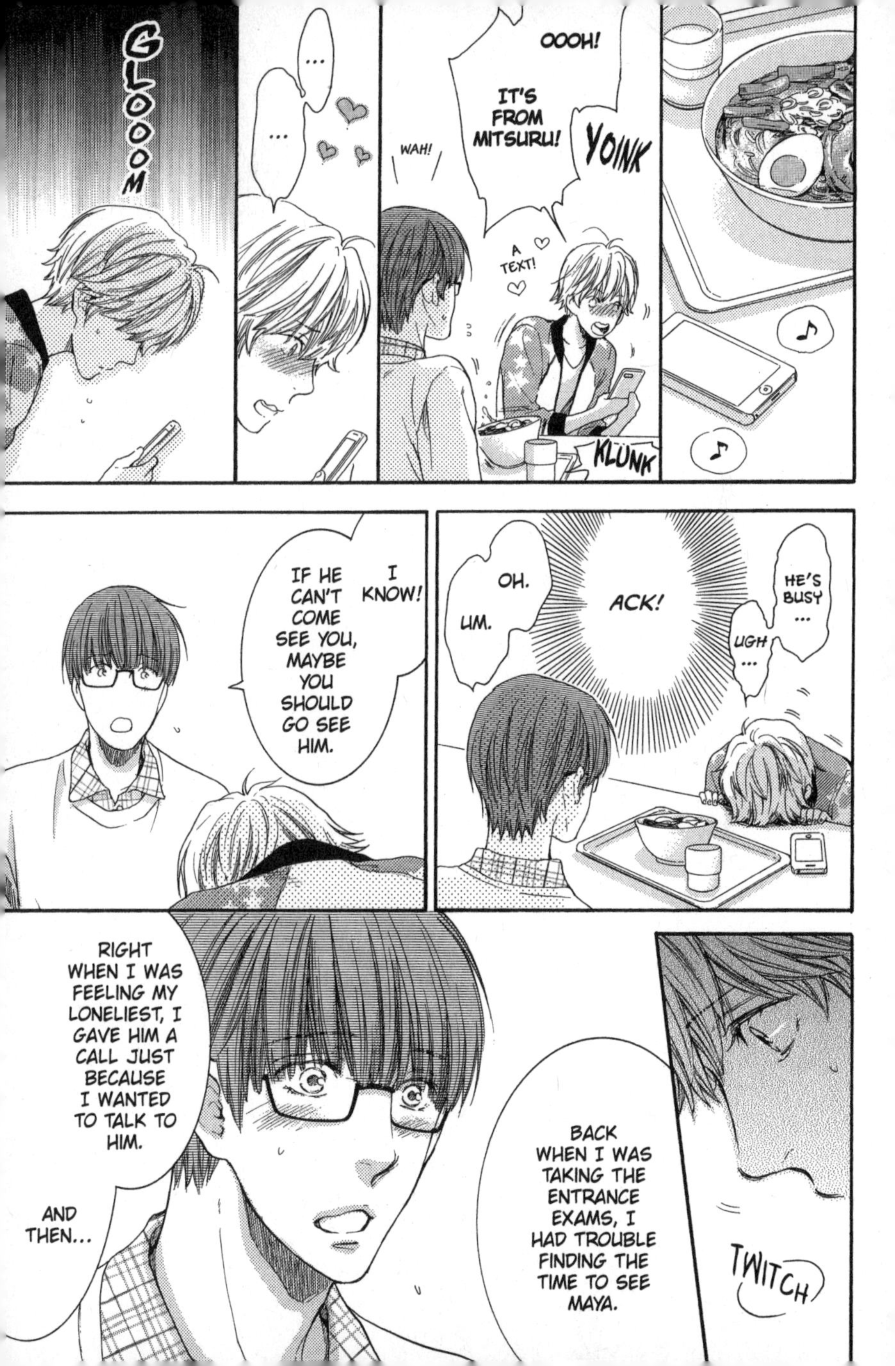
♪
♪
OOOH!
IT'S FROM MITSURU!
YOINK
WAH!
A TEXT!
KLUNK
...
...
GLOOOOM
HE'S BUSY...
UGH...
ACK!
OH.
UM.
I KNOW!
IF HE CAN'T COME SEE YOU, MAYBE YOU SHOULD GO SEE HIM.
TWITCH
BACK WHEN I WAS TAKING THE ENTRANCE EXAMS, I HAD TROUBLE FINDING THE TIME TO SEE MAYA.
RIGHT WHEN I WAS FEELING MY LONELIEST, I GAVE HIM A CALL JUST BECAUSE I WANTED TO TALK TO HIM.
AND THEN...

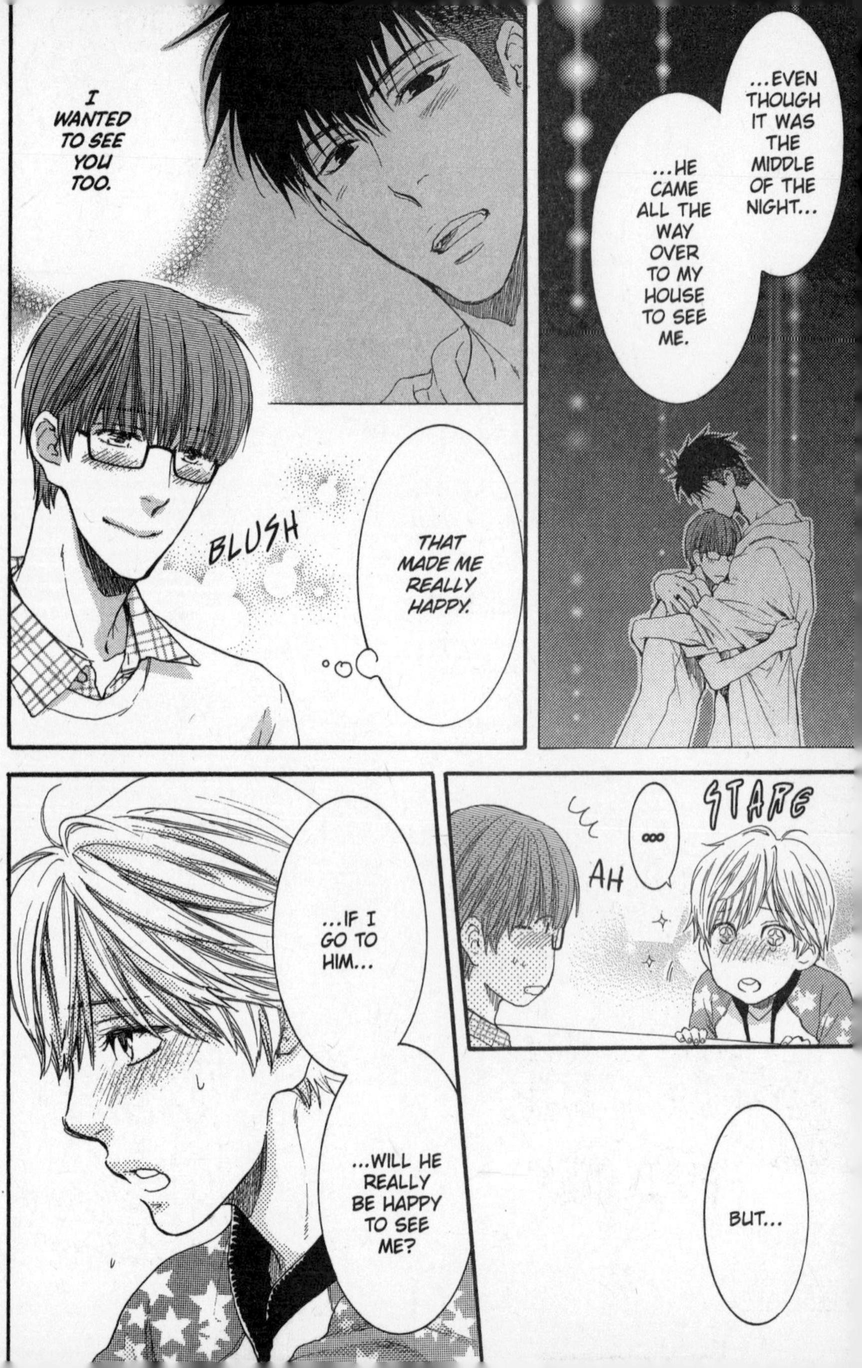
...EVEN THOUGH IT WAS THE MIDDLE OF THE NIGHT...
...HE CAME ALL THE WAY OVER TO MY HOUSE TO SEE ME.
I WANTED TO SEE YOU TOO.
THAT MADE ME REALLY HAPPY.
BLUSH
STARE
...
AH
BUT...
...IF I GO TO HIM...
...WILL HE REALLY BE HAPPY TO SEE ME?

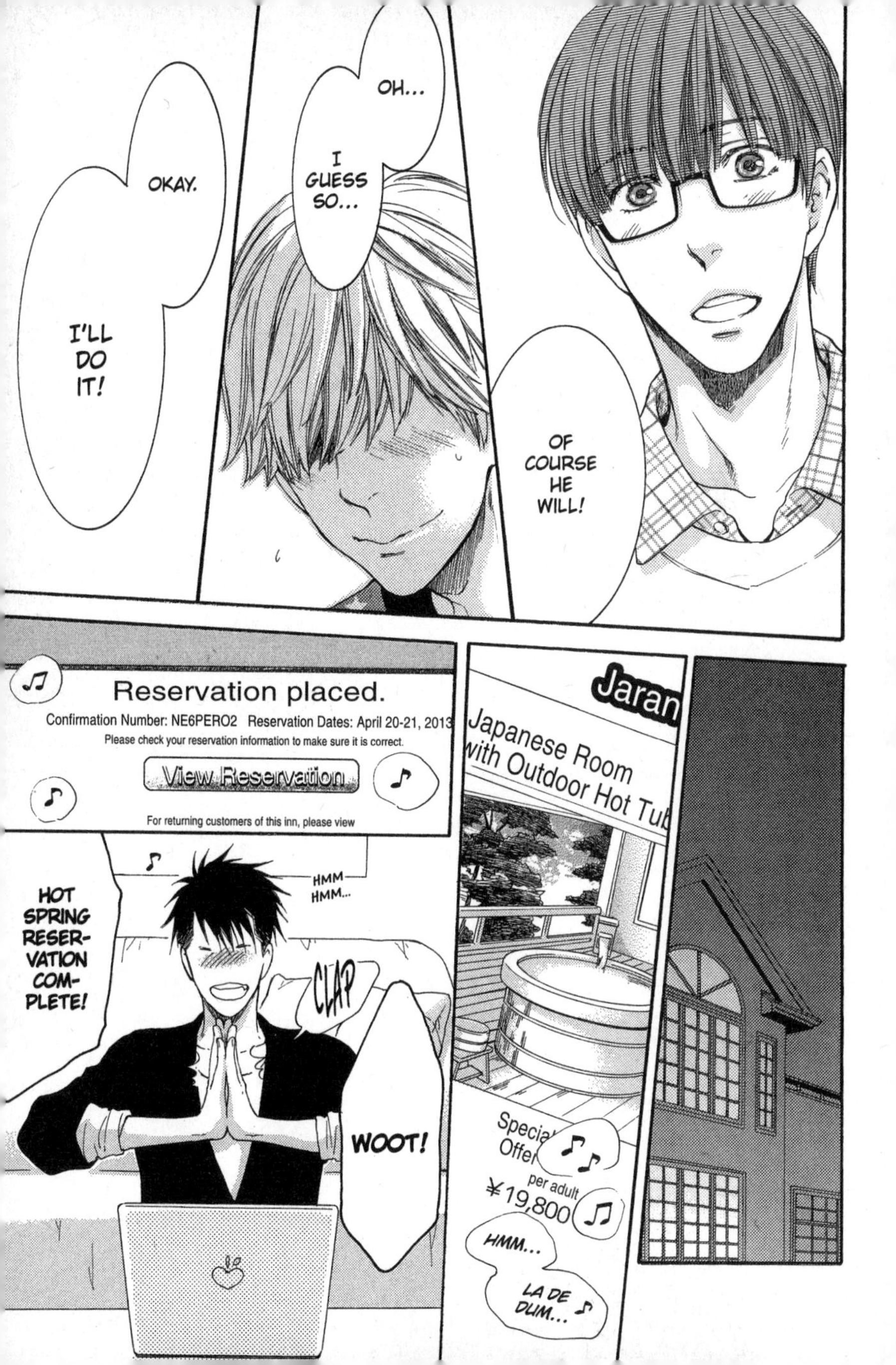
OF COURSE HE WILL!
OH...
I GUESS SO...
OKAY.
I'LL DO IT!
Jaran
Japanese Room with Outdoor Hot Tub
Special Offer
per adult ¥19,800
♫
♪♪
HMM...
LA DE DUM... ♪
Reservation placed.
Confirmation Number: NE6PERO2 Reservation Dates: April 20-21, 2013
Please check your reservation information to make sure it is correct.
View Reservation
For returning customers of this inn, please view
♫
♪
♪
♪
HMM HMM...
HOT SPRING RESERVATION COMPLETE!
CLAP
WOOT!

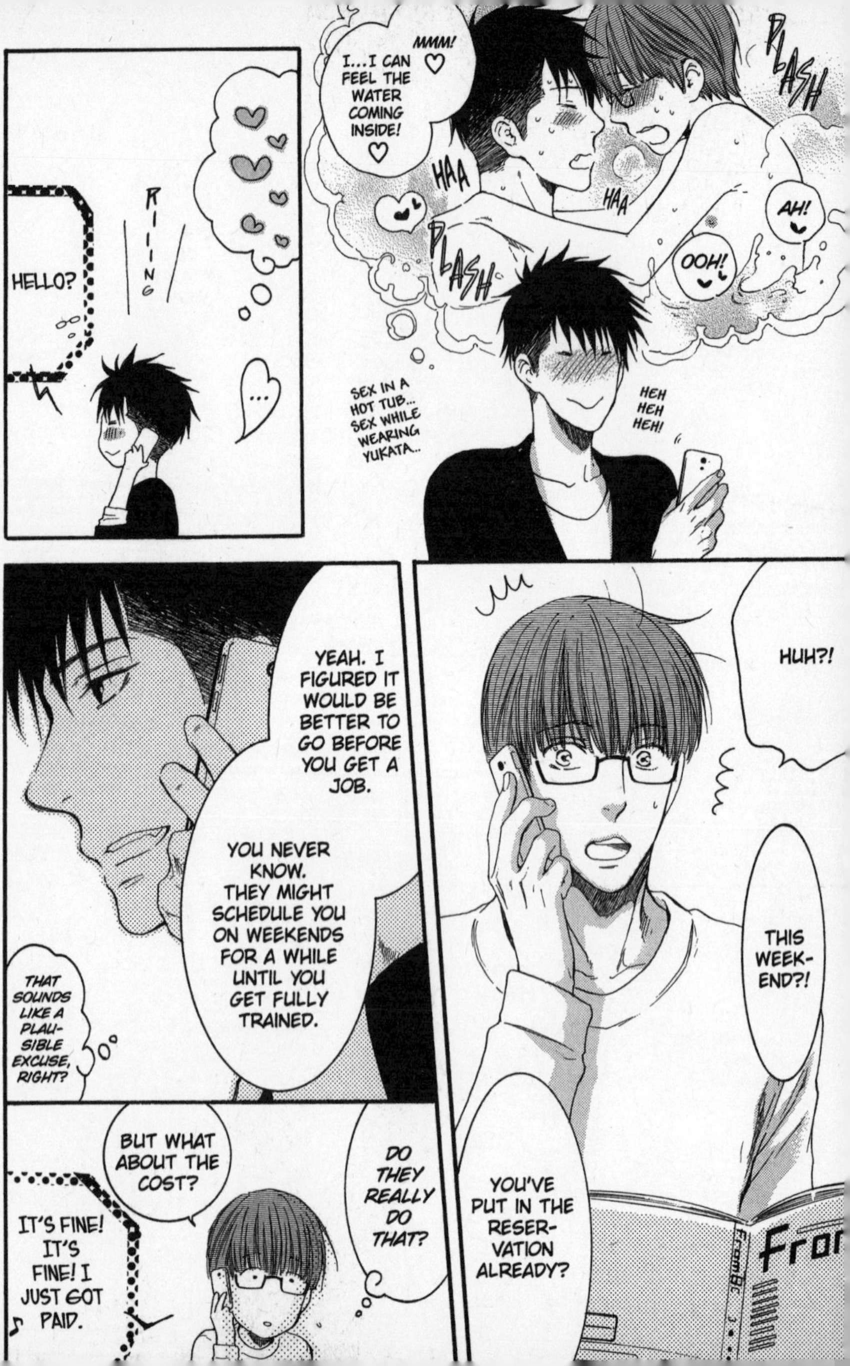
PLASH
MMM! ♡
I...I CAN FEEL THE WATER COMING INSIDE! ♡
HAA
HAA
PLASH
AH!
OOH!
HEH HEH HEH!
SEX IN A HOT TUB... SEX WHILE WEARING YUKATA...
RIIING
HELLO?
...
HUH?!
THIS WEEK-END?!
YOU'VE PUT IN THE RESER-VATION ALREADY?
YEAH. I FIGURED IT WOULD BE BETTER TO GO BEFORE YOU GET A JOB.
YOU NEVER KNOW. THEY MIGHT SCHEDULE YOU ON WEEKENDS FOR A WHILE UNTIL YOU GET FULLY TRAINED.
THAT SOUNDS LIKE A PLAU-SIBLE EXCUSE, RIGHT?
DO THEY REALLY DO THAT?
BUT WHAT ABOUT THE COST?
IT'S FINE! IT'S FINE! I JUST GOT PAID.
From

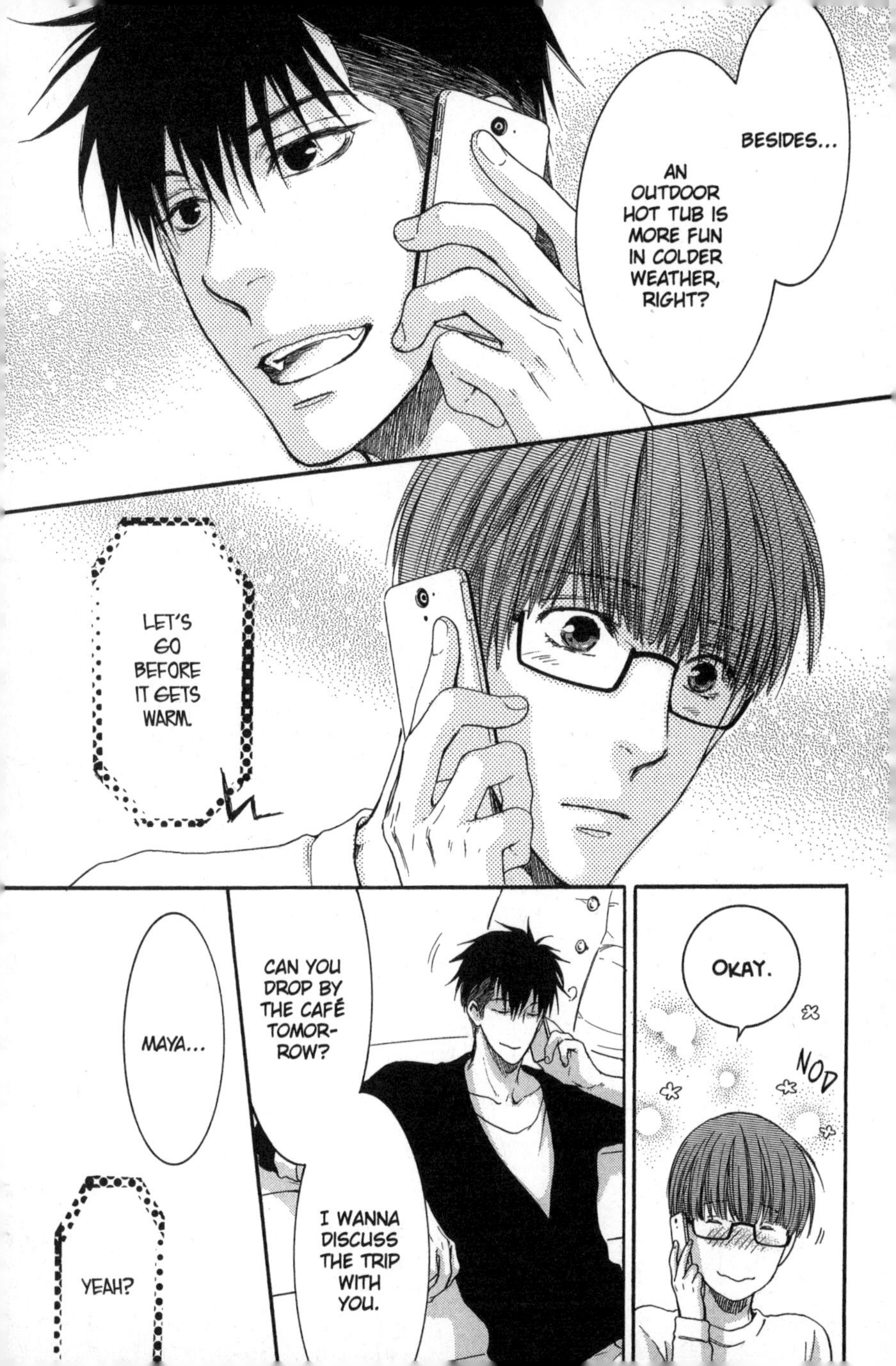
BESIDES...
AN OUTDOOR HOT TUB IS MORE FUN IN COLDER WEATHER, RIGHT?
LET'S GO BEFORE IT GETS WARM.
OKAY.
NOD
CAN YOU DROP BY THE CAFÉ TOMOR-ROW?
I WANNA DISCUSS THE TRIP WITH YOU.
MAYA...
YEAH?

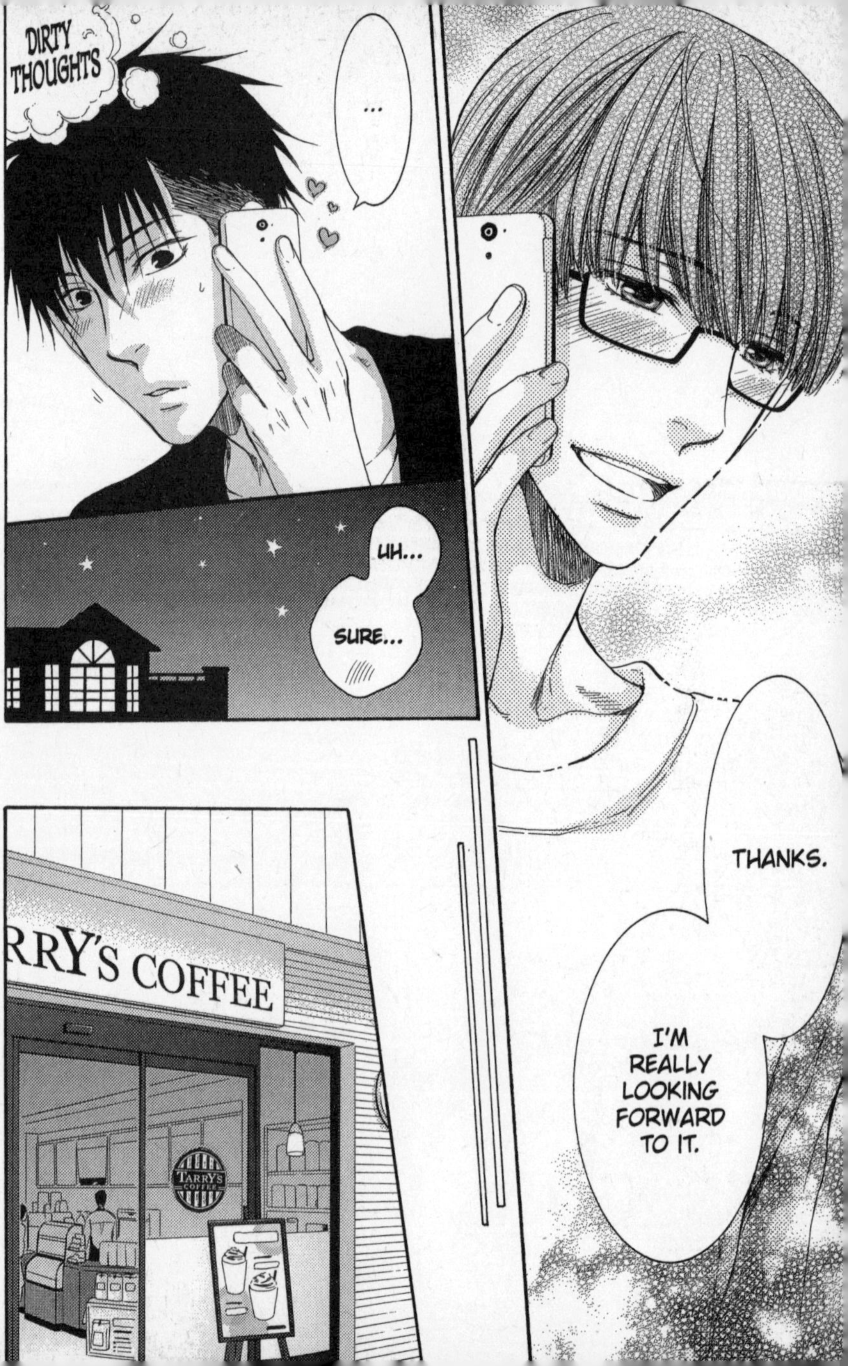
THANKS.
I'M REALLY LOOKING FORWARD TO IT.
DIRTY THOUGHTS
...
UH...
SURE...
RRY'S COFFEE
TARRY'S COFFEE

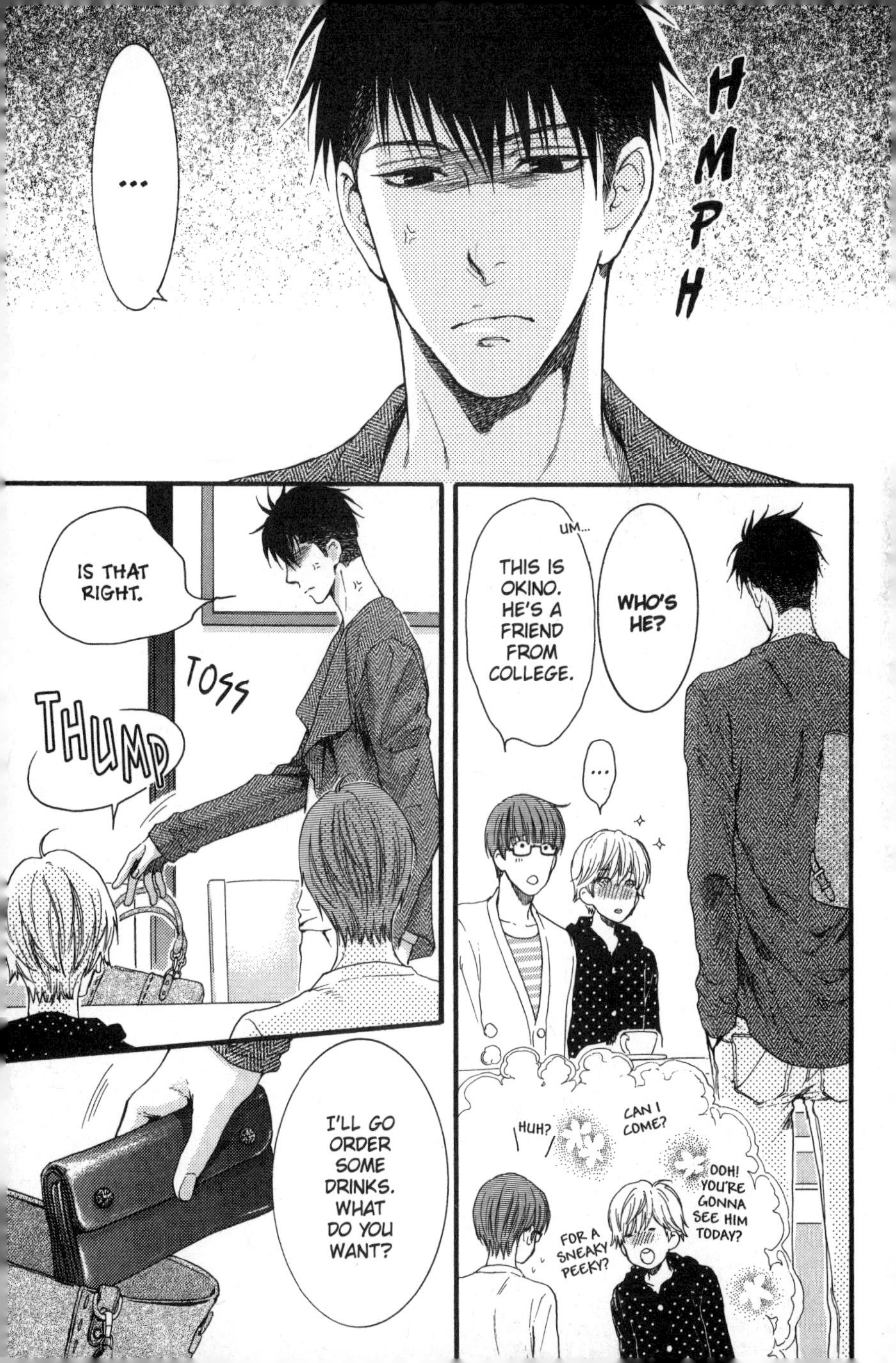
...
HMPH
WHO'S HE?
UM...
THIS IS OKINO. HE'S A FRIEND FROM COLLEGE.
...
OOH! YOU'RE GONNA SEE HIM TODAY?
CAN I COME?
HUH?
FOR A SNEAKY PEEKY?
IS THAT RIGHT.
TOSS
THUMP
I'LL GO ORDER SOME DRINKS. WHAT DO YOU WANT?

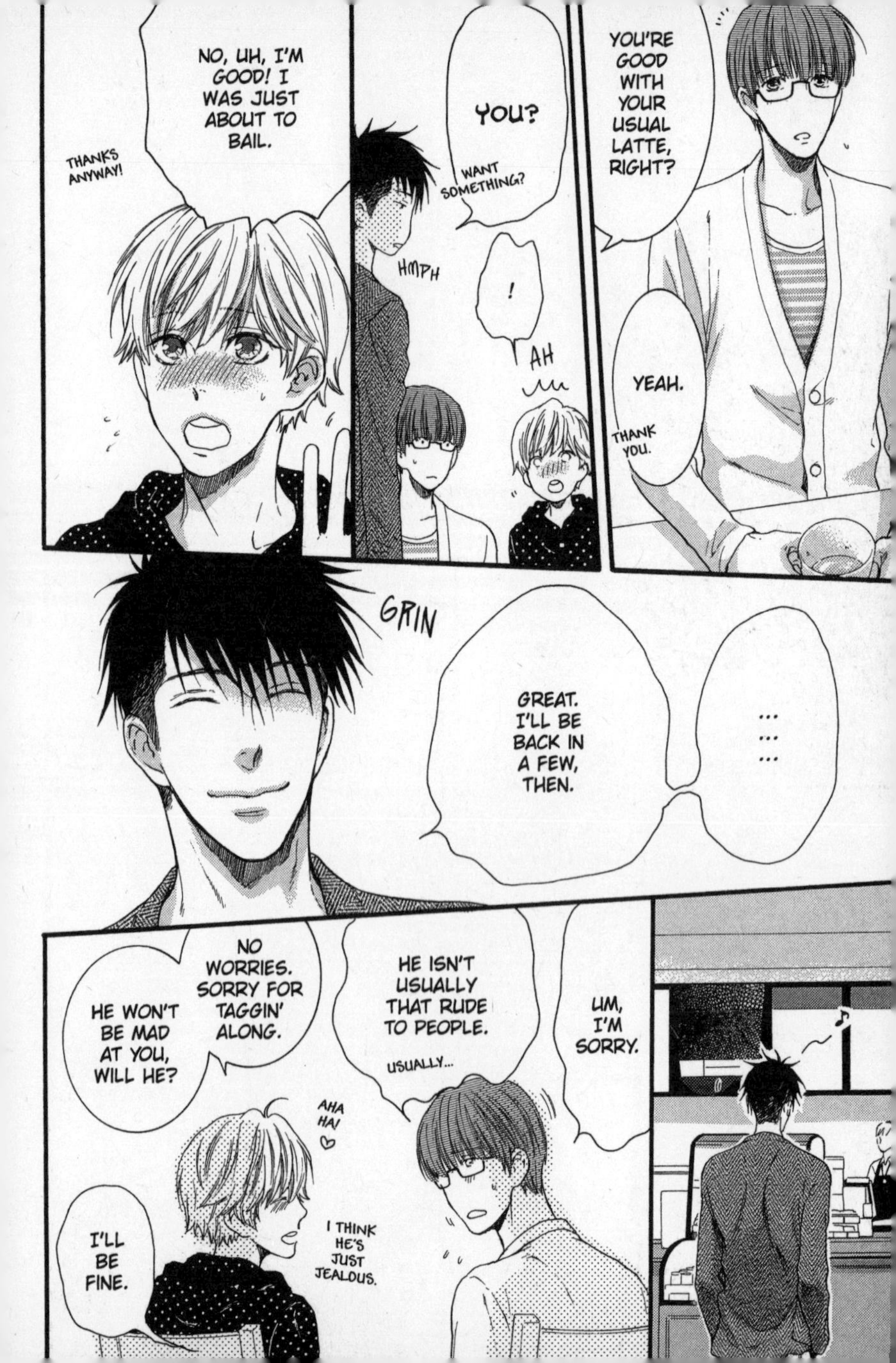
YOU'RE GOOD WITH YOUR USUAL LATTE, RIGHT?
YEAH.
THANK YOU.
YOU?
WANT SOMETHING?
HMPH
!
AH
NO, UH, I'M GOOD! I WAS JUST ABOUT TO BAIL.
THANKS ANYWAY!
... ...
GREAT. I'LL BE BACK IN A FEW, THEN.
GRIN
UM, I'M SORRY.
HE ISN'T USUALLY THAT RUDE TO PEOPLE.
USUALLY...
NO WORRIES. SORRY FOR TAGGIN' ALONG.
HE WON'T BE MAD AT YOU, WILL HE?
AHA HA!
I THINK HE'S JUST JEALOUS.
I'LL BE FINE.

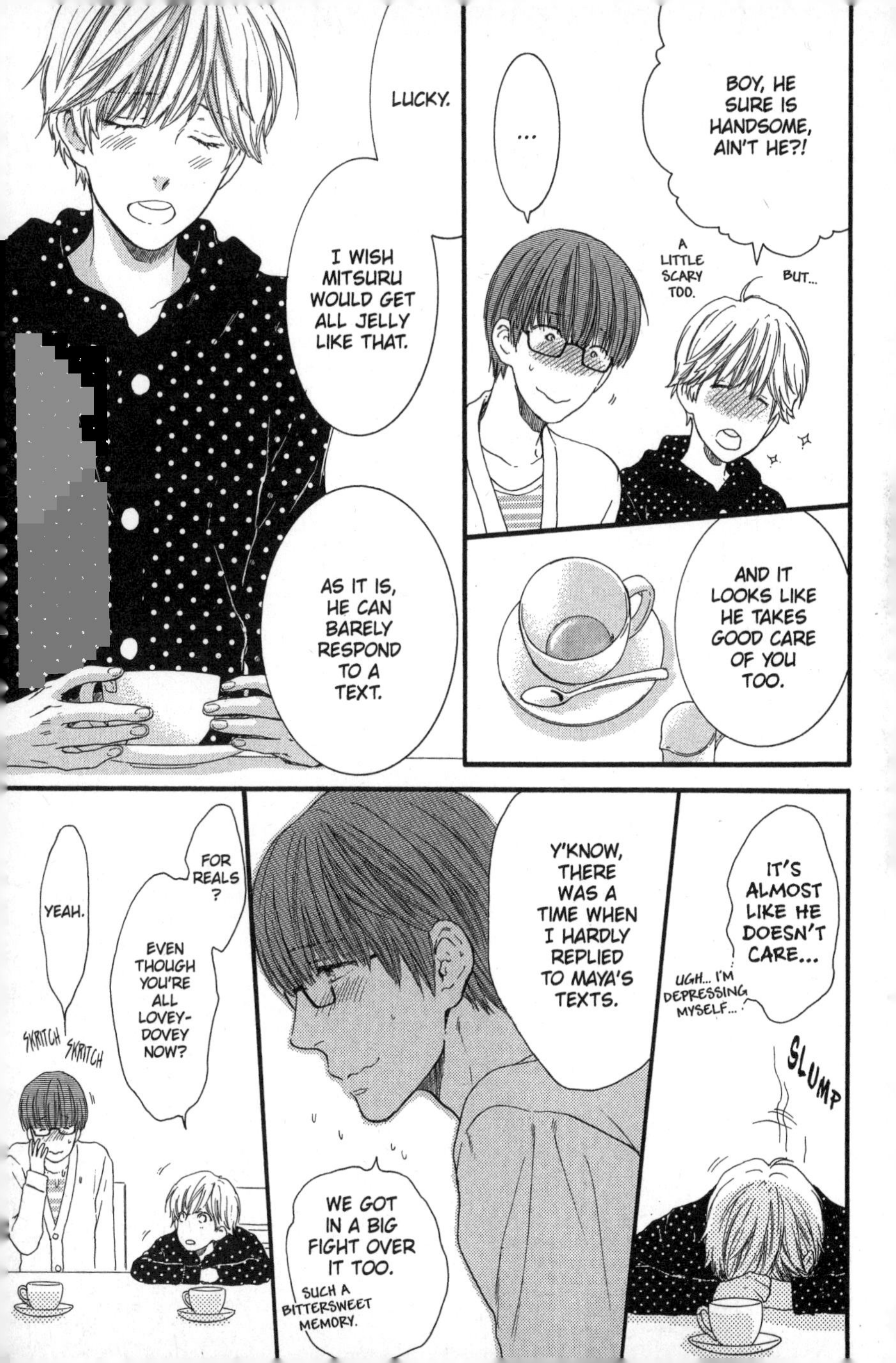
BOY, HE SURE IS HANDSOME, AIN'T HE?!
...
BUT...
A LITTLE SCARY TOO.
AND IT LOOKS LIKE HE TAKES GOOD CARE OF YOU TOO.
LUCKY.
I WISH MITSURU WOULD GET ALL JELLY LIKE THAT.
AS IT IS, HE CAN BARELY RESPOND TO A TEXT.
IT'S ALMOST LIKE HE DOESN'T CARE...
UGH... I'M DEPRESSING MYSELF...
SLUMP
Y'KNOW, THERE WAS A TIME WHEN I HARDLY REPLIED TO MAYA'S TEXTS.
WE GOT IN A BIG FIGHT OVER IT TOO.
SUCH A BITTERSWEET MEMORY.
FOR REALS?
EVEN THOUGH YOU'RE ALL LOVEY-DOVEY NOW?
YEAH.
SKRITCH SKRITCH

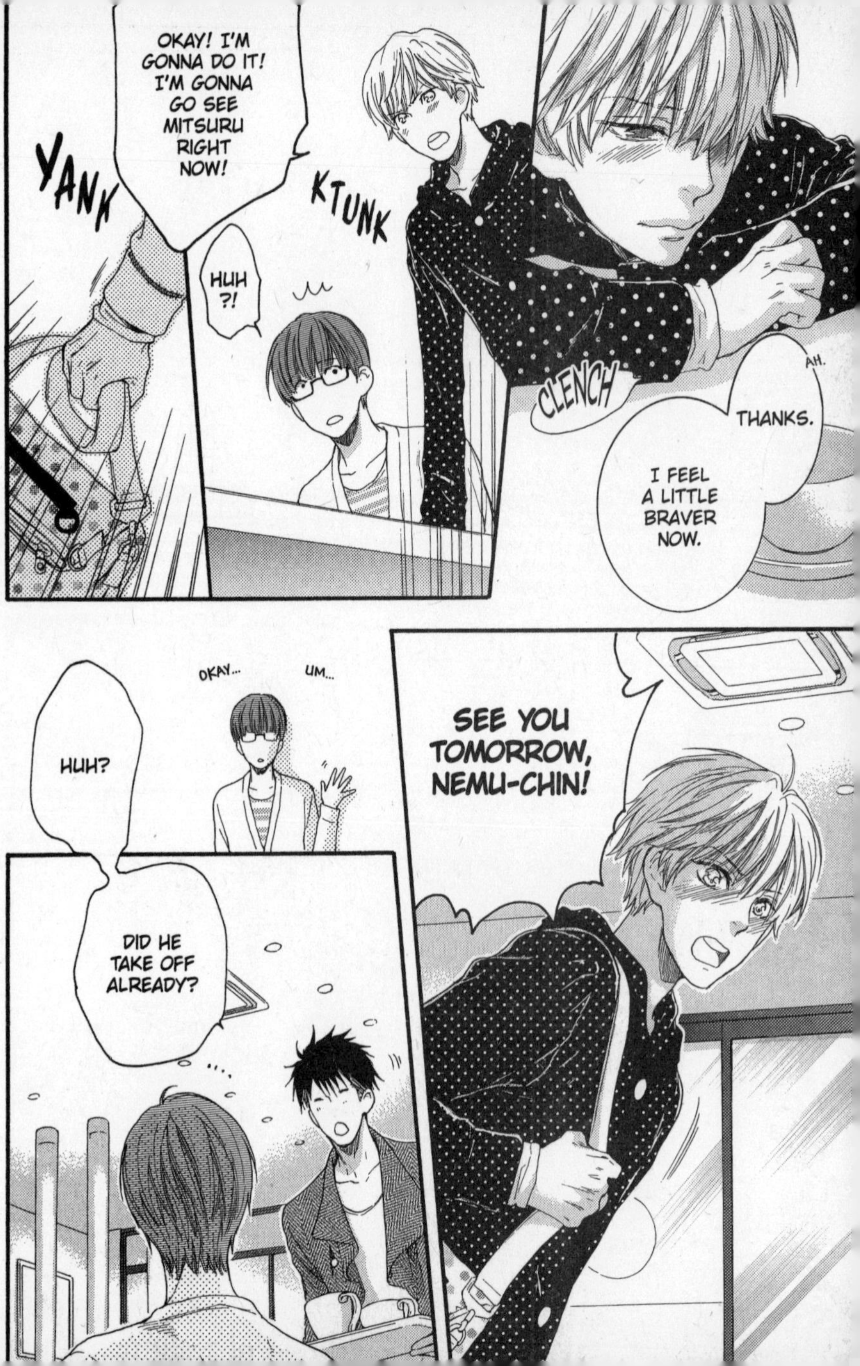

CLENCH
AH.
THANKS.
I FEEL A LITTLE BRAVER NOW.
OKAY! I'M GONNA DO IT! I'M GONNA GO SEE MITSURU RIGHT NOW!
KTUNK
HUH ?!
YANK
SEE YOU TOMORROW, NEMU-CHIN!
UM...
OKAY...
HUH?
DID HE TAKE OFF ALREADY?
...

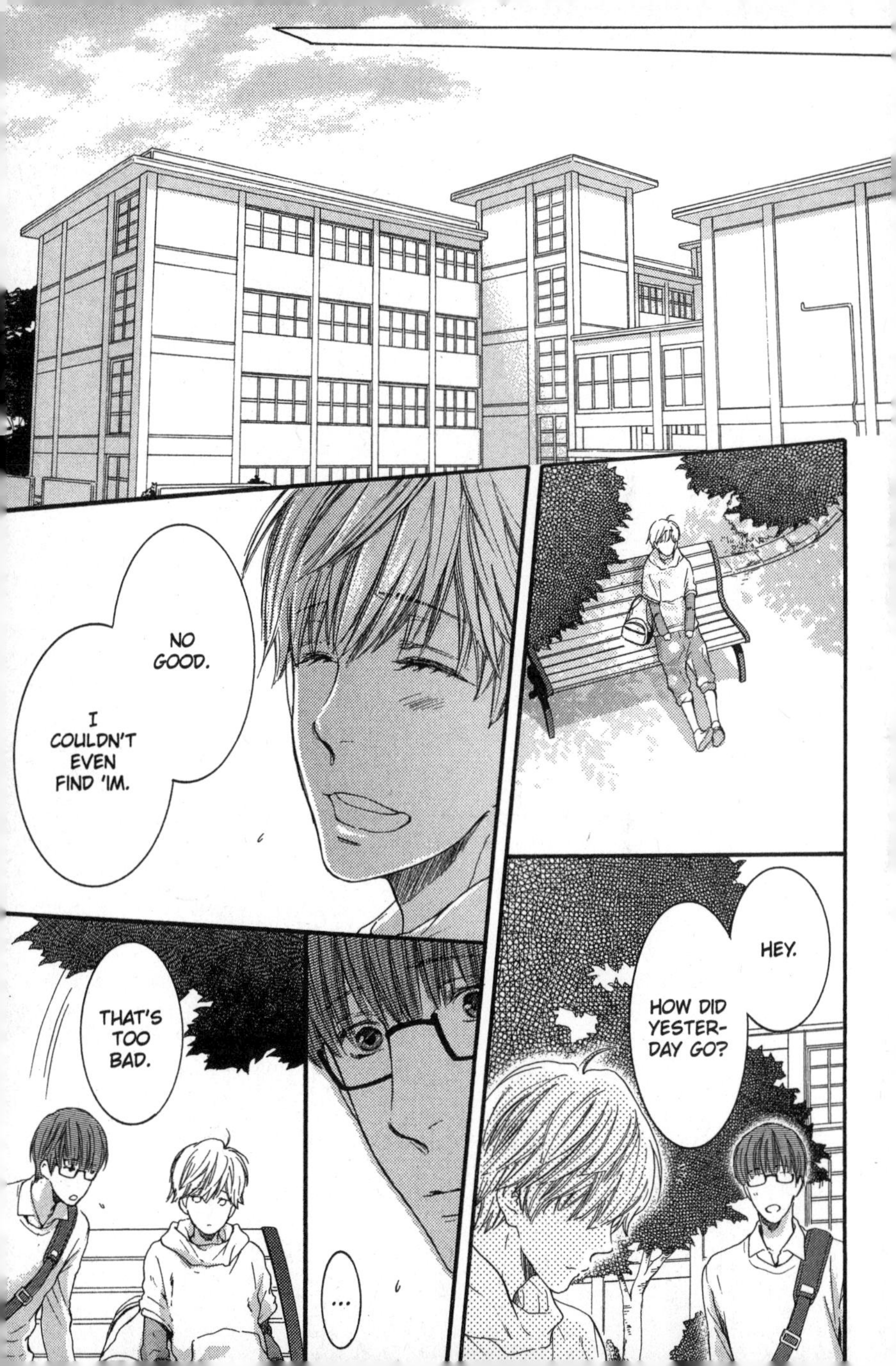
HEY.
HOW DID YESTER-DAY GO?
NO GOOD.
I COULDN'T EVEN FIND 'IM.
...
THAT'S TOO BAD.

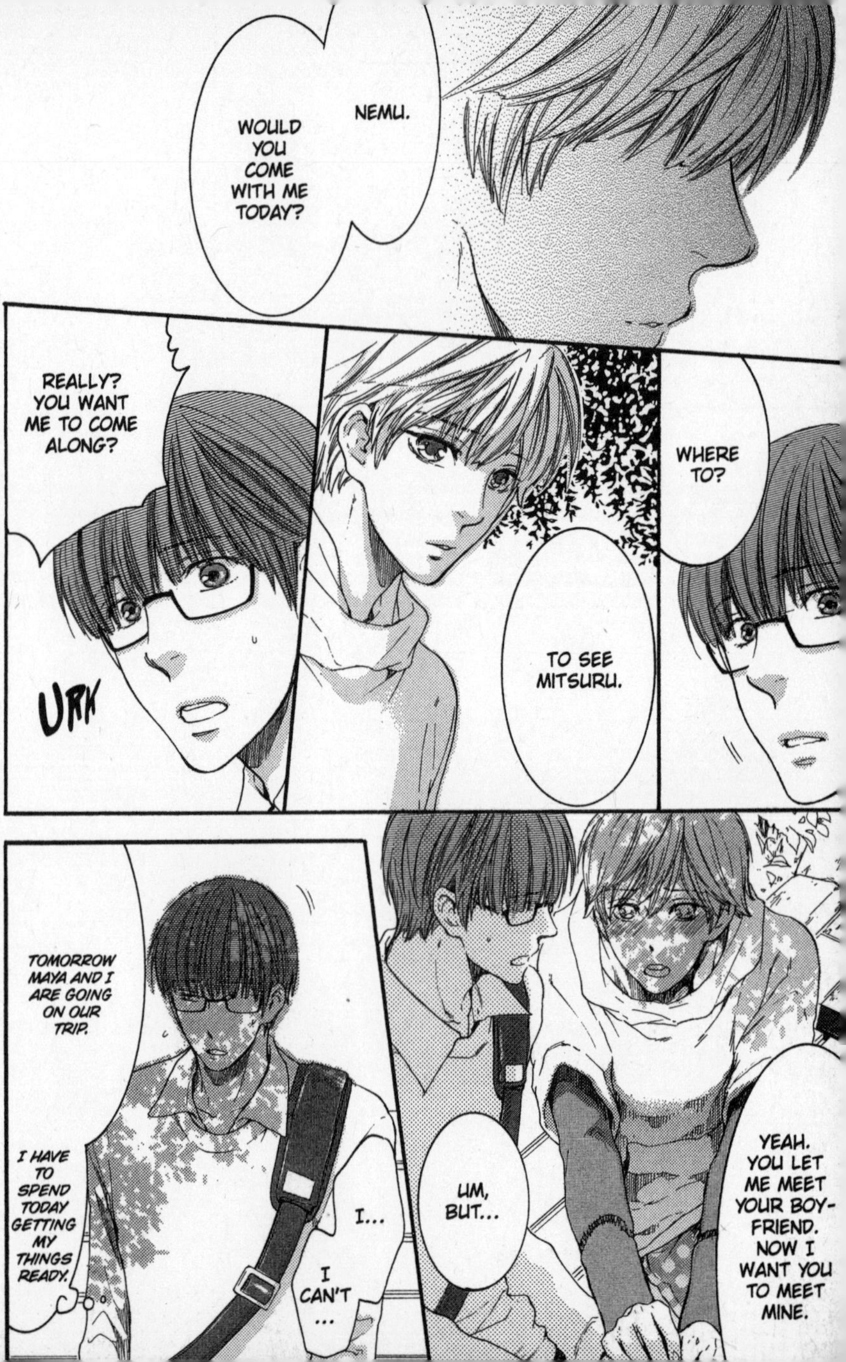
NEMU.
WOULD YOU COME WITH ME TODAY?
WHERE TO?
TO SEE MITSURU.
REALLY? YOU WANT ME TO COME ALONG?
URK
YEAH. YOU LET ME MEET YOUR BOY-FRIEND. NOW I WANT YOU TO MEET MINE.
UM, BUT...
I...
I CAN'T ...
TOMORROW MAYA AND I ARE GOING ON OUR TRIP.
I HAVE TO SPEND TODAY GETTING MY THINGS READY.

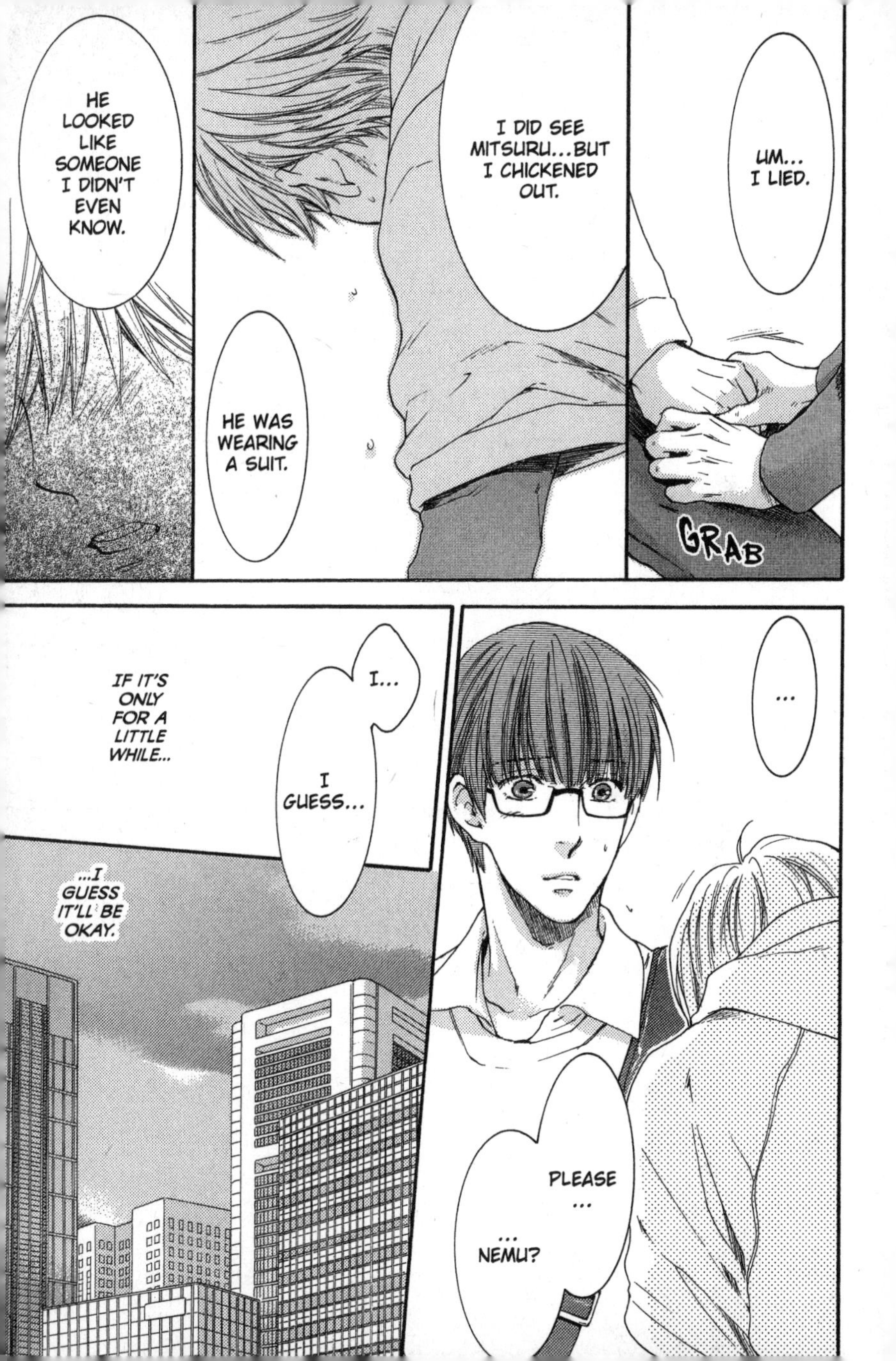
UM... I LIED.
GRAB
I DID SEE MITSURU...BUT I CHICKENED OUT.
HE WAS WEARING A SUIT.
HE LOOKED LIKE SOMEONE I DIDN'T EVEN KNOW.
...
I...
I GUESS...
PLEASE ...
... NEMU?
IF IT'S ONLY FOR A LITTLE WHILE...
...I GUESS IT'LL BE OKAY.

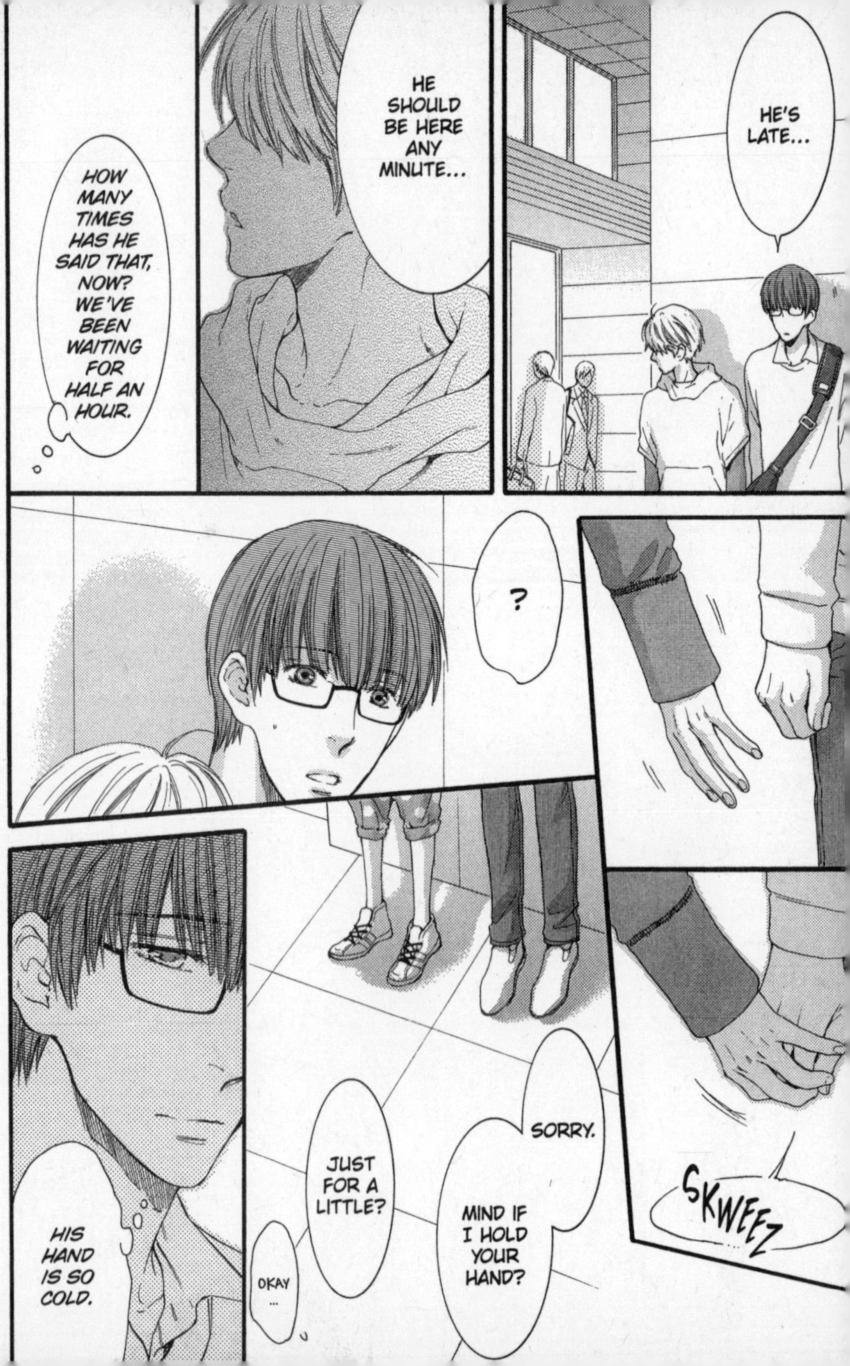
HE'S LATE...
HE SHOULD BE HERE ANY MINUTE...
HOW MANY TIMES HAS HE SAID THAT, NOW? WE'VE BEEN WAITING FOR HALF AN HOUR.
?
SKWEEZ
...
SORRY.
MIND IF I HOLD YOUR HAND?
JUST FOR A LITTLE?
OKAY ...
HIS HAND IS SO COLD.

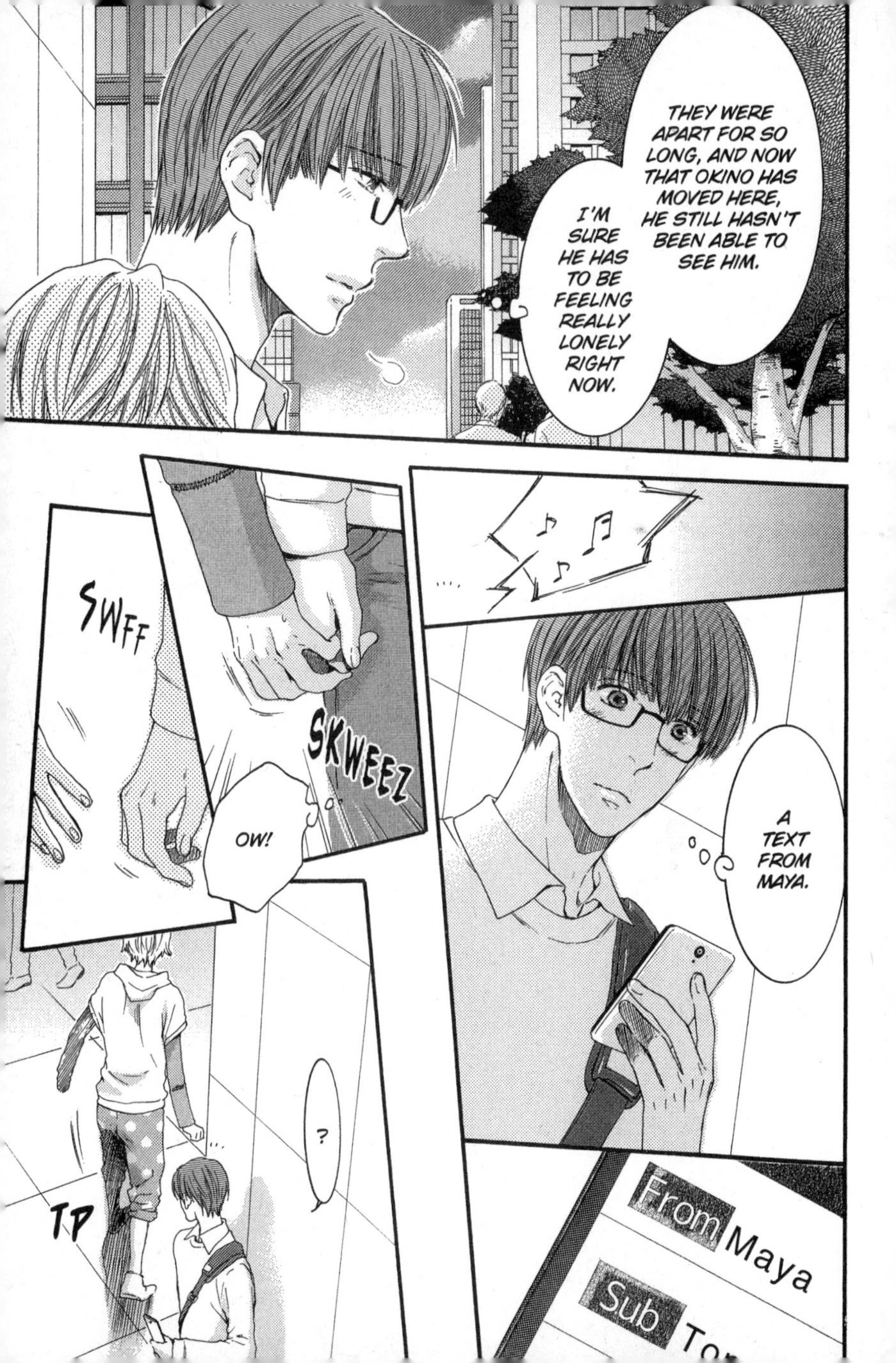
THEY WERE APART FOR SO LONG, AND NOW THAT OKINO HAS MOVED HERE, HE STILL HASN'T BEEN ABLE TO SEE HIM.
I'M SURE HE HAS TO BE FEELING REALLY LONELY RIGHT NOW.
♪ ♫ ♪
...
A TEXT FROM MAYA.
SKWEEZ
OW!
SWFF
From Maya
Sub
...
?
TP

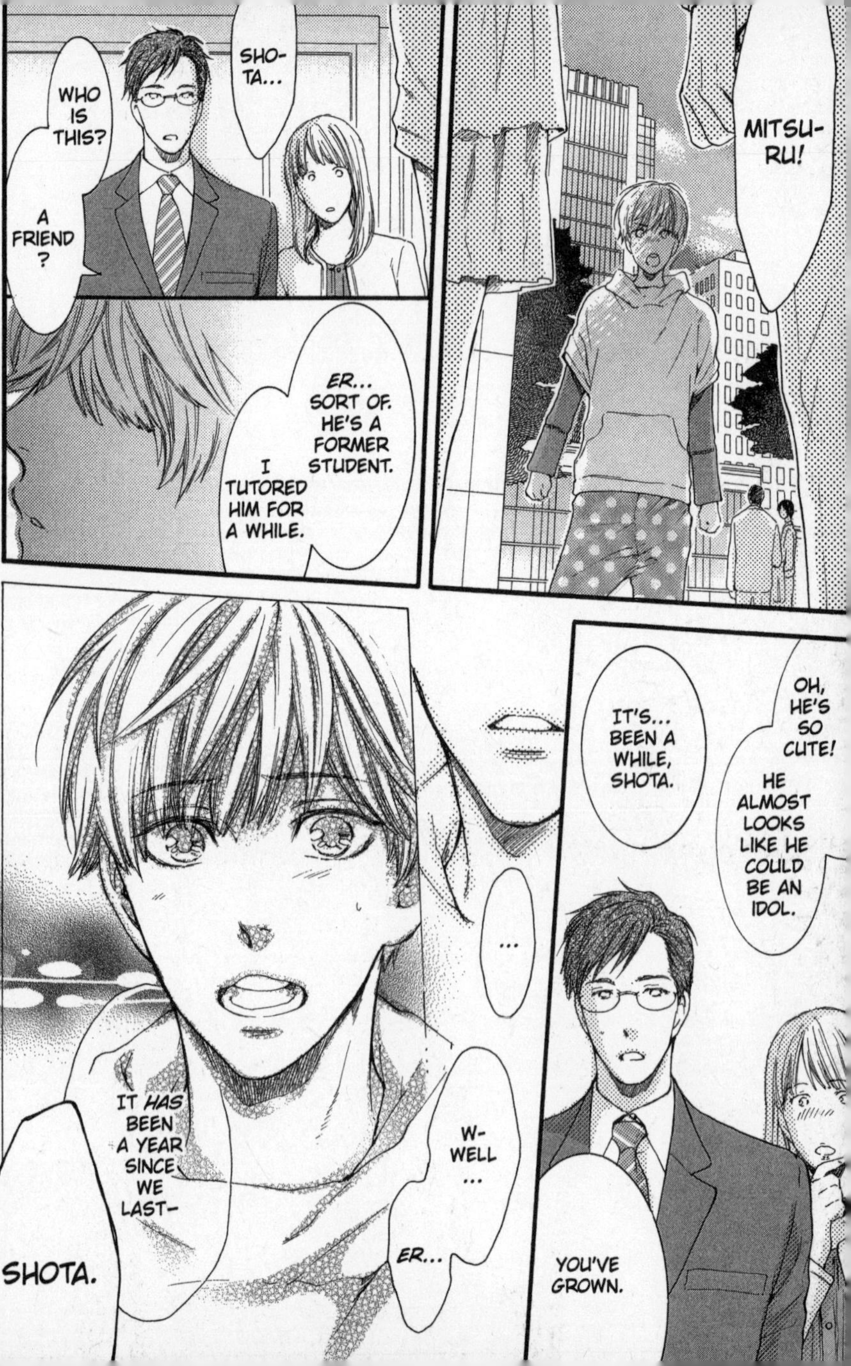
MITSU-RU!
SHO-TA...
WHO IS THIS?
A FRIEND?
ER... SORT OF. HE'S A FORMER STUDENT.
I TUTORED HIM FOR A WHILE.
OH, HE'S SO CUTE! HE ALMOST LOOKS LIKE HE COULD BE AN IDOL.
IT'S... BEEN A WHILE, SHOTA.
YOU'VE GROWN.
...
W-WELL...
IT *HAS* BEEN A YEAR SINCE WE LAST-
ER...
SHOTA.

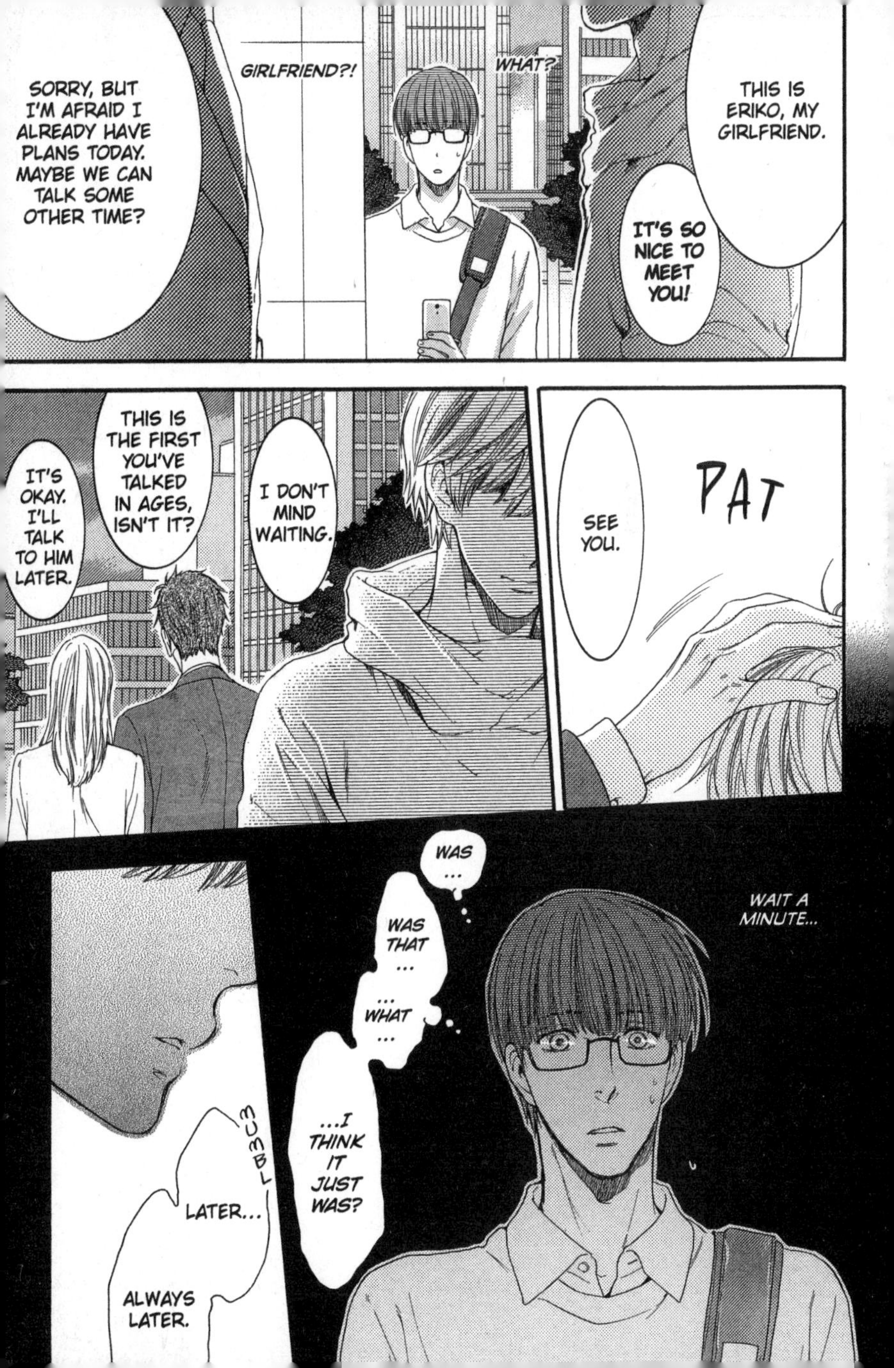
THIS IS ERIKO, MY GIRLFRIEND.
IT'S SO NICE TO MEET YOU!
WHAT?
GIRLFRIEND?!
SORRY, BUT I'M AFRAID I ALREADY HAVE PLANS TODAY. MAYBE WE CAN TALK SOME OTHER TIME?
SEE YOU.
PAT
I DON'T MIND WAITING.
THIS IS THE FIRST YOU'VE TALKED IN AGES, ISN'T IT?
IT'S OKAY. I'LL TALK TO HIM LATER.
WAIT A MINUTE...
WAS...
WAS THAT...
...WHAT...
...I THINK IT JUST WAS?
LATER...
ALWAYS LATER.

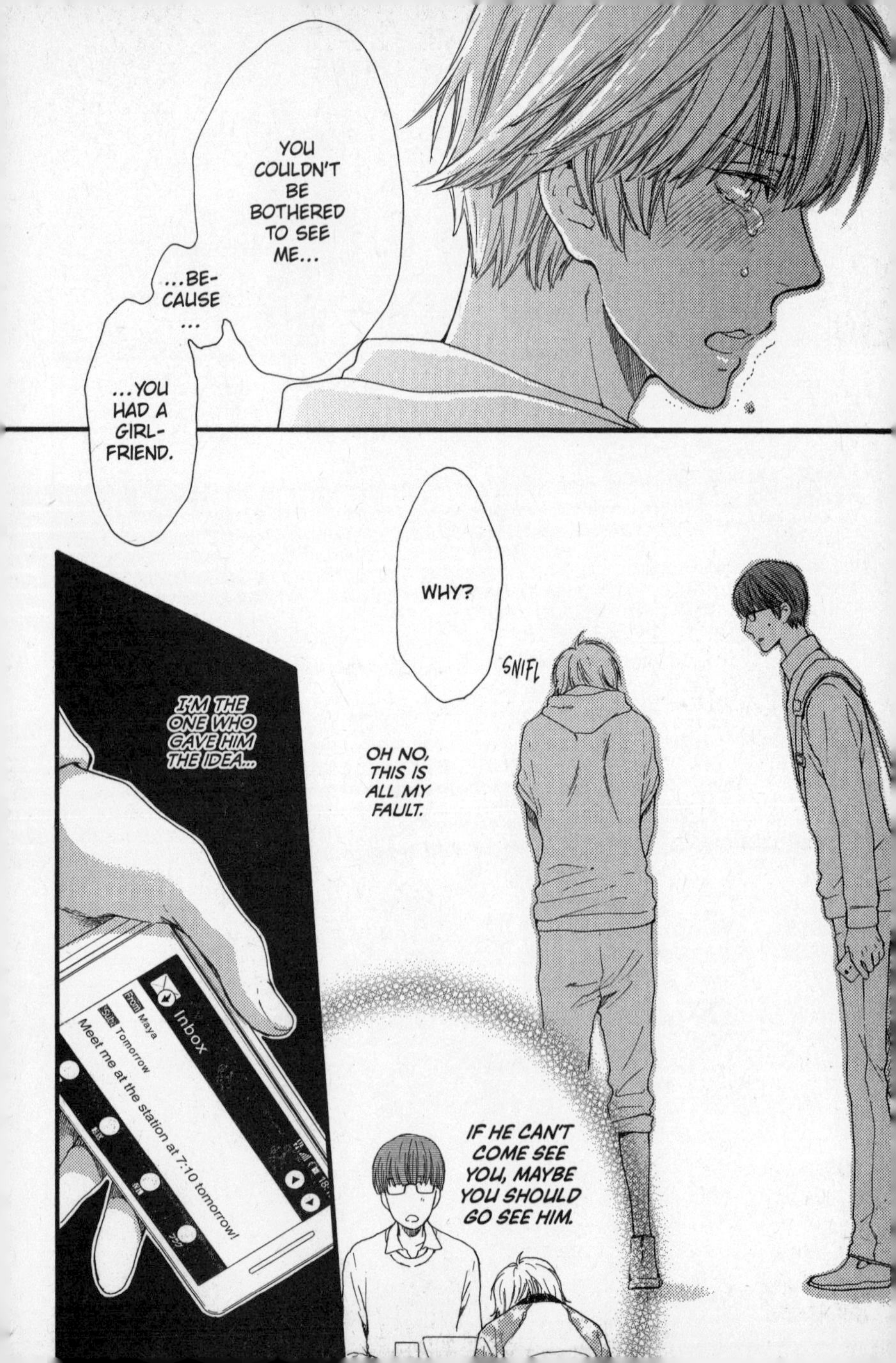
YOU COULDN'T BE BOTHERED TO SEE ME...
...BE-CAUSE...
...YOU HAD A GIRL-FRIEND.
WHY?
SNIFL
OH NO, THIS IS ALL MY FAULT.
IF HE CAN'T COME SEE YOU, MAYBE YOU SHOULD GO SEE HIM.
I'M THE ONE WHO GAVE HIM THE IDEA...
Inbox
Maya
Tomorrow
Meet me at the station at 7:10 tomorrow!

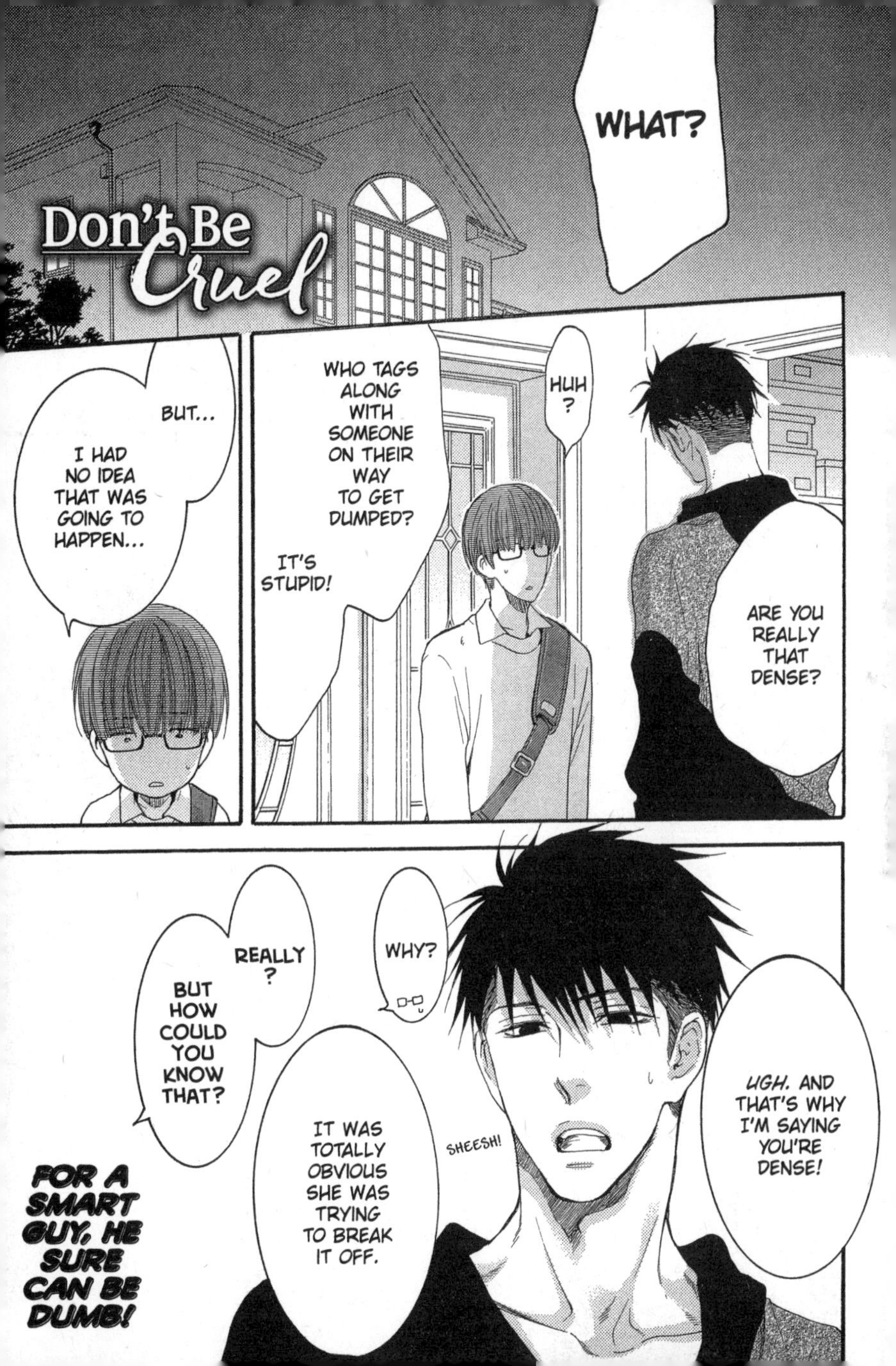
WHAT?
Don't Be Cruel
HUH?
WHO TAGS ALONG WITH SOMEONE ON THEIR WAY TO GET DUMPED?
IT'S STUPID!
ARE YOU REALLY THAT DENSE?
BUT...
I HAD NO IDEA THAT WAS GOING TO HAPPEN...
UGH. AND THAT'S WHY I'M SAYING YOU'RE DENSE!
SHEESH!
IT WAS TOTALLY OBVIOUS SHE WAS TRYING TO BREAK IT OFF.
WHY?
REALLY?
BUT HOW COULD YOU KNOW THAT?
FOR A SMART GUY, HE SURE CAN BE DUMB!

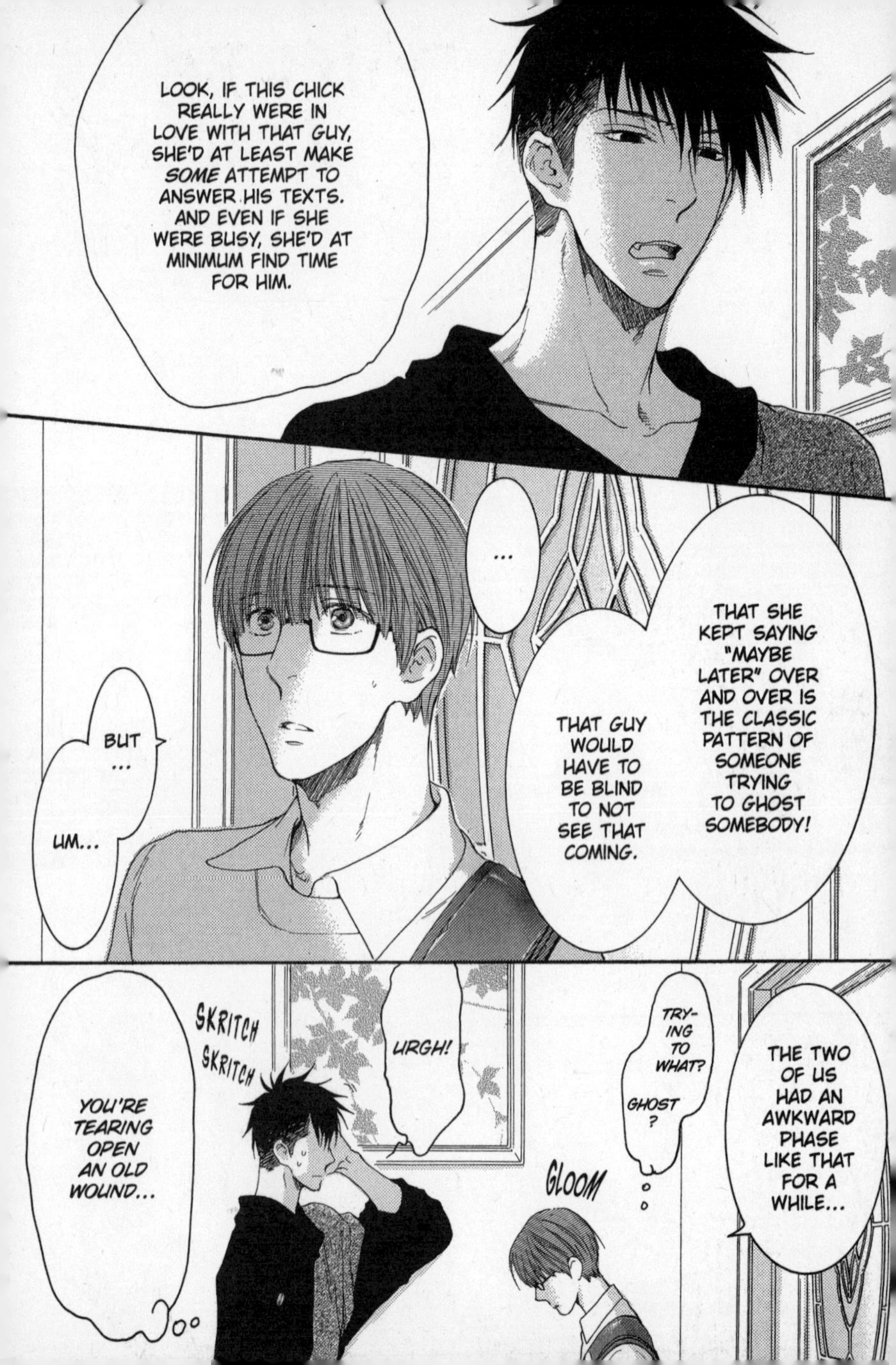
LOOK, IF THIS CHICK REALLY WERE IN LOVE WITH THAT GUY, SHE'D AT LEAST MAKE *SOME* ATTEMPT TO ANSWER HIS TEXTS. AND EVEN IF SHE WERE BUSY, SHE'D AT MINIMUM FIND TIME FOR HIM.
THAT SHE KEPT SAYING "MAYBE LATER" OVER AND OVER IS THE CLASSIC PATTERN OF SOMEONE TRYING TO GHOST SOMEBODY!
THAT GUY WOULD HAVE TO BE BLIND TO NOT SEE THAT COMING.
...
BUT ... UM...
THE TWO OF US HAD AN AWKWARD PHASE LIKE THAT FOR A WHILE...
TRY-ING TO WHAT? GHOST?
GLOOM
URGH!
SKRITCH SKRITCH
YOU'RE TEARING OPEN AN OLD WOUND...

Don't Be Cruel

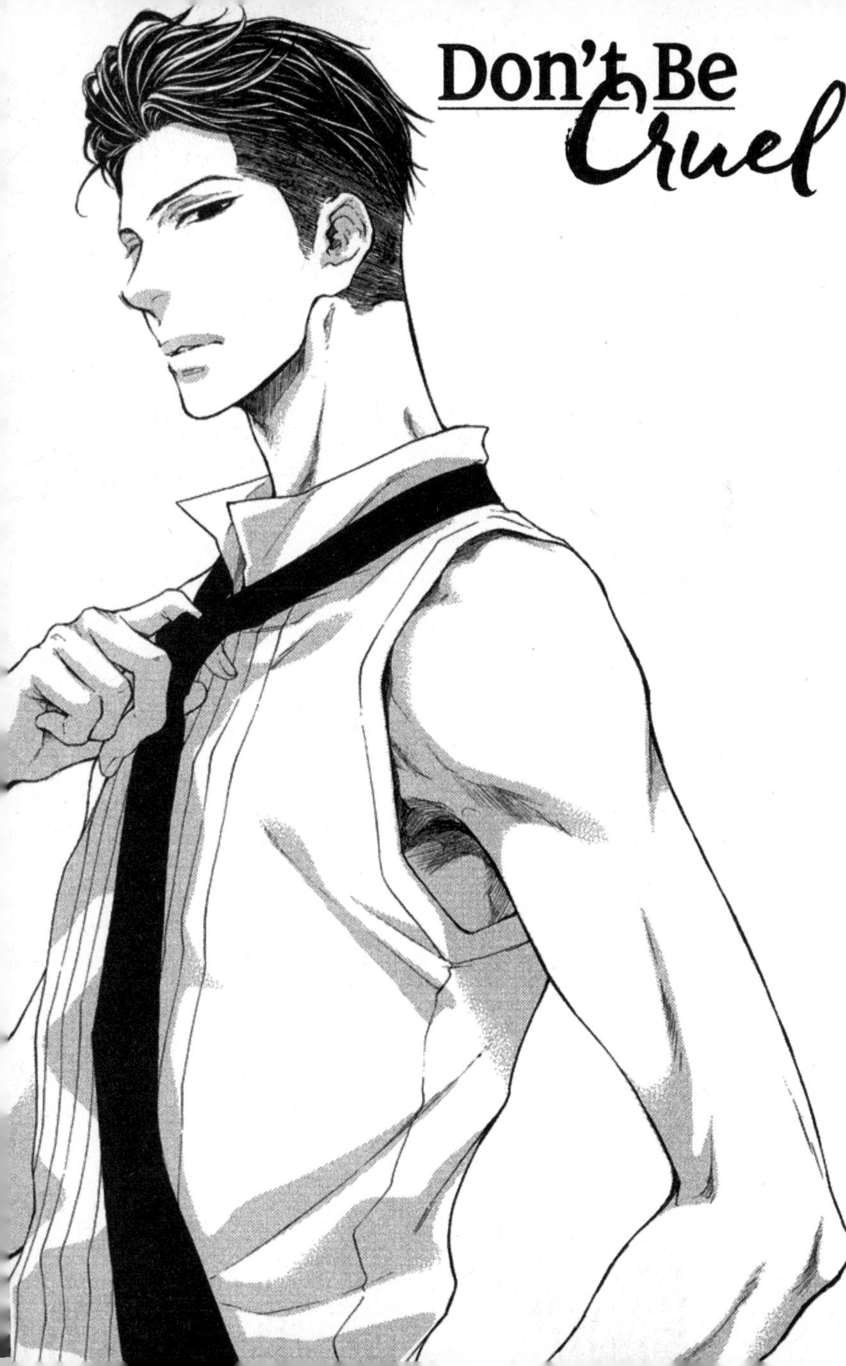

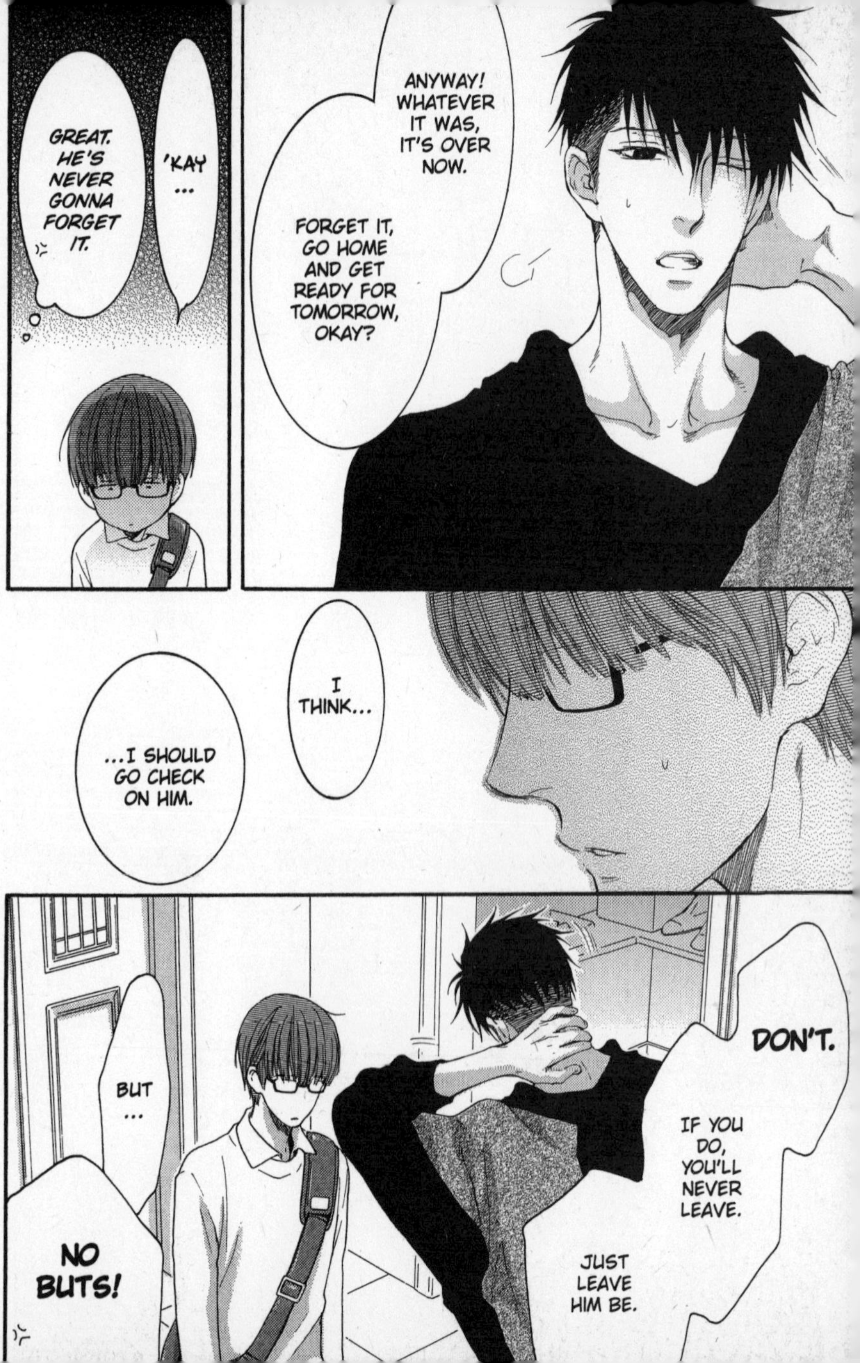
ANYWAY! WHATEVER IT WAS, IT'S OVER NOW.
FORGET IT, GO HOME AND GET READY FOR TOMORROW, OKAY?
'KAY...
GREAT. HE'S NEVER GONNA FORGET IT.
I THINK...
...I SHOULD GO CHECK ON HIM.
DON'T.
IF YOU DO, YOU'LL NEVER LEAVE.
BUT...
JUST LEAVE HIM BE.
NO BUTS!

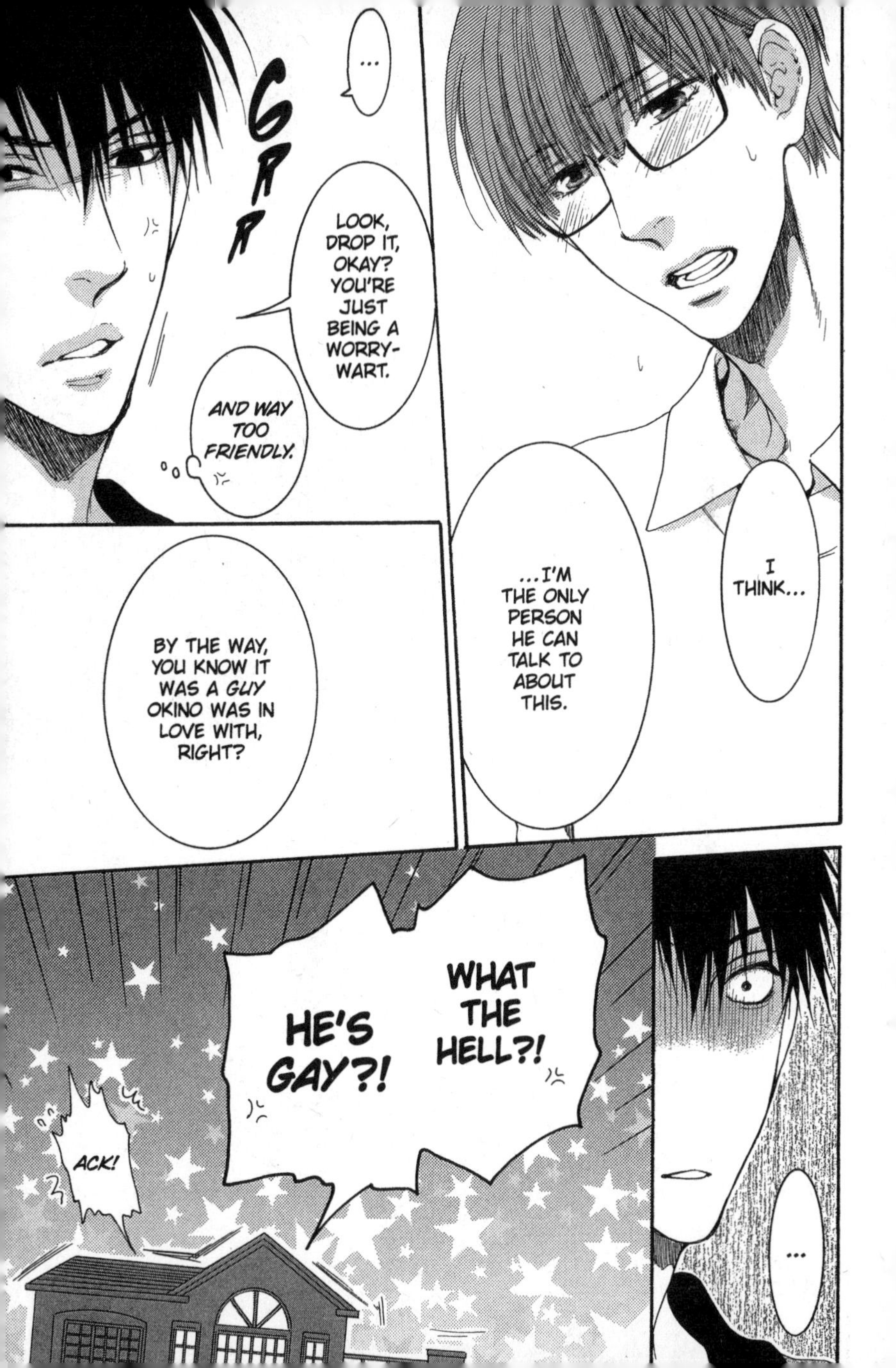
I THINK...
...I'M THE ONLY PERSON HE CAN TALK TO ABOUT THIS.
...
GRR
LOOK, DROP IT, OKAY? YOU'RE JUST BEING A WORRY-WART.
AND WAY TOO FRIENDLY.
BY THE WAY, YOU KNOW IT WAS A GUY OKINO WAS IN LOVE WITH, RIGHT?
...
WHAT THE HELL?!
HE'S GAY?!
ACK!

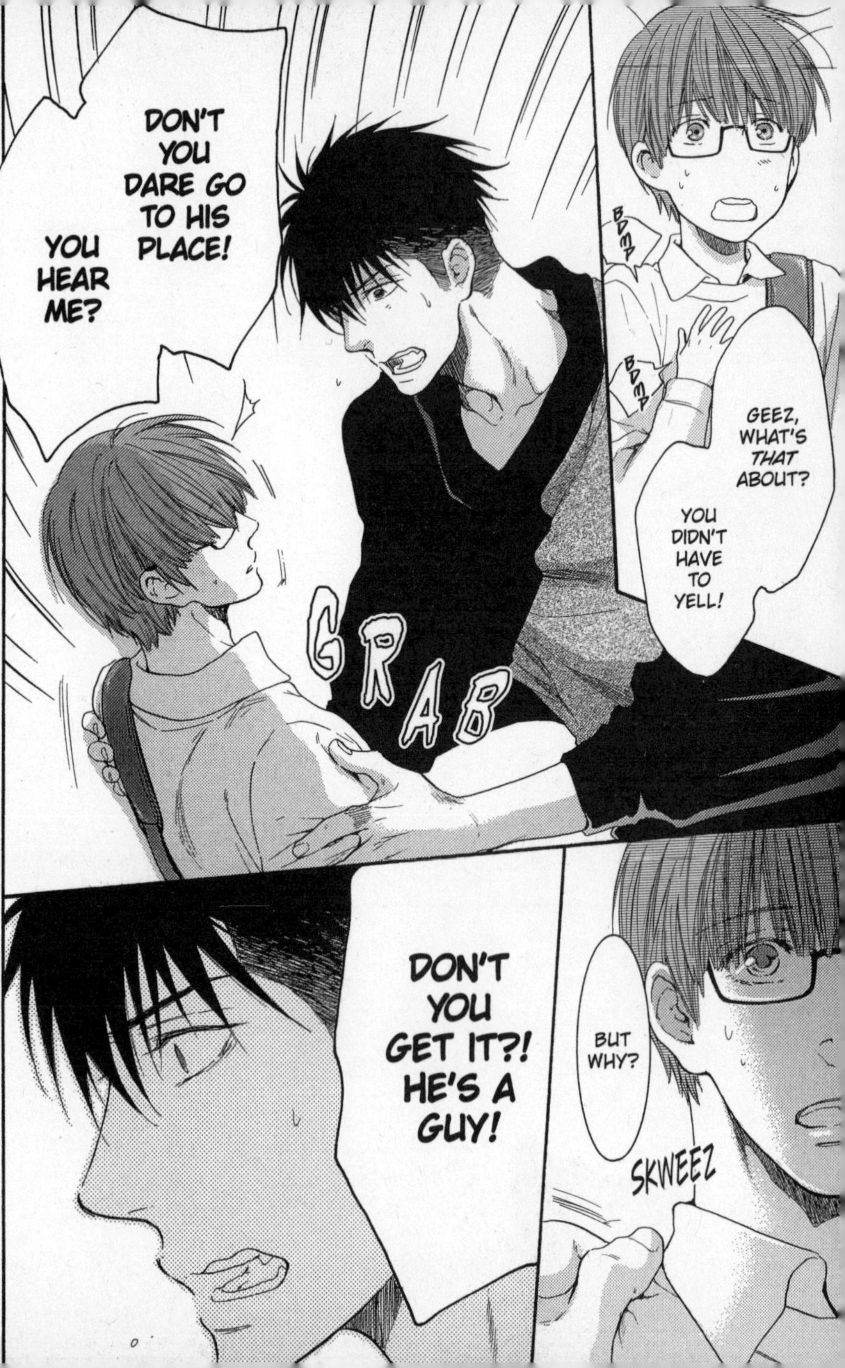
BDMP
BDMP
GEEZ, WHAT'S *THAT* ABOUT?
YOU DIDN'T HAVE TO YELL!
DON'T YOU DARE GO TO HIS PLACE!
YOU HEAR ME?
GRAB
BUT WHY?
SKWEEZ
DON'T YOU GET IT?! HE'S A GUY!

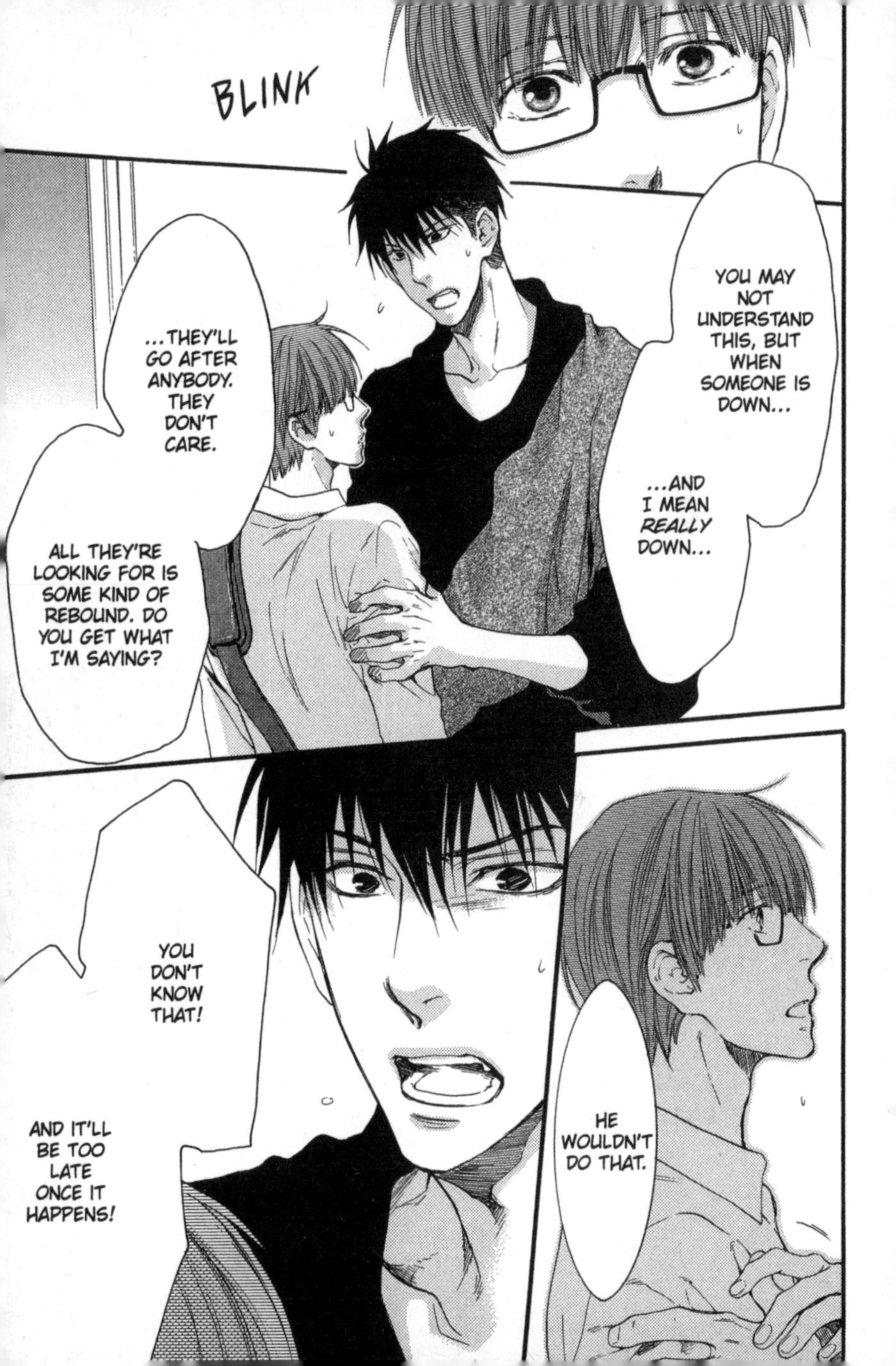
BLINK
YOU MAY NOT UNDERSTAND THIS, BUT WHEN SOMEONE IS DOWN...
...AND I MEAN *REALLY* DOWN...
...THEY'LL GO AFTER ANYBODY. THEY DON'T CARE.
ALL THEY'RE LOOKING FOR IS SOME KIND OF REBOUND. DO YOU GET WHAT I'M SAYING?
HE WOULDN'T DO THAT.
YOU DON'T KNOW THAT!
AND IT'LL BE TOO LATE ONCE IT HAPPENS!

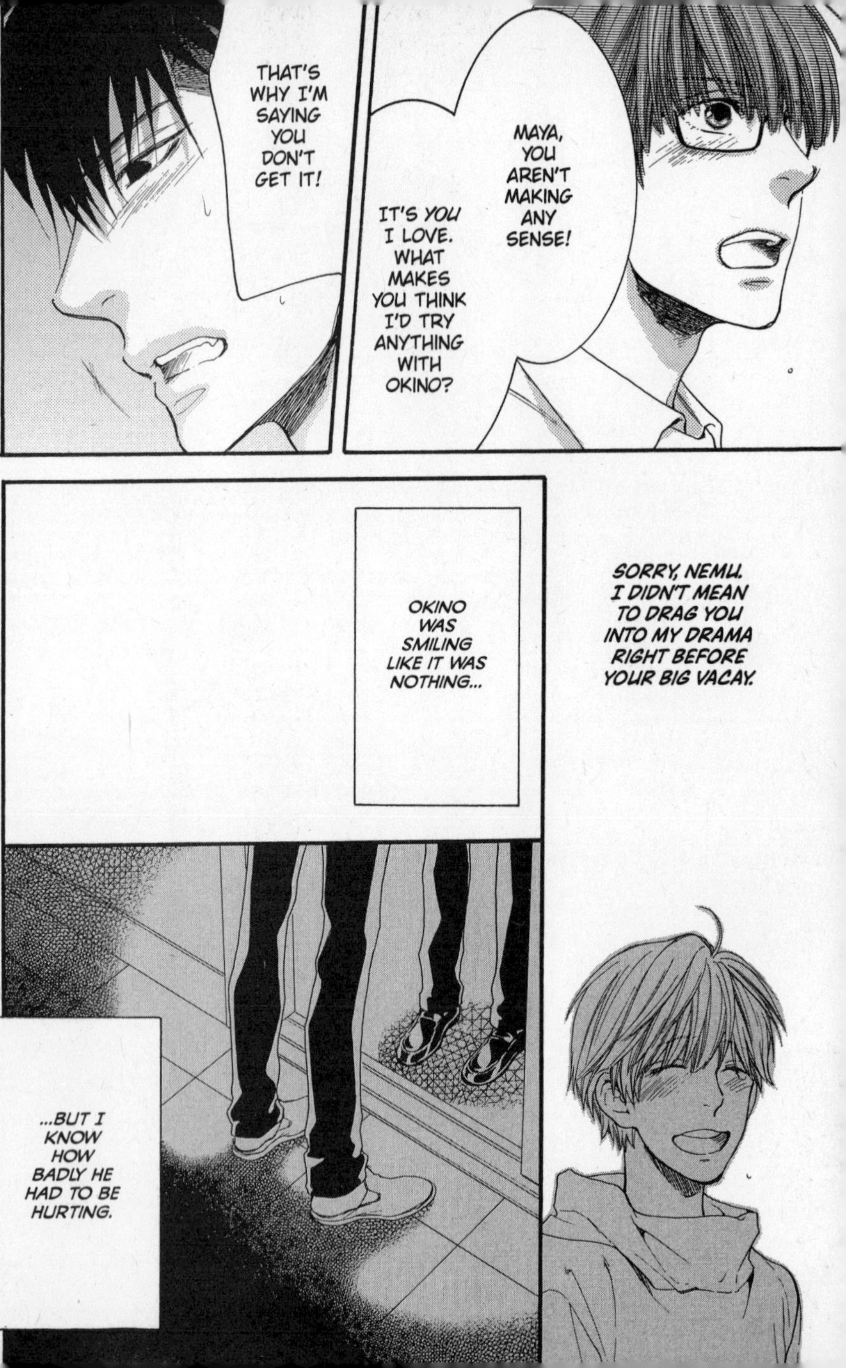
MAYA, YOU AREN'T MAKING ANY SENSE!
IT'S *YOU* I LOVE. WHAT MAKES YOU THINK I'D TRY ANYTHING WITH OKINO?
THAT'S WHY I'M SAYING YOU DON'T GET IT!
SORRY, NEMU. I DIDN'T MEAN TO DRAG YOU INTO MY DRAMA RIGHT BEFORE YOUR BIG VACAY.
OKINO WAS SMILING LIKE IT WAS NOTHING...
...BUT I KNOW HOW BADLY HE HAD TO BE HURTING.

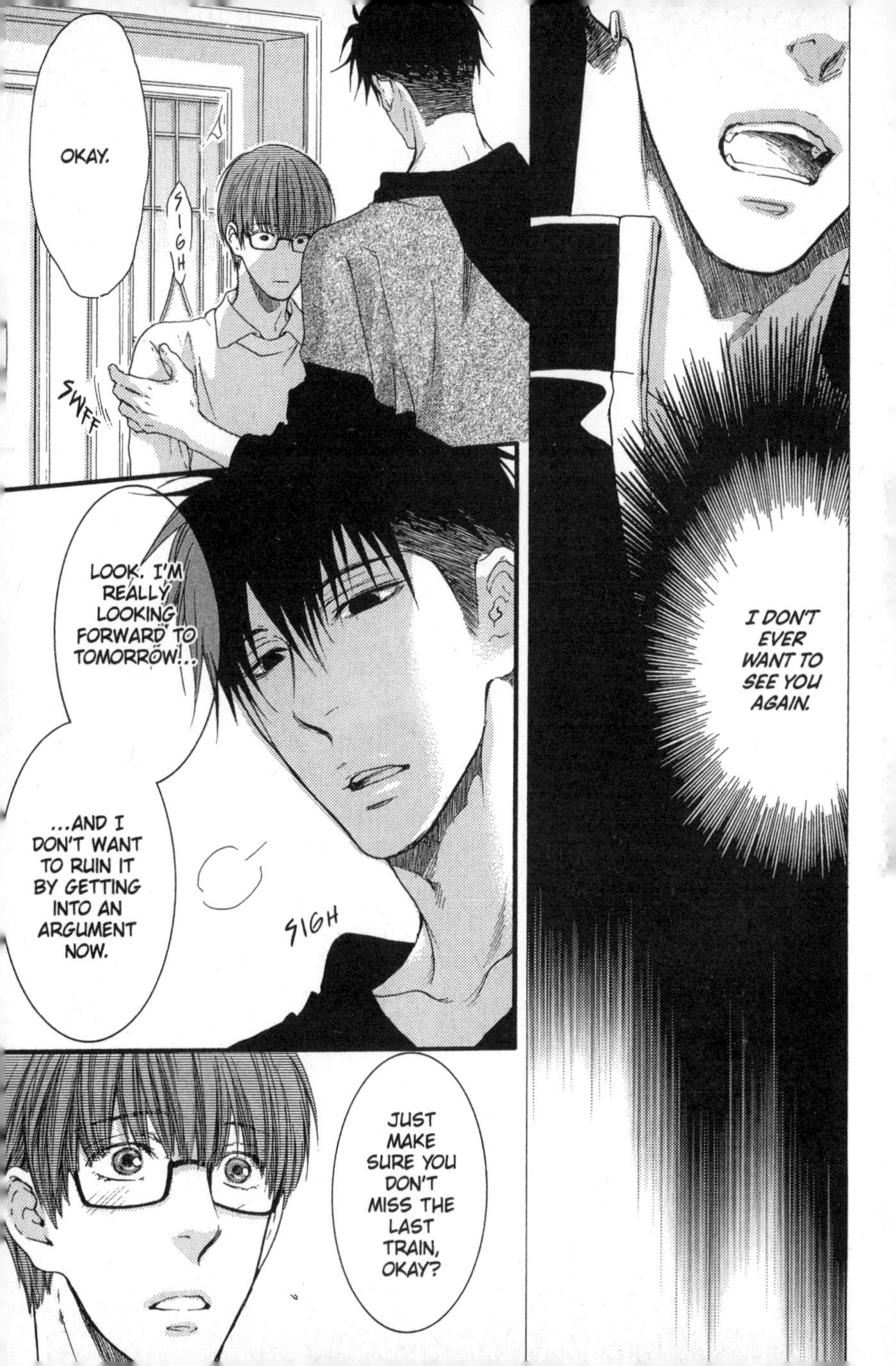
I DON'T EVER WANT TO SEE YOU AGAIN.
OKAY.
SIGH
SWFF
LOOK. I'M REALLY LOOKING FORWARD TO TOMORROW...
...AND I DON'T WANT TO RUIN IT BY GETTING INTO AN ARGUMENT NOW.
SIGH
JUST MAKE SURE YOU DON'T MISS THE LAST TRAIN, OKAY?

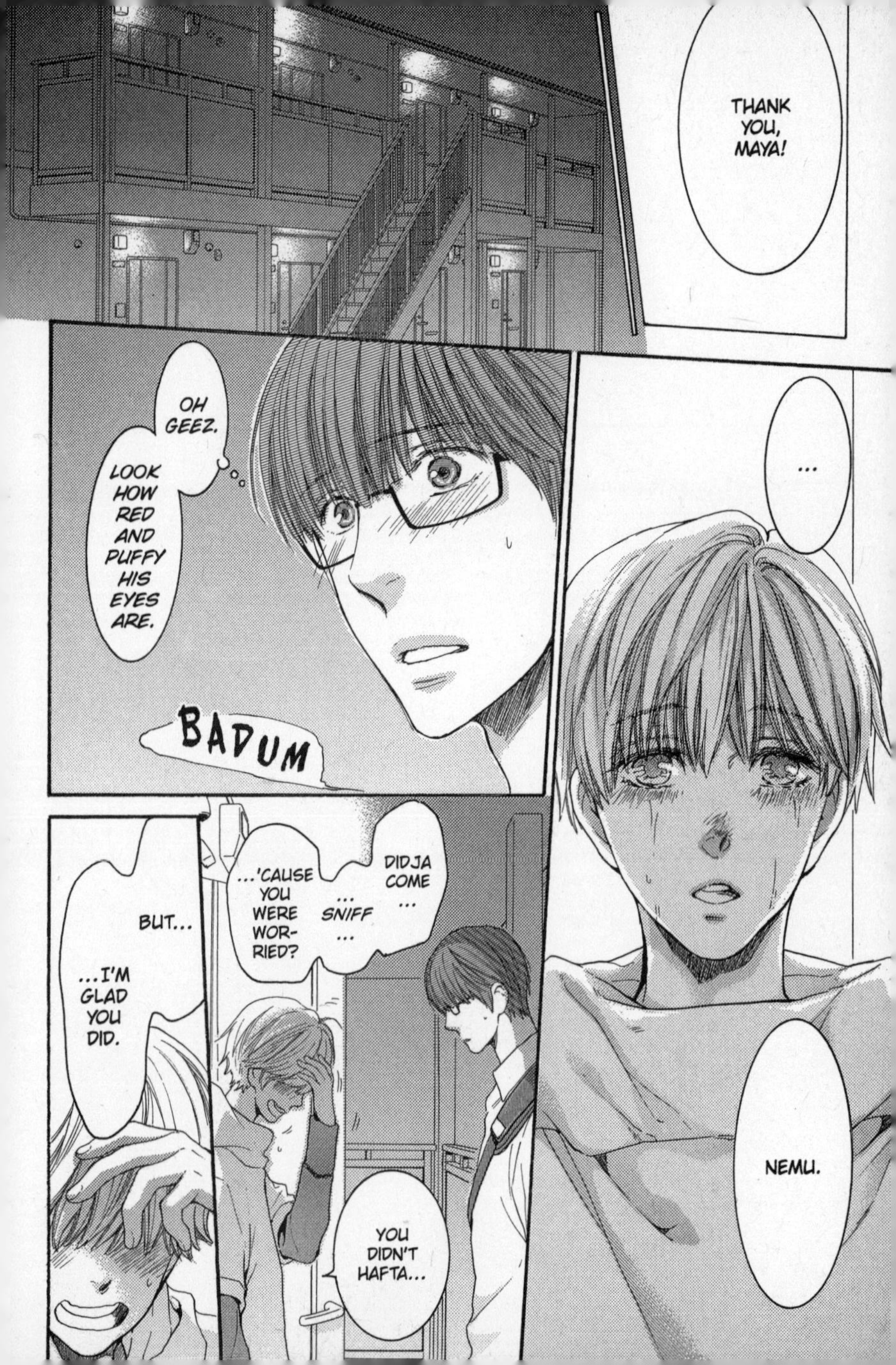
THANK YOU, MAYA!
...
NEMU.
OH GEEZ.
LOOK HOW RED AND PUFFY HIS EYES ARE.
BADUM
DIDJA COME...
...SNIFF...
...'CAUSE YOU WERE WOR-RIED?
YOU DIDN'T HAFTA...
BUT...
...I'M GLAD YOU DID.

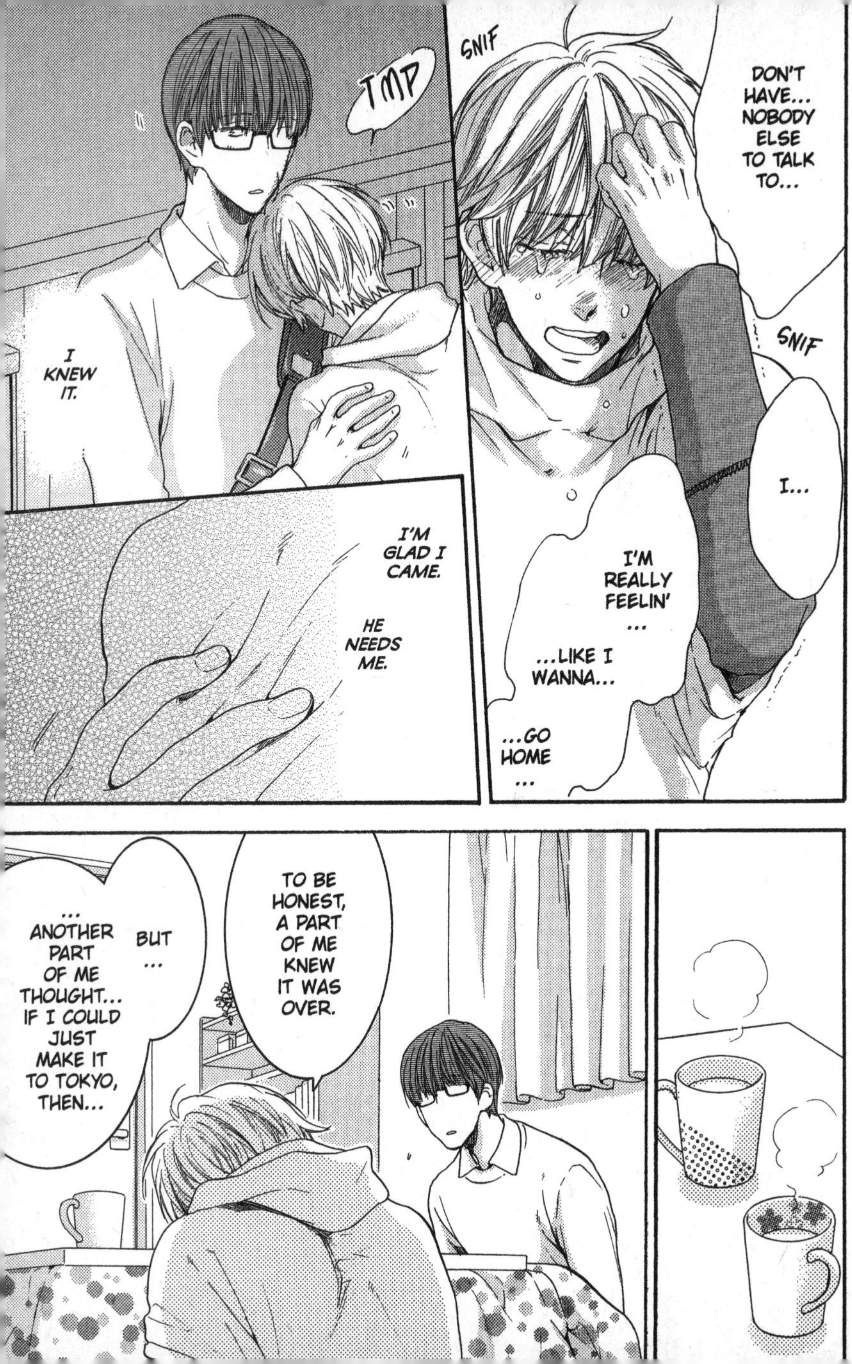
SNIF
DON'T HAVE... NOBODY ELSE TO TALK TO...
SNIF
I...
I'M REALLY FEELIN' ...
...LIKE I WANNA...
...GO HOME ...
TMP
I KNEW IT.
I'M GLAD I CAME.
HE NEEDS ME.
TO BE HONEST, A PART OF ME KNEW IT WAS OVER.
BUT ...
... ANOTHER PART OF ME THOUGHT... IF I COULD JUST MAKE IT TO TOKYO, THEN...

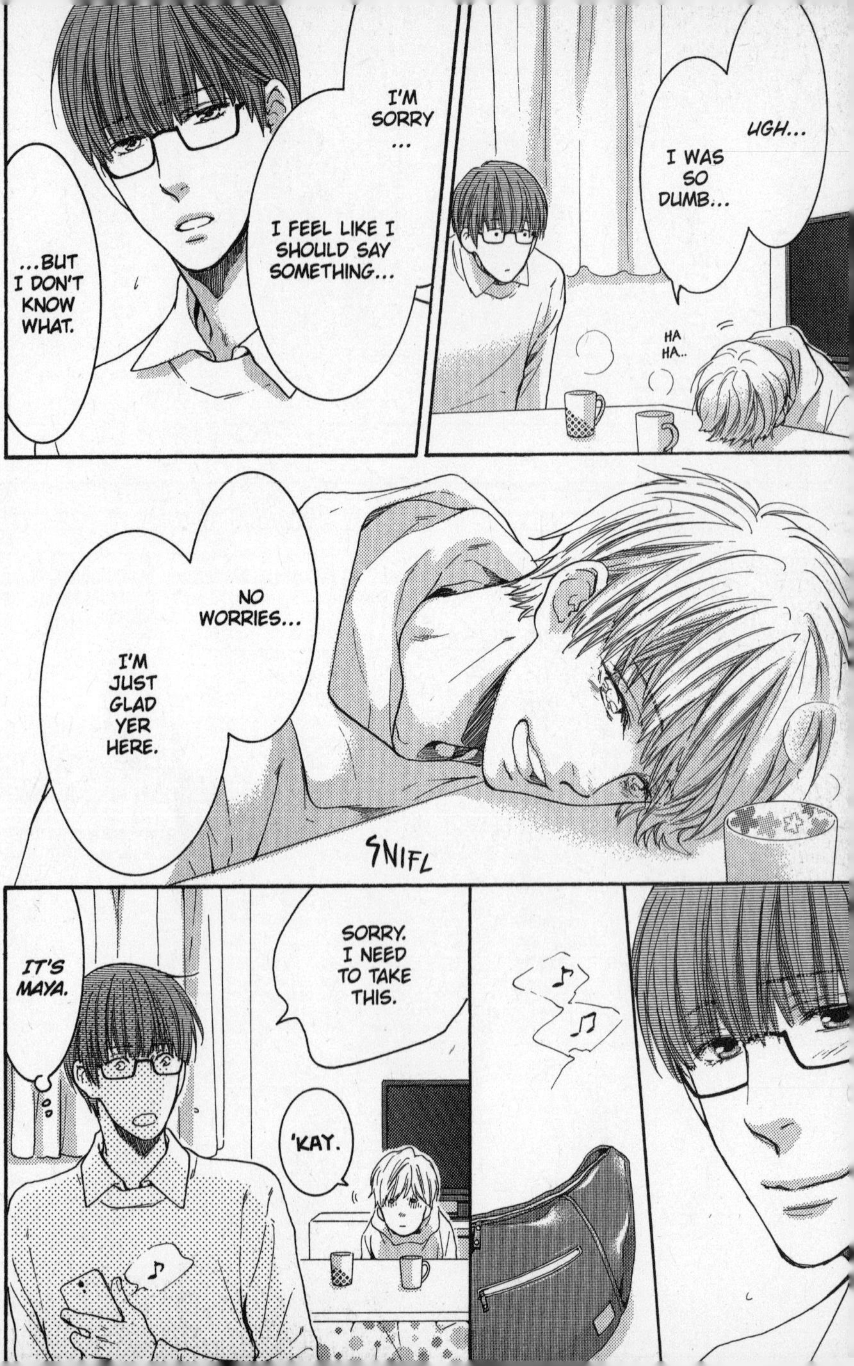
UGH...
I WAS SO DUMB...
HA HA..
I'M SORRY ...
I FEEL LIKE I SHOULD SAY SOMETHING...
...BUT I DON'T KNOW WHAT.
NO WORRIES...
I'M JUST GLAD YER HERE.
SNIFL
SORRY. I NEED TO TAKE THIS.
IT'S MAYA.
'KAY.

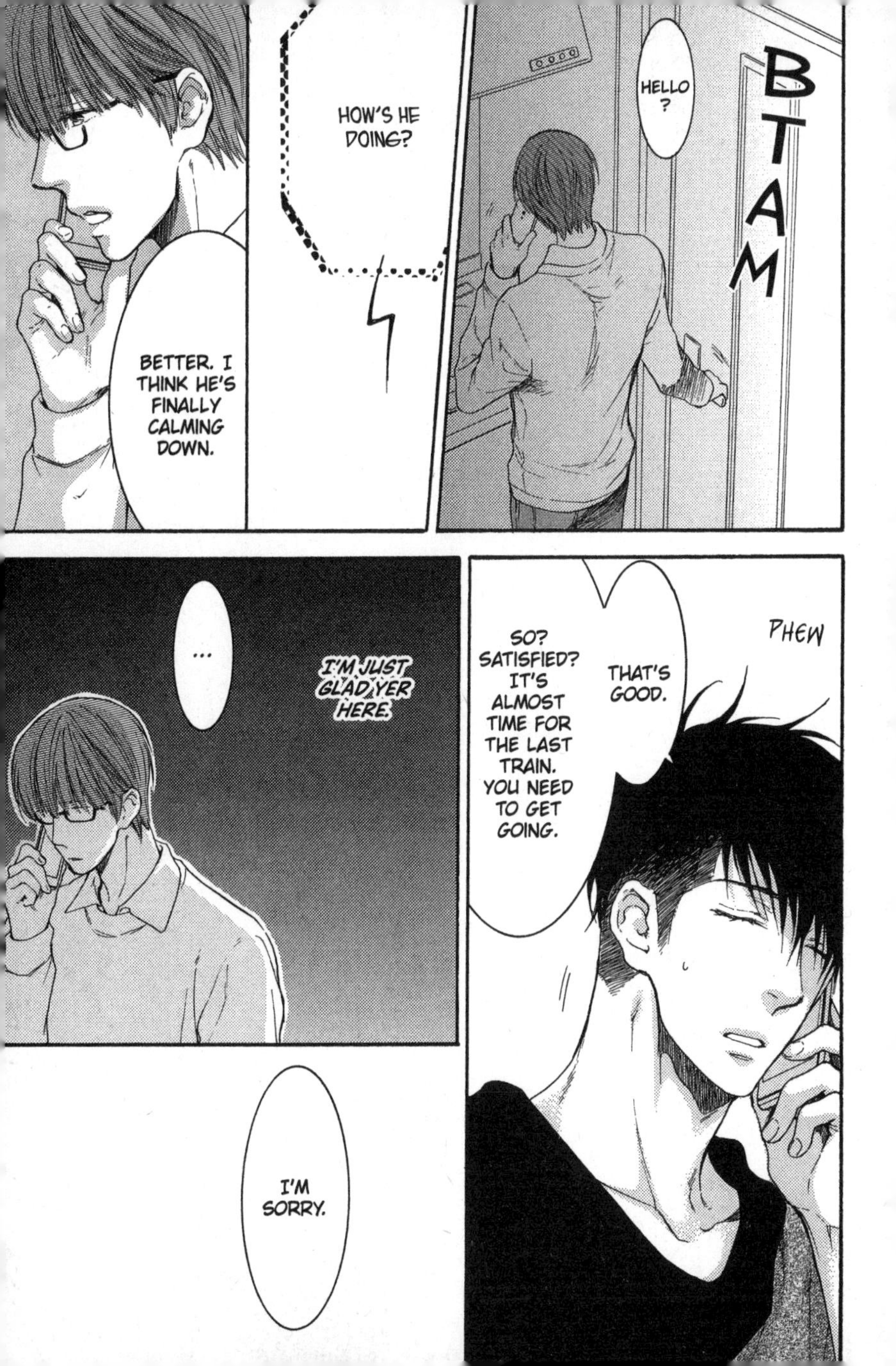
BTAM
HELLO ?
HOW'S HE DOING?
BETTER. I THINK HE'S FINALLY CALMING DOWN.
PHEW
THAT'S GOOD.
SO? SATISFIED? IT'S ALMOST TIME FOR THE LAST TRAIN. YOU NEED TO GET GOING.
I'M JUST GLAD YER HERE.
...
I'M SORRY.

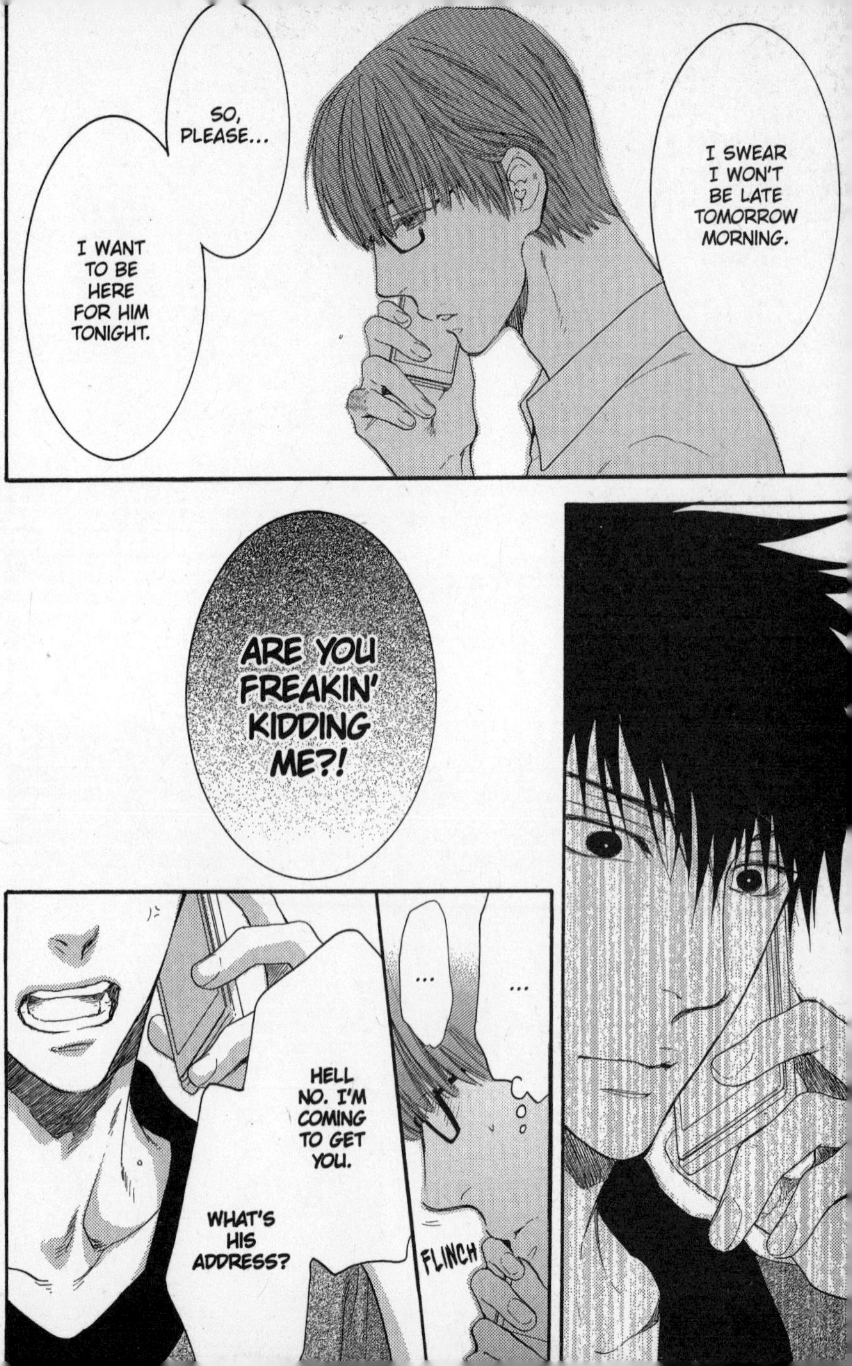
I SWEAR I WON'T BE LATE TOMORROW MORNING.
SO, PLEASE...
I WANT TO BE HERE FOR HIM TONIGHT.
ARE YOU FREAKIN' KIDDING ME?!
...
...
FLINCH
HELL NO. I'M COMING TO GET YOU.
WHAT'S HIS ADDRESS?

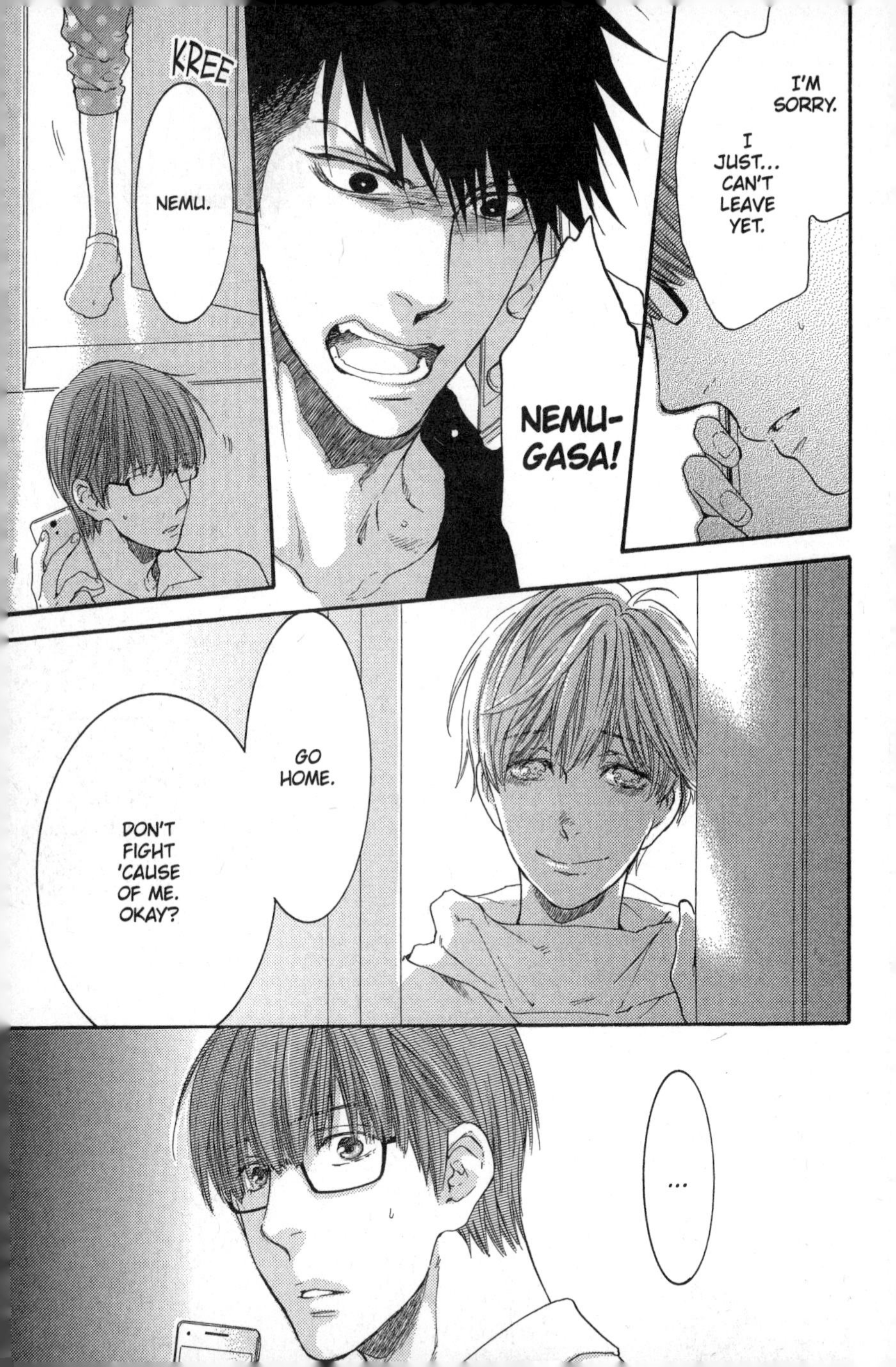
I'M SORRY.
I JUST... CAN'T LEAVE YET.
NEMU-GASA!
KREE
NEMU.
GO HOME.
DON'T FIGHT 'CAUSE OF ME. OKAY?
...

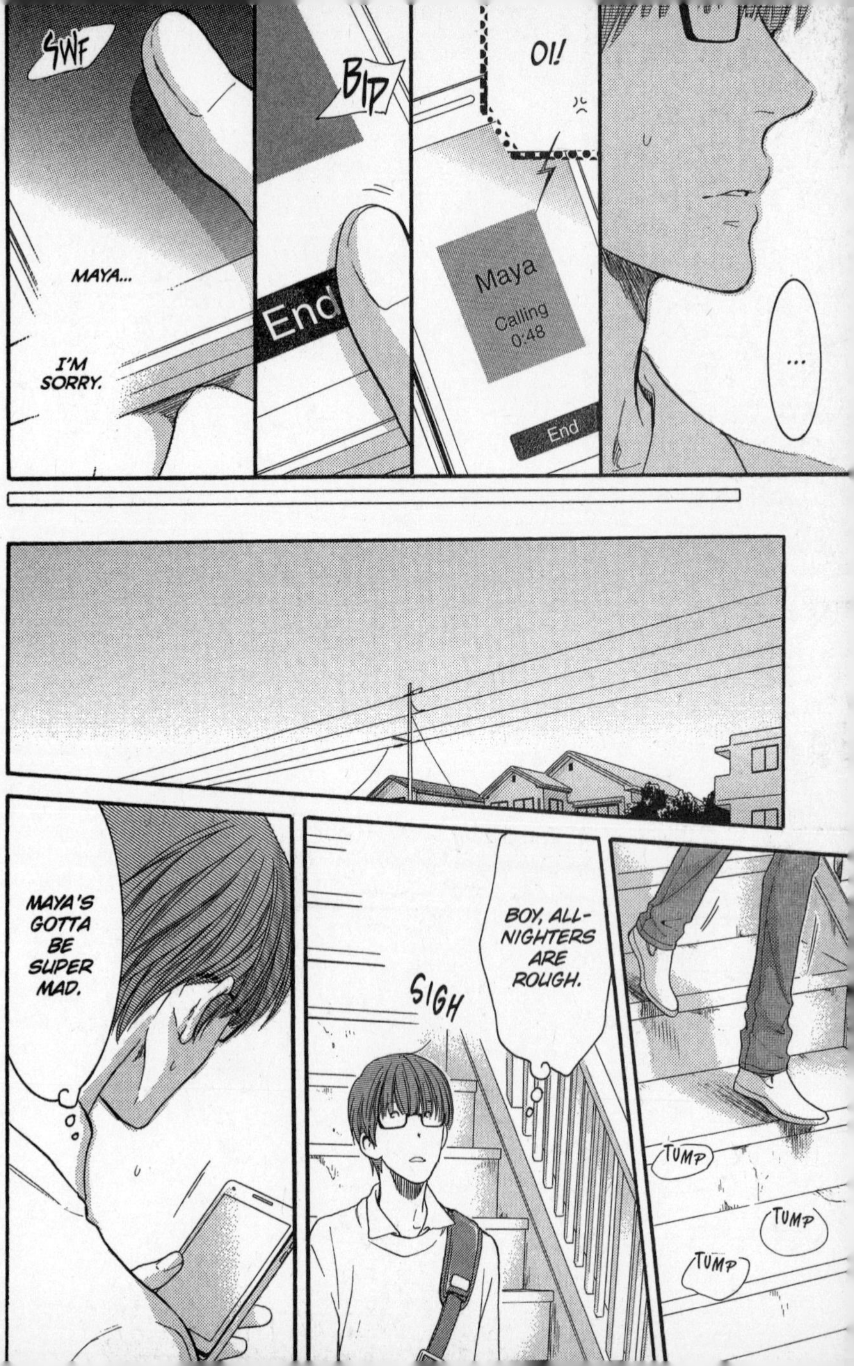
...
OI!
Maya
Calling
0:48
End
BIP
End
SWF
MAYA...
I'M SORRY.
TUMP
TUMP
TUMP
BOY, ALL-NIGHTERS ARE ROUGH.
SIGH
MAYA'S GOTTA BE SUPER MAD.

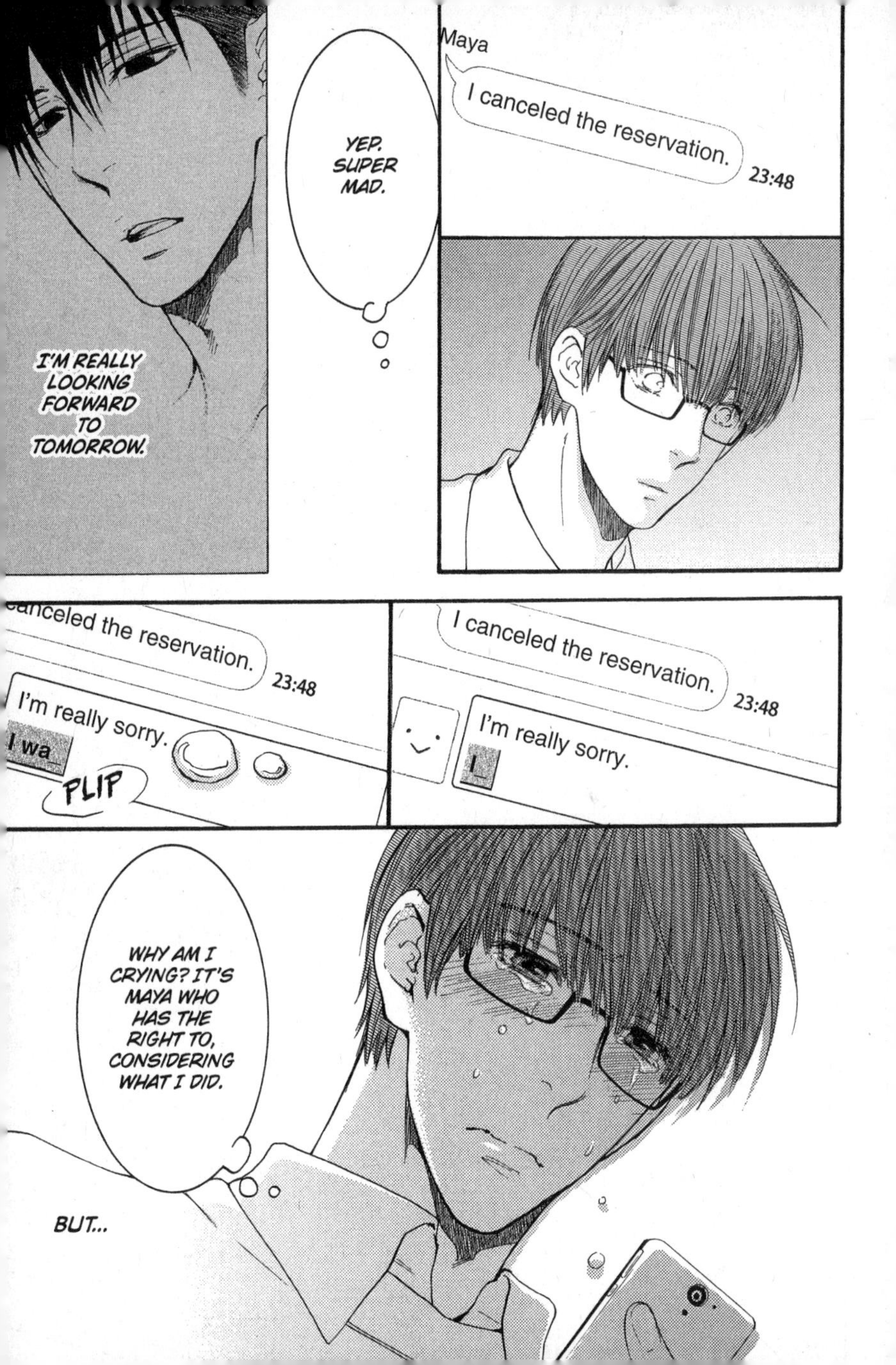
Maya
I canceled the reservation.
23:48
YEP. SUPER MAD.
I'M REALLY LOOKING FORWARD TO TOMORROW.
I canceled the reservation.
23:48
I'm really sorry.
I_
canceled the reservation.
23:48
I'm really sorry.
I wa_
FLIP
WHY AM I CRYING? IT'S MAYA WHO HAS THE RIGHT TO, CONSIDERING WHAT I DID.
BUT...

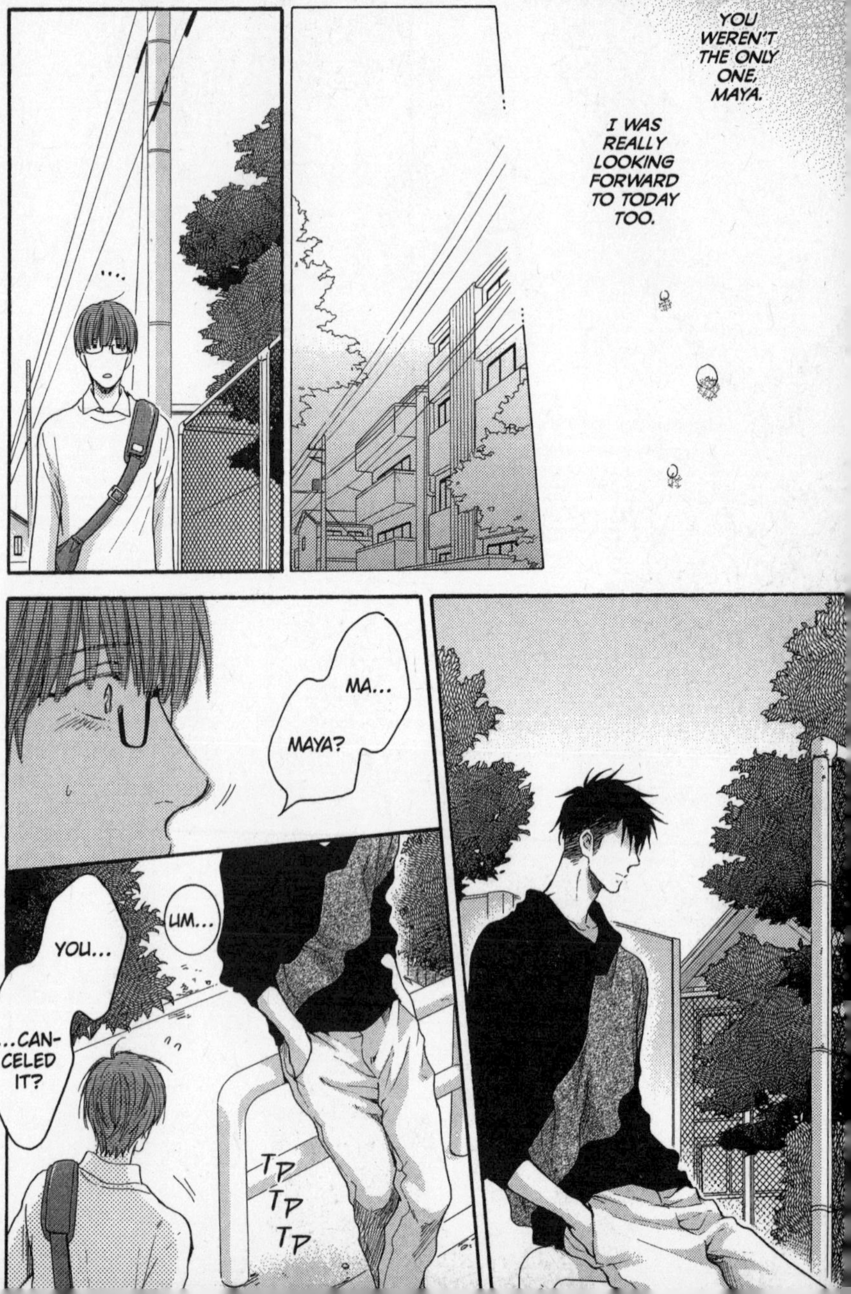
YOU WEREN'T THE ONLY ONE, MAYA.
I WAS REALLY LOOKING FORWARD TO TODAY TOO.
...
MA...
MAYA?
UM...
YOU...
...CAN-CELED IT?
TP TP TP

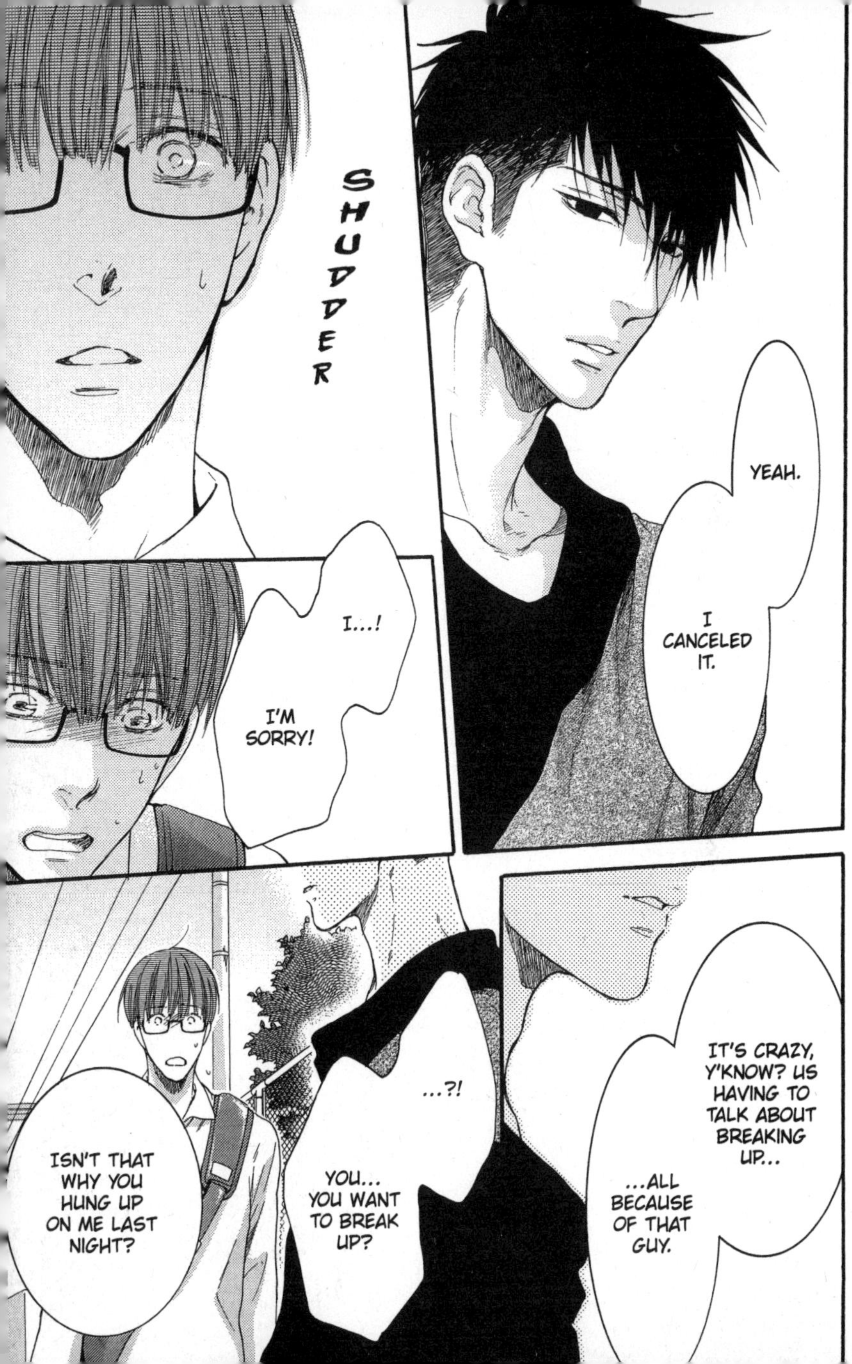
YEAH.
I CANCELED IT.
SHUDDER
I...!
I'M SORRY!
IT'S CRAZY, Y'KNOW? US HAVING TO TALK ABOUT BREAKING UP...
...ALL BECAUSE OF THAT GUY.
...?!
YOU... YOU WANT TO BREAK UP?
ISN'T THAT WHY YOU HUNG UP ON ME LAST NIGHT?

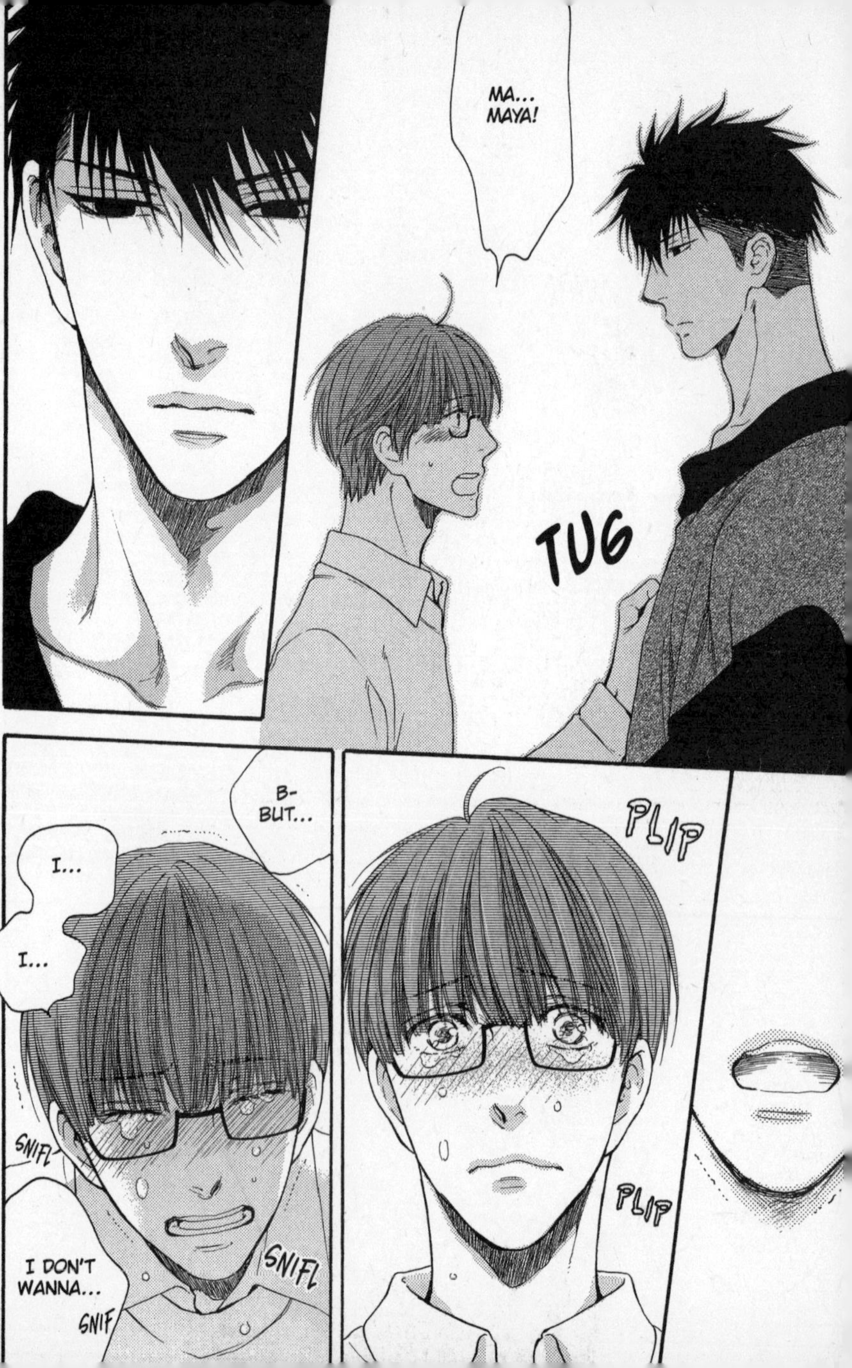
MA... MAYA!
TUG
PLIP
PLIP
B-BUT...
I...
I...
SNIFL
SNIFL
I DON'T WANNA...
SNIF

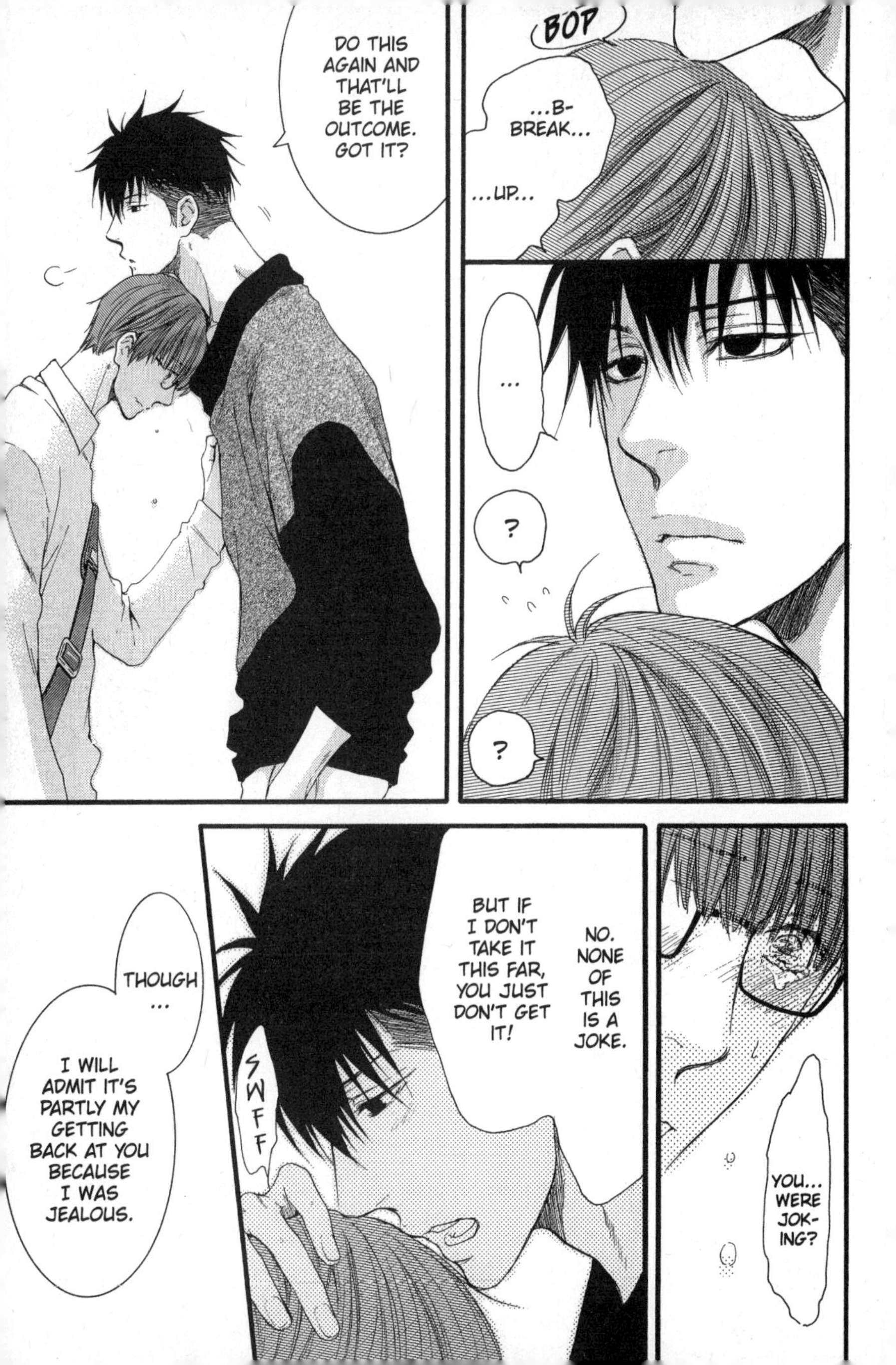
BOP
...B- BREAK...
...UP...
...
?
?
DO THIS AGAIN AND THAT'LL BE THE OUTCOME. GOT IT?
YOU... WERE JOK- ING?
NO. NONE OF THIS IS A JOKE.
BUT IF I DON'T TAKE IT THIS FAR, YOU JUST DON'T GET IT!
THOUGH ...
SWFF
I WILL ADMIT IT'S PARTLY MY GETTING BACK AT YOU BECAUSE I WAS JEALOUS.

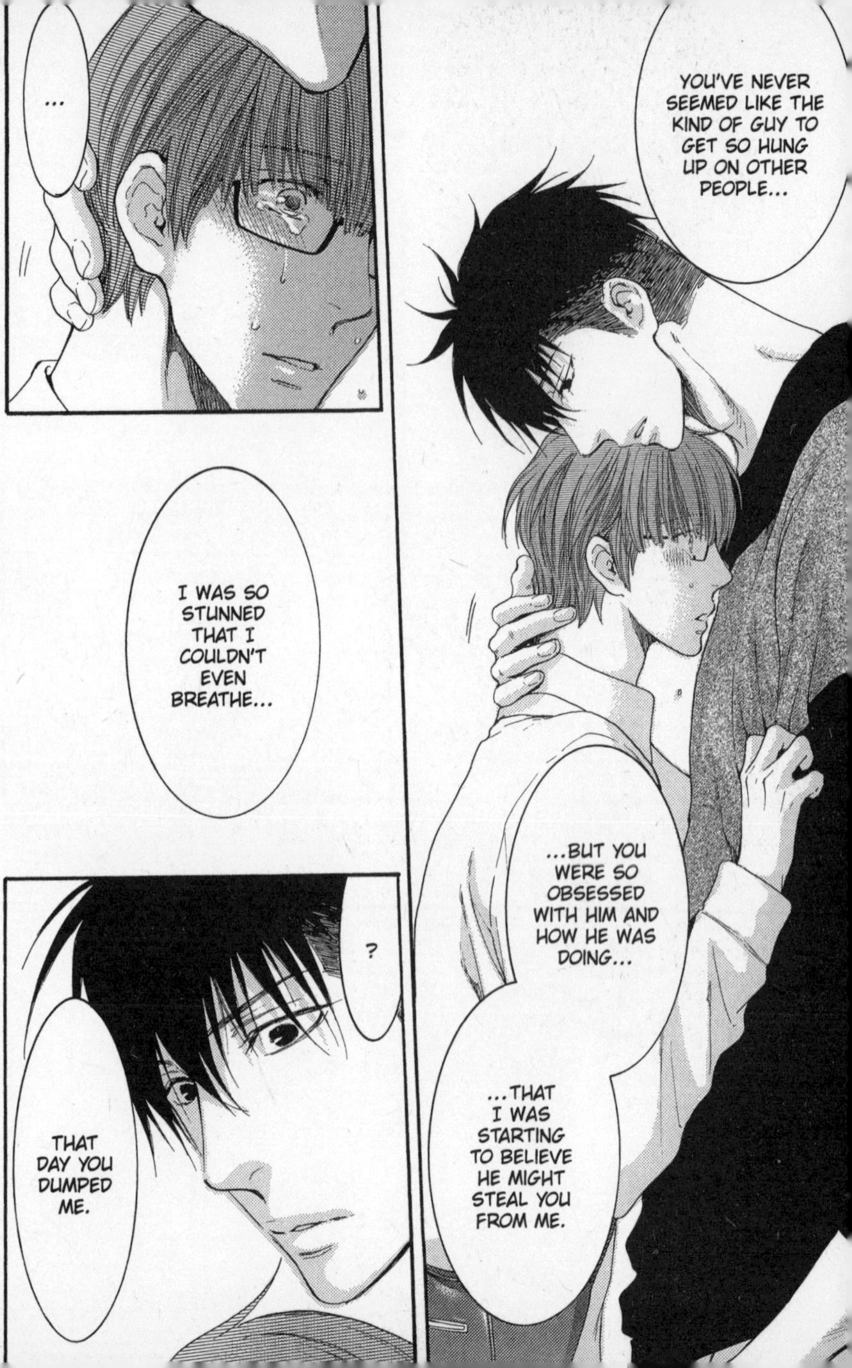
YOU'VE NEVER SEEMED LIKE THE KIND OF GUY TO GET SO HUNG UP ON OTHER PEOPLE...
...BUT YOU WERE SO OBSESSED WITH HIM AND HOW HE WAS DOING...
...THAT I WAS STARTING TO BELIEVE HE MIGHT STEAL YOU FROM ME.
...
I WAS SO STUNNED THAT I COULDN'T EVEN BREATHE...
?
THAT DAY YOU DUMPED ME.

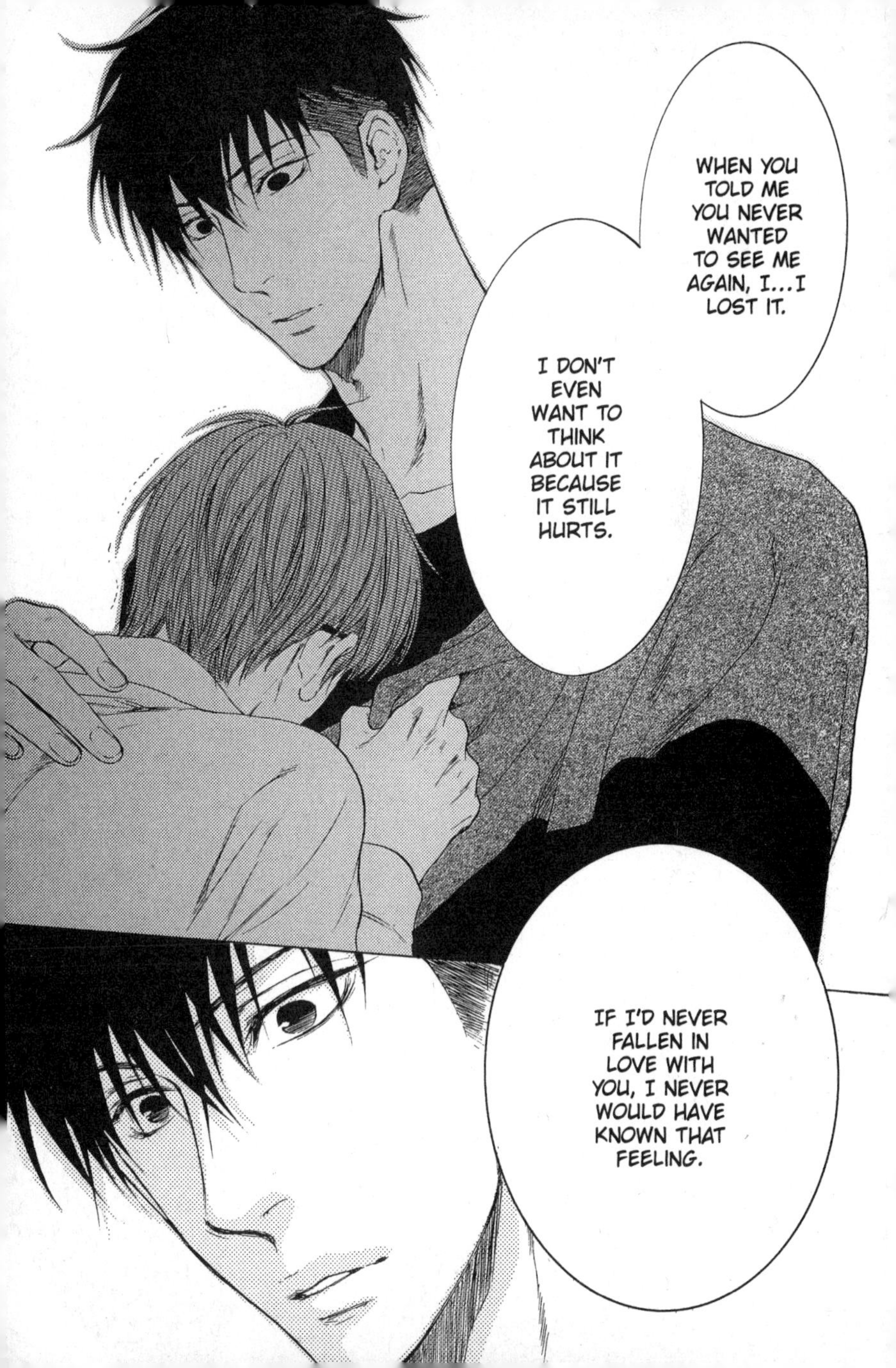
WHEN YOU TOLD ME YOU NEVER WANTED TO SEE ME AGAIN, I...I LOST IT.
I DON'T EVEN WANT TO THINK ABOUT IT BECAUSE IT STILL HURTS.
IF I'D NEVER FALLEN IN LOVE WITH YOU, I NEVER WOULD HAVE KNOWN THAT FEELING.

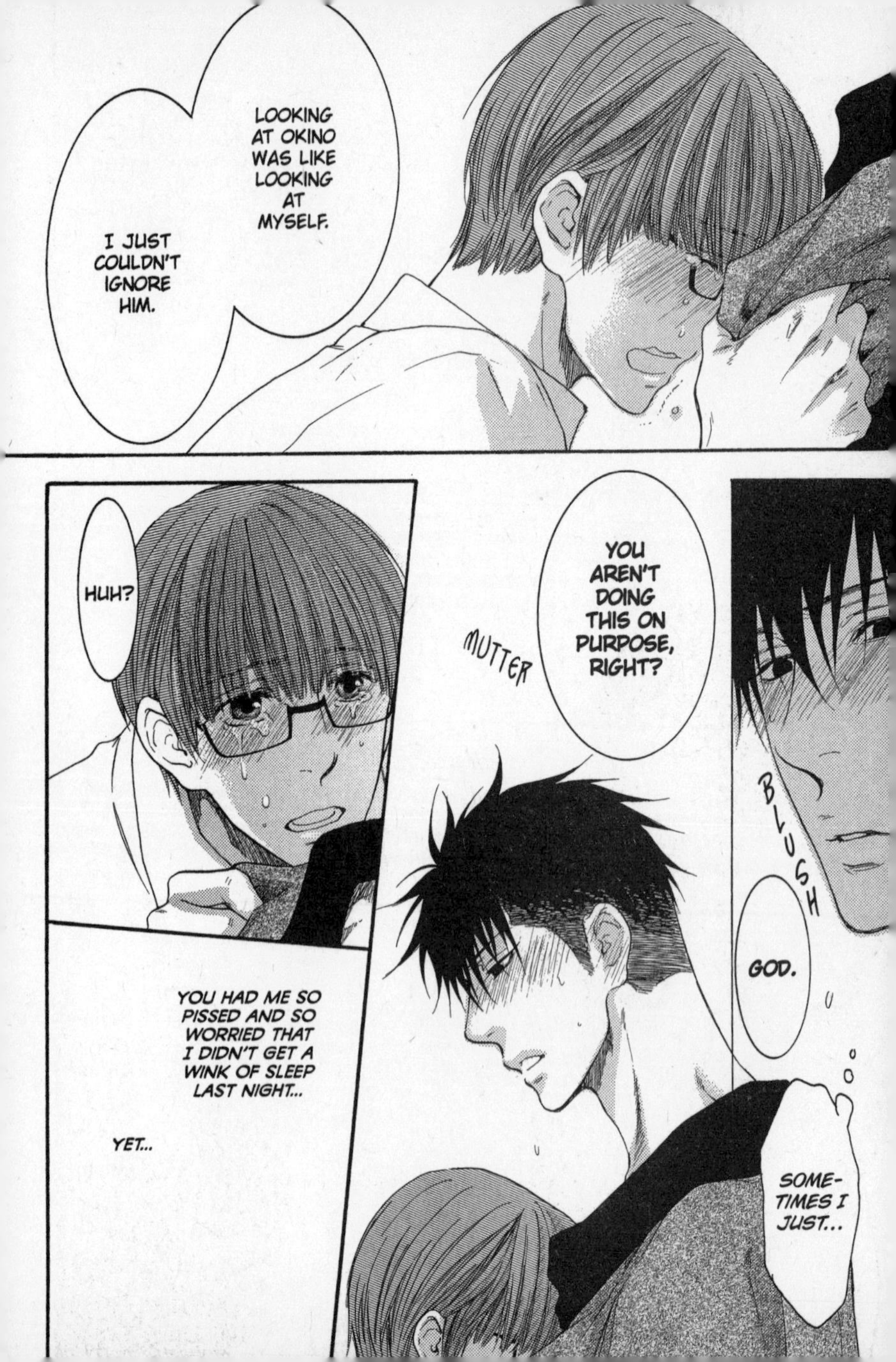
LOOKING AT OKINO WAS LIKE LOOKING AT MYSELF.
I JUST COULDN'T IGNORE HIM.
BLUSH
GOD.
YOU AREN'T DOING THIS ON PURPOSE, RIGHT?
MUTTER
HUH?
SOME-TIMES I JUST...
YOU HAD ME SO PISSED AND SO WORRIED THAT I DIDN'T GET A WINK OF SLEEP LAST NIGHT...
YET...

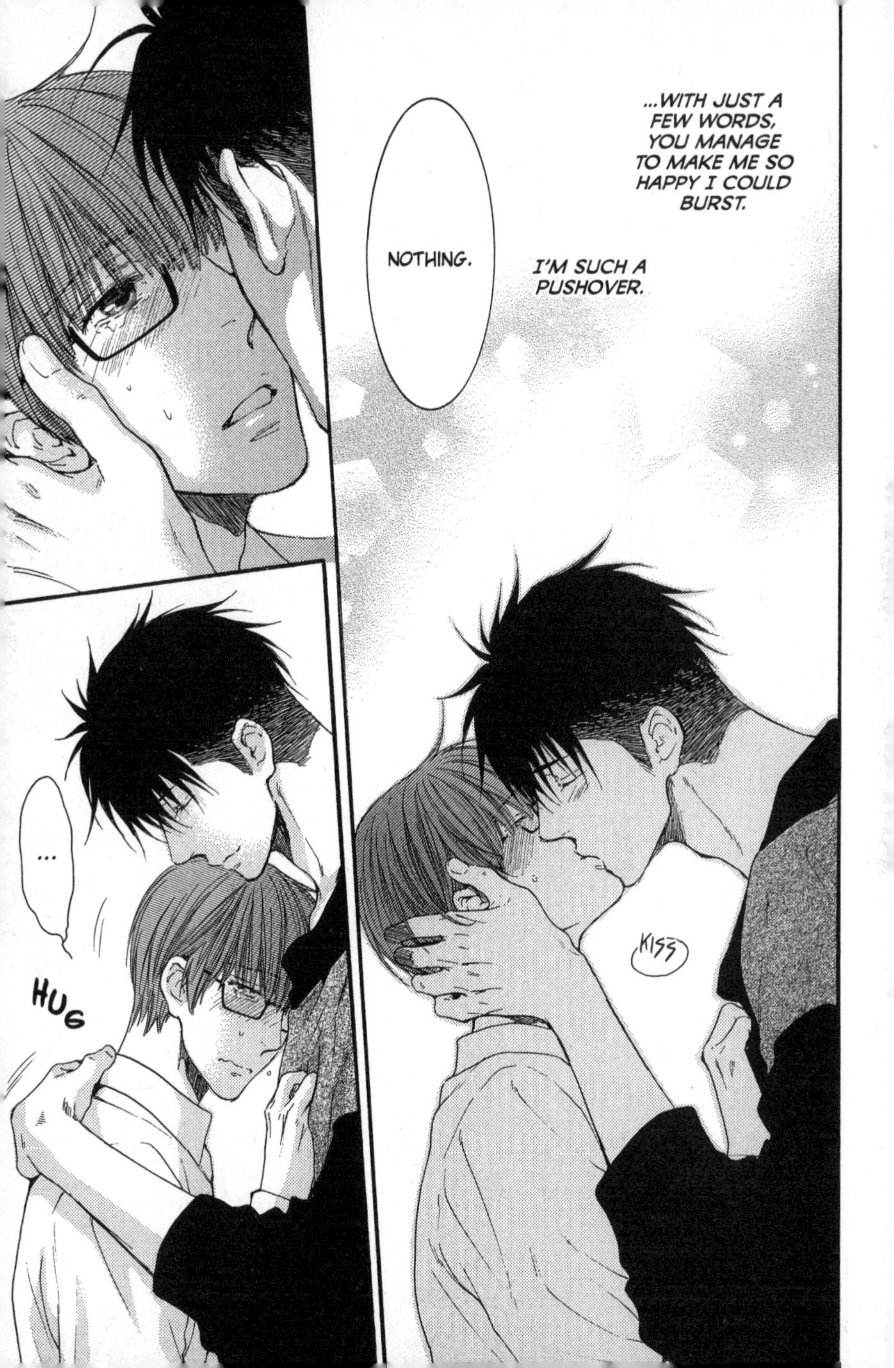
...WITH JUST A FEW WORDS, YOU MANAGE TO MAKE ME SO HAPPY I COULD BURST.
NOTHING.
I'M SUCH A PUSHOVER.
KISS
...
HUG

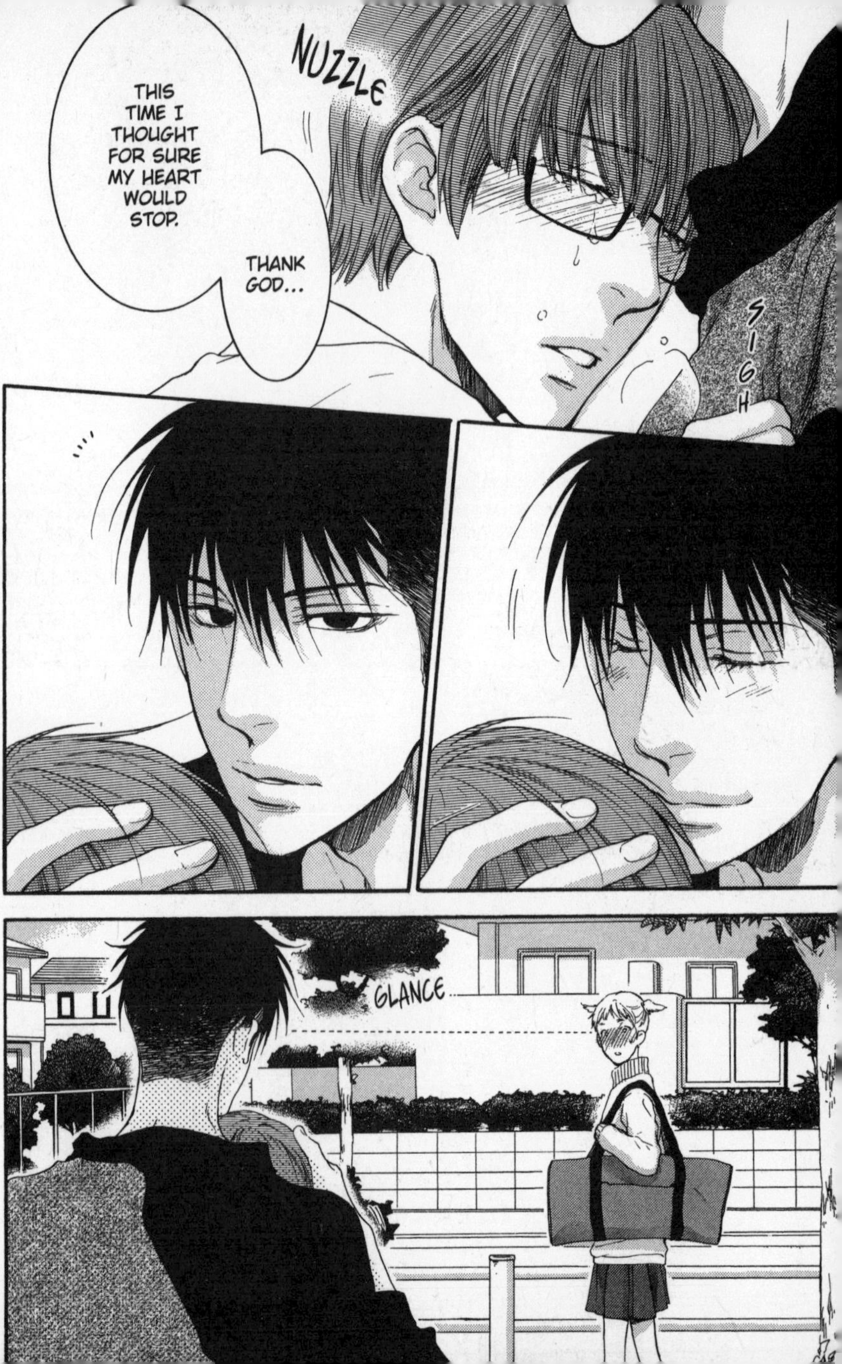
NUZZLE
THIS TIME I THOUGHT FOR SURE MY HEART WOULD STOP.
THANK GOD...
SIGH
GLANCE...

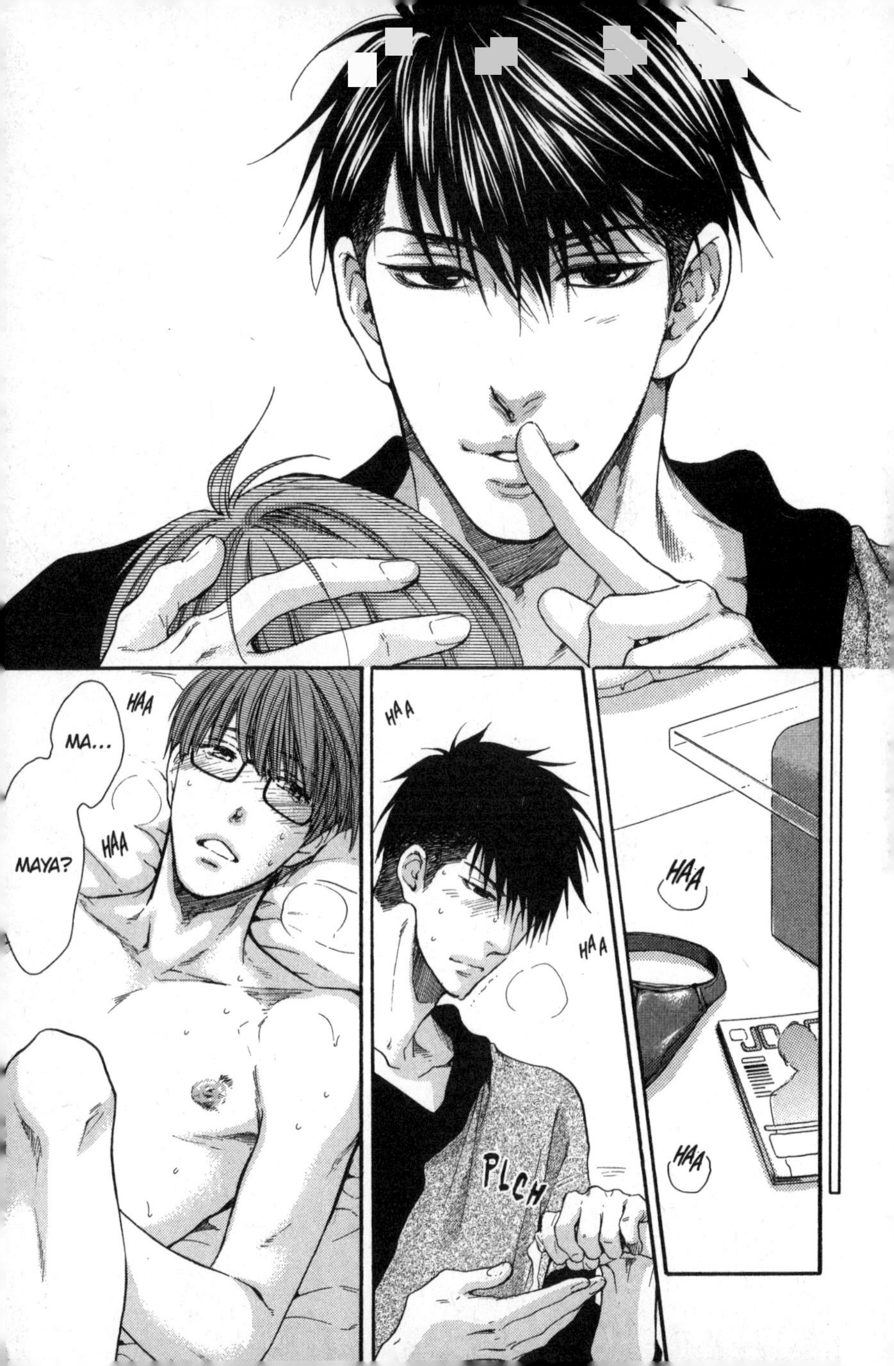
HAA
HAA
HAA
HAA
PLCH
HAA
MA...
HAA
MAYA?

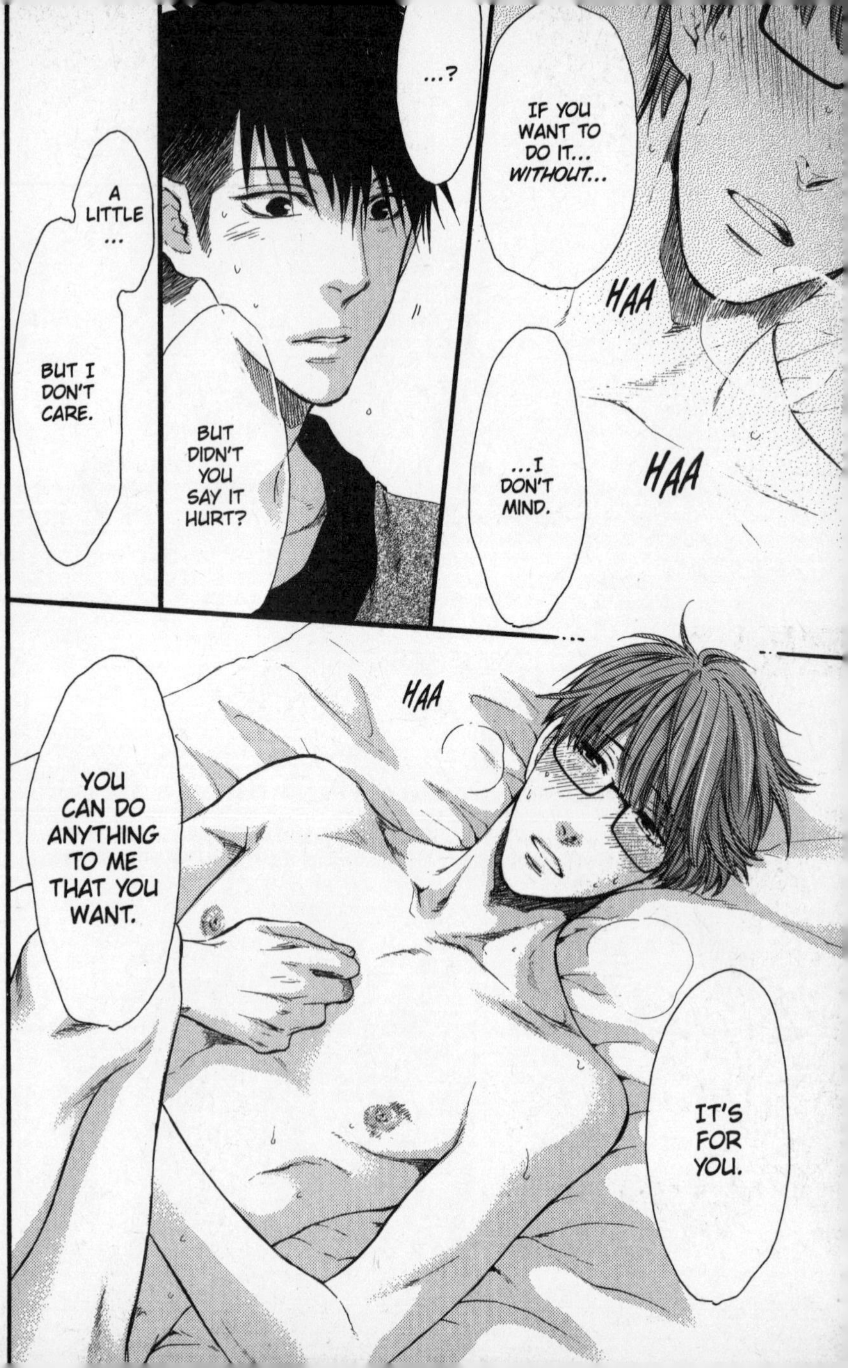
IF YOU WANT TO DO IT... WITHOUT...
HAA
...I DON'T MIND.
HAA
...?
BUT DIDN'T YOU SAY IT HURT?
A LITTLE...
BUT I DON'T CARE.
HAA
YOU CAN DO ANYTHING TO ME THAT YOU WANT.
IT'S FOR YOU.

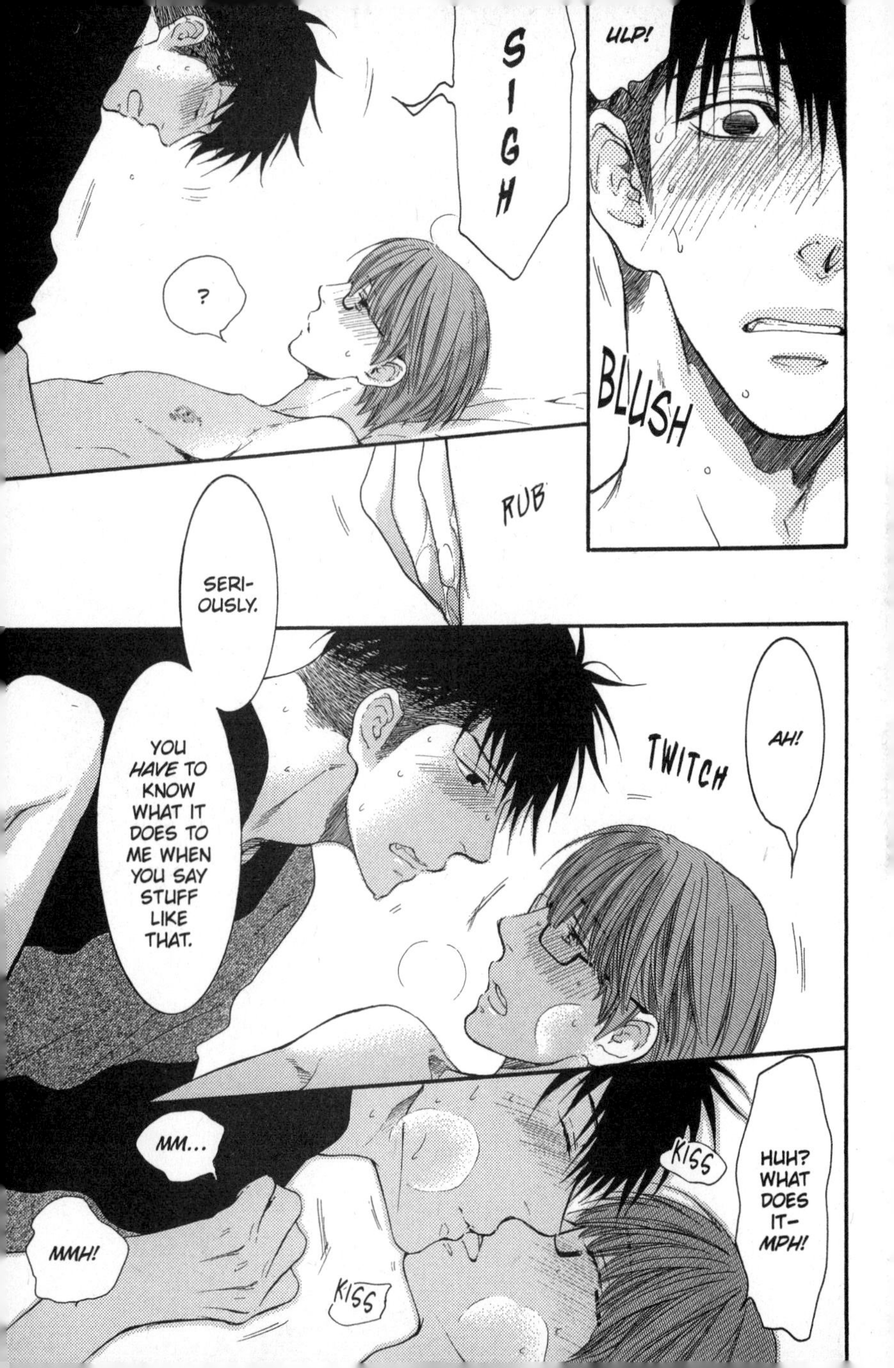
ULP!
BLUSH
SIGH
?
RUB
SERI-
OUSLY.
AH!
TWITCH
YOU *HAVE* TO KNOW WHAT IT DOES TO ME WHEN YOU SAY STUFF LIKE THAT.
HUH? WHAT DOES IT— MPH!
KISS
MM...
MMH!
KISS

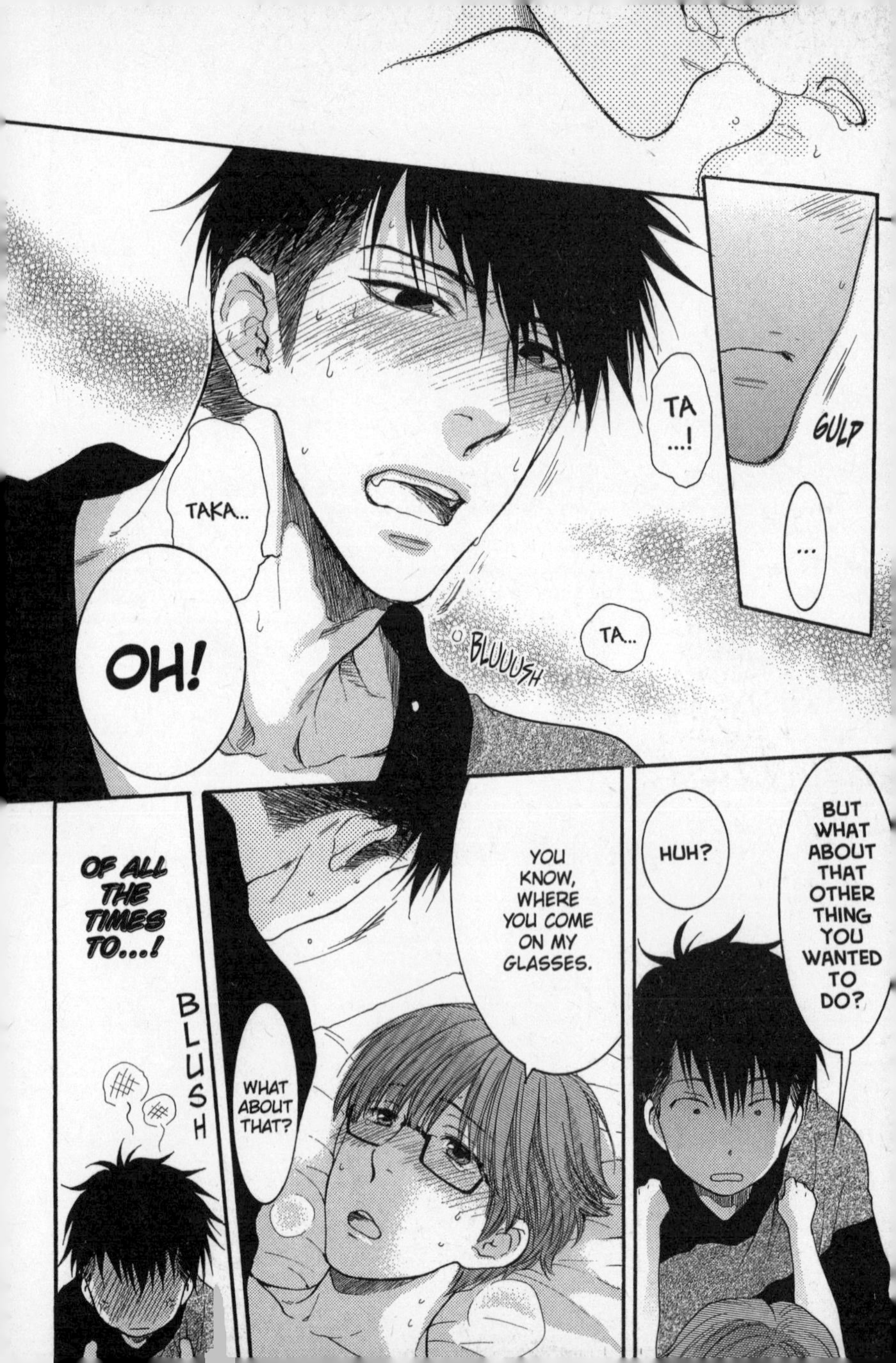
GULP
...
TA ...!
TA...
BLUUUSH
TAKA...
OH!
BUT WHAT ABOUT THAT OTHER THING YOU WANTED TO DO?
HUH?
YOU KNOW, WHERE YOU COME ON MY GLASSES.
WHAT ABOUT THAT?
OF ALL THE TIMES TO...!
BLUSH

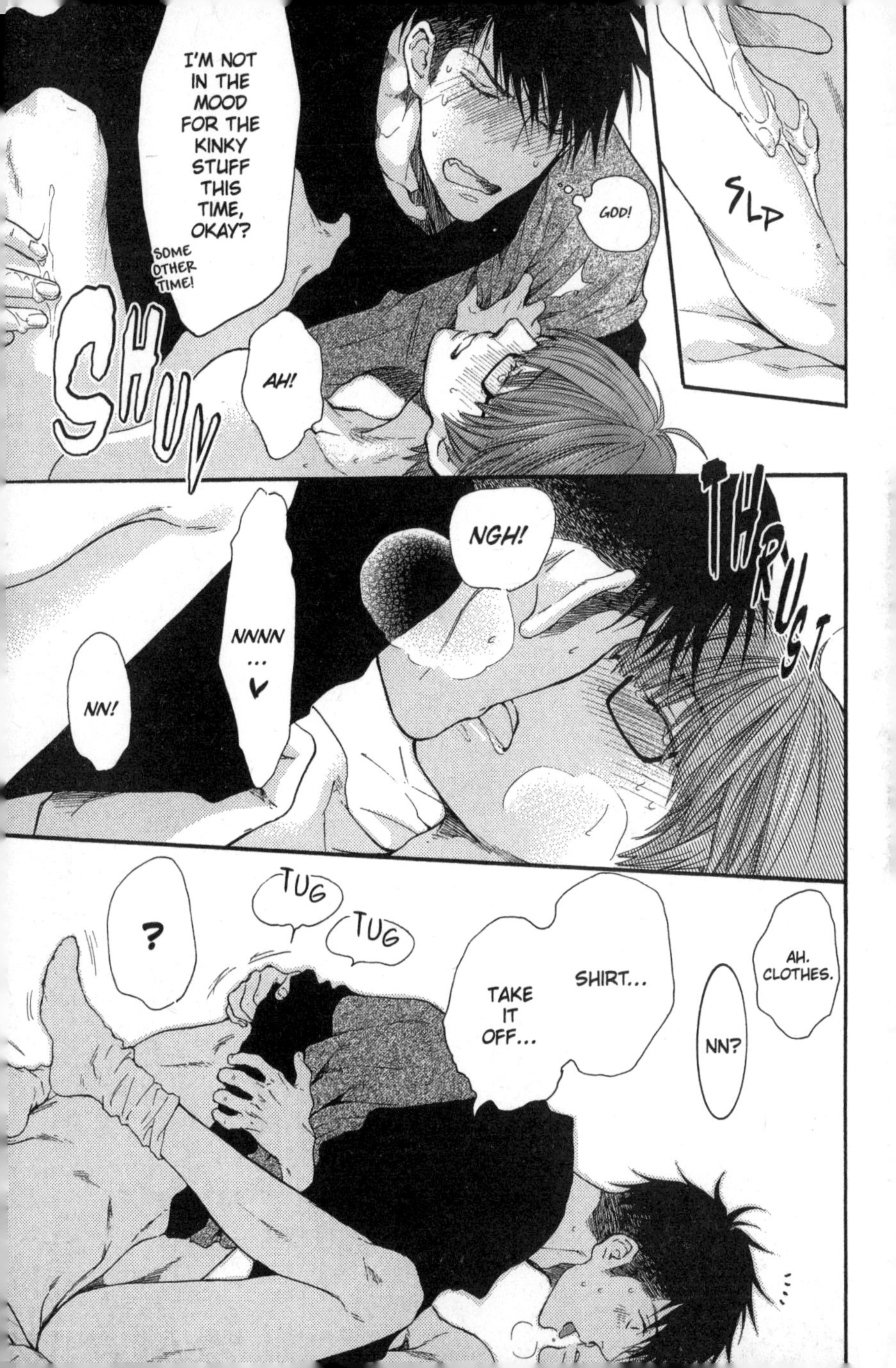
SLP
GOD!
I'M NOT IN THE MOOD FOR THE KINKY STUFF THIS TIME, OKAY?
SOME OTHER TIME!
AH!
SHUV
THRUST
NGH!
NNNN... ♥
NN!
AH. CLOTHES.
NN?
SHIRT... TAKE IT OFF...
TUG
TUG
?

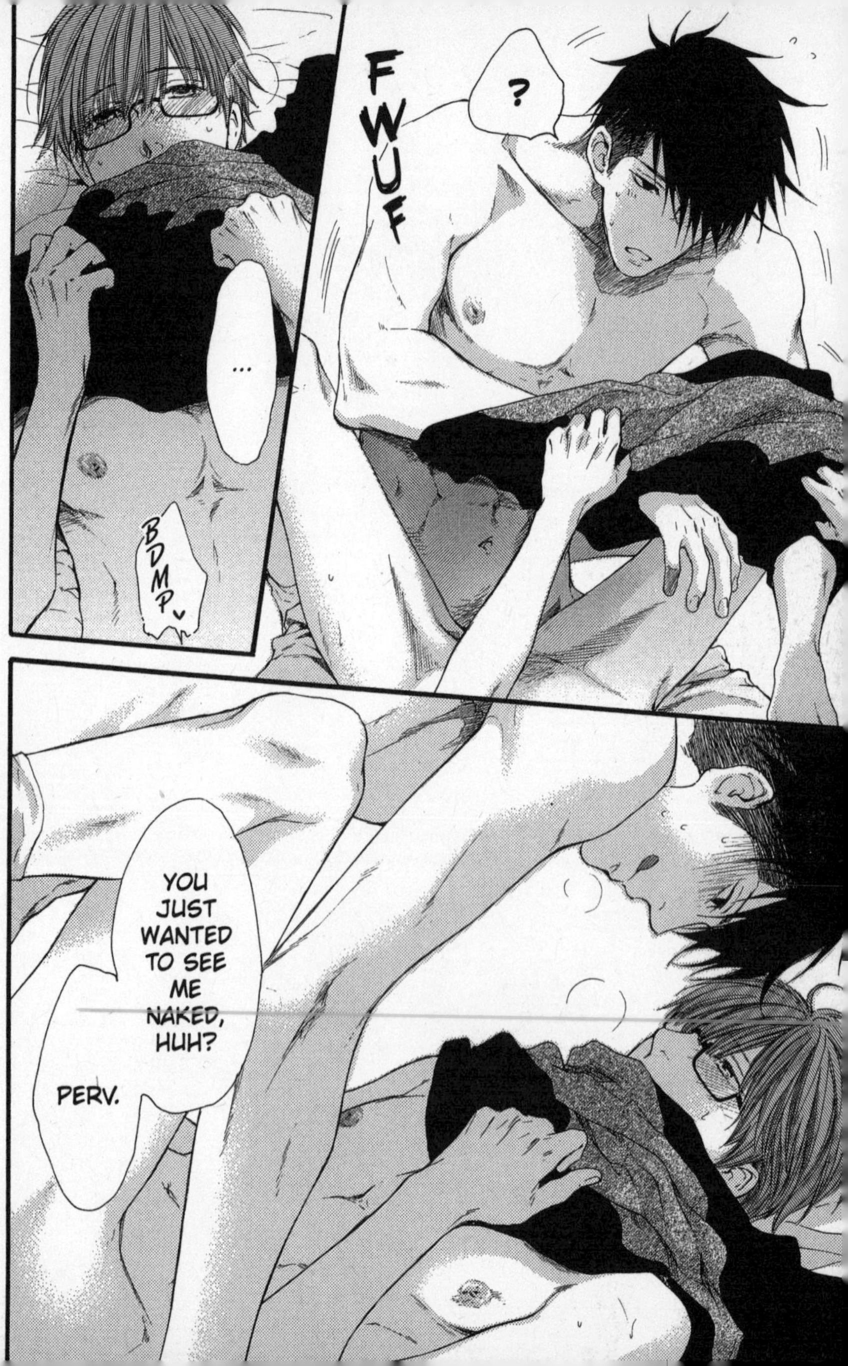
FWUF
?
...
BDMP
YOU JUST WANTED TO SEE ME NAKED, HUH?
PERV.

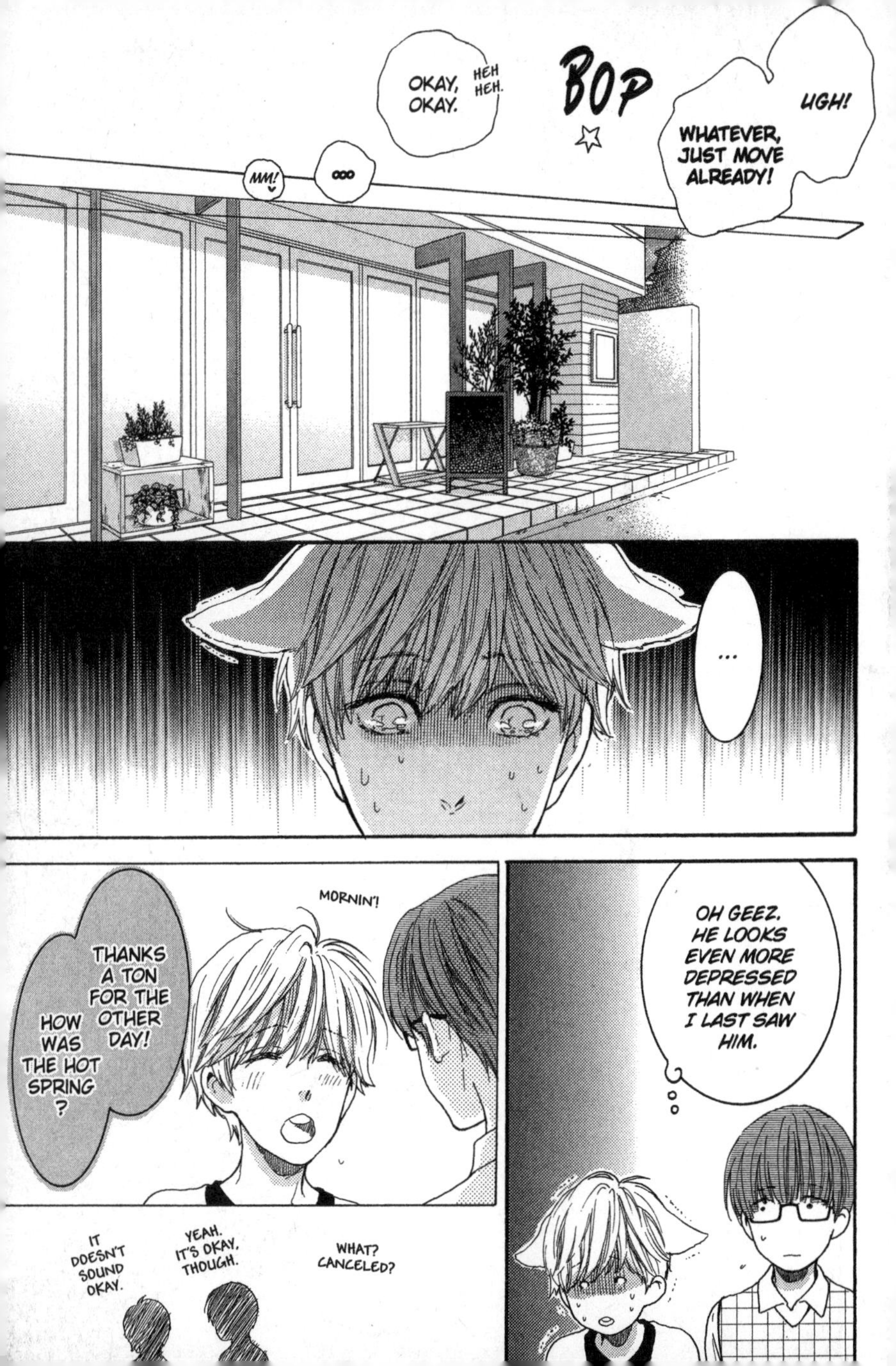
UGH!
WHATEVER, JUST MOVE ALREADY!
BOP
OKAY, OKAY.
HEH HEH.
MM!
...
OH GEEZ. HE LOOKS EVEN MORE DEPRESSED THAN WHEN I LAST SAW HIM.
MORNIN'!
THANKS A TON FOR THE OTHER DAY!
HOW WAS THE HOT SPRING?
WHAT? CANCELED?
YEAH. IT'S OKAY, THOUGH.
IT DOESN'T SOUND OKAY.

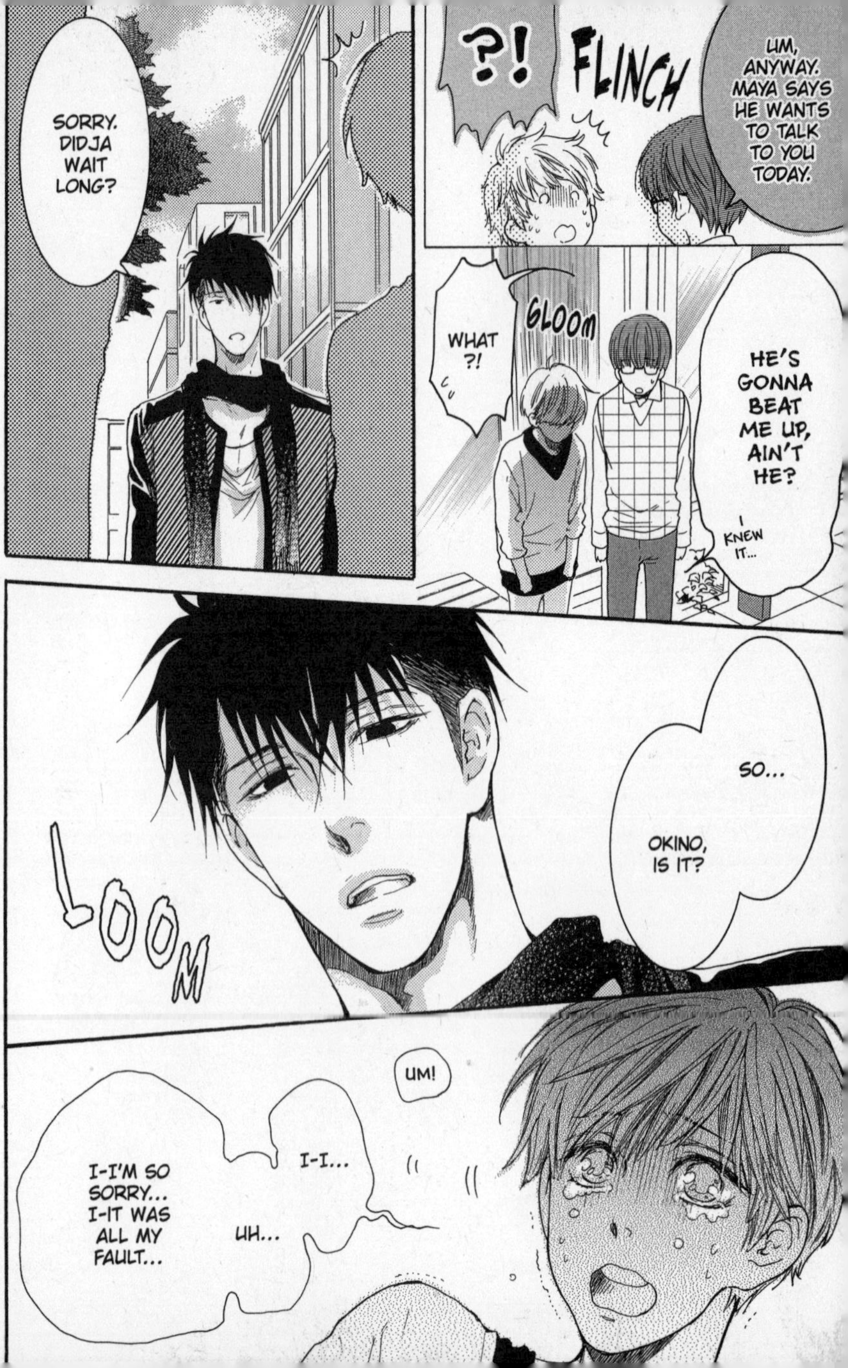
UM, ANYWAY. MAYA SAYS HE WANTS TO TALK TO YOU TODAY.
FLINCH
?!
HE'S GONNA BEAT ME UP, AIN'T HE?
I KNEW IT...
GLOOM
WHAT ?!
SORRY. DIDJA WAIT LONG?
SO...
OKINO, IS IT?
LOOM
UM!
I-I...
UH...
I-I'M SO SORRY... I-IT WAS ALL MY FAULT...

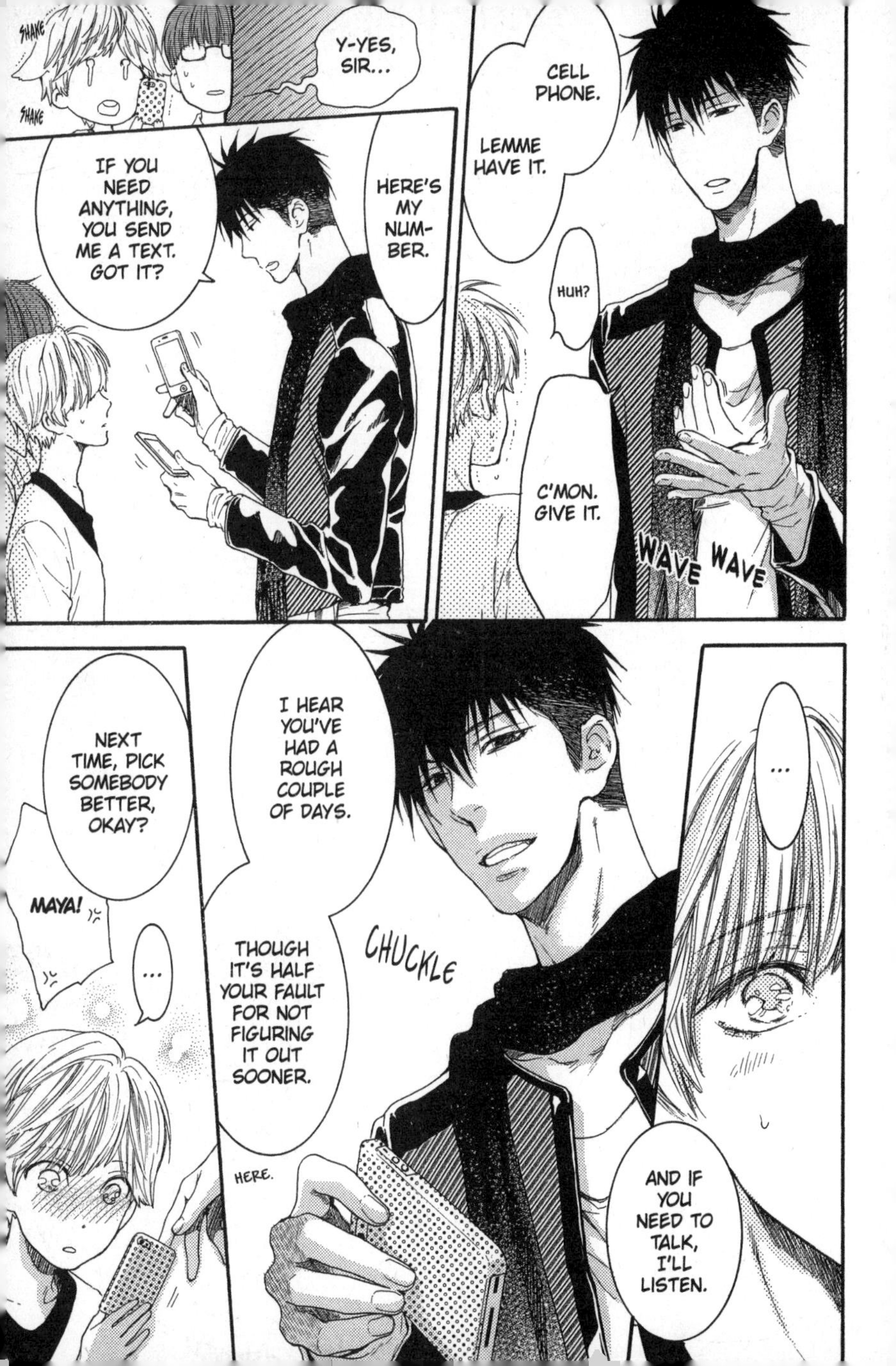
CELL PHONE.
LEMME HAVE IT.
HUH?
C'MON. GIVE IT.
WAVE WAVE
Y-YES, SIR...
SHAKE
SHAKE
HERE'S MY NUM-BER.
IF YOU NEED ANYTHING, YOU SEND ME A TEXT. GOT IT?
...
AND IF YOU NEED TO TALK, I'LL LISTEN.
I HEAR YOU'VE HAD A ROUGH COUPLE OF DAYS.
THOUGH IT'S HALF YOUR FAULT FOR NOT FIGURING IT OUT SOONER.
CHUCKLE
HERE.
NEXT TIME, PICK SOMEBODY BETTER, OKAY?
MAYA!
...

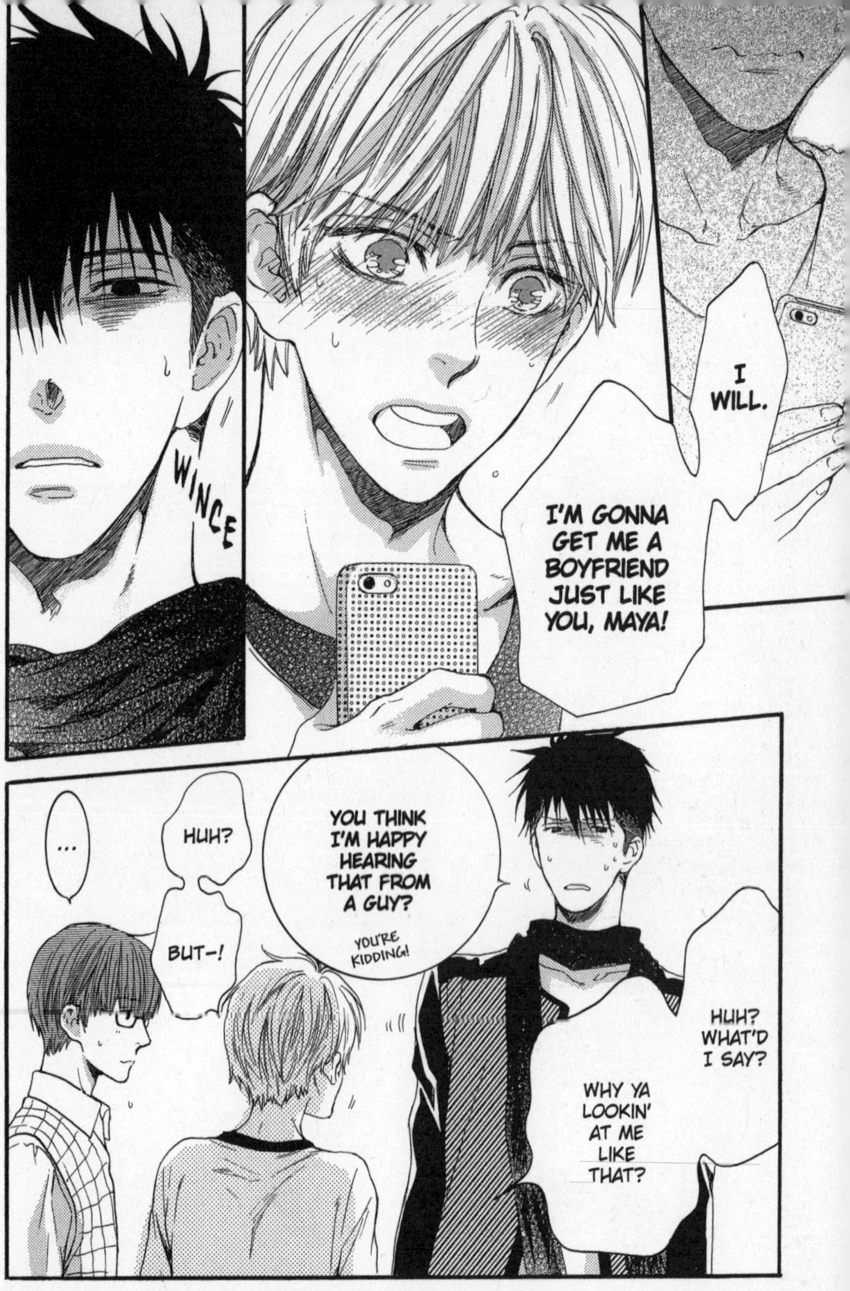
I WILL.
I'M GONNA GET ME A BOYFRIEND JUST LIKE YOU, MAYA!
WINCE
HUH? WHAT'D I SAY?
WHY YA LOOKIN' AT ME LIKE THAT?
YOU THINK I'M HAPPY HEARING THAT FROM A GUY?
YOU'RE KIDDING!
HUH?
BUT-!
...

Anniversary

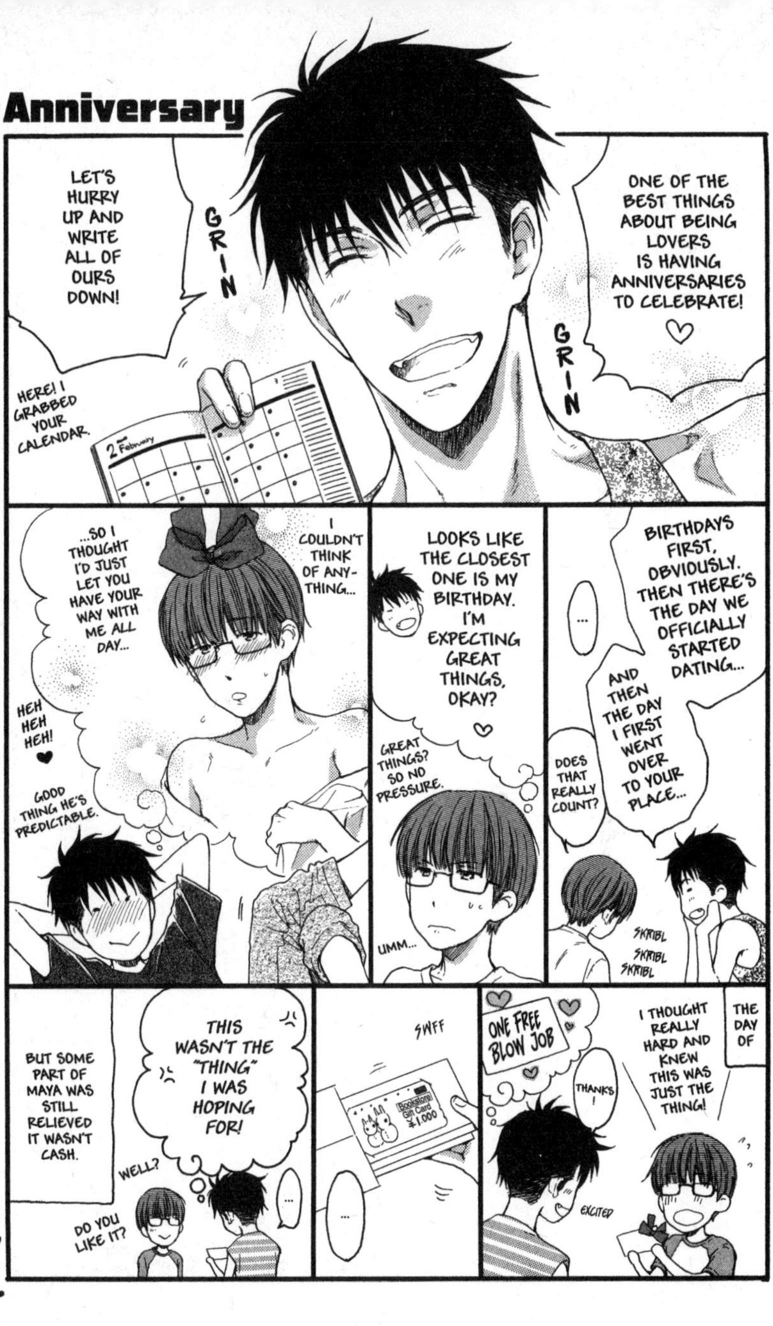
ONE OF THE BEST THINGS ABOUT BEING LOVERS IS HAVING ANNIVERSARIES TO CELEBRATE! ♡
GRIN
LET'S HURRY UP AND WRITE ALL OF OURS DOWN!
GRIN
HERE! I GRABBED YOUR CALENDAR.
2 February
BIRTHDAYS FIRST, OBVIOUSLY. THEN THERE'S THE DAY WE OFFICIALLY STARTED DATING...
...
AND THEN THE DAY I FIRST WENT OVER TO YOUR PLACE...
DOES THAT REALLY COUNT?
SKRIBL SKRIBL SKRIBL
LOOKS LIKE THE CLOSEST ONE IS MY BIRTHDAY. I'M EXPECTING GREAT THINGS, OKAY? ♡
GREAT THINGS? SO NO PRESSURE.
UMM...
I COULDN'T THINK OF ANY-THING...
...SO I THOUGHT I'D JUST LET YOU HAVE YOUR WAY WITH ME ALL DAY...
HEH HEH HEH! ♥
GOOD THING HE'S PREDICTABLE.
THE DAY OF
I THOUGHT REALLY HARD AND KNEW THIS WAS JUST THE THING!
ONE FREE BLOW JOB
THANKS!
EXCITED
SWFF
Bookstore Gift Card ¥1,000
...
THIS WASN'T THE "THING" I WAS HOPING FOR!
...
WELL?
DO YOU LIKE IT?
BUT SOME PART OF MAYA WAS STILL RELIEVED IT WASN'T CASH.

END

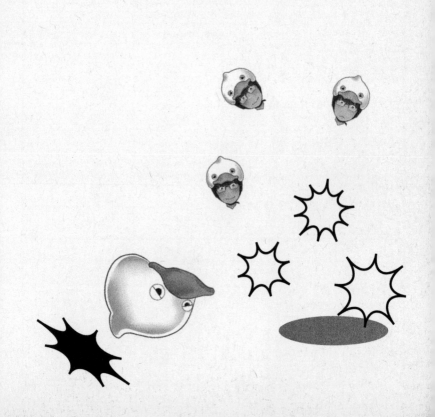

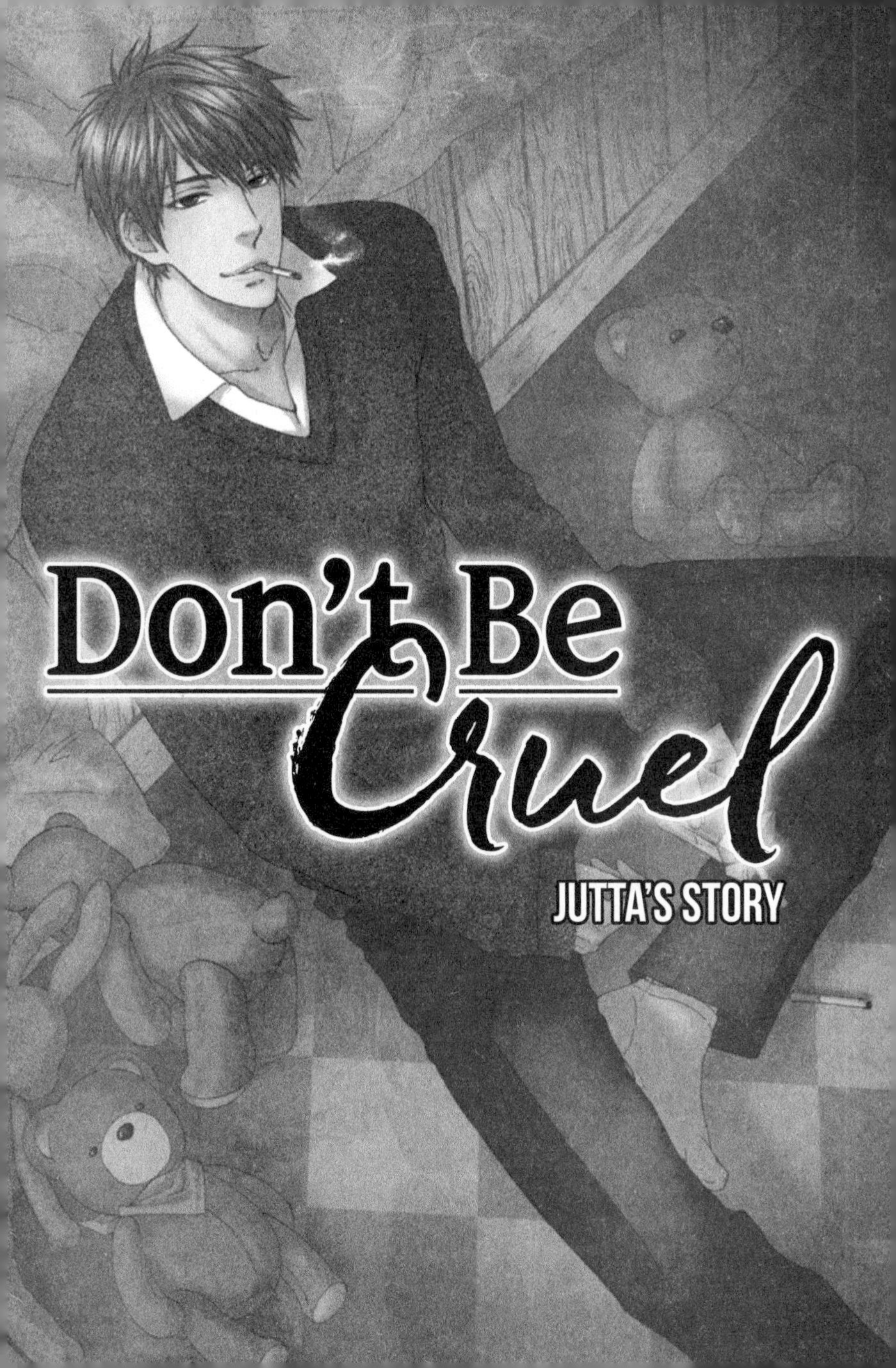
Don't Be Cruel
JUTTA'S STORY

Don't Be
Cruel

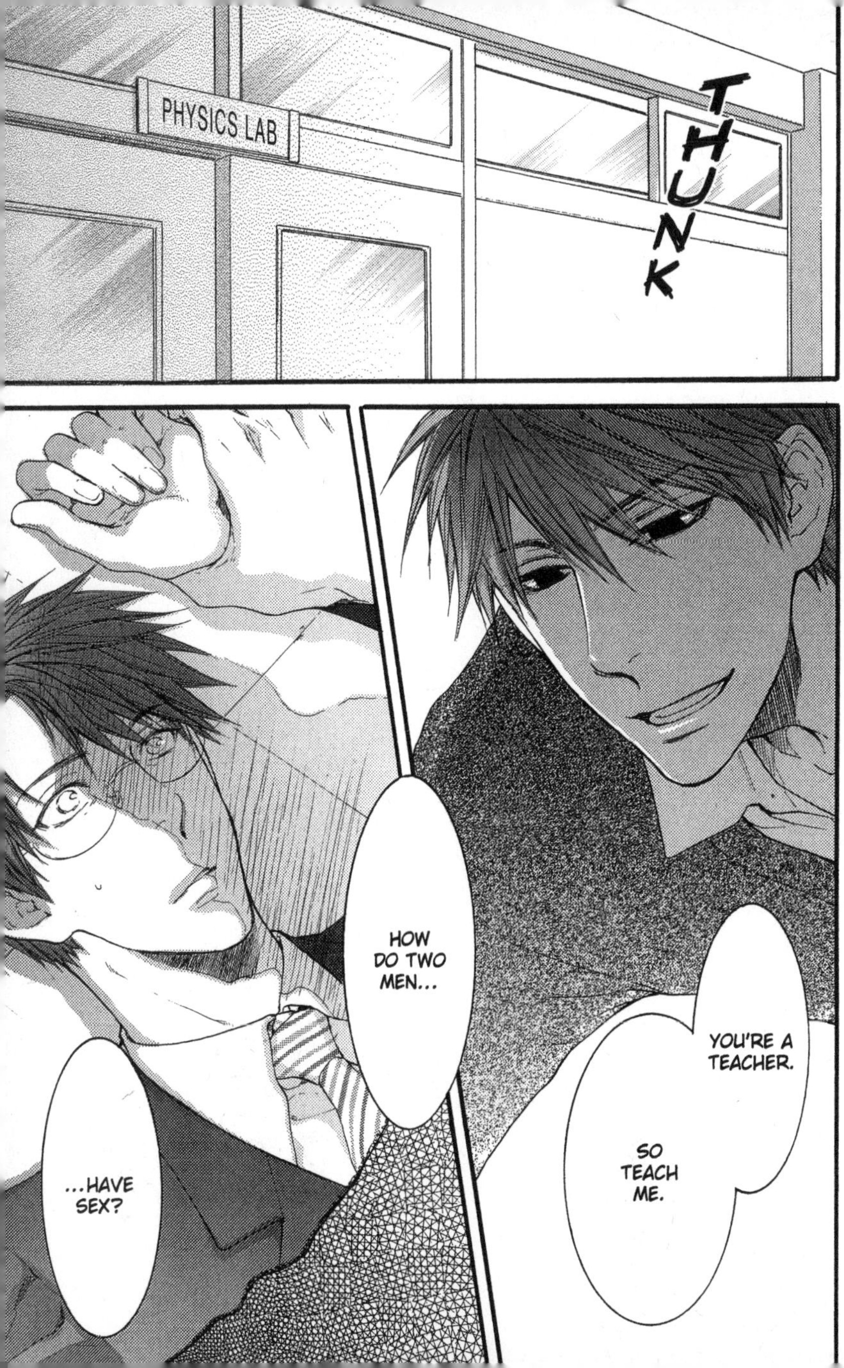
PHYSICS LAB
THUNK
YOU'RE A TEACHER.
SO TEACH ME.
HOW DO TWO MEN...
...HAVE SEX?

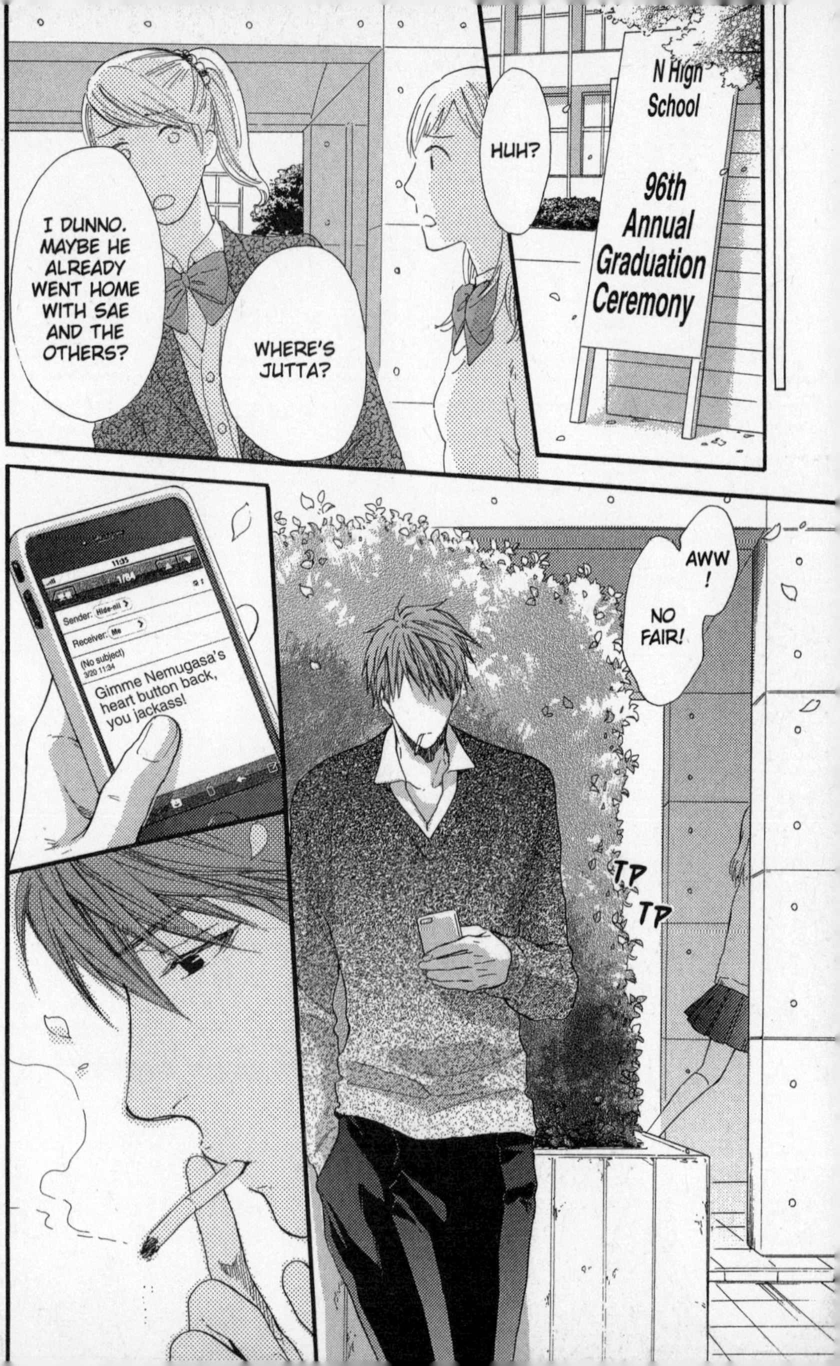
N High School
96th Annual Graduation Ceremony
HUH?
WHERE'S JUTTA?
I DUNNO. MAYBE HE ALREADY WENT HOME WITH SAE AND THE OTHERS?
AWW! NO FAIR!
TP TP
Sender: Hide-nii
Receiver: Me
(No subject)
3/20 11:34
Gimme Nemugasa's heart button back, you jackass!

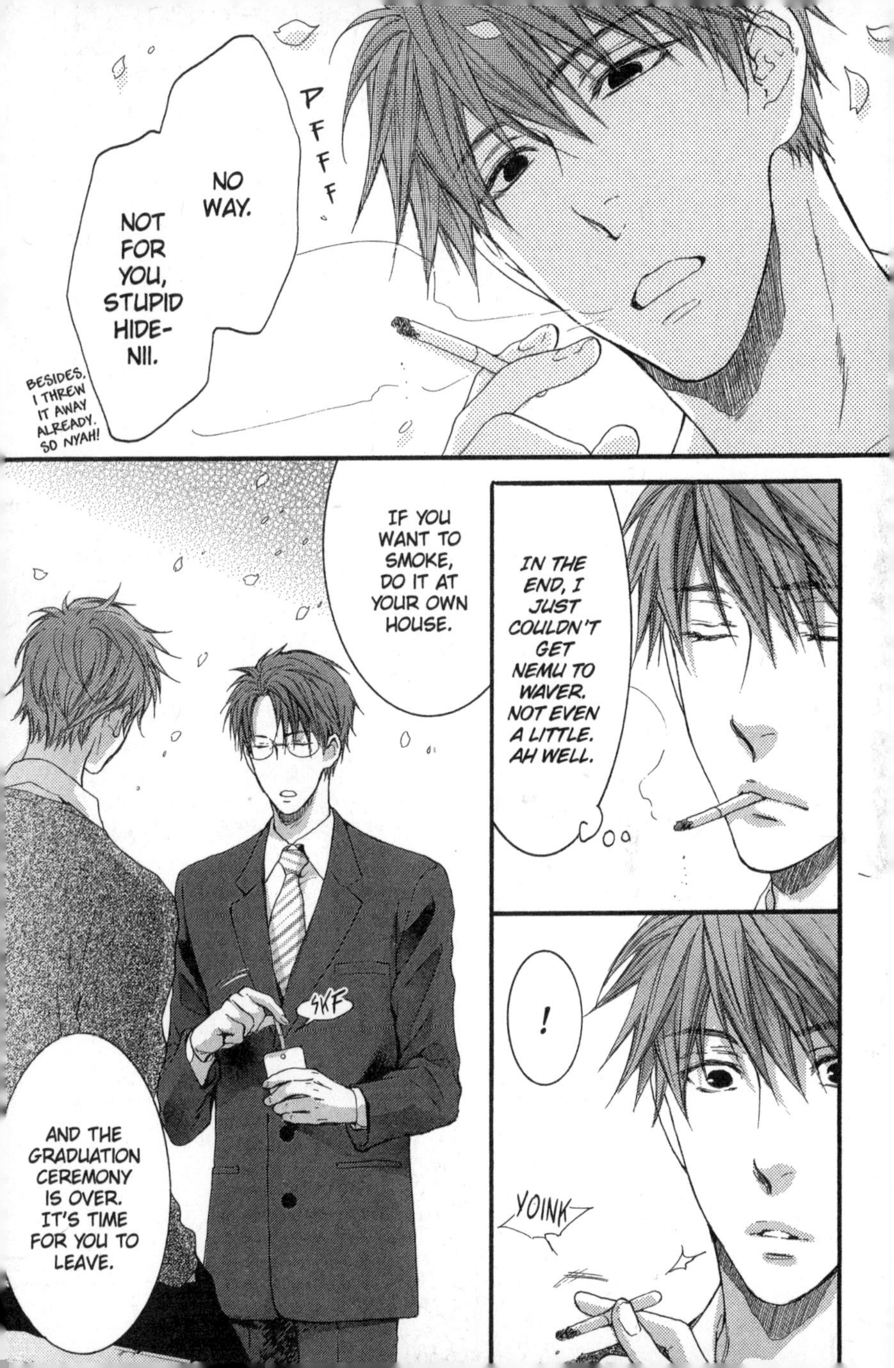
PFFF
NO WAY. NOT FOR YOU, STUPID HIDE-NII.
BESIDES, I THREW IT AWAY ALREADY. SO NYAH!
IN THE END, I JUST COULDN'T GET NEMU TO WAVER. NOT EVEN A LITTLE. AH WELL.
!
YOINK
IF YOU WANT TO SMOKE, DO IT AT YOUR OWN HOUSE.
SKF
AND THE GRADUATION CEREMONY IS OVER. IT'S TIME FOR YOU TO LEAVE.

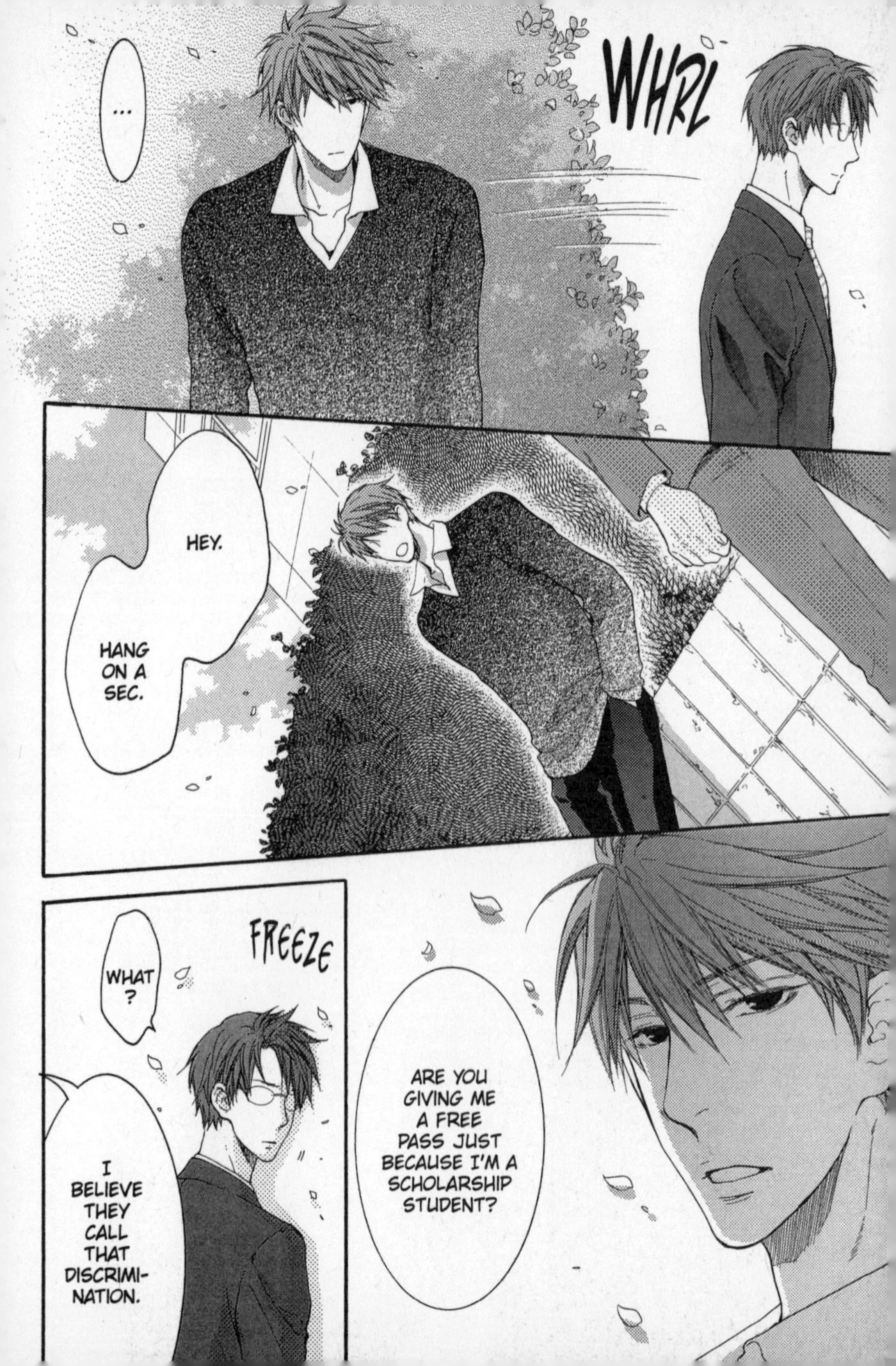
WHRL
...
HEY.
HANG ON A SEC.
ARE YOU GIVING ME A FREE PASS JUST BECAUSE I'M A SCHOLARSHIP STUDENT?
FREEZE
WHAT?
I BELIEVE THEY CALL THAT DISCRIMINATION.

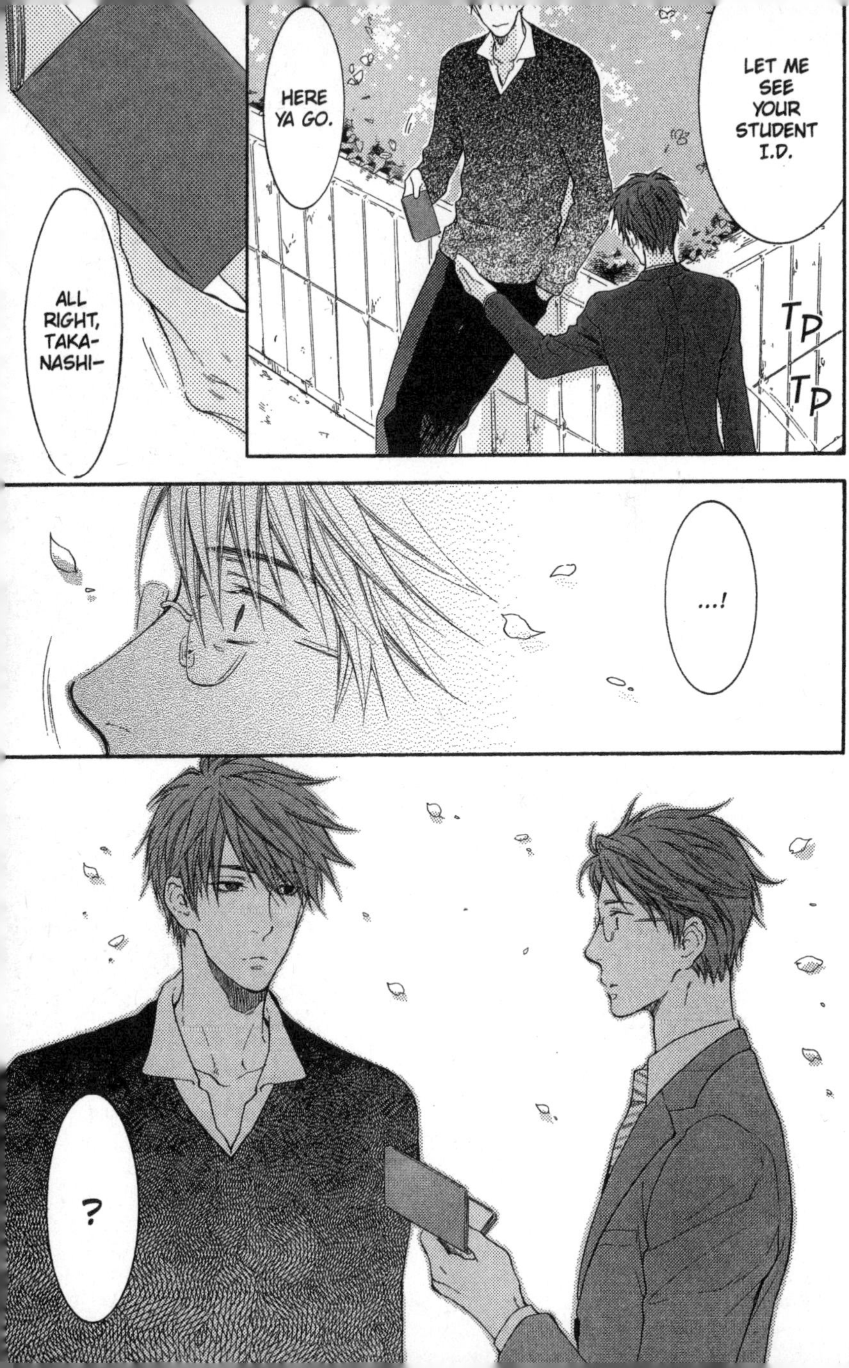
LET ME SEE YOUR STUDENT I.D.
HERE YA GO.
TP TP
ALL RIGHT, TAKA-NASHI-
...!
?

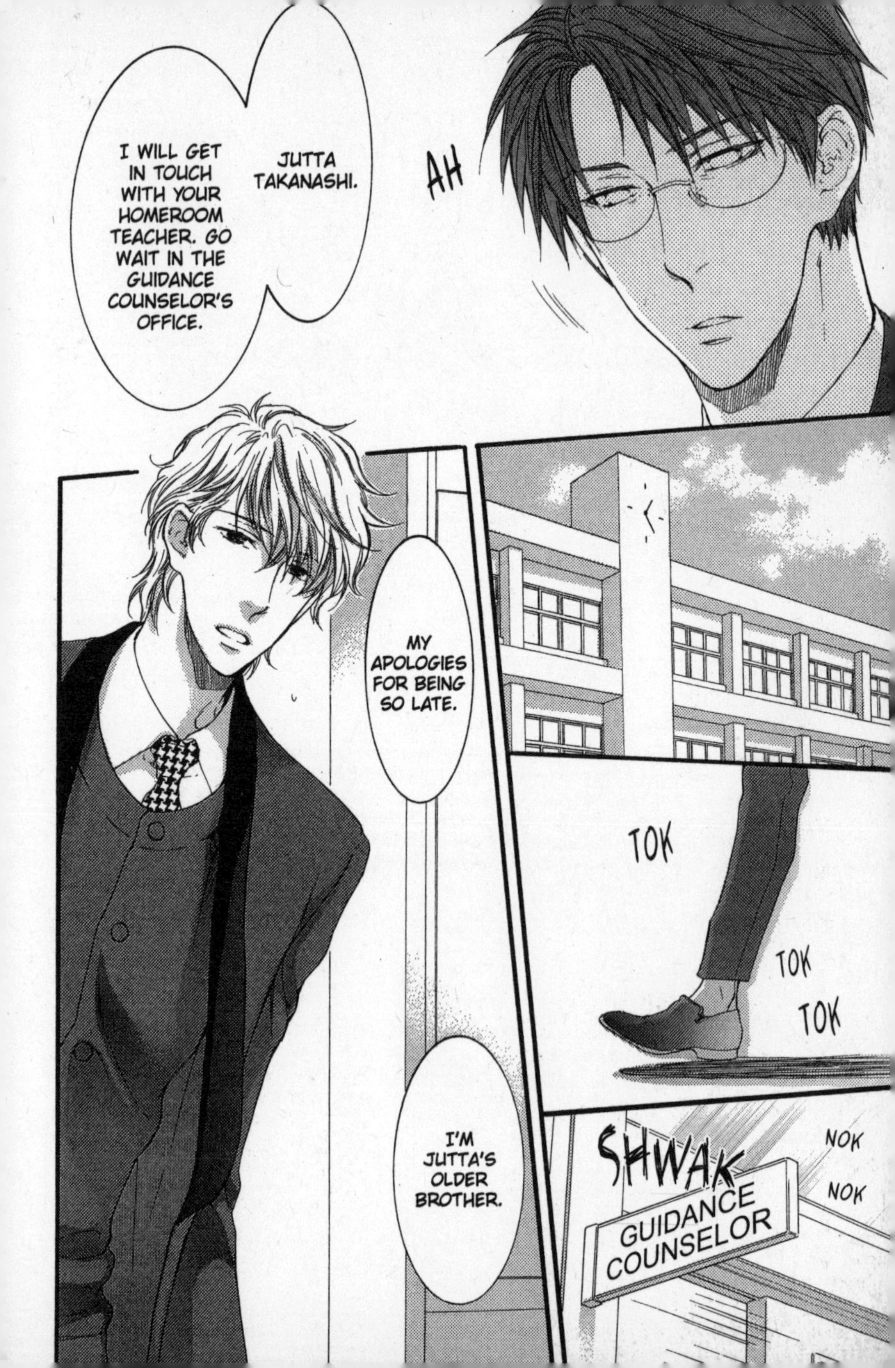
AH
JUTTA TAKANASHI.
I WILL GET IN TOUCH WITH YOUR HOMEROOM TEACHER. GO WAIT IN THE GUIDANCE COUNSELOR'S OFFICE.
TOK
TOK
TOK
NOK
NOK
SHWAK
GUIDANCE COUNSELOR
MY APOLOGIES FOR BEING SO LATE.
I'M JUTTA'S OLDER BROTHER.

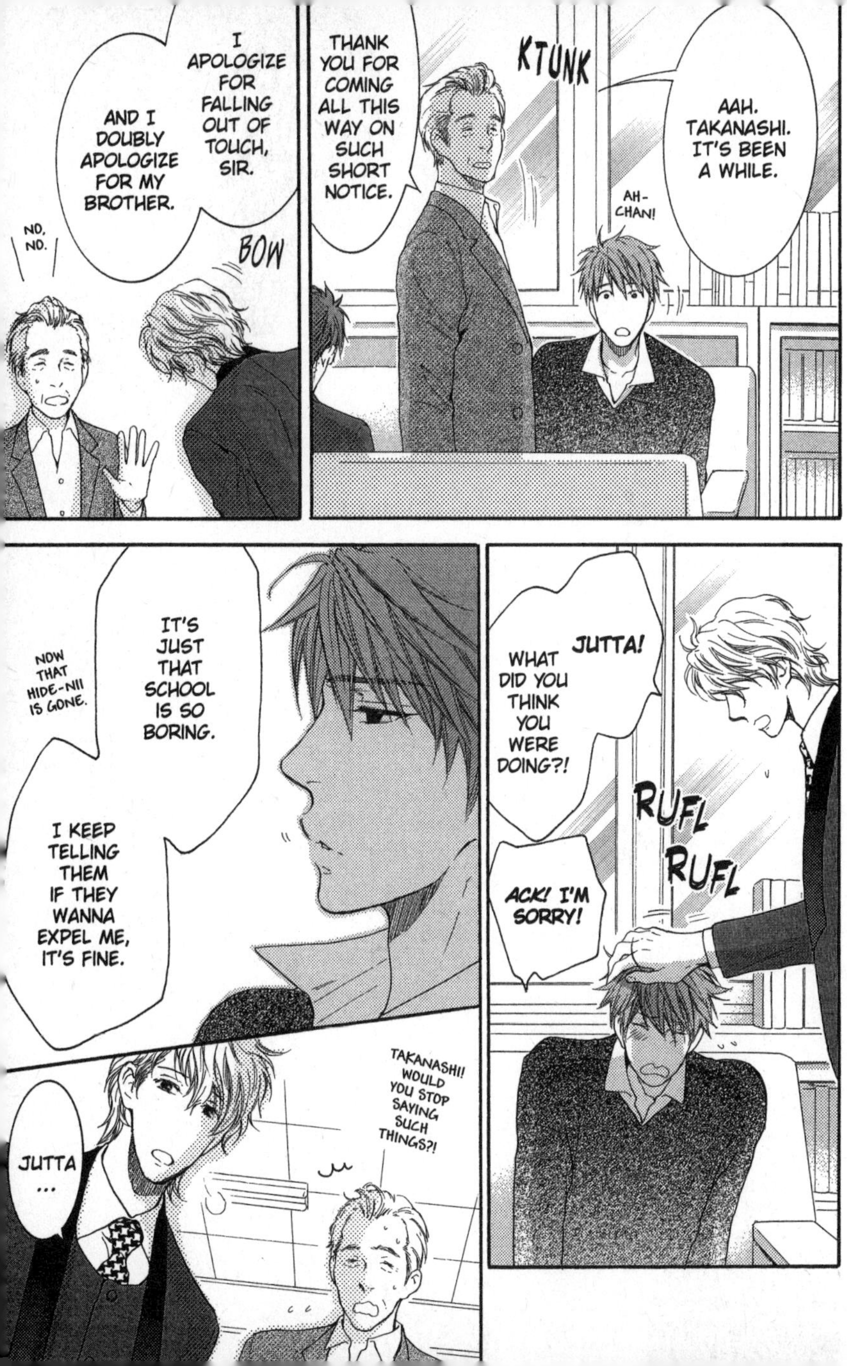
AAH. TAKANASHI. IT'S BEEN A WHILE.
AH-CHAN!
KTUNK
THANK YOU FOR COMING ALL THIS WAY ON SUCH SHORT NOTICE.
I APOLOGIZE FOR FALLING OUT OF TOUCH, SIR.
AND I DOUBLY APOLOGIZE FOR MY BROTHER.
BOW
NO, NO.
JUTTA!
WHAT DID YOU THINK YOU WERE DOING?!
RUFL
RUFL
ACK! I'M SORRY!
IT'S JUST THAT SCHOOL IS SO BORING.
NOW THAT HIDE-NII IS GONE.
I KEEP TELLING THEM IF THEY WANNA EXPEL ME, IT'S FINE.
TAKANASHI! WOULD YOU STOP SAYING SUCH THINGS?!
JUTTA ...

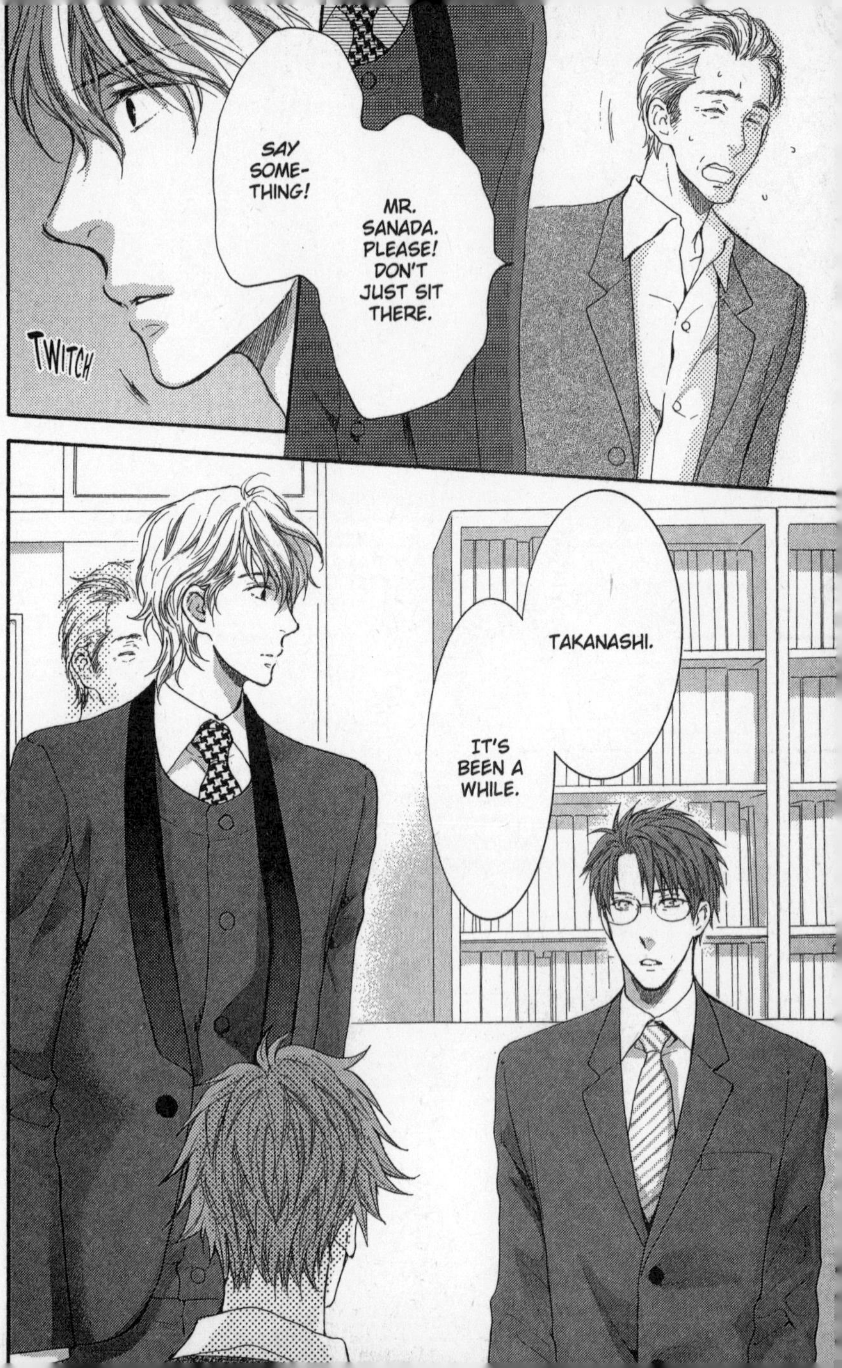
MR. SANADA. PLEASE! DON'T JUST SIT THERE.
SAY SOMETHING!
TWITCH
TAKANASHI.
IT'S BEEN A WHILE.

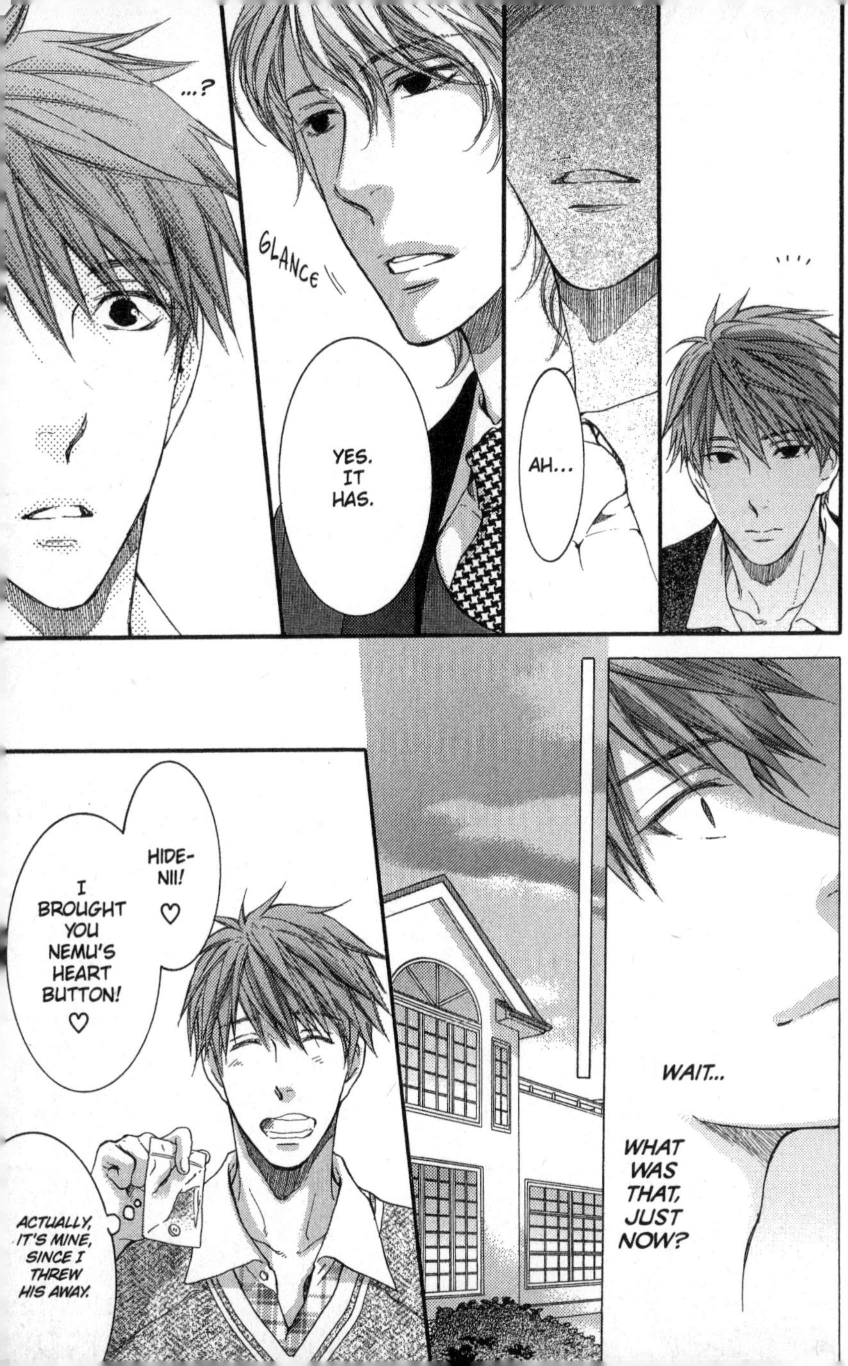
AH...
YES. IT HAS.
GLANCE
...?
WAIT...
WHAT WAS THAT, JUST NOW?
HIDE-NII! ♡
I BROUGHT YOU NEMU'S HEART BUTTON! ♡
ACTUALLY, IT'S MINE, SINCE I THREW HIS AWAY.

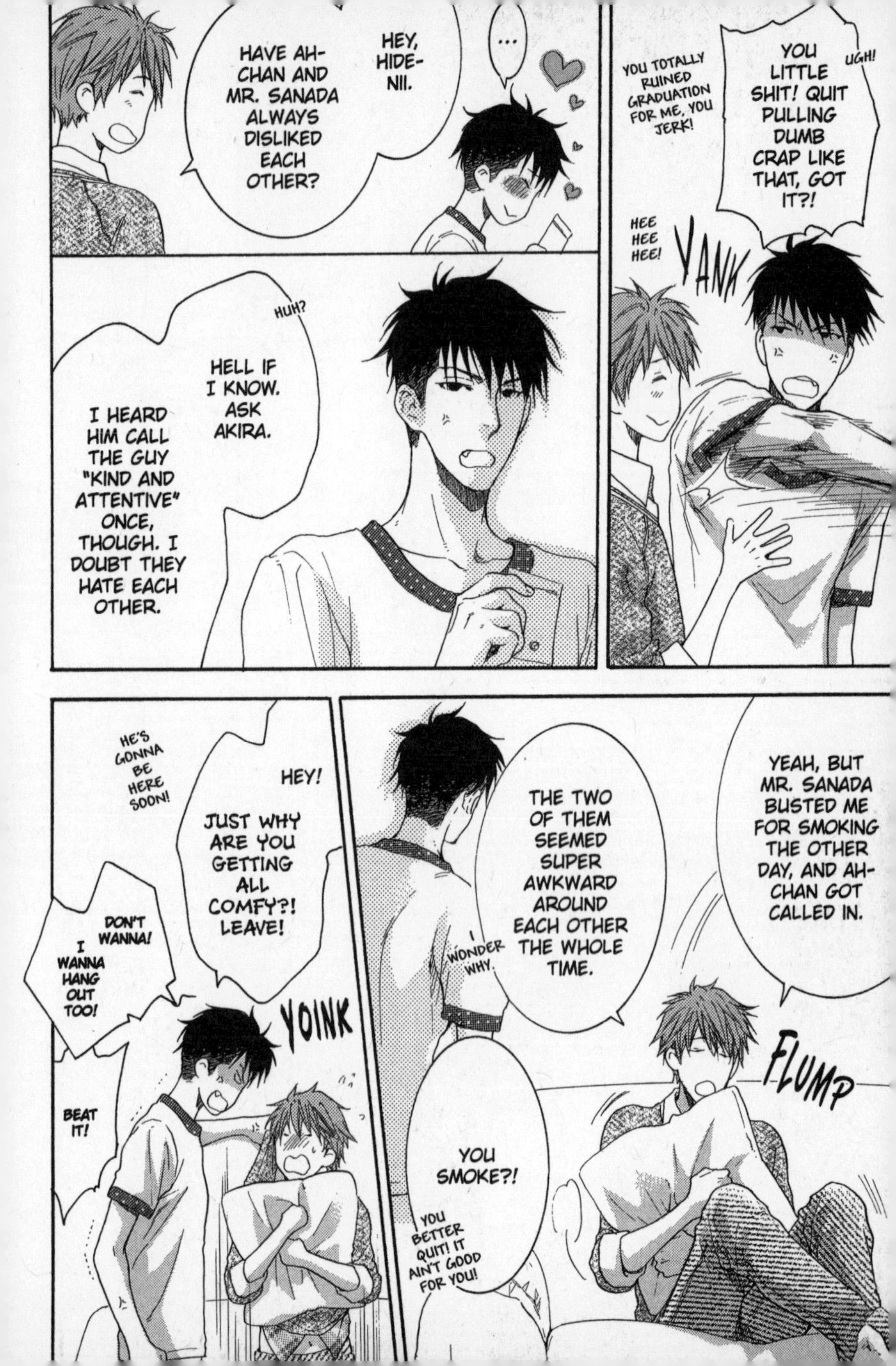

YOU LITTLE SHIT! QUIT PULLING DUMB CRAP LIKE THAT, GOT IT?!
UGH!
YOU TOTALLY RUINED GRADUATION FOR ME, YOU JERK!
HEE HEE HEE!
YANK
...
HEY, HIDE-NII.
HAVE AH-CHAN AND MR. SANADA ALWAYS DISLIKED EACH OTHER?
HUH?
HELL IF I KNOW. ASK AKIRA.
I HEARD HIM CALL THE GUY "KIND AND ATTENTIVE" ONCE, THOUGH. I DOUBT THEY HATE EACH OTHER.
YEAH, BUT MR. SANADA BUSTED ME FOR SMOKING THE OTHER DAY, AND AH-CHAN GOT CALLED IN.
THE TWO OF THEM SEEMED SUPER AWKWARD AROUND EACH OTHER THE WHOLE TIME.
I WONDER WHY.
FLUMP
YOU SMOKE?!
YOU BETTER QUIT! IT AIN'T GOOD FOR YOU!
HEY!
JUST WHY ARE YOU GETTING ALL COMFY?! LEAVE!
HE'S GONNA BE HERE SOON!
YOINK
DON'T WANNA! I WANNA HANG OUT TOO!
BEAT IT!

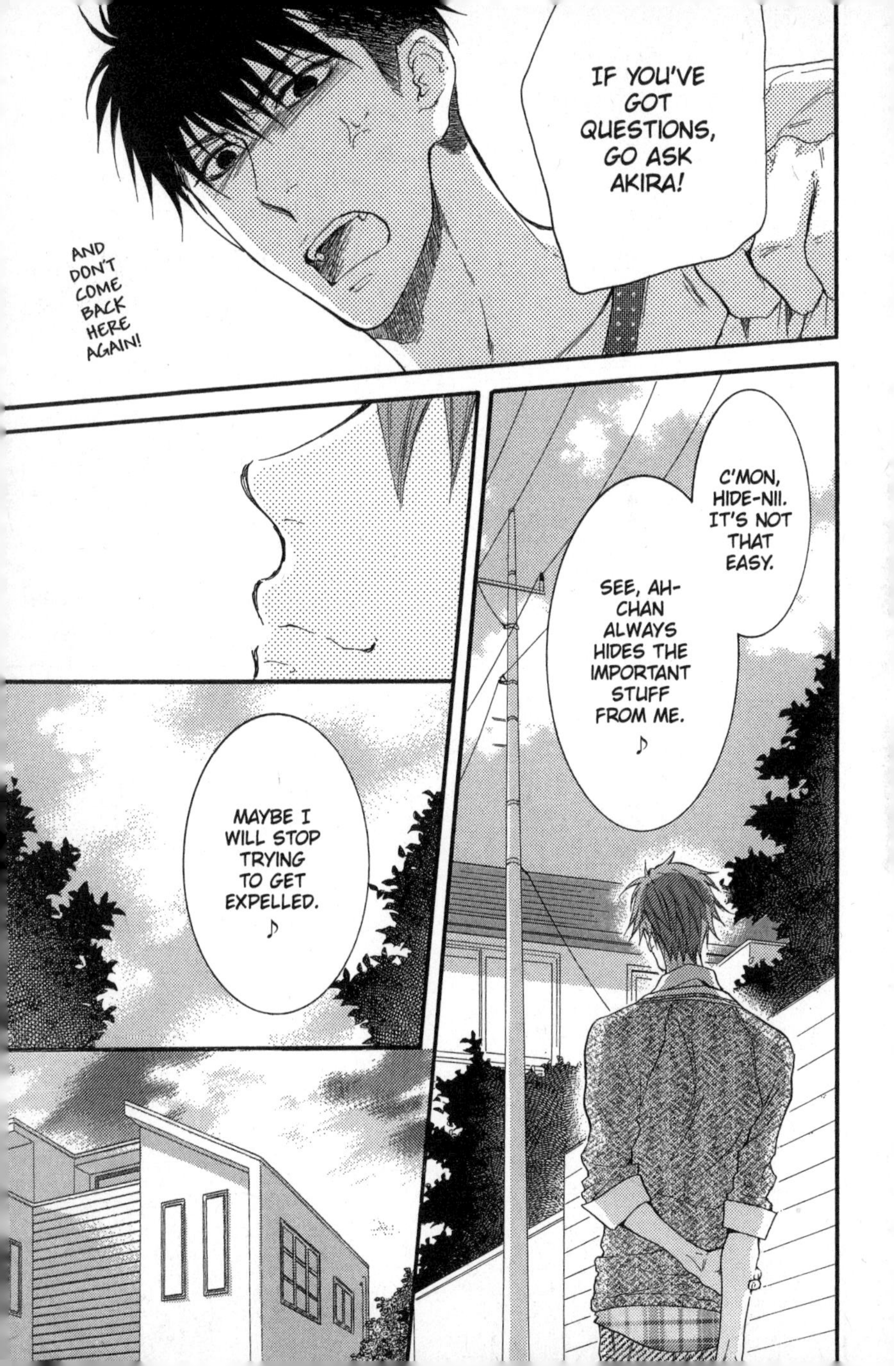
IF YOU'VE GOT QUESTIONS, GO ASK AKIRA!
AND DON'T COME BACK HERE AGAIN!
C'MON, HIDE-NII. IT'S NOT THAT EASY.
SEE, AH-CHAN ALWAYS HIDES THE IMPORTANT STUFF FROM ME. ♪
MAYBE I WILL STOP TRYING TO GET EXPELLED. ♪

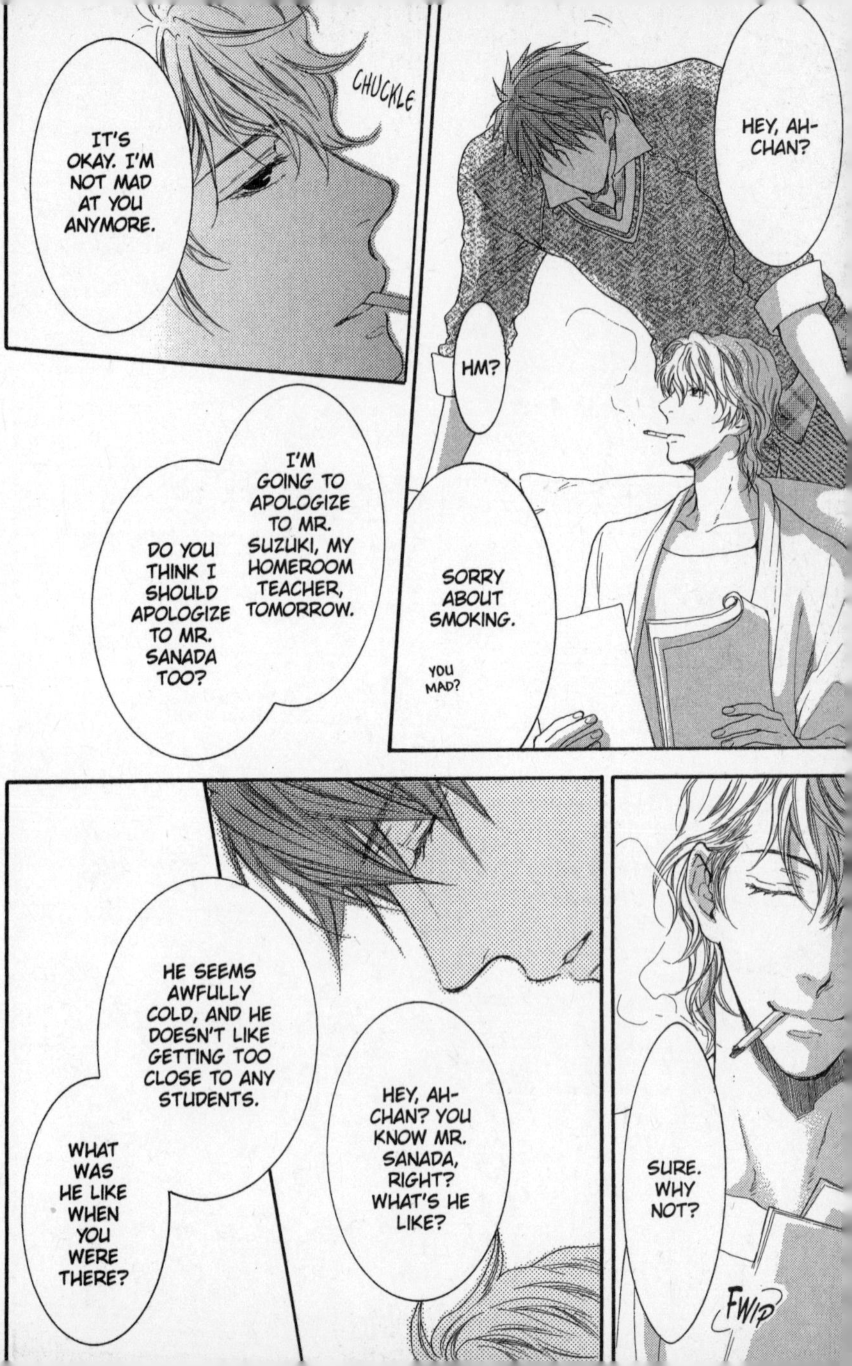
HEY, AH-CHAN?
HM?
SORRY ABOUT SMOKING.
YOU MAD?
CHUCKLE
IT'S OKAY. I'M NOT MAD AT YOU ANYMORE.
I'M GOING TO APOLOGIZE TO MR. SUZUKI, MY HOMEROOM TEACHER, TOMORROW.
DO YOU THINK I SHOULD APOLOGIZE TO MR. SANADA TOO?
SURE. WHY NOT?
FWIP
HEY, AH-CHAN? YOU KNOW MR. SANADA, RIGHT? WHAT'S HE LIKE?
HE SEEMS AWFULLY COLD, AND HE DOESN'T LIKE GETTING TOO CLOSE TO ANY STUDENTS.
WHAT WAS HE LIKE WHEN YOU WERE THERE?

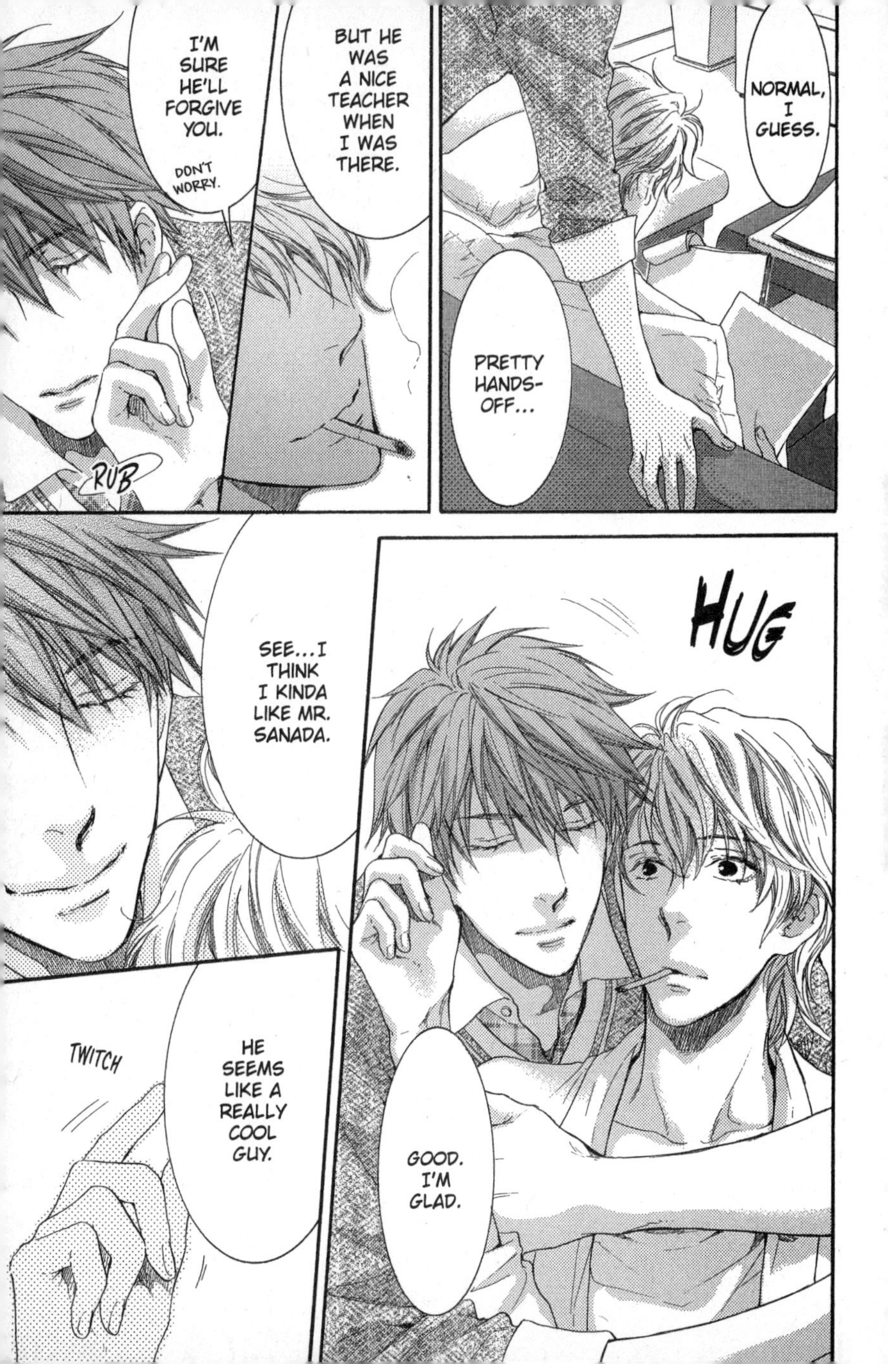
NORMAL, I GUESS.
PRETTY HANDS-OFF...
BUT HE WAS A NICE TEACHER WHEN I WAS THERE.
I'M SURE HE'LL FORGIVE YOU.
DON'T WORRY.
RUB
HUG
GOOD. I'M GLAD.
SEE...I THINK I KINDA LIKE MR. SANADA.
TWITCH
HE SEEMS LIKE A REALLY COOL GUY.

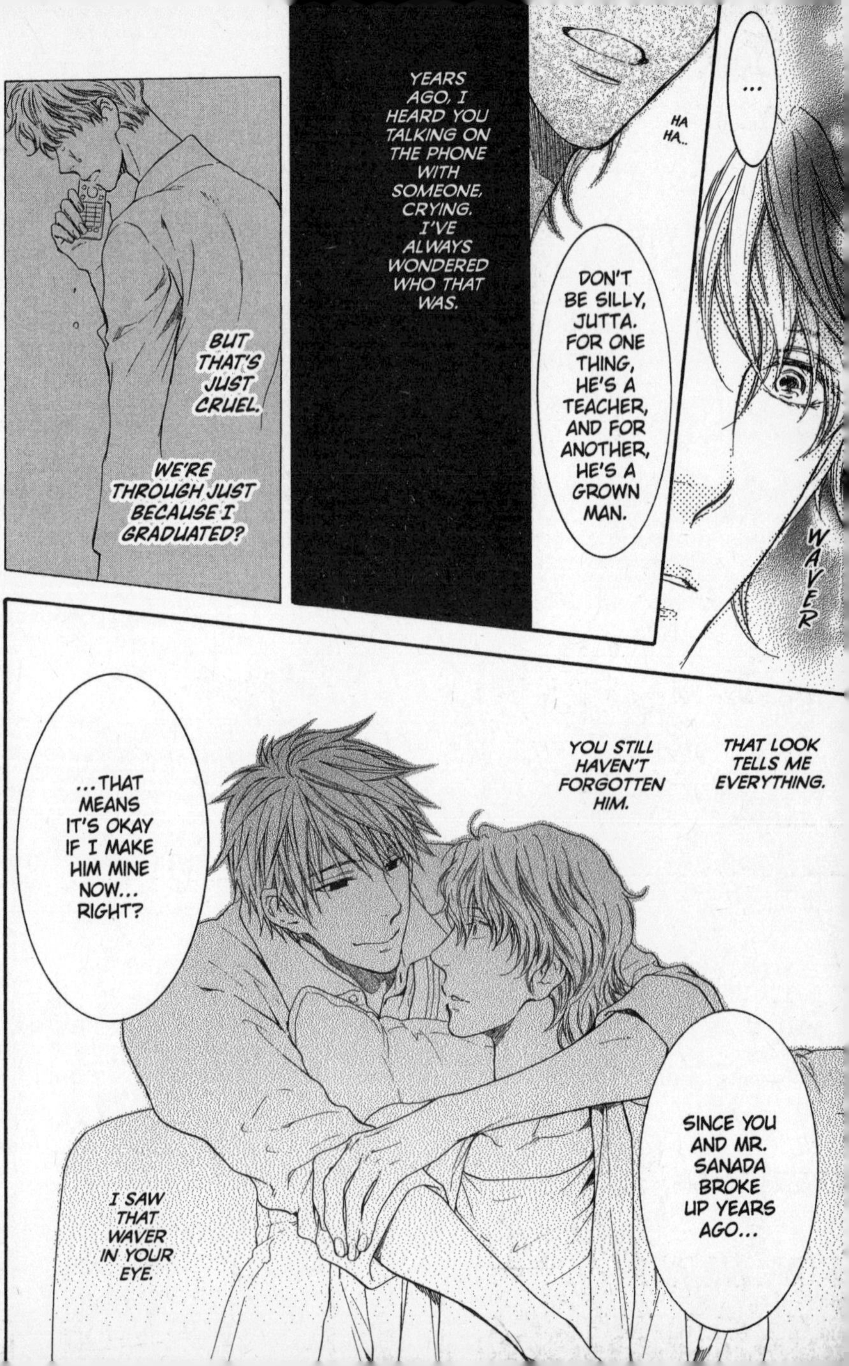
...
HA HA..
DON'T BE SILLY, JUTTA. FOR ONE THING, HE'S A TEACHER, AND FOR ANOTHER, HE'S A GROWN MAN.
WAVER
YEARS AGO, I HEARD YOU TALKING ON THE PHONE WITH SOMEONE, CRYING. I'VE ALWAYS WONDERED WHO THAT WAS.
BUT THAT'S JUST CRUEL.
WE'RE THROUGH JUST BECAUSE I GRADUATED?
THAT LOOK TELLS ME EVERYTHING.
YOU STILL HAVEN'T FORGOTTEN HIM.
SINCE YOU AND MR. SANADA BROKE UP YEARS AGO...
...THAT MEANS IT'S OKAY IF I MAKE HIM MINE NOW... RIGHT?
I SAW THAT WAVER IN YOUR EYE.

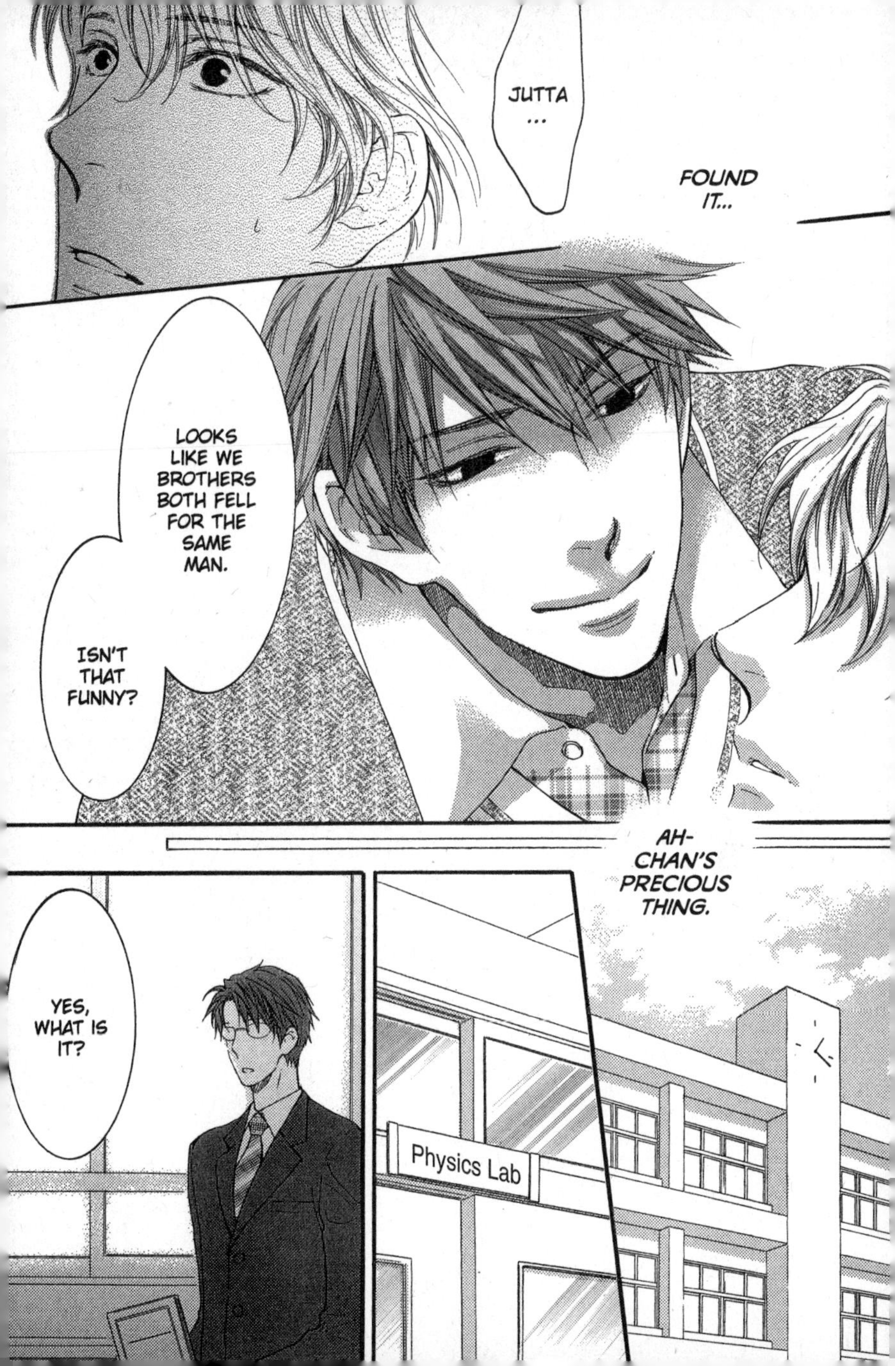
JUTTA ...
FOUND IT...
LOOKS LIKE WE BROTHERS BOTH FELL FOR THE SAME MAN.
ISN'T THAT FUNNY?
AH-CHAN'S PRECIOUS THING.
Physics Lab
YES, WHAT IS IT?

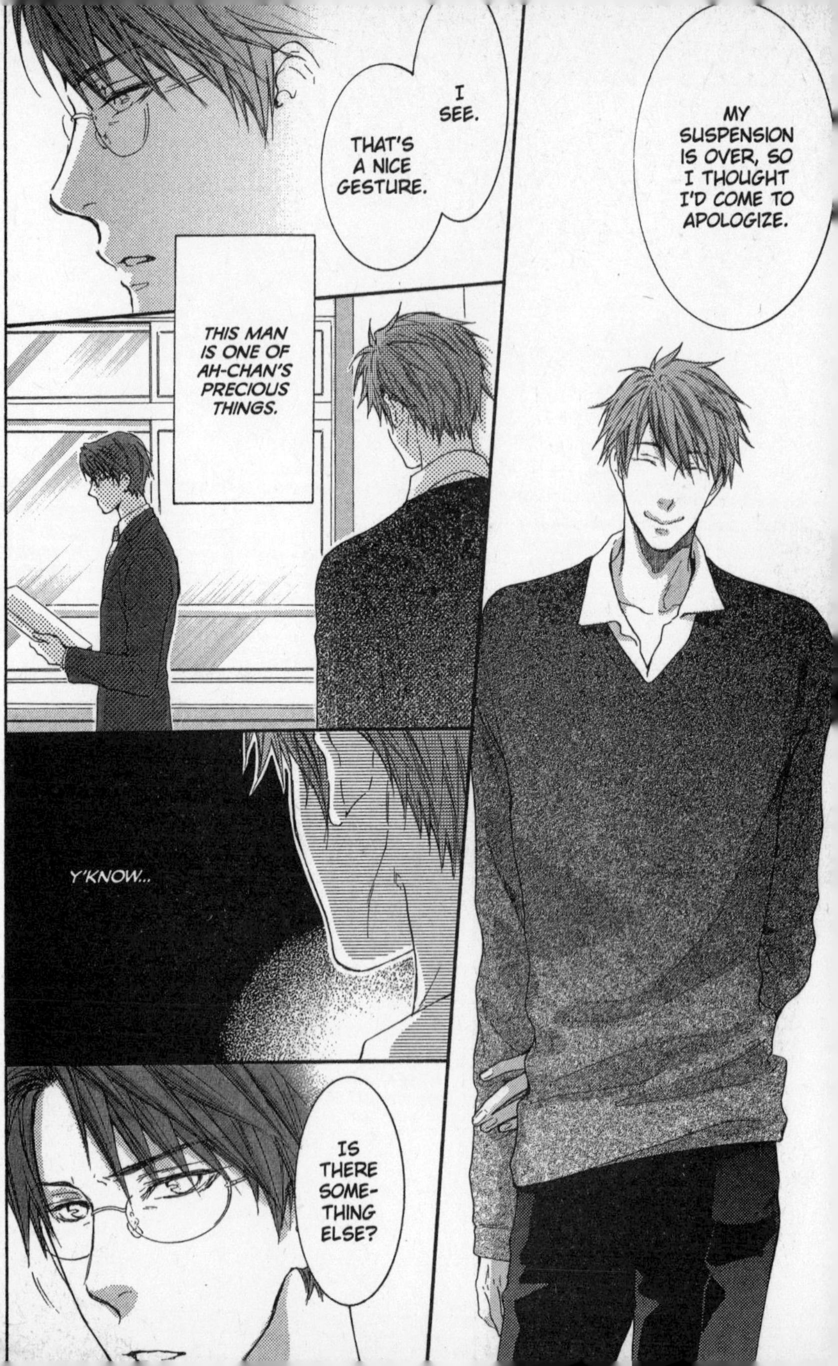
MY SUSPENSION IS OVER, SO I THOUGHT I'D COME TO APOLOGIZE.
I SEE.
THAT'S A NICE GESTURE.
THIS MAN IS ONE OF AH-CHAN'S PRECIOUS THINGS.
Y'KNOW...
IS THERE SOME-THING ELSE?

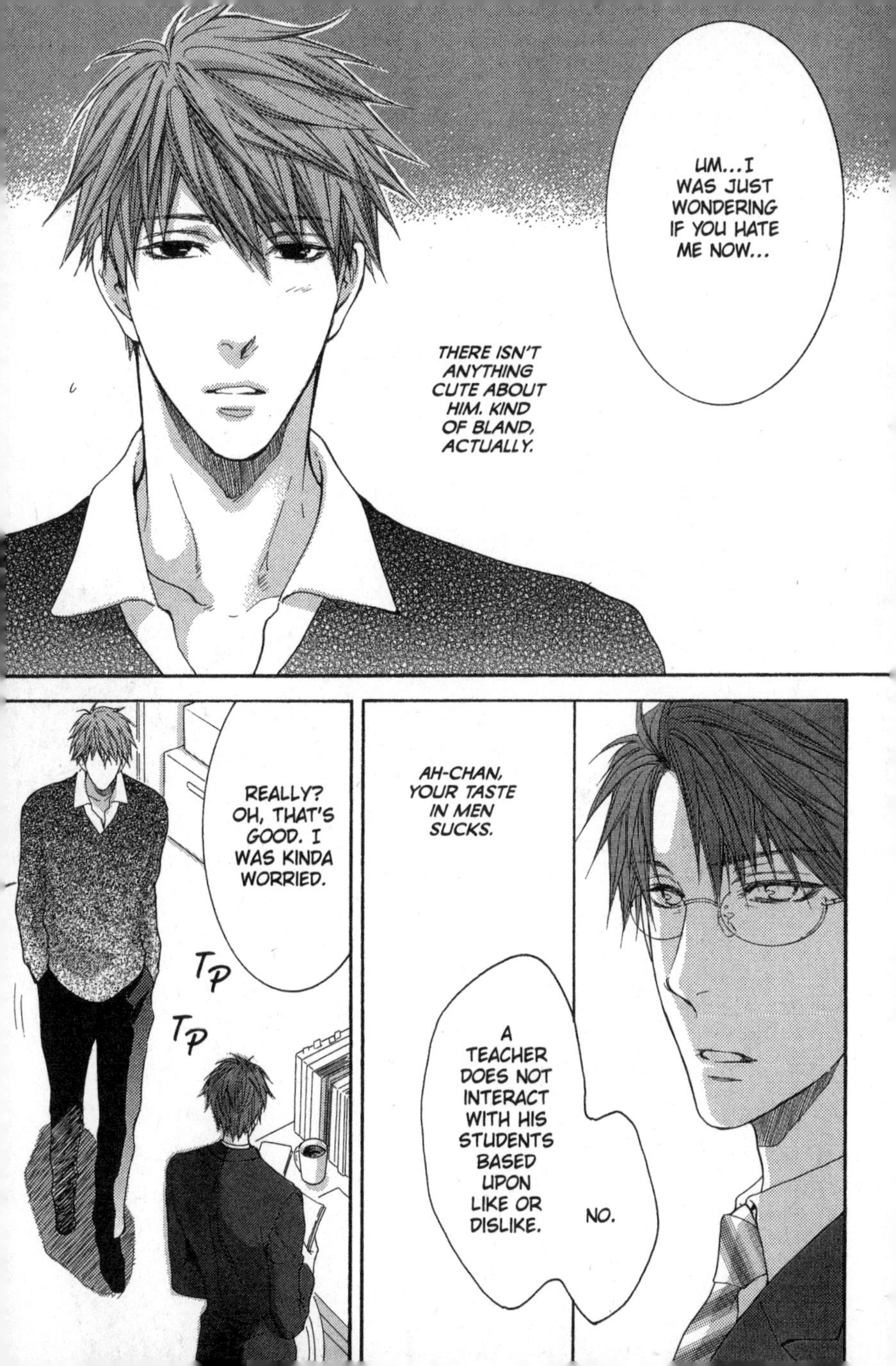
UM...I WAS JUST WONDERING IF YOU HATE ME NOW...
THERE ISN'T ANYTHING CUTE ABOUT HIM. KIND OF BLAND, ACTUALLY.
NO.
A TEACHER DOES NOT INTERACT WITH HIS STUDENTS BASED UPON LIKE OR DISLIKE.
AH-CHAN, YOUR TASTE IN MEN SUCKS.
REALLY? OH, THAT'S GOOD. I WAS KINDA WORRIED.
TP
TP

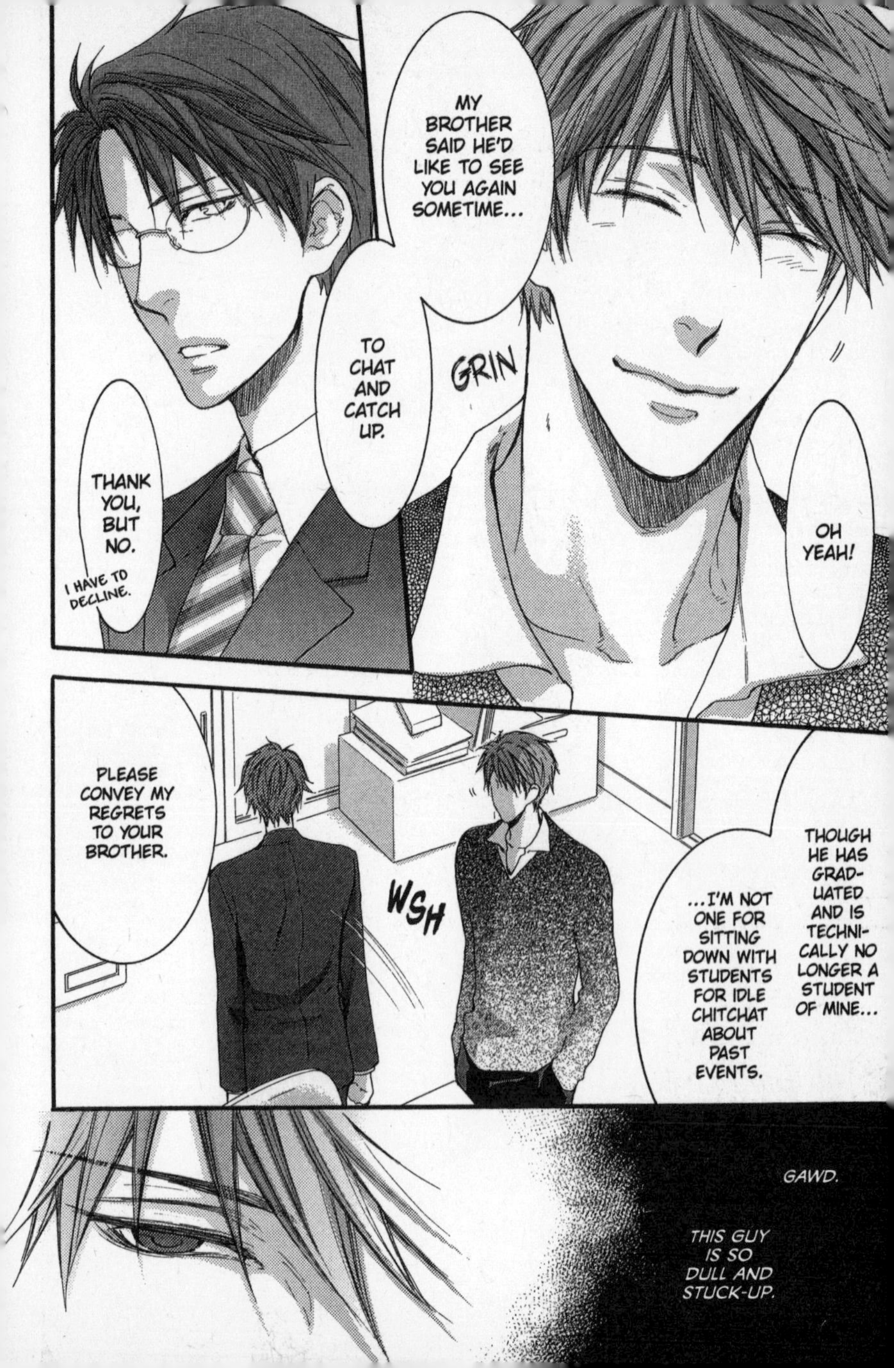

OH YEAH!
MY BROTHER SAID HE'D LIKE TO SEE YOU AGAIN SOMETIME...
TO CHAT AND CATCH UP.
GRIN
THANK YOU, BUT NO.
I HAVE TO DECLINE.
THOUGH HE HAS GRAD-UATED AND IS TECHNI-CALLY NO LONGER A STUDENT OF MINE...
...I'M NOT ONE FOR SITTING DOWN WITH STUDENTS FOR IDLE CHITCHAT ABOUT PAST EVENTS.
WSH
PLEASE CONVEY MY REGRETS TO YOUR BROTHER.
GAWD.
THIS GUY IS SO DULL AND STUCK-UP.

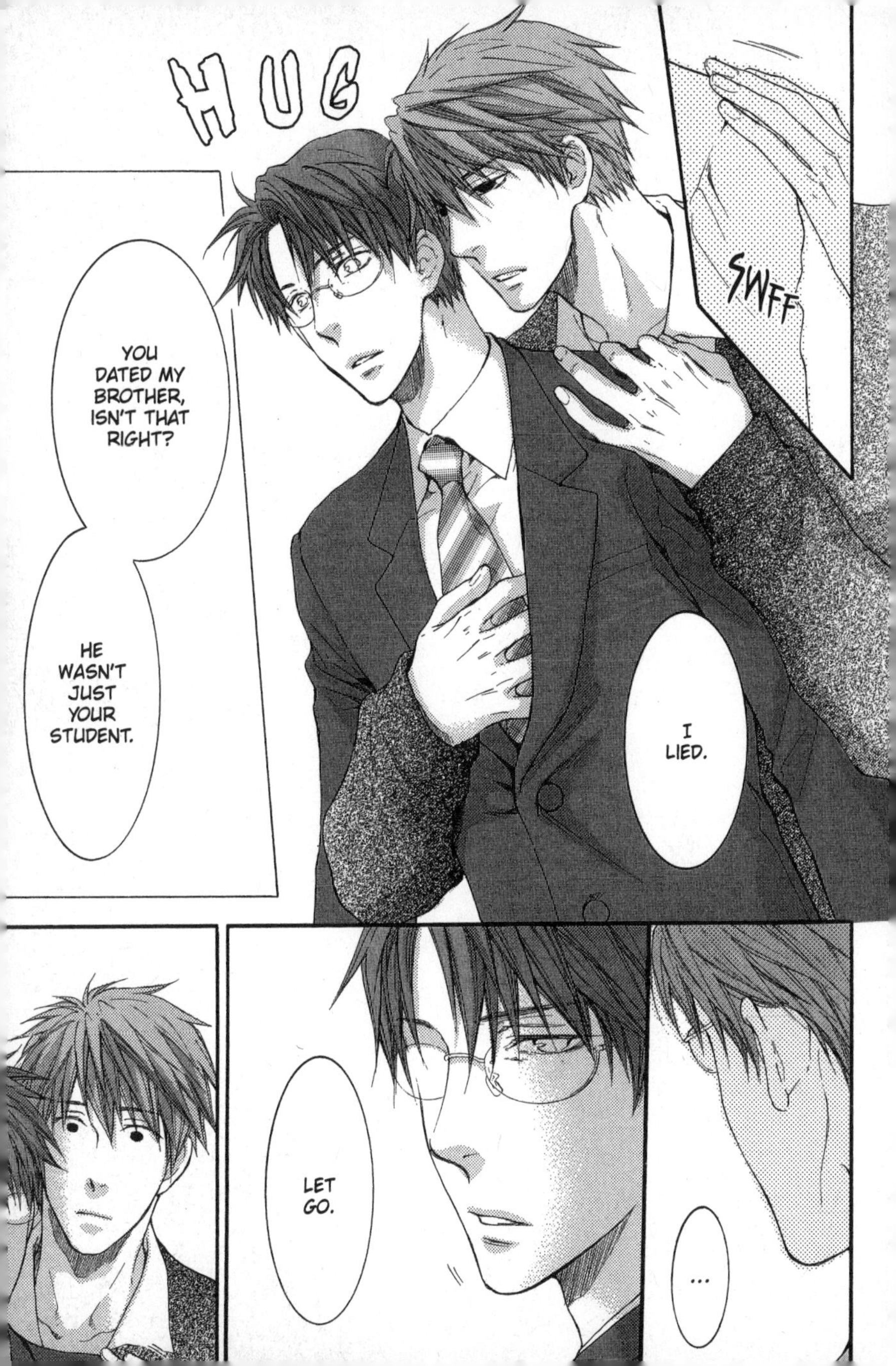
SWFF
HUG
I LIED.
YOU DATED MY BROTHER, ISN'T THAT RIGHT?
HE WASN'T JUST YOUR STUDENT.
...
LET GO.

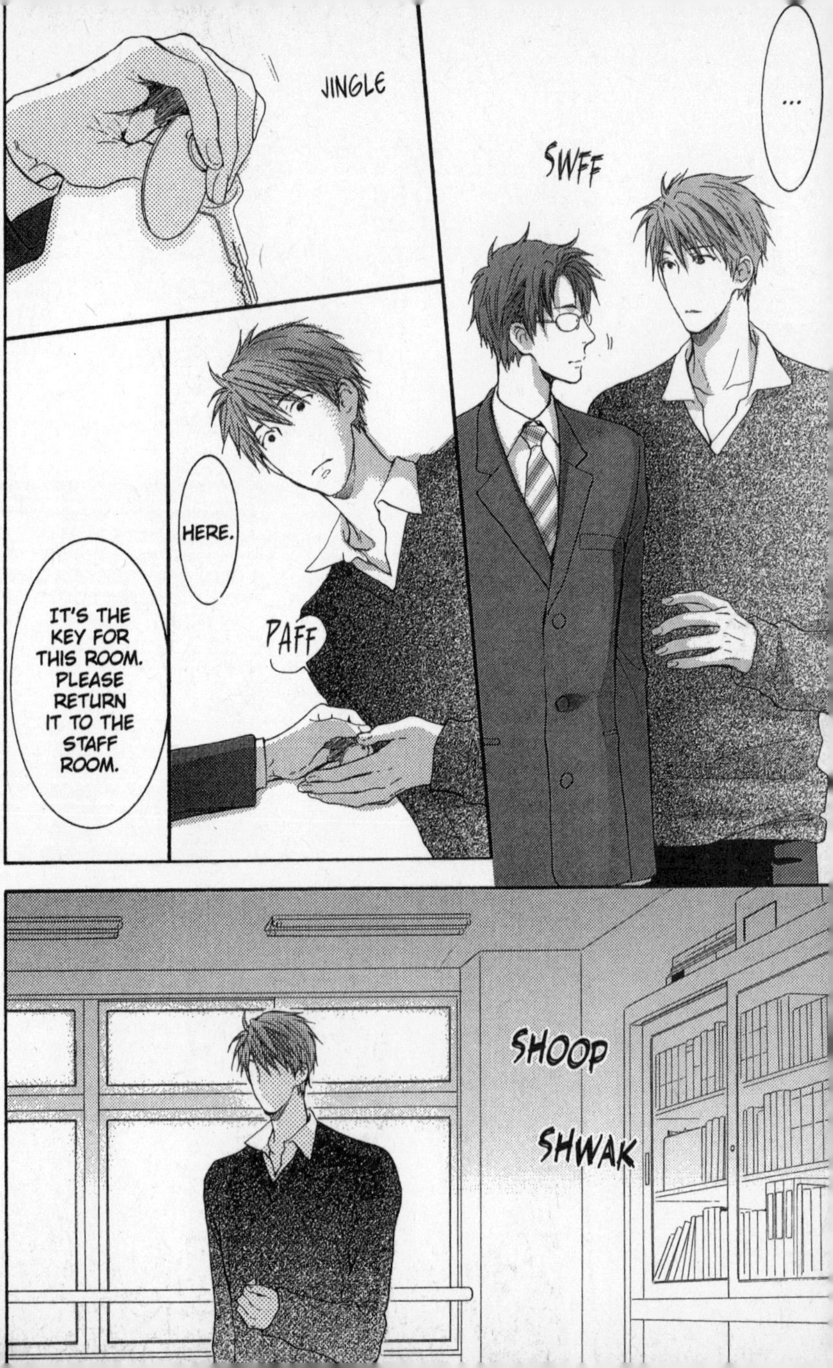
...
SWFF
JINGLE
HERE.
IT'S THE KEY FOR THIS ROOM. PLEASE RETURN IT TO THE STAFF ROOM.
PAFF
SHOOP
SHWAK

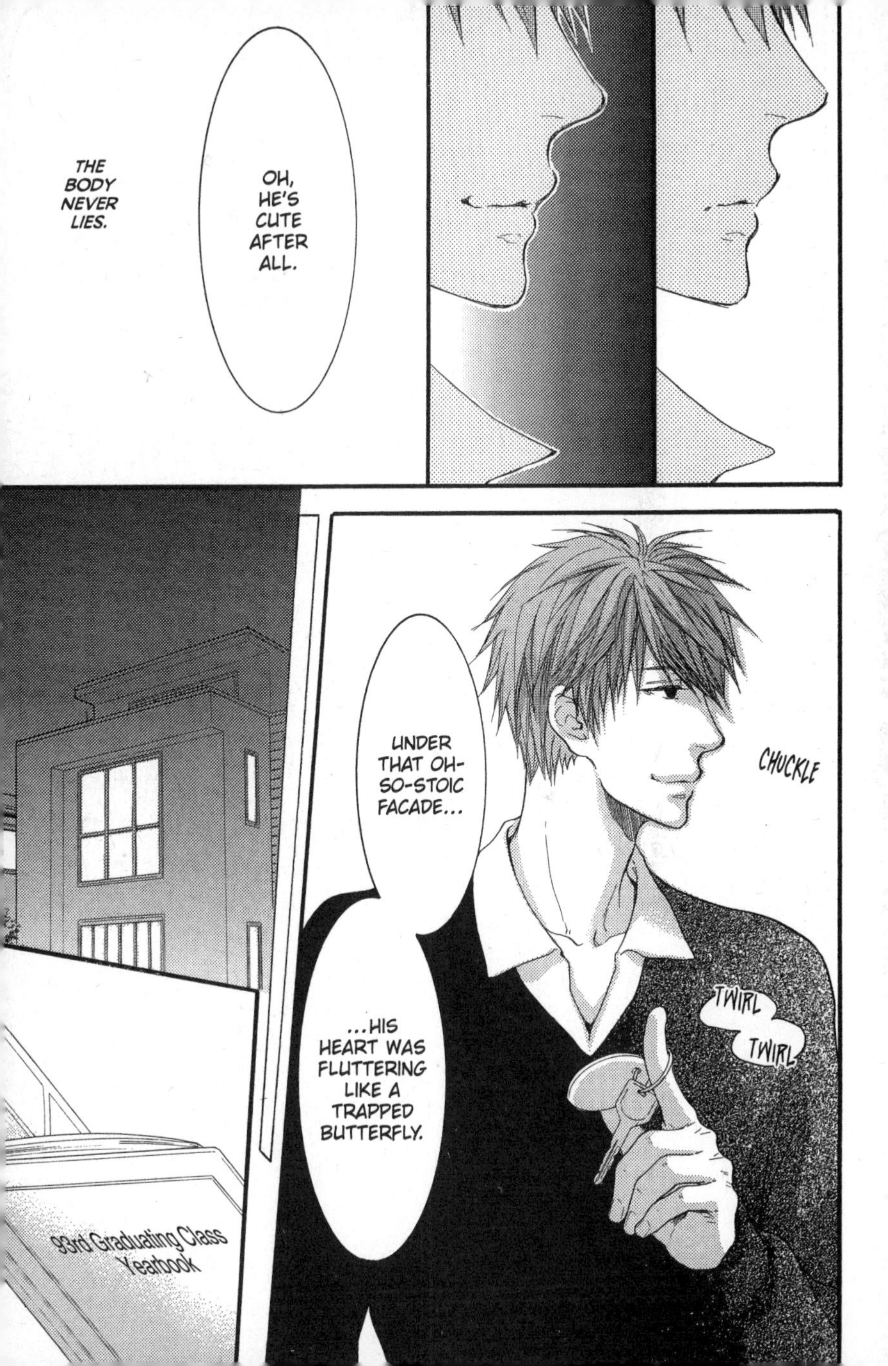
OH, HE'S CUTE AFTER ALL.
THE BODY NEVER LIES.
UNDER THAT OH-SO-STOIC FACADE...
CHUCKLE
...HIS HEART WAS FLUTTERING LIKE A TRAPPED BUTTERFLY.
TWIRL
TWIRL
93rd Graduating Class Yearbook

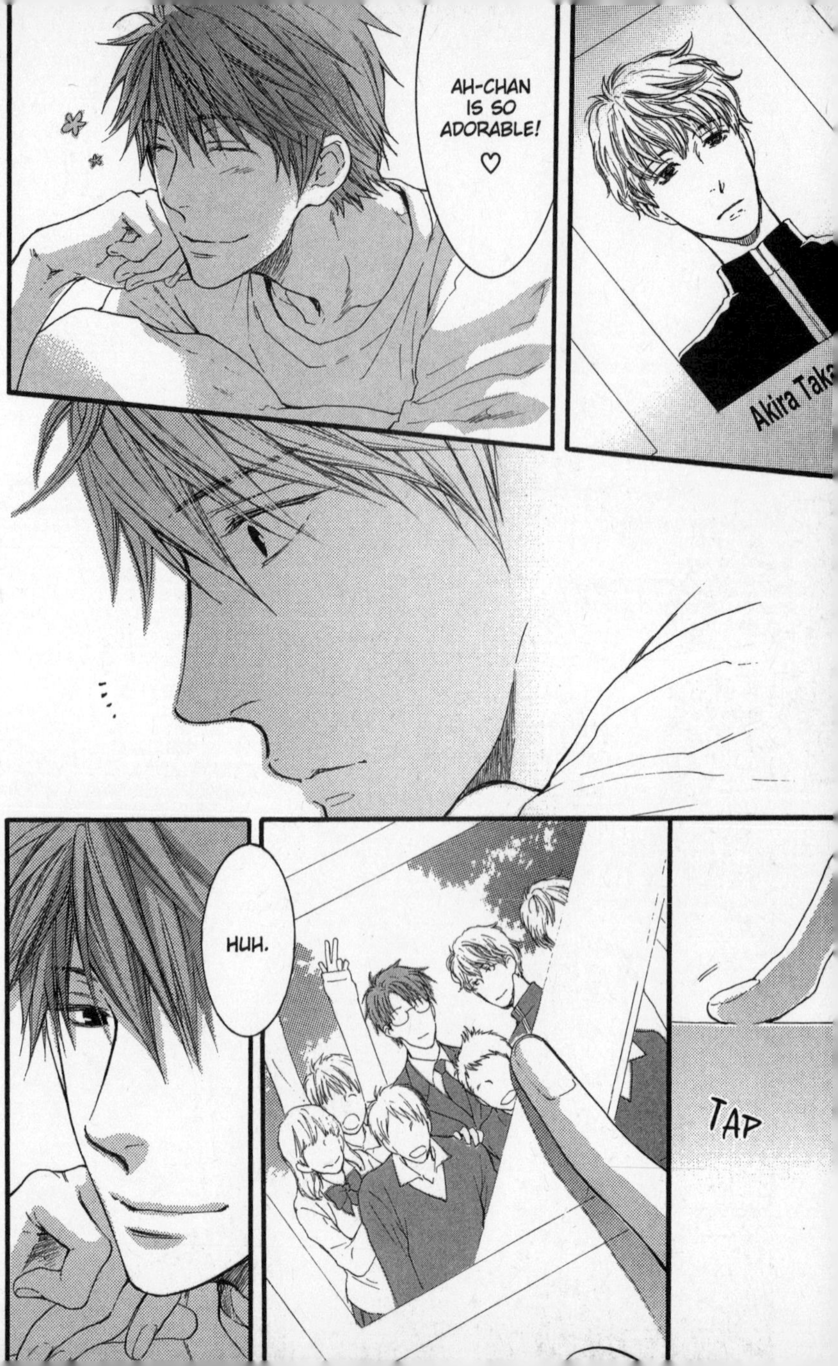

Akira Taka
AH-CHAN IS SO ADORABLE! ♡
...
TAP
HUH.

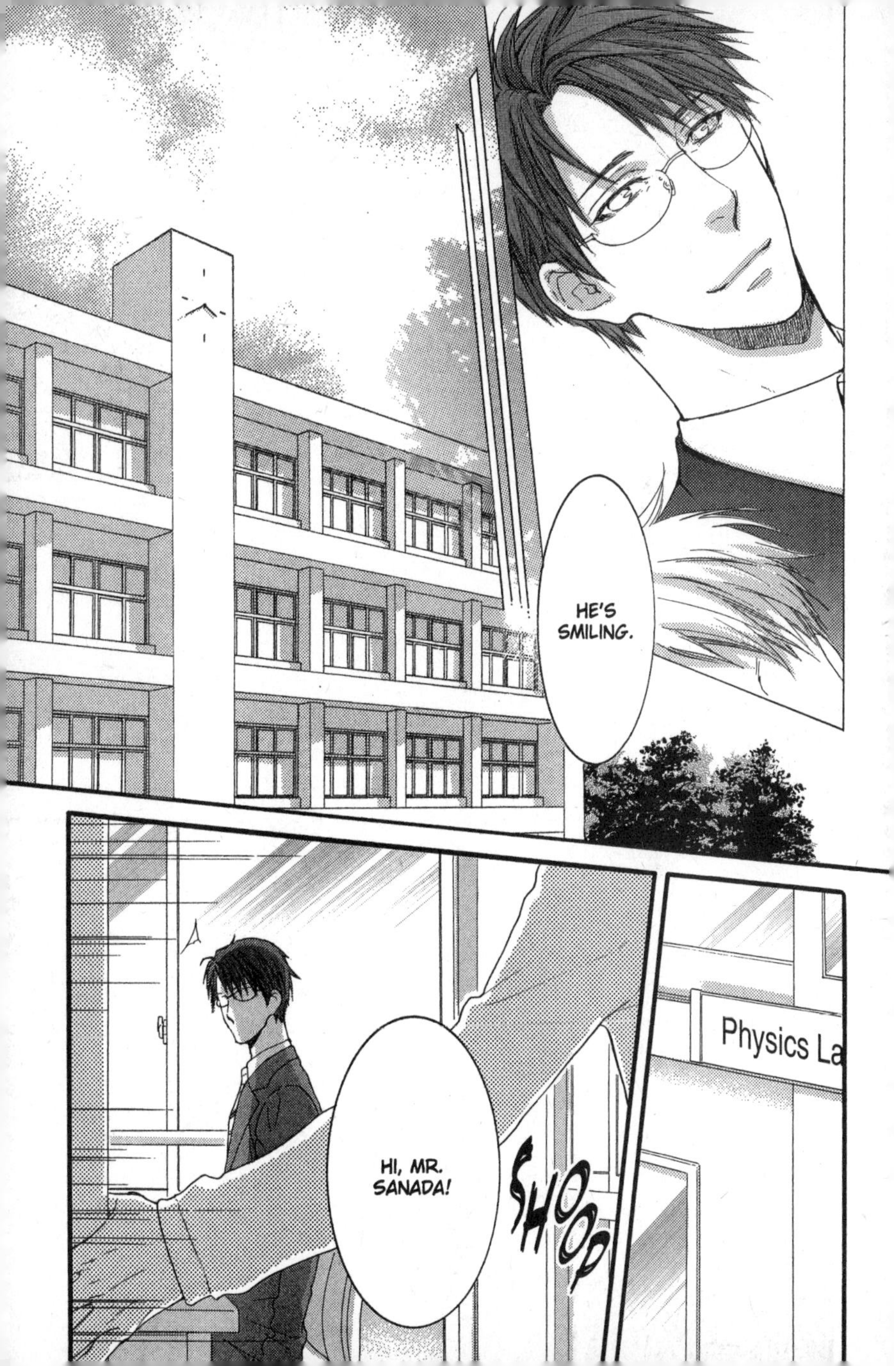
HE'S SMILING.
Physics La
HI, MR. SANADA!
SHOOP

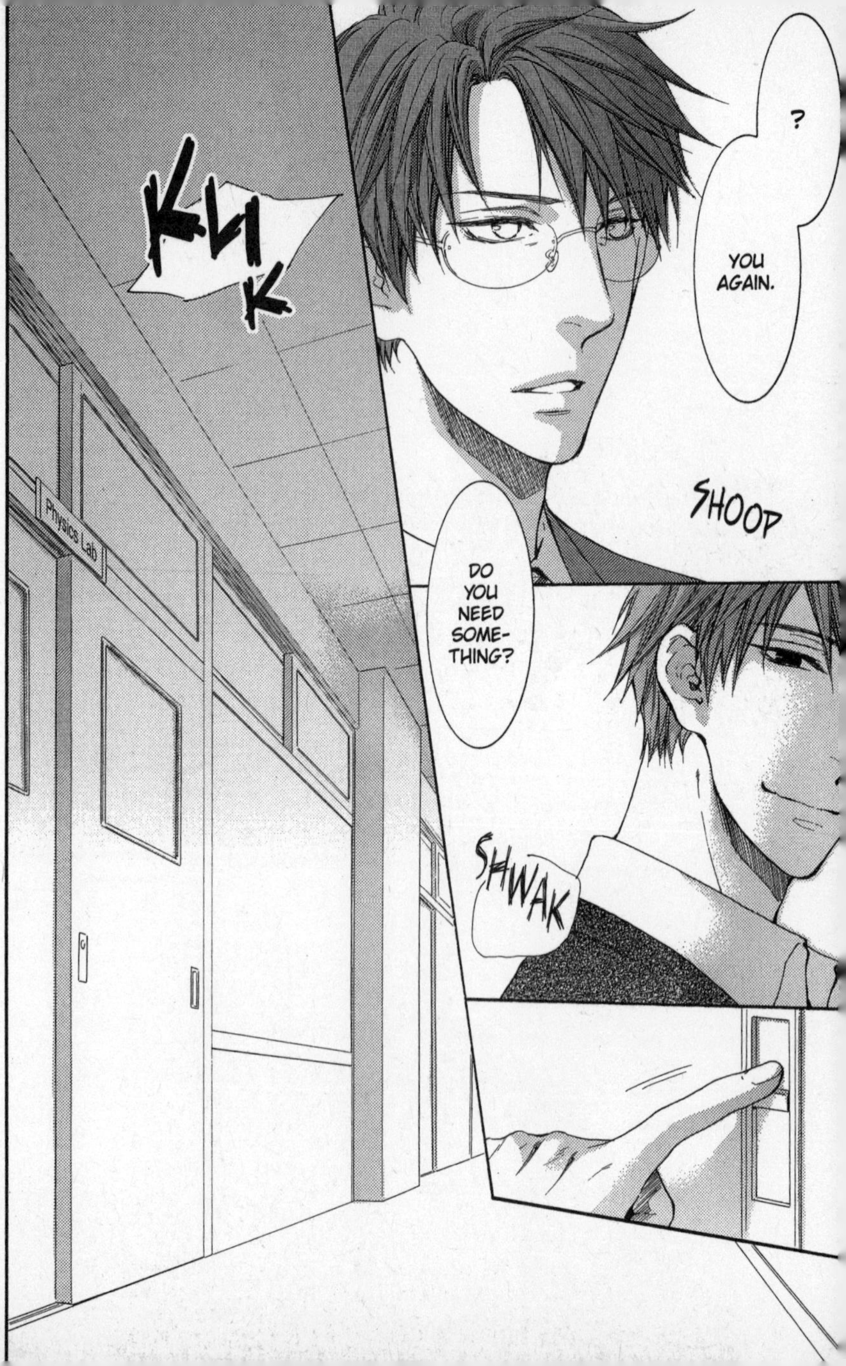
?
YOU AGAIN.
SHOOP
DO YOU NEED SOME-THING?
SHWAK
KLIK
Physics Lab

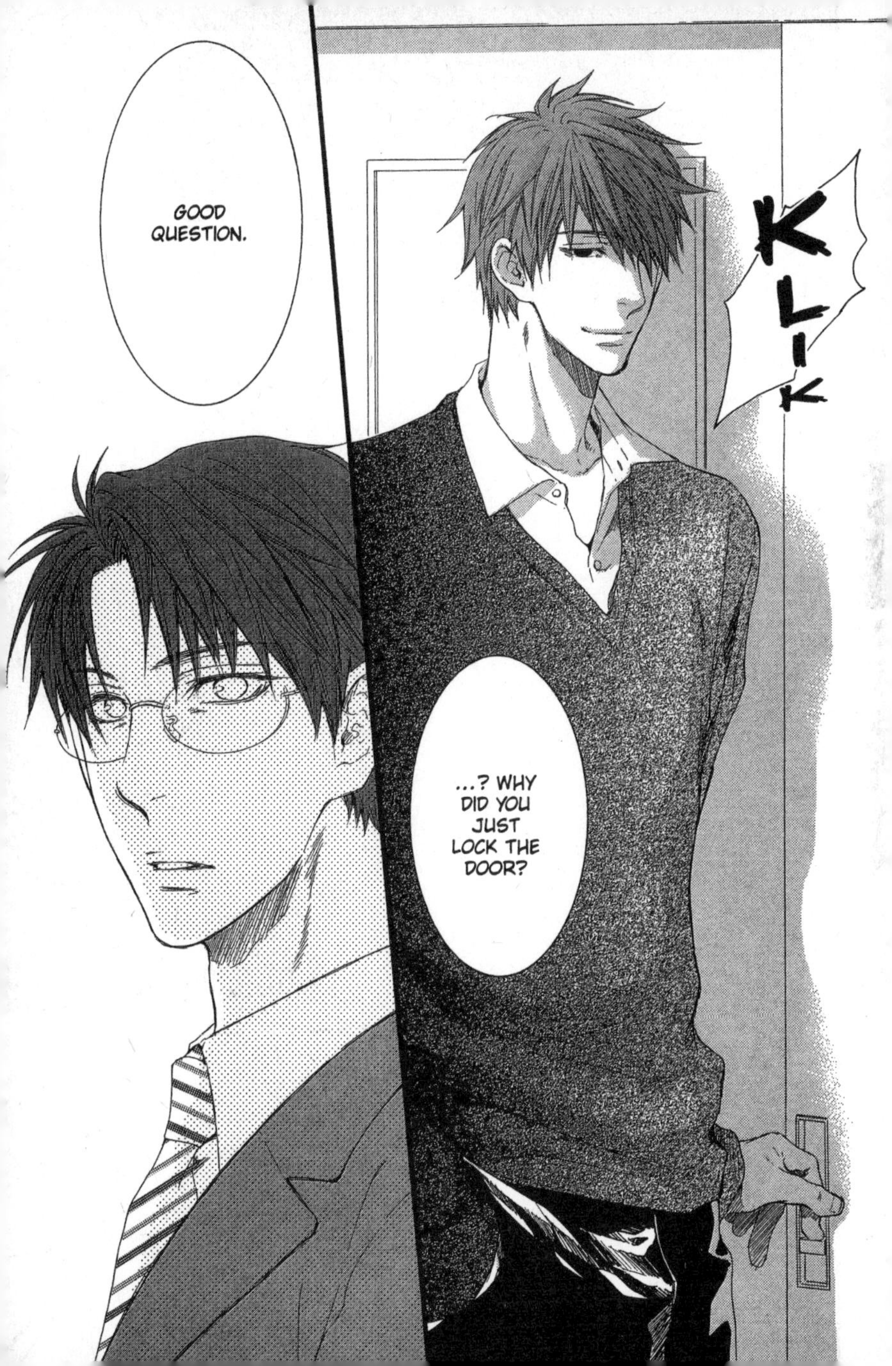
KLIK
...? WHY DID YOU JUST LOCK THE DOOR?
GOOD QUESTION.

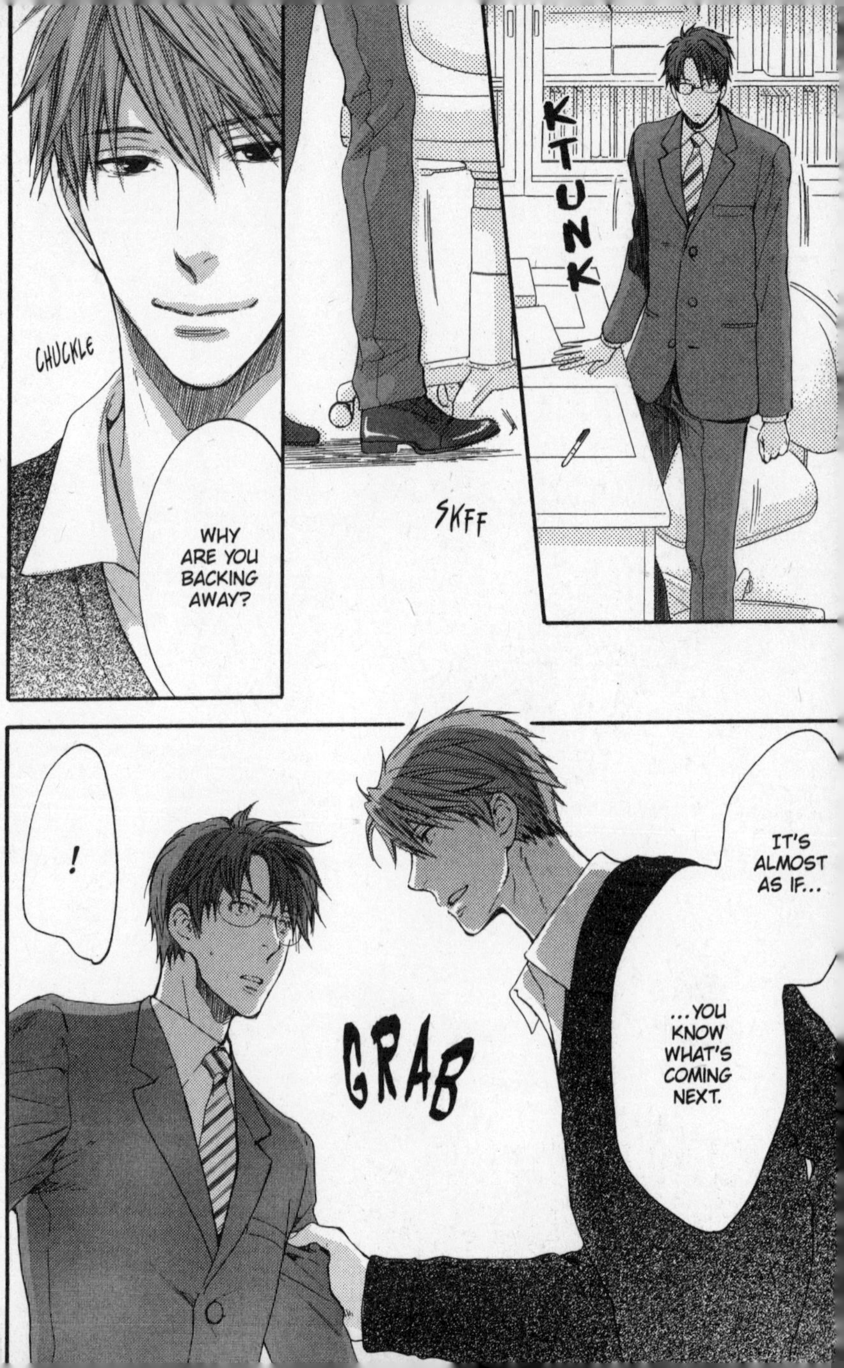
KTUNK
SKFF
CHUCKLE
WHY ARE YOU BACKING AWAY?
IT'S ALMOST AS IF...
...YOU KNOW WHAT'S COMING NEXT.
GRAB
!

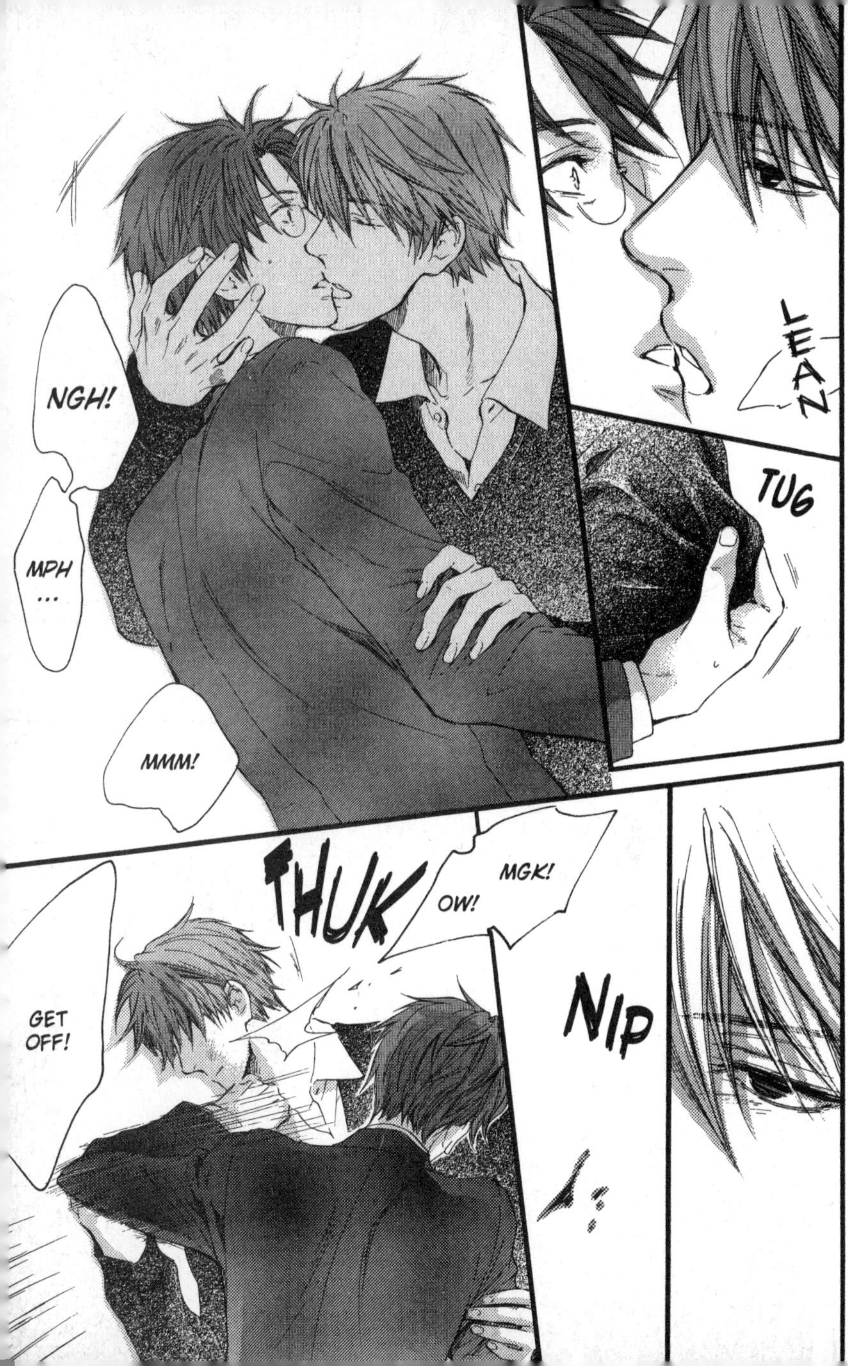
LEAN
TUG
NGH!
MPH ...
MMM!
NIP
MGK!
OW!
THUK
GET OFF!

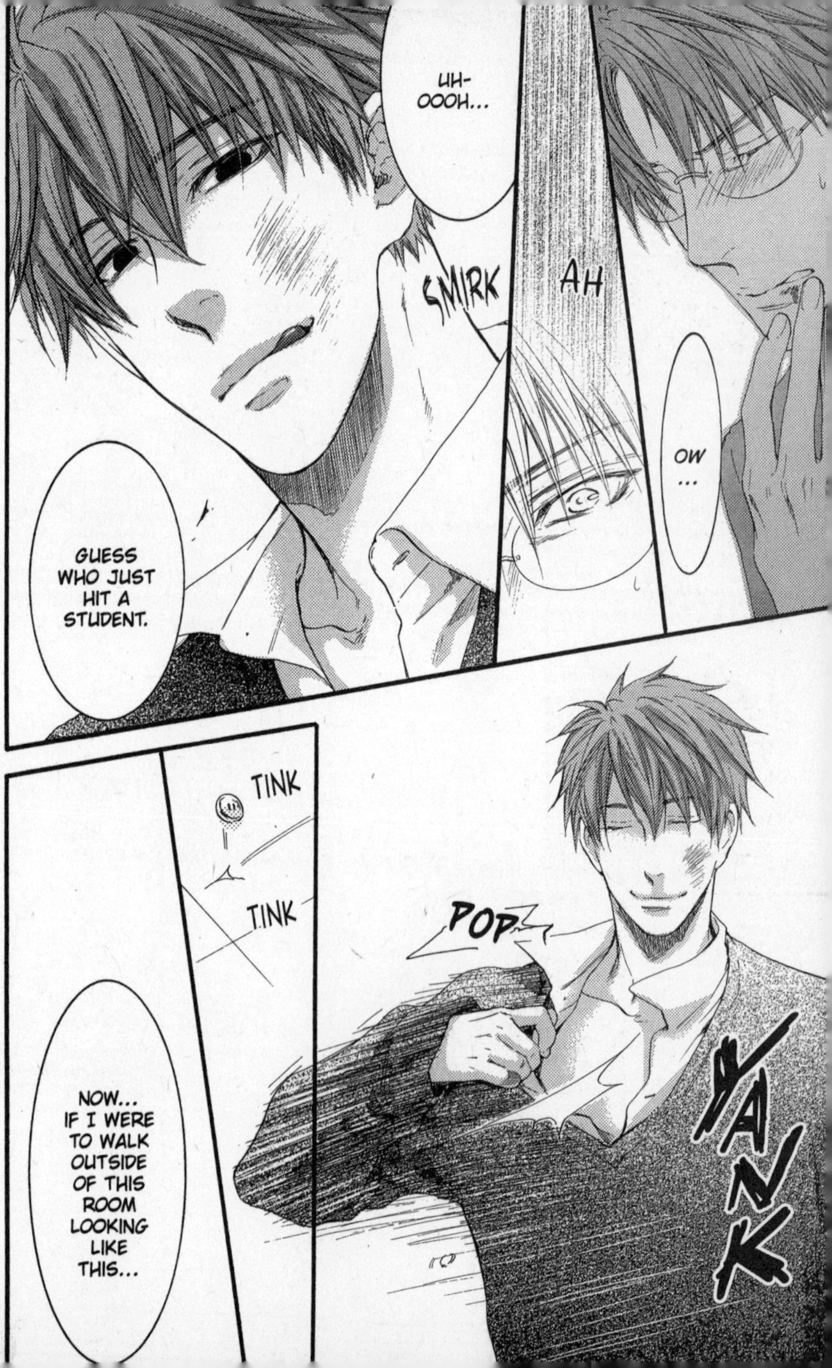
OW ...
AH
UH-OOOH...
SMIRK
GUESS WHO JUST HIT A STUDENT.
POP
YANK
TINK
TINK
NOW... IF I WERE TO WALK OUTSIDE OF THIS ROOM LOOKING LIKE THIS...

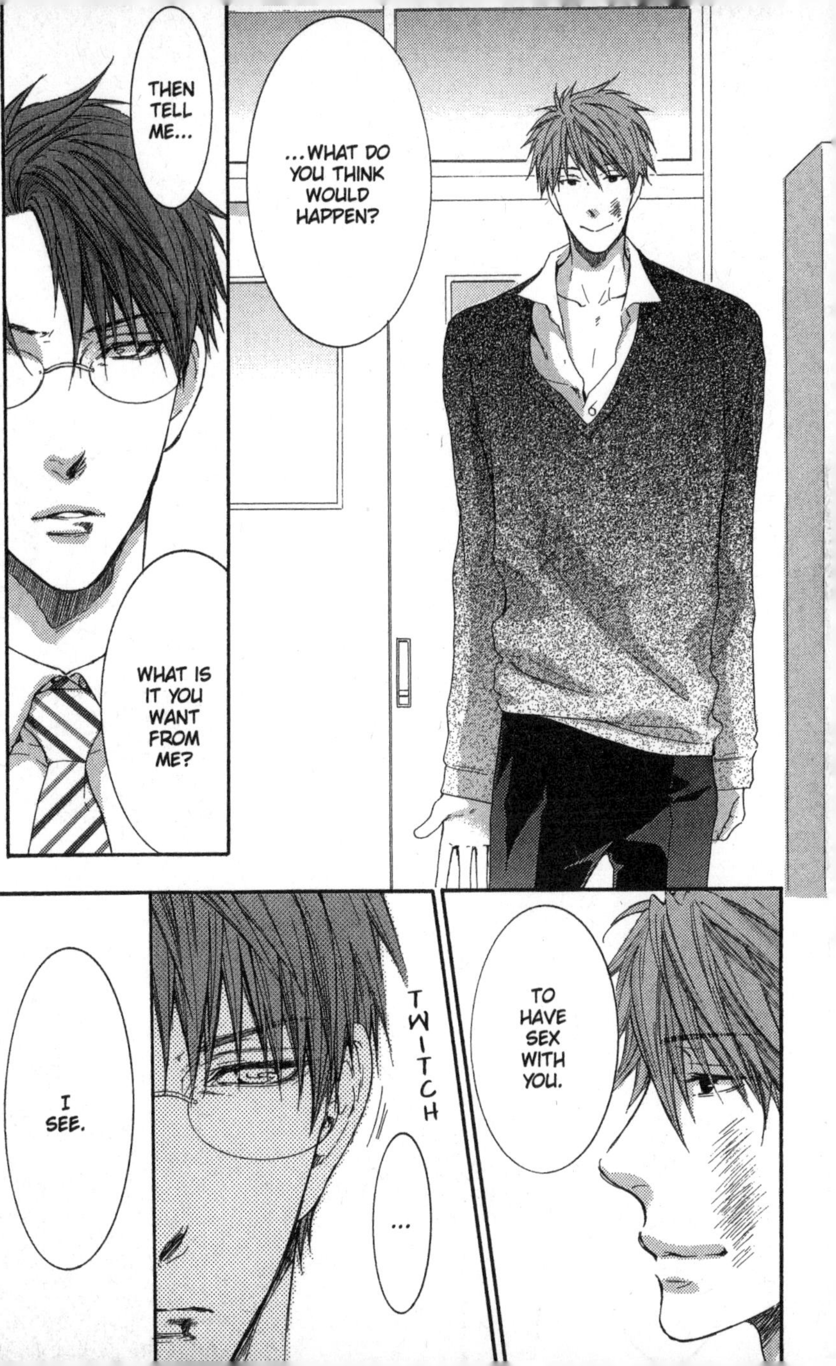
...WHAT DO YOU THINK WOULD HAPPEN?
THEN TELL ME...
WHAT IS IT YOU WANT FROM ME?
TO HAVE SEX WITH YOU.
TWITCH
...
I SEE.

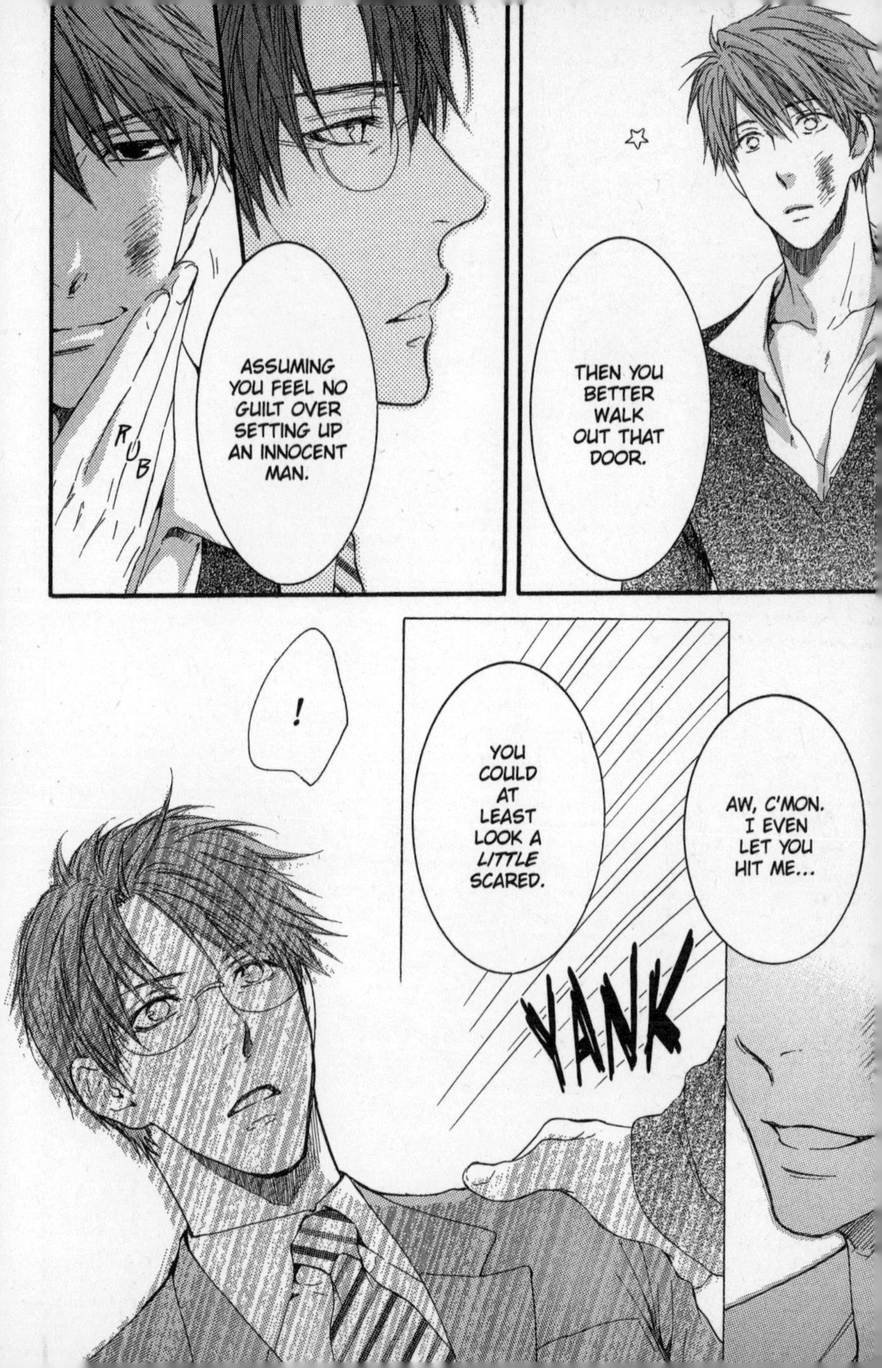
THEN YOU BETTER WALK OUT THAT DOOR.
ASSUMING YOU FEEL NO GUILT OVER SETTING UP AN INNOCENT MAN.
RUB
AW, C'MON. I EVEN LET YOU HIT ME...
YOU COULD AT LEAST LOOK A *LITTLE* SCARED.
YANK
!

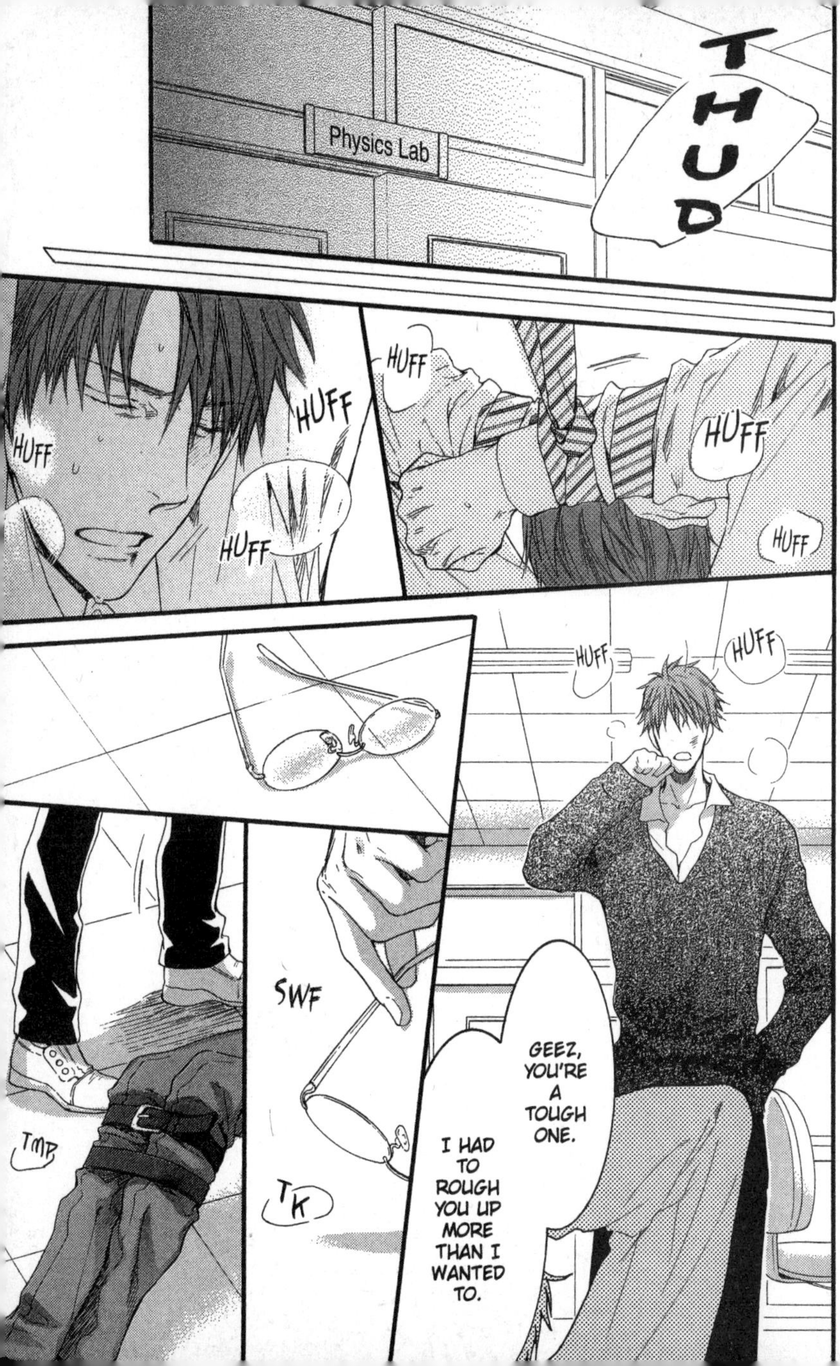
THUD
Physics Lab
HUFF
HUFF
HUFF
HUFF
HUFF
HUFF
HUFF
HUFF
GEEZ, YOU'RE A TOUGH ONE.
I HAD TO ROUGH YOU UP MORE THAN I WANTED TO.
SWF
TK
TMP

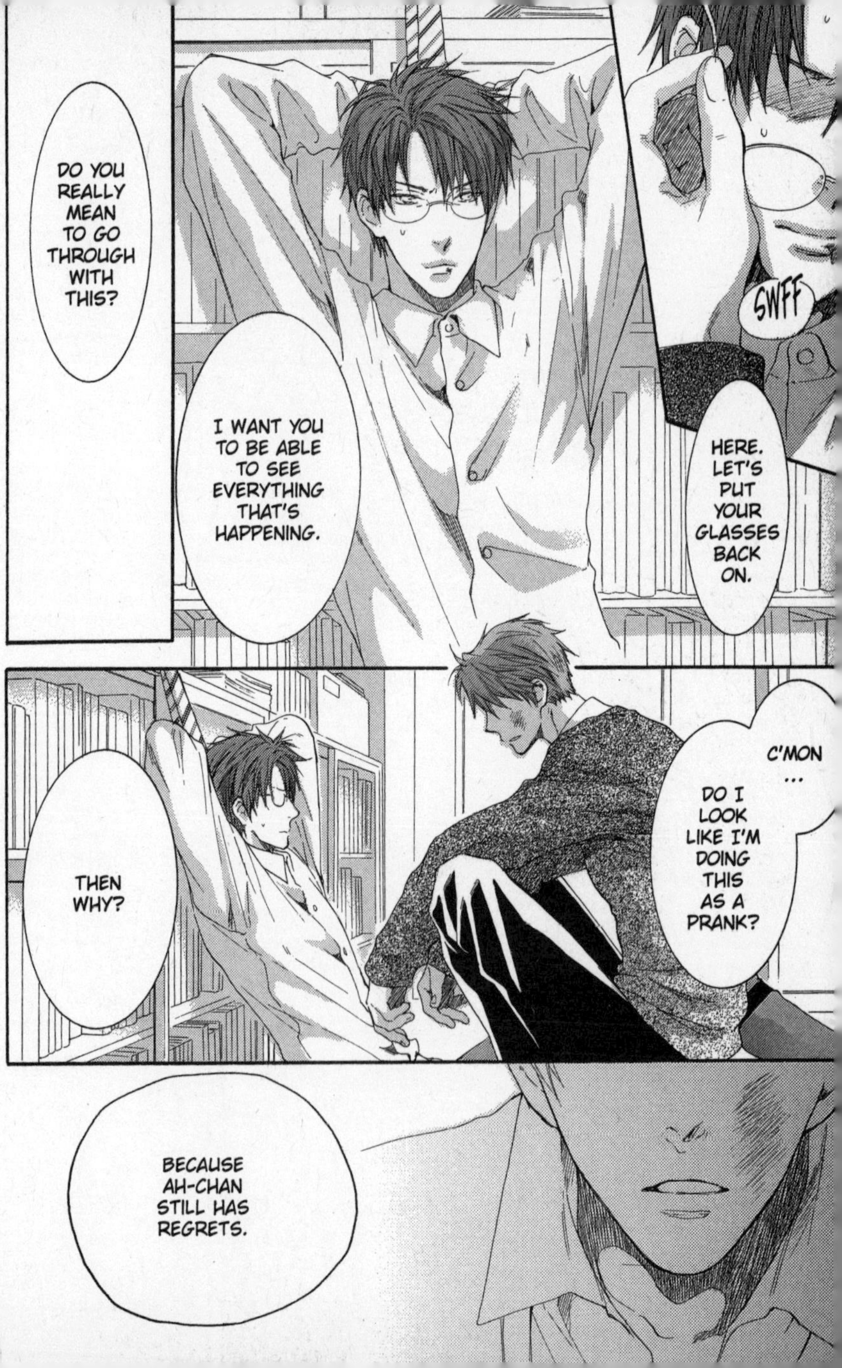
SWFF
HERE. LET'S PUT YOUR GLASSES BACK ON.
I WANT YOU TO BE ABLE TO SEE EVERYTHING THAT'S HAPPENING.
DO YOU REALLY MEAN TO GO THROUGH WITH THIS?
C'MON ... DO I LOOK LIKE I'M DOING THIS AS A PRANK?
THEN WHY?
BECAUSE AH-CHAN STILL HAS REGRETS.

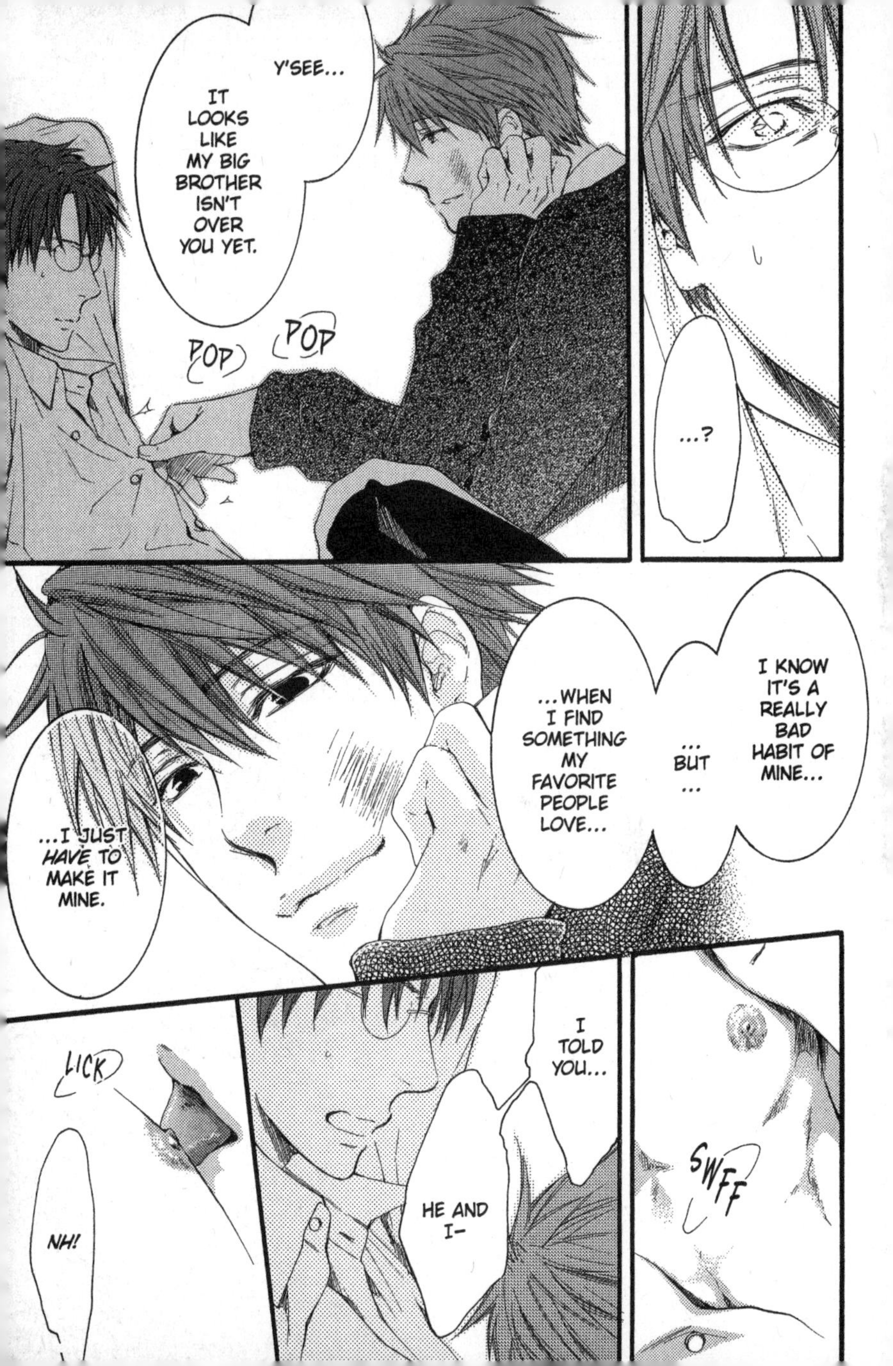
...?
Y'SEE...
IT LOOKS LIKE MY BIG BROTHER ISN'T OVER YOU YET.
POP
POP
I KNOW IT'S A REALLY BAD HABIT OF MINE...
...BUT...
...WHEN I FIND SOMETHING MY FAVORITE PEOPLE LOVE...
...I JUST *HAVE* TO MAKE IT MINE.
SWFF
I TOLD YOU...
HE AND I–
LICK
NH!

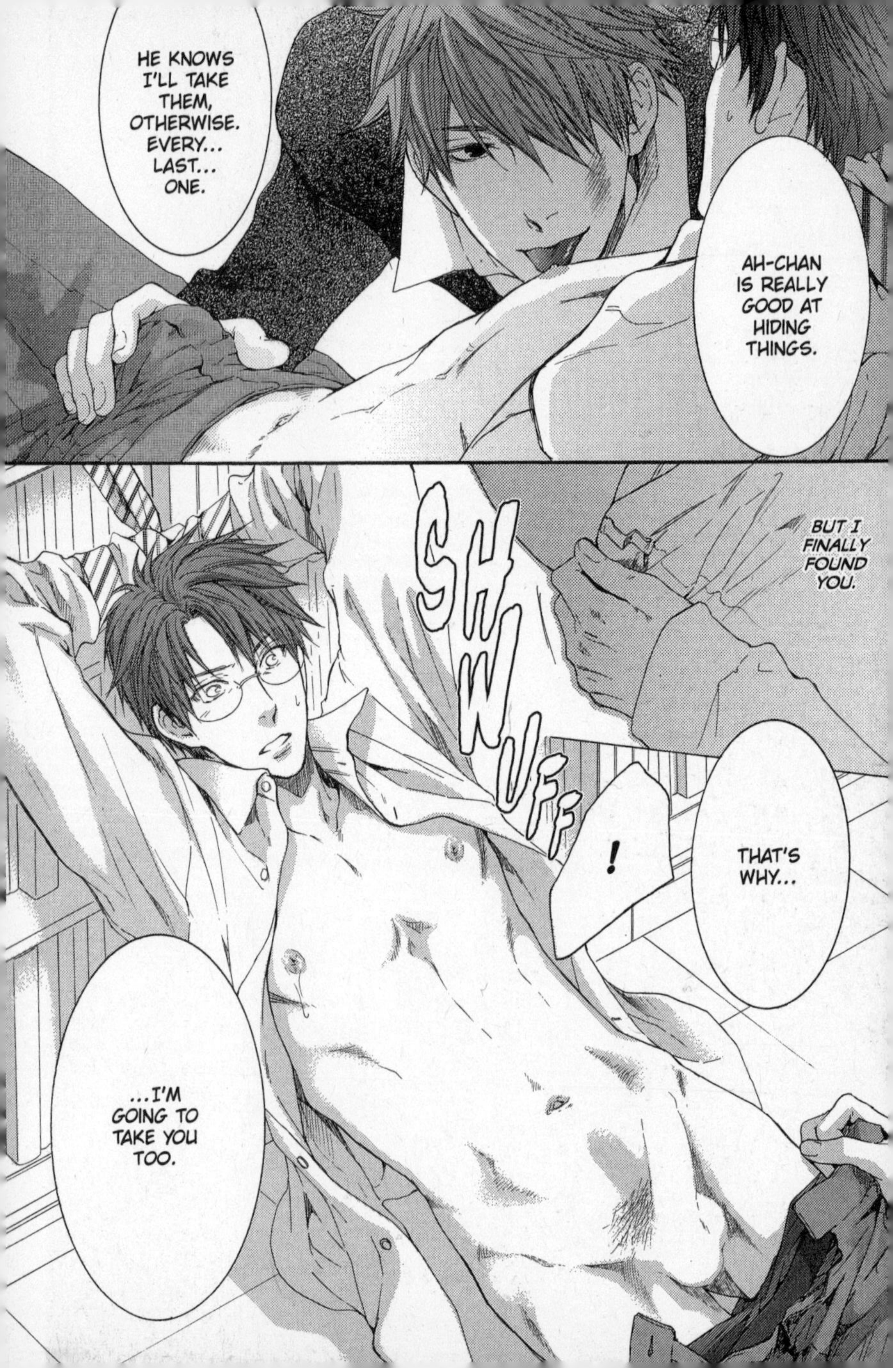
AH-CHAN IS REALLY GOOD AT HIDING THINGS.
HE KNOWS I'LL TAKE THEM, OTHERWISE. EVERY... LAST... ONE.
BUT I FINALLY FOUND YOU.
SHWUFF
!
THAT'S WHY...
...I'M GOING TO TAKE YOU TOO.

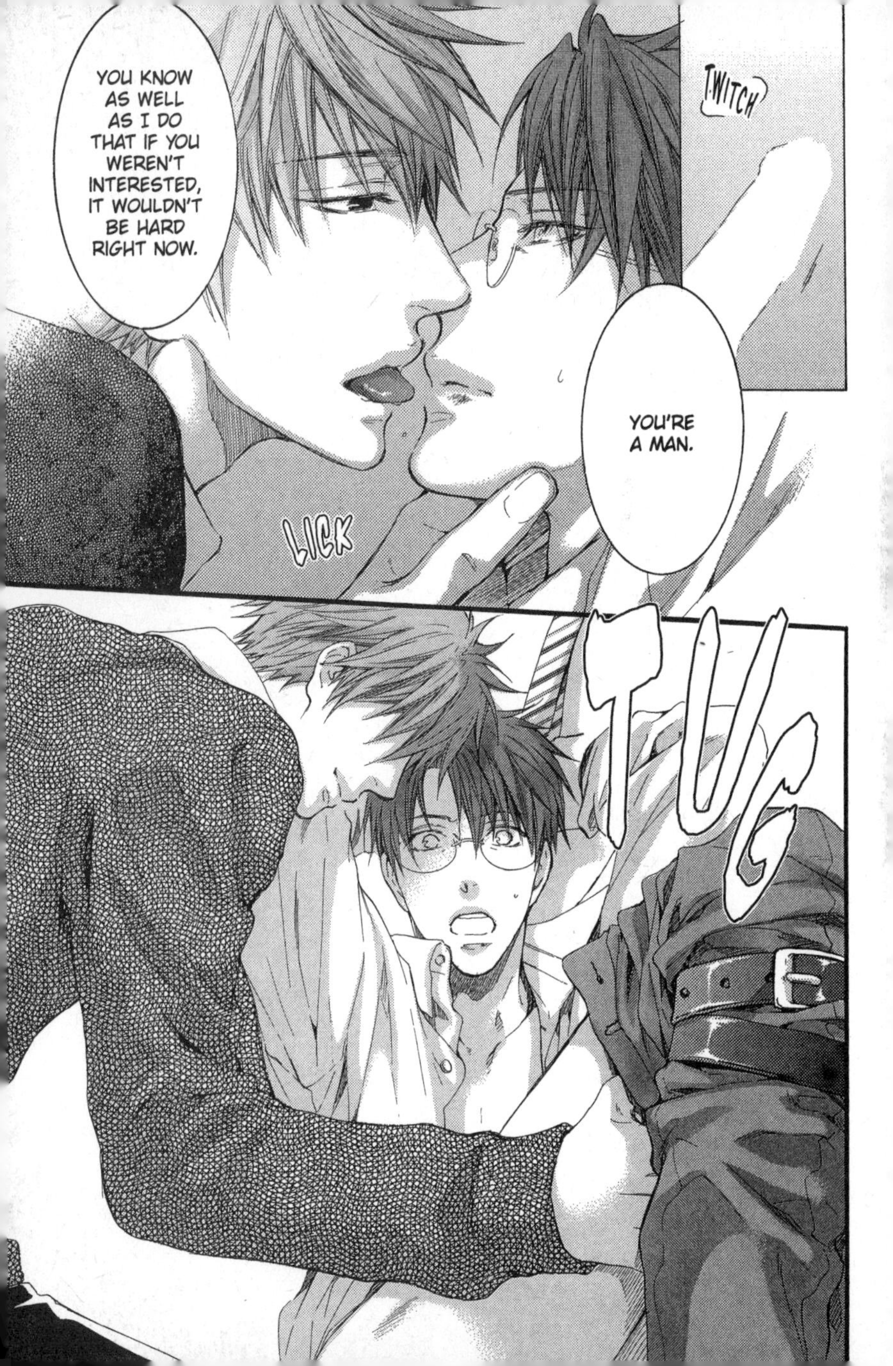
TWITCH
YOU KNOW AS WELL AS I DO THAT IF YOU WEREN'T INTERESTED, IT WOULDN'T BE HARD RIGHT NOW.
YOU'RE A MAN.
LICK
TUG

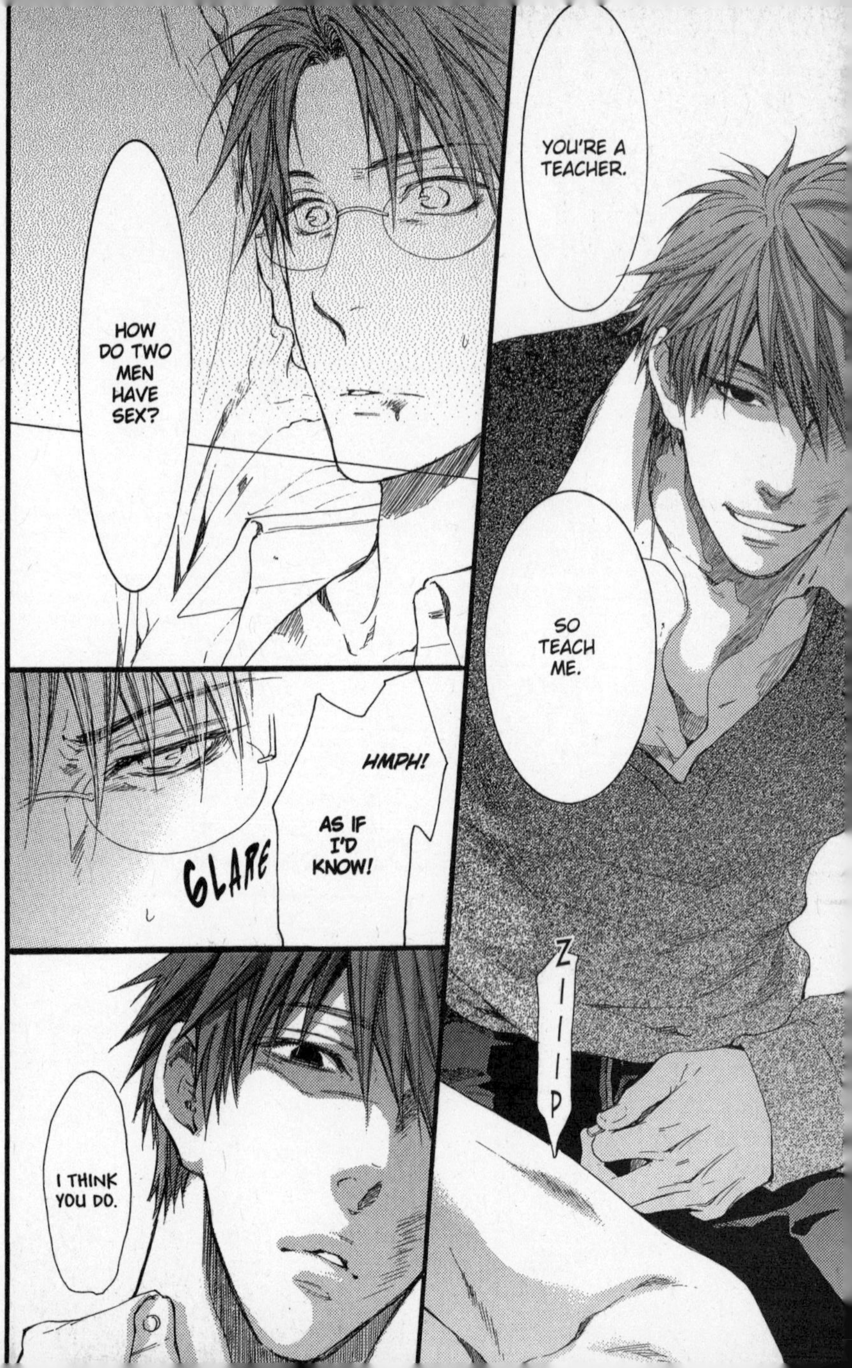
YOU'RE A TEACHER.
SO TEACH ME.
ZIIIP
HOW DO TWO MEN HAVE SEX?
HMPH!
AS IF I'D KNOW!
GLARE
I THINK YOU DO.

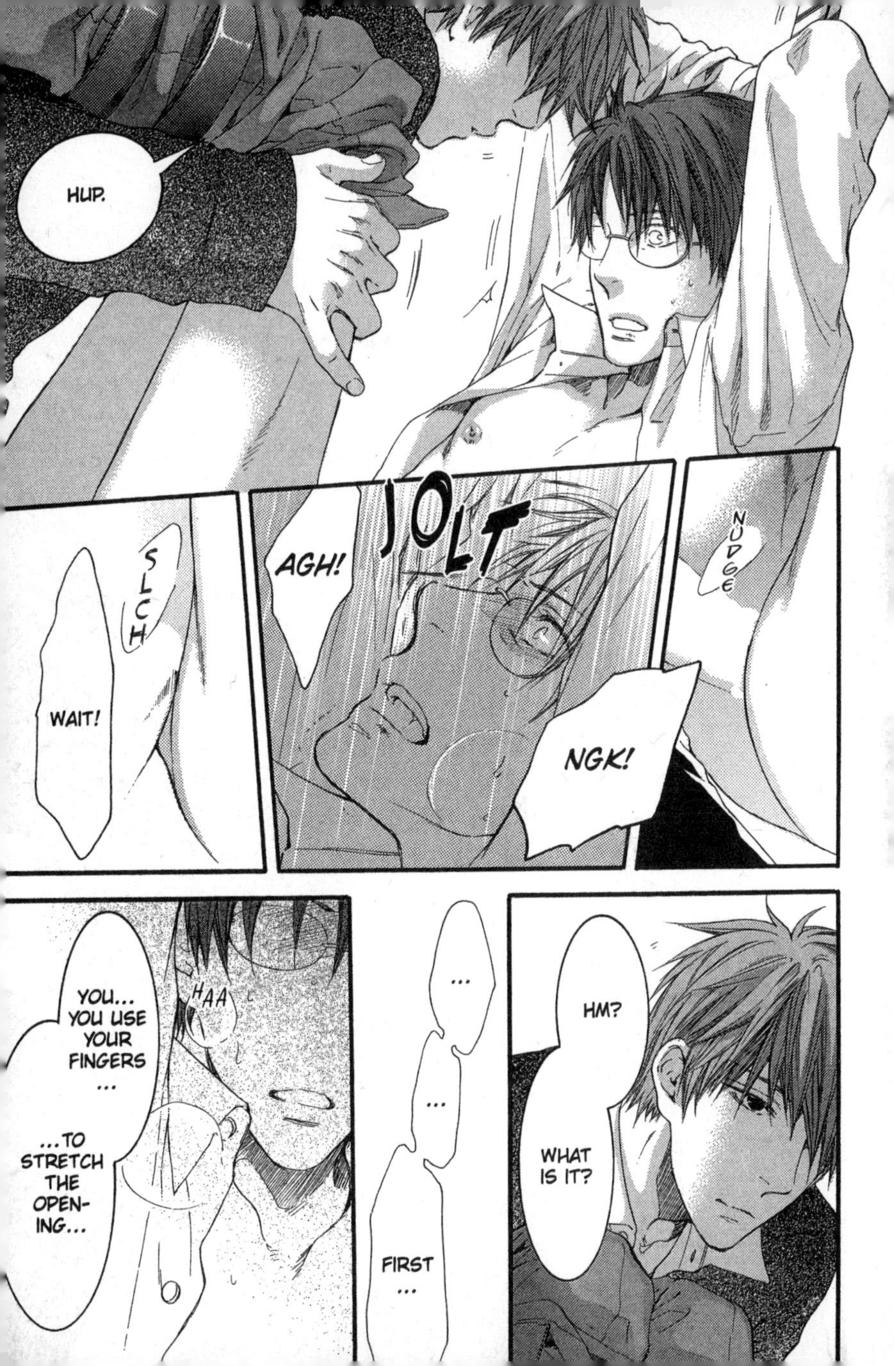
HUP.
NUDGE
NGK!
JOLT
AGH!
SLCH
WAIT!
HM?
WHAT IS IT?
...
...
FIRST ...
YOU... YOU USE YOUR FINGERS ...
...TO STRETCH THE OPENING...
HAA

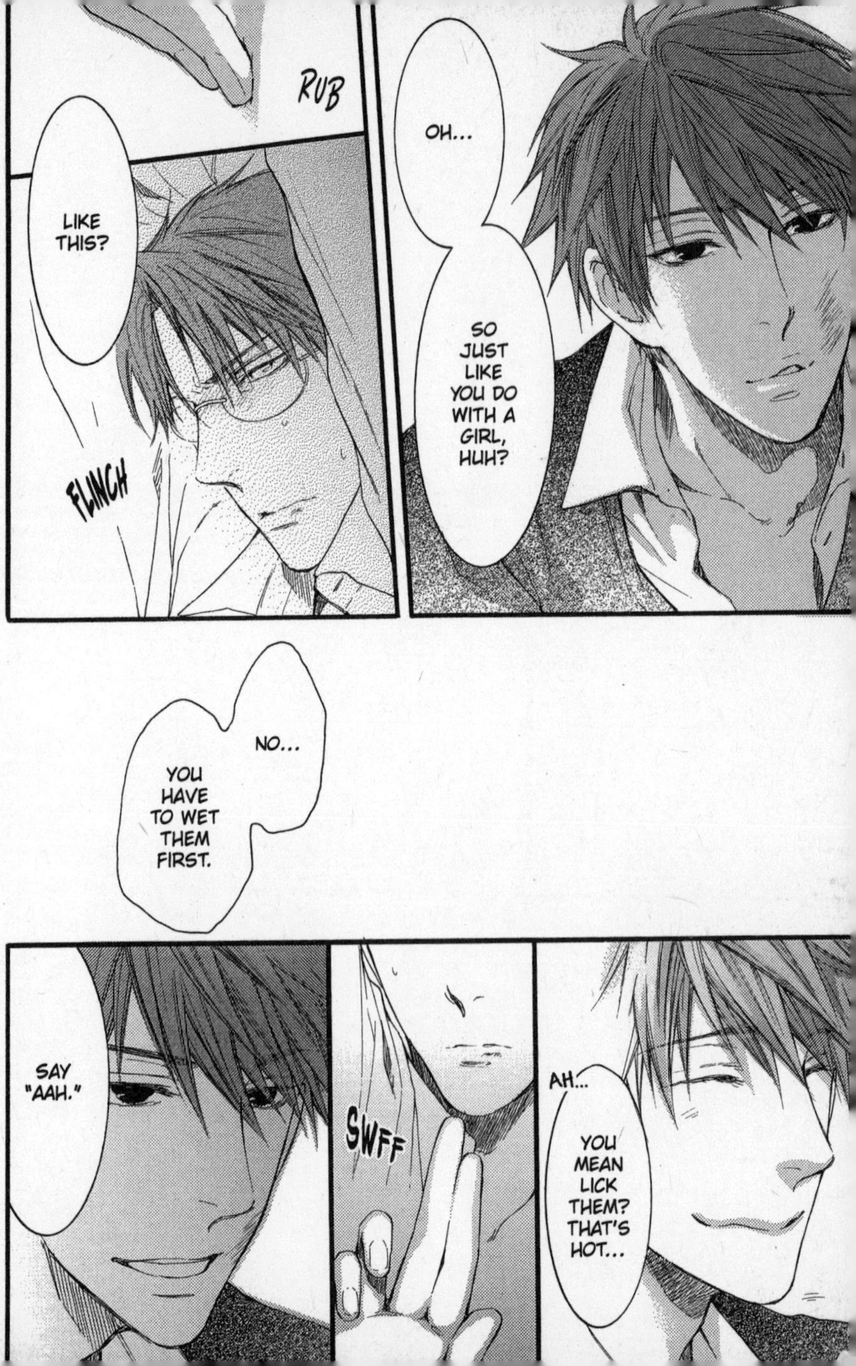
OH...
SO JUST LIKE YOU DO WITH A GIRL, HUH?
RUB
LIKE THIS?
FLINCH
NO...
YOU HAVE TO WET THEM FIRST.
AH...
YOU MEAN LICK THEM? THAT'S HOT...
SWFF
SAY "AAH."

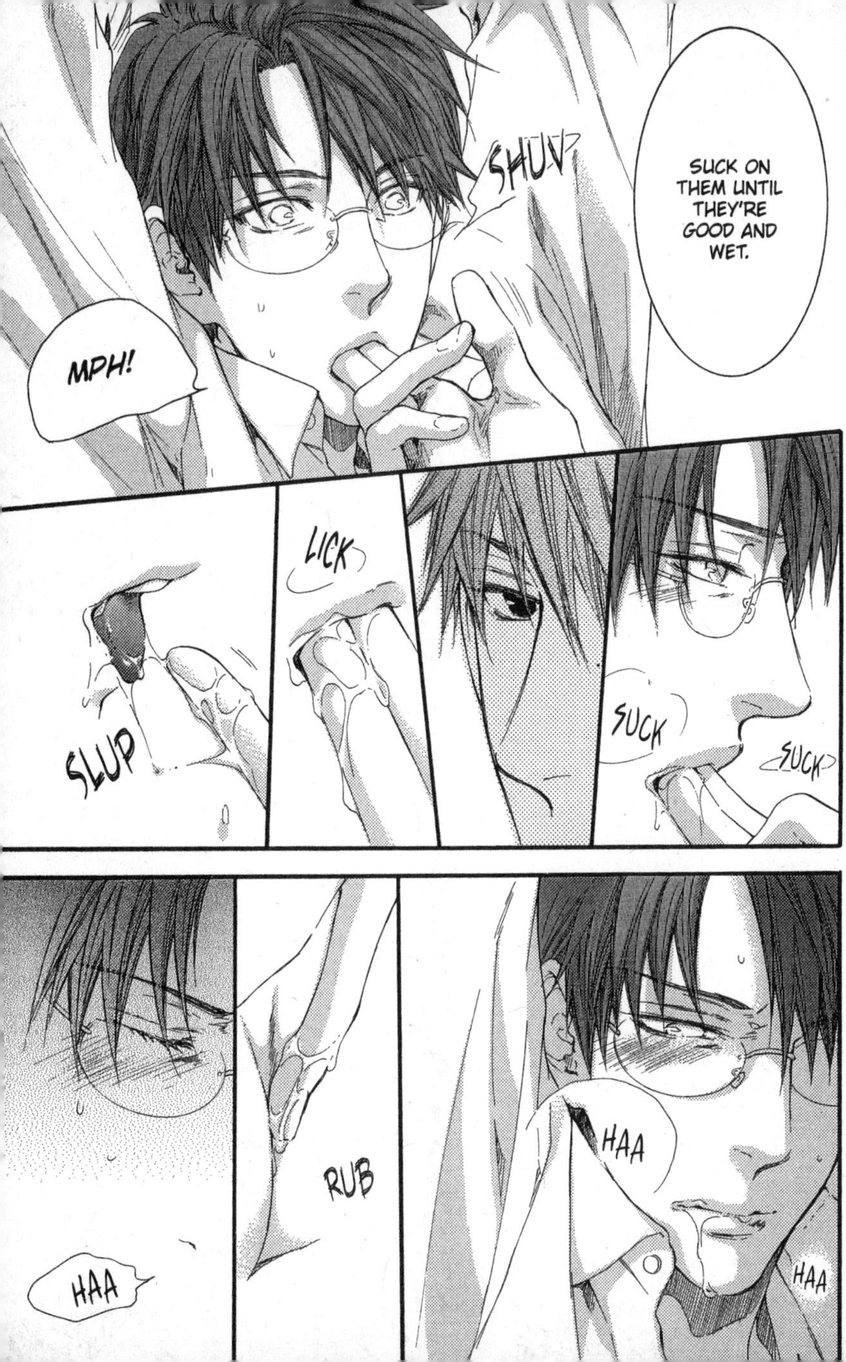
SUCK ON THEM UNTIL THEY'RE GOOD AND WET.
SHUV
MPH!
SUCK
SUCK
LICK
SLUP
HAA
HAA
RUB
HAA

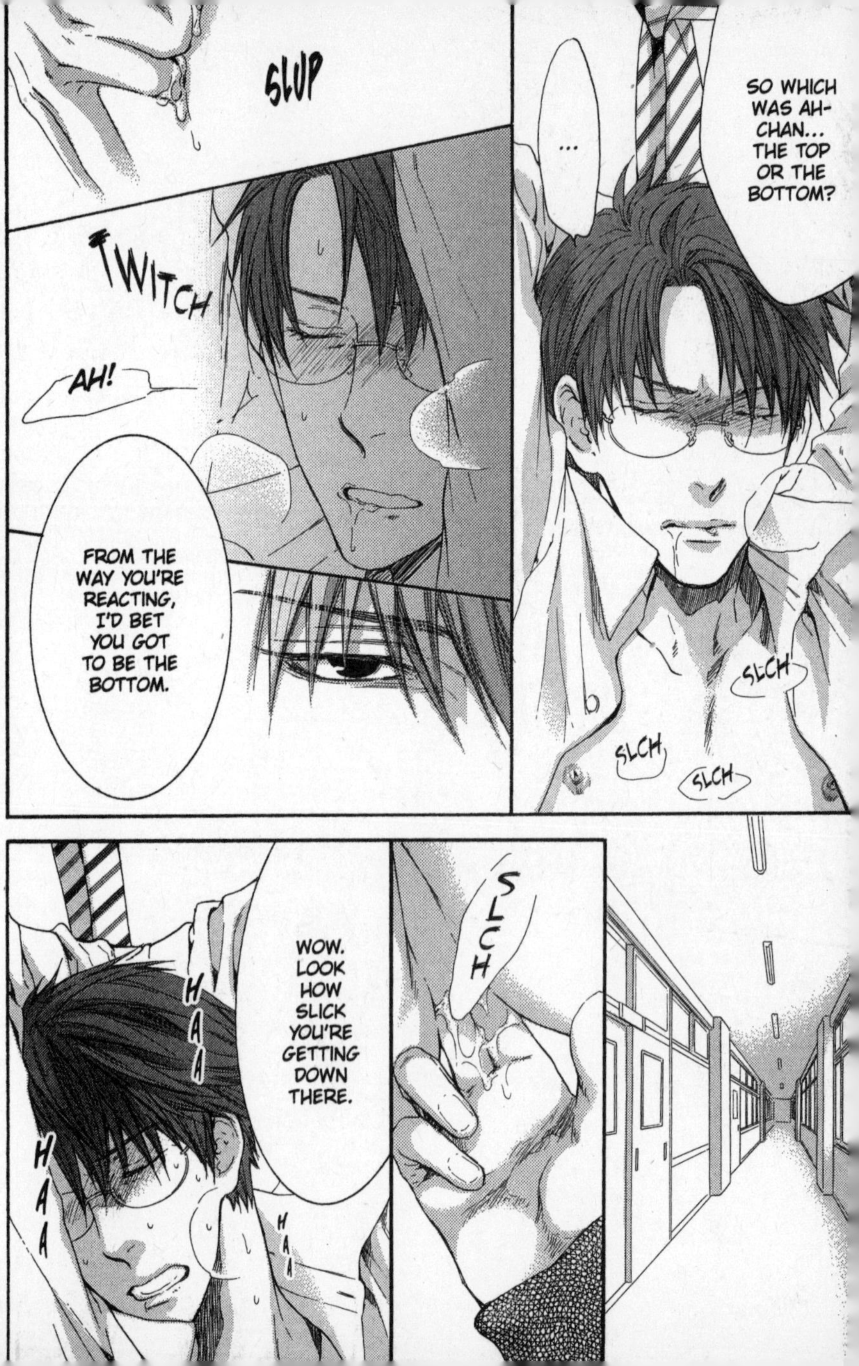
...
SO WHICH WAS AH-CHAN... THE TOP OR THE BOTTOM?
SLCH
SLCH
SLCH
SLUP
TWITCH
AH!
FROM THE WAY YOU'RE REACTING, I'D BET YOU GOT TO BE THE BOTTOM.
SLCH
WOW. LOOK HOW SLICK YOU'RE GETTING DOWN THERE.
HAA
HAA
HAA

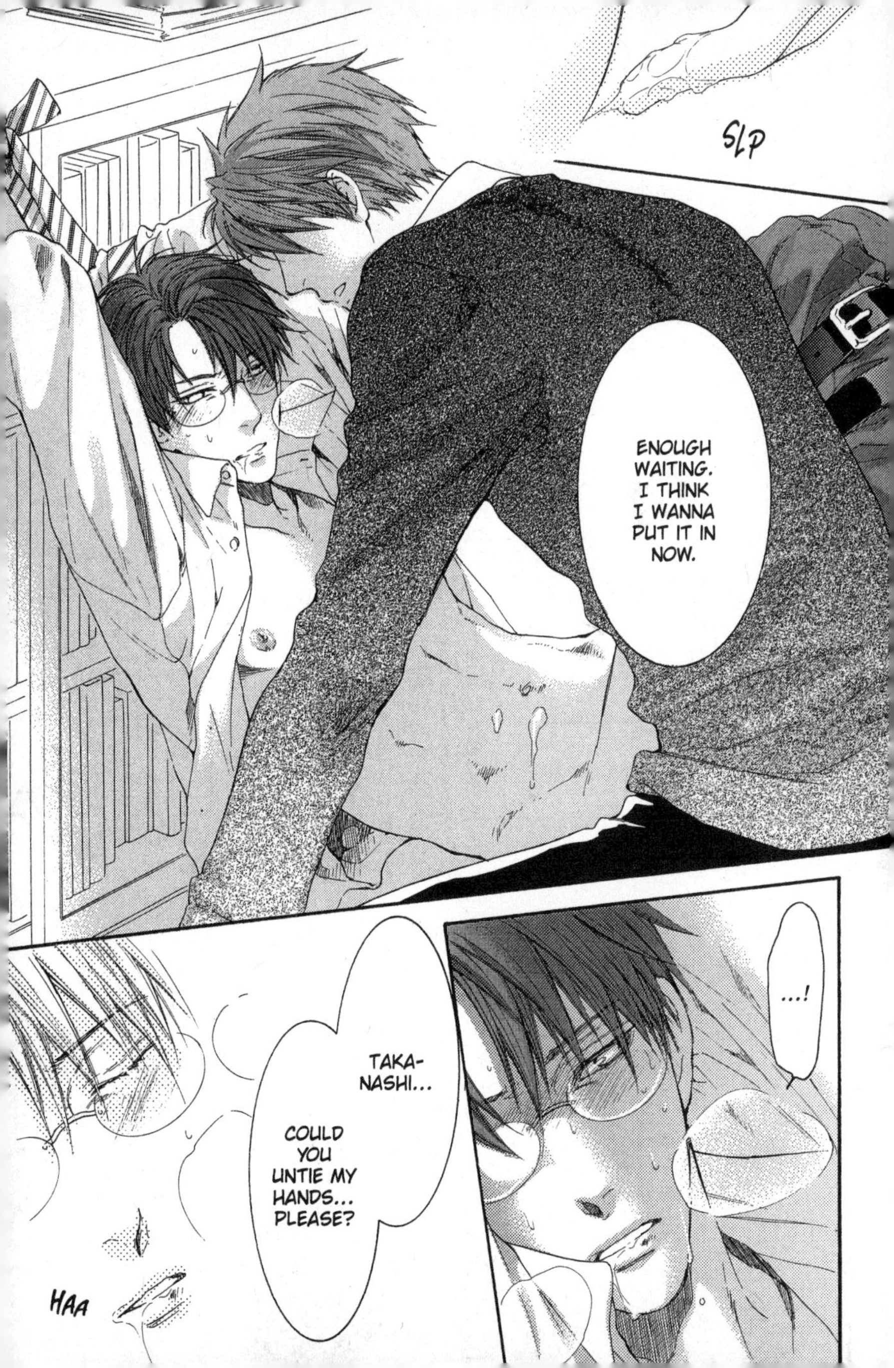
SLP
ENOUGH WAITING. I THINK I WANNA PUT IT IN NOW.
...!
TAKA-NASHI...
COULD YOU UNTIE MY HANDS... PLEASE?
HAA

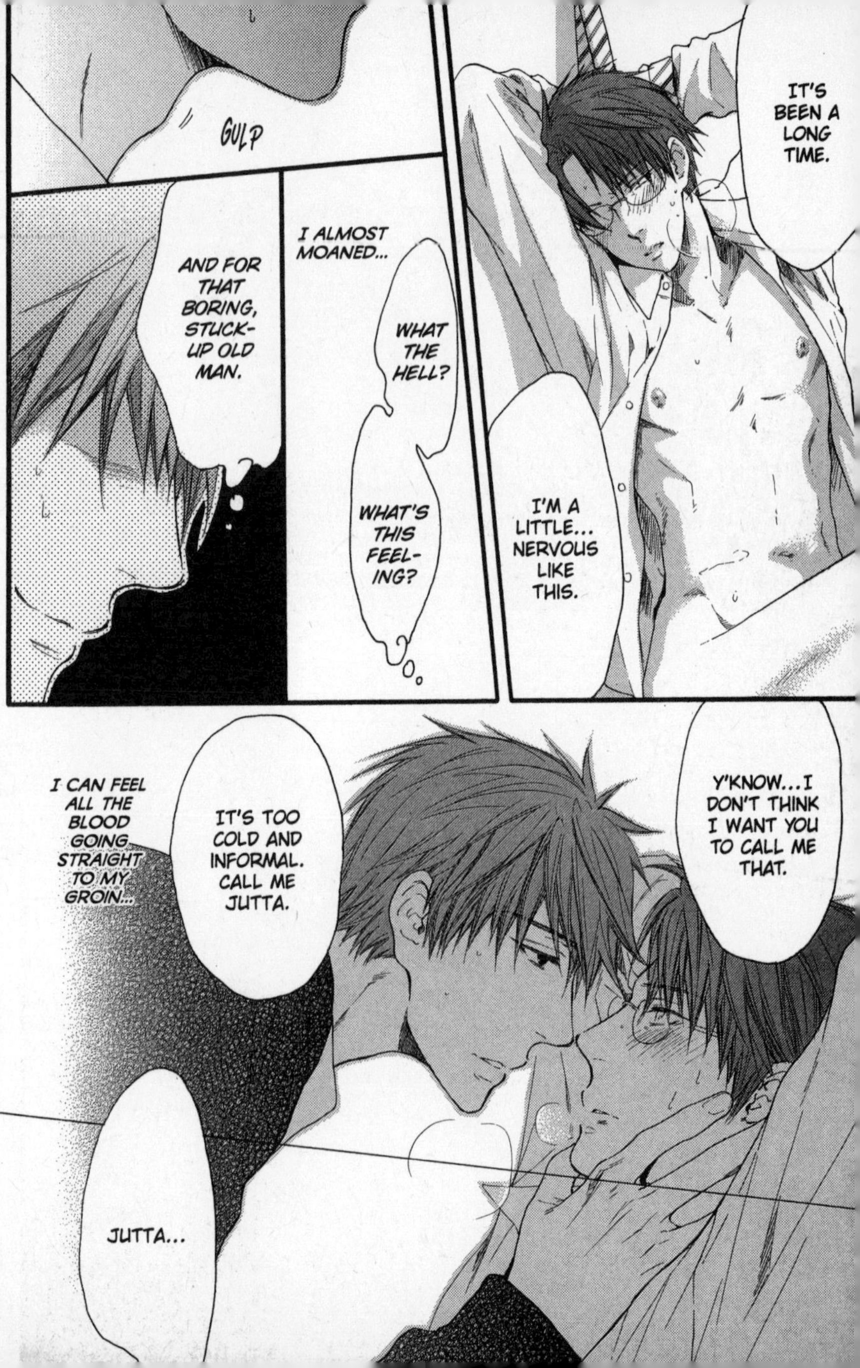
IT'S BEEN A LONG TIME.
I'M A LITTLE... NERVOUS LIKE THIS.
GULP
I ALMOST MOANED...
WHAT THE HELL?
WHAT'S THIS FEELING?
AND FOR THAT BORING, STUCK-UP OLD MAN.
Y'KNOW...I DON'T THINK I WANT YOU TO CALL ME THAT.
IT'S TOO COLD AND INFORMAL. CALL ME JUTTA.
I CAN FEEL ALL THE BLOOD GOING STRAIGHT TO MY GROIN...
JUTTA...

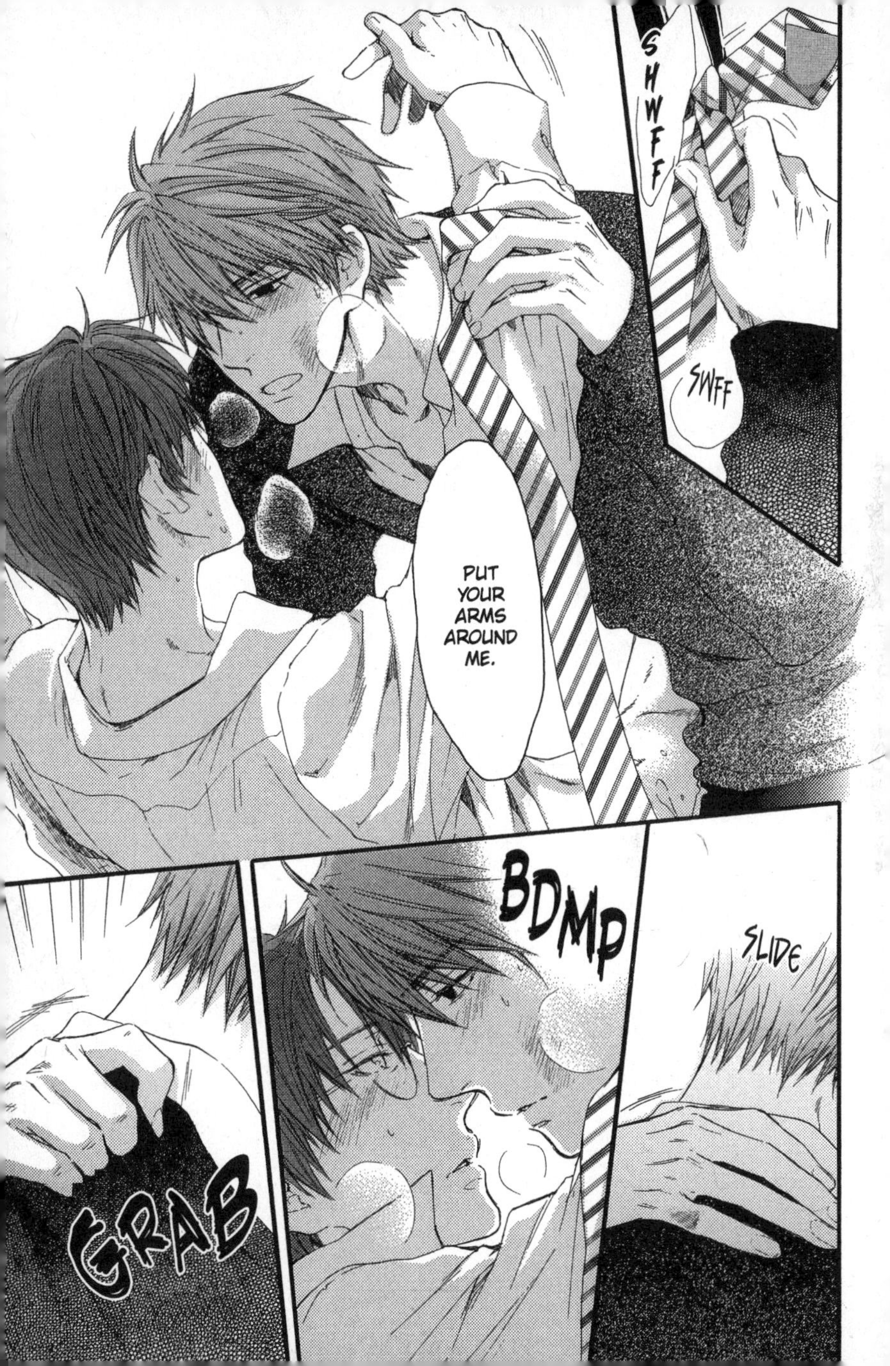
SHWFF
SWFF
PUT YOUR ARMS AROUND ME.
SLIDE
BDMP
GRAB

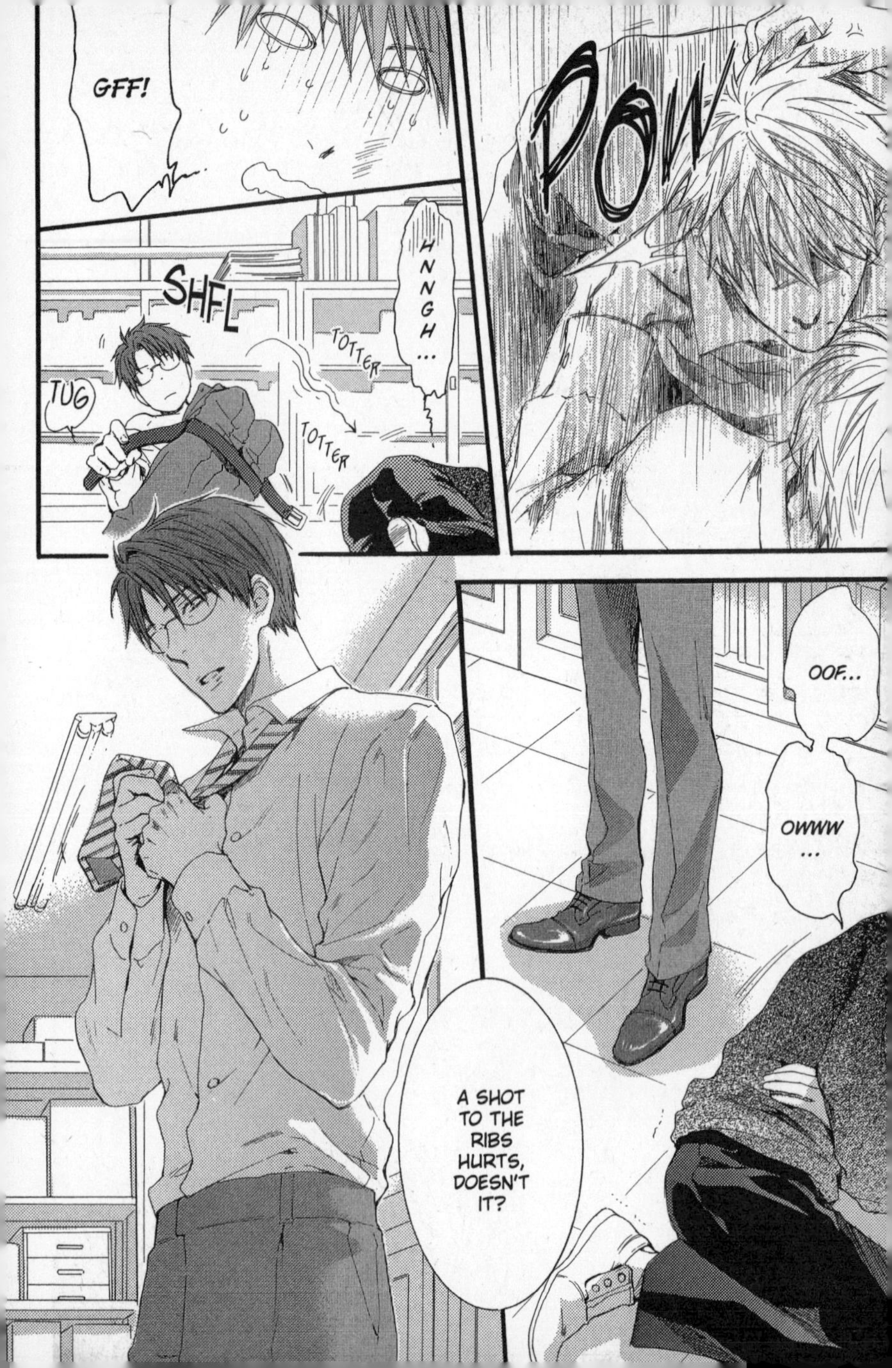
POW
GFF!
HNNGH...
SHFL
TOTTER
TOTTER
TUG
OOF...
OWWW...
A SHOT TO THE RIBS HURTS, DOESN'T IT?

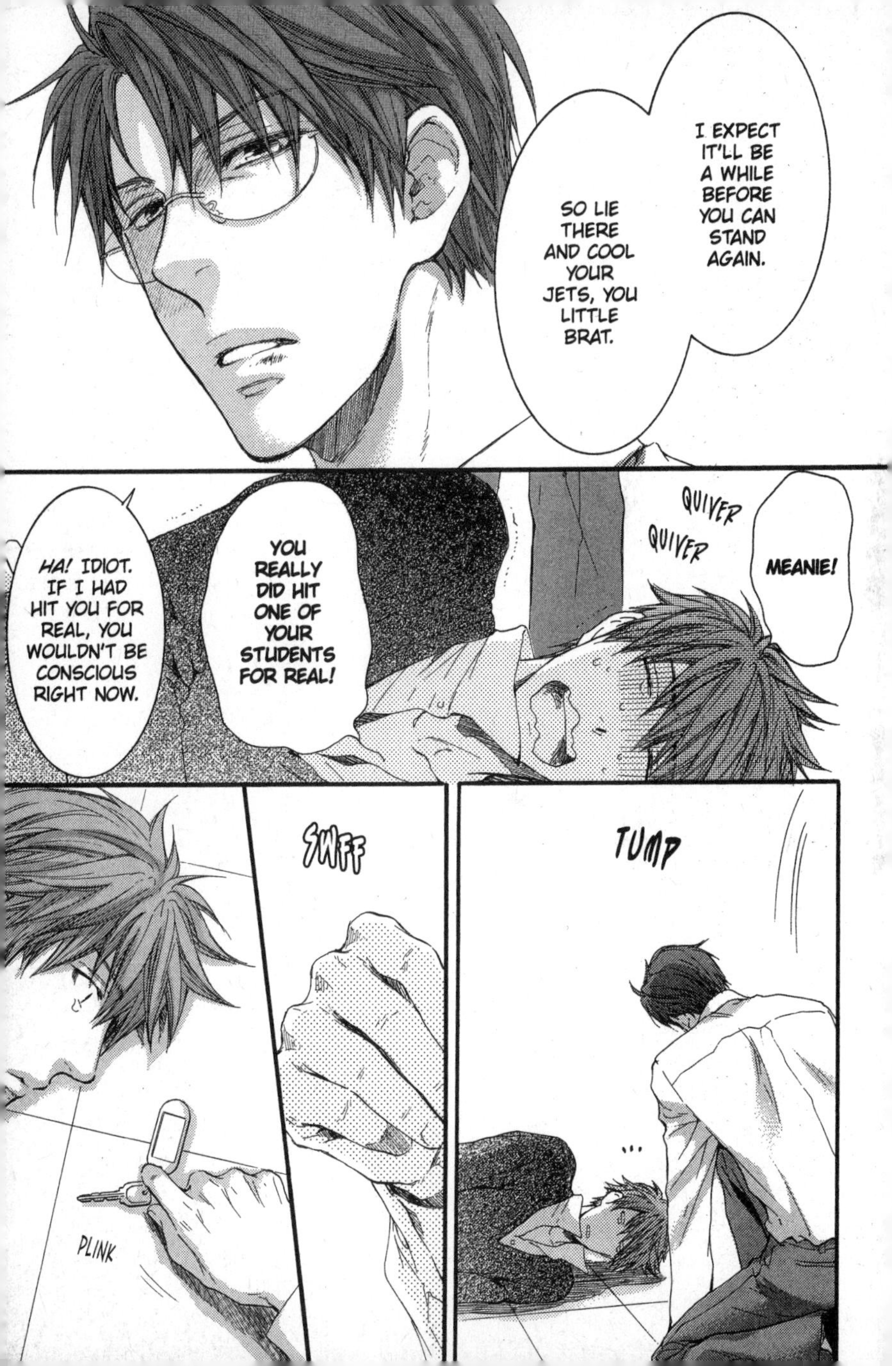
I EXPECT IT'LL BE A WHILE BEFORE YOU CAN STAND AGAIN.
SO LIE THERE AND COOL YOUR JETS, YOU LITTLE BRAT.
MEANIE!
QUIVER QUIVER
YOU REALLY DID HIT ONE OF YOUR STUDENTS FOR REAL!
HA! IDIOT. IF I HAD HIT YOU FOR REAL, YOU WOULDN'T BE CONSCIOUS RIGHT NOW.
TUMP
...
SWFF
PLINK

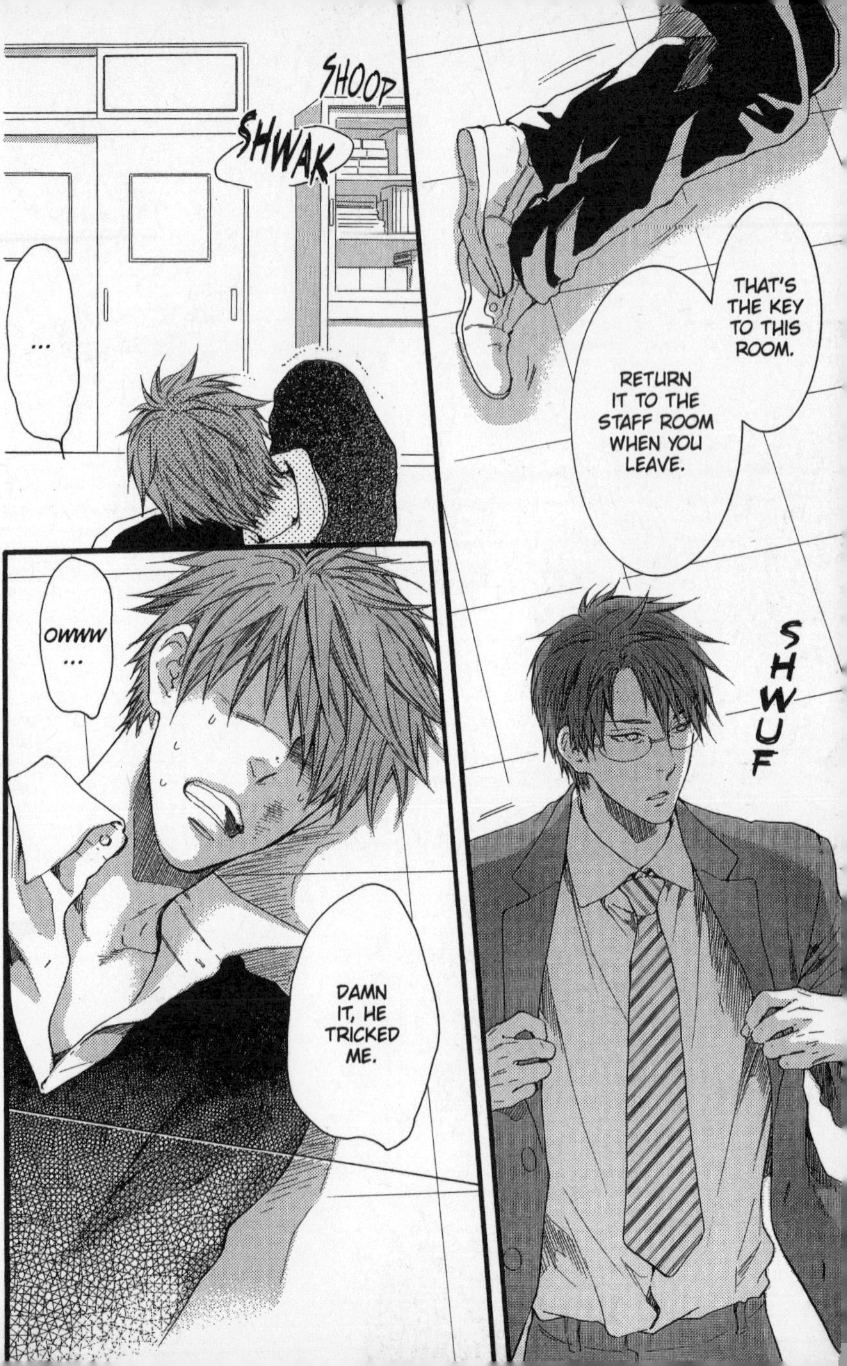
THAT'S THE KEY TO THIS ROOM.
RETURN IT TO THE STAFF ROOM WHEN YOU LEAVE.
SHWUF
SHOOP
SHWAK
...
OWWW ...
DAMN IT, HE TRICKED ME.

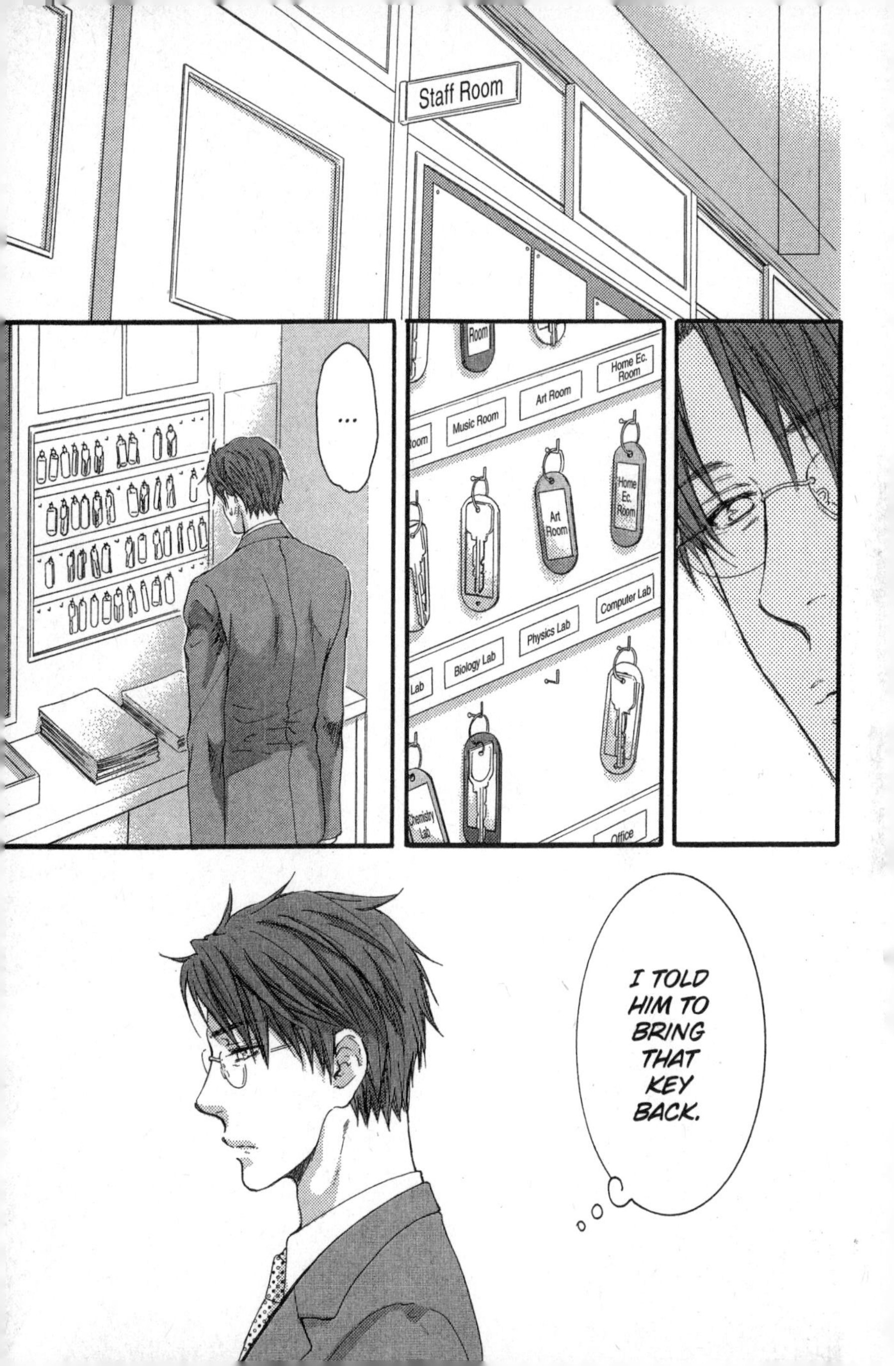
Staff Room
Room
Home Ec. Room
Art Room
Music Room
Home Ec. Room
Art Room
Computer Lab
Physics Lab
Biology Lab
Lab
Chemistry Lab
Office
...
I TOLD HIM TO BRING THAT KEY BACK.

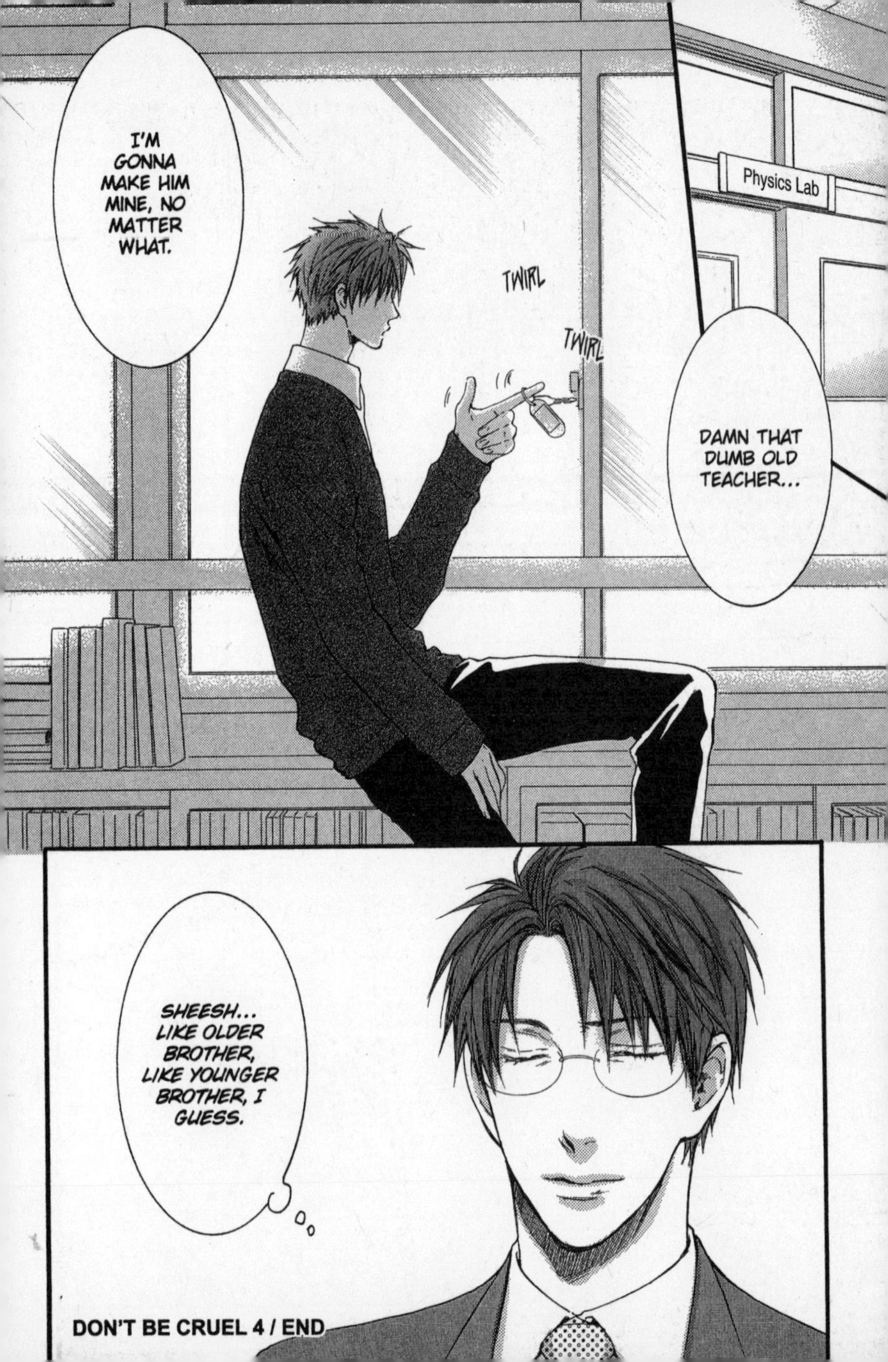
Physics Lab
DAMN THAT DUMB OLD TEACHER...
TWIRL
TWIRL
I'M GONNA MAKE HIM MINE, NO MATTER WHAT.
SHEESH... LIKE OLDER BROTHER, LIKE YOUNGER BROTHER, I GUESS.

DON'T BE CRUEL 4 / END

A: I Want to Take Your Yukata Off

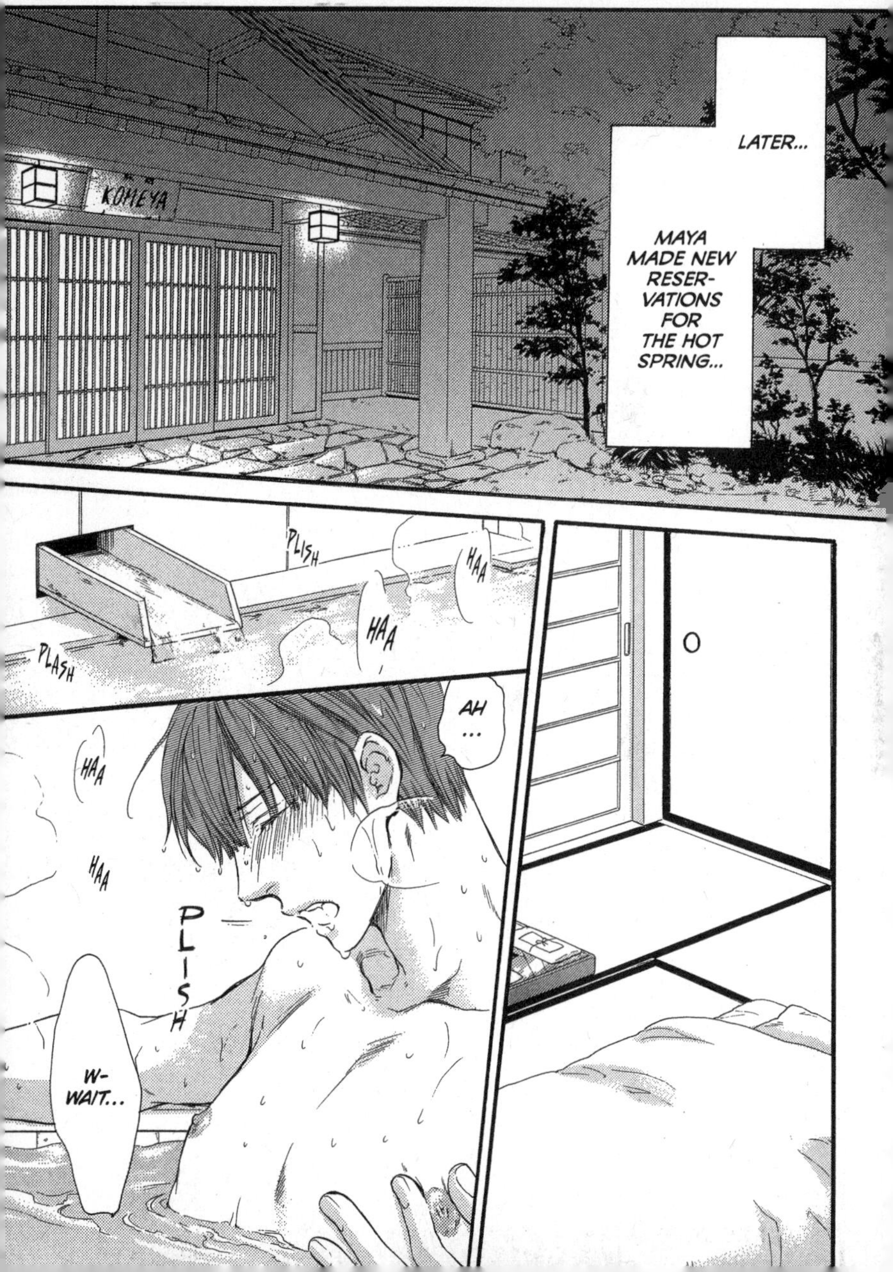
KOMEYA
LATER...
MAYA MADE NEW RESER-VATIONS FOR THE HOT SPRING...
HAA
PLISH
HAA
PLASH
AH...
HAA
HAA
PLISH
W-WAIT...

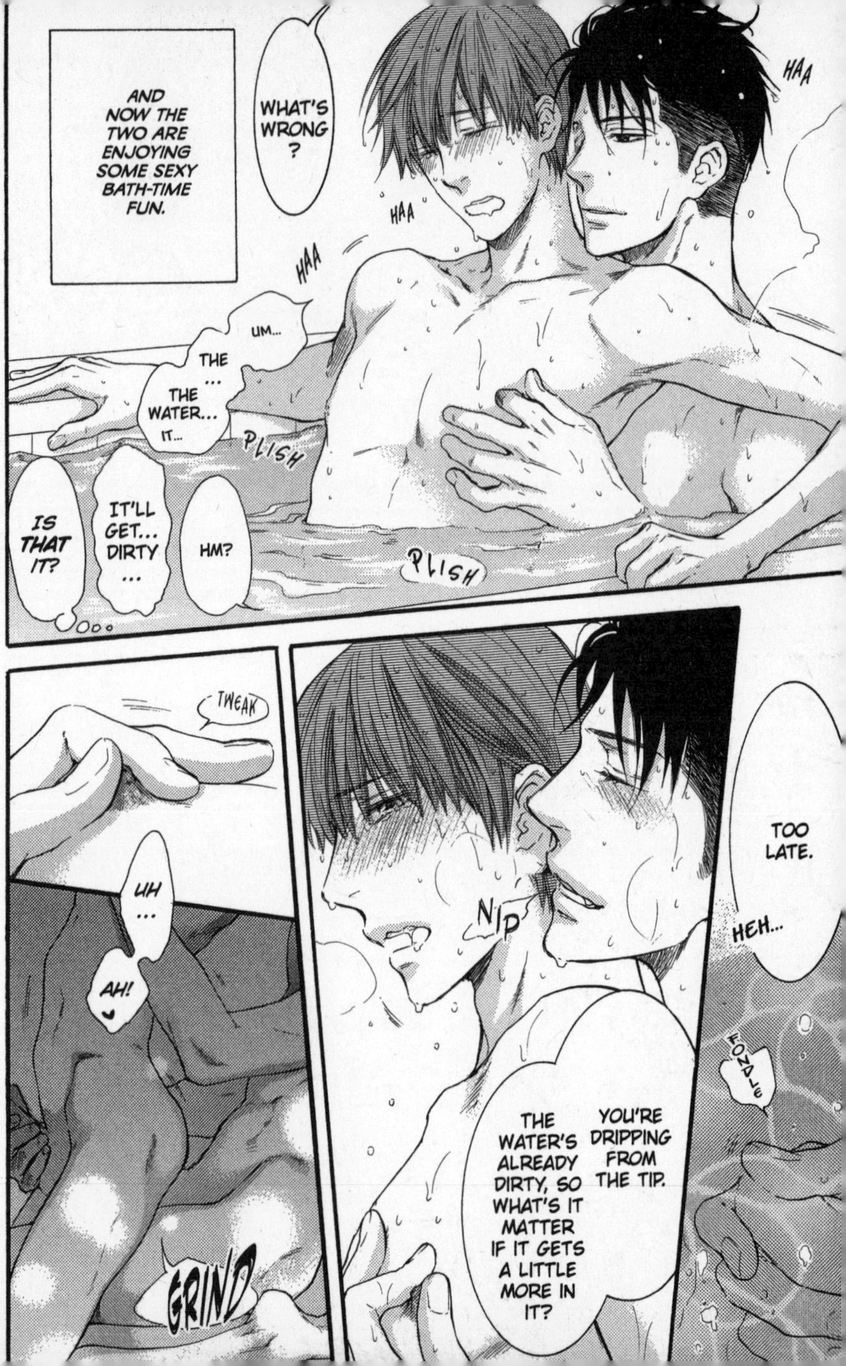
HAA
WHAT'S WRONG?
AND NOW THE TWO ARE ENJOYING SOME SEXY BATH-TIME FUN.
HAA
HAA
UM... THE... THE WATER... IT...
PLISH
HM?
IT'LL GET... DIRTY...
IS THAT IT?
PLISH
TOO LATE.
HEH...
NIP
FONDLE
YOU'RE DRIPPING FROM THE TIP.
THE WATER'S ALREADY DIRTY, SO WHAT'S IT MATTER IF IT GETS A LITTLE MORE IN IT?
TWEAK
UH...
AH!
GRIND

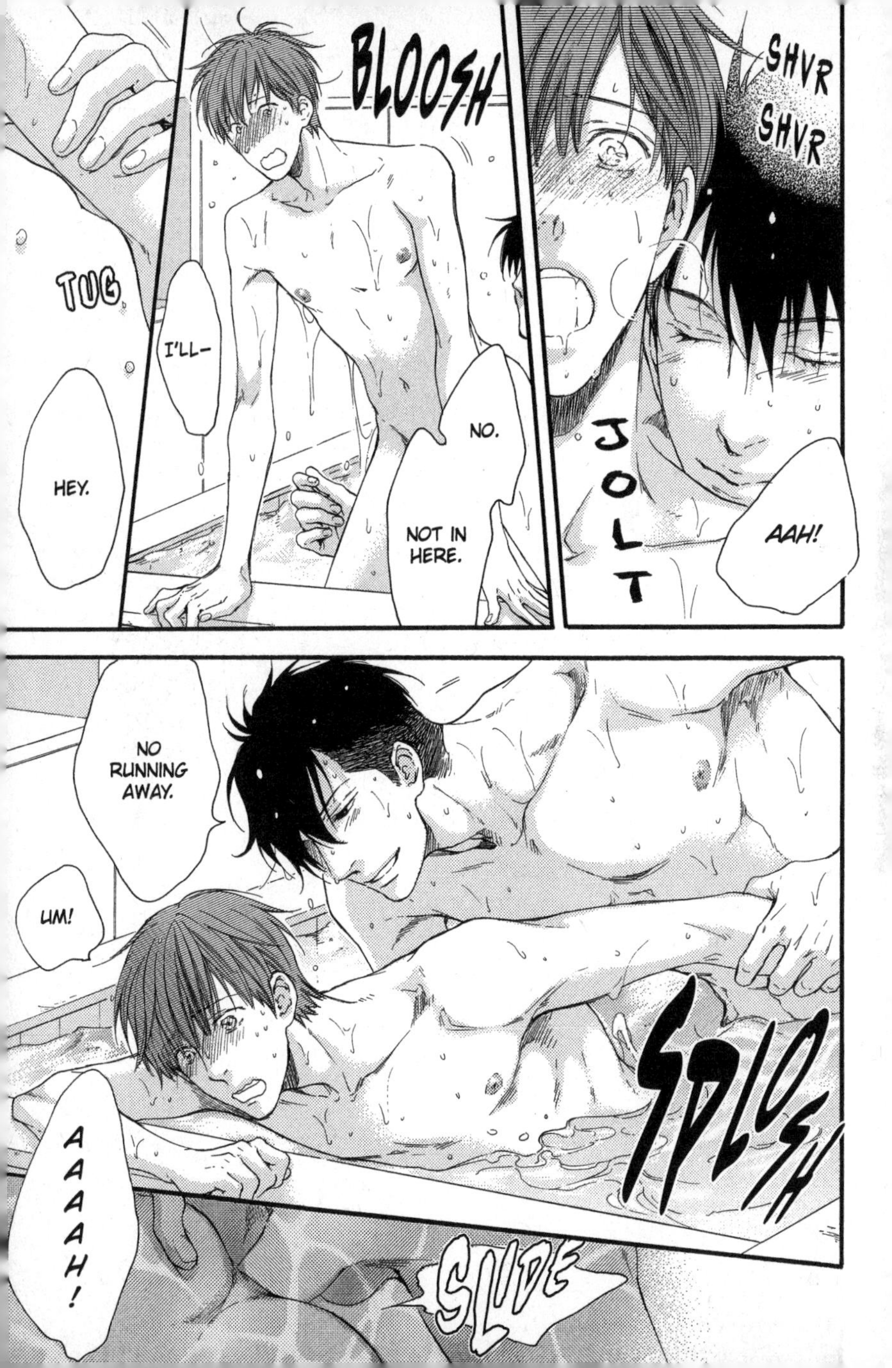

SHVR SHVR
JOLT
AAH!
BLOOSH
NO.
NOT IN HERE.
I'LL—
TUG
HEY.
SPLOSH!
NO RUNNING AWAY.
UM!
SLIDE
AAAAAH!

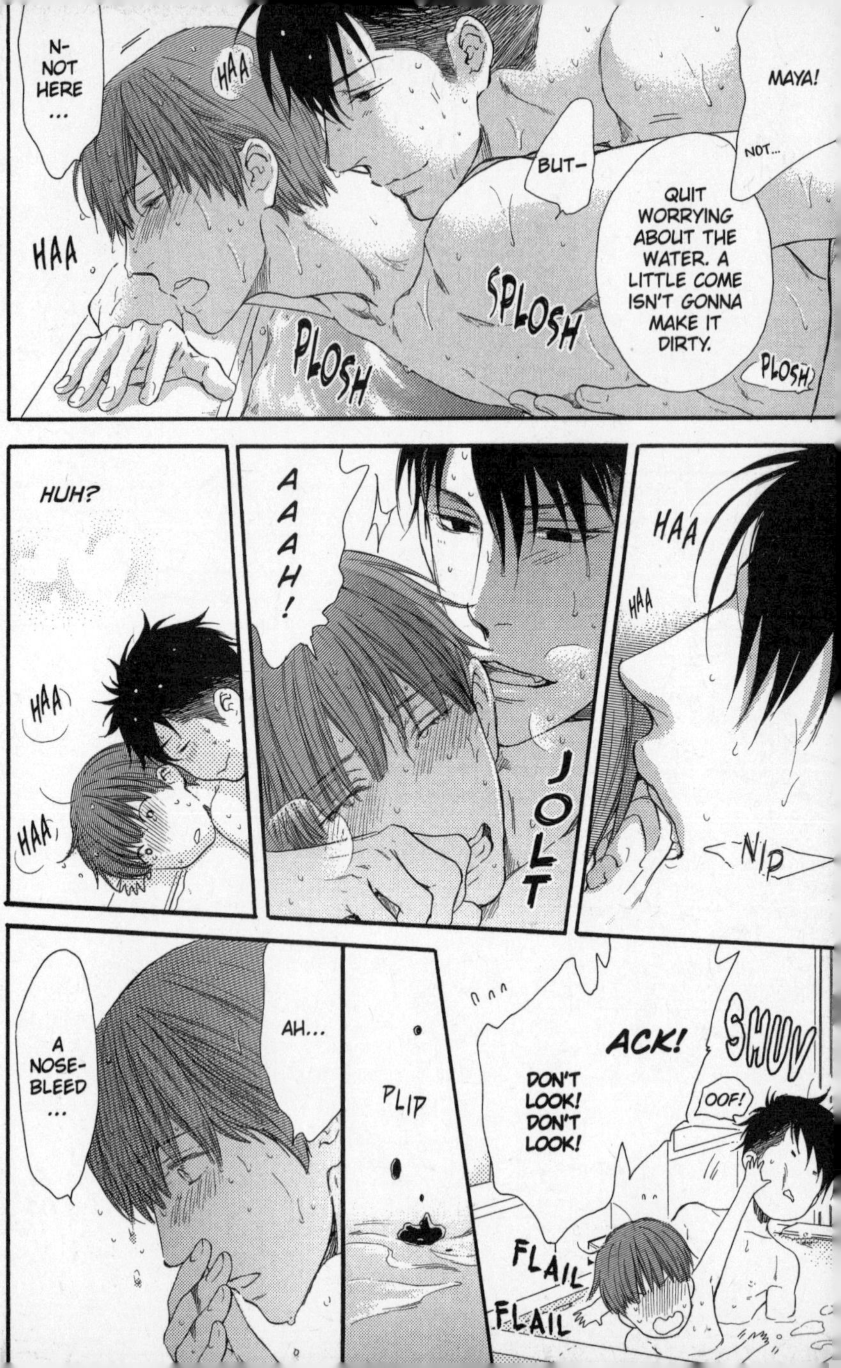
MAYA!
NOT...
BUT–
HAA
N-NOT HERE...
QUIT WORRYING ABOUT THE WATER. A LITTLE COME ISN'T GONNA MAKE IT DIRTY.
SPLOSH
PLOSH
PLOSH
HAA
HAA
HAA
NIP
AAAAH!
JOLT
HUH?
HAA
HAA
SHUV
ACK!
OOF!
DON'T LOOK! DON'T LOOK!
FLAIL
FLAIL
AH...
PLIP
A NOSE-BLEED...

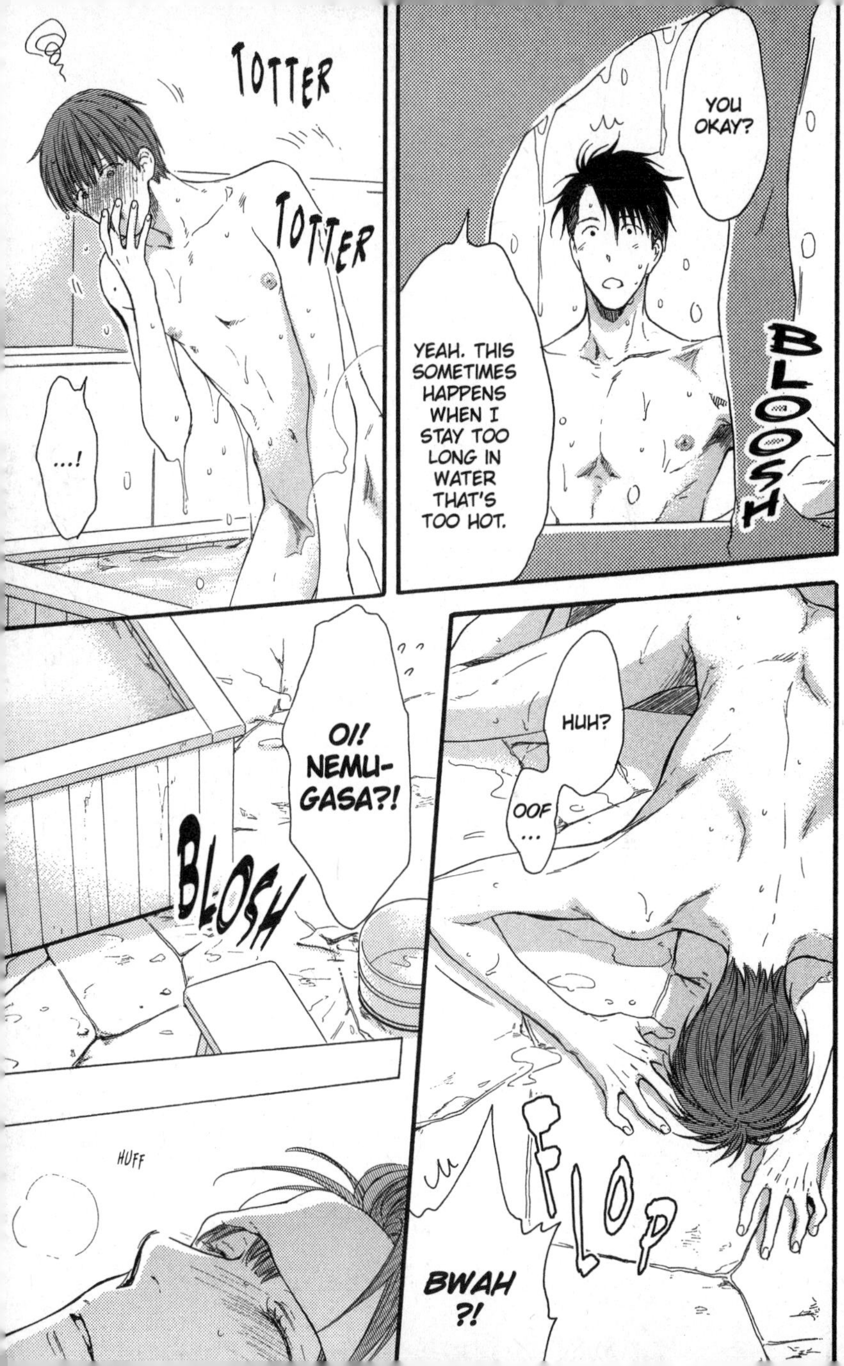
YOU OKAY?
BLOOSH
YEAH. THIS SOMETIMES HAPPENS WHEN I STAY TOO LONG IN WATER THAT'S TOO HOT.
TOTTER
TOTTER
...!
HUH?
OOF ...
FLOP
BWAH ?!
OI! NEMU-GASA?!
BLOSH
HUFF

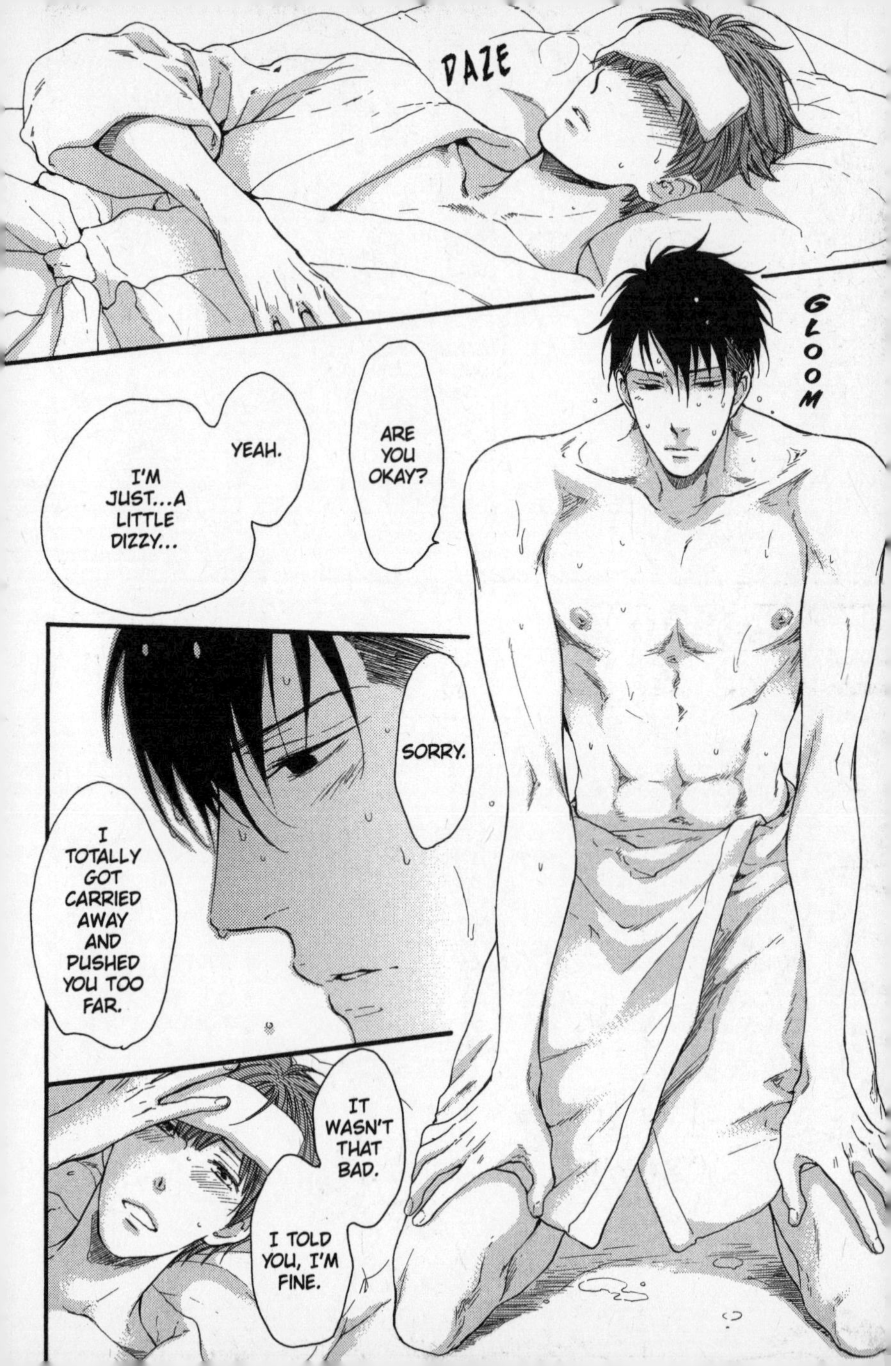
DAZE
GLOOM
ARE YOU OKAY?
YEAH.
I'M JUST...A LITTLE DIZZY...
SORRY.
I TOTALLY GOT CARRIED AWAY AND PUSHED YOU TOO FAR.
IT WASN'T THAT BAD.
I TOLD YOU, I'M FINE.

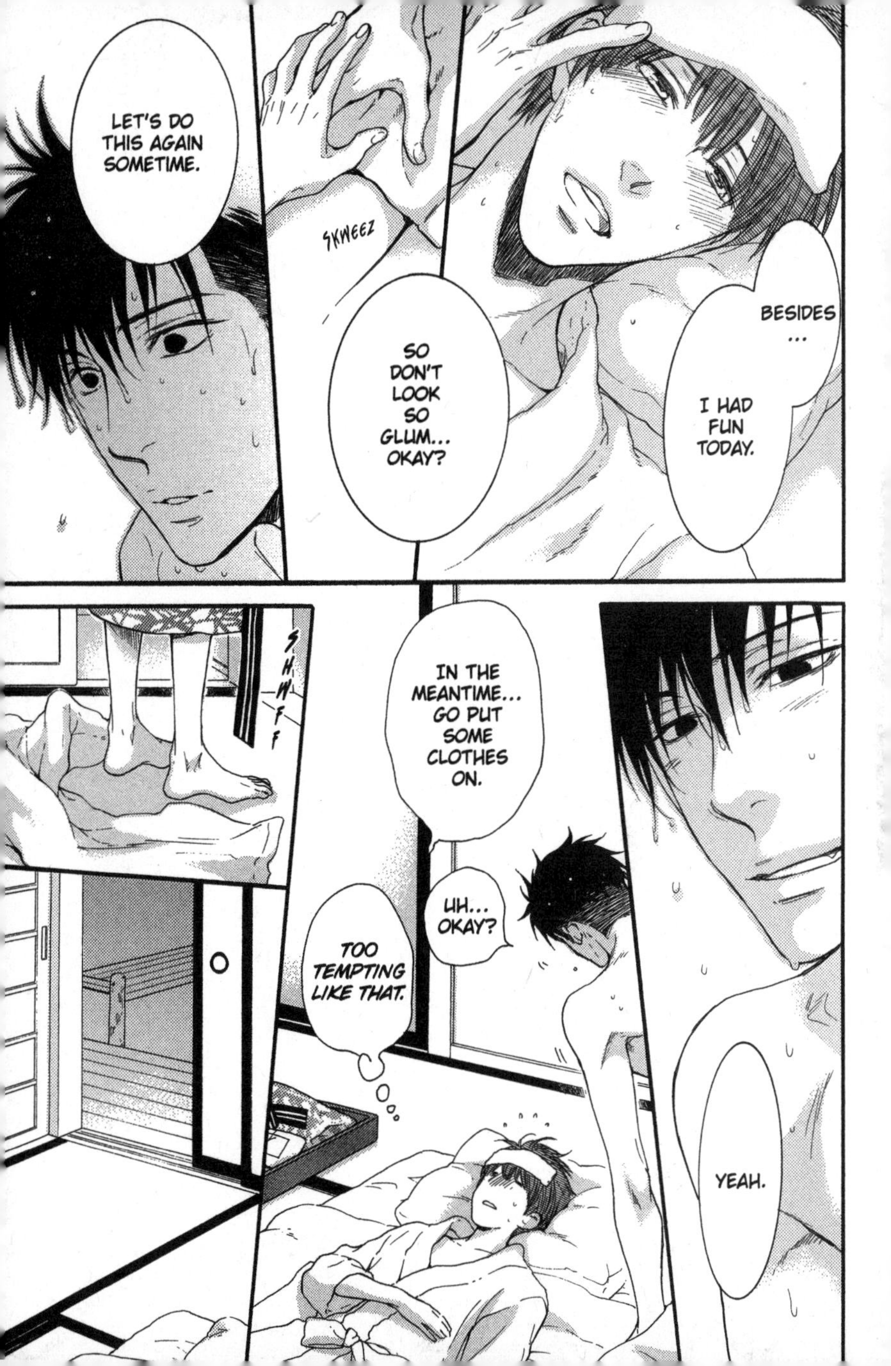
BESIDES...
I HAD FUN TODAY.
SO DON'T LOOK SO GLUM... OKAY?
SKWEEZ
LET'S DO THIS AGAIN SOMETIME.
YEAH.
IN THE MEANTIME... GO PUT SOME CLOTHES ON.
UH... OKAY?
TOO TEMPTING LIKE THAT.
SHWFF

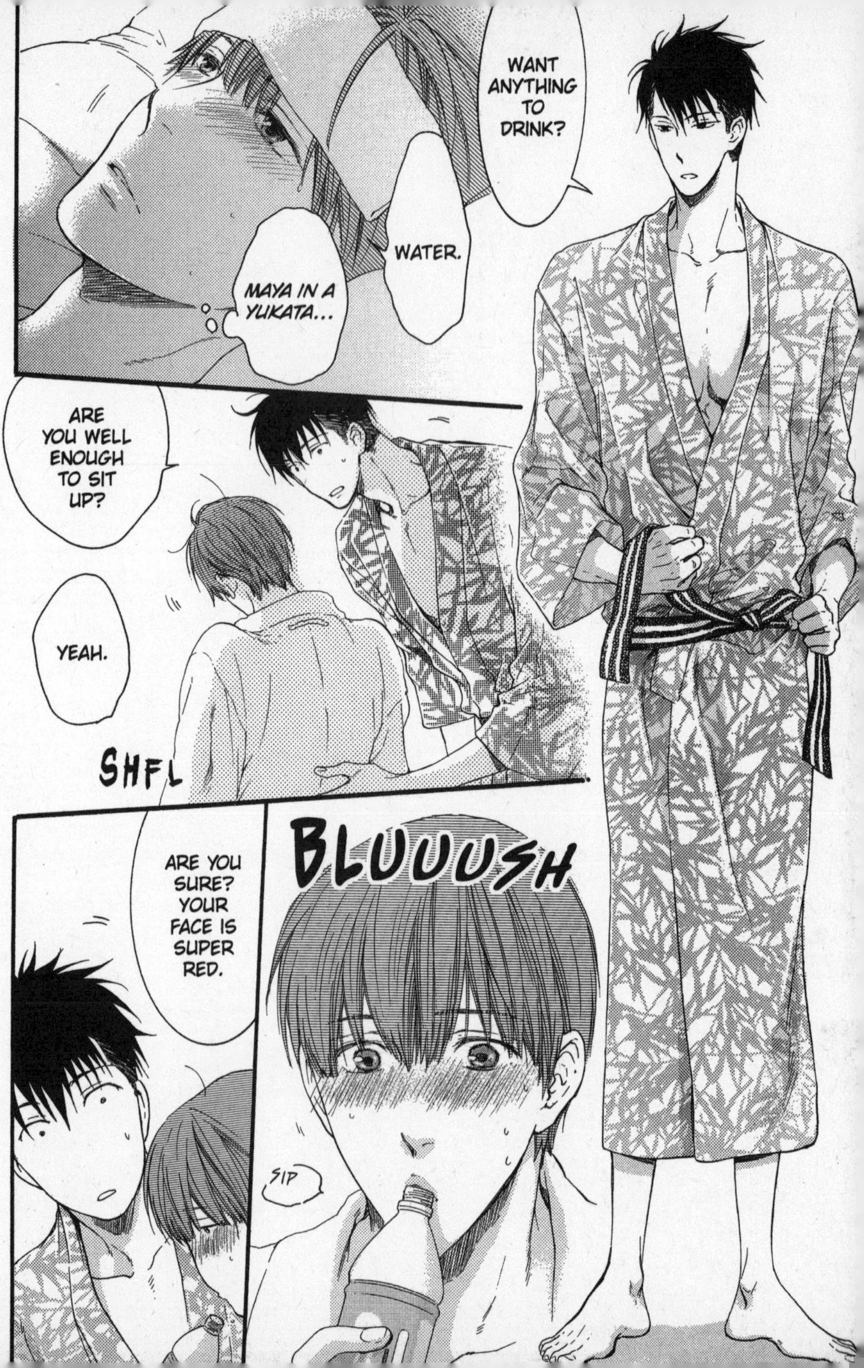
WANT ANYTHING TO DRINK?
WATER.
MAYA IN A YUKATA...
ARE YOU WELL ENOUGH TO SIT UP?
YEAH.
SHFL
BLUUUSH
SIP
ARE YOU SURE? YOUR FACE IS SUPER RED.

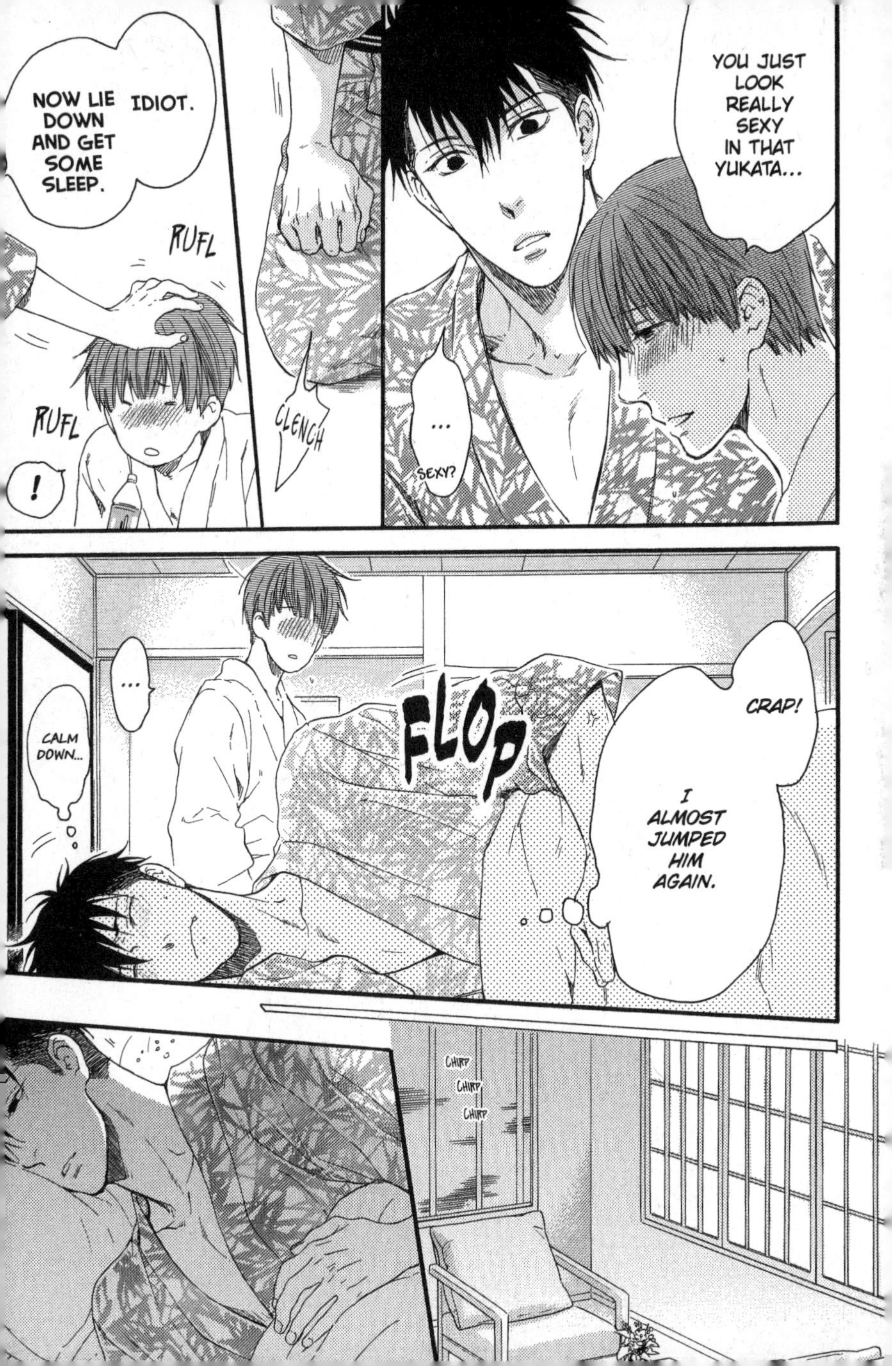
YOU JUST LOOK REALLY SEXY IN THAT YUKATA...
...
SEXY?
CLENCH
IDIOT.
NOW LIE DOWN AND GET SOME SLEEP.
RUFL
RUFL
!
CRAP!
I ALMOST JUMPED HIM AGAIN.
FLOP
...
CALM DOWN...
CHIRP
CHIRP
CHIRP

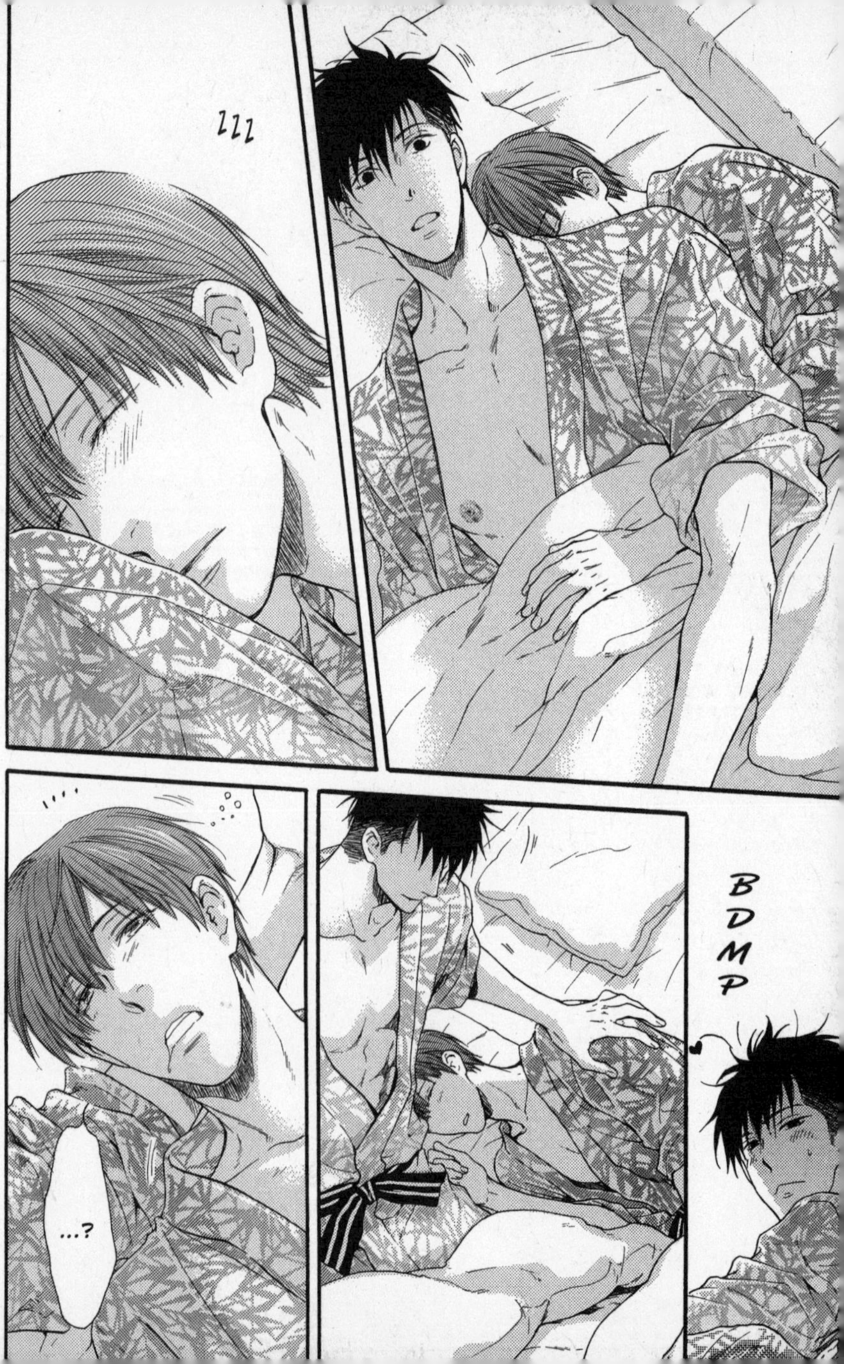
ZZZ
BDMP
...?

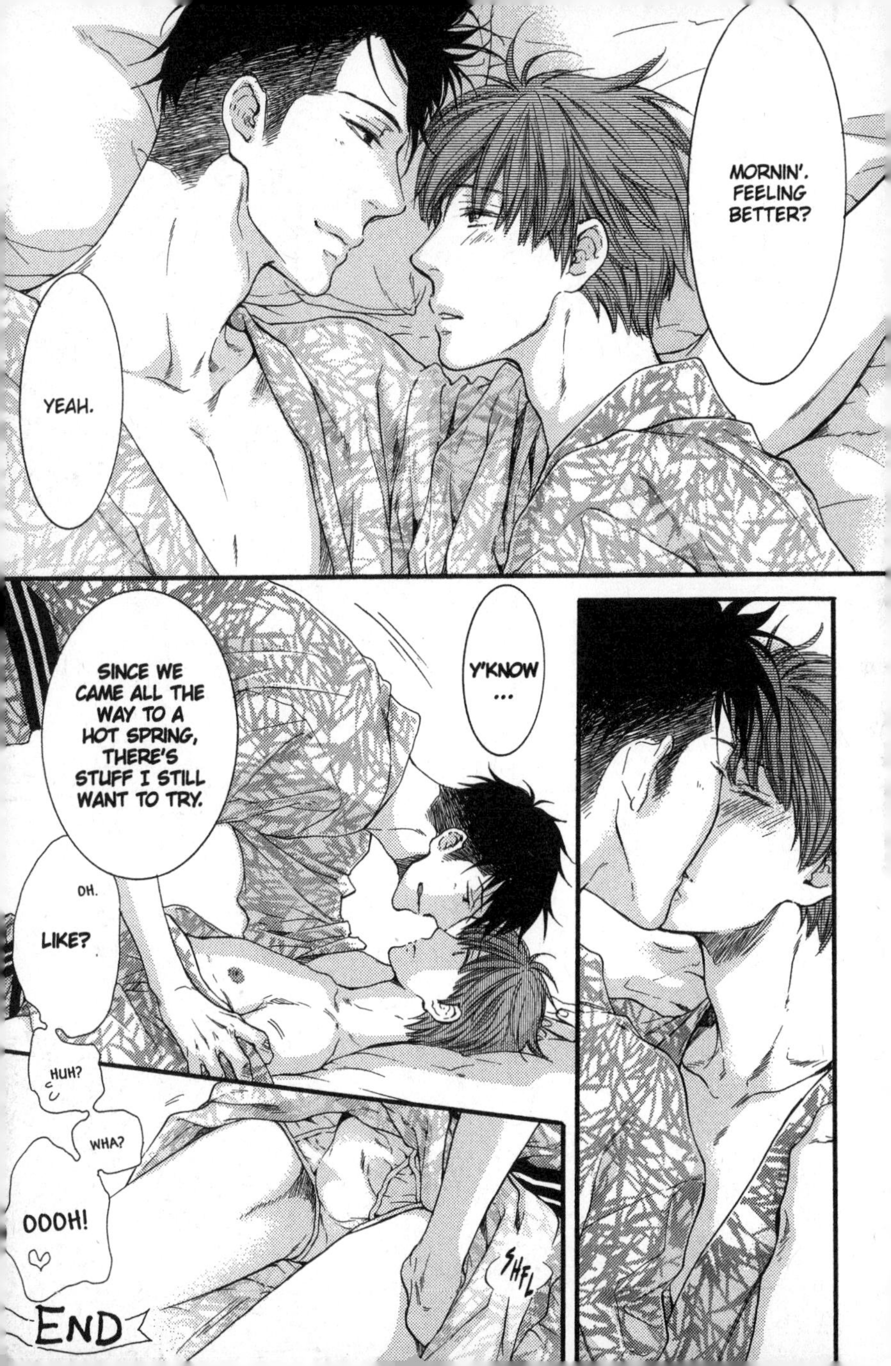
MORNIN'. FEELING BETTER?
YEAH.
Y'KNOW ...
SINCE WE CAME ALL THE WAY TO A HOT SPRING, THERE'S STUFF I STILL WANT TO TRY.
OH.
LIKE?
SHFL
HUH?
WHA?
OOOH!
END

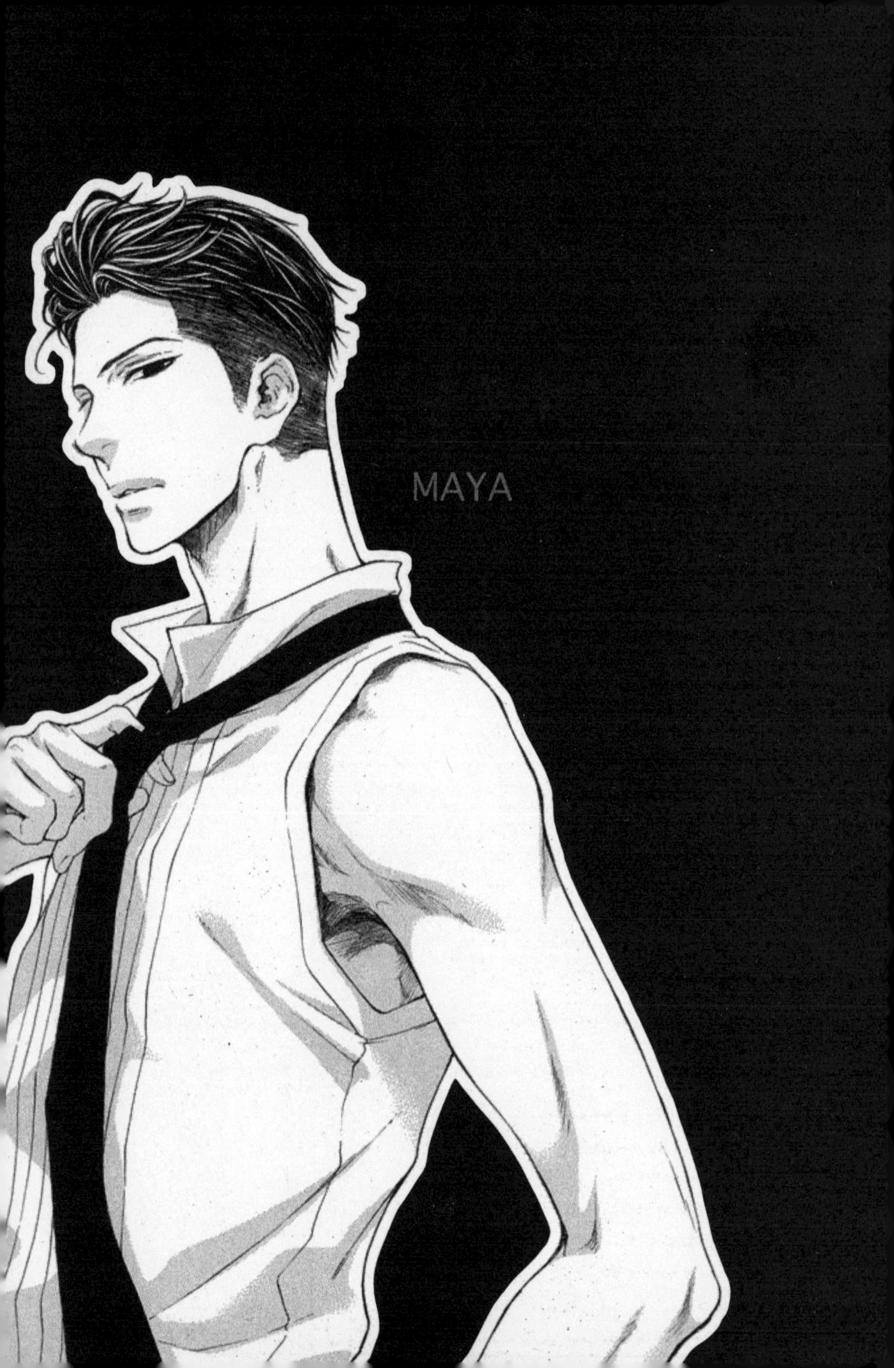
MAYA

AFTERWORD

Start

WELCOME TO VOLUME 4! MAYA AND NEMUGASA ARE COLLEGE STUDENTS NOW. I WANTED TO HAVE NEMUGASA DO ALL KINDS OF NEW THINGS, LIKE GET A PART-TIME JOB AND JOIN A CLUB, BUT I HAVEN'T GOTTEN THE CHANCE TO DRAW THEM.☆ YET, THAT IS. I'M HOPING TO ADD THEM IN BIT BY BIT AS THE STORY CONTINUES TO GROW. AND THEN THERE'S MAYA! HE STARTED SHOWING FLASHES OF MATURITY IN VOLUME 3, AND AFTERWARD I GOT FAN MAIL TELLING ME THAT THEY MISSED HIS PRIDE AND EGOCENTRIC ATTITUDE A LITTLE. BUT Y'KNOW? EVEN THE ROWDIEST OF ROWDY BOYS WILL, UPON REACHING A CERTAIN POINT IN THEIR LIVES, GROW INTO MATURE MEN. I HOPE YOU ALL WILL ENJOY WATCHING MAYA AS HE GOES THROUGH THAT TIME IN HIS LIFE.

OH! SPEAKING OF MAYA, THE ILLUSTRATION OF HIM AT THE START OF THE THIRD CHAPTER WITH HIS HAIR SLICKED BACK GOT A REALLY POSITIVE REACTION WHEN IT FIRST RAN IN THE ANTHOLOGY. I HAD FUN DRAWING IT TOO. LOOKS LIKE I'VE FOUND SOMETHING NEW I CAN PLAY WITH AS I WORK THROUGH THE SERIES. OOH! THEN THERE WAS THE COUPLE-EATING-PIZZA SHOT!♥ IT STARTED OUT A LOT MORE NORMAL WHEN I WAS WORKING THROUGH THE STORYBOARDS, BUT MY EDITOR SAID SHE WANTED THEM TO BE MORE LOVEY-DOVEY, SO I ADDED IN THE PART WHERE MAYA WORRIES NEMU IS ADDING TOO MUCH HOT SAUCE. THAT LITTLE TIDBIT DID NOT GO UNNOTICED BY THE FANS, IT SEEMS. I COULDN'T HELP BUT GRIN AT ALL THE SQUEES.

→ AND FINALLY, THE HOT SPRING TRIP. MANY FANS WERE WORRIED THAT NEMU AND MAYA WOULDN'T GET THE CHANCE TO GO AND ENJOY THEMSELVES, SO FOR THE BONUS CONTENT I DREW A LITTLE *OMAKE* SHOWING THAT, YES, THEY DID GET THEIR HAPPY VACATION. I WAS HOPING TO SHOW OFF MAYA LOOKING HOT IN A PROPER YUKATA, BUT GIVEN HOW TALL HE IS, THEY'D ALL BE TOO SHORT ON HIM ANYWAY. BUT I DID GET TO DRAW HIM LOOKING AS GUILTY AS A NAUGHTY PUPPY, SO I'M HAPPY.♪ OH! OH! AND THEN THERE'S JUTTA AND THE TEACHER. IT SEEMS A LOT OF YOU FANS THOUGHT HE AND AKIRA WOULD GET BACK TOGETHER (!). THE CONCEPT I HAD FOR THE COUPLE WAS AN OLDER, MORE MATURE *UKE* WHO WOULDN'T LET HIMSELF GET CARRIED AWAY BY HIS *SEME*. I'M HOPING TO CONTINUE WITH THEIR STORY A LITTLE BIT HERE AND THERE WHENEVER I CAN, BUT...DOES ANYBODY WANT TO SEE IT? (WHO KNOWS?) ANYWAY, EVERYBODY SEEMED TO LIKE THE GUT PUNCH THE TEACHER LANDED, SO I'M HAPPY.

NOW THEN...THANK YOU ALL SO MUCH FOR STICKING WITH ME THIS LONG. ♡

YONEZOU NEKOTA

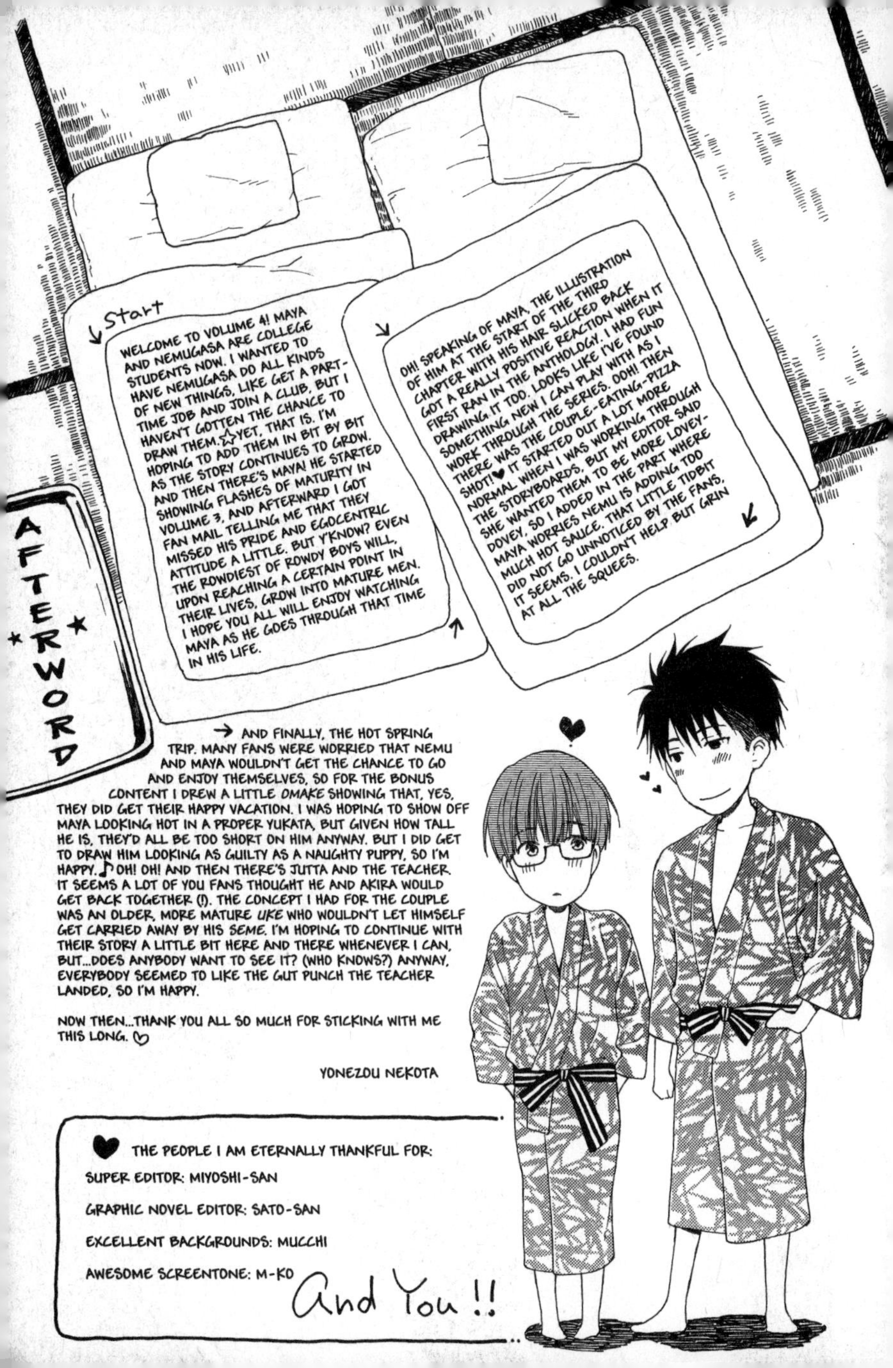

♥ THE PEOPLE I AM ETERNALLY THANKFUL FOR:

SUPER EDITOR: MIYOSHI-SAN

GRAPHIC NOVEL EDITOR: SATO-SAN

EXCELLENT BACKGROUNDS: MUCCHI

AWESOME SCREENTONE: M-KO

And You!!

“At the same time this volume came out, *Core Magazine* released volume 3 of my series *Mousou Elektel*. It's a simultaneous release!

My new avatar picture above is a rejected sketch from when I made an animated GIF of Maya licking his lips. On another note, by the time this volume comes out, I'll be off on another overseas trip. I've been going on a lot of those lately. This time I've been invited to attend an event in Italy. See you there!”

About the Author

This may be **Yonezou Nekota**'s first English-language manga, but she is already well-known for the Japanese release of her title *Mousou Elektel* (Elektel Delusion). A prolific *doujinshi* (independent comics) creator, she was born in Tokyo in August and is a Leo with an A blood type. You can find out more about Yonezou Nekota at her website, **kmy.blog.jp**, or her Twitter page, **@yonekozoh**.

Don't Be Cruel
Volumes 3 & 4
SuBLime Manga Edition

Story and Art by **Yonezou Nekota**

Translation—**Adrienne Beck**
Touch-Up Art and Lettering—**NRP Studios**
Cover and Graphic Design—**Fawn Lau**
Editor—**Jennifer LeBlanc**

Hidokushinaide ③④ © 2012-2013 Yonezou Nekota
Originally published in Japan in 2012-2013 by Libre Publishing
Co., Ltd. Tokyo.
English translation rights arranged with Libre Publishing Co.,
Ltd. Tokyo.

Printed in the U.S.A.

Published by SuBLime Manga
P.O. Box 77010
San Francisco, CA 94107

10 9 8 7 6 5 4 3 2 1
First printing, September 2016

 PARENTAL ADVISORY
DON'T BE CRUEL is rated M for Mature and is
recommended for mature readers. This volume
MATURE contains graphic imagery and mature themes.

www.SuBLimeManga.com

For more information

on all our products, along with the most up-to-date news on releases, series announcements, and contests, please visit us at:

Downloading is as easy as:

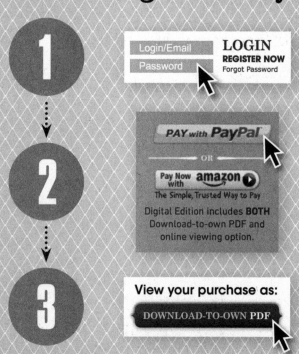

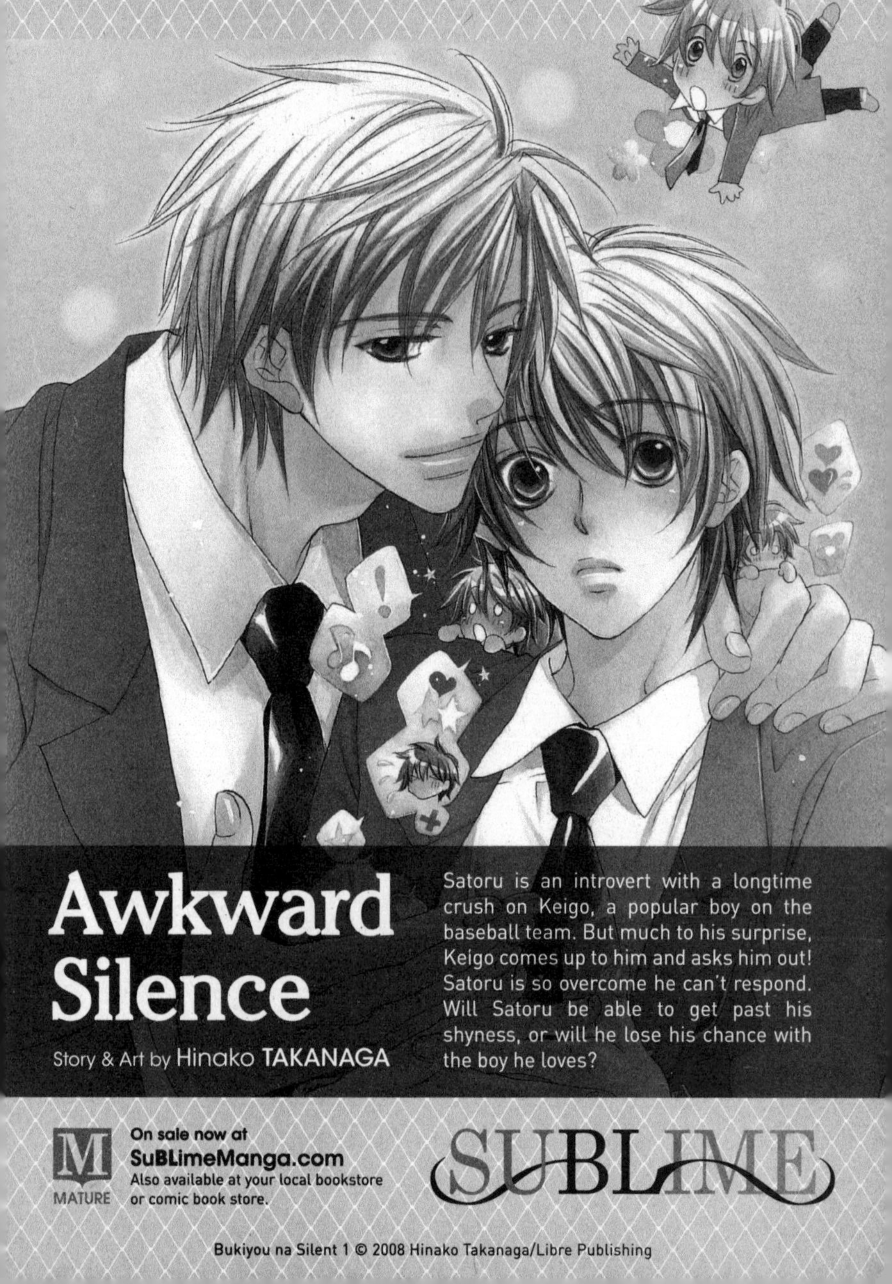